Manifest the Highest Point
in Your Horoscope

In the 1980's there is an increasing and widespread interest among astrologers and psychologists alike in the works of C.G. Jung. The number of speakers on such topics as Archetype and Myth increases every year at various conventions and conferences, and the lectures are well attended. This growing interest among astrologers in the Unconscious is a good indicator that a book such as this is very much needed today.

Kathleen Burt has given the reader a deeper look at astrology as it relates to Jungian Archetypes. The technique offered in the book is based upon the integration of the esoteric rulers of the signs with their opposites. This technique will help you to understand your instinctual behavior, enhance your creativity and modify the negative energies in your horoscope.

By understanding myths and archetypes, you can attain the potential of your birth chart—your life map—and gain conscious control of the instincts that rule you. With this volume you can change the instinctual patterns that seem to have you locked in, and become healthier and more productive.

Anyone who is studying astrology and archetypes—counselors, professional astrologers and even novices—can benefit from this information. You can bring out the higher octave of your sign and manifest it in your life, and learn to help others do the same in your practice as a counselor. By drawing on Jungian concepts, this long-overdue book can help you to help others as well as yourself. Reading it will take you on a fascinating and revealing journey through the signs.

About the Author

Kathleen Burt was born September 12, 1943 in Ottawa, Illinois. She is a longtime student of astrology, raja yoga, and the psychology of C.G. Jung. An astrologer in private practice for eighteen years, Kathleen has taught many classes and workshops both locally and throughout the Northwest. Her article "Attraction and the Ninth Harmonic" appeared in *News From 33 North*.

Kathleen completed her coursework for a doctorate in South Asian Studies at the University of Chicago, and was awarded a Fulbright grant to India for research. She has taught Indian History at Roosevelt University, Chicago, and at Mira Costa College in Del Mar, California. Kathleen also participated in "Patterns in Health," a two-year study program for counselors on the Jungian Archetypes, Myth, Ritual, Dream Interpretation and Active Imagination.

Kathleen and her husband Michael reside in Solana Beach, California. Their hobbies include meditation and travel. Among their favorite places visited they list India, Thailand, Greece and the Yucatan.

To Write to the Author

If you wish to contact the author or would like more information about this book, please write to the author in care of Llewellyn Worldwide, and we will forward your request. Both the author and publisher appreciate hearing from you and learning of your enjoyment of this book and how it has helped you. Llewellyn Worldwide cannot guarantee that every letter written to the author can be answered, but all will be forwarded. Please write to:

Kathleen Burt
c/o Llewellyn Worldwide
P.O. Box 64383-088, St. Paul, MN 55164-0383, U.S.A.

Please enclose a self-addressed, stamped envelope for reply, or $1.00 to cover costs. If outside the U.S.A., enclose international postal reply coupon.

Free Catalog from Llewellyn

For more than 90 years Llewellyn has brought its readers knowledge in the fields of metaphysics and human potential. Learn about the newest books in spiritual guidance, natural healing, astrology, occult philosophy and more. Enjoy book reviews, new age articles, a calendar of events, plus current advertised products and services. To get your free copy of *Llewellyn's New Worlds of Mind and Spirit*, send your name and address to:

Llewellyn's New Worlds of Mind and Spirit
P.O. Box 64383-088, St. Paul, MN 55164-0383, U.S.A.

THE LLEWELLYN MODERN ASTROLOGY LIBRARY

Books for the *Leading Edge* of practical and applied astrology as we move toward the culmination of the 20th century.

This is not speculative astrology, nor astrology so esoteric as to have little practical application in meeting the needs of people in these critical times. Yet, these books go far beyond the meaning of "practicality" as seen prior to the 1980's. Our needs are spiritual as well as mundane, planetary as well as particular, evolutionary as well as progressive. Astrology grows with the times, and our times make heavy demands upon Intelligence and Wisdom.

The authors are all professional astrologers drawing from their own practice and knowledge of historical persons and events, demonstrating proof of their conclusions with the horoscopes of real people in real situations.

Modern Astrology relates the individual person to the Universe in which he/she lives, not as a passive victim of alien forces but as an active participant in an environment expanded to the breadth, *and depth*, of the Cosmos. We are not alone, and our responsibilities are infinite.

The horoscope is both a measure, and a guide, to personal movement—seeing *every* act undertaken, *every* decision made, *every* event, as *time dynamic*: with effects that move through the many dimensions of space and levels of consciousness in fulfillment of Will and Purpose. Every act becomes an act of Will, for we extend our awareness to consequences reaching to the ends of time and space.

This is astrology supremely important to this unique period in human history, when Pluto transits through Scorpio and Neptune through Capricorn, and the books in this series are intended to provide insight into the critical needs and the critical decisions that must be made.

These books, too, are "active agents," bringing to the reader knowledge which will liberate the higher forces inside each person to the end that we may fulfill that for which we were intended.

Carl Llewellyn Weschcke

Forthcoming books by Kathleen Burt

Myths of the Chinese Zodiac

Astrology of the Rig Veda

The Llewellyn Modern Astrology Library

ARCHETYPES
OF THE ZODIAC

Kathleen Burt

1993
Llewellyn Publications
St. Paul, Minnesota 55164-0383, U.S.A.

FIRST EDITION
Fifth Printing, 1993

Cover art and interiors by Martin Cannon

Library of Congress Cataloging-in-Publication Data
Burt, Kathleen, 1943-
    Archetypes of the zodiac.

    (The Llewellyn modern astrology library)
    1. Zodiac. 2. Archetype (Psychology)—Miscellanea.
I. Title. II. Series.
BF1726.B87   1988   133.5'2   87-45743
ISBN 0-87542-088-5

Llewellyn Publications
A Division of Llewellyn Worldwide, Ltd.
P.O. 64383, St. Paul, MN 55164-0383

*This book is dedicated to
Swami Sri Yukteswar Giri,
with love and gratitude.*

Acknowledgements

I would like to thank, above all, my husband Michael, who patiently devoted many hours of his time and who contributed many good ideas to *Archetypes*, particularly to the questionnaires.

A special debt of gratitude is owed to the late Mircea Eliade, Professor of Comparative Religions at the University of Chicago; to Goswami Kriyananda (Dr. Melvin Higgins) of the Kriya Temple, Chicago, and to Sri Kriyananda (Reverend J. Donald Walters), founder of the Ananda Community in Northern California.

For their help in typing and proofreading I would like to thank Dagny Bush, my secretary and my friend and fellow astrologer Anne Neighbors.

For their work on the format and production of *Archetypes* I would like to express appreciation to Terry Buske and Emily Kretschmer. I am especially grateful to the artist, Martin Cannon, for his paintings, and to Carl Llewellyn Weschcke, who encouraged me to pursue the initial concepts which resulted in this mammoth undertaking.

My appreciation is also extended to many others, too numerous to mention by name—members of the San Diego Friends of Jung, fellow astrologers in the United States and India, students from the astrology classes at Mira Costa College, and my many friends and clients.

Contents

Preface

These essays on the signs of the zodiac and their rulers, esoteric and mundane, have been compiled from the transcripts of a workshop called "Archetypes of the Zodiac." The workshop series was presented through Mira Costa College's Community Service Program, Del Mar, California, 1982-85.

The workshop theme itself sprang into being, like the goddess Athena from the brow of Zeus, when an intermediate astrology student asked one day, "How can we *work with* the energy pattern in our horoscopes? How can I use my free will to consciously direct the 'Taurus within me' instead of going through life unconsciously 'reacting like a Taurus'?"

The idea came. "Let's do a workshop. Let's experiment with the 'higher' energy, the esoteric ruler of each of the twelve signs as well as the energy and meaning of the mundane ruler, which most of us express instinctively (unconsciously) every day. Let's also examine the 'balance point' for each of the signs and strive for that inner equilibrium it represents." Perhaps by tuning in to the higher meaning of our rulerships we could discover ways of using the energy of the signs more constructively.

The esoteric rulerships had interested me since the 1960's, when I had first read Alice Bailey's *Esoteric Astrology.* For the purposes of the workshop esoteric rulers for each sign were taken from her later book, *Labours of Hercules.* The myths have been collected from many sources over many years. The students, well versed in Jung, Oriental religions, Edgar Cayce, etc., made the symbolism come alive through their participation.

The workshop was, I think, exciting, but neither it nor these essays is intended to be the last word on zodiacal archetypes.

Introduction

Since some of you have come from a background in astrology, some from a study of C.G. Jung's psychological works and others from the Oriental religions, it might be a good idea to review the major concepts we'll be using before we begin with the first of the personality archetypes, Aries.

The first term is *archetype*. Most of us are familiar with its nonpsychological meaning: any model or prototype. For our purposes in this workshop though, its psychological definition would be preferable. Jung defines archetype many different ways in his various works. We read, for instance, that an archetype is ". . . an instinctual pattern of behavior contained in the collective unconscious." It is "transcendent." In other words, archetypes are not just part of an individual's personal unconscious, but something greater. They transcend the individual and have an independent form of existence on the collective level.

Jung also tells us that an archetype is "like a crystal in its form," and that the archetype is "like an empty envelope" having within it "modes of behavior the same everywhere and in all individuals." Jung says that within this pattern a conscious individual can give form to the archetype; he can choose to participate in its positive rather than in its negative energy.

As long as we have the empty envelope of the Goddess, the Cancer archetype or Jung's *Magna Mater*, for instance, we have a clean crystal, a transparent container. Yet, we have no form. We could call this empty envelope "The Womb," as in the *Rig Veda*, but an individual would have difficulty worshipping it or relating to the *Magna Mater* in this state. Various cultures give form to *Magna Mater*, the Great Mother, some of which are positive and some of which are not (such as the Devouring or Terrible Mother). It is the *forms* that are worshipped. For the worshipper, the envelope is no longer empty and the crystal container is no longer pure.

Joseph Campbell pointed out in *Occidental Mythology* that a

Catholic would be unlikely to knowingly kneel and say a prayer at a shrine of the Goddess Isis. As soon as art gives individual forms to the Goddess and the local cults are embellished with myth and ritual, each culture personalizes the archetype. *Magna Mater* comes in many forms, from the merciful Kwan Yin of China to Terrible Mother Kali of India, who wears skulls around her neck and snakes in her hair and has a protuberant tongue. Within the archetype there are many forms. We are free, like the Catholic passing through Egypt, not to kneel at some of the shrines if we prefer.

Every horoscope has many archetypes. Most of us are familiar with our Sun sign, but the Moon and the rising sign (Ascendant) may not be in the same archetypal envelope at all. A person could have a fiery Sun, an earthy Moon, a watery Ascendant. Or a Sun sign that hangs on to the past, a Moon sign that craves novelty and wants to rush ahead to the future, and an indecisive rising sign that mediates between the energy of Sun and Moon. The horoscope is the most personal tool we have for individual growth. It seems important to understand the archetypal energies and integrate them if we are serious about the individuation process Jung discusses, or if in our search for enlightenment we just want to be happy people until we reach our goal.

If we explore the archetypes and observe their instinctual behavior patterns, we will come to understand ourselves and others better. For one thing, our tolerance will increase. If in reading the myths illustrating the various archetypes we like what we see—if the patterns of action and reaction make us happy—fine! But if we identify with the hero or heroine whose journey is arduous and painful, or whose outcome is not as we would have liked it to be—if perhaps we hear an echo of the complaints our spouse or co-workers or our boss have made about us over the years, then maybe we would like to wipe off the crystal and find more appropriate, more positive uses for the energy contained in the archetype. Why be unhappy as a Terrible Kali when one could be happy as a Kwan Yin?

Myth is the second term to be defined. In taking one form, the idea (archetype) goes through a story development process. The Leo king has to reclaim his throne; the Aries hero goes off to fight his battles in the outer world. The Scorpio hero descends into himself (the inner world) to fight his demons and rescue his Persephone. Taurus encounters his/her obstacles to create a comfortable, secure world, or has to let go of his world once he creates it solidly. There are many definitions of myth. In *Myth and Reality*, Mircea Eliade says that "a myth is a sacred history which explains how the world came to be the way it is (for a particular culture) and why we are the way we are. Myth is truth; it concerns us directly, today." We often recreate it in ritual to restore ourselves, even if it is only reliving a memory or repeating our wedding vows on anniversaries.

There are many fine definitions of myth that distinguish it from legend fragments or fairy tale, but my preference is: myth is not something that happened once upon a time, long ago and far away, to *others*; myth is something that happens over and over again, every day, right here and now, *to us*. Eliade's emphasis on the sacred in his definition of myth is important, I think, for our purposes. Each of the signs has a symbol—an animal, a god, a book (scripture)—that was worshipped somewhere on Earth in some age. There is a very real element of the sacred here.

For those of you well versed in archetypes and myth as a result of long immersion in Jung—a word about some of these astrological terms which may be new to you. You probably know the basics, like the names of the twelve signs and the ten ruling (mundane) stellar bodies. But please memorize which planets relate to which signs. And please also remember that astrological symbolism has evolved over the centuries. There were not always twelve signs. Leo/Virgo was once undifferentiated and represented by the Sphinx in Egypt. Across the wheel from the Sphinx, the Cup represented the combined symbol of Aquarius/Pisces. It was a Cup that overflowed each year when the flood season brought fertilizing rains to the Nile delta. Some say that a 13th sign, Orphiacus, will wedge itself between Scorpio and Sagittarius in the next millennia. The forms change, though not in the lifespan of an individual.

What is the difference between mundane and esoteric rulers? Most people can easily identify *mundane*. Usual. Ordinary. Everyday, common garden variety. Boring is often implied when the word mundane is used. Jungians who know the myths of Aphrodite (Venus) easily associate Libra as the mundane ruler, observing the instinctive behavior of Libra and Libra rising friends. "Vanity, thy name is woman." (Models who look like the Venus de Milo, etc.) If you know an Aries who is argumentative, daring, impetuous, an adventurer, compare him with Mars, the mundane ruler and god of war. Capricorns are saturnine personalities (Saturn-ruled) and wise old men as they get older. The newspaper astrology columns have told you already that Cancers are Moon children. Here, the most feminine planet rules the most feminine sign. The Moon has many phases, corresponding to the many moods of Cancer. The associations are easy to make for Jungians who already know the myths and then learn the signs.

The word *esoteric* is usually defined as hidden knowledge or hidden information that is of interest to only a few specialists. Alice Bailey does not actually define her use of esoteric, but she says that "the esoteric ruler of the Sun and the Ascendant. . . indicate subjective life purpose." The disciple or initiate learns from the esoteric rulers what he's doing here in this lifetime, the old karma to be finished and the new lessons to be learned. Whereas the mundane and ordinary rulers of the Sun and Ascendant are descriptive of the work we do in the outer world or the types of problems we encounter in our environment. Objective reality equals mundane. Subjective reality equals esoteric.

Exaltation is the last term we need to define. A planet that is exalted in a sign of the zodiac is more powerful than another planet would be in that same sign because the energy of the planet accords with the energy of the sign and enhances it. There is a synergistic relationship between planet and sign. Thus, exalted planets are always strong but not always positive in the sense of being easy to deal with. Some of the planets in their exaltation sign are "inflated" or somewhat overwhelming to people who live with the exalted person's horoscope on a daily basis. An example would be the Sun (planet) in Aries (sign). The I AM planet is the Sun; the I AM sign is Aries. We would not get the same confident, impetuous, assertive energy if we looked at any of the other eleven Sun signs because the sun wouldn't be exalted in them.

For Taurus, the Moon is the exalted planet. If you know someone who has his Moon in Taurus, you will note I POSSESS coming through because the Moon represents attachment and possessiveness. The Moon is family, so attachment extends to the lives of the children. If they are artistic Taurus types, they will possess books, manuscripts and other collectibles. You can barely move around in some of their homes because of the priceless collections.

Exaltations were traditionally assigned to the seven planets discovered before the telescope was invented—those that the ancients could see and identify with the naked eye. For Uranus, Neptune and Pluto, different astrologers have different speculations about the signs of exaltation. In this book, I'll mention my own ideas on the outer planets' exalted positions. For now, here is a table on the esoteric and mundane rulers as well as the exalted planets in each sign. My suggested exaltations are in parentheses.

	Mundane Ruler	Esoteric Ruler	Exaltation
Aries	Mars	Mercury	Sun, (Pluto)
Taurus	Venus	Vulcan	Moon
Gemini	Mercury	Venus	(Uranus)
Cancer	Moon	Neptune	Jupiter
Leo	Sun	Sun	(Neptune)
Virgo	Mercury	Moon	(Uranus)
Libra	Venus	Uranus	Saturn
Scorpio	Mars	Mars	————
Sagittarius	Jupiter	Earth	————
Capricorn	Saturn	Saturn	Mars
Aquarius	Uranus	Jupiter	Mercury
Pisces	Neptune	Pluto	Venus

There is another important concept: integrating the opposites or polar extremities across the zodiacal wheel. Both C.G. Jung and the esoteric astrologer Alice Bailey emphasized the importance of balancing the personality by uniting the opposites. In astrology, we have twelve signs—or six polarities. (See diagram). Across from every dynamic, active, outspoken Fire sign lies a thoughtful, reflective Air sign. Across from every grounded, realistic Earth sign lies a Water sign that wishes cruel reality would disappear, but which also offers its earthy polarity the gifts of intuition, imagination and sometimes psychic powers to fertilize the dry soil.

Unlike the Jungian model of the opposites, astrology does not oppose the thinking and feeling functions, or the Masculine and the Feminine. My own belief is that the astrological system of masculine and feminine derives from Alchemy, where Saturn could be feminine as *Mercurius Senex*. (Where else could Capricorn (Earth) have been feminine? Or Scorpio (Water) feminine?)

I have included within each chapter a section on the Sun's progression from the original sign into the following signs. Spiritually and psychologically, the progressed Sun is an important factor in personality growth and evolution. If you are unfamiliar with this subject, here is an easy way to find out when your progression will take place.

If you know the degree and sign of your Sun at birth, count ahead one degree as one year. When you reach 30 degrees, the Sun will be entering the next sign. An example would be a natal Sun position of 18 degrees Scorpio. In 12 years that person's Sun would have progressed to Sagittarius. Follow this method for determining your own Solar progressions.

One final word before closing: remember that the Sun sign is not the only archetype in an individual's horoscope. When we begin to speak of the Aries archetype, we are not limiting ourselves exclusively to people with the Sun in Aries. Suppose that a chart has an Aries Sun and five planets (a stellium) in Taurus. Does he participate in the Aries or the Taurus archetype? Both! If his Moon or Ascendant is in Gemini, then we have all three archetypes to consider for this person. Even apart from the Sun, Moon, and Ascendant, any three or more planets in a particular sign will cause the individual to manifest archetypal characteristics of that sign.

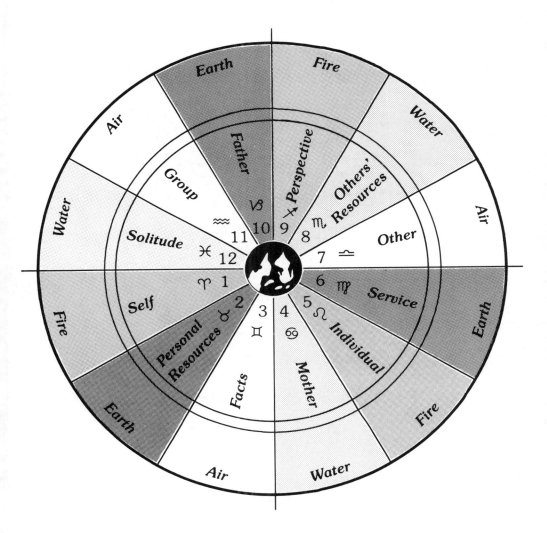

**Houses of the Natural Zodiac by Element
and Keyword**

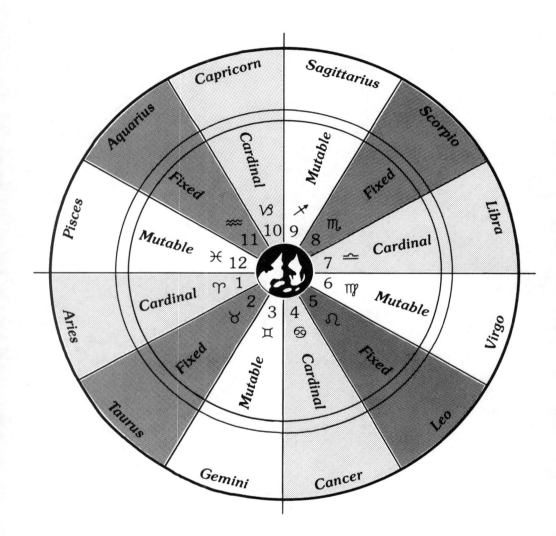

The Six Polarities

1 ARIES:
The Search For a Separate Identity

The Age of Aries is a solar, or masculine age. It is the Age of the Ram, of Mars and of the Hero. In the Late Bronze Age, Hellenic heroes in Greece and Aryan invaders in India attacked the sacred groves and grottoes of the Great Goddess. These heroes on horseback, these princes in their Solar Chariots, wrested control from the local rulers. They also destroyed the fertility cults whose priestesses and oracles supported the old dynasties.

The Earth Mother under her various names and forms, goddess of the preceding ages, had demanded tribute through ritual sacrifice of young princes and warriors to assure the continued fertility of the land. In India, priests of the conquering Aryans married local goddesses to the male deities of the Vedic Pantheon and tried to outlaw human sacrifices. In mainland Greece, heroes like Perseus I, King of Mycenae (1292), invaded the sacred shrine of Medusa, protectress of Lady Athene, destroyed her ritual masks, broke the statuary and drove out her priestesses. They had succeeded in ending ritual sacrifice of young princes, and by substituting a sacrificial sheep or lamb for the prince, had protected the institution of kingship. Patriarchy replaced Mother Right in the late Bronze and early Iron Age and priests replaced priestesses. Heroic myths about warrior-princes defeating dragon-lady monsters reveal that they believed they were delivering the countryside from bloodthirsty demonesses who laid waste the land. They believed that power had passed from the older goddesses to their own newer divinities and that their Solar, or masculine world view was more orderly and rational. But for the local

1

people in Mycenae, India, and elsewhere, power still remained with the Earth Mother, though foreign heroes had done violence to her sacred places and married her to their strange foreign gods.

Perhaps what Joseph Campbell called the "sociological trauma" of the late Bronze Age (Occidental Mythology, p. 152) is to us an example of the limitations of fighting fire with fire or responding to one type of violence (human sacrifice) with another form of violence (making war on the Great Goddess). One cannot really destroy the archetype; she just settles into our unconscious in a more frightening form. What we accomplish in the outer world of Aries activity (kingship, for instance) has its price in the inner, subjective world—the mass unconscious of our age. Sweet Medusa became a demoness and blissful Mother Kali of the earlier Upanishads became a truly Terrible Mother.

The Age of Aries, then, brought about a dramatic change in symbolism from the Lunar (feminine) to the Solar (masculine). The Aryan Age was a period of violent heroic activity, of feats of derring-do. We experience some of the energy of the Age of Aries every year at the time of the Vernal Equinox, when spring is bursting out all over. In the temperate zone, we emerge from the doldrums of late Pisces, which Shakespeare called the Ides of March. We then celebrate the Astrological New Year close to March 21, though Leap Year and other fluctuations sometimes alter the date slightly.* It seems to us, after the long winter, that nature has suddenly gone wild.

In the temperate zone, the four Cardinal signs traditionally marked the changing seasons, and the passing of each season was celebrated with rites and festivals. In pre-Christian times, springtime was a season of renewal—a rebirth of plant and animal life. It was a time of hope, of optimism, of confidence in good times to come. Christians later chose that time close to the Vernal Equinox to celebrate their festival of hope and renewal—Easter. It is a fitting time of year to celebrate the resurrection of a Messiah and the birth of the hero personality.

Aries' energy is like the Sun's rays—clear or conscious, frank, direct, obvious, full of light and heat and visible to all. Though all three Fire signs are solar in nature, Aries is the most exuberant, just as spring is the most exuberant season. Thus, astrologers say that the Sun is exalted in Aries. An exuberant planet in an exuberant sign leads to an exalted personality. The Sun is the only I AM planet; Aries

---

*See Llewellyn's Astrological Calendar or Daily Planetary Guide for exact dates.

is the I AM sign. The archetypal Aries takes pride at being on Earth in that physical form or body, pride in him/herself and his/her creative capacity, his/her drive to fulfill his desires in the outside world. Observe a very small Aries child, one too young for society to have curbed his/her enthusiasm, and you may see the Aries archetype manifest—excitement, pride, drive, supreme self-confidence, a strong sense of discovery and impatience to experience the world around him. Like Icarus in the myth, s/he is ready to disregard his/her father's rules, glue on his/her wings and fly as close to the Sun as s/he can. S/he feels no sense of danger. S/he does not want to be taught to fly. S/he wants to *do* it. Aries wants to go and do.

Let us consider the glyphs for Aries and for Mars, the mundane ruler. Aries is the ram's horns and the battering ram. Aries makes a place for himself in a crowd or in a waiting line. He lets the restaurant hostess know, "I'm here." Aries represents the "Irresistible Force," as Dane Rudhyar put it. This is the power of the ram's horns. He can also be a fearless ram on the outside ("I'll volunteer for the front lines of battle!") and be timid inside. He can be a sheep in the subjective world of personal relationships.

Aries is spontaneous in falling in love, but is often unable to find the romantic vocabulary to express his feelings. "My Aries husband takes the initiative so quickly in the outer (business) world, but at home he leaves all the decisions to me," complains Aries' mate. "He may make the effort to praise and encourage his employees at the office, but he never says anything encouraging to me."

Aries, remember, is outward drive and Logos. Aries is the ruler of the head in medical astrology, and part of the work on planet Earth for Aries is knowing when to use logic and when to proceed from the emotions—Eros. Aphrodite (Eros) is opposite Mars, just as Aries is 180 degrees across the wheel from Libra. An undeveloped Aries—a young child or one who hasn't studied or observed others' social behavior—will use the word "I", a solar and a Mars word, too often. One example is the case of the Aries tourist who said to 25 other people in his group, "Let's go back to the hotel. I'm tired." Aries matures as he becomes more aware and uses the word "we" more frequently and "I" less often. His logic will work well for him in the business world where his assertive Mars and his competitive Cardinal nature also serve him well.

The Aries who is a battering ram in his career relationships will often be a gentle lamb at home—a true innocent when it comes to

relating to the opposite sex. He will learn that his spouse doesn't appreciate his logic when she asks him a rhetorical question such as, "How do you like my new fur coat?" Mars may come up with the instinctive, spontaneous reply, "Well, to be honest, dear, it makes you look fatter." The spouse, who has just purchased the coat and is delighted with it, is not impressed with his honesty. To an Aries, every question deserves an honest, logical answer. Mars is passionate, but not exactly tender or aware of others' feelings! He has a good deal to learn about relating to others without thoughtlessly bursting their balloons.

The Eros sign, Libra, 180 degrees away, holds the balance here. Mars needs to temper Logos with Eros. Mars is independent, but 180 degrees away, Venus ruled Libra wants to be liked, wants to make a good impression. She can help Mars to curb his spontaneity, to think before speaking, to broaden his *I*-thinking to *we*-thinking.

The glyph for Mars (♂) is the biological symbol for the male sex. Many people whose Aries energy manifests at the mundane level alone identify with Mars—with the libido and the senses, with the body's drives and instincts. This has prompted astrologers over the centuries to observe that for many an Aries the life lesson involves distinguishing between lust and love. Here the Libra polarity provides the balance. In the myths, Mars is identified with Cupid, son of Venus/Aphrodite, ruler of Libra. Cupid/Mars learned about love from Aphrodite, who is also an expert in finesse, popularity and charm. The Seventh House, the Other, is Aphrodite's House and is the House of consideration, reciprocity, and sharing. The First House, the Self, from which Aries symbolically proceeds, needs to balance its independence with an awareness of reciprocity. No man is an island.

It's a good idea to locate Venus/Aphrodite in the chart of Aries Sun sign or Aries rising. Is she in a positive dialogue with Mars? If not, the Arian may prefer independence to relationship. The exalted Aries may even look down on women as inferior. This tends to be true not only of Aries/Aries rising men, but women as well.

Just as in the Age of Aries, when the hero looked down upon the feminine and sought to slay the dragon goddess, today we can still observe a sort of masculine arrogance and lack of respect for the feminine in the macho Mars man, the Aries/Aries rising personality. There is a sense that the man of the species is destined to greatness, while the "little woman" should be at home performing the menial tasks which are hers by biological destiny. One sees this heroic masculine ideal in television commercials like the beer commercials where men are competing in some athletic event in the great outdoors without a single woman in sight. (The women are probably off in the background making coffee and sandwiches.) The implied message seems to be this is man's world, and a great one, at that.

Women who complain of masculine arrogance and disrespect (chauvinism) often cite as examples such Mars men as the traffic policeman who stops them and, while writing the ticket, mutters, "women drivers," or the plumber or mechanic who hands them his bill but refuses to explain it because, "this mechanical stuff is over your head, little lady." He acts as if her role is to submissively pay him so he can get on with his work. Or, a woman with briefcase in hand rushes past a construction site on her lunch hour and hears a wolf-whistle. A liberated woman, she is astonsihed that such old-fashioned behavior still exists and looks up into the scaffolding to see a construction worker wink appreciatively at her, hoping she enjoyed the compliment. The fact is, if she were an Aries woman in touch with her passionate instincts through her Mars, she probably *would* enjoy it!

Aries, then, likes the rugged life, the great outdoors and especially to work with his tools, his gun or motorcycle, his wrench and screwdriver, his hammer and saw—the metal implements of Mars. The Aries/Aries rising man usually feels good with these things in his hands. Mars, Aries and the First House of the chart are about the body, and the mundane Aries is very likely going to keep his in good shape all his life. Many can be found working out with weights (heavy metal) at the gym, getting in shape for the local ten kilometer run or the office softball competition. Mars rules adrenalin, and the true Mars type is an adrenalin junkie. He feels better after a workout, which releases the day's frustrations. Even if his job is physically demanding, he usually has energy left over. He may need only four or five hours of sleep a night. Archetypally, we think of Mars as a sports car driver or even a professional racer in the Indianapolis 500. Mars seeks to "go where no man has gone before," which is perhaps why so many Aries Sun sign test pilots signed on to train as astronauts— outer space pioneers.

Many of my Aries male clients have a high risk hobby such as hang gliding, cliff diving, or scuba diving in uncharted, dangerous waters. Others have hobbies that might one day put them in the

Guinness Book of World Records, if they survive. Still others are involved in the martial arts. A great many have served in the military, the traditional heroic career that enables them to "defend the kingdom." They also look handsome in uniforms, have the competitive opportunities to prove that they have the right stuff, enjoy the company of "real men" and, if they become officers and draw wealth and power, will satisfy their Mars need to attract beautiful, sexy women.

What then is the archetypal Aries woman like at the mundane, instinctual level? I mentioned above that she would enjoy a wolf-whistle. She is usually athletic and keeps herself in good physical shape and she appreciates a man who notices it. Her attitudes are somewhat masculine, to the point that other Aphrodite-like women may not appreciate her at all. One Aries woman said, "Men find me dynamic, magnetic, fun. Other women don't seem to like me as well as men do. I have a lot of energy and I am assertive, downright aggressive, in fact! I like to dance. At the military base where we live, I go to parties while my husband is overseas and, well, I don't want to just sit there demurely like a phony while everyone else is having a good time. I go over and ask men to dance—even other women's husbands! I guess their wives don't appreciate it. What can I say? These coy women get on my nerves. I'm direct, honest in saying what I mean. They think I'm rude at times, but who cares? Certainly not me."

The military base attracts many Aries/Aries rising, Angular Mars people, both men and women. Domestic battles often break out at the end of a social evening like the one the Aries woman described. "How dare you dance with *her* when I, your wife, was sitting there? I'm furious. . . " She throws things, and he responds, and the neighbors call the police. Sometimes he ends up in the brig. Living life through Mars' passions, instincts, and desires certainly provides an exciting lifestyle. He goes off to defend the kingdom, returns, and passion flares up between them again. Energy bursts out all over, like flowers shooting up in springtime, but it is often energy out of control.

Traditionally, Aries/Aries rising women had little in the way of a career outlet for their passionate, competitive spirits, so their Mars was lived out vicariously on the domestic scene. Mars played out its sense of danger through the husband's career, and he was often a handsome man in a high risk occupation. The first marriage of an Aries woman client is often to a soldier, policeman, professional athlete, or professional gambler. One Aries woman married two firefighters in a row! She has since found an outlet for her energy, her need for excitement and sense of discovery in her own career. Her *inner* exploration of Jungian psychology, the I Ching, and metaphysics has brought the stimulation and progress along life's journey that the Aries heroine requires. Aries needs to *move forward*, not stand still or fall back.

Aries with Mars linked to Mercury often have very good reflexes and dexterity. My last three seamstresses were self-employed Aries women who were very quick and precise in their use of such metal objects as scissors and needles. All three were a bit impulsive, anxious to cut into the cloth, and each time I brought in a new piece of material I found myself saying, "Now, be sure to make it large enough in case I gain a pound or two. It's harder to add cloth than to cut it off, so if you make it too big at first, it's fine." They were restless spirits and kept moving on to new horizons. I seemed to be constantly seeking a new tailor, but they were all talented at executing the chosen design, and at doing so on short notice. Aries men and women with positive Mars/Mercury aspects, then, can be found in careers such as sports, requiring quick reflexes, or in work that involves dexterity with tools. As they grow older, they may teach their skills to a younger generation of sportsmen, tailors, cabinet makers, or cosmetologists.

Thus we have the Aries/Aries rising or Angular Mars individuals with their automatic attunement to Mars, the instinctual ruler. What, then, distinguishes the spiritual or esoteric Aries from the mundane? The Aries at the esoteric level has begun to work consciously with Mercury (Logos), his/her spiritual ruler. In Greek mythology, particularly in Homer's epics, Mercury's thinking, counseling role as wise Messenger God was played by Hermes or Athene, two almost interchangeable Logos symbols. Zeus dispatched them to the hero in time of need. Aries as Conscious Seeker, like Hermes and Athene, has developed and disciplined his intellect so that it controls his restless, angry Mars. Hermes or Athene knows the appropriate uses of Mars' energy. They are able to put the immediate situation on hold, distance themselves from spontaneous anger and reflect: Is this emotion constructive or destructive? Am I just letting off steam today at the wrong person? At the wrong time?

In the *Upanishads* and the *Bhagavad Gita*, the Solar Chariot and its horses refer to the inner quest of the Seeker—control of the restless senses (horses) by the mind. In astrology, Mercury/Hermes, the mental planet, or Logos, is the charioteer, the hero who holds the horse's reins. Aries energy has been represented by an innocent, gentle lamb in many sculptures of Greece and Rome. Hermes was the protector of the lamb (the good sheperd) and also the guide of the instincts, of the headstrong ram. If the prudent mind, Mercury/Hermes, was followed, the ram would be safe. This is the meaning conveyed by the beautiful statue of ram-carrying Hermes in the Acropolis Museum of Athens, by Roman statues of a lamb curled up asleep at Hermes' feet, and by many columns with the same motif throughout mainland Greece and in Ephesus, Turkey. The instincts need a thinking function, Hermes/Mercury, to rein in the sensory wild horses of Diomedes.

Aries/Aries rising and Angular Mars people who have spent many years in academia may, however, reach a point as objective scientists or researchers where they stand back too far and filter Mars' emotions too thoroughly. If this is the case, they may dream of animals (instincts) that are trying to tell them something. Unlike the Aries sportsman who is in touch with his body and trusts the information Mars provides through it, the Aries scholar may be repressing Mars to the point that he leads a passionless or colorless life, feels a lack of energy (Mars rules adrenalin), loses his sex drive, or even loses interest in his project. Or the preoccupied academic may bump his head (the Aries part of the body) as a warning to pay attention. There is a story about Athene throwing rocks at Aries' head. She was probably trying to tell him, "Wake up! Be conscious of what you're doing!" Athene is not a colorless goddess. As Nike, she is Goddess of Victory and patroness of the city of Athens. Homer, in the *Iliad*, calls her "Athene of the flashing eyes," and she certainly flashed them at Achilles on the eve of battle when the situation called for her appearance. Achilles was ready to take out his sword and kill King Agamemnon on the spot. Suddenly Athene appeared:

> Homer tells us, "He was deep in this inward conflict, with his long sword half unsheathed, when Athene came down from heaven. . . She stood behind him and seized his golden locks. No one but Achilles was aware of her, the rest saw nothing. He swung round in amazement, recognized Pallas Athene at once—so terrible was the brilliance of her eyes—and spoke out to her boldly: 'And why have you come here, Daughter of Aegis-bearing Zeus? Is it to witness the arrogance of my Lord Agamemnon? I tell you bluntly, and I make no idle threats, that he stands to pay for this outrage with his life!'
> 'I came from heaven,' replied Athene of the Flashing Eyes, 'in the hope of bringing you to your senses. . . Come now, give up this strife and take your hand from your sword. . . Here is a prophecy for you. The day

Shall come when gifts three times as valuable as what you now have lost
will be laid at your feet in payment for this outrage. Hold your hand,
then, and be advised by us!

'Lady,' Achilles the great runner replied, 'When. . . goddesses command, a man must obey, however angry he may be. Better for him if he does;
the man who listens to the gods is listened to by them!" *(Iliad, Book I)*

Listening to the intellect (one's Mercury or Athene) and to god is
important for a quick-to-act hero like Achilles and for those who
belong to the heroic Aries archetype. Though his anger was justifiable, for King Agamemnon had not acted fairly, his reward was not to
be immediate. He had to wait. Listening and waiting are very difficult
for anyone with a strong Mars.

It is interesting that Athene replaces the ram as symbol for Aries
on several Nabatean zodiacs in Palestine and appears seated on the
ram in others. Some authors theorize that Athene was selected
because goddesses represent fertility, so a goddess was required to
connect Aries, the Vernal Equinox sign, with the fertility of spring. It
seems to me that a ram was just as effective a fertility symbol as a goddess. Also, if just any Great Mother would do to symbolize fertility,
why choose Athene, a masculine Solar goddess? Why not select a
Lunar goddess like Demeter, who would *clearly* signify fertility?

It seems more likely that the Nabateans consciously chose
Athene because she belonged to Aries. As a Solar goddess who
sprang full-blown from the brow of Father Zeus, Athene represented
all the qualities of Logos—thinking, planning, strategizing, organizing. Athene seated on the ram symbolized the power of Logos to control the instincts, the same point Homer repeatedly makes in the *Iliad*.
Her mythology demonstrates that she is just as courageous as Aries,
the Greek Mars, but wiser. Homer informs us in the *Iliad* that she was
dispatched by Zeus to restrain Aries from impulsively creating havoc
during the Trojan War. She carried out the will of God (Zeus) with
prudence and confidence. She was unafraid on the battlefield of life.
Her courage is admirable. Many people with Mars intercepted or in
the Twelfth House could benefit from this courage to say no directly,
mean it, and stick to it when the mind and the instincts tell them
to do so.

As Logos, Athene tempers Mars' impulses to gratify his immediate desires with her reason and her discrimination. She proves a
wise counselor to Telemachus, the young hero of the *Odyssey*. The
Aries/Aries rising individuals who exhibit her prudence under fire,
who are well-organized and calm, who read and improve their minds,

who control their tempers and their instincts, who sublimate the passion of the moment to more important future goals, are Athene-like.

Some young Athenes, or little Aries girls, excel at sports but may not be encouraged by adults to compete. They are told, rather, that they must be ladylike, dress in ribbons and bows and develop their domestic skills. For children with mental curiosity, quick minds and restless bodies, this is sad. It's fortunate that as we enter the New Age Athene will be as valued as the other goddesses. Already girls' athletic programs are being funded and skilled coaches provided, similar to those available for boys.

The natural competitive and leadership talents of Aries girls can then be tested and refined—and some of the Mars' restlessness released in sports. Legend has it that sculptors at the Parthenon were told to clip the wings of Athene/Nike's statues so that she could never leave Athens. If the wings of little Aries girls are not clipped in childhood they are less likely to drop out of school and run away with a dangerous man who acts out their Mars for them, sometimes in violent or abusive ways, or to connect with a James Bond-type fantasy man.

So many Aries women have told me of violent people in their environment, or of abuse they seemed to attract from the opposite sex, or from life itself. The exalted Aries Sun with several passive Pisces planets often manifests as a passive-aggressive horoscope. Aries passion will stir up a reaction in others who respond with physical or emotional abuse. The Pisces planets then react as a victim or martyr. "How could you hurt my feelings like that? Poor little me!" Or, "You hit me! How could you hit a defenceless woman?" The passive-aggressive needs to develop Athene's discrimination. If she has a pattern of physical or emotional abuse, she might ask herself, "What am I doing or saying to provoke violent emotions in others?" Or, "Where have I been going to connect with this abuse?" If she has been attending heavy metal rock concerts or going to dangerous bars this could be *her* contribution to the pattern. Athene is the goddess of wisdom and one who is attuned to her might ask, "Is it wise?"

Aries often seems to spark confrontations with others. The exalted Sun (ego) is very powerfully placed. Aries may be unconsciously treating others, especially women, disrespectfully. Aries of both sexes who complain of having very few women friends may discover that they do not make much effort in this direction. Women are usually powerless and are therefore not always going to seem as interesting to Aries as men. For this reason, Aries parents might listen to the unconscious signals they are communicating to their daughters. The same is true of Aries grandparents and their granddaughters.

Recently an Aries grandma was overheard remarking to her son within earshot of her young grandchildren, "Lisa gets better grades than Bobby. It's such a shame when the girl inherits the brains in the family. I mean, she's just going to get married when she grows up." Grandma herself is a successful businesswoman. She has few women friends. She constantly recounts the stories of her son's success, but seldom those of her equally successful daughter.

Athene women can be well-organized housewives when they so choose. Athene introduced domestic arts, as well as tools, to the Greeks. Aries women who have good Mercury/Mars aspects are often quite talented in crafts. Some of them even use the loom, Athene's favorite domestic tool. (The weaving art is probably also symbolically connected with "weaving strategies.") Logos, however, can mean the restless mind! Many an Aries woman becomes claustrophobic in the home when her children are babies and she longs to put her competitive mental skills to use in the marketplace. Pisces and Cancer mothers tend to enjoy the years when their children are cute, cuddly, dependent babies, but Aries women usually tell me that the years they most enjoyed were those in which their children were in junior high and older. "It was so interesting to see the way they developed as people, to watch them perform in sports and school plays, to see who they chose as friends and what they wanted to do in life when they grew up." Those Aries women whose personalities are low in the Water element are not nurturers as such and tend to foster independence in their children. They do not seek to keep them home forever!

What of the Aries woman who has a square, a negative aspect, between her esoteric and mundane rulers, Mercury and Mars? She may communicate sarcastically, let her temper have free rein, or she may communicate in a loud voice. Like an Aries drill sergeant, she can be a tyrant. Like the drill sergeant, she may not care what people think of her. Athene rules education, the process of developing the mind. In our times, she may well rule the business seminars on effective communication, too. As Athene told Achilles, listening is an important part of communicating.

In *Goddess In Everywoman*, Jean Shinoda-Bolen says that those Athene-women whose fathers have given them moral support to achieve their educational goals tend to go far in both business and academia, but that once they've arrived at success, they tend to support the values of the patriarchy, become conservative, oppose the Equal Rights Amendment and side with the men in management against other women. Mental strategies that win attention in academia often deny the feeling function, too. Serving on committees where she'll be noticed, for instance, helps Athene obtain tenure at the university, but also may overdevelop the solar, masculine side of the personality at the expense of the lunar, feeling side.

In the chart of one Athene woman whose feeling function (Water element) was low, I really felt what Shinoda-Bolen calls Athene's armor! She had erected a strong defence against any relationship that might render her job vulnerable to attack. Her company did not keep its employees on the payroll once they were married to each other. Though she met interesting men from other companies at sales seminars she could not date them. If she did, her own company might decide that she was no longer trustworthy, because she was too close to the power structure and knew too many secrets the competition would have liked to discover. She did not really want to marry within the power structure and had little respect for flirtatious Aphrodite women who did. "I am not some weak, simpering female," she told me. "I did not get where I am by flirting with management. I owe my success to intelligence and hard work. I want to belong to the power structure on my own merits, not to marry into it, leave my job and wash diapers." This seemed very strong armor, indeed!

The Parthenon, the temple that has for centuries been a landmark on Acropolis hill overlooking the city of Athens, is dedicated to Athene Parthenos, Athene the Virgin. Many Aries/Athenes in academia, the business world, and religious life correspond to Athene Parthenos. She was invulnerable to Aphrodite and Cupid. Because this sort of esoteric Aries woman seems so totally in control of the instincts, she sometimes seems to the staff she leads quite cold and lacking in compassion. "Working for my Aries woman boss is harder than working for the man she replaced," said one executive secretary. "I could call the male boss and tell him I was sick and he would be quite kind about it. But she says, 'Oh, I suppose it's female problems again? I never call in sick for those so why should you? What are you really going to do today, go to the beauty shop?' She seemed to lack female hormones."

Aries women with Water, particularly Cancer Water in the chart, seem to get along better with other women. They are not as identified with the patriarchy—the values of the male management. Cancer planets usually mean she's also subject to moods and feminine problems, too. Aries women, like Aries men, often fail to realize that the other eleven signs may lack their energy, stamina, vitality, and even (on the highways) their quick reflexes and coordination. Mars has little patience with failure, or weakness. Pisces planets, in the chart of the Aries/Aries rising, add a dimension of compassion. They tend to feel guilty after a confrontation and apologize, for instance. For the Aries personality the mental filtering process, the aloof distancing followed by Athene-like analysis of the reasons behind his/her anger in the situation, is quite important.

In medical astrology, Aries the head, is opposite Libra, the kidneys. The kidneys' function is to filter out impurities from the bloodstream before they cause problems in the body. Through the process of filtering out negative emotions, and separating the constructive emotions from the destructive, Aries can save himself migraine headaches, bumps and cuts, and kidney-related diseases. Though I have found more Aries women with kidney and bladder ailments than men, this polarity is important to consider in reading a chart.

So many Neptune in Libra generation Aries have an opposition to the Sun or Ascendant from an obscure and hard-to-diagnose planet, Neptune. I have found that many of them exhibit Libran filtration symptoms in life. They may not be dealing appropriately with their emotions; they may be venting anger at the wrong people or under the wrong circumstances. (Being angry at home when the spouse has done nothing to deserve it and being tactful at work when management doesn't deserve it! Or treating the men in the environment with tolerance and dumping on the women, who are powerless.) Or, like the Athene-in-defensive-armor, sacrificing romance (Neptune in Libra) to make things work, pragmatically, through Aries logic, in the career area.

When we think of Cardinal Fire (Aries) we think of the competitive drive toward success, of the quest in the outer world, because Mars is the sign's mundane ruler. The courage of Mars' Aries children is often amazing to behold; more than one cautious Earth sign client has remarked over the years, "these Aries are so foolhardy!" Actually, Mars bestows on the Aries wonderful confidence. Give an Aries an opportunity to try something new—a task, an approach, a skill—and he's likely to respond, "Sure, I know I can do that!" His inventive, initiating, pioneering side, combined with the mental ingenuity of a well-developed esoteric ruler (Mercury/Hermes), i.e., with the proper education and technique, will take him far in life. He'll be finished with introductory astrology and hanging out the "Astrological Consultant" shingle on his office while a more inhibited, less confident and less courageous student of astrology is still saying, "Actually, astrology is a hobby thing. I've only studied it for ten years. I don't know enough to try to read a horoscope!" Aries would be inspiring instructors of assertiveness training to those horoscopes low in Fire or where Mars is weakly placed.

If s/he has few or no inhibitions, what then prevents the mundane or Mars-ruled Aries from succeeding on his/her quest? Temper. Impatience. Coming on too strong around shy or quiet people, who think s/he is rude rather than frank or direct. Desire for immediate gratification of wants or goals. Digging up the seeds s/he has just sown for one of his/her projects before they've had a chance to germinate and annoying the gardener s/he depends upon. Example: an Aries client writes up a grant proposal for his/her departmental science project. S/he mails it to several funding sources, but s/he can't wait to see if his/her contacts at each organization liked the idea. S/he calls them every day to see if they've read it yet. This makes them very irritated with the Aries because bureaucratic temperaments don't like to be rushed.

One way the Jason myth reflected Aries energy was Jason's sowing seeds which instantly sprout. Instant realization is what impatient Mars craves. Logos, the Aries mind, wants to *know* the outcome so s/he can move on to the next phase. S/he *acts first* (sows the seeds), but then s/he digs the seeds up; s/he has lost interest in the project because a newer idea has come to him/her. Mars enjoys a new project more than the current venture which has become boring or frustrating. It's easy for Aries to get sidetracked from his/her quest. Sometimes the Aries client comes to a session feeling like Don Quixote tilting at windmills. Doubt has set in and s/he begins to wonder if maybe those others who did not volunteer for the front lines of the company's marketing battlefield knew something s/he didn't know. Perhaps, after all, this *is* "Mission Impossible?" "What does the astrologer think. . . ?" he asks. The Fixed signs, including Fixed Fire, are more likely to persevere after the first few dragons have been slain, but the Cardinal Mars native tends to lose interest.

This brings to mind an old saying that seems appropriate for Aries: "Don't change horses in the middle of the stream (of life)." The horse is an important symbol for the Age of Aries, or the Age of Heroes, because without horses to pull their Solar Chariots, the Aryan and Hellenic tribes might not have been able to conquer the Indus Valley or Greece and replace the Mother Right with the patriarchy. Though the horse is also associated with Sagittarius, another solar or masculine Fire sign, this adage about changing horses in mid-stream seems particularly fitting for impetuous Aries. Aries' spontaneity, initiative and enthusiasm in the initial stages of projects are legendary, but when the first of the obstacles has been met and conquered, "burnout" often occurs for Aries' Fire. Aries, mounted on horseback in mid-stream, longs for a faster vehicle, a different horse, a new direction. Mars' energy is well-suited to short-term ventures, but unlike Fixed Fire, Leo, Aries tends to lose interest and move on too soon. Many come to consult astrologers on the timing of new ventures, and some are told, in effect, "Hold your horses!"

Mars, of course, is an ambitious planet and Mercury, the esoteric ruler, is a strategist. Yet, both are fast-moving, somewhat restless rulers. Where then do so many of the Aries' leaders among my clientele derive their staying power? A few Aries self-starters do, of course, go from job to job or change careers frequently, but others tend to "hang in there" for the duration, especially the more educated Aries with a strong and well developed Mercury. Many of them are also drawn to centers of power in business, academia, and the military. Power and influence, making an impression and accomplishing personal (First House) goals seems more interesting to them than making money. "The job title is fine, but the power to do things I want to accomplish is more important," is the impression one often gets from a session with Aries.

Pondering this for many years in connection with my study of planetary exaltations, I eventually concluded that there is a second planet besides the Sun exalted in Aries—Pluto. (The three outermost and most recently discovered planets have no set and determined exaltations as of yet, but it is certainly interesting to speculate about them.) In the horoscopes of Aries who had built their own businesses, who were successful administrators, or scientists involved in research and discovery I noticed that Pluto was often Angular (in Houses 1, 4, 7 or 10) and/or made a strong aspect to Mars. In the more esoteric charts (and some of the more devious, too) it contacted Mercury, the thinking function and esoteric ruler. Thus, I began to take Pluto very seriously in the charts of Aries and to check out its aspects, noting first of all whether they were positive or harsh in nature (squares and oppositions versus trines, sextiles, etc.).

As ruler of Scorpio, Pluto brings fixity of purpose and will to power to the Mars personality. Pluto has Scorpio's strong points which enhance Mars' dynamism and ambition but also Scorpionic weaknesses which bring out Mars' negative qualities. Pluto, for example, is a reclusive planet which can, in the chart for a scientist, help Mars sublimate sexual energy into the work of discovery. Pluto and Mars together can go off into a laboratory for long periods of time. Pluto offers control and the ability to keep fighting old habits and obstacles over time. It strengthens the Mars battering ram with steady perseverance when it otherwise might lose interest and go on too soon to a new and greener seeming field. For instance, Aries women whose fathers have encouraged them to succeed, but have been unable to help them financially, who possess strong Pluto/Mars or Pluto/Mercury aspects, have worked to put themselves through school. The combination of Pluto's will and powers of concentration with Mars' physical energy enabled them to take many courses while simultaneously holding a full-time job.

Again, through sublimation of the Libran polarity—Eros, for a number of years—Mars and Pluto together with Mercury can accomplish marvels. Pluto's magnetism enhances that of Mars; people really tend to notice an Aries with a strong Mars/Pluto aspect. Pluto's intensity and determination offsets Mars' restlessness when the two are in positive aspect.

In the case of the negative Mars/Pluto aspects, one often finds manipulation, deceit, ruthless drive to power, a vengeful desire to destroy the competition, and in relationships, a sadistic, cruel approach to women, a desire to vent frustrations upon them—that helpless sex.

Pluto in the First House (Aries in the natural zodiac) also plays an exalted role. Placed close to the Ascendant, Pluto seems to have a great deal more magnetism than any other planet in the same position. There is an underlying aura of confidence to the Pluto in the

First House person that he or she will win out in the end, that the inner resources are there to meet any challenge life sends along, however long one must endure to achieve an important goal. However, there's also a sort of intuitive power to determine when to move on, to make changes, to try a new venture. These people are quite good at dissolving the obstacles to power in the outer world, and some are also good at dissolving their own inner obstacles—the bad habits that get in the way of the goal. Pluto is very strong for transcending and transforming. However, at relationship readings the person without Pluto in the First House may complain that the Pluto person is self-absorbed, or even self-obsessed. It's important to check the aspects to determine how Pluto functions in an Aries chart, especially the Pluto/Mars, Pluto/Mercury aspects.

Thus, though I have never met a client with Pluto in Aries, I feel from its First House influence and its influence upon my Aries clients, that this must be its position of exaltation. This accords, too, with the esoteric tradition in which Pluto is the higher octave planet for Mars. The planet Pluto was discovered in 1931, and even if we placed it into the charts of clients who lived before it was discovered, the client would have to be quite old as it last left Aries in 1851.

We come now to the myths for Aries. Both are solar, heroic stories about young, naive, independent, supremely confident heroes. In the first story *Hercules* learns the importance of tuning in to Hermes/Mercury, his esoteric ruler. In the second, *Jason* learns the need to acknowledge at least the principle of Eros, child of Goddess Aphrodite, if not also the need to sacrifice his restless independence to Eros and settle down with a mate.

In the *Labors of Hercules*, Alice Bailey recounts the myth of the Aries Quest, the first of Hercules' famous labors. Hercules is told to go through the Gate (the twin columns of Duality that are the symbol of entry into the world of delusion) and tether the wild mares of Diomedes, the war horses that the king bred. It is interesting that in this myth the most dangerous were the female horses (mares) who "devastated the land." It seems appropriate for an Aries Quest to have Logos (thinking) struggling against the destructive side of the feminine, just as Perseus fought the Dark Goddess who was laying waste the land. Yet, Hercules did not think or plan. He rushed headlong into the fray with full confidence, then stopped briefly when he saw the odds were against him; there were a great many wild mares snorting and pawing the ground. He thought of his friend, Abderis, "whom he greatly loved," and called out for help. Together the two devised a plan to corner and tether the mares. When they had completed the task, Hercules became bored and restless. Rather than stay with Abderis, he was in a hurry to move on to the next task. He left all the mares with his friend and instructed Abderis to drive them back through the gates. Why should the solar hero stay around and complete an old project? A leader must move on to more important work. A follower like Abderis ought to be able to carry through with the task at hand. His friend, however, did not have the courage to harness and control the mares. They realized this and turned on him. He was trampled to death. The mares then escaped into the remoter, wilder regions of the unconscious, Diomedes' Kingdom.

Hercules' exalted pride was humbled; he was grief-stricken and wiser afterwards, according to Alice Bailey's account. He returned to his task, rounded up the mares and drove them through the gate.

Several themes stand out in this myth. Often we assume that what comes easily to our personality also comes easily to others. For Aries, courage, confidence, and facing the challenge of an exacting project comes easily. It therefore surprises Aries when others do not possess these same qualities. Poor Abderis! He probably lacked Hercules' quick reflexes as well as his fearlessness. Hercules said, "Here, I'll show you just once; watch carefully now. This is easy. Here's how to tether up the wild mares. Now just proceed and finish up here for me, will you?" Then he vanished and Abderis was trampled to death by the instincts. He had to start anew on the same old task as well as suffer the loss of his friend.

The second theme is pride, or exaltation of the Sun in Aries. It never occurs to Hercules that Abderis might fail, or that he, through Abderis, might fail. If we are too confident, things look too easy for us. We then have to start all over again on the same boring project rather than go on to the next. A leader has to be aware not only of his own limitations, but of his associates' shortcomings as well. Learning to anticipate, for others as well as him/herself, is important for Aries. Pride often "goes before a fall" or results in wasted energy.

Thoughtfulness seems the most important theme in the story. The saddest part of the Aries Quest for Hercules was not his partial failure in his task, but the loss of a friend. Even more important than being guided by Logos (conscious awareness or Hermes/Mercury) is incorporation of the Libran/Seventh House polarity. The independent Self, House One, lies across the wheel from the interdependent Other, or Eros, House Seven. Mars' independence opposes Venus/ Aphrodite's sense of reciprocity. Someone who has several planets in the First House is centered in the personality. Someone who has many planets in the Seventh is aware of the interdependency of his/ her own life with that of others.

Often after a loss, such as Hercules' loss of Abderis, the client with many First House planets or many planets in Aries will remark, "You know, I never realized how much work so and so did until s/he retired." Or, "I never realized how much my wife did for me till after her death. I guess I took her for granted. I always thought of myself as such a capable, independent person. I'm beginning now to see how dependent I really was, and I wish I had expressed more gratitude in the past. . . "

Jason's Quest

Jason's quest for the Solar treasure, the Golden Fleece and the throne that is his birthright, is not intended just for those of us with Sun, or Ascendant in Aries, but is the quest of everyman and every-woman for the Self, the divine birthright. In the myth, the fleece is the gift of the esoteric ruler, Hermes, and is sacred to Father Zeus (Jupiter). All of these implications surrounding the fleece reveal it to be a very important treasure. It is fragile and delicate and golden, or sun-colored. Sheeps' wool also has to it the meaning of innocence. Jason begins the quest innocent and enthusiastic, seeking the treasure in the outer world. Possessing the treasure, the Self would bring freedom, peace and contentment on the throne, and the responsibility to serve the kingdom with wisdom.

Jason, however, like most of us, is not aware in the beginning of how difficult the quest for the ephemeral fleece, the impossible, is to be. He sets sail with eleven trusted friends on behalf of his Uncle Peleus, from whom the fleece has been stolen, to retrieve it for Greece. He lands in Colchis and discovers that the rumors were correct, the fleece is there under guard. The King of Colchis has no intention of parting with such a treasure, but is too old to fight Jason personally and does not want to lose face. He instead offers Jason a task: "Do the impossible and I will certainly willingly yield the fleece." The task is to harness two fire-breathing bulls to a plow made of dragons' teeth and sow a field. However, as soon as Jason would finish sowing, the dragons' teeth would spring forth as warriors ready to kill him in defense of the fleece. Since this is an Aries myth, and Aries often attempts what others would consider impossible, Jason, participating in the archetype, says, "Of course. I can do it!"

The King of Colchis thought this task likely to discourage our young hero and cause him to lose interest in the quest. Of course, a hero does not appreciate delay, and Jason does have a temporary bout of faintheartedness. This is not a problem Mars can solve in its own style—independently. This is not a problem to be solved with sheer force of energy, enthusiasm, or bluffed confidence. It requires a strategist and some sort of skill or technique. It requires: 1) reflection and 2) outside help.

The heroic individualist needs an ally, and Jason prays to the Goddess Aphrodite. The Goddess of Love sends Cupid (Eros) with his bow and arrow, and he shoots first Jason and then Medea, the sorceress daughter of the King of Colchis. Medea suddenly appears in the field prepared to help the dejected Jason. They immediately fall in love.

Medea has a vial of oil which she pours on the dragons' teeth as Jason finishes his plowing so that the teeth will not become warriors. Together the two complete the task for the king and, theoretically, the Golden Fleece is now Jason's.

Life, however, is full of complications. Jason discovers that he still has to fight a pitched battle against Medea's father. By the end of the story, when Jason, his friends, and Medea sail off with the Golden Fleece, Medea feels that she has betrayed her family. Her aid to Jason has resulted in the deaths of father, brother, and cousins. Her use of soothing oil has resulted in violence.

In one of the biblical parables about the kingdom, the phrase, "and the violent shall bear it away" is used. Often, it seems the gates of heaven are stormed by courageous Fire signs. It seems to be a karmic pattern. There is anger and courage and a fight for the birthright—the Father's Throne, the gift of the inheritance (Golden Fleece), the Kingdom that is *mine* to possess. In living up to the expectations of Father Zeus (Jupiter), and often even exceeding them, the Fire sign accomplishes his quest.

What happens to the Hero when he reaches his natal place with Medea and the fleece? Does the tyrant, Peleus, surrender the throne with grace and resignation? No. There follows a subtle battle, a period of intrigue orchestrated by Medea, resulting in Peleus' death by subterfuge. Then, Cupid's love potion wears off for Jason and

Medea, while Glauce, the Princess of Corinth begins to appeal to him—and her kingdom becomes his new quest. As a Mars personality, Jason doesn't really want to settle down at home with Medea. He is restless; he wants to keep moving, keep questing.

When Jason tells Medea that she is expendable and he now loves the Princess of Corinth, she shrieks, "What? After all I've done for you—betrayed my family and my country—after all the blood on my hands because of helping you. . . !" And he says, logically, "Oh, no. I don't owe you anything, Medea. It's the Goddess who helped me. Aphrodite answered my prayer by sending you along and making you fall in love with me. It's Aphrodite who aided me, not some mere mortal sorceress!"

Thus, by the end of the story, Medea was feeling vindictive and vengeful. She was beginning her evolution into a Terrible Mother who would one day devour her own children.

Liz Greene, in *Astrology of Fate* (Aries, p. 179), makes the point that if we consider Medea his *anima*, his feminine side, Jason certainly did cast her off, abandon her. In his old age he probably became a tyrant no better than his Uncle Peleus. Certainly, he did not try to integrate his polarity (Libra/Eros) to settle down in a committed relationship and enjoy the peace of his kingdom and mete out justice to his subjects like a Libran. He used the gift of Hermes (the fleece), his esoteric ruler, and the magic sent by a Hermes person—Medea the sorceress. (Hermes, as we shall see later, rules sorcery, alchemy, magic and people who suddenly appear from nowhere, as Medea did. See Chapter 6, Virgo.) But he did not learn thoughtful discrimination or Hermes' wisdom in his old age. Yet, one thing about the myth was satisfying: he did honor Aphrodite. He admitted that she had helped him. He had needed someone else; he had prayed and she had responded. For an independent Mars person, that much expression of gratitude to another is significant.

At this point several Aries/Aries rising readers may be thinking, "This isn't me. I just can't relate to any of this. I married quite young, gladly sacrificing my independence to Eros. I have had a long and happy relationship. My spouse and I discuss everything. I listen attentively to what the spouse says and often change my mind to the spouse's opinion and act on it. I have a good many women friends and take their views as seriously as those of my men friends. I care a lot about whether my co-workers and my staff like me. I have had an office partner several years and we get along just fine. I don't wish I had a private office. I see myself as a 'team player' in the game of life. I enjoy coziness and constancy. People consider me pretty diplomatic, not at all abrasive. I wouldn't join the army on a bet; I'd sooner run off to a foreign country. I can't stand the military. I would never cut into a line using my elbows as a battering ram."

If you would respond in agreement with over half of these statements you may be living your life at the Libran polarity. If you are an Aries Sun sign person, you may have been born close to sunset on your birthday and have Libra, your polarity sign, rising. You may also have several planets in the Seventh House, and experience the Libran polarity that way. Or, Venus/Aphrodite may be in a strong House (1, 4, 7, or 10) with Mars in a weaker House. Your chart may be dominated by artistic/aesthetic aspects. Are you an Easter poster lamb, a gentle Libran/Aries? If so, you may be in a Libran career—library work (Libra is 'the Book'), fashion, the florist industry, architecture, photography, beauty products, and so forth. Many Taurus cusp Aries tend toward the Aphrodite/Libra polarity. Romance (Eros) is more important to them than sex; love is more important than lust.

You may still exhibit Aries restlessness—the tendency to dig up the seeds before your projects can germinate or sprout. Your relationship partner may complain that you are constantly returning from the grocery store with the items *you* need, but without the items the partner requested you to bring, when you yourself don't use them! These qualities tend to manifest in even the gentle Easter poster lamb. You will likely benefit from reading the questionnaire on being in touch with Mars, the mundane ruler, as Venus is probably stronger in your horoscope.

What, then, does the Aries lifetime mean in the long journey of the evolutionary soul? The Aries incarnation is so often seemingly spent in restless questing for adventure's sake, or for discovery's sake. So often it's a lifetime of going, doing, and taking action to prevail against mediocrity and sameness. It is, however, an important lifetime. In this lifetime the ego-identity crystallizes and learns to set boundaries, to develop a sense of separateness by developing the mind (Logos). The Sword of Discrimination, the intellect, learns to distinguish the opposites and quantify them. Time and space, for instance, are measured by the Aries mathematician, geographer, or astrologer. The intellect gathers together the dry facts and looks at them in new and different ways. Sometimes Aries scientists, establishing boundaries and categories, are able to come up with miraculous discoveries. They symbolically hit a hard rock with their magic wand (mind) and produce living water. But it is often alone on the quest, in the isolation of the laboratory, that the scientist makes the discovery, or that the archaeologist finds his treasure, far from the company of his fellow man.

Many Indians believe that the Divine created a diversity of life forms, including human ego-identities, in order to enjoy a variety of experiences over time. If so, what joy God must take in the Aries who lives life to the fullest, courageously, eagerly, exuberantly, and in total self-confidence. During the Aries lifetime, the soul experiences inner resourcefulness and self-reliance. Even those Arians who have integrated the Libran polarity through a long and happy marriage never seem to lose their sense of selfhood, of individuality. Though they are thoughtful, and use the "we" rather than the more selfish "I" vocabulary, there is still an inner sense of reserve about them. Their souls are their own. If the partner puts Aries down or threatens his self-esteem, Aries, barring a stellium in the Seventh House, or a merging Ascendant/Moon sign, is quickly on his way to a more positive environment. Not every Aries, by the end of the lifetime, is aware that the I AM is the Self, but nearly every Aries/Aries rising, Angular Mars personality has pride in, and respect for, the uniqueness of his ego-personality.

Aries seems to correspond to the *separatio* phase of the inner alchemical process. In *Anatomy of the Psyche*, the *separatio* chapter, Edward Edinger discusses the importance of this alchemical stage of establishing boundaries. In this phase, the ego sees itself not just as God's heir and son, but as the only child of the Divine, and values its own uniqueness. In this phase, Logos, the intellect, constantly defines and compares, and sets limits. This is the sharpening of logic, or of the Sword of Discrimination, which Edinger calls "the cutter." It quantifies and measures the dual worlds of time and space with clocks, compasses and other tools, and takes refuge in facts, limits, categories, and boundaries. It develops an independent perspective which Edinger compares to the line in Robert Frost's poem, "Mending Walls." "Good fences make good neighbors." Here, the bounds of Logos are opposite the merging of Eros, whose perspective is, in the same poem, "something there is that does not love a Wall." Logos, or *separatio*, then, is the cutter or the sword, while Eros or *conjunctio* is the glue. The glue is ruled by Aphrodite, mother of Eros (Cupid). Aries tends to move toward the *conjunctio*, or towards integrating the feeling function through marriage. In his/her earlier years s/he may have reclusively remained in his/her ivory tower, laboratory, or monastery. S/he might have been a traveler restlessly wandering in the outer world instead of in his/her own head. But the advent of the Taurus progression inclines him/her towards Aphrodite, and towards the anima (or in the case of Aries women, the animus, the wise old man—the mentor in religious life, business, academia, or the marriage mate).

If during this cycle progressed Venus contacts the Sun, or the Aries Ascendant, romance is usually not far behind. For the Aries woman, this motion of progressed Venus may not be as important. Her Mars progressing towards natal Venus though may have the same effect. Or the same can be felt with natal Mars or Venus changing from retrograde motion to direct. The "cutting edge" of Logos may develop pliancy and yield to the "glue" of Eros.

The Taurus progression lasts 30 years. Aries' impatience and impulsiveness wanes, and in some cases, ambition seems to wane. Taurus is a sign that builds slowly, and can be complacent. Many Aries who enter this progression in their late twenties lose some of their interest in exercise, for instance, and develop a Venusian taste for fancy and fattening desserts. Yet, in most cases they adjust to the energy and realize they feel better when they're physically active. Most tend to return to running, or some other exercise—often solitary, rather than a team sport. A natal Aries has a very strong desire nature, but he fixes or focuses it in Taurus. Things of substance (Earth) like property or stability in relationships, as well as loyalty and constancy and comfort, begin to appeal more. This does not happen overnight, of course, but gradually, over the years. Many Aries who were born in the early degrees of the sign appear to be confirmed bachelors but marry shortly after the Sun enters Taurus, to the surprise of their parents and friends. The stability of the Fixed sign can be a real asset to the achievement of Mars' goals. Often, it is important to remind the Aries client to attune to the things he considers positive about Taurus, such as perseverance and the ability to build solidly in many areas of life, otherwise some of the Taurean inertia may catch him/her unaware. In the first few years of a new progression, we always need to look at the strengths and weaknesses of the sign we're entering and be on the alert.

In reading natal charts, I have found that clients whose cutters (Mercuries) are retrograde tend to turn the blade in upon themselves and analyze their every thought, feeling, possible motive, so that the ego cuts and bleeds. This endless self-analysis does not further growth in self-esteem. Developing the feeling planets helps people with retrograde Mercury, for Eros, Edinger tells us, is also the glue that patches the poor, wounded ego. (*Anatomy of the Psyche, separatio.*) Aries is one of the signs that goes at life through the head, and frequently benefits from its contacts to the heart planets in the chart. In many charts where Mars and Mercury are retrograde (the mundane and esoteric rulers of the head, Aries) medical problems may develop as a result of emotions which are repressed and never released into the outer world. The head does too much filtering. In the case of Mars retrograde, Aries/ Aries rising often turns his/her anger and frustrations against himself/herself, rather than appropriately confronting the people in the outer world directly about issues that really bother him. I have often connected retrograde Mars, afflicted, to the migraine headache in charts of Aries Sun sign people. The instincts and feelings, as well as the intellect, deserve to be honored.

One change I've noticed in my battering ram clients after ten years of progressed Sun in Taurus is a dwindling of the vehemency with which they formerly argued politics or religion. Mars, ruler of the natal Sun, loves a good fight, but Venus, ruler of the progressed Sun, has more finesse in social gatherings and has learned when to keep quiet, or be diplomatic. I often think of Eris, the Goddess of Discord, sister of Ares. She once took a golden apple, labelled it "the fairest of all," and threw it into the midst of a Mt. Olympus wedding. The apple was so lovely that the goddesses decided it simply had to be awarded to the fairest, which meant that a beauty contest had to be held and the goddesses compared to one another. Soon they were at odds. Poor Paris had to judge them. He got his payment in the form of Helen of Troy and war was the final result. We all know people like Eris, those with Mercury/Mars afflictions who can't wait to sow discord. Well, I note in the Taurus progression, the peace-maker side of Venus comes through and many Eris-like Aries tend to put away their apples, cease stirring things up, and try to keep things harmonious. "Make peace, not war" is one message Venus tries to give Mars/Aries children in this progression. Many of them seem to mellow by the end of the 30-year cycle.

After Aries concludes his journey through Taurus, the 30-year cycle of Gemini begins. Because Gemini is ruled by Mercury, planet of logic and facts, this cycle may enhance his attunement to Athene, Goddess of Wisdom. The Taurus period of groundedness (house-holdership, obligations to employer) and responsibility has helped stabilize Aries and s/he is now ready to explore new facets of his personality and talents in this highly versatile progression. Aries people enter Gemini anywhere from their forties to their sixties, and nearly all of them see it as an exhilarating fresh start—the beginning of a cycle less boring than the Taurus progression.

The restlessness of Gemini tugs at the natal Aries horoscope. Many plan to relocate near a child or a grandchild or in a warmer part of the country. This is a cycle to look forward to, a new adventure. While their contemporaries in the other eleven signs complain of aches and pains, Aries, who has kept him/herself in good shape, thinks, "What old fogies! I feel quite young, actually!" Some experience Gemini at the more mundane level and pursue learning in the *outer* world—reading about Age of Aquarius scientific discoveries (from the space program to the heart transplant) and discussing them. Others turn inward and read of explorations in consciousness, afterlife experiences, techniques for realization of the Self. Gemini flexibility enables Aries to let go of any Taurean tendencies to be stuck and helps Aries to adjust to new circumstances drawing upon his natal positive thinking. Sometimes Aries attempts to live with a brother or sister in this cycle (Gemini refers to siblings) but it usually does not work out as Aries is such an independent personality. Those Aries who have long been truth-seekers are often regarded as Wise Old Men or Wise Athenes by the young people around them in the community.

Though I know very few Aries who have progressed into Cancer—they are quite old by then—a few generalizations can be made. Traits quite uncharacteristic of Aries manifest in the personality—moodiness, nostalgia, concentration on the past, hypersensitivity to slights. These new qualities really confuse friends and family members who remember Aries as so outspoken and direct. "We used to be able to say *anything* to Uncle Harry. We had such interesting intellectual arguments. Now he's so sensitive! What on earth has happened?" Or the spouse will say, "You've never been romantic in your life! Why are you suddenly remembering songs from our courtship days 50 years ago?"

Many Aries seem to develop a particularly strong attachment to family members and cling to the body itself in the last few years of their lives. Attachment is a major issue in this sign. Often, for instance, Aries' spouse will observe, "S/he used to be so independent, but now s/he seems so dependent! I wonder what will happen if I die first? Before it always seemed *I* was the dependent person. What would I do if I outlived my Aries?" Cancer, however, seems an appropriate sign in which to conclude life's journey. In Plato's system of philosophy, Cancer was Mother Earth, to which our earthly remains returned, yet she was also the Great Lunar Goddess who would give us our new, stronger, healthier form! Platonists believed that souls journeyed to the Moon, received new forms and then dropped back to Earth to fulfill their remaining desires, taking on new personalities as they dropped through the zodiac along the ecliptic on their way back.

The Aries lifetime is likely to be valorous and therefore, in the case of many spiritual seekers, victorious in the end. Hope springs eternal in this Fire sign! Attitude is paramount for the Spiritual Seeker, and Aries' optimistic spirit is infectious. Aries has the power to motivate and inspire others to believe in themselves, to believe that there is light at the end of the tunnel, to carry on and move forward even in life's darkest moments.

Questionnaire

How does the Aries archetype express itself? Though this relates particularly to those with the Sun in Aries or Aries rising, anyone could apply this series of questions to the house where his/her Mars is located or the house which has Aries (or Aries intercepted) on the cusp. The answers to these questions will indicate how in touch the reader is with his/her Mars, his God of War, his Aries instincts.

1. My communication style is direct and forceful.
   a. Usually.
   b. Most of the time.
   c. Seldom.

2. I usually take the initiative, suggest the project, consider it my own, and act on it with enthusiasm.
   a. 80-100% of the time.
   b. 50-80% of the time.
   c. 25% or less of the time.

3. I fail to see the value of such negative virtues as humility, patience, diplomacy, prudence, and obedience to the rule book.
   a. Most of the time.
   b. 50% of the time.
   c. 25% of the time or less.

4. Among my better qualities I include optimism, self-esteem, courage, vitality, and the ability to motivate others.
   a. Usually.
   b. About 50% of the time.
   c. 25% or less of the time.

5. Among my negative qualities I would probably list rashness. I sometimes move impulsively on a new idea and take undue risks. For instance, if I had waited a few days I probably would not have bought a certain stock, car, or time-share apartment, but I didn't wait. I make impulsive decisions.

    a. 80% of the time or more.
    b. 50% of the time.
    c. 25% of the time or less.

6. My greatest fear is
    a. losing my independence.
    b. bankruptcy.
    c. loss of my spouse.

7. The greatest obstacle to my success comes from
    a. my competitors and/or circumstances beyond my control.
    b. within myself.

8. I feel the weakest part of my body, the part that causes me the most trouble, is
    a. Head (migraine or other headaches, sinus problems, eye problems).
    b. The throat area (thyroid, loss of voice, sore throat).
    c. The kidneys, or lower back pain.

9. Important to my life are such Mars activities as sports, sex, fast cars, and the latest in mechanical equipment.
    a. Very important.
    b. Moderately important.
    c. Not important at all.

10. I consider myself accident prone. I bump my head
    a. seldom.
    b. more often.
    c. often.

    Those who have scored five or more (a) answers are highly in touch with their instincts. Those who have scored five or more (c) answers are moving to the polar extremity on the instinctual level. Their Mars is not allowed to express itself properly. One symptom of a frustrated Mars is that a person tends to "attract" accidents. Those who answered (c) on question 10 should review their natal Mars. Is it in the Twelfth House? Is it retrograde? Is it intercepted? It is important for them to work consciously with the planets aspecting natal Mars to help Mars express its positive instincts—courage, confidence, self-esteem, direct communication, vitality, assertiveness.

Where is the balance point between Aries and Libra? How does the Aries integrate Self and Other? Though this relates particularly to those with Sun in Aries or Aries rising, all of us have Mars and Venus *somewhere* in our horoscope. Many of us have planets in the First or Seventh House. For all of us the polarity from Aries to Libra involves learning to relate to others without losing our sense of self.

1. My spouse says I only appear to listen when he or she communicates an opinion on a joint decision matter, that I appear to agree with my spouse but then the next week I do exactly what I want as if we had never had the discussion. I hear this
   a. never.
   b. half the time.
   c. most of the time.

2. When I stop at the store for an item I need myself I remember my spouse mentioning that he or she needed an item which I personally *never* use. I purchase the item for my spouse
   a. 25% of the time or less.
   b. about 50% of the time.
   c. 80—100% of the time.

3. Competition is a lot more important than cooperation!
   a. 25% of the time or less.
   b. 50% of the time.
   c. 80% of the time or more.

4. Both at home and at work others find my temper hard to take, but in my opinion it's much better to flare up and clear the air than to hold a grudge.
   a. Seldom to never.
   b. About half the time.
   c. Almost always.

5. I hate to be dependent on others. It's so much faster and easier to "go it alone." This is true
   a. about 25% of the time.
   b. about 50 % of the time.

c. most of the time.

Those who have scored three or more (b) answers are doing a good job with personality integration on the Aries/Libra or Self/ Other polarity. Those who have three or more (c) answers need to work more consciously on developing natal Venus in their horoscopes. Those who have three or more (a) answers may be out of balance in the other direction (weak or undeveloped Mars). Study both planets in the natal chart. Is there an aspect between them? Which one is stronger by House position, or location in its sign of rulership or exaltation? Is either of them retrograde, intercepted, in fall, or in detriment? Aspects to the weaker planet can point the way to integration.

What does it mean to be an Esoteric Aries? How does Aries integrate Mercury into the personality? Not every Aries will have an aspect between Mercury and Mars but every Aries will have Mercury somewhere in his or her chart. The answers to the following questions will indicate the extent to which Aries is in touch with Mercury, his or her esoteric ruler. Remember that Mercury refers not only to the thinking function but also to thoughtfulness.

1. I see the importance of reflection, getting all the facts, and considering the possible results of each alternative before making my decision and taking action.
   a. Almost always.
   b. 50% of the time.
   c. Hardly ever.

2. I consider myself a thoughtful person. I take others' opinions into consideration before making a decision that affects them.
   a. Almost always.
   b. Sometimes.
   c. Hardly ever.

3. I work in an occupation that requires patience and precision such as technical work, teaching, sculpting, or one of the arts.
   a. True.
   b. I would like to.
   c. False.

4. I make an effort to keep up with the latest information in my field. I read or attend schools and seminars
   a. whenever I have the opportunity.
   b. sometimes.
   c. not if I can get out of it.

5. My Aries' sense of adventure is fulfilled in a field that involves scientific research and discovery.
   a. True.
   b. No, but I would like it to be.
   c. False.

Those who have scored three or more (a) answers are in touch with the esoteric ruler. Those who scored three or more (b) answers need to work more at integrating Mercury according to its house location in their natal chart—they need to stop, think, and plan before taking action through the House where Mercury resides. Self-help books and seminars dealing with the House where Mercury resides are often helpful. Those who scored three or more (c) answers may lack an aspect between Mercury and Mars. Mercury may also be intercepted, in fall, or in detriment. To integrate the esoteric ruler objectivity can be developed through study of the sciences and psychology. Objectivity and discrimination are valuable keys to developing and integrating the esoteric ruler.

References

Alice Bailey, *Esoteric Astrology*, Lucis Publishing Company, New York, 1976

Alice Bailey, *Labours of Hercules*, Lucis Publishing Company, New York, 1974

Joseph Campbell, *The Hero with a Thousand Faces*, Princeton University Press, New York, 1968

Joseph Campbell, *Occidental Mythology*, Penguin Books, New York, 1982

Edward Edinger, *Anatomy of the Psyche*, "Separatio," Open Court, La Salle, 1985

Edward Edinger, *Ego and Archetype*, G.P. Putnam's Sons, New York, 1972

Michael Grant, *Myths of the Greeks and Romans*, Mentor-New American Library, New York, 1962

Liz Greene, *The Astrology of Fate*, Sam Weiser, Inc., York Beach, 1984

Edith Hamilton, *Mythology*, "The Quest for the Golden Fleece," Mentor Books, New York, 1969

Joseph L. Henderson, "Ancient Myths and Modern Man-Heroes and Hero Makers," in C.G. Jung (ed.), *Man and His Symbols*, Doubleday and Co., Garden City, 1969

James Hillman, "Ananke and Athene," in *Facing the Gods*, Spring Publications Inc., Irving, 1980

Homer, *Iliad* (Book I), "Athene Counsels Achilles," Penguin Books, New York, 1982

Homer, *Iliad* (Book XV), "Ares and Athene," Penguin Books, 1982

Homer, *The Odyssey* (Book I), "Athene Visits Telemachus," Penguin Books, New York, 1978

Jolande Jacobi, *The Way of Individuation*, Harcourt Brace and World, New York, 1967

C.G. Jung, *The Integration of the Personality*, Kegan Paul Trench Trubner and Co. Ltd., London, 1948

C.G. Jung, *Symbols of Transformation*, "The Origin of the Hero," Princeton University Press, Princeton, 1967

Karolyi Kerenyi, *The Heroes of the Greeks*, H.L. Rose translator,

Thames and Hudson, London, 1959

F.R.S. Raglan, *The Hero: A Study in Myth, Tradition and Drama*, Methuen, London, 1936

Jean Shinoda-Bolen, *Goddesses in Everywoman*, "Athena," Harper and Row, San Francisco, 1984

2 TAURUS:
The Search for Value and Meaning

As symbols for the Age of Taurus we have the bull, the goddess, and the Buddha. Venus/Aphrodite is the mundane ruler and Vulcan/Hephaestus the esoteric. A good source for bull and lunar goddess symbolism is Joseph Campbell, *Primitive Mythology* (pages 37 and following). Campbell provides illustrations of the Cretan Goddess and her bull-consort. He mentions Europa and the bull in mainland Greece, Inanna and her bull in Sumeria, and of course, Parsiphae, the wife of King Minos, falling in love with Poseidon's Heavenly Bull in Crete. The Minoan story of the Minotaur in the maze is perhaps the most famous myth of the goddess and her fertility consort. Campbell mentions that "the Taurean corner of the world" extended in the early to middle Bronze Age from the Indus Valley in India through Iran, to Crete and Mycenae on mainland Greece and as far west as Stonehenge in England.

The connection between bull and goddess is very important for the astrologer because the glyph for Taurus (♉) is composed of a round bull's head with an upside-down crescent Moon on top. There is a double-feminine influence in Taurus—the mundane ruler is Venus and the Moon is exalted in the sign. With the double-feminine influence we have the receptivity of the Earth Mother herself which Isabel Hickey has described as, "the freshly plowed earth of springtime, ready for the seed." Passive, patient, and placid, Taurus earth is fertile and fecund sexuality. As the mundane, instinctual ruler of Taurus, Venus, the principle of attraction, has a strong physical magnetism. As Linda Goodman has said in *Sun Signs*, "Taurus," this energy is not sexually aggressive but prefers to attract others rather than pursue them. Taurus is associated with biological reproduction and other types of creativity. This association of Taurus with the feminine may seem odd to us in the Twentieth Century. Today when we think of bulls, our first associations are likely to be masculine. We tend to think of stud bulls and macho bullfighters. In our times the bull has a definite masculine authority that is no longer associated with the Mother.

In South India, the Tanjor Temple has a giant statue of Nandi the Bull, who is now known as vehicle of the male divinity, Lord Shiva. In pre-Aryan times, the Age of Taurus, Nandi was consort to Sati, goddess of married love and loyalty. His Tanjor statue, like many contemporary Bronze Age bull statues, has a sweet expression—gentle and almost feminine. The temple is filled with phallic-shaped *lingas*, symbols of fertility and biological creativity. Nandi is the masculine side of the Earth Mother. Goddess Durga, riding her lion-vehicle, chased and put to death a wild bull in ritual sacrifice to assure the Earth's fertility. The rites on bull sacrifice or bull-baiting in India are mentioned in the *Markandaya Purana* and *Chandi Purana*. Some of the illustrated editions of the purana stories reproduce in small scale the striking wall paintings of Goddess Durga, the dark phase of the Moon, astride her ferocious lioness, in pursuit of the bull who is to be the ritual sacrifice. On the mundane level, this sacrifice of a powerful, sexually potent animal was intended to fertilize Mother Earth with his blood for the next planting season. Spiritually, this issue of the Age of Taurus sacrifice has continued down to the present to be pertinent for seekers on the Taurus/Scorpio axis. Do they try to kill their desires, especially their sexual desires, in a monastery? Must they be celibate in order to get in touch with their Taurean creativity? Must they go to the extreme of the Scorpio polarity recluse who sublimates his energy entirely into his work? Or can they please God and also be artistically creative, "whole" people in the social scene to which Venus/Aphrodite, ruler of Taurus, calls them? Perhaps the Cretans, with their view of "riding" or taming the physical Bull of the Mother, the body and its instincts, had the right idea. Zen Buddhists, with their approach to the ox or Bull of the Mother, had a similar approach and also, like the Cretans and the Persians, possessed techniques for controlling the bull.

The highest Age of Taurus mythology is perhaps that of Lord Krishna and the gopis, the cow maidens of North India. In *Gnostic Circle*, Patrizia Norelli-Bachelet states that Krishna was the Avatar (Messiah) of the Age of Taurus in India. In art and myth he was con-

stantly surrounded by young women who yearned for the sound of his flute as the soul longs for realization of the Divine or Spirit. The constancy and loyalty, as well as the receptivity of the gopis seem characteristic of the Moon in Taurus ideal, its symbolic exaltation. The Moon reflects the light of the Sun, and the gopis' souls reflected Spirit, Lord Krishna. Though so many Moon in Taurus individuals reflect the Taurean concern for emotional and financial security in their desire nature and in their behavior, there are a few who disdain the world and seek only to please the Divine, as the gopis did. There are many others whose lunar nature reflects the inertia, or as the Hindus call it, the *tamas* of Taurus. They sacrifice the bull of their own creative talents to the schedules and routines of others for the first half of their lifetime. Then, they begin to feel vaguely dissatisfied. They have given much of themselves through their nurturing professions, often in healing or learning environments, or through support, either financial or moral, to family members. Often at mid-life Moon in Taurus as well as Sun in Taurus/Taurus rising people feel quite disappointed that little effort, over the years, went into the development of their own creative, psychic or spiritual talents. "Who gave *me* support for *my* gifts?" is too often the question. "Did you ask them for any?" is, of course, part of the answer. There is a definite inertia in Taurus, the sign of Ferdinand the Bull, quietly grazing away as the years pass. Yet, Taurus feels frustrated, unappreciated, sometimes even unnoticed by those to whom he has given so much and to whom he is so attached. (Moon in Taurus is a doubling of attachment to people, places, and things, because the Moon in Taurus reflects the qualities of the I POSSESS nature.)

Listening to the complaints of Taureans over the years who at mid-life experience the outer planets (especially Saturn, or Father Time) that oppose Taurus and dwell upon "what might have been," I am reminded of the Chinese saying, "the Moon does not know its own beauty." Serving others seems part of the karma of Earth signs for the first half of the lifetime. Most Moon in Taurus people do it well. But as the oppositions occur from that Scorpio introverted/introspective polarity, Taurus is likely to ask, "To what have I sacrificed the bull of my desires? of my personal life? or of my creativity?" The social energy of Aphrodite that took them into the extroverted, active world wanes and the Plutonic, Scorpionic, reclusive energy and passion pulls them inward. They need fewer people and want to spend more time alone. The Taurean Moon person, in particular, wants to discover his or her own beauty in relationship with one other person, or sometimes, totally alone on the current Pluto/Neptune withdrawal transits. "For everything there is a season under heaven." This is so often demonstrated watching the Taurus/Scorpio individuals swing back and forth from amassing possessions, to renunciation, to collecting, and so forth.

The psychic, or spiritual meaning of the Taurus bull, and especially of the Moon Goddess and the bull, comes through the association of the Apis bull of Egypt with prophecy. The Bronze Age civilization of the Nile Valley in Egypt is very similar to that of the Indus Valley in India, Stonehenge in England or the Minoan culture of Crete. The Goddess reigned supreme over the fields with her creatively potent consort, the bull. Around 1600 B.C. in Egypt the Egyptians worshipped a bull said to have been born at midnight in the dark of the Moon (New Moon phase), and therefore is represented artistically as having a crescent Moon between his horns. The actual Apis bull used for fertility rites was chosen because he had a crescent Moon on his flank. He was black like the dark of the Moon. Sometimes he had an eagle shape on one flank. Some sources say the lunar Apis bull was sacrificed and others say he died of old age, but all agree that after his death he became known as resurrected Osiris. This very special bull was considered an oracle. If he licked an astronomer's clothing, for instance, the man's death was said to be not far away. Thus, symbolically there was a strong connection between the lunar bull and the gift of prophecy.

Many Taurus Moon people have psychic gifts as well. Some, with no prior study whatsoever, can let their eyes go out of focus and see colored auras around others, even around animals. One man asked me, "Couldn't *anyone* do that if s/he tried?" Possibly anyone could develop the skill through long practice of a technique, but not spontaneously, from childhood, whenever he felt like it. Thus, in Taurus Moon people there is a lot of psychic talent as well as spiritual receptivity, devotional potential to be opened and artistic ability latent in Taurus, Taurus Moon and Taurus rising. However, first Taurus must sacrifice his/her inner insecurities and inhibitions and believe in his/her own talent without the constant reassurance of some other human being to encourage him/her. It helps a great deal when childhood has been a positive experience—when Mother (symbolically, the ideal exalted Taurean Lunar Goddess) has believed in and encouraged the gifts of the Taurean child. If this has not been the case, very likely a Hephaestian cycle of inner work is necessary, developing the person's ability to believe in his lunar intuitive and creative, feminine gifts, before s/he can actualize his/her talents. This will be discussed below in terms of Hephaestus' role as esoteric ruler.

It's interesting that later, in the patriarchal Age of Heroes, even the solar bull, Amen-Ra, an incarnation of the sun god, was known as "the bull of his mother." We have, for instance, this lovely hymn:

... to Amen-Ra, the bull in Heliopolis
who presides over all the gods,
beneficent god, beloved one,
the giver of the warmth of life to all beautiful cattle.

Hail to thee, Amen-Ra,
Lord of the thrones of. . . Thebes
Bull of his mother,*
Chief of his fields. . .
Lord of the sky,
eldest son of the earth,
lord of the things which exist,
establisher of things
establisher of all things.

* (emphasis added)

The bull was thus symbolic of fertility and strength, which in Egypt and elsewhere eventually became associated with kingship and the masculine; but in the early Bronze Age he was either the consort of the Goddess, or the Bull of his Mother, and stood with her in art just as he did in the Cretan frescoes (Jack R. Conrad, *The Horn and the Sword*, pages 82-83). The Moon and Aphrodite (dual feminine energy) seem to dominate the Bronze Age worldwide.

One interesting thing about the Taurean civilizations—there is a Venus presence in the arts, from the grace and beauty of the frescoes in Crete and Mycenae to the lines of the palace in Knossos. The gold work in the jewelry from Crete in the Athens Historical Museum has a real Venusian delicacy, a feminine feeling. There are no hordes of warriors (heroes on horseback) riding roughshod in the Age of Taurus. The countryside is relatively quiet. The island of Crete, for instance, is isolated and free of invaders, except of course, from those invaders beneath the surface—volcanoes and earthquakes. It was an earthquake that supposedly devastated the palace of King Minos (the site of the Minotaur myth). Legend had it that Vulcan, or Hephaestus, the ugly, lame smith at his forge beneath the Earth, destroyed the comfortable world that belonged to the Goddess and her bull in Crete. The Minotaur-monster is a sort of Vulcan image, too. The ugly beast is partially divine and must not be slain; he must be left alone to stamp his hooves in his labyrinthine prison and shake the earth with his strength. Nikos Kazantzakis, author of *The Life of St. Francis*, says in his last book, *Report to Greco*, that as a child in Crete, when there would be a tremor underground and he would be frightened, a relative would tell him very seriously, "It's the Minotaur. It's Minos' bull stamping and snorting under the earth." The myth lives on in his native land.

Aphrodite was married by Zeus to Hephaestus/Vulcan—Beauty married to the Beast. The mundane ruler of Taurus married to the esoteric. The dwarf god whose hammer brings abrupt change (even chaos) married to the goddess of harmony, peace, and order. Ask any Taurean how s/he would feel if there were an earthquake that devastated his home and all his "collectibles"—his beautiful possessions. The exalted Moon in Taurus collector would likely respond more vehemently than Sun in Taurus from a deeper, more emotional attachment to comfort, security, and beauty. Sudden destruction of one's structures, so carefully and solidly built, feeling them all pulled down around him/her—this is Vulcan's impact on Taurus.

Hephaestus works beneath the surface of the career of the Taurean "good provider" businessman. An astrologer often meets a Taurus man for the first time when the boss has pressed early retirement upon him or when bankruptcy looms ahead. Vulcan has been at work.

If we look on the materialistic/mundane side of Aphrodite ruling the Earth sign Taurus we do see some decadence, rather like the decadence of the last stages of Bronze Age art in Crete—the ladies wearing luxurious jewelry and rich fabrics at the Knossos Court, as depicted in the frescoes. Sometimes complacency in the successful Taurus almost seems to invite Vulcan to do his work against the forces of inertia. The structure seems to collapse suddenly from within. And the Taurean good provider feels emotionally devastated. Aphrodite is a very emotional ruler.

One such Taurean man said, "I don't understand it. My wife met an even more affluent man at the country club and wants to leave me for him. She thinks I neglect her to make money. She doesn't seem to understand that I work all those long hours building a business for her and the children so they can have a real quality life, the best of everything that money can buy. Just when I finally think I've achieved that for my family I've lost them, for reasons I can't figure out. I'm stunned!"

Aphrodite is a goddess that likes quality—the best. The difficulty comes for Taureans in understanding what quality means. If the quest on the mundane level takes all of their resources of time and energy, then there's not much left of themselves to give; Vulcan erupts on some transit to Venus/Aphrodite and threatens the security of Taurus' relationships, whether personal or financial.

The esoteric ruler is very Scorpionic about his beneath the surface explosions. His power to cause turbulent change is reminiscent of the polar extremity sign. Both Taurus and Scorpio have to do with resources, inner as well as material, and with resourcefulness. The issue then becomes whether or not a Fixed Earth person can keep his or her structures flexible enough to withstand Vulcan's changes. Can he or she design a life like the architects design buildings for the San Andreas Fault zone—so that the buildings sway from side to side with the quake? Can Taurus deal with the complacent, lazy, satisfied-to-be-comfortable side of Aphrodite, once he or she thinks, "I've got it made"? Can the Taurean work on the inner quality of life as well as the material/outer quality? These are some pertinent questions. Venus as ruler of the Second House in the natural zodiac, the house of personal values, needs satisfaction intrinsically, as well as in the outer, material world.

Another question, more for Moon in Taurus individuals, would be: Do my possessions own me? Can I take a long trip without worrying about them? Could I sublet my house to a stranger if my company sent me to the Mideast for six months? Am I free or am I bound to the material world? Am I a dependent personality? Do I possessively hold on to my boyfriend or to my children instead of giving them freedom to make their own mistakes in life? If we think of Taurus as *prima materia* (prime matter or modelling clay) and the Moon as form (which Plato called her), we may have the impression of a double dose of receptivity in the Taurus Moon. We may find a support person who becomes dependent on the other or others and whose clinging dependency may alienate the other and may cause claus-

trophobia.

Many of these same questions involving possessiveness, dependency relationships and not allowing others sufficient freedom would apply to individuals with Taurus rising. In the case of Mars ruled Aries, there was a spontaneous rushing forth of energy. The fiery hero faced direct confrontation on the quest and enjoyed it. But Taurus, ruled by Aphrodite, reflects her gentler, quieter, more feminine influence. Taurus communicates displeasure indirectly. Aphrodite does not want to make a scene—how rude and inharmonious that would be. We will see this again when we meet her in Libra.

You may have read Linda Goodman's *Sun Signs*, in which she discusses the Taurean boss. In that book, the Taurean boss hires a new employee who likes to take two hour lunches. He looks sullen for a few months but doesn't say anything. The new employee is supposed to notice his look of displeasure but does not, and continues to do this. She also becomes careless about proofreading her typing. One day, she finds him in front of her desk tossing papers about, shouting, stamping his feet like the Minotaur. After he fires her and she's packing the contents of her desk, she shakes her head in bewilderment and says, "Why didn't he say these things bothered him? Yikes! How was I s'posed to know? I mean, who'd have thought he cared?" "Beware the anger of a patient man," says the proverb. A volcano does not erupt often; it builds up over the years and then explodes. This is often how Taurean anger manifests as well.

Here Taureans could learn from the ruler of their polar-extremity sign, Scorpio. Scorpios are often indirect communicators, too. But a Scorpio in charge will usually let you see his or her Mars (temper) if you are late *every* day to work. As with all the signs, the more conscious the Taurean, the more he or she strives to integrate the polarity sign and to work consciously with the power of the esoteric ruler, the better! If Taurus is consciously attuned to Vulcan/Hephaestus then s/he's less likely to explode from beneath the surface, exhibiting the rage of a mad bull. How then can Taurus attune to the positive qualities of Hephaestus?

Through sacrificing the bull of attachment and removing the veils of Goddess Inanna, we leave behind the dry, parched Earth (Taurus) as Inanna did to enter the mysterious unknown, the deep Scorpionic waters of the unconscious. Often bankruptcy, divorce, or the "empty nest feeling" as the last child leaves home to marry (the denial of a strong desire by the outer world on a Volcanic-like transit) will precipitate Taurus' descent into the Scorpionic depths. Sylvia Brinton Perera put it well in *Descent of the Goddess* when she said that energy released from one part of the psyche by releasing an outward form—an attachment—will be liberated and will eventually re-emerge in another part of the psyche. Life is not a fixed or stationary thing but a process of constant change and growth.

It is frightening to let go of the old persona. "I am a much needed mother of five." "I am a bank president." "I was soon to be an M.D. or Ph.D." The sacrifice, however, removed Taurus from the peg where he or she was stuck (fixed) Inanna-like in the unconscious. When after rest and relaxation in the quiet introverted cycle—on transit of Neptune or Pluto—the Taurean Inanna comes out into the daylight again, and there is no telling what creative powers will be his or hers.

Inanna went to the underworld to observe the sacrifice of a bull and was accompanied by several scorpions, so the myth seems to accord well with integration of this polarity, in its social and reclusive cycles—its concentration upon matter and upon spirit at different times during the course of life. For Inanna, the bull seems to have served as scapegoat for her unfulfilled desires. She had wanted to marry someone other than the Sun God's choice for her, but acquiesced to his masculine decision without objection. She sacrificed her own feelings, intuition, and values; this required the descent and the re-energizing and healing. Taureans who follow the voice of the Sun God—the rational mind—at the expense of their subjective values, feelings, and intuitions are seldom happy. This is a double-feminine sign.

The Bull of Inanna, as one of my astrology students put it, is also "the balls of Inanna"—her courage, her decisiveness, her anger, her ability to fight back at life. Impaled on a peg (phallic symbol), she seems to have recovered her fight. I often hear of passive-type Taureans stuck in a negative cycle who have violent dreams, or dreams of taking off their clothes—their old personas—so that all can see them as they are. In the outer world, too, Taurean complacency is often shattered after such a dream series begins. The final result of the Scorpionic death and rebirth cycle is usually positive, however, and sometimes dramatically so, when Taurus has long been in a negative, complaining, *tamasic* state.

How, then, can Taurus consciously attune to the *positive* qualities of Vulcan/Hephaestus? How can Taurus avoid the volcanic blow-ups in the outer world that frustrated desires attract? In *Symbols of the Transformation*, C.G. Jung tells us that Hephaestus is an archetypal Wise Old Man. Like Inanna, however, his wisdom came through a long and painful process, a descent into the Underworld, during which he let go of a good deal of bitterness, resentment, and anger. (It is interesting that the goddess, the feminine, first had to get in touch with these feelings—admit she had them—whereas the masculine god revelled in these emotions—brooded over them quite consciously—in the beginning of the story.)

Hephaestus did not have a happy childhood. At the time of his birth, Hera, his mother, was furious with Zeus, her husband. Zeus had proceeded to sire a child without any help from Hera or for that matter, womankind at all. Athene had been delivered from his head. Hera decided that if women were not necessary to Zeus, men would not be necessary to her either. She gave birth to Hephaestus by parthenogenesis. Much to her dismay, however, he did not turn out as well as Zeus' child, Athene. Hephaestus was a very ugly dwarf with crooked feet. Hera threw him from Mt. Olympus in horror and went on her way. Hephaestus brooded in the underworld. Why was he an orphan when everyone else had parents, or at least a parent, who loved them? He hated Hera with all his strength. He tried to create useful objects for awhile, then he tried to create artistic objects, but he was blocked by his own negative emotions. He felt his deformity too strongly to believe he had talent, and the gods in the underworld avoided him as much for his melancholy disposition as for his appearance.

In the underworld he did make a few women friends, for his was a feminine spirit. He was a Mother's son, just as Athene was a Father's daughter. He belonged in the creative unconscious. For a long time, though he lived in the creative underworld, he could not recognize the source of creativity within himself, within his own soul. In his dark and melancholy state he plotted revenge upon his mother. He would let her know what it felt like to be abandoned. He fashioned a throne for her and when she sat in it, clamps bound her. She became imprisoned suspended in mid-air on a type of swing. He left her in limbo, neither up nor down, and totally alone. That would fix her. This, however, only made Hephaestus feel worse. He had tied up and suspended his own creativity, his feminine side. I have seen many a Moon in Taurus client do this out of stubborn resentment—suspend his relationship with a woman relative (very likely another creative person with whom he could discover much in common) because of an old wound. He would have to let Hera go and let go of his bitterness, quit blaming her for his nonexistent childhood and get on with the process of being an adult artisan and of becoming a genuine artist, as well as a craftsman.

Dionysius, on one of his annual journeys to the underworld, felt compassion for Hephaestus, whom he must have recognized as a kindred spirit, another feminine, artistic soul whose inspiration came from the quiet of the unconscious. Compassionate Dionysius knew that many gods had tried to approach Hephaestus about forgiving Hera, but to no avail. He was a really hard case, but Dionysius never gave up hope. He would trick the smith into an altered state of consciousness, and then convert him to a change of heart. *In vino veritas* (in wine is truth) was Dionysius' motto. He succeeded. He took the sleeping dwarf out of the underworld and up to Mt. Olympus—to the heights of awareness—slung on the back of a humble mule.

When Hephaestus awoke to the Light of Olympus he felt much better. He felt drained of all his negative emotions and full of the bliss of Dionysius' sacred cup. He loosened Hera's bonds and immediately discovered, to his surprise, that he had loosened the bonds and obstacles to his own creativity as well. From that time on Hephaestus made beautiful artistic objects that actually looked alive (art imitating life) like Achilles' shield, which Homer describes at length in the *Iliad*. He also made useful objects for the gods and goddesses.

Murray Stein thinks that Hephaestus fell in love with Athene when she came in looking for one of his practical objects—a new spear—and that she was his soul mate. He was a feeling or feminine-type god, and she was a thinking, masculine-type goddess. In Stein's view, they would have been a well-balanced couple, had Athene not been completely aloof with Hephaestus. (She was cool to everybody.) Stein also thinks that Aphrodite and Hephaestus were not a balanced couple because they were both feminine souls.*

In ascending to Olympus to complete his healing process, Hephaestus also completed his initiation and took his place as an equal among the gods and goddesses. Of the Olympians, only vain Aphrodite was unimpressed with his transformation. She looked at him through her aesthetic snobbery and saw only the same old deformed body, not a beautiful soul. Perhaps it was to promote Aphrodite's growth

---

*see Stein's "Hephaistos, A Pattern in Introversion," in *Facing the Gods*, p. 79.

that Zeus arranged their marriage, but who can fathom the will of the gods? Perhaps she did eventually learn to appreciate Hephaestus' constancy and dependability, but her immediate reaction was to have an affair with Hephaestus' brother Ares, the handsome war god. Some sources contend that Aphrodite's son Eros (Love or Cupid) was fathered by Hephaestus rather than Hermes.

According to Stein, Hephaestus was "of the Earth" and because of his close connection to the Earth Mother, his feminine side, he was a "natural intuitive." When he had released all his "fixated" emotions—in astrology we would say Fixed—he began to tend his inner forge-fire properly, and from that point on there was nothing Hephaestus could not fashion beautifully, useful tool or objet d'art. There is a good deal in his story that corresponds to the life journey of my Sun in Taurus, Taurus rising, or exalted Moon in Taurus client who is a seeker and a spiritual aspirant. They have within the forges of their own souls a good deal of his talent and also of his inner struggle, his stubborn refusal to let go of outer obstacles and get on with it.

Since Taurus is the first of the Fixed signs (Fixed Earth or prime matter), this might be a good place to look at the symbols for the theme of fixity, which is power. The wild bull and the lion are two land animals to be reckoned with. The same is true of the eagle. No other creature could overwhelm it in the air. And the fourth Fixed sign is symbolized by the enlightened man, the Bodhisattva, or the Messiah, who also stands alone in his domain. Artists use these power symbols derived from the Fixed signs of the zodiac and they also appear frequently in heraldry. In the Middle Ages, Dionysius took on the shapes of bull and lion. The four symbols of the Fixed signs can also be found on stained glass windows representing the four Christian evangelists.

In the temperate zone, we begin the astrological year with a Cardinal sign, Aries, and set our festivals and our seasonal rites for the other Cardinal points, the Solstices and Equinoxes. But outside the temperate zone, in dry lands where the Fixed signs overhead are the harbingers of the monsoon season and fertility, calendar and festivals are set for the Fixed signs. In the Mayan Yucatan, for instance, a Venus Ephemeris was used for the calendar of rituals. Venus' orbit may have also been used to determine planting and harvesting for the maize culture, or so Rodney Collin speculates in *The Theory of Celestial Influence* (pages 276 and 298). We do know for certain that the calendar year began for Mayans when the Pleiades, a constellation in Taurus, was visible in the night sky overhead. When the Pleiades came into view, the rains were not far behind. Plutarch tells us that the same was true of the Greeks—that twenty-seven days after the Vernal Equinox, the bull-driving ceremony was held and sowing and plowing began. An old cameo representing the bull with the three graces on its horns and the Pleiades as seven stars overhead is now on display in the Hermitage Museum in Leningrad. (Jane Harrison, *Epilegomera and Themis*, page 205, figure 53.)

The Pleiades are a mystical constellation in Egypt, India, and the Mayan world as well as classical Greek mythology. The power of the Pleiades to bring the spring rains was an outward, mundane sign of their spiritual power. As Alice Bailey tells us in *Labours of Hercules*, the power of Taurus and of Aphrodite to attract abundance extends beyond the realm of physical, material substance. This power of attraction is centered in Alcyone, the galaxy's Grand Central Sun, said to be located in the Pleiades. Alcyone exerts a steady and continuous pull of our Sun and the planets orbiting it. To the ancients, Alcyone's attraction symbolized the power of spirit to attract matter; Alcyone's attention held the worlds in position, Spirit attracted and animated Matter. Orion, the Hunter or Seeker, is also located in Taurus, as is Aldebaran, the eye of the bull.

The issue is one of the power of the elements—cold weather in the temperate zone or dry weather relieved by rains in the rest of the world. Power was connected with the seasonal changes, the power of the forces of nature. Thus, powers of fertility, strength and endurance were associated with Taurus. Taurean stamina is the stamina of Mother Earth herself into which the crops were planted every spring to be watered by Father Sky. This endurance or loyalty is, to me, more characteristic of Taurus than any other quality—even the stubbornness, greed or attachment we come across in stories about the less attractive side of the mundane ruler, Venus, from whose name we derive the word "venal"—like the legendary King Midas, a truly venal character. Taurus/Scorpio have endurance in common—the inner resources to hang on regardless of a temporary trauma or set-back. The Fixed polarities have inner self-control as well as physical strength.

Taurus and Scorpio are esoterically associated with concentration or single-pointed focus. To the yogi, the bull's eye or the third eye of meditation is the esoteric meaning of Taurus. The Buddha has often been called the Bull, and legend places his birth in Taurus. He was spoiled as a child at his father's court, but was not satisfied with the material joys of a world that offered only suffering, illness and death in the end. He went out in search of enlightenment, and through concentration released the yogic power within. Buddha sat in his Immovable Seat under the Tree of Knowledge until enlightenment came. If Taurus can be complacent (Aphrodite can be lazy at the mundane level), Taurean inertia or the ability to sit can work well for him on the spiritual path. While a Fire sign might be too restless, a Taurean can sit in a relaxed posture for a long time. He has the stamina and the loyalty to stick to his path.

In Chinese Buddhism the bull represents truth in action. There are ten steps to realization of one's inner nature—10 Ways of the Bull—which were depicted in art by a Zen master, Kakuan, writing in the 10th century on true values, or true quality (Aphrodite). Each was illustrated with a wooden block print. Kakuan's wood block prints, along with commentaries on each, are reproduced in *Zen Flesh, Zen Bones* (Chapter 10, "10 Bulls").

Also interesting are the illustrations of Mithra, the Persian initiate (Figures 26, 27 and 28 in Franz Cumont's *Mysteries of Mithra*). Mithra rides the bull barebacked after capturing him in the wild, being dragged by him, and finally subduing the animal in a cave. In the Mithrus legends, there are the two levels already discussed—the mundane and the esoteric. The mundane is the usual story of springtime sacrifice of the bull so that its blood would fertilize the ground and Mother Earth would produce a new crop next year. The esoteric level refers to taming the bull in terms of subduing the desires and thoughts in the manner of the Chinese Buddhist in the "10 Bulls" chapter. The cult of Mithrus was solar rather than lunar in nature, but included seven levels of initiations of which the two most important were the bull and the lion. Each esoteric initiation and technique involved stripping away another of the seven bodies or planets known in Mithrus' time. The hymns have been lost but art describes the esoteric initiations. Especially interesting are Cumont's illustrations of Mithrus on the bull in the center of the wheel with the zodiac and its symbols around them in the outer circle. According to Cumont the initiate sought the Light, or illumination, while the uninitiated simply saw the bull imagery as part of the annual fertility cycle. In addition to the sacrificial bull with a wheat staff growing from his spine, there was an immortal Heavenly Bull, who was to return one day with Mithrus. Mithrus was known as the Judge of the Dead; an eagle, symbol of death or darkness, appeared on his shoulder in some of the carvings along with a serpent at his feet.

If we view Taurus esoterically, if we think about its receptivity to the Divine Light that is prime matter, the powers of concentration inherent in that stubborn or Fixed sign, about the search for enlightenment—the third eye or eye of the bull—the life force, stamina, loyalty and perseverance of Taurus, there is a good deal to admire. But with the Venusian tendency to inertia, or the tendency of an Earth sign to take this transitory world too seriously, there's a real need for Taurus to integrate the dark, watery side of Scorpio. If Taurus represents light and life—Venus as the bright morning star worshipped by the Mayans, as the fertility of springtime—then autumnal Scorpio represents darkness and death, followed by the rebirth experience of the Eighth House. Perhaps that is why, in so many cultures, the bull was sacrificed and reborn for the prosperity of the land and the people. It served as a reminder, too, that nothing is permanent; spring is followed by autumn, youth by old age, death by rebirth or immortality.

If we think of Houses Two through Eight as a values axis, then in order for Taurus to find his peace and contentment or the bliss of the ten bulls, it seems s/he must first die to personal desires (2nd House) and be reborn with a more enlightened value system in the 8th House (others' values). Aphrodite, as the value planet and quality seeker, appears quite subjective and personal in Taurus. She lacks the objectivity she possesses as ruler of airy Libra. On the mundane level, many born in Taurus attempt to overcome that subjectivity and transcend desire as the Buddha did, by a type of renunciation. Often they are not conscious that this is what they are doing when they say such things as, "I can develop my own creative talents later; at this point I must provide a quality life for my spouse and children (others)." Or "I'd like to continue my singing career but my children need me at home. Maybe when they are in college. . . "

Others follow a path of conscious renunciation, giving up job security as the Buddha did his earthly kingdom to search for Truth, to return to school and study philosophy, or to travel abroad, living in physical discomfort in cheap hotels, seeking they know not what truth. This, like the Taurean who sacrifices for spouse and children, is a movement toward others' values (8th House) at the expense of personal comfort and desire—but here the teaching represents others' values—the "values of the patriarchs," as the author of "10 Bulls" called it. Having gained perspective or objectivity later in life, the Taurean may return to satisfy his/her own strong emotions and desire nature, his mundane ruler—earthy, sultry Aphrodite. This has been my experience with esoteric Taurean clients. The first half of the lifetime is lived for or through others' values or philosophies and the second half of life is concerned with romance and the personal quest for earthly joy.

Taurus, in most textbooks, is associated with the key words I POSSESS. But the key words I BUILD are also important because the esoteric client, attuned to Vulcan/Hephaestus, is often a builder. Vulcan, the fashioner or toolmaker of the gods, as Alice Bailey called him, is at work deep within Taureans and is discontented if some sort of creative project is not underway. In Taurus, we have the builder of a company who tunes in esoterically, retires early and spends his/her time on humanitarian pursuits. Several esoteric Taureans of my acquaintance have sacrificed financially, "ridden the bull" or sublimated personal desires in order to build structures such as wholistic healing centers or homes for runaway children in both rural and urban spiritual communities, where seekers can live and learn with like-minded people.

Unlike the mundane Taurean energy, which builds for itself or its own children and hangs on miser-like to its wealth, these esoteric Taureans have found real joy. They also seem to have found Aphrodite's white dove of peace. Peace is elusive if Vulcan is not working constructively with his tools, whether the tools be artistic, craft-connected, financial, or meditative. Hatha yoga has been a favorite tool of many Taureans to facilitate riding the bull—controlling the body. Zen and other techniques, such as *pranayama*, have been helpful tools for controlling the mind and emotions. Through use of his tools, Taurus attunes consciously to Vulcan and cooperates with his esoteric ruler, making it less likely that he will be hit with Vulcan's hammer on the more difficult transits of the trans-Saturnian planets.

A Taurus who is a successful rider of the bull reaches a state of bliss where "nothing can distract him; he no longer needs the patriarchs, and he mingles among men and is a vehicle for their enlightenment." ("10 Bulls," page 186.) A modern Buddha. This seems to be the message of the Mithrus cult in Persia, the Way of the Bull of the Chinese Zen master, and most likely, of the Cretan bull riders pictured on the frescoes. The Apis bull, with its annual sacrificial death and rebirth symbolizing the fertility of spring and the death of the Earth in fall and winter, seems to have more to do with the alchemical integration of Houses Two and Eight. Here we seem to have the Second House, as substance, or Prime Matter (*prima materia*), losing its structure, experiencing chaos or upheaval, and then after a sense of loss—darkness, depression or inner death, becoming reborn in the Eighth House after the solitude and dormancy of late autumn in Scorpio when the Phoenix rises from its ashes. The Apis bull is not only symbolic of Taurean springtime and life, but the eagle on its flank reminds us of autumn, of Scorpio, of death and rebirth.

Jung, in a study on the alchemy of integrating the opposites, refers to Prime Matter and the Phoenix, to Light and Darkness, and to Life and Death; and one cannot help but think of the natural zodiac—of integrating the hopefulness of Spring, teeming with life and fertility, with the more depressing late Fall season, barren, dead Scorpio. I would highly recommend that anyone interested in integrating the Taurus/Scorpio energy read Volume XIV of Jung's Collected Works, *Alchemical Studies*, and ponder the illustration from the German alchemical manuscript on the frontispiece. It is a Scorpionic dragon with several heads, including the Sun-head and the Moon-head. The wedding of Sun and Moon, Masculine and Feminine, Light and Dark within us all was associated with Taurus in the alchemical writings— Taurus, where the Moon and Venus function well together. The exaltation of the Moon in Taurus is not mentioned specifically by Jung, but he does say that "Diana is the bride" in the wedding of Masculine and Feminine, which occurs in Taurus at the delicate time of the New Moon. The frontispiece says that the glyphs for Venus (♀) and the Moon (☾) combine to form the glyph for Mercury (☿), ruler of alchemy. Thus, Mercurius, the elusive alchemical guide who leads the medieval seeker to the secret of the philosopher's stone of inner transformation—to the changing of base human nature into gold— appears at the New Moon in Taurus.

Jung says in *Alchemical Studies* that integrating Darkness and Light is difficult—that the two really back away from each other. It is difficult for the light to shine in the darkness, for the unconscious (8th House or Scorpio) to become conscious. The astrologer would call this resistance fixity, because on this axis we deal with two Fixed signs or Fixed houses. Still, the receptivity of Taurus, its dual-feminine side, gives that sign an opening which other signs, or other seasons of the year, might not have. Scorpio is also a receptive sign in the sense that Water is receptive. Scorpio has funerary associations—Osiris' coffin, mummies, death—but it also has the Phoenix. If Taurean prime matter can undergo change or transformation, then the energy of Spring that is Taurus need no longer remain rooted to the ground (Earth), but can fly like a Phoenix and be free. It may be difficult for Taurus to appreciate the dark, instinctual side of Scorpio—the unconscious side. In actual cases involving clients who had a good deal of Taurean energy, what they said of Scorpio revealed that they thought of themselves as the Light, and the Scorpios they encountered as dark, chaotic, mysterious, reclusive, and irrational. If Taurus makes demands on Scorpio that Scorpio is not ready to accept, Scorpio will often put Taurus through a trauma or upheaval, thus showing Taurus its own shadow. Taurus could respond by integrating the insight and saying thanks to Scorpio or by withdrawing and concluding that Scorpios are sarcastic, nasty people to be avoided in the future. Through integrating some of the darkness of its unconscious Scorpio polarity, Taurus could learn to sprout wings like the Phoenix, to drop its insecurities and fly like the winged bull of Assyrian art.

As Taurus opposes Scorpio, Aphrodite opposes Mars, the ruler of Scorpio. We have Ariadne of the Minotaur myth, a bit of a social or cultural snob, sometimes perceiving Mars as too coarse or too physical. Here again I'm reminded of lovely Aphrodite being forced to marry Hephaestus, the seemingly ugly dwarf. She was forced to confront her superficial view that beauty is skin deep. In reading Taurean Sun sign charts, I have encountered Aphrodite the socialite angry at her mate, who has Scorpio planets, because he is not in the mood to go to a party. "Why does he need all that solitude?" she wonders. Yet Taurus can learn from Scorpio's quiet courage. Aphrodite can learn from Mars to take risks—to allow Vulcan to forge ahead. Mars can teach her to welcome change and sexuality—to let her own springtime energy find release. Both Scorpio and Taurus are intuitive and possessed of strong will. They have a good deal to learn from each other if they can but move beyond the stubborn resistance of fixity. An esoteric, spiritual Taurus is open and receptive to God. The Myth of the Minotaur is about the issue of receptivity. In the myth, King Minos is stubborn and unreceptive to Neptune (God). Minos' greed and attachment for a bull "fit to be owned by a god" cause him to do damage to his entire lineage. Minos lives in the world of the senses (lower Aphrodite) to the exclusion of all else. He reminds us of Taureans we know who keep asking, "What should we eat today?" "Where should we go and shop today?" "What should we do for entertainment today?" They never seem to ponder the esoteric questions of Aphrodite. "Where can I find lasting value?" "What is the meaning of life?"

Myth of Minotaur

On the island of Crete there lived a king who was himself a divine child of the lineage of the bull—King Minos. Minos descended from Zeus in the form of the bull, and therefore the bull was a symbol of his kingship. To assure the continued prosperity of his people, Minos was regularly sent a bull to sacrifice from the god known as the Earth Shaker—Poseidon (Neptune). Neptune, as you know from astrology, was a renunciant god who did not look with favor upon greed or attachment. One year, to test Minos, he sent a particularly beautiful, rare white bull.

Such luster, such sheen! Minos had never seen a bull like it. A bull fit for a god—or for King Minos? He was aware of his responsibility to his family and subjects to do the will of Poseidon and sacrifice the same bull he was sent. (As an archetypal Earth sign, Minos had much responsibility.) Yet, his greed triumphed. He kept the Heavenly Bull of Poseidon and switched a smaller white bull for the sacrifice.

A series of catastrophes ensued. His wife Parsifae, to whom Minos, as a warm and passionate Taurus, was deeply attached, fell in love with the Heavenly Bull. Daedalus, the architect, built her a wooden cow so that she could disguise herself and unite with it. The result of their union was a monster—half man and half bull—the Minotaur. Because it was a partially divine being, Minos was not supposed to kill it. So Daedalus went to work again and built a maze, a labyrinth to contain it. With his wife, whom he loved, imprisoned in her room and a noisy Minotaur racing about in the labyrinth, there was little joy left in Minos' life.

He thought of ways to get rid of the monster. There was, some sources say, a ritual on Crete every seven years to pay tribute to Minos from other islands and mainland Greece. Young warriors were sent to ride the bull—wild bulls were captured and naked heroes would attempt to grab the horns and vault over them onto the animals' backs, hang on and ride. Frescoes depict the riding of the bull as a ritual, with court ladies looking on. When it was time for tribute to be sent, Minos thought of advertising on the mainland for a hero willing to slay the Minotaur. Then King Minos would not be responsible for killing a partially divine beast. His son went to the mainland to recruit heroes for the task and was killed by a bull in the city of Marathon.

Minos had thus lost his wife to the Heavenly Bull and his son to the Marathon bull. The rest of the story is probably more familiar to you. Theseus came and volunteered for the task. He was not a Cretan and did not know the skills for riding the bull. Yet, he was successful at the bull-riding ritual and decided to take on the Minotaur. He thought the major problem with the task would be finding his way back out of the labyrinth—not slaying the Minotaur—and he was right. However, Ariadne, daughter of Minos (from whose name we get the term for spider—arachnid), fell in love with the hero and came to his aid with her thread. He used it to find his way out of the maze and back to Ariadne. There was an earthquake and a fire following the death of the divine Minotaur and Ariadne sailed away from Crete with the "coarse" people from the mainland. As she looked back at her burning palace she wondered what she had done in aiding the barbarian Greeks. She had an argument with Theseus and he and his shipmates put her ashore on an island; they were apparently tired of her complaints. Poseidon/Neptune took pity on her, compassionate god that he is, and placed her in the sky as a constellation for all of us to see. In other versions of the story, Neptune/Dionysius married her, and then placed her in the heavens. In any case, it was a sad ending for the Minoan dynasty, which ultimately was destroyed by earthquake and fire, all resulting from the short-sighted greed of its rulers.

There is a balance point for Taurus in dealing with responsibility. Minos did not take his responsibilities seriously enough and let his greed overwhelm him. Others who participate in the archetype of Taurus are so bound by responsibilities that they never take vacations, or they complain, "My family always leaves all the planning and all the work to me. They are so helpless." Aphrodite works harder in Taurus than she does as ruler of Libra. It is important for Taureans to find the balance point and let others in the family or the office carry their own share of the burden so there is time for the Taurean to work out his/her own growth—also, so that Taurus does not build up resentments.

In Aries, we had the need to control our instincts as wild horses. In Taurus, we have the rider of the bull—of our passions. We confront our instincts, our desires, our emotions, even our inertia, amidst a changing world. Many Taureans take the bull by the horns as in the Cretan rite or the Mithrus rite in Persia and exert such willpower and such control over the emotions that Aphrodite and her consort, Vulcan, are unhappy. Both are creative energies; neither of them wants to live that structured or controlled a life.

Taurus gains insight during the 30-year Gemini progression, but not always the type of insight the spouse hopes s/he'll gain. So often during astrology classes on progressions, a woman married to a wheeler-dealer Taurean businessman will ask, "Does the Gemini progression mean he'll want to come to metaphysical classes with me? I've been reading about Gemini as a real learning cycle. Will he change, open up to new things?" It's more likely that he'll take practical seminars on computer programming, income-tax law, or if he has some natal air, sales-oriented classes related to his work, than develop an interest in the metaphysical, at least until the end of the progression. She should hang on for his Cancer cycle.

Others have asked, "Will my Taurean spouse be less stubborn on the Gemini-adaptable cycle? It's Mutable, after all. It's also analytical; Mercury rules Gemini. Will he analyze his behavior and work at changing?" The odds are that for the first few years of it, at least, he's likely to notice (gain insights into) how others around him should change—the spouse, the children, the boss. This is an habitual, Fixed sign. Most likely, if he has Gemini planets, the progressed Sun cross ing them will become critical of others for a number of years before it begins to introspect about changing himself/herself. Here other factors enter into the picture as well. Is natal Mercury in Gemini or has it entered Gemini too? How is natal Mercury aspected? If it is retrograde, he or she will have a habit of introspection about personal motives and behavior, as well as that of others. But the insights about changing long-standing Taurean habits do not come overnight.

One positive side effect of this cycle is Gemini's love of talking about things. Those Taureans who have been quiet types prior to this progression will want to communicate more. In particular, the spouse of someone with planets on the Taurus/Scorpio axis will notice this and find it easier to raise sensitive issues. Behavior changes may not happen, though, in Gemini. It is fun to analyze and talk about things, to theorize and discuss, but even for the Fixed signs with natal Mercury in Gemini behavioral carryover does not immediately follow intellectual understanding. "Oh, yeah, I'm like that. It drives other people crazy. Isn't that interesting!" is the common reaction of progressed Gemini. There is also a good deal of inertia in Taurus.

The 30-year Gemini progression gives Taurus a chance to try out his versatility. Those who are low in Air may stay with the old profession—business, or music, or a supportive, practical line of work which gives them a sense of security. Taureans with many Air planets, or an Air sign rising, often become confused during the first few years of the progression, as they become aware of the variety of talents connected to communication and self-expression. (Gemini refers to getting the word out either in print or verbally). One mother referred to her college-age daughter, a Taurus Sun sign who had just progressed into Gemini, this way: "I hope you can help her sort all this out. She changed her major four times last year and her father and I can't afford to keep her in school forever. She used to be so practical. She wanted to get a credential and have a solid skill when she graduated. I worry that she won't be employable."

The daughter said, "Till last year I was unaware I had all these talents. Mom said, 'Get a teaching credential. You'll always have teaching to fall back on when you get married.' And it used to sound practical to major in Secondary Education. But last year I had a really good teacher for journalism. She sent us out into the community to interview interesting people. I decided I'd love to work on a newspaper. Then I took some creative writing courses. I discovered I have a gift for writing dialogue. I decided to write stage plays. But then my older brother came to visit; he talked of how well he was doing in marketing, which is a communication field, too, and I decided to shift majors to business communication. I plan to get an MBA and follow in my brother's footsteps."

Her problem was too much feedback from the cosmos. Good teachers who encouraged her many talents; her mother, her brother all tried to influence her in this mutable progression. It helps if the astrologer can resist the temptation to add to the information glut. Otherwise, when the astrologer finds three *other* communication career possibilities, the client leaves the session more confused than when she arrived. I try to ask the Aphrodite questions, the questions emphasizing value and meaning. "What do you really enjoy most? Going home after a day of practice teaching that went especially well, basking in the warmth and satisfaction that resulted from working with young people? Or, going home from the interview with the mayor feeling mentally stimulated, sitting down at the typewriter and organizing the interview material?"

In the first few years, many fields are interesting for a short time;

the Taurus feels a bit like a natal Gemini. But one can ask, "What do you visualize yourself doing for a long time and liking most?" The Earth signs are long-term planners. The underlying issue of what's practical is always important to consider. The client will be a progressed Gemini for 30 years, but a lifelong natal Taurean! This particular young lady tried the MBA, her brother's choice, but it did not work out for her. She was not happy. Eventually, she went back to school and became a nurse. Venus, in her case, found meaning in healing, nurturing, and helping others. It was a useful, practical choice, but, unlike marketing, she felt there were deeper rewards beyond the material. Healing careers often appeal to Taurus at the end of the Gemini (mental) cycle, as Taurus prepares to progress into nurturing Cancer.

Another major issue for Taurus during the Gemini progression, if they have older brothers and sisters, is the issue of following in the sibling's footsteps. Karma with brothers and sisters is important in the Gemini phase. Many a client progressing through Gemini has said, "I'd like to major in my brother or sister's career area" or "I'd like to marry someone just like the person my brother or sister married." This often actually leads to dating the sibling's brother-in-law or sister-in-law. Sometimes it works out (in South India, cross-cousin marriages are common, or two brothers married to two sisters), but sibling's horoscopes are usually very different where talents and taste are concerned. There is another problem, too. If the confused person progressing through Gemini opts for the sibling's career-choice, he will set him/herself up for a lifetime of comparisons with the sibling's career progress. The older sibling has several years head start, too. "How many insurance policies did you sell last year, dear?" asks Aunt Ruth. "Oh, your older brother sold twice as many. My, my." I usually attempt to raise these issues in the course of the session. If the sibling's career choice fits the client's chart and the client has thought about that career for a number of years, it might work out, but it is still interesting to compare the sibling's horoscope talents with the client's and shed whatever light on their differences one can.

Aphrodite's interest in the good, the true and the beautiful is present in the unconscious of Taurus. The goddess seeks to provide warmth and love to others. She could do it through healing, music or the arts, marriage, entertainment, a florist's shop. But her satisfaction is subjective; she should find joy in her workday. In this sense, Venus ruled Taureans have more in common with Libra than with the other two Earth signs. They take a less objective view of their work. The people Taurus encounters are less important than the material. This is not as true for the other Earth signs.

The Cancer progression is much more familiar to Taurus. It's a conservative cycle. One can enjoy what he or she has built earlier in life. One can enjoy home, family, possessions, and the familiar stability. The water progression is important in the chart of Taurus as it brings out the feminine side, the intuitive sensitivity. In the beginning year or two of the 30-year cycle, Taurus may even find that the body seems hypersensitive. Toxic chemical allergies are common, symptomatic of the new openness of the Taurean nature. It helps to visualize the protection of the Spiritual Master as a white light, to purify the diet, order pure drinking water (Cancer refers to liquids) and be tested sometimes for allergies to dairy products.

Though many Taureans are in psychic or nurturing careers during this cycle, it is also important that they find time to nurture the inner child, to meditate, rest, and get away for weekends with family members. Often the spiritual Taurean has built for others in the first half of the lifetime and the more mediumistic Cancer cycle is a shift towards building a soul, building *within*, strengthening Aphrodite's quest for beauty, meaning, personal value. Home and hearth may replace commuter travel as the restlessness of the Gemini cycle winds down. Purchasing or adding to property becomes important as Taurus may decide to work out of his home, and because he now spends a good deal of time there, he wants it comfortable. Karma with one's parents and older living relatives often is worked through in this cycle, as by this point parents are usually quite elderly and need attention. If there are old, painful issues, resentments, or negative memories from childhood (like those of Hephaestus) Taurus often is able to release them from the unconscious in Cancer, practicing healing techniques on himself as well as on others. This is facilitated by the fact that the elderly parent herself may become a needy child, a fragile human being. Taurus will often say, "Mom (or Dad) did the best s/he knew how with us. I've lived long enough to realize that I made my own share of mistakes in life, so I can be more understanding and forgiving with others."

Another karmic area for the spiritual Taurus would be the karma with legitimate religion, or Holy Mother the Church. Many a Taurean in the Cancer cycle seeks to return to the womb of the spiritual mother organization from whom he separated early in life.

"I was very stubborn and opinionated as a young man," said a Taurus in the Cancer progression. "I had a terrible fight with the orthodox rabbi in my little town. He was an equally stubborn, opinionated fellow who didn't approve of my choice of brides. I told him it was none of his business. He refused to perform my marriage. So I joined a reformed temple. But you know, my bride is long since dead and the rabbi is long since dead. I'd like to go 'home' to orthodoxy now. This discussion group modern junk in the temple I've been attending makes me uncomfortable."

Or, "I'm so mad at the church! When I applied to them to have my first marriage annulled back in 1946, did they grant the annulment? No. Now, in 1986, I have to stand by and watch them give out annulments as if the things were lottery tickets anyone could buy. I'd still like to have an annulment, to have the children of my second marriage legitimized by the church, even though they don't care at all. They have grown up and even have teenage children of their own. I guess what it really means is that I'd like to make my peace with the church, to be buried in consecrated ground. . . "

This quest for legitimacy, or to return to the roots, to one's own religious tradition, seems to be emotionally charged for many a Taurean in the Cancer cycle. Making peace is also an issue for Aphrodite, whose symbol is the dove. Not every Spiritual Mother, every religious institution, of course, will take the progressed Taurus back home, especially if he is still stubbornly dictating his own terms. Yet, when Taurus approaches the authorities with an open heart, good motives and willingness to be flexible about the terms, he seems to find his own inner peace regardless of any inflexible bureaucrats he may encounter.

Spiritually, the Cancer issue is one of letting go of attachments—in some cases, even attachments to religious organizations. Taurus often goes at communication, and at life, indirectly. But at the end of life, s/he may realize a direct connection between him/herself and the Divine, rooted not in an intermediary organization, but within his/her own soul. Many Taureans have, during this progression, become less dependent on the legitimacy conferring institutions and have found the inner peace, Aphrodite's dove, in their own inner feminine, the anima, or soul.

Taurus is usually blessed with physical stamina and endurance. Many live on into the Leo progression. Those who have grandchildren really enjoy them, and especially enjoy encouraging their creativity and teaching them new things. The Sun, progressed or natal, belongs to Leo, so this is often a joyous cycle of personal growth as the Sun shines upon Taurus. If s/he has been generous with his/her resources, rather than stingy or greedy, blessings are returned by family and community and his/her last years are full of love, warmth and gratitude. He may be a respected Wise Old Man/Woman in the community. If s/he has not learned flexibility in the Gemini cycle, change may, however, hit him/her hard, especially if his/her mate should die before him/her. (See Chapter 5, a Lion needs a mate.) For those Taureans who have worked at Hephaestian change and growth, this is a pretty stable, happy period. Taurus feels blessed. Younger people often introduce him/her to new hobbies, talents, interests. This may well be the best time in his/her life in terms of self-esteem, warmth, and joy.

Questionnaire

How does the Taurean archetype express itself? Though this relates particularly to those with the Sun in Taurus or Taurus rising, anyone could apply this series of questions to the house where his Venus is located or the house which has Taurus (or Taurus intercepted) on the cusp. The answers to these questions will indicate how in touch the reader is with his Venus, his "goddess of peace and love," his Taurean instincts.

1. When the conversation becomes too direct or confrontational I become uncomfortable
   a. most of the time.
   b. 50% of the time.
   c. 25% of the time or less.

2. When I am given a project at work, I can be depended upon to see it through to its conclusion. Among my strong points are loyalty, practicality and perseverance
   a. usually.
   b. 50% of the time.
   c. not often.

3. I prefer constancy and stability to uncertainty and change
   a. 80% of the time or more.
   b. about 50% of the time.
   c. 25% of the time or less.

4. Among my negative qualities I would probably include stubbornness.
   a. I am extremely stubborn.
   b. I am stubborn 50% of the time.
   c. I am not stubborn at all.

5. Financial and emotional security are
   a. extremely important.
   b. moderately important.

  c. not very important.

6. My greatest fear is
  a. bankruptcy or poverty in my old age.
  b. loss of my independence.
  c. my deepest darkest secret will be found out.

7. The greatest obstacle to my success comes from
  a. within myself, self-doubt.
  b. the outside world—circumstances beyond my control.

8. I feel the weakest part of my body is
  a. the throat, jaw bone, vocal chords or thyroid.
  b. head and sinuses.
  c. the alimentary canal.

9. Important to my life are such Venus concerns as social life, social status, the savings account, and material possessions.
  a. These are very important.
  b. Moderately important.
  c. Not important at all.

10. When asked to perform before large or unfamiliar audiences I have a tendency to develop sore throats or sudden laryngitis no matter how hard I've rehearsed. This happens
  a. seldom.
  b. about 50% of the time.
  c. often.

  Those who have scored five or more (a) answers are highly in touch with their instincts. Those who have scored five or more (c) answers are moving to the polar extremity on the instinctual level— their Venus is not allowed to express itself properly. One symptom of a frustrated Venus is that the native freezes up when he is required to perform in unfamiliar social circumstances. Those who answered (c) on question 10 should review their natal Venus. Is it in the Twelfth House? Is it retrograde? Is it intercepted? It is important for them to work consciously with the planets aspecting natal Venus to help Venus express its positive instincts—warmth, grace of self-expression, social comfort, artistic expression, and charm.

Where is the balance point between Taurus and Scorpio? How does the Taurean integrate personal resources with the transformation? Though this relates particularly to those with Sun in Taurus or Taurus rising, all of us have Venus and Mars somewhere in our horoscope. Many of us have planets in the Second or Eighth houses. For all of us the polarity from Taurus to Scorpio involves learning to balance personal security with change and transformation.

1. When my spouse bows out of a planned social event that is important to me, I graciously accept his/her need for solitude
   a. 25% of the time or less.
   b. about half of the time.
   c. 80% of the time or more.

2. When I stop at the store, I pick up the brand of the item my spouse or roommate asked for rather than what I feel to be a better choice
   a. 25% of the time or less.
   b. 50% of the time.
   c. 80% of the time or more.

3. It's easy for me to say no to somebody who asks me to do a favor when I don't really want to do it or when I really don't have time to do it
   a. most of the time.
   b. about half the time.
   c. hardly ever.

4. I practice passive resistance rather than argue, say no, or openly compete
   a. 25% of the time or less.
   b. about 50% of the time.
   c. 80% of the time or more.

5. Others find me stubborn and demanding when it comes to change regarding a project in which I have an interest
   a. 25% of the time or less.
   b. about half the time.
   c. 80% of the time or more.

Those who have scored three or more (b) answers are doing a good job with personality integration on the Taurus/Scorpio or personal resources/transformation polarity. Those who have three or more (c) answers need to work more consciously on developing Mars in their natal horoscopes. Those who have three or more (a) answers may be out of balance in the other direction—they have not developed Venus enough. Study both planets in the natal chart. Is there an aspect between them? Which one is stronger by house position or location in its sign of rulership or exaltation? Is either of them retrograde, intercepted, in fall, or in detriment? Aspects to the weaker planet can point the way to integration.

What does it mean to be an esoteric Taurean? How does Taurus integrate Vulcan into the personality? Remember that Vulcan is the archetype of Volcanic change. Every Taurean will at some time in his life have to deal with Vulcan (upheaval in finances, relationships, organizations, loyalties). Mutability rising and/or planets in mutable signs lend resiliency to the natal chart and help the Taurean adapt to Vulcan's changes. The lesson of Vulcan is—*without change there is no growth*. The answers to the following questions will indicate the extent to which Taurus is open to change and is in touch with Vulcan, his esoteric ruler.

1. I consider myself an adaptable person
   a. 80% of the time.
   b. 50% of the time.
   c. 25% of the time or less.

2. When hit with sudden and catastrophic change in my finances, my relationship, or an organization to which I belong, I adapt
   a. very well.
   b. fairly well.
   c. poorly; I resist change.

3. When required to move on in life by outer circumstances such as retirement, job transfer, divorce or death of a loved one, my ability to let go of the past is
   a. very good.
   b. fair.
   c. poor.

4. Having been through a major crisis or upheaval I can now understand and appreciate the way in which the change was necessary to my growth and transformation.
   a. Definitely.
   b. Maybe.
   c. Not really.

5. Because of my inner resourcefulness, my co-workers, family, and friends come to me for support in times of upheaval.
   a. Always.
   b. Sometimes.
   c. Never.

Those who have scored three or more (a) answers are in touch with the esoteric ruler. Those who scored three or more (b) answers need to work consciously at being receptive and adaptable to change. Those who have three or more (c) answers may be low in mutability in the natal chart. Fortunately, Taureans evolve and develop through their thirty-year progression in Gemini, a Mutable sign. An important lesson for Taureans is that those who resist change often have change forced upon them. Since esoterically the Second House is the House of Values, Taurus represents spiritual receptivity or openness to Divine Grace. It is this grace which sustains Taurus and facilitates growth during times of Volcanic upheaval.

References

Alice Bailey, *Esoteric Astrology*, Lucis Publishing Co., New York, 1976

Alice Bailey, *Labours of Hercules*, Lucis Publishing Co., New York, 1977

Joseph Campbell, *Occidental Mythology, Masks of God III*, Penguin Books, New York, 1982

Joseph Campbell, *Primitive Mythology, Masks of God I*, Viking Press, New York, 1959

Rodney Collin, *The Theory of Celestial Influence*, Samuel Weiser, New York, 1954

Jack R. Conrad, *The Horn and the Sword*, Mac Gibbon and Kee, London, 1959

Leonard Cottrell, *The Bull of Minos*, Grosset and Dunlap, New York, 1962

Franz Cumont, *The Mysteries of Mithra*, Dover Publications, New York, 1956

Mircea Eliade, *The Forge and the Crucible*, University of Chicago Press, Chicago, 1978

Linda Goodman, *Sun Signs*, "The Taurean Boss," Taplinger Publications, New York, 1968

Jane Harrison, *Proglegomena to the Study of Greek Religion*, Meridien Books, New York, 1955

Jolande Jacobi, *The Psychology of C.G. Jung*, Rutledge and Kegan Paul, London, 1951

C.G. Jung, *Alchemical Studies*, Princeton University Press, Princeton, 1967

C.G. Jung, *Symbols of the Transformation*, Princeton University Press, Princeton, 1967

Nikos Kazantzakes, *Report to Greco*, Simon and Schuster, New York, 1965

C. Kerenyi, *The Gods of the Greeks*, "Hephaestus," Thames and Hudson, New York, 1951

Larousse Encyclopedia of Mythology and Religions, "The Apis Bull"

Patrizia Norelli-Bachelet, *The Gnostic Circle*, Aeon Books, Panorama City, 1975

Pausanius, *A Guide to Greece, Vol. I and II*, trans. Peter Levi, Penguin Classics, New York, 1979

Sylvia Brenton Perera, *Descent to the Goddess, A Way of Initiation for Women*, Inner City Books, Toronto, 1981

Murray Stein, "Hephaistos," in *Facing the Gods*, Spring Publications, Irving, 1980

E.A. Wallis-Budge, *The Egyptian Book of the Dead*, "Hymn to Amen Ra," Dover Publications, New York, 1967

Zen Flesh, Zen Bones, compiled by Paul Reps, Charles E. Tuttle, Rutland, 1983

3 GEMINI:
The Search for Variety

We have examined Cardinal Fire and Fixed Earth. Now we reach the light and breezy sign of Gemini. Gemini is cheerful, playful, and somewhat glib, like its ruling planet Mercury/Hermes. Hermes was known to the Greeks as Guide to the Three Worlds, Dweller of the Twilight, Lord of the Shepherds (esoteric ruler of the ram), Patron of Merchants, Patron of Thieves. He was informally known as patron of magic, sorcery and alchemy, ruler of good fortune at the crossroads, maker of mischief in the lives of those who lacked discrimination. He helped heroes and people in search of a quick solution. He is the only one of the Greek Pantheon who had no home on Olympus but was always in transit among the three worlds. He was the Guide and Messenger for Olympus, Earth and Hades.

Hermes was forever young—a perpetual adolescent. Sometimes Hermes' statues presented him as a young man with a pointed beard, and sometimes he was beardless, but he was nearly always young. The Romans and later the medieval alchemists called him by the name familiar to us from astrology—Mercury. *Mercurius alchemius.* In astrology, he rules Gemini and Virgo. It is interesting that people with these two signs on the Ascendant tend to appear several years younger than they really are. The Ascendant is the attitude, and Hermes' gifts to Gemini and Virgo include a Mutable or flexible attitude towards life's changing circumstances; the ability to analyze one's errors and adapt one's behavior; a sense of humor about oneself, and a lively mental curiosity about life. Versatility is also a Hermes gift. A Fixed sign rising might see only one way to react in a certain circumstance and hang on rigidly to that pattern; Mercury provides the Gemini Ascendant a variety of options—several possible ways to react to change. Jung tells us that in alchemy the "astrological Mercury" was the fluid, mobile, quicksilver mind. The mind by itself (apart from the rest of the psyche) is dual and amoral. It can lead us in either a positive or a negative direction. Hermes is "of two minds," especially as ruler of Gemini. In dreams, says Jung, the man with the cap and a black pointed beard was seen as the devil; Mephistopheles in Faust was a negative guide to the soul. (Jung, *Psychology and Alchemy*, Dream #14.) Mental curiosity can lead to brilliant discoveries or to experiences with painful consequences.

This is why the medieval alchemists prayed for the power to discern between good and evil, to ". . . purge the darkness of our minds." (Jung, *Alchemical Studies*, p. 250.) The Hindus have a similar prayer, "Lord, lead us from the Darkness to the Light." Jung points out that western civilization has forsaken the humble prayer of the alchemists, and in deifying reason, has seemingly forgotten the darker side of the dual mind. In the 18th century, he reminds us that "enlightened" French philosophers crowned the Goddess of Reason in Notre Dame Cathedral. Worship of reason continued in the two centuries that followed, emphasizing the positive, progressive, inventive and scientific power of the mind. (*Alchemical Studies*, pp. 228-229.)

In *Puer Aeternus*, Marie Louise von Franz discusses the dangers of living exclusively in one's head. She says that according to Jung, the feeling-type is more likely than the thinking-type to be in touch with his or her own creative gifts, uniqueness and his or her own value system. While the feeling type is able to invest him- or herself emotionally and wholeheartedly in a relationship, the thinking-type tends to hold back and analyze him or herself, his or her partner, life, and usually, as von Franz puts it, s/he "finds a hair in the soup." Jung attributes this to the intellectual's tendency to think statistically, which is depressing. He thinks, "There are thousands of people just like me, with my identical background, in the city where I live. There are thousands of people who go off every morning to jobs just like mine. I think I'm in love with a unique woman (or man) but there are really thousands out there just like him/her, too! How boring!" This does not help a person to find meaning, happiness, or even contentment in his work or his relationship. Further, the *puer/puella* also tends toward low vitality, a weak libido; s/he usually sees his body as frail and unable to accomplish the things that others are able to achieve in life. S/he may therefore sleep late, smoke a lot, take drugs to escape into an altered state of consciousness, dream and fantasize about the

future, view the present moment as something transitory to be lived through, and think that the future offers greater possibilities than the present.

In Gemini, we deal with Mutable Air which represents observation, analysis, rational classification of data, and objectivity. We have the conscious mind (Mercury) processing information. In Virgo, another Mutable Hermes sign, we will meet *Mercurius psychopompous*, or Hermes as Guide to the Underworld, and sorcerer's apprentice, the magical healer who wields the Caduceus.

As the fluid mind, Hermes himself seemed happiest when in motion. He preferred not to remain too long in the same place. If he stayed, he might become rooted to it. The situation around him might crystallize with its bonds and obligations, routines and structures, and life would then become quite dull. Without new gossip and experiences, life would no longer be exciting, fun or informative. His dreams for the distant future might never be realized. If his perfect ideal were to vanish, Hermes would be stuck with a very imperfect reality. Hermes corresponds to Peter Pan, the Eternal Youth (*Puer Aeternis*) who refused to grow up and take on responsibility. For this reason, Jung perceived the puer as the opposite of *Senex* (Saturn)—as the child who refuses to grow up and be grounded, or settle down (to become a Saturnine personality). The puer looks to the future and avoids commitments in the present; he strongly resembles Hermes and the airy Gemini archetype. Gemini tries to avoid boring reality as long as possible. Geminis whose horoscopes are low in Earth and high in Air will, for instance, tell the astrologer, "I haven't many Earth sign friends. I find them heavy, serious, and to be honest, boring people." Gemini is a very inventive, imaginative sign—imagination is also a characteristic of Hermes' myths—and grounded Earth seems too structured to be creative from Gemini's perspective. Gemini, then, collects facts and puts them together in inventive, new and experimental ways.

Often, a Gemini child is bored in school and, because of his/her intelligence, says to the parent, "I want to quit after high school graduation and experience life. I'm intelligent, you know that, Mom. It's only a temporary, short-term decision. I'll eventually return to school and get my degree." But short-term decisions have long-term consequences.

In this case, Mom may agree with Gemini, "S/he will go back to school. S/he's my brightest child. S/he was always the first to learn the new educational game; s/he loves learning. S/he'll take off a few years and return to college (9th House—higher education) and by then s/he'll know what s/he wants as a major. S/he'll be more mature later."

An astrologer might say to Mom, "Yes, s/he was the first to learn the new educational game, but s/he was also the first to become bored with it. Many who drop out of high school or after the first two years of college never do return. The temporary decision does indeed have long-term consequences. This may not be wise (Jovian). Why not encourage her or him to see a vocational counselor at the college who may be able to find an apprenticeship program that seems more challenging than the classroom, or can help him or her find some variety in elective courses with more interesting teachers?"

Beyond such practical considerations as learning skills that prepare Gemini for employment, the 9th House has an expansive role to play in the development of an analytical young mind. The two Hermes signs, Gemini and Virgo, need to move from the specific to the general, from the concrete fact to the larger picture. Liberal arts requirements generally have a broadening effect. Jovian-type courses include philosophy, foreign languages, pre-law, history of foreign cultures and civilizations, travel programs (such as junior year abroad), literature and great Books courses which expose the student to a wide variety of ideas as well as to good writers who use the English language with great flair. These are all worthwhile ways of integrating the 9th House.

Finally, an educated person has mastered the art of studying; he enjoys learning. He can always occupy his mind in a positive manner. Because he likes school he can always fill in free time by taking courses in new and different subjects. Through his love of learning he can participate in the Sagittarian archetype directly rather than vicariously, from the letters of the traveling spouse or conversations with the student spouse. If Gemini enjoys learning, s/he will pursue it, rather than depend on the spouse to come home and stimulate his mind. It has been my experience that many people born in the Gemini archetype are married to travelers—for instance—salesmen, military or airline personnel, diplomats, or professors on sabbatical. When the traveling spouse is gone, Gemini has a lot of time on his/her hands. "An idle mind is the devil's workshop," the old adage goes. Air signs tend to feel boredom acutely. School is an outlet for the boredom. The educated Gemini who has developed his/her mind and his/her inner resources is less likely to give in to temptation (Mephistopheles, or the darker side of the mind) and have an affair than the uneducated. So, even ethically, education helps to develop Gemini's alternatives—and the 9th House polarity provides a great many varied options for this mentally inquisitive personality.

When she speaks of her therapy sessions with the puer personality, though, von Franz warns that this archetype is not inclined to take advice—especially advice that requires work, settling down or living within boundaries. (Hermes, we recall, was the out-of-bounds god who helped the traveler in transit.) School is a restrictive structure for the young. Gemini/Gemini rising needs to be in touch early in childhood with the stimulation reading offers, the inner resources that can be discovered and developed by a controlled mind. Von Franz also warns that puer/puella is most skillful at convincing the therapist that he or she has already completed the inner work, is finished with the therapy. Gemini masters the vocabulary, the jargon of any therapist readily and is quite precocious. Gemini is gifted with considerable verbal talent. One can almost hear the Gemini puer speak, "Oh, yes, I've released my 'special' creativity; I've integrated my positive shadow aspects, fought it out with the negative shadow side, dealt with the mother complex—I'm done!"

Von Franz says that she puts energy into catching them at it. She asks, "What did you do this morning? What time did you get up? What time did you get home for lunch? What do you have to show for this afternoon's work?" Otherwise, the puer's mental fantasies and his sense of reality tend to blend together. C.G. Jung thought that puella should be home with young children, which for her is hard work and should ground her. I have tried recommending this to Geminis in the Cancer progression—usually not before. Most of them seem highly insulted, unless they have several natal Cancer (maternal) planets for the progressed Sun to conjunct. In *Puer Aeternus*, von Franz thinks that Jung is right about this as a solution for sexually active Gemini women, but doesn't say whether any of them listened to the advice. My own puella clientele consists mainly of academic women with a high percentage of planets in Air, many of whom have Gemini Sun or Gemini rising. I have several very high strung Sun/Uranus conjunction clients who are perennial students, and when it comes to actually doing the work of their chosen field, find a "hair in the soup" and return to graduate school. Von Franz mentions that Jung's puer is a nervous type. This describes the

Gemini/Gemini rising type as well.

It's interesting that Jung's puer, the Hermes-type perennial adolescent, has a Geminian literary talent. Two examples usually cited in
Jungian texts and lectures on the Eternal Child are Antoine de Saint-
Exupery and Harry Crosby, both of whom not only flirted with danger
and defied death, but also thought of themselves as literary people,
literary artists. Crosby retained his high-spirited prankster nature till
the day of his suicide, while St. Exupery split off his childish side into a
shadow figure, the Little Prince. The Prince was naive, innocent,
spontaneous, and able to express his feelings, his needs, which St.
Exupery could not do. St. Exupery flew back and forth to spend a few
weeks at a time with his moody wife, smoked opium with his girlfriend
and wrote to his mother, who preferred to see him with the opium-
smoking girlfriend than with his wife. St. Exupery also left behind a
beautiful, if sentimental book full of charming, child-like pictures of
his shadow, his special prince, and an account of the puer's journey to
wholeness. His own journey was aborted by a fatal airplane crash in
the desert. We will return to the Little Prince later.

One hundred eighty degrees away from Gemini is wisdom, the
power to put facts in perspective—Sagittarius. Jupiter, ruler of Sagittarius, was Hermes' father in the myth. Hermes was a scribe of Jupiter
(though the scribe image may fit Virgo and Virgo rising more than
Gemini), and in Babylonian mythology, Nebo, the Hermes equivalent, was a scribe of Marduk, the Babylonian Jupiter. This polarity
from Gemini to Sagittarius means that facts help lead Gemini to wisdom if Gemini can put them in proper perspective—can learn to synthesize. To be a scribe is not a very exciting goal, although taking a
series of unrelated courses may be great fun for the Gemini perennial
student. (Jupiter rules the 9th House, academia, opposite the 3rd
House or Gemini, the concrete facts and study habits.)

Jupiter was the classical ruler of Pisces before Neptune was discovered. Thus mythologically the same gods ruled the axis from the
sixth to the twelfth sign—Hermes (Virgo) to Father Jupiter (Pisces),
but there is a greater emphasis on *logic* versus *intuition* from houses
six to twelve. In the case of both Hermes ruled signs, integrating the
polarities would involve learning what to do with the facts. This is
often the dilemma Hermes' children present when they come to their
astrologer. "I have six good reasons to quit my job and go back to
school," says logical Hermes, "and six good reasons not to quit." "I

have six good reasons to move to New York and six to stay in California." "I think my boyfriend is the right one to marry, but I have six good reasons why it might not work out." This is the crossroads of decision-making for our first Air sign. Our next Air sign, Libra, will face the same indecision dilemma in a less nervous modality. As ruler of Mutable Air, Gemini, Hermes is restless and very high strung.

Gemini stands at a crossroads and seeks a guide. The glyph for Gemini (♊) is the symbol that resembles the Roman numeral II—the principle of duality, as the Hindus call it in the *Upanishads*. The Greeks called the glyph the Gates of Hercules, the gates to the world of opposites. Recently in Ephesus, Turkey, our guide asked us to walk in silence through the so-called Gates of Hercules. "Are you any wiser?" she asked. But none of us admitted to greater wisdom or to any more discrimination in making choices. In Gemini, there is a certain lack of emotional attachment to the idea; ideas are sought and admired for their own intrinsic value—for sheer mental stimulation.

Hermes, the logical mind, is there to give the quick solution, but he doesn't pretend that it is necessarily a wise solution. C.G. Jung saw him as a prankster or a trickster and he does have that side to his personality. He is pictured on vases as sometimes giving a husband a sleeping potion and leading the man's wife off to be with her lover—other times as reuniting two separated partners.He is amoral. Hermes/Mercury operates in the context of a specific, concrete situation (3rd House). He evaluates the particular circumstances and determines an appropriate course of action. The Sagittarian archetype 180° away represents a moral or ethical imperative (9th House). Jupiter (Father Zeus, the judge of men, gods and demi-gods) acts with fiery determination based upon his perception of truth, ethics and absolute morality applied to the particular situation. Hermes/ Gemini reflects and Jupiter reacts.

Hermes as prankster also appears in peoples' dreams when they become too pompous or stuffy, too Saturnine in their social roles (personas) in the outer world. In Jung's *Man and His Symbols*, there is a humorous account of a Bishop dressed in all his embroidered splendor, sitting upon his throne holding aloft his mitre (Hermes' shepherd's crook) at a solemn ritual, perhaps a confirmation. Suddenly a ceiling tile right over the Bishop's throne comes loose, falls, and hits him on the head. The adults in the congregation inhale sharply in shock, while a small group of altar boys bursts out in spontaneous giggles. Things like this happen in dreams and waking-state life alike in order to remind us, through our embarrassment or humiliation, to keep our sense of humor, our childlike spontaneity and joy; to act appropriately in the situation rather than always playing out a social role or wearing an authoritative mask.

An example of the polarity from Gemini to Sagittarius which the astrologer often encounters is that of a short-term decision with long-term consequences. A case in point would be the encounter between the author St. Exupery and his character, the Little Prince. When the Little Prince, a special, golden-haired child from a tiny asteroid appeared suddenly to him in the desert, St. Exupery made a short term decision to put him off for the time being. He did not yet know whether the apparition was a positive or negative Shadow, a helpful figure who would point him toward future growth or one who would get him stuck in his childhood. St. Exupery's situation clearly called for getting rid of the Child and fixing the engine so that the stalled plane would fly again before he ran out of water in the desert. And St. Exupery was not talented at such practical things as airplane mechanics.

He could not resist showing his two childhood drawings to the Prince. All his life he had carried these with him, hoping to find someone who could glance at them and recognize his boa-constrictor trying to digest his elephant, someone who could explain why the drawings frightened him. The Prince (who was, of course, part of St. Exupery himself) at once told him what the creatures in the drawings were, but not what they meant. Instead, the Prince asked him to draw a sheep so that the Prince could take it home with him to the asteroid. St. Exupery, thinking about his dwindling drinking water, quickly tried three sheep, none of which satisfied the Prince. He explained that he might have become a real artist if only the adults around him had encouraged his talent in boyhood, but they hadn't, and as a result he wasn't good at drawing sheep.

"That sheep is too old. That one is a lead ram; see its horns!" said the Prince.

So, St. Exupery said, "Here's a box with air holes in it. The sheep is inside, you can't see it, but it's in there, take it and go." He went back to his instruction manual. The Prince believed him temporarily, "Oh, it's asleep in the box, I see, I'll come back later. I'll need a muzzle so it won't eat my rose. You can draw me a muzzle next."

The hallucination of the Little Prince from the tiny asteroid is similar to the archetypal dream of the Child. Is the dream figure a positive or negative Hermes? Does it come from the Self to guide us? Or is it a part of ourselves to be faced and then released? Is it going to present some negative trait we see in others but don't want to look at in ourselves?

When the Prince returned to get the drawing of the muzzle to put in the box with the sheep, he told St. Exupery about life on the asteroid. The author continued working on the plane. There were two active volcanoes and one inactive volcano on the asteroid. Every morning, before breakfast, the Little Prince cleaned them out so they would not erupt. (The mind cleans out the *libido*.) There was one beautiful rose there; to the prince she was the only rose in existence, as he had never seen any others. She was sensitive to draughts and caught cold easily. He was responsible for her, but he had watered her well and left her, looking for a sheep to bring home. The rose was a moody creature (like St. Exupery's wife) in touch with her feelings and seemingly quite demanding; she had definite values. They had had a fight. His trip to Earth—the desert— was apparently a sort of vacation from the rose. He didn't know whether he would go back to her or not. St. Exupery told the Prince that there are many species and colors of roses, not just one rose. The Prince wept. How sad his rose would be to know that. How sad *he* was to know it! He rolled in the desert sand, saying, "I am not much of a Prince. I am only Lord of one rose and three volcanoes, one of which is inactive, at that."

St. Exupery had not finished the drawing of the muzzle for the sheep, so the Prince wandered off. He met a yellow snake (a death-wish; the snake offered the possibility of his death and return to his asteroid and his rose). The Prince made an appointment to meet the snake later, partake of his venom, and go home with the drawings. He also met a crafty and cunning fox. "You could tame me. You could stay here, now, on this planet," said the fox. But the Prince did not listen. He thought of his rose and wanted to go home. First, though, he wanted the muzzle to protect his rose from the sheep.

St. Exupery looked up to see the Prince was back, as he was nearing completion on the engine work. He shook his head. "Back again, and I still don't have your muzzle." (The inner child is very demanding in dreams, too; it seems to keep returning.) Suddenly, St. Exupery took a moment to ask the Child why it needed the sheep and gained insight into its character and insight into the puer character as well. "Oh, so I won't have to do any more work! The sheep can do my job for me." said the Prince. "You see, on the asteroid, we have these baobab trees which, if allowed to grow to maturity, will push their roots right through the asteroid and split it in two. This actually happened to a neighboring asteroid—it was destroyed by trees. I have to work to chop down the young shoots, but a sheep could easily eat them instead, and then I would be free all day."

This is a theme dear to the heart of the puer, freedom from mundane, routine work. Like the Little Prince and his sheep, the puer invents many good theories to avoid work. But probably in this case the special Prince Shadow reflected St. Exupery's puer ideal. In that event, the Prince is not a guide who represents the Self, but a more negative Shadow sent to show the puer his dark side. The Prince had a puer-like death wish; he wanted to leave the Earth and return to an ideal world—the Unconscious—to be free.

St. Exupery next asked the Prince if he would like to take the drawing of the elephant—his boyhood favorite—with him to the asteroid? Perhaps it could eat the shoots instead of the sheep? But the Prince said, "No! My asteroid is not solid enough to bear the weight of even one elephant!" This seems to mean that St. Exupery should try doing ordinary sheeplike work, following others' less glamorous trades for awhile, instead of endangering himself flying over the desert. Von Franz sees the elephant as representing St. Exupery's mother complex. This accords well with the Asian interpretation of the elephant as symbol for the Mother Goddess. St. Exupery had felt caught in his own childhood between a boa-constrictor and a devouring mother. He escaped into the air as a pilot. The Prince lived on an asteroid where the ground was not solid. (There was no groundedness.) The asteroid would split or break easily, in fact its double, another asteroid, had already done so. The Prince had given St. Exupery a very real warning. Though he resisted his job chopping down tree sprouts and was very childish, the Prince had nonetheless brought an important message. If St. Exupery did not change occupations, do something ordinary or return to his rose (wife) of his own volition, his airplane could split like the asteroid.

St. Exupery finally had the drawing nearly finished; he had only a strap to put on the muzzle for the sheep in its box. His plane was ready to be airborn, but as he approached the Prince, the yellow snake bit his little Shadow, who by this time, had seemed to take on a real physical body, so strong was the vision. St. Exupery took the Prince in his arms and wept, but could not bring him back to life. He missed him very much, and continued to seek him everywhere until the day he crashed and died.

The issues of Senex—practicality, work, ordinary hum-drum life, commitment to the spouse, responsibility, are running rampant in the story, even though the drawings are childlike and the language sentimental. Groundedness and finishing one's efforts are especially important themes. St. Exupery, for instance, wondered if out on the asteroid the muzzle had come off the sheep and had eaten the rose, because he never finished drawing the strap.

The point of the dream vision when Gemini stands at the crossroads point would seem to be that the intellect must not be too quick to accept the Hermes messenger as coming directly from the Self, nor must it be too quick to reject Hermes. He is a trickster, but he probably also has a valid message. The short-term, facile drawing of a box with air holes to put off the Messenger worked. He returned later and the dreamer was able to reach a clearer understanding of his nature and his motives, as well as of his message. In a dream series or a vision series we may think, "There's time—I'll reconnect with the guide later." In real life (waking-state) we do not always have the interest or the opportunity, however. Short-term decisions may become long-term solutions by default.

The snake is an interesting figure in the Little Prince story. Clearly, through its powerful venom it was a deliverer when the Prince was ready to go home. The Prince's death wish was likely St. Exupery's, too, because the author did not give up flying dangerous missions and crashed. Von Franz elaborates on the puer fear of *senex*—old age. The puer does not want to live too long, to become old and stiff. S/he does not long to be a wise old man or woman, but prefers to be thought of as a perpetual fair-haired child with great potential, with an exciting future ahead of him. A dream snake, then, can be a death wish for the puer, especially at mid-life, when s/he is aware of changes, a limiting of options and opportunities, of the body's aging. Mid-life, according to von Franz, is very hard for the puer/puella.

My puer clients do not often mention grim dreams of snakes or fear of growing older. However, in contrast to the other eleven signs nearly every Gemini does bring up the issue of the siblings. This karmic bond seems a very important part of the life journey that is distinctly Gemini's. Even the *Little Prince*, the archetypal sourcebook on the puer, was probably inspired by the death of the author's younger brother. (Von Franz thinks the Prince was a version of the child who died, and that the scene of abject misery at the end, where the author holds the dying Prince and feels so helpless at his inability to revive him, is connected to the actual death of St. Exupery's child-brother.)

In astrology, death and transformation go together. Sometimes, Hermes holds his snake-wand, his caduceus, over Gemini when he is at life's crossroads and seems to beckon a sibling to come along with advice or help. In other cases, the snake-wand seems to mean the death of a sibling and an almost immediate transformation of Gemini's life from puer to senex, often an almost overnight change, as my clients have experienced it. One Gemini rising puella, who had tried three careers but failed to find her niche, heard of her older brother's death on the eve of a qualifying exam. The next time I saw her, all her puella carefree cheerfulness had been replaced by a serious Saturn expression and a vocabulary of "shoulds" and "oughts."

"I took my brother's chair at the Board meeting in the family business. I wish I had listened to him discussing the business over the years, but I was never interested in it. . . I had my own talents and plans. . . now, well, it's a challenge, but I'm a fast learner. Nobody else is in line for the job, so I guess I have to do it. The family expects it of me. . . "

Later, when the initial challenge of learning about the products and contacts had worn off, she said, "I feel so burnt out. So fatigued. Like the Greek God Atlas felt when he had the weight of the world on his shoulders." The mutable signs complain often of burn out, of low vitality. I recommended that she find a project within the business— or even totally outside it—something stimulating to energize her mind, her will to live. Making more money might have been an exciting challenge for her brother, but was much too mundane for Gemini. She seems to like the newly formed research and development division, and the opportunity to meet interesting people in connection with it, at least for the present.

Gemini has a sensitive nervous system. The pressures of responsibility can lead Gemini to smoke too much. Astrologically Gemini/ Gemini rising is associated with the lungs, so this is cumulatively very hard on the body. Or, like Harry Crosby, the archetypal Gemini puer, Geminis tend to relax with alcohol, and finally lose all interest in their work. Or, like St. Exupery, and his opium, drugs make them feel more creative. None of this is good for a sign that really needs to strengthen the body. Geminis have very good minds at birth (unless Mercury is badly afflicted); there's no need to "improve" the mind with any artificial substances. It's the body that needs attention.

When Gemini steps into the shoes of the deceased sibling, or the disabled sibling, and takes on his/her financial obligations or his/her dependent children, the pressures build. Fresh air and exercise, as well as healthy fun, can be neglected. The playful puer or puella within wants an outlet for its spontaneity, its prankster side. Too often personal life (the marriage) suffers from the over-structuring that occurs when puer becomes senex. Here, we have an archetypal case in point—our only Gemini U.S. President, John F. Kennedy, who assumed his brother's role in fulfilling parental ambitions after his sibling's wartime death. Boyish and charming, as the media described him, Kennedy's puer side apparently came out in extramarital affairs. This instability in relationship tends to plague Geminis who are living out a sibling's role, or who live too structured a life through attunement to natal Saturn in an angular position in the horoscope. (See Capricorn, Chapter 10.)

Many Geminis seem to begin life as puer or puella, but to move toward a practical Saturnine lifestyle, to settle down close to the age of 30, the Saturn Return year. Often, as Mutable signs, they feel that circumstances beyond their control have propelled them down a certain path in a crossroads year. Many cite family destiny, with which they tend to identify if the planet Saturn is strong in the horoscopes. Family aspirations, expectations, and ambitions become personalized. My typical Gemini rising client seems to resist groundedness longer than the Gemini Sun sign; perhaps attitudinally he is more of a Peter Pan—less karmically bound to family and siblings than the Sun sign Gemini. Transiting Saturn's aspects to the Gemini Ascendant, however, are important in developing the desire to settle down, in career or marriage.

Mercury, or Hermes, appears in the heavens at twilight, when the *Upanishads* tell us that things are not what they seem; this is the time of day when a rope is easily mistaken for a serpent. If the Moon is full, Hermes is hard to distinguish overhead because he hides; he shines with a dimmer light than the Moon. He also appears to go backwards on his orbit three times a year, on the average. In ancient times when people observed the travel of the planets this lent an aura of mystery to the nocturnal god. He is said to have materialized out of nowhere, with his magical caduceus—two snakes he hypnotized and entwined to form his staff. He made his sandals out of myrtle tree limbs and attached wings for rapid flight. He carried a shield and wore a cap of invisibility, which he sometimes loaned to needy heroes. He was free with short-term advice to the hero, but he did not address the deeper ethical issues of the quest.

Those of you who have Gemini prominent in your horoscopes may enjoy reading Hermes' myth-fragments in *Pausanius' Guide to Greece, I & II*, Penguin Paperbacks, or in Wallace Otto's *The Homeric Gods*. These stories are more like myth fragments because they are not long and involved, like Jason and the Fleece, or Theseus and the Minotaur. Nonetheless, they are complete and make the same point about the human mind as the *Upanishads* and Patanjali's *Yoga Sutras*. If we were really to examine our motives and monitor our own thoughts—our "mind's moods," as Liz Greene called them (*Astrology of Fate*, "Gemini"), we would be amazed at the duality we found within us—the shades of light and darkness that our thoughts reflect.

The myths of Hermes seem to me as brief as the attention span of a small Gemini child. In the first story, Hermes is still in his cradle. He is clever, glib and precocious. He is said to be Jupiter's smartest child, and Jupiter had quite a large progeny. Hermes, in the myth, crawls from the cradle into the forest and steals Apollo's cattle, hides them, and returns to the cradle to pretend sleep. When Apollo discovers the cattle missing, he goes at once to Jupiter to demand that they be found and returned, and that the thief be judged. Hermes is called before the Tribunal of All Highest Zeus (Jupiter) and responds to the accusation with clever stories. He is curious to find out whether he can get away with it or not. Apollo is furious. Jupiter laughs until the tears run down his cheeks and then he says, "Do you not understand that Apollo is the god of prophecy? How could he not know who has stolen his own cattle?" Jupiter set a date for their return. On the appointed day, while Apollo was waiting for him, Hermes stole his bow and arrow. He then fashioned a beautiful lyre which he would trade Apollo for the bow and arrow.

Hermes received many titles on the basis of this short story— patron of thieves, patron of merchants (for the bargain with Apollo), finder of lost objects (the cattle), and liar. There is also a story in which he teaches his son, Autolycus, how to tell convincing lies. It's all in fun.

There is very seldom any meanness to Hermes or Gemini. You may meet him as the practical joker on your office staff, a cheerful, good-natured fellow who is well-liked.

Hermes is generous with his services. He likes to travel among the three worlds and keep up on all the gossip. He does his best for the traveler in need of help, but in making the crossroads decision, Jupiter's wisdom (Sagittarius) or kindness (Pisces) might be of greater aid. Gemini often asks help at life's crossroads. The pros and cons s/he has listed do not really add up to a proper decision, s/he feels. There is still an unknown element. One can never collect all the facts. While s/he sits at Hermes' pillar, waiting for inspiration, s/he consults a career counselor in the morning, an astrologer in the evening, and a therapist in the afternoon. After all this advice from professionals, s/he is likely to listen just as seriously to his barber the next day. It's all a process of gathering data. Each of us has his input for Hermes' child.

Objectivity, like discrimination, is an important Gemini virtue. Hermes may be of two minds, but he is always open minded. As a Mutable sign, Gemini is receptive to the Companion on the Road, Hermes, in his many disguises. Hermes rules the journey itself and may appear as a foreigner—Sagittarius, a "godsend" (messenger of Jupiter) who will offer Gemini a magical opportunity in his time of need. To the Greeks, chance encounters with foreigners or strangers were considered meetings with Hermes himself, and had the aura of fate—or divine timing.

In the *Iliad*, for example, the Trojan King Priam, despondent after hearing of the death of his son, Hector, on the battlefield, prayed to Jupiter to arrange the return of Hector's body for proper burial rites. Only then could a Trojan father have peace of mind. It seemed an impossible request because the body was held in the enemy camp by Achilles, a Greek general who despised Trojans.

Jupiter dispatched Hermes to Priam with these interesting words (from the last book of the *Iliad*)—"Hermes, for you above all other gods, it is dearest to be man's companion." It is as if Zeus had said, "Go forth—they like you down there on Earth. Represent me; use your magic staff and do the impossible!" Hermes invented a story to authenticate his credentials with King Priam, who asked immediately, "Who are you, and what is your parentage?" Hermes lied creatively, "I'm a noble from Achilles' province in Greece (a foreigner). My father is quite rich. I'm a seventh son of a seventh son. I can make you invisible with my cap, speed your journey to the enemy camp, and sneak you in against all odds by putting the sentries to sleep with my magic wand. Then, you'll be persuasive with Achilles (in spite of his hatred for Trojans) and I'll arrange for him to return Hector's body. He'll even agree to stop the war for twelve days for the burial. Then I'll sneak you out with Hector's body before the guards awake or King Agamemnon arrives at camp and kills you. I'll fly you back here to your own camp to bury Hector. Then your peace of mind will be restored and Hector's soul will be at rest."

Priam tested Hermes with a bribe—a golden cup. Hermes refused it. Priam then accepted this "impossible opportunity" offered by the "godsend" in the form of the beautiful young foreign noble. The magic worked. The long epic ends in that same chapter with Hector's burial.

What seems so intriguing about the Gemini archetype is the number of clients who have, over the years, not only been spokesmen or intermediaries for foreigners (translating, tutoring, etc.), but who have been asked to help foreigners illegally, "Will you take this package through customs for me? Will you hide someone from Immigration for the sanctuary movement?"—literally render someone invisible, as Hermes did Priam until he got Priam past the sentries. Often the opportunity in the fateful encounter involves a bribe, like the golden cup Priam offered Hermes, which would compromise Gemini. This issue is a real test of ethics, discrimination and objectivity. The circumstances differ slightly in each client's case, but the objectivity of the Air element is their best defense. Emotional identification with the needy stranger is the danger—(that would involve other watery archetypes in the client's chart, not Gemini planets). The ethical tests can be very subtle. Jupiter offers good karma, especially in areas like the sanctuary movement, where the ethical-legal issues are complex. Priam asked good questions of Jupiter's messenger. He was unaware that he was dealing with Hermes until the very end of the story. Safely home with Hector's body, Priam must have heaved a great sigh of relief.

Not all encounters with Hermes turn out as well as Priam's. Beware especially a solution that looks too facile. Will Gemini be loyal rather than fickle? Dependable? If fixity is also prominent in the horoscope s/he tends not to veer off course ethically. This is usually true if s/he has positive Mercury/Jupiter aspects in his or her chart or if s/he has integrated the ethical standards they're exposed to in the early childhood environment. Children born in crafty, precocious Gemini need to be watched carefully and caught when they are too inventive with the truth, as Jupiter caught Hermes! It's very helpful when Hermes' children have ethical parents.

Hercules, for instance, was not constant in following the guide. Alice Bailey, in the Gemini task, has Hercules abandoning his guide impulsively for a false teacher he's just met. He ends up being tied hand and foot to a sacrificial altar for a year because of his lack of constancy. Most Geminis seem to do better than Hercules (Bailey, *Labours of Hercules*, p. 27). They may wear a tragic mask when you see them in the morning and a comic mask by evening, but as the years go by, they still look youthful. Though they may intellectualize incessantly, Geminis manage not to take life or their own mistakes too seriously.

Hermes, then, as a symbol for the amoral, dualistic mind, can attract either good or ill. He gave the Fleece, a great treasure, to Jason's ancestors. In his honor, Greeks in ancient times generously left food and beverages at Herms, or Hermes' pillars (boundary stones), for his protoges, the weary travelers. But let the travelers beware, for Hermes' other favored children, the robbers, were on the road at night, too. Conscious awareness and alertness seem to be required of those who deal in Hermes' energy.

This awareness is especially important after an encounter with playful Hermes, the Trickster. The mind, the *Upanishads* tell us, can attract either what it fears or what it wants. Even a very intelligent Hermes-type, a Gemini with an extremely good mind, will occasionally meet a convincing trickster or thief along the way. Later, when Gemini regains his objectivity, s/he thinks, "How could I have been so stupid as to have believed that person?"

This leads to more reserve and caution in his next Hermes-encounter. Sometimes it leads to bitterness. Mercury humor turns to sharp, sarcastic wit and Gemini slams the door to new companions for awhile. This is sad because s/he misses opportunities—what Kerenyi called, new "joys, delights and revelations" along the Way. (C. Kerenyi, *Hermes, Guide of Souls*.)

Astrologers occasionally meet older Geminis who have become cynical as a result of negative encounters, especially those who have progressed into Virgo. It's unfortunate, because they seem to have lost their openness and resiliency—and the opportunity to learn through relationships. Learning is a major part of the journey for the Hermes sign.

Hermes-the-Trickster has long been associated with accidents on the road. People who are apprehensive and whose lives include no creative mental projects as an outlet for Gemini energy are vulnerable to accidents of the fender-bender or paper cut type— or sometimes of even greater magnitude on transits of Mercury. Dislocated shoulders, whiplash or injured arm, which affect the Gemini body areas, are common. Alertness in traffic, regardless of preoccupations, is important for Gemini, especially on days of difficult transits. We can often deal with the Trickster (Hermes' nervous mental energy) on these transits, by (1) checking the ephemeris, and (2) giving him an alternative—a project to study, or write, or a lecture to organize—but not in the car. *After* we reach our destination! Commuter travel is a 3rd House or Gemini area of life opposite long distance travel (9th House).

Discrimination should also be used in regard to impulsive purchases during retrograde Mercury, for those with Gemini Sun, Moon or Ascendant. Department stores seem to have a lot of sales when Mercury is in retrograde phase. This must be one of Hermes' tricks. If you are an impulsive Gemini, try to avoid these. If you buy a new gadget or appliance, chances are it won't work when you get home— and sale items are non-returnable. If you buy a bargain dress, chances are it's inappropriate for the occasion you had in mind—only swim suits or blue jeans will be worn to that one. Or, you go to a bookstore on retrograde Mercury—Gemini loves books—and buy books which you later discover only repeat in a slightly new way information already on your shelves.

Hermes is a catalyst; a messenger. He communicates information and brings people together. That's why in medical astrology Gemini rules the nervous system; it functions as a network to carry messages from the senses to the brain. In social situations, the Gemini archetype is also a catalyst. This involves two factors, of course— positive and negative (dual). In the positive sense, Gemini friends are good at circulating your business card at social events. Give them a stack of cards to add to their gardener's, hairdresser's, caterer's. seamstresses'. But, in the negative sense, beware of the gossip tendency. Remember that Hermes, in constant transit through the Three Worlds, talked with many gods, heroes and men. Therefore, if you have Scorpio-privacy tendencies yourself, don't entrust your deepest secrets to Hermes' children. He doesn't always report the story accurately. Hermes likes to improvise, create and entertain.

The Third House, Gemini, in the natural zodiac, deals with communication, close relatives (especially siblings) and the neighborhood. Gemini mothers often leave the children with close relatives or a neighborhood friend and go to work. Geminis crave adult company and conversation; it's hard for them to be at home with children under the age of six. Gemini reciprocates and tutors and babysits for relatives, too, though she may not always be patient about it and is creative about doing the tutoring *her* way. Hermes babysat for several of the gods. He was not, however, very good for very long with his own son, Pan. Though Pan was an ugly child his father adored him at first. Eventually Hermes became bored with fatherhood and took him to Dionysius to raise. I have observed Mercury-in-the-5th House women, many of whom had communications (sales, teaching, advertising, etc.) or writing as a profession. When we discussed children as a meaning of the 5th House in their lives, they tended to respond, "Well. . . I think I'm too nervous and high-strung to want children of my own. I enjoy teaching them, you understand. I like kids. But noisy little ones at home at night after teaching all day? No. . . I don't think so, unless I had a relative who lived in the neighborhood and could help, so I could continue working." A babysitter/relative would do it. I thought of Hermes and Pan. Geminis serve on neighborhood commissions, are alert to the need for improvement and changes, and of course, if you are looking for your Gemini friend, try her neighbor's house. She may be there, having a chat.

Carolyi Kerenyi, in his *Hermes, Guide of Souls*, makes an interesting point about the Messenger God. Wherever Hermes happened to be, whatever he needed at the moment, would materialize for him in the immediate environment. This is something Geminis have often remarked upon, too. They seem to know that, regardless of where they are, if they are alert and ask around, the very thing or information they require will appear.

Kerenyi gives us an example of Hermes caught in a situation which brings tension into the lives of many Geminis—deadline pressure. Zeus had decreed that on a certain day Hermes must face the wrath of the Sun God, Apollo, and return the stolen cattle. Apollo had not taken this slight lightly; an infant godling had embarrassed him and caused him to lose face with the rest of his peers in the Pantheon. He had been successfully tricked by the Prankster. A gift was required to put him in better humor, but what kind of gift? Maybe something to bring out his creativity, since Apollo was a Fifth House God.

Hermes instinctively went to his mother's house. Crawling across her threshold was exactly what he needed—a tortoise. Apollo liked music and probably had a hidden talent for it. Hermes quickly snatched the tortoise, scraped out the shell and fashioned an instrument, history's first lyre, for the Leo God. Apollo was delighted. The inventive mind had triumphed; the environment had provided for him. I often think of this story when a client with many planets in Gemini says, "I need this item by Monday for a project. I cannot afford to put a lot of money into it though. But I know there will be one at the swap meet this weekend."

Wouldn't this happen for all of us, we might ask, the way it does for Gemini, if we were more alert? It might. Their alertness is part of the Hermes magic, but their inventiveness is also part of it. Many of us, for instance, would have looked at that ugly tortoise and chased it away instead of making a connection between the tortoise and the problem at hand—how to placate the Leo God. Would *we* have seen how the tortoise could become something Apollo might like even better than his sacred cattle?

Hermes gave Pandora her voice as well as her box, and communication professions appeal to his children—sales, teaching, advertising, journalism, receptionist work. They can meet the public and also be free to arrange the day—a variety of subjects, projects or tasks at the desk. They hate to sit and want to move around the room, or move through town in the car. The mental restlessness of Gemini seems to generate physical restlessness reminiscent of Aries. Gemini often enjoys being the office messenger or delivery person.

Gemini is the most versatile archetype. Hermes, as inventor of the lyre, was patron of instruments and crafts. Many Geminis are creative craftspeople. Some are even ambidextrous. Others are so well coordinated that they can sew a dress, watch TV, talk on the phone (using a neckrest for the instrument) and time dinner in the oven simultaneously. As ruler of Gemini, Hermes is capable of artistic perfection in the crafts, while as ruler of Virgo he is adept at detailed precision paperwork. Virgo, however, usually can be observed sitting all morning at his desk engrossed in one project, while Gemini takes lots of breaks and would prefer to start three different projects before noon. Finishing by the deadline is a problem for both the Hermes ruled signs. Gemini becomes very nervous as Christmas approaches and his gift projects for relatives must be completed. Virgo is equally nervous as deadlines set by the IRS, the boss, or the publisher approach. To be complete, Virgo has to make several additions at the last minute. Hermes' children often are found burning the midnight oil the week before the deadline.

To Gemini Hermes gives his cheerful wit and communication skills, his young-at-heart philosophy, versatility, and dexterity. The Hermes gift that at first glance seems of dubious or even negative value is the dual mind. In a sense, Gemini has a head start, though, where consciousness is concerned, because s/he is aware of duality. Hindu philosophy holds that all of us must first become aware of the illusion of Maya or the duality in nature—cold and heat, light and dark, pleasure and pain, like and dislike—in order to transcend our preferences and aversions. Gemini is perhaps best equipped to analyze the thoughts, to observe the light and dark ideas flitting across the cerebral cortex. Of course, the next step—*transcending* duality, walking through the Gates of Hercules and emerging on the other side with Wisdom (Sagittarius)—still remains to be taken. Gemini is constantly collecting idea input from his/her environment (3rd House) and storing the data (if it's logical) in his memory bank. Gemini acts much as the *Upanishads* describe; he stands back from his/her thoughts, registering them as logical or illogical, and does not identify with them. S/he is very slow to label ideas "mine." They are on file till he encounters their polar opposite—the other side of the story—at which point Gemini balances out both ideas. S/he is on the lookout for the larger truth (Sagittarius) instinctively, but he sometimes thinks that adding up all the facts/opinions on file will give him truth. Hermes, the Quicksilver Mind, does not personalize; he objectifies.

It's interesting to watch Gemini clients deal with the dark side or Shadow, which, as C.G. Jung has said, "all of us have but few of us want openly to acknowledge." (*Archetypes of the Unconscious*, CW V.9, 284f.) Unless a Gemini or Gemini-ascending has many planets in water (a personalizing element), I have found that when his dark side is brought up s/he will say, "Yes, I'm like that! I noticed those tendencies years ago." Usually there's no attempt to deny it, or guilt expressed about it. The dark side is a fact. Gemini is quite conscious of what goes on in his life and in his thoughts.

Yet, often, in a session with Gemini, if the astrologer brings up another of Jung's points about that Shadow—that it is a perfectly normal instinct, appropriate to express in certain circumstances or even that it can be creative and perhaps ought to be given scope (C.G. Jung, *Aion*, CW V.9, 266)—the Gemini's eyes become thoughtful and Hermes' nervous wrinkle appears on his brow. "It's not rational. It's not logical behavior." One Gemini woman, low in Fire and the product of a private school education, said, "A lady doesn't behave like a fishwife! When I blow up over something, it's embarrassing. It's not normal behavior for me. I have a peaceful disposition." I was thinking of her void in Fire, her retrograde Mars, and her tendency not to communicate resentment/anger, but to let it build and explode over minor incidents. What bothered her most about communicating anger *directly* to others at the time they upset her was that, "It's not rational behavior. A person needs to think (Hermes), to reflect on whether it's worthwhile to be upset about your teenager and his friends destroying the house while you were away for the weekend. So, I stood in the doorway in shock and then decided to come in and unpack and think about how to handle him. Then two days later, I yelled at him for spilling something on the rug—which he does all the time." The instincts know how to handle the situation in a fiery, direct, immediate, spontaneous way. But a Hermes-type will often reject what appears as a dark or irrational instinctual reaction. To some extent, this applies to all the Air signs because Air is a thinking element. The spontaneity of the Fire sign across from the Air sign gives a key to the appropriate type of action. Sagittarius is the most blunt communicator in the zodiac and it's opposite Gemini.

One more word on duality. Literal, physical twins also participate in the archetype of Gemini. They are working with understanding the Shadow, the dark side, of their own personality. But, as Liz Greene has pointed out in her "Gemini" section of *The Astrology of Fate* (p. 190), it is often easier for them to project the dark side outward than to confront it within. Having conveniently handy a person who is a physical replica, a type of mirror image, is an opportunity for

the "good" twin to project upon the "bad." I have watched twin clients struggle with the dark side or Shadow issue over the years and listened closely to what they said about it. Male twins looked at each other as the dominant or successful and the weaker or unsuccessful. When transits brought down the successful from a lofty peak of attainment to a rocky valley of misery, he remarked that he suddenly understood his twin much better. . . success wasn't the only value in life. Women twins regarded each other as the playful and the responsible/professional. There were several cases of this. When working on a project with a psychologist, I had administered the Myers-Briggs personality test to twins, among other people. Several twins were fascinated to learn the differences between their personalities. One lady called and said, "I came out a 'perceptual' and she came out a 'judgment'—I just knew it! I am the one who is playful—she is the workaholic."

Gemini seeks a good guide at the crossroads, as Alice Bailey has remarked. At the shadow crossroads, my twin clients often find a relative (3rd House) to be the arbiter or guide. They call Aunt May and ask, "I'm right, aren't I? That man is wrong for my twin? That other job is better for her. . . ?" The astrologer has to struggle, sometimes, against being cast in the role of Aunt May when the dear lady is out of town.

Twins have a protracted battle with their dark side, a struggle which often involves jealousy and the pain of identity separation in adulthood (after the Saturn return). Yet, they also have a strong motivation to overcome the pain and keep alive their special bond. This motivation is what Mitchell Walker, in his article for *Quaternary Magazine* (1975), calls "The Double Archetype." The double concept seems similar to the Hindu idea of the soul mate—to experience oneness with someone not only through the same mental wavelength, but through the same feelings, on the empathy level, too. Most of us at some point in our lives have longed for a friend who truly understands us as we are. "As angry as I have been at my sister—or as jealous of her—I have always loved her more than anyone! And I have always known that if one of us ever really needed the other— regardless of how intent she or I were on our own lives at the time— we would be there for each other," a woman who is a twin once remarked. A male twin said, "Though my brother and I see each other about once a year—we live in different parts of the country—when we get together it's as if we had just left off talking the day before. One of us begins a sentence, stops for a breath, and the other finishes it."

The search for the double, especially for mental understanding from another, seems a truly Gemini search. Physical twins are born with the other—the friend already on the scene, but Walker points out examples of professional collaborators who, in the process of creating musical scores or plays or novels, attained the double wavelength. The work flowed when they were both present in the office or studio. Energy circulated in the room; stimulation happened for those couples as it had not happened for either of them with anyone else.

The Mitchell theme most interesting to me, however, aside from mental understanding and creative flow, is androgyny. He says that the double works only between people of the same sex. Over the years, I have thought of androgynous Hermes and Mercury of alchemical fame (see Virgo) as the perpetual adolescent. Eternal children always in flux—free to travel the three worlds. But until reading Mitchell's article, I had never really connected the Gemini archetype and Hermes with my gay clients. Once the connection was made, though, it was amazing the number of gays I observed on the Gemini quest for that mental friendship—the perfect collaborative relationship. How many creative people are looking to reconcile duality and participate in the Gemini archetype—through Sun, Moon, Ascendant, or the 3rd House, the Hermes' careers in communication of ideas (including his merchant or sales career), and close attachments with relatives? I have seen several clients with Gemini as a major chart theme go through a period of involvement in gay relationships, often during the same years they considered the peak time for their creativity. This generally coincided with transits or progressions through the 5th House—love and creativity. There may be something in the double archetype for the astrologer to ponder. Hermes, after all, is the only androgynous ruling planet; the other gods and goddesses are decidedly either male or female.

VENUS/APHRODITE
Esoteric Ruler

How, then, does the restless Gemini mind resolve its choice of options—concentrate its energy and go forward on the quest? The goal might be to write the epic of our times, the *Gone with the Wind* of the 1980's; to become travelling salesman of the year; to finish the afghan in time for Christmas; to find the double; fight or integrate the creativity of the Shadow; or, most interesting for esotericists, go through Hercules' Arches and transcend duality! Sagittarian focus, fiery inspiration and energy are part of the solution. But Air needs to relate as well as to create. Each Air House in the natural zodiac (Houses 3, 7 and 11) is about a different type of relating.

Gemini begins with the sibling relationship and continues throughout life to learn from relatives—listening to their problems and giving logical, objective advice, babysitting, or entering into family businesses. But, even with close relatives and good neighbors (3rd House), something is still missing without a partner. Yet as a puer, Hermes often compromises in order to keep his freedom. He could write the epic novel while his wife flew the friendly skies as a flight attendant. She could maintain the freedom to take courses, teach, organize someone's office, counsel, create while he traveled with the armed forces or for his corporation. Marriages with a lot of room for roving, physically and mentally, are often a good compromise for Hermes. He does not want to be bound in the present. He is living in the future. He wants to be mentally free. The difficulty with relationships where one spouse travels a great deal is apparent to those of us who work with Gemini clients—the opportunity for a love triangle to develop. With the freedom there is risk.

With Vulcan away, Aphrodite and Hermes were able to have an affair. Hermes, ruler of Gemini, remained free to transit the three worlds. Aphrodite, though, got into trouble with her husband, Vulcan. The disappearance and reappearance of the traveler-spouse seems a source of excitement to many Gemini clients. "It's like a courtship all over again," said one military wife. "When he comes home, we have so much to discuss. It's so stimulating! I think if we were together all the time, like other couples, it would be terribly boring!" One could almost see Hermes the Messenger in the wings, smiling at her. He, too, likes to catch up on all the news and gossip.

But the client has come not so much to talk to the astrologer about the stimulation or the positive side of the marriage, but about the affair. Such a paradox, thinks the astrologer. The affair seemed grounding or earthy to the Eternal Child, the Gemini, but commitment doesn't seem grounding. Responsibility seems scary. They might not be free for the quest—the tilting at windmills or the impossible dream. So many spouses of Gemini Peter Pans have asked, "But what does s/he think I'm keeping him/her from?" The Gemini very often doesn't know the answer—only that there is a quest—that there is something out there that one must be unencumbered to do.

What, then, is the higher or spiritual meaning of Hermes meeting Aphrodite; what was it all about esoterically? At first, it seems incongruous—the airy sprite, Hermes, falling in love with the most physical of the goddesses, the sexiest lady in the Pantheon, sultry Aphrodite? If we view Aphrodite as a symbol of the physical, as an Earth Goddess (ruler of Taurus), vain about her body, lazy, relaxed (ruler of Libra), and Hermes as the nervous mental energy that gives us insomnia at night, we can see the grounding of Hermes and the coming together of two worlds—Air and Earth. Also, the thinking (Hermes) and feeling (Aphrodite) polarities which complete the personality—symbolically, the masculine and feminine, when the Eternal Airy Child meets the Goddess of Love. It is such a meaningful union that their androgynous offspring, the Hermaphrodite, has been over the centuries an important subject for artists. It is an archetype of wholeness—a symbol of the Self.

In *Labours of Hercules*, Alice Bailey amplifies Aphrodite's role as esoteric ruler when she reminds us that she is harmony—the Eros' power to reconcile opposites, to heal all misunderstandings and transcend duality in all its forms. She is the unity principle that spans the Gates of Hercules.

I hope all of you will take time to look at the picture (in J.E. Circlot, *Dictionary of Symbols*, page 146) of Ishwara. This, to Hindus, represents transcendence—passing through the Gates of Hercules, passing beyond Maya's tricky world of illusion. Because when one has the vision of Ishwara, one has transcended the polarities of hot/cold, night/day, pleasure/pain, and most important, male/female. There is only the Soul and the Divine. The rest is illusion.

In the Western tradition also, Jung tells us that for the alchemists Mercurius has "a more or less secret connection with the Goddess of Love." (*Alchemical Studies*, p. 216.) In the Egyptian *Book of Krates*, for instance, Aphrodite appears holding a vessel from which flows a stream of quicksilver, the Hermes metal. Elsewhere in the alchemical literature the seeker descends into an underground cave where he enters the bedchamber of Venus, asleep on her couch. Thinking (Mercury) or the Masculine descends into the Unconscious to meet Feeling, the Goddess of Love, Aphrodite, who is in Jung's interpretation his anima or guide. Wholeness is the result of their hermaphrodite union.

Suppose the quest for someone with Gemini energy is not the Divine Vision on the other side of Hercules' Gates, but simply to finish a current project—get focused, get the creative juices flowing? Then Aphrodite will still help to reconcile the divided mind of Gemini, which is stuck by the wayside at a crossroad intersection and cannot decide upon its course. Look to the House where Venus sits wanting to be comfortable and secure, but not wanting to work too hard either. She has her talents. Look at her aspect dialogues with the other planets, especially planets in Gemini. What is the greatest treasure, the pearl of great price for Venus? She will help you focus your energy in order to fulfill herself in that house of your chart or in one of the houses she rules (Taurus or Libra). You'll enjoy working with her, especially if she offers a few harmonious, rather than discordant, links to the other planets in your horoscope. Consciousness (Hermes) and love (Venus and Eros) combined form a very intuitive, creative partnership. Most important, however, in my experience with Geminis who have developed their Venus (or esoteric ruler), is the warmth they project to others. Others in their lives feel loved, as well as analyzed.

Gemini's mercurial nature seeks variety; his/her curiosity and dilettante spirit carry him/her down many different paths as s/he moves explorer-like through the avenues of his/her own mind during his/her first 30 years. Facts are like food to Gemini, and his/her friends are used to depending upon him for company when they attend lectures and workshops. Suddenly, Gemini goes through a change and they ask each other, "What's happened to him? The only courses he's interested in are things like gourmet cooking and refinishing antique furniture? Can you imagine? He used to be such an idea person. Then, too, he's become so moody. He spends so much time on the phone with his mother."

Or, in the case of a Gemini woman, "What's wrong with Angela? The only book she's read in a month is about real estate. She's bought a condominium and wants to sell them to other people. Last week I invited her to hear an exciting speaker at Unity Church. We used to go to the lectures together every Thursday night. This week she said, 'I am sitting by the fire cozy and content in my new apartment, wrapped in an afghan my mother made me. I am enjoying the company of the dogs, drinking hot chocolate and finishing a box of cookies. I don't really want to go out tonight.' Imagine! I reminded her that we are what we eat, and that when she thought facts were food she was a lot thinner than she is now."

These two Geminis have progressed into Cancer, the zodiac's most domestic sign. Cancer is concerned with nurturing oneself and others. Food is one form of nurturing; calling one's mother, if she is a positive influence, is another. Or, if Mother is a negative person, Gemini can spend part of the Cancer progression discussing childhood and the mother complex with the therapist and coming to terms with dependency. This would be nurturing and developing the Inner Child, the Hermes within.

If Gemini has some natal planets in Cancer, the progressed Sun will conjunct them over the 30-year cycle and psychic or imaginative talents will usually emerge. Intuition improves, with the exception of those few Geminis (usually men) who deny they have a feminine side at all. Purchasing and furnishing a home, or selling homes to others, is a way of nurturing, of providing a nest or hearth. Finally, for puer or puella the major Cancer issue of whether or not to have children is faced. Here there seems to be a real difference between the client who has natal planets in Cancer, for whom parental obligations seem easier and more natural, and the high-strung Gemini with a stellium in his Sun sign (5 or more planets). This person usually prefers to develop the Cancer progression by shifting toward a nurturing or an imaginative career rather than having children of his/her own. I have among my clientele several medical doctors with the Gemini stellium and very little Water (no Cancer) in their horoscopes. They have shifted their focus from large, impersonal hospitals, or from clinical research, toward smaller, more personal, family-oriented clinics. One has changed his field to work exclusively with pregnant women and new mothers. There are many ways to experience the archetype.

The Cancer progression is Moon ruled. This means that the unconscious, the lunar nature, is quite powerful and seems to lead Gemini/Gemini rising toward satisfying its inner needs in the outer, career world. For instance, a Gemini Sun sign man who had never even cared to read fiction, a writer of technical manuals, suddenly announced that he was taking several creative writing courses in the Cancer cycle. "I can't bear the thought of having to write one more dry computer manual!" He admitted that this statement would have seemed ridiculous to him just two years before when natal Mercury and natal Sun were still in Gemini.

The Cancer progression may put Gemini in touch with old childhood memories and with his personal past. He may recall an old slight from a Christmas dinner many years ago, brood over it, and then begin to take remarks made to him in the present quite personally. Family members may ask, "What happened to the prankster? Where is his sense of humor? Why is he so offended at my joke?" To them, he seems to be losing objectivity during a subjective cycle. However, the water signs in the family may begin to like Gemini better in the Cancer cycle. "I think he's much less superficial, much deeper now," or, "he doesn't hurt my feelings anymore with his analytical, sarcastic wit. I think he's kinder, more sensitive. He talks less and listens to us more." The water element has its good and bad points as it emerges in Gemini. The progression changes are subtle. It sometimes helps to read about the progressed character traits in a Sun sign book, to tune in to the positive and become aware of the negative points.

Cancer is often a time when Gemini loses one or both parents to death, to Father Time, the enemy. It is painful to let go in this watery, attached phase as the unconscious seems to resist healing, to hang on. It is so much better if Gemini has sorted out his own identity and goals from those of the parent/parents ahead of time. And if there is disharmony with one or both parents at the end, it helps if Gemini has a meditation technique or affirmation for letting go of his or her own emotions, and if s/he can come to realize that no human being really understands another human being perfectly—only the Divine can do that.

The search for the goddess is part of the Cancer cycle for most of my Gemini clients, though they might not choose to call it that. (Von Franz would call it, perhaps, the puer's mother complex.) To me, it seems a tendency to project the goddess on the most unlikely people in the outer world. Many times, for instance, a gay client with bulging muscles, a young Adonis, will complain of his Gemini/Gemini rising partner, "He wants me to be his mother, to take care of him. I'm sick and tired of it. I'm looking for an adult to relate to. I'm moving out." To the outsider, it seems amazing that the progressed Cancer could project Mother onto this handsome young man who lifts weights. The Hindus say, "Divine Mother is within." Jung has said something similar: "The *anima*, the inner feminine, is the soul." We cannot find anything but disappointment projecting her upon others in the outer world. We find wholeness when we find her within and follow her guidance.

The Leo progression is more conscious, therefore more comfortable for Hermes ruled Gemini in many ways. Confidence is strong, and physical vitality usually improves. Gemini feels active, rather than passive. Leo magnetism enhances Gemini's original thinking. Leo warmth attracts positive people. Leo fixity stabilizes the nervous system. Like Cancer, Leo is an emotional sign. Through trusting intuition as well as Hermes logic in Cancer, Gemini developed inward. In Leo, an extroverted sign, Gemini expresses emotion spontaneously and outwardly. Leo courage reinforces Gemini's hesitant decision-making. Leo comes through to others as sincere, direct and genuine, rather than as the mercurial strategist, as the cunning Hermes-mind of Gemini's early years. Leo enjoys adult nieces, nephews and often, grandchildren. Many Geminis appreciate the Jungian path to individuation when they reach Leo. Devised by Carl Jung, himself a Leo, the Path of Individuation offers techniques to achieve integration of the opposites and transcend them. This is also the Hindu goal—transcendence of the illusory opposites. In esoteric astrology this is the Gemini task, directly related to the dual glyph and the journey of the Twins.

The Sun rules the Leo progression. It is a time when Gemini can really shine. These years offer many Geminis a chance to renew the spontaneity, enthusiasm, joy, and even occasionally the prankster side of their youth. Leo is a conscious awareness sign, connected to the Sun center, or *ajna* chakra. The natal hermetic logos attitude is fostered as Gemini enters this 30-year cycle.

I have not met many Geminis who lived long into the Virgo progression. This is a double Hermes influence and therefore very mental, as Mercury rules both the natal and progressed signs. Mercury is a worrisome ruler. S/he wants badly to communicate and the absence of relatives to communicate with is difficult for him/her when the family lives a long distance away. I would imagine that this progression could produce some chronic complainers, given the Hermes cynical wit. But, there are some very serviceful Gemini/Virgos too! Former teachers, for instance, volunteer their services to the less fortunate, the learning impaired. People who give of their minds and their hearts to others receive great inner rewards. Hermes, after all, is the Friend to Mankind.

Our inner work in spiritual astrology involves letting the soul come forward to lead the personality. In Gemini's youth the developing intellect would have freedom to explore many different avenues as a variety-seeking dilettante. During the Cancer progression, the intuition would emerge, particularly if Gemini had watery planets prominent in the horoscope, or planets in the psychic houses (4th, 8th, or 12th). The unconscious may have become as interesting a realm as the conscious, waking-state awareness of Hermes, its mundane ruler. In Leo, the emphasis would shift towards personality integration—wholeness, growth in the emotional depths of the personality as well as mind and intuition. Aphrodite as esoteric ruler may have begun to play her role in introducing warmth, relationship, (Eros) to balance Hermes Logos—feeling to balance Hermes' thinking. Integration of the personality may have taken Gemini toward its polar extremity, Sagittarius—a spiritual search, foreign philosophies, travel abroad. Finally communication of values (Aphrodite/Eros) to others is a function of the Virgo progression, which is serviceful, practical, and works well with either the spoken or printed word. Gemini always liked to chatter, and in Virgo, at the close of the lifetime, s/he often has something quite worthwhile to say.

Questionnaire

How does the Gemini archetype express itself? Though this relates particularly to those with the Sun in Gemini or Gemini rising, anyone could apply this series of questions to the house where his Mercury is located or the house which has Gemini (or Gemini intercepted) on the cusp. The answers to these questions will indicate how in touch the reader is with Mercury, the "messenger of the gods," his conscious mind and his powers of communication.

1. My ability to communicate my ideas and concepts to others is
   a. superior.
   b. very good.
   c. not very good.

2. Among my strong points I would list sense of humor, objectivity, versatility, cheerfulness and adaptability
   a. 80% of the time.
   b. 50% of the time.
   c. 25% of the time or less.

3. I get along well with people from all types of social, educational, and economic backgrounds. I consider myself broadminded
   a. 80% of the time or more.
   b. 50% of the time.
   c. 25% of the time or less.

4. Some people see me as a restless person who is unlikely to see a project through to its conclusion. This is probably true
   a. 80% of the time or more.
   b. 50% of the time.
   c. 25% of the time or less.

5. When under the pressures of deadlines I tend to be accident-prone. My hands, fingers and arms tend to be bruised
   a. 25% of the time or less.
   b. 50% of the time.

   c. 80% or more of the time.

6. My greatest fear is
   a. my dark (Shadow) side will be visible to other people.
   b. bankruptcy.
   c. that I will be blamed unjustly for something I didn't do.

7. The greatest obstacle to my success comes from
   a. my competitors and/or circumstances beyond my control.
   b. within myself.

8. I feel the weakest part of my body—the part that causes me the most trouble is
   a. lungs, stiff neck, tension felt in shoulders and upper back.
   b. heart and circulatory system.
   c. sciatic muscle, hip or thigh.

9. Important in my life are such Mercury-related areas as friendship with siblings, seminars and workshops, reading and conversation. These are
   a. very important.
   b. moderately important.
   c. unimportant.

10. Like Mercury the Messenger God, I like to move around a lot during the day. My day involves
   a. a lot of travel time.
   b. some travel.
   c. hardly any commuter travel.

Those who have scored five or more (a) answers are highly in touch with their mundane ruler, Mercury, the conscious mind. Those who have scored five or more (c) answers need to develop Mercury's conscious awareness. Mercury's versatility, dexterity, and communication skills may need to be developed. One symptom of a frustrated Mercury is that a person tends to be accident prone—attracting cuts and bruises. Those who answered (c) to question (5) should review their natal Mercury. Is it in the twelfth house? Is it retrograde? Is it intercepted? It is important for them to work consciously with the planets aspecting natal Mercury to help Mercury express itself constructively—courses involving one or more practical skills, development of body coordination, as well as courses in public speaking or data analysis can be helpful.

Where is the balance point between Gemini and Sagittarius? How does the Gemini integrate the concrete situation and the general perspective? Though this relates particularly to those with Sun in Gemini or Gemini rising, all of us have Mercury and Jupiter somewhere in our horoscope. Many of us have planets in the Third or Ninth House. For all of us the polarity from Gemini to Sagittarius involves the ability to analyze and to synthesize—to go from specific information to the whole picture.

1. I consider myself a strategist. I sort through the facts and decide how much information to give to whom. I do this
   a. never.
   b. some of the time.
   c. most of the time.

2. Because I can see two sides to every issue I am comfortable with "situation ethics"
   a. never.
   b. sometimes.
   c. usually.

3. I like to travel
   a. overseas—long distances.
   b. both short and long distances.
   c. short distances only (mainly in my own country).

4. I am more interested in the spirit of the law than the letter of the law
   a. most of the time.
   b. 50% of the time.
   c. I don't distinguish between the two.

5. My higher education includes
   a. a graduate degree.
   b. a bachelor's degree.
   c. some education beyond high school.

Those who have scored three or more (b) answers are doing a good job with personality integration on the Gemini/Sagittarius polarity. Those who have three or more (c) answers may need to work more consciously on developing natal Jupiter in their horoscopes. Those who have three or more (a) answers may be out of balance in the other direction (weak or undeveloped Mercury). Study both Mercury and Jupiter in the natal chart. Is there an aspect between them? Which one is stronger by house position, or location in its sign of rulership or exaltation? Is either of them retrograde, intercepted, in fall, or in detriment? Aspects to the weaker planet can help point the way to its integration.

What does it mean to be an esoteric Gemini? How does Gemini integrate Venus, its esoteric ruler, into the personality? Every Gemini will have both Mercury and Venus somewhere in the horoscope. The well-integrated Venus adds warmth and kindness to mercurial Gemini. The answers to the following questions will indicate the extent to which Gemini is in touch with Venus.

1. I go beyond the techniques of my trade and make of my work an art form
   a. often.
   b. occasionally.
   c. rarely.

2. I try to temper my speech with kindness
   a. most of the time.
   b. some of the time.
   c. hardly ever.

3. I consciously try to be loving as well as analytical in my personal relationships.
   a. Most of the time.
   b. Some of the time.
   c. Hardly ever.

4. I am considered not only witty and intelligent but a caring person by
   a. most of the people I know.
   b. about half of the people I know.

    c. very few people.

5. If a co-worker presents a report in which a few of the facts are inaccurate
    a. I refrain from criticism and give him the benefit of the doubt.
    b. I refrain from criticism at the time but gossip later.
    c. I criticize him mercilessly.

Those who have scored three or more (a) answers are in touch with their esoteric ruler. Those who scored three or more (b) answers need more work at integrating Venus according to its house, sign and aspects in their natal chart—approach situations more from the heart rather than just from the head through the house where Venus resides. Those who scored three or more (c) answers should study their natal Venus. Is it intercepted, retrograde, in fall, in detriment? Developing and integrating Venus softens the cutting edge of Mercury's sarcasm, cynicism, and bitterness as the years go by.

References

Alice Bailey, *Esoteric Astrology*, "Gemini," Lucis Publishing Co., New York, 1976

Alice Bailey, *Labours of Hercules*, "Gemini," Lucis Publishing Co., New York, 1977

Norman O. Brown, *Hermes, The Thief*, University of Wisconsin Press, Madison, 1947

Paul Carus, *The Gospel of Buddha*, Open Court Publications Co., La Salle, 1973

Jean and Wallace Clift, *Symbols of Transformation in Dreams*, "The Trickster," Crossroad Publications, New York, 1986

William Doty, "Hermes," in *Facing the Gods*, James Hillman ed., Spring Publications, Irving, 1980

Marie Louise von Franz, *Puer Aeternus*, Spring Publications, Zurich, 1970

Marie Louise von Franz, "The Process of Individuation," Part 3, in *Man and His Symbols*, C.G. Jung ed., Doubleday and Co. Inc., Garden City, 1969

Liz Greene, *Astrology of Fate*, "Gemini," Samuel Weiser Inc., York Beach, 1984

Jane Harrison, *Mythology, Our Debt to Greece and Rome*, M. Jones printer, Boston, 1924

Joseph L. Henderson, "Ancient Myths and Modern Man-Symbols of Transcendence," Part 2, in *Man and His Symbols*, C.G. Jung ed., Doubleday and Co. Inc., Garden City, 1969

James Hillman, *Puer Papers*, "Senex and Puer," and "Peaks and Vales," Spring Publications Inc., Irving 1979

C.G. Jung, *Aion*, Princeton University Press, Princeton, 1959

C.G. Jung, "Alchemical Studies," transl. R.F.C. Hull, Princeton University Press, Princeton, 1967

C.G. Jung, "Approaching the Unconscious," Part 1, in *Man and His Symbols*, C.G. Jung ed., Doubleday and Co., Garden City, 1969

C.G. Jung, "Psychology and Alchemy," transl. R.F.C. Hull, Princeton University Press, Princeton, 1968

C. Kerenyi, *The Gods of the Greeks*, "Hermes," Thames and Hudson, London, 1951

Karl Kerenyi, *Hermes, Guide of Souls*, Spring Publications, Zurich, 1976

Swami Prabhavananda, *How to Know God: The Yoga Aphorisms of Patanjali*, Christopher Isherwood ed., Mentor Books, New American Library, New York, 1969

The Thirteen Principle Upanishads, transl. by R.E. Hume (2nd revised ed.), Oxford University Press, Oxford, 1931

Pausanius: A Guide to Greece, Vols. 1 and 2, "Hermes," transl. by Peter Levi, Penguin Classics, New York, 1979

Jean Pierre Vernant, "Hermes and Hestia," in *Mythes et Pensées Chez les Grecs*, 3rd ed., Editions la Decouverte, Paris, 1985

Mitchell Walker, "The Archetype of the Double," *Quaternary Magazine*, 1975

Donald Ward, *The Divine Twins: An Indo-European Myth in Germanic Tradition*, Folkstore Studies #19, University of California Press, Berkeley, 1968

Geoffrey Wolff, *Black Sun: Brief Transit and Violent Eclipse of Harry Crosby*, Random House, New York, 1976

4 CANCER:
The Search for the Mother Goddess

Cancer, the Cosmic Womb, is also the first Water sign. The connection between Cancer and water is really important. As the physical birth process involves the breaking of waters, so also does the process of Cancer involve creativity. Of course, there are often complications during the birth process; some of our creative ventures do not flow as smoothly as others. In order to release Cancer's creativity, we must first cut the umbilical cord which binds us to family karma and leave the safe womb of the home and choose our own direction in life.

The glyph for Cancer (♋) is the male and female seeds. The archetype of Cancer is the Cosmic Womb in which the seeds of creativity grow and burst forth in diverse ways—biological, artistic or intuitive creativity, imaginative creativity, even business creativity. There is also, at the esoteric level, mystical creativity—giving birth to the Divine Child within. The *Magna Mater* is the most ancient personal manifestation of divinity found around the world.

This archetypal symbolism can be studied through creation myths. How did the Earth come into being? we ask. "The land separated from the water," we are told, and "the firmament from the earth." (*Old Testament*, "Genesis," Ch. 1). That which was wet or rain-producing (the firmament) separated from that which was dry. Or there was a Goddess named Padma (Lotus) who sat in a stream (water) while the Earth sprang from her navel. Or, in Sumeria, the Goddess Inanna gave birth to the world. Or the Earth hatched from the yolk of a cosmic egg. Symbols of the waters, the womb of a goddess, an egg; the creation myths are replete with Cancer symbols. The Summer Solstice is a time of year when the Earth itself is ripe. Cancer

113

lies opposite the Winter Solstice (Capricorn), where the land lies fallow, dry and barren. The Mother Goddess opposes Old Man Winter. In the Chinese Taoist mystical text we are told that the Tao is the "Mother of all things; she pervades everything, but she is nowhere visible." She is the force and energy behind life itself.

Power, energy, or *Shakti* are titles of the Great Goddess in India. Indians have only to look at the night sky to see Kali, the dark mother. They have only to look at the Moon to see Goddess Lakshmi, "born of the moon." If we were all to close our eyes right now and visualize the night sky with the pale Moon overhead on its black background, we would have an image of the Dark Goddess—mysterious and nocturnal. All sorts of creatures come out during the night in India. A tiger emerges from a jungle in the Northeast. A viper drops from a tree in the South. Or Kali's least conscious devotees, the thugs—robber castes—may appear. It is easy to see how the Dark Goddess might be feared by those of primitive awareness. For the educated, Kali is a time goddess. An entire Yuga is named for her—Kali-Yuga, the Age of Kali. Kali, by means of her dance at Chidambaram Temple has the power to bring creation in and out of existence. Hindus also believe that every life form has its appointed length of time (or number of breaths) and when its appointed day to change its form arrives, Kali will devour it. Through her cosmic womb, she will give it a new form for a new lifetime.

In the myth of Kali's dance there are two other important points. The first is that the womb gives form or shape to the entity. The Moon, Cancer's ruler, has been called in both India and the West (in Plato's writings, particularly) the Giver of Form. The Moon itself can be observed to pass through so many shape changes—the Full Moon, the quarterly moons, the dark or New Moon, etc., that the ancients connected it with the birth and death of form and planted their crops according to its phases. The many moods of the Moon were also observed in connection with the 28-day transiting Moon, the physiological changes in women's bodies associated with the lunar orbit, and the emotional moods connected with that cycle. The goddess and her priestesses and oracles were deemed capable of mysterious insights and intuitions, such as the power of trance mediumship. The Moon was a bestower of the gifts of feeling, of intuition, and of nurturing instincts which men did not seem to possess. During the Bronze Age, cults of the Fertility Goddess developed and were led by priestesses who were believed to have occult powers over life and death.

This issue of life and death (Hindus would say life, death and rebirth) is important, because we have the 4th House, the root of the horoscope, the Alpha and Omega point in the chart to consider as well. Cancer is the 4th Sign and the 4th House of the natural zodiac. Cancer is the cornerstone House, and planets in a person's 4th House describe a good deal about his karma—the circumstances around him at the beginning and the end of his lifetime. They indicate the nature of family karma. Transits of the trans-Saturnian planets over the Nadir often leave a person feeling shaken as if he or she had a near encounter with Kali, the Dark Goddess. As if he were fortunate to have survived the encounter and to still be on Earth.

To review the symbolism, we have the seeds (Cancer's glyph), the womb, Shakti (or power over life and death), and the Moon, the giver of form, as mundane ruler. The Moon represents feelings and emotions. She is an instinctual, intuitive, nurturing planet, but also a planet that fosters emotional attachment to the form she provides. We have already encountered lunar exaltation in Taurus as the attachment to emotional and financial security. The Crab, the creature that tenaciously hangs on with its claws, is an appropriate symbol for Cancer attachment. Within the Great Mother archetype are two distinct personalities—the Gentle Mother like Kwan Yin the Merciful and Compassionate of Chinese Mythology, and the Terrible Mother, like India's Kali Ma and the Greek Medusa.

In "The Dual Mother," (*Symbols of the Transformation*), C.G. Jung discusses the light and dark sides of the Great Mother Goddess, with reference to Indian and Greek mythology. The light and dark phases of the Moon are connected to the individual's experience with his mother, which in turn are at the root of his positive or negative mother complex. Sometimes Mother did not herself participate in building the complex—it was the child's own projection upon or fantasy about her. Other times, she did participate actively. He also refers to Nokomis, the grandmotherly mother, in Longfellow's poem, Hiawatha. Though Nokomis had died and gone to the Moon, "the land of the grandmothers," she was still part of Hiawatha's psyche, of his anima. As a young hero, he undertook impossible tasks to appease her, and to avenge her honor as he saw it.

In *Symbols of Transformation*, Jung also quotes Ms. Miller's hero fantasy as a source on the Great Mother. Ms. Miller did not have the courage to cut the umbilical cord and leave her own Mother, but she fantasized a hero, a courageous American Indian named Chiwantopel, who said, of Mother's Love:

"Not one who understands me, not one who resembles me or has a soul that is sister to mine. There is not one among them who has known my soul, not one who could read my thoughts—far from it, not one capable of seeking the shining summits with me, or spelling out the superhuman world of love." He left home and went upon a journey in search of her.

It is this superhuman world of love that my clients miss upon the death of the positive mother, for nobody will ever replace her, will ever love them that much again. Jung, in the same book, goes on to discuss mother's love, "understanding," in English or "comprendre" in French, or in German "begreifen." "Erfassen" originally meant "to seize" in one's hands, then "grip tightly in one's arms." This is what the positive side of the Goddess/Mother does—seize and grip. Though he did not analyze the English word "understand" that he quoted from Ms. Miller's fantasy, it is a word my clients with watery planets use so often. "I want a partner who understands me. . . " I think it connects with the idea we have of Mother, or Cancer people, as supportive as well as sympathetic listeners. Understand or stand-under, I think, is a reference to supporting someone's development, talents, and goals. This can go too far and probably has if it means that Mother continues to provide financial support to her 40-year old jobless child and/or his/her family.

The positive Cancer mother can be seen in action when her toddler is taken off for his first day of kindergarten. She says, "I cried. He cried. The teacher finally pushed me out and slammed the door. I watched the clock all day, counting the minutes till I could go get my first born. I expected him to run up and grab me. I would hold him tightly in my arms. Reunited again after this awful day. Well, the three hours seemed an eternity. I went to the kindergarten to find him playing contentedly in his sandbox with the others. He said, 'Ah. Want to finish making my castle.' I had to tug at him to get him out of there!" But she didn't lecture him, "Didn't you miss mommy?". . . or make him feel guilty. She dealt well with her own hypersensitivity. Later, when it became harder and harder to tear him away from school projects, she accepted that she was no longer the only star in his sky, the only goddess in his pantheon.

Devouring Mothers are often powerful women who "rule the

roost" with firmness. In "The Process of Individuation" (*Man and His Symbols*), Marie Louise von Franz speaks of a mother who was always telling her little boy to be less energetic, less ebullient, "Don't slam the door. Don't get dirty. Don't use that toy in the house." He can grow up quite effeminate, or to be a Don Juan, always returning from his love affairs to live with Mom. Home seems to have the same effect as Calypso's island on Odysseus—spellbinding. He proves unable to remain away for long. Many gays with Cancer rising seem to have had this sort of Siren Mother whose song kept calling them home. No other woman could compete or measure up to Mother.

A positive mother can, however, build a positive anima in a young man. Later in life she may appear as a spiritual guide or as a Wise Old Woman in his dreams. It is easier for him to relate positively to his inner feminine if his mother was supportive, but not devouring. He may see Kwan Yin or the Virgin Mary as a positive, trustworthy, anima guide in his dreams. Beatrice proved to be such a guide for the poet Dante in "Paradiso." If we reflect on gentle Kwan Yin or the Virgin Mary standing on the crescent Moon in Durer's painting, we have a sense of the Feminine as a nurturing, sympathetic, understanding guide to the Self. In Catholic theology, the Virgin Mother is known as Mediatrix of all Grace. This seems an appropriate title for such a powerful intercessor as the Goddess. As the Bengali poet Ramprasad Sen has said, a child often feels more comfortable praying to a Mother Goddess than a more strict, austere Father Deity. This is particularly true in India where children are fond of the maternal household Goddess, Lakshmi, who provides a cornucopia of blessings. In various regions of India, the Great Mother is worshipped under various names and forms.

Kali is the most powerful of the Great Mothers. Her Shakti goes beyond the force theologians have deemed appropriate for a Goddess in the West, since the Age of Aries patriarchy put Medusa in her place and Zeus dispatched the Dragoness Typhon. By the time of the Age of Heroes (late Bronze Age), the Goddess had been stripped of her sacred groves, her priestesses driven out, and her sacred masks and statues destroyed. Terrible Mothers like Medusa, Durga the Destroyer, Hera, and devouring Medea began to express their fury in mythology.

Kali, too, became more fierce. One day, while sitting in the Tamil language class, an insight occurred to me about all the anger, frustration and occult power projected upon Kali in South India. We were

reading through a list of Tamil proverbs, the general tone of which
was sad. But one, in particular, stood out:

> In childhood a woman is subject to her father; after puberty,
> to her husband, and after widowhood, she is subject to
> her son.

Such "subjection" after the Aryan invasion must have resulted in an
increase of not only Kali's power in the collective unconscious, but
that of local smallpox and malaria goddesses. During epidemics, men
as well as women hurry to the temple of the local goddess to suppli-
cate and propitiate. In the view of many Indians, her power is greater
than that of Shiva or Vishnu; hers alone is the power over life and
death. Hers is the Alpha and Omega point—the Nadir of the chart.

While in South India in 1979, I read in the back of a newspaper
of a human sacrifice in a remote village. It was done to placate the
Great Goddess during drought. A few weeks later, I traveled to
Chidambarum Temple of Kali pilgrimage fame. As I admired the
sculpture of Kali dancing in her creative rite upon the prostrate form
of her consort, Lord Shiva, a Brahman came up to me. "Interesting,
isn't it?" he asked. "Have you also seen the *yonis*, the receptacles, the
vase-like structures that symbolize Mother Kali in the inner sanctum?
I have always wondered what Freud would have thought of us here in
India. While at University, I was reading his very Western theory of
penis envy. If that is what you have in the West, then surely in India we
must have womb envy.

Outside this temple is a structure called a Godown, a shed-home
for the sacred cow, who is also a symbol of Kali-Ma. Her milk and ghi
(butter) are distributed at mealtimes as a *prasad* (sacred offering) to
nurture and sustain. There is no greater wealth in India than the
wealth of milk and ghi. But all of these are feminine symbols. Surely
we must be very different from you." Of course, there are also Shiva
temples of the Lingayid sect with phallic pillars in South India, but the
sense of power (Shakti) is not the same. The Lingayids do not propitiate Shiva as Kali is propitiated.

There are so many levels of Kali worship—so many "Kalis," one
could say, in India. The Kali of the Thug caste for robbers who practice bloody sacrifice, the Kali of frightened villagers, who is a fertility
goddess, a Kali for the university educated who enjoy the dance and
art connected with her mythology, and the Kali venerated by Yogis.
Kali-Ma was the beloved of Ramakrishna, perhaps the most famous

of her twentieth century devotees. His little room in Dakshineswar Temple, Calcutta, is visited by thousands of followers every year from all over the world. The great yogi gives this description of Kali and of what she meant to him:

> When there were neither the creation nor the sun, the moon, the planets, and the Earth, and when darkness was enveloped in darkness, then the Mother, the Formless One, the Maha-Kali, the Great Power, was one with Maha-Kali, the Absolute.
>
> Shyama Kali has a somewhat tender aspect and is worshipped in Hindu households. She is the Dispenser of Boons and the Dispeller of Fear. People worship Raksha Kali, the Protectress, in times of famine, earthquake, drought and flood. Shmashana-Kali is the embodiment of the power of destruction. She resides in the cremation ground, surrounded by corpses, jackals, and terrible female spirits. From her mouth flows a stream of blood, from her neck hangs a garland of human heads, and around her waist is a girdle made from human hands.
>
> After the destruction of the universe, at the end of the great cycle, the Divine Mother garners the seeds for the next creation. She is like the elderly mistress of the house who has a hotchpotch-pot in which she keeps different articles for household use. . . After the destruction of the universe, my Divine Mother, the embodiment of Brahman, gathers together the seeds for the next creation. After this creation, the Primal Power dwells in the universe itself. She brings forth this phenomenal world and then pervades it. . .
>
> Is Kali, my Divine Mother, of a black complexion? She appears black because she is viewed from a distance; but then intimately known she is no longer so. . . Bondage and liberation are both of her making. By her Maya worldly people become entangled in 'women and gold' and again, through her grace, they attain their liberation. She is self-willed and must always have her own way. She is full of bliss.

For Ramakrishna, as for many yogis, the quest was bliss. His was a Lunar Path of receptivity, surrender, obedience and devotion. The yogi on the Lunar Path awaits in humility Shakti (the transforming power of the goddess) and is receptive to her approach. She roots out all the habits, all the unconscious behavior patterns that stand between him and the goals of bliss, joy, peace. Shakti awakens him. But in Ramakrishna's case, he had to break his image of Kali, literally break her statue, his attachment to her physical form, in order to experience the bliss he sought with the Formless Divine.

All this is relevant to our study of Cancer because its mundane ruler, the Moon, has traditionally represented not only attachment to form, but also our unconscious habits. If a client asks the astrologer when is a good time to give up smoking or find the willpower to lose ten pounds, what does the astrologer look for? An aspect from transiting Saturn (discipline) to the Moon, or progressed Moon to natal Saturn, because of the traditional connection of Moon and habit. "Begin the fast, or the diet, or giving up the habit of smoking, on the Saturn/Moon date, or transiting Moon (new phase) to Saturn," we say. Here we are trying to gain control of an unconscious craving or instinct, with the help of Saturn, a conscious planet of discipline.

The Moon stands in strong contrast to Hermes, ruler of Gemini. In Gemini, Hermes' sign, the mind is consciously active, while in this archetype Cancer works on a psychic, instinctual, unconscious feeling level. Similarly, through our Sun sign, we are used to analyzing our behavior. "Today I am acting like an impatient Aries," or "Today I'm acting like a bored and restless Gemini." But we don't stop and think, "Today I'm coming on like my possessive Taurean Moon," or "Today I've been feeling guilty for things that aren't even my fault, like my Pisces or Cancer Moon!" The lunar part of us is very often like a familiar child—we feed it when it's hungry, but we don't pay much grown-up analytical attention to it; we're busy with the adult business elsewhere in our charts. When we do take a look at its behavior patterns, usually there's a Saturn transit conjunct, or square, or opposite it, or a lunar progression that causes others to point out to us that our habits are driving them to lunacy.

If we're not interested in the Lunar Path of Ramakrishna or other *bhaktas*, we can always wait for our transits and progressions to work on our habits. We don't have to invoke Kali's help actively, as he did. One final word on Kali. Westerners have seen her as a shadow figure, as an ugly nightmare vision, but to the Indian she's a normal part of life. She represents the cycle of life, death and rebirth. As he walks past a vulture eating a carcass in his native village, the Indian is aware that the wild tiger and the gentle deer inhabit the same nearby forest. Hunter and prey are both part of the cosmic *Lila*, or drama, that Kali performs as she dances in Chidambarum, inventing the world of Maya, or illusion.

The Greek goddess that I perceive as closest to the archetype of the Great Mother is Demeter, Goddess of the Grain Harvest. When Persephone, her daughter, was abducted by Hades and taken to the underworld, Demeter sat and pined away by her sacred well in Eleusis till the Earth itself suffered; the crops failed. Here we have a clear indicator of Demeter's power, which to me is an essential part of the Cancer archetype. She was able to ruin the harvest. Father Zeus, who up to that point had not taken particular interest in Persephone's fate, became aware that his human worshippers were angry and had lost their patience with the Olympian gods. He dispatched his messenger Hermes to Hades to fetch Persephone and bring her home to Mother.

In the Demeter myth we have a behavior type characteristic of many a Cancer client—emotional blackmail. "If you won't do what I want, God (Zeus), I'll just sit here and sulk and refuse to do my work; *that* will force you to come around!" Jean Shinoda Bolen says that the behavior of Demeter at the well was passive-aggressive, and that Demeter had gone on strike to get Zeus' attention. (See Jean Shinoda Bolen, *Goddesses in Everywoman*, pages 190-191, on Demeter's "strike.") While reading Bolen on Demeter's withdrawal, an image came to my mind of the Cancer crab pulling its head back into its shell-home and refusing to come out till the world cooperated again. In the shell-home, Cancer is safe and protected and has everything comfortably arranged. Cancer is in control at home, too. The Great Mother wants to be home with her children, and later, with her grandchildren around her.

Many Cancer archetype parents fear that a child will be abducted like Persephone and as a result are overprotective, overwatchful. It's interesting for each of us to check the cusp of the House in our own chart where Cancer is located to see if we have a sort of apprehensiveness or anxiety that the children of this house will be abducted. Children, of course, are not always biological. We could worry that our ideas will be stolen by plagiarists, or that we will lose our investments, depending on the House cusp the devouring Goddess rules.

For Cancer parents, emotions and feelings tend to be stronger than logic. They know, for instance, that the University two hundred miles away would offer their child a wider selection of courses and that living in the dormitory with other freshmen would be a maturing social experience for her. But, says the Cancer partner, "She seems so young. We don't want to lose her yet." So they send out signals to their daughter that, while it is a good university, true, she might prefer to live at home and attend the local junior college for two years first, which would save the family so much money.

Then there is the attachment of Cancer mother for her son. Most of us know an archetypal case—a Cancer mother client has a 35-

year-old bachelor son who keeps moving back in with her. "Gosh, I've lived in those cold and dreary apartments," he says. "It's not as comfortable as home. Mom always fixes my eggs just the way I like them. And she does my laundry perfectly. And then, it's so much cheaper." Why grow up and move away when life is so good at home?

Cancer mothers will sometimes tell the astrologer that they sacrificed so much of their own creativity for the children, that they gave them every advantage, and now, when the children are adults, they feel victimized. What was the purpose of it all when there's "no such thing as gratitude?" Suzie is moving across the country with her husband, who has been transferred, and Arnold hasn't even taken her along on the last three vacations he took with his wife and children.

Then there's the Cancer professional (or Cancer Midheaven)— "Look at the ingratitude! After all the hours I spent training Anna, she quit after only eight years. And these clients. I work so hard with them and they are so fickle. If I'm out with a headcold for a weekend, they change therapists."

This nurturing archetype invests emotional energy and expects a return on the investment. The same is true in the marriage relationship. Cancer wants a dependable husband, a responsible man who would be a good parent to her children. Cancer rising also wants a successful man. (She would define that according to her own social standing.) She has Capricorn on her 7th House cusp, and the "talented" man, whose ego she enjoys nurturing or building up with her supportive Ascendant, often fall short in the eventual success test of Capricorn. The type of partner drawn to her mothering Ascendant is not always the type her Capricorn partnership house can respect. If she ends up with a Peter Pan (See Gemini, Chapter 3) she often makes the best of it and sighs a lot. Her children will respect her more for doing all the parenting work herself and her power increases in the home.

My favorite Cancer definition of the family comes from a session with a double Cancer client fresh out of college. She said, "In sociology class, we had to read such really silly definitions of what the family unit meant. Why didn't the text just say that it consists of a woman with her children around her and a man to provide for them financially?" Demeter taking care of Persephone. . . it seemed so simple, and yet I couldn't imagine any other astrological sign giving quite that same definition of marriage.

When Cancer speaks of finding a dependable, responsible parent for his or her unborn children, it brings to mind the Capricorn polarity one-hundred eighty degrees away from Cancer. This is also a parenting sign, just as the Moon and Cancer symbolize the Magna Mater, Capricorn and Saturn (*Senex*, Chapter 10) symbolize Father. And what is Capricorn but the dutiful, dependable, responsible if somewhat strict and austere parent? I know several couples who participate in this parental archetype—Cancer and Capricorn—who have had long and happy marriages to each other. Sometimes the woman is the Capricorn, of course, and the man is the Cancer. In that case, she takes her children seriously—they are one of her careers. But at the same time, she usually admits to others that she would have had one or two fewer children "if it had been up to me. I wanted to get back to work sooner—at least part time." The 10th House beckons. But she deferred to her Cancer husband, who wanted more children. Something deep within the Cancer archetype longs to create or take care of helpless things—children, foster-children, animals, birds, etc.

Both Cancer and Capricorn parents are good at providing structure for the children, organizing the trips to their various lessons and sports events, serving on the Board of the PTA, etc. Quite often, Daddy, the Cancer, is a master chef. (The Capricorn mother doesn't cook unless she *has* to in several of these archetypal marriages. Catering services are helpful.) The more traditional marriage would be a Capricorn father and a Cancer mother. They are both prudent, serious, thrifty, cautious. They appreciate old-fashioned legitimacy and church weddings—none of this modern living together outside marriage for that archetype. The children's futures are too important. They like old things usually and joint projects include fixing up an old house, refinishing old furniture, going to antique shows and shopping together for bargains. They are very proud of one another in the home (which is the woman's domain) and he doesn't advise her much unless she asks him questions. She's the home manager and he is the breadwinner. Each is the Cardinal authority figure in his or her domain. These roles might seem old-fashioned to many of us, but to those who participate in Cancer and Capricorn archetypes heavily, the roles feel right—that is, to people with several planets in Cancer/Capricorn.

The meaning of this parenting axis, Houses 4 and 10, is important for any parent to understand. If a single parent is, for instance, a

Cancer type (and this includes many fathers in the 1980's; more and more Cancer daddies are winning custody suits), he or she can err on the side of love and really spoil the child. He or she really wants to keep the child home, not have the child develop a preference for the divorced parent he visits on Saturdays. Discipline—saying no and meaning it, is an area where Cancer parents, especially single parents, need work. If on the other hand a parent is on the Capricorn polarity, his child experiences Saturn's discipline and high expectations and is left alone more to develop independence. (A 10th House value, independence is the last thing an archetypal 4th House person would try to develop in a child.) More time spent with the child and more affection are important here; give the child a hug and let him know it's all right that he didn't do as well as expected on the arithmetic test.

I have come to understand the archetypal exaltation of Jupiter in Cancer, and in the 4th House, through listening to Cancers discuss the quality of life they want for their children. Jupiter is best known as the planet of abundance and of generosity. There's a bit of a paradox here though, as Cancer is such a conservative, frugal sign for the expression of Jupiter, the abundance planet. Jupiter, like Venus/ Aphrodite, wants the best, and for Cancer parents it usually translates to "the best that's out there for my kids" and "I'll economize on other areas of life such as *my* art classes in order to pay for theirs, or *my* trip to Europe for their trip to the Grand Canyon." Or "we'll get bicycles for the boys instead of replacing the vacuum cleaner this year."

Cancer/Cancer risings who are not parents tend to expand (Jupiter) in the business area and to spoil the clientele. In the beginning years, as they establish the business, they cannot afford to give Jupiter full scope for his grandiose decorating desires, but his quality side manifests as tastefulness. Energy, if not money, is put into designing waiting rooms that make the client feel as loved and comfortable as at home, to provide a nurturing environment for him. The difficulty here is that the client becomes a sort of spoiled child; he feels so much at home with his tutor or counselor that he often is lazy about doing his homework, academically or psychologically. "Mother" is doing the work and is properly sympathetic with all those problems that keep coming up to make him late for the session/lesson. "Mother" readjusts *her* schedule and squeezes in the student/patient/client at the person's convenience. Dependency of client on astrologer or therapist can become like the dependency of a child on a parent.

One client has a Cancer boss. "He is so kind and understanding when we're out sick. He always sends flowers to the hospital or comes and visits when his employees are in accidents. But you know, though he's a really good boss in a lot of ways (we enjoy going to work for him), he hasn't given anyone a raise for a long, long time." Jupiter's exaltation often falls short in the area of financial generosity. Cancer's thrift dominates, and he thinks, "Well, I do things for my employees that most employers wouldn't do. Why give raises too? There are so many fringe benefits in working for me. . . "

During the astrology session, complaints about money or lack of opportunity for advancement often mask the real issues: dependency, feelings of ingratitude or neglect, lack of sensitivity to others' feelings or others' progress. Archetypally, Jupiter's exaltation in Cancer seems to mean that Cancer views itself as the model, nurturing employer, whose staff are an extension of his/her family, and like his/her children, are living on beneficent allowance money. "I know this is a small, quality operation, not a big, impersonal company," said one Cancer business owner. "Gizelle knows that too. All these years I was a shoulder for her to cry on. I offered bonuses and loaned her money. Now, she suddenly quits to move to a firm that's offered twice the salary she had here. What, after all, is money?" Gizelle had accumulated twice the original responsibility, but had received only several small step raises in recognition for her efforts. "I was his little girl, we had an interdependent relationship, like parent and child. But he would have never paid me what I was worth, because he couldn't see me as an adult who could have handled a supervisory title, authority, and an appropriate salary. So I had to leave the nest," said Gizelle.

In social environments like restaurants one can observe the quality of Cancer's generosity. Does it extend beyond his/her immediate family, to others at the table? After you have finished eating with Cancer and his/her spouse and five children, does s/he reach for the check with serious intentions of paying? Or does s/he wait and see what *you* will do? Will you treat all seven of them? Does the Jupiter within him work merely for self-aggrandizement and for his/her own family or is its scope larger? If Cancer's benevolence extends beyond the nuclear family, Jupiter is truly functioning positively, spiritually, opening his personality beyond the confines of Cancer.

The Cancer parent wants the best in life for his/her children, but like the Cancer professional, s/he often tries too hard. "Gosh," said the child of one Cancer mother, "I wish she had taken those art courses and that trip to Europe and bought that vacuum cleaner back in 1968. But you know something? I don't think she really wanted to go to Europe. Dad and she have plenty of money now and they've never done it. She likes to go back East and visit her family on all the holiday vacations. I think she enjoyed baking the cookies for my Brownie troop more than she would have enjoyed those art classes at night. She feels like a martyr for reasons I cannot understand. None of us asked her to give up anything for us!" The girl's brother said, "Mom says she just wants us to be happy (jovial or Jupiterian) but there's more to it than that. She wants to be proud of us. She wanted us to marry the girl next door and buy a house down the street from her. She wants me to stop quoting my wife to her. She says I never listen to her anymore, only to my wife."

When the Cancer mother's youngest child has reached his teens and is ready to leave the nest, Cancer often sees an astrologer for the first time. What will she do? If she is in her thirties, she could still stay home and have another child. She knows that she is perfectly competent to find work in the business world. That isn't a problem. Cancer women frequently tell me that anyone as organized and efficient as they are would be a valuable asset to any company—and they are right. Cancer is a cardinal sign and for many a Cancer, business is the strongest creative outlet in the horoscope. But Cancer is looking for fulfillment for the Moon, for something that is nurturing to do, for people who need help. She will say, "Of course, I could get a job making costumes for the repertory theater. Anyone who can make seven elaborate Halloween costumes in a week can outfit a theater group." Or, "Of course, I could take a job as manager of one of my family's restaurants. I'd be a good hostess. I have had all kinds of experience organizing meals for large numbers of people. I could even open a catering service." Or "I could open an antique shop; I have rooms and rooms of furniture I've refinished and with the children gone, there's no reason not to sell it."

Still, she hesitates to leave the nest. She is safe there, and even more important to the Kali-Shakti part of her—her power base is there. It's very hard to leave her domain at midlife and take a position where someone else would have the authority, where someone else would be the boss.

Sometimes we discuss self-employment in the home as a possibility. There on her own terrain with her crab-shell still intact and familiar things around her she will not feel vulnerable. She can proceed with a business on her own terms, at her own rate. Tutoring, daycare work, or even opening a pre-school if she has the training and background—the antique shop she had suggested could be opened in the gate house. The family restaurant chain is a possibility, too, though it's a step removed from the home. It has the advantage of working with people who already know her competence and efficiency as a manager. (How she can juggle schedules for carpooling, after dinner sports events, individual children's lessons, etc. Relatives have seen her work under pressure and know she would be a good, capable worker.)

Cancer often brings up the possibility of returning to school to finish an old credential or to begin working toward a new one. This often seems threatening. "All of those young people in classes with me." (She's only 35.) Or, "I haven't taken a class in years. . . I don't know. Yet, when I quit college to marry John, I thought that I had been preparing for a useful career—working in a hospital as a nurse (or dietician), making decisions that would help a lot of people." Here we have Jupiter exalted in Cardinal water. She wanted to make decisions (Cardinality) that would help (Water) a lot of people (Jupiter). It even integrated the Capricorn/Earth polarity—a useful career. Or, "My therapist tells me that I have a lot of empathy and intuition. Sometimes, it seems clear to me in my dreams that I ought to finish my social work credential. I could intuitively feel what the client's real problem was—what she was *not* telling me."

This, then, is lunar or personal fulfillment, with the exalted perspective of Jupiter in Cancer wanting to reach a lot of people, understand, and help. She needs to be needed. Theoretically, I could open up the whole gamut of imaginative/intuitive professions here. She could study fiction writing like those famous Cancers Hesse, Orwell, Hemingway. Theoretically, that would be personally fulfilling. She could read Tarot cards or interpret dreams, right? She could do Japanese brush paintings or silk screens; that would be very creative. She has already mentioned that her husband certainly doesn't need for her to make any money; as a breadwinner, he is doing a fine job. He wants her to "be creative."

The Moon could find personal, emotional satisfaction in many ways, but it is also a restless planet. Though the Moon is said to be prominent in charts of writers and psychics, the successful creative writer seems to be able to sit alone for hours at a time, shutting out the family, tuning inward to his Muse and working on his novel. Hemingway and many other Cancer writers achieved personal fulfillment this way, but my Cancer/Cancer rising clients are not Hemingway. They are not used to sitting alone attuned to the Muse within. They are used to sitting across a desk from another human being tuned in to the needs of *that* person. Or in many cases they don't sit still at all; they move about gracefully all day like Luna in the night sky. They move about the kitchen making sandwiches, calling other mothers to organize the Cub Scout meeting, driving around the city and suburbs to stores and schools and banks and to gyms delivering forgotten running shoes.

I once loaned a Cancer client a copy of a biography written about Hemingway by one of his ex-wives. The Cancer returned it and said, "My, what a selfish man. I could write brilliant novels, too, if I wanted to treat the people I love the way he did." I thought that was a telling Cancer comment on the difference between potential and realized talent. For the astrologer it was also a telling comment about the difference between the textbook Cancer and the real Cancer. Doing things for others seems to be the major source of fulfillment I've observed in lunar types. Life seems so much more satisfying for those Cancers who are tuned in to their feminine, feeling nature, who are able to recognize and fulfill the need to be needed, than for those who deny the feminine.

In our society, power (Shakti) is associated with earning power out there in the business world. In the last fifteen years, many Cancers have turned to real estate. One woman, having struggled through the licensing program, had sold her first house and received her first commission check. She called me, elated, with the news. "There is nothing so fulfilling as this, apart from giving birth. I've just matched a family with the perfect old house for them. When they get it fixed up, it will be such a lovely home. And look at this check. Teaching never paid this well. I finally feel like a valued member of society." Real estate—what a perfect 4th House profession.

Many Cancer/Cancer rising men have developed their lunar nature through careers in social work, counseling, the arts, design. Those who have a particularly strong attunement to Jupiter have expanded their interest into the community, given of their time, energy and lives to the homeless—immigrants in their own country or the sick and hungry abroad. Some are involved in the ministry, while others promote the arts, scholarship funds, or local civic work. Providing for others' basic needs such as food, clothing, shelter or medicine is an archetypal Cancer function. A Cancer businessman who operates mainly through the solar, thinking function in his career derives a great deal of his inner, personal satisfaction from helping others and thus fulfilling his lunar nature.

Sadly, some Cancer men seem reluctant to acknowledge the feminine side of themselves, the relating side, the side that is creative and intuitive (though their business timing is largely derived from this lunar energy). Perhaps they feel that other men would think them weak, dependent or sentimental. They remain close to Mother, to daughters, and tend to choose an ultra-feminine wife who is fragile, lovely, gentle—often a patroness of the arts—to carry the feminine for them. If, however, they have never worked with developing the lunar side of themselves they may feel an emptiness at midlife; they may sense that there must be more to life than making money and providing for children who are grown up, who have moved away. It is here, at midlife, that they meet the astrologer or the analyst for the first time asking, "What else is there in life, when the family is dispersed, and my Mother is gone?"

Stomach ailments, calcium assimilation problems, milk allergies often develop in Cancers who, at midlife, are learning to rechannel the nurturing energy from the outer world toward the Self, the inner source of creativity, in Cancers who may be feeling emotionally starved, neglected, or abandoned. Another symptom is eating vast amounts of ice cream, creamy pastries, rich desserts. Cancer tends to eat when the Inner Child is feeling deprived, and especially to crave milk products. Mother's milk is of course the earliest source of nourishment that the unconscious recalls. In women who are used to nurturing others, the female organs are symptomatic of the shift from the outer to the inner self-nurturing process at mid-life.

So many, many Cancer/Cancer rising women between ages 40-55 first develop anxiety as a symptom. "Do I need a mastectomy? Does it show up in my chart? I won't feel 'whole,' yet I'm afraid something will have to be cut out of my body soon. It's a definite premonition." We tend to attract to ourselves things we dwell upon, worry about. I usually ask, "Has something been cut out of your life, your home recently? Is your youngest about to marry? Graduate? Join the army? Relocate?" So often the answer is yes. It seems a shame to keep cutting up the body. I feel intuitively certain that many, many unnecessary hysterectomies are performed on women in this age group whose loving nature has been so outer-directed that they cannot tune in to who they are. They cannot sit still and meditate, or say the rosary with concentration, or practice the devotional techniques of their religion, or let go of their anxiety and find peace.

Cancer is attached to the past—tradition, home and hearth. Often Cancer's husband retires and announces, "We're moving to Florida; it's too cold here." Or, "I'm buying a motor home and going off to see the country." If she is recovering from surgery, or a series of surgeries, it's harder for him to make his changes, to buy the motor home, sell the big house she lives in and move on into the future he's been planning for twenty years. Sometimes he moves on without her, leaving her daughter who lives nearby to give her love and attention. She stays in her crab-shell, her beloved home.

Astrologically, the motion of the progressed Moon can provide a clue to the direction the Unconscious is taking, and the astrologer can help Cancer to become more aware of why he's eating all the dairy products or why she's fearful about needing reproductive surgery. This is an important indicator in the horoscope of intuitives in general and of Cancer/Cancer rising in particular. Many years ago Derek and Julia Parker said in the *Compleat Astrologer* that Cancer people tend to live their lives in 2-year to 28-month cycles, in the rhythm of the secondary progressed Moon as it changes signs and Houses. I have asked Cancer/Cancer rising and Cancer Moon clients about this and far more of them have agreed than disagreed. They seem closely connected to the Unconscious and may discover its needs during their lunar progressions.

I usually follow Noel Tyl's suggestion and identify the quadrant of the horoscope (a slice of the pie that involves three Houses, beginning with an Angular House and ending just before the next Angular House) that the Moon is progressing through. Is it putting them in touch with personality? (First quadrant) Skills? (Second Quadrant) Cooperation/joint resources? (Third Quadrant) New goals/psychic resources? (Fourth Quadrant). The astrologer can locate the quadrant at a glance; after awhile the eye automatically goes there. This is the area where the personality is currently developing and often, where old habits are challenged. Will they get stronger, more en-

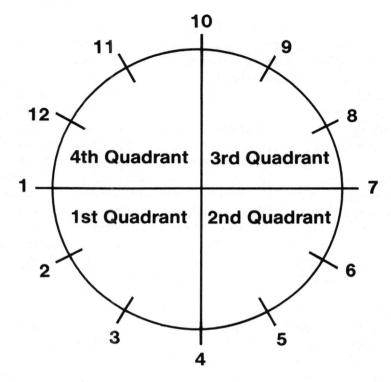

trenched, or will they loosen up? I look at the modality; mutability does well with change; cardinality is happy trying something new; but, fixity wants the status quo. I look at the quadrant as a 7-year learning cycle in the inner, subjective, personal life area, as the individual relates to Mother in particular, women in general, and if he is interested in spiritual development, with the anima, the inner goddess.

Where are the cravings, the childish lunar desires and moods going to pop up? In the House that the progressed Moon occupies for the 2-year to 28-month cycle, the sign through which it passes and according to the nature of the natal planets it contacts. (If it passes over Mars or squares Uranus, the mood will be restless, touchy, volatile, and if Water is involved, hurt.) To what sort of person will the Cancer/Cancer rising be receptive? (4th house)-Parent? (7th house)-Spouse? (9th house)-Minister? If it passes through the Ninth, the astrologer can discuss what would interest Cancer, at the level of awareness where Cancer is happy. That is, if Cancer is interested in grandchildren the astrologer can say, "This is a really good year to take them along on your vacation. The progressed Moon is in your Ninth, activating your natal Grand Trine." Or, if Cancer has no grand-children, but is very religious, he might ask, "Ask at your parish if some-one is taking a group to Lourdes or Rome this year. You would be very receptive to a pilgrimage tour, quite open to the blessings right now." (Other years she would probably be too frugal to want to go, or prefer to stay home and wash the altar linens.)

Personal, inner satisfaction, then, is connected with the lunar progressions. I spend time on it with intuitives, as well as Cancers. They may already know what I'm going to tell them before I say it, however, especially if the Moon is about to leave a quadrant and enter the next. They "feel" its motion strongly. Looking back seven years is another good technique to apply when the progressed Moon is changing quadrants. I usually ask outright, "Now that the Moon is about to enter the Tenth House, do you feel as if you've 'peaked' in one area of life, as if you're about due to begin a new cycle of change?" I almost invariably receive the response, "How did you ever know that? I drag myself off to work every day wondering why my body is still going there. My soul is done with that environment, with those lessons, and yes, I did take that position seven years ago. This is uncanny."

As astrologers we are not of course trying to amaze, frighten or intimidate sensitive Cancers with our "uncanniness"; we try to help. The Unconscious wants to do something different when the Moon enters a new quadrant. Helping a person sort out what the new direc-tion might be is, I believe, more useful than telling them particular events that lie ahead. The trend, the seven-year direction, is impor-tant to intuitive and feeling types. It may also allay someone's fears, nervous premonitions, or forestall the trip to the surgeon until he or she has had the time to look at alternative meanings of the physical symptoms. Sensitive Water signs like Pisces and Cancer have sensi-tive bodies—bodies that pick up on a message from the frustrated unconscious before the conscious mind can figure it out. Our science lends clarity and objectivity and helps either to confirm the intuitions or put them into proper perspective.

Saturn, with its practical, realistic and grounded nature, is ruler of the polarity sign—Capricorn. It is also an important planet for gain-ing objectivity. The progressed Moon will tell us what the uncon-scious craves, is tired of, wants to establish, and so forth, but not whether or not in the real world it will, in effect, be able to meet its needs at this particular moment in time. Shiva and Kali—Saturn and the Moon—are a pair. They deal with creative change (the Moon) in the world of finite time (Saturn). Saturn, like the progressed Moon, spends approximately seven years in a quadrant. So, the astrologer's eye travels toward the quadrant Saturn transits, where the aspirations, ambition, events, and challenges are likely to be centered. Then, after looking at the quadrant he considers the House and the sign through which Saturn moves. If the progressed Moon is, for instance, entering the Tenth house and Cancer asks, "Will I be able to pass my real estate licensing exam," Saturn's transits clarify the situation. Saturn transiting the Third or Sixth, for instance, would help with disciplined concentration. However, if Saturn were to transit back and forth in retrograde motion over her Mercury, she might have to retake the exam, which would be discouraging. It helps to understand both Saturn's positive (discipline) and negative (delayed results) meanings.

Many fine astrologers including Noel Tyl (*The Expanded Present*) and Alexander Ruperti (*Cycles of Becoming*) have noted that both Saturn and the Moon have an orbit cycle connected to the number 28. Transiting Moon takes 28 *days* to circle the horoscope and pass through all twelve signs. Natal Saturn takes 28 *years* for its return to its Sign, House, degree of longitude. The Moon symbolically moves through its secondary progressed orbit around the chart in 28 years as well. Thus, our inner, personal life planet, the progressed Moon, and our outer, ambition fulfillment planet, Saturn, are juxtaposed, and analyzed every 28 years, and often the balance between them is redressed at that point. People close to 30 will often remark, "I want it all—a solid career and a solid marriage," inner and outer satisfaction. Close to 56 they may say, "I was too one-sided. Too much outer development in business (Saturn/Tenth House), too little inner fulfillment (Fourth House)". Or in the case of many traditional Cancer mothers, vice versa. The individual who thinks, in retrospect, that she was too lunar in the first part of life longs for outer fulfillment; the person who was too Saturnine in the first cycle longs to stay home, cook, decorate, play with the grandchildren, and work on hobbies of a creative nature.

Spiritually and psychologically though, there is more to it than this shifting of energies at midlife. Karmically, a strong lunar type—an individual with a Moon-Ascendent conjunction, a Cancer/Cancer rising, will think about family in a deeper way during these periods. Mother is a mirror of self; Mother's approval or disapproval of the way life has developed mirrors a person's own analysis. If Mother was concerned with her biological role (having children) and daughter was not, then the 30's are a time when her own lack of children may bother daughter. She may go into therapy about it; sift through her childhood memories Cancer-like. Or among younger generation women, perhaps Mother was a successful businesswoman and daughter is a Cancer who preferred to stay home with her children. Close to age 30, this too bothers her. Should she get a part or full-time job? In spite of the fact that she'd feel guilty leaving the little ones with a babysitter? What is fulfillment all about for a 1980's lunar person? I usually remind Cancer/Cancer rising that there's plenty of time. Enjoy the little ones, the inner lunar fulfillment. The second half of life doesn't begin till the 40's.

Positive and negative Mother complexes often come up at the return of the progressed Moon. Touching one's home base and connecting with one's roots are often important issues for Cancer as the progressed Moon crosses the Ascendant or Nadir. Cancer may think about returning to the past, perhaps even the home town, the natal place where the horoscope took shape, for a family or school reunion. It is psychically stimulating for Cancer to reconnect with women from the past, in particular on these progressions. Cancer men have encountered old loves, aunties who adored them as children, or the woman who taught them English literature in high school and believed them destined to write the great American novel of their generation. "When I met her she seemed so old, so discontented with her own life. My goddess fell from her pedestal," one man commented. "And my sweetheart, my childhood anima figure, is no one I would care to date now. How taste changes."

Another woman remarked, "I almost stayed home because, you know, I haven't done great creative things. Then I thought, well, maybe they haven't either! I haven't exactly read about them in the headlines over the years. Then I thought, should I dress like a Californian, which I have been for 20 years, or buy something suitable for fall in Boston, something wool and chic, that'll sit in my closet in California forever?" She went and had a good time in her Boston outfit. A third Cancer said, "I agonized about going to the reunion. I love my past memories as they are, though—as memories. I want to remember everyone as young, full of hope for the future, handsome and attractive. I'd rather keep my old photo albums than see them in their 40's and hear that their marriages failed or other sad things about them."

One Cancer woman, whose Ninth and Tenth House planets took her into business rather than into domesticity said, "I don't know what I'll say to my sisters if I go to the wedding. All they talk about on the phone is their kids. Our family placed so much emphasis on children as a woman's role. . . yet, I'm glad I broke out of the collective mold and moved on in life. I'm glad I didn't follow the mass consciousness and drift through life unaware of anything but biological destiny." She also chose not to go home on progressed Moon over the Nadir. If she had, as an intuitive she may have benefited. By hindsight, the past usually brings clarity to the present. A new closeness and mutual respect might have emerged from a personal meeting with her sister which would have been very different from the cold, impersonal phone calls over the years. She has good aspects to her Third House Moon (sisters).

When Cancer calls with his data to make an appointment, I usually mentally note whether the birth year would place Cancer in the first or second half of life. If the new client is under 40, this means that Cancer has young children at home in whom he or she has deep interest. So, I usually ask, "Are there children about whom you'll have questions at the session? If so, could you please provide their birth data in advance, so that I can have their charts ready when you arrive?" This usually generates enthusiasm, for Cancer, nine times out of ten, cares more about what's going on in the children's life than his/her own. Cancer fathers usually have a question or two about business or property, but then, high on the list, comes a question about daughter. There is a special karmic bond between Cancer/ Cancer rising or Cancer Moon men and their little girl, even if she is 50 years old by the time of the reading.

If the new client is a rare Cancer who is childless, I usually say, "You know, there's a karmic bond between Cancer and Mother. If your Mom is still living, you might want to ask some questions about your interaction this lifetime. . . " Nine times out of ten the person is very glad to have the insights. The tenth person often has what Jung would call a negative Mother complex (see "Dual Mother" in Jung's *Symbols of the Transformation* and also "The Mother Complex" in *Archetypes of the Collective Unconscious*) and at first, doesn't want to think about her but will usually call the night before the reading and say, "This has been on my mind all week. I did get mom's data, and I do want to spend part of the session looking at our inter-action, astrologically."

In the second half of life, I meditate on inner growth and creativity emerging for Cancer. I look at the progressed Moon, as well as Eleventh House (personal goals, hopes, dreams and wishes) planets in the chart.

Spiritually, Cancer and the Fourth House are very important for all of us. In reading the esoteric section we might consider our own Fourth House cusp, the planet that rules it, and the planets that inhabit it.

Neptune: The Esoteric Ruler
The Lord of the Sea meets the Mother of Form

This chapter began with Kali, the Dark Goddess, dancing on the inert form of Shiva, her consort. We have now come full-cycle back to Kali. She's still dancing, creating new life forms within the limits of time and space. Shiva appears to be asleep, but is really in a yogic trance at one with the formless Divine. Shiva is beyond space, time and the limitations of ordinary consciousness. Ages pass; forms are born, die and are reborn. Still Shiva continues his meditation.

Shiva is Lord of the Seas, Dissolver of Forms. Were he suddenly to awaken and lift up his trident, all of Kali's work would dissolve into the ocean of formlessness. He is the most impersonal of the gods and she the most personal. The two are cosmic polar opposites: male and female, passive and active, temporal and eternal.

In Greek mythology, Poseidon (Neptune), God of the Seas, was also a great dissolver or destroyer, and he, too, used a trident to bring down attachment. If form resists change when the time has come for Shiva to wake, or Poseidon to demand sacrifice, then squalls quickly arise on the ocean of our lives. It's very similar to a Taurean encountering Vulcan on land.

The struggle between the Mother of Form and the God of the Sea is indeed a birth process—a Fourth House cusp process of inner death and rebirth. Shiva and Poseidon would make us more impersonal, more unselfish, and wiser. But if we resist, then the birth process is more painful; the "waters" should break naturally. We should not try too hard. Creativity, spiritual or artistic birth is more a matter of quiet (Shiva's trance) attunement to the universal, formless reality.

Family is a particular attachment for the Moon Child, whether Sun, Moon or Ascendant participates in the Cancer archetype. It is hard when the children go off to first grade, graduate, depart for college and marry. A son's disappearance into the army or a cross-country move is painful. It's hard for Cancer to stand back with Neptunian impersonality and watch them make mistakes. But if a Moon Child can do that; if he or she can enjoy watching his or her child "change form"—grow up to become an interesting adult—that's quite a feeling of fulfillment.

Another danger, especially for a Cancer parent with frustrated creativity, artistic or spiritual, is the attempt to live vicariously through the children. Having provided them with every opportunity, as Mother sees it, it is hard not to be, as the *Gita* puts it, "attached to the fruit of our labors." This sort of vicarious living is hard on a child who needs to express the talents in his, rather than his parent's horoscope, and results in feelings of frustration for both parent and child. Sometimes there is a particularly talented child, to whom much is given and of whom much is expected. A Cancer would ordinarily not come out and say, the way a Capricorn parent might, "I expect you to join my law firm when you graduate, then go into politics and eventually run for Congress." But Cancer, especially as Mother, wants creative, happy, well-adjusted children who earn enough money to have a quality life by the time she is ready to start in nurturing her grandchildren. That is a heavy emotional burden to carry, for both parent and child—even if the child himself has two or three planets in Cancer and enjoys fulfilling mother's expectations and being placed on mother's pedestal. A day will come when Neptune's waters will lash out at the pedestal's base and threaten to dissolve the "image" of the child if not to take away the child itself.

Alice Bailey said something quite interesting on the subject of Cancer twenty years ago: "Is the house you are building yet lit? Is it a lighted house or a dark prison? If it is a lighted house, you will attract to its light and warmth all who are around you." (*Esoteric Astrology*, page 343.) If you develop your own inner temple, others, including children, will always come home to it. Neptune/Poseidon will not dissolve the connection between parent and child in his adulthood.

Those of us who perceive Neptune as a spiritual planet may have noticed that when we took an initiation or began to practice a meditation technique we had esoterically attuned to the Dissolver of

Form. Suddenly, the outer world appeared very different. Many of us noticed a sudden sensitivity to the environment; it felt uncomfortable to go on living as we were at that time. Alice Bailey says that this heightened sensitivity to our surroundings is a sign of Neptune's presence. At first we might have had a vague, intuitive feeling that we had outgrown our comfortable crab shell, that things were going to change for us. The more venturesome moved on to take up new challenges; but others among us hung on to the outworn shell till the outer world dissolved it for them, till a spouse announced an intention to leave and grow in a different direction, or an employer fired us from our secure job.

At points like that in our lives, it seems as if Shiva stands at the Nadir of our chart and waves his trident. Courage is required to walk through the Gate on the Nadir, sometimes alone, into the unknown, leaving the empty shell, the empty womb, behind.

Yet, standing on the threshold, we become aware of new opportunities in the mundane world because new doors open even as the old doors are closing. Through Neptune's transits, increased intuition sheds new light on everything—career, ways of relating to daughter, son, to Mother. Neptune is the planet of faith, and faith is needed to let go of the past and open up to the future, rather than attempt to hang on to outworn forms with crab-like tenacity. For those who can willingly sacrifice the old way, the old role, the old career, the old attachments, to Neptune; for those who dare to create, to use their imagination, to trust their intuition, Neptune is a liberator. Remember— Poseidon does not dissolve anything we still need. He only prevents a Seeker from clinging to that which limits him, or stands in the way of his growth.

Eventually, on the Neptunian journey which opens up our intuition, expands our creative capacity and frees us from self-imposed limitations, we reach a vantage point where we gain a more universal (Neptunian) perspective. Through increased sensitivity to others, it becomes easier to transcend our habits and control our more negative instincts. We react with less emotionality and with greater sensitivity. We also see our own horoscopes in a new and clearer light. As we become aware of new ways to use the old talents, we take some risks. We try writing rather than reading charts for a while, or we enter the business world and sell real estate over the protests of our family, who argue, "You come from a background of teaching and nursing women—business is a man's world." It's a liberating experience when we take risks and the new creative venture really flows. If the experiment of using the talent in a new way has been successful, perhaps we can take other risks, too.

During the 30-year progression of the Sun through Leo, Cancer seems to exude some of the confidence of this magnetic, self-assured Fire sign. Gone are some of the doubts that characterized his early years. (Cancer rising progressed into Leo seems to gradually lose its timidity as well.) The Sun moves more slowly and steadily than the Moon so that its co-rulership of the personality lends a fixed stability to Cancer during this progression. The fixity also tends to carry over to Cancer's opinions, which become firmer, and often more rigid. This is the cycle during which Cancer sinks down strong roots into the neighborhood. If the spouse is transferred or tries to move the Cancer, Cancer will not be easily uprooted. On the whole, it is a happy, rewarding time. Cancer feels in control (Leo is concerned with being in charge) at home or at work.

Cancer may be chosen Head Nurse, Chief Dietician, or voted pre-school teacher of the year. In business, the magnetism and persuasive power brings promotions. The Fifth House investment meaning of Leo often carries over into this progression. Cancer seems to do well in investments, especially in fields that benefit the needy or in property. New ventures in the entertainment or food and beverage area are often successful, too. Both Cancer and Leo are warm, emotional signs involved with children and young people. Cancer may have been comfortable at home, decorating its crab-shell and cooking gourmet dinners before the Leo progression, but in this cycle the Cancer homemaker is more likely to be found in the PTA, center-stage, making strong statements, or as a den mother for the Cub Scouts, or as a neighborhood watch organizer. Anything that helps make the world a safer, happier place for children appeals to Cancer in this cycle. Those who have natal Leo planets may discover in the years that progressed Sun conjuncts Leo an enthusiasm for community theater, for dance, for taking children to the ballet.

Many traditional Cancers surprise their own parents by dramatically changing religions in this cycle. If raised in a conservative region, but forced to put down roots in a new area as a result of a job transfer, Cancer may well decide a parochial school offers greater advantages for the children than a public school, or if Cancer him/herself went to a denominational school, that the Montessori School now provides better opportunities. Many also discover Jung's individuation process (a Leo approach) in this growth-oriented progression. They may leave a traditional religion that suddenly seems conceptually narrow, or that interferes with personal freedom of decision. In *The Interior Castle*, St. Theresa of Avila speaks of leaving behind old habits, outworn rooms in the inner soul castle. In our age, the religion of one's childhood may come to seem a very small, very old room. Often listening to Cancers talk of this in readings I am reminded of the poem "Chambered Nautilus" in which a sea creature like the Cancer crab built "more stately mansions" for its soul.

Cancer, however, is close to parents and grandparents. It's difficult to explain to them moving beyond the traditional religion or not enrolling the children in the public school, or later on, in the *alma mater*. In the Leo cycle, Cancers usually express sadness over loss of family traditions, but also a positive Leo attitude, "Progress is what's important. We want what's best for the children. They need to be educated for the future, not the past, however beautiful our own memories may be. Perhaps one day Mother will come to understand this." There is often a sort of subliminal choice between Mother's good and the good of one's own children. The astrologer thinks, also, of Christ's words to the young man: "Leave mother and father and follow Me." Here Cancer is leaving Mother to follow the road of Individuation, if not for herself, for her children. She may experience sadness about leaving the past, as she sees it, behind.

Leo is physically stronger, and has more stamina than natal Cancer. If one says to a natal Cancer whose chart is low in Fire, "Let's do some rigorous exercise today," Cancer is likely to say, "No, you go on ahead. I'll take a nap and see you later!" But, in Leo, Cancer seems gradually to develop an interest in keeping fit through a favorite sport as he gets deeper into the progression. The sport may not be really demanding on the body, but he usually practices it regularly, and finds he feels good as a result. In *Symbols of Transformation*, Jung said that the first two signs of the zodiac, the Spring signs Aries and Taurus, have a lot of energy, but after the Solstice begins to wane there's a lull, a devitalizing period. I think it comes between mid-Cancer and mid-Leo and this is why Cancer has a fatigued feeling till the energy waxes again in Leo. This is easy to visualize if one considers the Nadir of the chart as Cancer and Leo, immediately after the Nadir, as energy on the rise. Leo is the heart in medical astrology. The body, as well as the emotions, are strengthened in Leo. Solar energy is very positive and much more extroverted than Lunar Cancer.

Courage comes out if progressions of Mercury, as well as the Sun, cross natal Leo planets. The time is often right for Cancer to work on his or her own creativity rather than simply foster that of the children. With added stamina, Leo-cycle Cancers may decide upon a part-time job in an area that they're excited about, if indeed it doesn't interfere with the needs of family and can be worked around the children's schedule. Cancers with planets in the Zenith area of the chart may not feel guilty about leaving small children with babysitters. They may nurture others in their work or nurture a business with Leo originality. Most Cancer women, however, use the Leo style in career only after the youngest is out of school. Courses may focus on creative approaches to teaching gifted children, or children with learning problems. Cancer wants her own children to excel in this Leo period of her life and will find them whatever tutors or aids are deemed necessary.

Spiritually, I am reminded of what Paramahansa Yogananda said about the "Us four and no more" attitude as Cancers progress through Leo. For most Cancers, the natal emphasis on home and children is emphasized in Leo, the sign of the 5th House (children). Cancer tends to focus her attention on children's activities and the immediate family becomes her main concern. She may later feel guilty at the death of an older woman relative, "I neglected poor Aunt Ruth. I'd wish we didn't live so far away from her."

For many Cancer clients, the Leo progression has meant a growth in conscious awareness. Leo is the Sun Center, or Ajna chakra. In Leo, many Cancers begin to ask more conscious questions, such as, "After Mother's death I began to think, is this all there is to life? First we detach from home and mother; we move away with our husbands. Then we become attached to our children. Then we have to detach again as they grow up and move away. Finally we grow old and have to detach from life itself. We die and we reenter the unconscious only to have to be reborn in another body and start all over again. It seems all of life is letting go. There must be more to this than biological destiny."

The Cancer glyph represents the seed of the Divine in the center of the soul (psychic 4th House). As the esoteric Cancer grows older, he or she feels an inner need to connect to the Self as psychic center and integrate life around it. There is a need to water the seed through meditation or other inner work, watch it grow and sprout, strengthening the natal intuitive gifts. Many a Cancer client has become interested in Jung's Path of Individuation during this progression and has become proficient at interpreting her own dreams and those of others. When the ego can connect with the Self, it touches upon a tremendous source of healing power. Cancer usually begins applying his/her healing touch to loved ones and then, in the Virgo progression, extends it to others as a service.

Virgo is the sextile sign for Cancer, and is concerned with nutrition, healing, and communication, both verbal and written. At the beginning of the Virgo cycle Cancer reads, lectures, and sometimes writes about diet and nutrition. Yet, at home, Cancer continues to consume those gourmet desserts high in cholesterol. The physical energy of Leo fire tends to wane in Virgo, and I usually ask my Cancers in this cycle if they *really* adhere to the exercise routine that they recommend to others in classes and newspaper columns. (Cancer is a media-related sign and many disseminate ideas in the press or on radio and television in the Virgo communication cycle.) Cancer usually looks puzzled and replies, "It's the oddest thing. I used to do hatha yoga (or aerobics, or run my 5 miles a day) a few years ago, but somehow it hasn't fit into the schedule lately." The word "schedule" is a key to the fact that Cancer is now thinking like a routinized Virgo; if it is in the schedule, the exercise program happens, if not, it usually doesn't—especially if it's a physically demanding or time-consuming activity.

Though nutrition and practical health topics appeal to Cancer, the sextile energy from the progressed Sun in Virgo to Cancer natal planets is more likely to bring out psychic talents. Virgo is an Isis energy (see Chapter 6) well-suited to healing intuitionally, as through herbs, chants, and affirmations, prayers and other techniques. Cancer is also the crystal ball psychic and many have the trance medium talent. More and more Cancer clients are asking about psychic healing, gemstones and crystals lately. The double-feminine influence of Cancer and Virgo (the Moon is the esoteric ruler of Virgo), however, leaves them feeling somewhat drained after lengthy counseling or massage sessions with sick people who leave behind a lot of negative energy in the office. It is important to remember to give the karma and the leftover energy to god, goddess or guru. Virgo is connected (especially in Egypt) with ritual. It would be helpful to have a purification rite that could could be done in the healing room each day in this progressed cycle.

For Cancers in this progression who are new to meditation, it is important to read about the chakras and to connect with a spiritual teacher who can answer questions and help with techniques. A Cancer who has developed her psychic gifts may find herself considered the Wise Old Woman in Virgo. Certainly, discrimination improves in this Mercury-ruled cycle and Cancer is less concerned with asking the teacher, or the analyst, to explain things. She has more confidence in her own thinking function. (Though Leo was a solar-masculine progression, it too proceeded emotionally rather than logically in making its decisions.) Mercury is a restless ruler, and Cancer may find herself traveling more than she would like, away from the peace of her home, her kitchen, her sewing table. She has skills that others need, and often children or other relatives living in distant places call upon her help.

What of those Cancers who are not interested in psychic or intuitive healing, or inner spiritual work? What happens to them during the Virgo cycle? Some perform services at church or at non-profit corporations, or repair items for hospital thrift shops, or tutor children in need. Those who have no giving or nurturing outlet tend to exhibit some negative Virgo traits; they become fussy, irritable, nervous; they worry about finances and may open a small business after retirement to supplement their fixed income. Extra income from a small upholstering, catering, or tailoring business covers Christmas gifts to the grandchildren and builds the savings account for the rainy day or the Great Depression. Cancer often worries about health (Virgo) and the possibility of medical expenses as the body gets older. Cancer men usually have quite a bit of money coming in from investments such as property. They are worried about the future too, and may use their financial skills (Virgo progression) to prepare taxes for friends and neighbors.

The Libra cycle is usually the last for Cancer. During these years Cancer often really gets to know the spouse for the first time, since Libra refers to the marriage relationship. Many traditional Cancers, for instance, called their spouse Mother or Dad in front of the children, so identified were they with the parenting role. But after the children are gone Mother and Dad are a couple once more, becoming re-acquainted as romantic partners. Often Cancer's spouse is happy to have Cancer show interest in him/her, as s/he would often half-listen to him/her and give most of his/her attention to the children while s/he spoke. Or, Cancer daddy was preoccupied with business first, with the children next, which left the spouse (Mother) a smaller percentage of his attention. "Who are we without the children?" Cancer clients wonder early in the Libra progression. The spouse may become ill and Cancer will devote himself or herself to the familiar nurturing role previously played with children or business.

The Libra cycle is more conceptual than any other. It's the first objective Air sign that this subjective natal personality has progressed through. Many Cancer grandparents will actually remark, "I must be careful not to spoil my grandchildren. I think I may have done too much for my children. I noticed that my neighbors do not have their married sons coming home for loans, or to have Mother do their laundry. They do not suggest that she keep the grandchildren for the entire summer. . . I may have been too lenient."

Objectivity will help Cancer to be a better in-law, too. Jung pointed out in *Symbols of Transformation* that Demeter would have been a very difficult mother-in-law. The only way Persephone could escape home and marry was to be abducted by Pluto. Then, Demeter forced her son-in-law to agree to let Persephone spend summers with mother every year. Sons and daughters of Cancer parents often know that they'll find an understanding, kind, sympathetic ear on the other end of the telephone whenever there's a quarrel with the spouse. Libran objectivity and balance, if Cancer can tune in to them, become real assets.

Cancer begins with a karmic bond to Mother, then usually develops one with children, and at the end of life, in Libra, concludes karma with the spouse. It is a lifetime of relating, a lifetime in which Eros, rather than Logos, is stronger. Surely those whose development is conscious contribute much that is positive to those they love. The intuitive gifts, if consciously developed, help Cancer proceed from the soul in the outer world and go deeper within as well.

Questionnaire

How does the Cancer archetype express itself? Though this relates particularly to those with Sun in Cancer or Cancer rising, anyone could apply this series of questions to the house where his Moon is located or the house which has Cancer (or Cancer intercepted) on the cusp. The answers will indicate how in touch the reader is with his natal Moon (nurturing, emotional needs, sensitivity, instinctual cravings).

1. My family is
    a. the most important thing in life to me.
    b. more important than many things to me.
    c. not as important as my profession to me.

2. Among my strong points I would list
    a. nurturing and caring.
    b. discipline.
    c. versatility and adaptability.

3. In making an important decision I rely on
    a. my feelings most of the time.
    b. cold logic most of the time.
    c. what others tell me.

4. Among my negative qualities I would have to list
    a. moodiness and hypersensitivity.
    b. over-strictness.
    c. insensitivity.

5. Financial and emotional security are
    a. extremely important.
    b. moderately important.
    c. not important at all.

6. My greatest fear is
    a. something will happen to my children or my house.

    b. I would not get recognition when deserved.

    c. being thought of as a boring person.

7. The greatest obstacle to my success comes from
    a. within myself.
    b. others outside myself.

8. I feel the weakest part of my body is
    a. my digestive system.
    b. my knees.
    c. my nerves.

9. I think I am over-cautious
    a. 80% of the time.
    b. 50% of the time.
    c. 25% of the time or less.

10. A real delight for me is
    a. entertaining friends and family with a gourmet dinner in my home.
    b. watching my business grow.
    c. traveling whenever I can.

Those who have scored five or more (a) answers are highly in touch with the Moon—the feeling nature. Those who have scored five or more (b) answers are moving toward the polar extremity. The Moon's nurturing qualities may need more room for expression. More energy may be going into the professional rather than the personal life. Those who scored five or more (c) answers are out of touch with the mundane ruler. Is the Moon intercepted, in detriment, in fall, in the twelfth house? It's important to work with the creative imagination when it comes to the Moon. Any sort of work that involves the co-operation of the unconscious will bring inner personal satisfaction and a positive expression of the Moon's receptive energy.

Where is the balance point between Cancer and Capricorn? How does Cancer integrate his/her inner and outer worlds? Though this relates particularly to Sun in Cancer or Cancer rising, all of us have the Moon and Saturn somewhere in our horoscopes. Many of us have planets in the 4th or 10th houses. For all of us the polarity from Cancer to Capricorn involves balancing nurturing with discipline, personal satisfaction with satisfying others, personal life with professional responsibility.

1. When I am in an argument with my mother over something that I really want to do
    a. I do what seems best to me without really considering mother's objections.
    b. I consider what mother says carefully but in the end make my own decision.
    c. I feel that I defer to mother if her disapproval is really strong.

2. In relationships with close family and friends
    a. I think respect is most important.
    b. I feel that love and respect go hand in hand.
    c. I feel that love is most important.

3. From my earliest childhood memories
    a. I remember mother as a strong disciplinarian.
    b. I remember mother as loving but firm.
    c. I remember mother as meaning well but not really "together."

4. As a parent I would
    a. put discipline uppermost.
    b. combine love with discipline.
    c. put love ahead of discipline.

5. If I were an employer I'd value uppermost in my employees
    a. loyalty, organization, and conformity to company image.
    b. loyalty, dependability, reasonableness.
    c. loyalty, sensitivity and compassion.

Those who have scored three or more (b) answers are doing a good job with personality integration on the Cancer/Capricorn polarity. Those who scored three or more (c) answers may need to work more consciously with developing Saturn in their horoscopes. Those who scored three or more (a) answers may be out of balance in the other direction. They may have a weak or underdeveloped Moon. Study both the Moon and Saturn in the natal chart. Is there an aspect between them? Which one is stronger by house position or location (its sign of rulership or exaltation)? Is either of them intercepted, in fall, or detriment? Aspects to the weaker planet can point the way to its integration.

What does it mean to be an "esoteric Cancer?" How does Cancer integrate Neptune (spirituality, letting go of attachment). How can Cancer attune to Jupiter (Guru, abundance), its planet of exaltation, positively? Conscious awareness can be developed during the Leo progression. The answers to these questions will indicate the extent to which Cancer is in touch with Neptune, his esoteric ruler, and the wisdom of exalted Jupiter.

1. At a restaurant with family and friends, when a check comes I
   a. reach for it.
   b. pay my fair share.
   c. wait to see if someone else will pay it first.

2. My response when told that I must make a drastic change in my home environment is
   a. welcoming change with faith that it is for the best.
   b. accepting it in a relatively short time and carrying on with life.
   c. brooding over it awhile and then resigning myself to it.

3. My ability to let go of the past is
   a. good.
   b. fair to poor.
   c. practically non-existent.

4. When it comes to charity, community service, or volunteering my time and energy
   a. I serve wherever and whenever I am needed.
   b. I find the time to serve in my children's organizations.
   c. I feel charity begins at home and that is where I serve.

5. In the Moon's house and/or the house with Cancer on the cusp
   a. I am unafraid for the future and non-attached.
   b. I have reservations but am conscious of them and am working in that area of my life.
   c. I worry and feel at times overwhelmed.

Those who have scored three or more (a) answers are in touch with their esoteric ruler. Those who have scored three or more (b) answers need to work more consciously at attunement to Neptune and Jupiter. Those who scored three or more (c) answers need to let go of unconscious fear and worry. Attunement to Neptune and Jupiter will liberate Cancer from unconscious fear through developing faith. When Neptune dissolves the status quo, Jupiter offers opportunity for growth. Those who answered (c) to questions 1 and 4 need to attune to Jupiter as Cosmic Wisdom. Generosity relates to wisdom in the sense that it brings expansiveness and abundance. The cosmic law of abundance is that it's more blessed to give than receive. Having faith and giving attracts both spiritual blessings and material security. If we expect good things to happen we draw them; if we are afraid of loss we tend to draw what we fear.

References

Alice Bailey, *Labours of Hercules*, "Cancer I and II", Lucis Publishing, New York, 1974

Bruno Bettleheim, *A Good Enough Parent: A Book on Child Rearing*, Alfred Knopf, New York, 1987

John Blofield, *Bodhisattva of Compassion: Mystical Tradition of Kwan Yin*, Shambhala Publications, Boston, 1977

The Book of the Goddess Past and Present, Carl Olson ed.. Crossroads Publications, New York, 1986

Marie Louise von Franz, "The Process of Individuation," Part 3 of *Man and His Symbols*, C.G. Jung ed., Doubleday and Co. Inc., Garden City, 1969

Joseph L. Henderson, "Ancient Myths and Modern Man," Part 2 of *Man and His Symbols*, C.G. Jung ed., Doubleday and Co. Inc., Garden City 1969

C.G. Jung, *The Archetypes and the Collective Unconscious*, "The Mother Complex," Princeton University Press, Princeton, 1959

C.G. Jung, *Mysterium Coniunctionus*, Princeton University Press, Princeton, 1976

C.G. Jung, *Symbols of Transformation*, "The Dual Mother," Princeton University Press, Princeton, 1956

W.C. Lawton, "Hymn to Demeter," in *The Successors of Homer*, Cooper Square Publications Inc., New York, 1969

Erich Neumann, *The Great Mother*, Ralph Manheim transl., Princeton University Press, Princeton, 1955

Sylvia Brinton Perera, *Descent to the Goddess: A Way of Initiation for Women*, Inner City Books, Toronto, 1980

Alexander Ruperti, *Cycles of Becoming*, C.R.C.S. Publications, Davis, 1978

Ramprasad Sen, *Grace and Mercy in her Wild Hair*, transl. by Leonard Nathan, Great Eastern Publications, Boulder, 1980

Jean Shinoda Bolen, *Goddesses in Everywoman*, "Demeter," Harper and Row, New York, 1984

Noel Tyl, *The Expanded Present*, Llewellyn Pubs., St. Paul, 1976

Marion Woodman, *The Pregnant Virgin: A Process of Psychological Transformation*, Inner City Books, Toronto 1985

5 LEO:
The Search for Being and Wholeness

Our archetypal journey moves on from Cancer to Leo, from the nocturnal, lunar world into the daylight of conscious awareness. This transition from night to day is perhaps easier to understand if, for a moment, we shut our eyes and visualize the night sky, with its dark, starry background and pale, crescent Moon hanging overhead. Now, suppose we change the scene. Suppose we visualize the noonday sky in midsummer. In Cancer, we witnessed the power, potential and mystery that belong to the Feminine, to Shakti, symbolized by the light of the silvery Moon as she undergoes her many moods or phases. In Leo, we arrive at the solar, or Masculine principle—the confident energy of the Sun. Gone are the subtleties of Cancer; we are now directly experiencing the golden rays of the Sun.

There is a constancy to the Leo archetype which seems to be derived from the orbit of Sol himself. The ancients knew that they could depend upon Helios Apollo or Ra to appear every morning at sunrise, bringing the warmth and light which the Earth required for survival. Many myths involved the orbit of the Sun in its fiery chariot, moving across the sky from the East, setting in the West. In Greece the path of Helios Apollo was central to many myths including the Icarus story. In Egypt, the Sun God Ra had two boats, one for morning and one to take him below the horizon at the twilight hour. His Disc is our present astrological glyph for the Sun ($\odot$), and the Egyptians have also provided us the lion's tail glyph for Leo (Ω). The constellation looked like a tail hanging over the Nile Valley. The lion's appearance is mentioned in *Gilgamesh* as the crucial season of the year which brought the floods to the delta. (*Gilgamesh*, as told in *Ancient Myths*, Goodrich, page 34.)

153

The Sun, then, was dependable; one could count on it. It was always the same orange disc; it didn't change its shape or go through phases. The Egyptians had hymns to Ra which conveyed their feeling for this, their most important and essential god:

> Hail, thou Disk, thou lord of rays who risest on the horizon day by day. . . Homage to thee. . . who art the self-created; when thou risest on the horizon and sheddest thy beams of light upon the lands of the North and of the South thou art beautiful, yea beautiful, and all the gods rejoice when they behold thee, the King of Heaven. . . And I have come before thee that I may be with thee and behold thy Disk every day. May I not be shut up in the tomb; may I not be turned back; may the members of my body be made new when I view thy beauties, even as all thy favored ones, because I am one of those who worshipped thee on earth. May I come in unto the land of eternity; may I come even unto the everlasting land; for behold, oh my lord, this hast thou ordained for me. . .
>
> Homage to thee, O thou, who risest in the horizon as Ra, thou resteth upon law unchangeable and unalterable. Thou passeth over the sky and every face watcheth thee and thy course, for (at night) thou hast been hidden from their gaze. . . the number of thy red and yellow rays cannot be known, nor can thy bright beams be told. May I advance, even as thou does advance, may I never cease to go forward, even as thou never ceasest to go forward even though it be for a moment; for with strides thou dost in one little moment pass over the spaces which would need millions and millions of years (for men), this thou dost and then thou dost rest below. Thou puttest an end to the hours of the night and thou dost count them, even thou, thou tendest them in thine own appointed season, and the earth becomes light. . .
>
> Grant, thou, that I may come into heaven that is everlasting. . . where dwell thy favored ones. . . that I may be joined into these Shining Beings, holy and perfect, who are in the underworld, and may I come forth with them to behold their beauties when thou shinest at eventide and goest to thy Mother Nu. Then thou dost place thyself in the West and my two hands are raised in adoration to thee when thou settest as a living being. . . I have given my heart unto thee without wavering, to thou who art mightier than the gods. A hymn of praise to thee, O thou who risest like unto gold, who dost flood the world with light on the day of thy birth. Thou dost give light unto the course of the disk.
>
> Oh, thou great Light, who shinest in the heavens, thou dost strengthen the generations of men with the Nile-flood, and thou dost cause gladness in all lands, and in all cities, and in all temples.
>
> Oh, thou mighty one of victories, thou who art Power of Powers, who dost make strong thy throne against evil fiends; who art glorious in majesty in the morning and evening boat, make thou me glorious through words which when spoken must take effect in the underworld, and grant that in the netherworld I be without evil. . .

> Homage to thee. . . when thou riseth, a cry of joy cometh forth to thee from the mouth of thy peoples, . . . in every place every heart swelleth with joy at thy rising forever.
>
> Oh, thou god of life, all men live when thou shinest, thou art crowned king of the gods. . . thou King of Right and Truth, thou Lord of Eternity, Sovereign of all the gods, thou god of life. Peoples long dead come forth with cries of joy to see thy beauty every day. . . souls of the East follow thee, souls of the West praise thee. . . thou hast joy of heart within thy shrine, for the serpent fiend Nak hath been condemned to the fire, and thy heart shall be joyful for ever.

(Quoted from the "Papyrus of Nekht," sheet 21, in E.A. Wallis-Budge, *Gods of the Egyptians*, V. I, pages 337-9.)

This beautiful hymn from the Sun religion of Egypt leaves an impression of awe, majesty and luminescence. There is here, I believe, a special sense of what Leo or Fifth House magnetism really means in such lines as: "Make thou me glorious through words which when spoken must take effect." The Egyptians believed that speech, when used with concentration, is causative—a creative, transforming force. Symbolically, Ra's magic is the persuasive power behind Leo's words.

This hymn collection gives a good indication of the two levels at which the sun operates in ruling Leo—as mundane and as esoteric ruler. If we are to read it as the reciter who asks Ra for strength, courage, or confidence in facing his/her enemies, (as Ra kept the evil fiend or serpent away from his own throne) or so that the mundane seeker could live a good, ethical life and enjoy his/her position in the afterlife in the company of the Shining Ones, we would have a good text for the mundane Leo going forth on his/her quest for the throne in the outer world—to be in the limelight, to draw followers, to seek applause, to shine.

We could also read the hymns, however, as an appeal for enlightenment, an appeal to Ra as Lord of Light, one of his titles. Esoterically, the sun represents illumination, and in India, the Sun Center or point between the eyebrows is the area where a yogi concentrates during his meditation as he seeks enlightenment. A vision of light is an indicator of spiritual adeptness in many ancient cults. In either quest, the words that to me, personally, most invoke Leo would be: ". . . May I advance, even as thou dost advance. . . May I never cease to go forward." This captures the spirit of so many of my Leo clients.

The joy that typifies Fifth House planets and clients with Sun or Ascendant in Leo also comes through the hymn. It is the joy and freedom of full-blown summer, when the Sun is overhead and people are out on the beaches soaking it up. The light-heartedness of the season, the entertainment House (the Fifth), and Leo are all to be found in Shakespeare's play, *A Midsummer Night's Dream*. In that play, there is no serious plot, but there are lavish costumes, lots of confusion about romance (Fifth House) and the fun of midsummer madness. The sun is past its Solstice point (around June 21st, when Sol, the Sun, makes his station overhead—or seems to stand still, bringing on long days and short nights) and seems to be advancing enthusiastically across the day sky, bringing with it both warmth and heat. During Leo, we know we're experiencing a Fire sign. We have only to look at the thermometer.

As the Sun climbs from the Nadir point of the natural zodiac and moves through the Fifth House, the energy shifts from family responsibility and building foundations, to entertainment, sports or trips to the race track. When we think of the Fifth House in all its meanings, we can picture the family at a summer fair. The father is looking at a sports car (Fifth House sports); the children are wandering off by themselves in the amusement section, riding the ferris wheel and the merry-go-round, and the mother is looking at a new exhibit of something that interests her. Individualism. Neither parent worries, as it gets dark, about whether the children are up too late for the rules they themselves have set, or whether maybe the children would have been better off in a structured camp or summer school, as a Capricorn parent might. Neither is concerned that an adult ought to be watching the children every second, as a Cancer parent might. They enjoy the day and their kids, whom they respect as children rather than as miniature adults. If Leonine parents err, it's not on the side of conservative parenting, but by magnanimity, liberality and generosity. If Leo's parents didn't give Leo enough time at the fair when s/he was young, s/he will overcompensate to give it to his or her children.

Yet, the Leo parent is an individualized adult, too. If given a challenge such as the opportunity that a cross-country transfer would offer, s/he would probably enthusiastically accept. S/he would not be likely to turn it down because s/he knows the local high schools might not be as fine. He would think, "Schools are good in this town, but they might be even better in the new city. And after all, the kids are still in pre-school and first grade. It's a long time to be planning ahead for their high school years." S/he will draw the children along into his/her orbit rather than orbiting around his/her children, as a Cancer parent would tend to do. This is the solar pattern.

In Greece, Helios Apollo ruled the Fifth House, and we can picture flirtatious Aphrodite there beside him. The Fifth House is associated not with married love but with courtship. (The Seventh House refers to committed or contractual married love.) Aphrodite was married, apparently against her will, to ugly Haephestus by Zeus (Jupiter). Jupiter, perhaps, wanted to settle her down and squelch her vanity with Haephestus' ugliness. She was unhappy and had many affairs with mortals as well as gods. Keeping Aphrodite satisfied is a major Fifth House issue; keep romance in your marriage. It's important to find an outlet for one's Fifth House planets.

We have already seen that when Hermes gave the lyre to Apollo he played beautifully. (See Chapter 3, Gemini.) Music is a possible outlet for anyone with Venus or Neptune in the Fifth. Natal Saturn there indicates administrative/supervisory talent and is not as vulnerable to Cupid's arrows. . . although I have even seen cases of dependable Saturn-in-the-Fifth House clients straying from marriages when boredom and restlessness set in under such mid-life transits as Saturn opposite Saturn or Uranus opposite Uranus. If you're married it's quite important to have an outlet for your Natal Fifth House planets in mid-life just to keep Aphrodite and Apollo, those romantics, at bay.

If your natal Pluto is in the Fifth, you have probably already come in contact with psychology; you may have been a patient or have become a therapist. A background in psychology will help you understand the sense of fate you feel at first encounters, the sense of mystery and intrigue you experience when you meet an old friend from a past life, even if you're already married this time. It's important to keep romance, intrigue and mystery (Pluto) in your marriage.

Having several Fifth House planets is similar to having a Leo Sun or Leo rising. Once I attended a lecture with some of my students. The speaker ascended the stage to the lectern and assumed her throne. She had a magnetic aura, strong stage presence, authority of bearing and when she spoke the power behind her words was pure lioness. "She's a Leo, isn't she?" asked a student. "No," I said, "she hasn't a single planet in Leo. Yet she really exudes Leo energy. She has five planets in her natal Fifth House. She is totally comfortable and confident sitting there before her subjects."

We can think of our natal Leo planets or our planets in the Fifth House as our personal, inner lions. In his *Eranos Lecture*, "The Thought of the Heart," James Hillman cites a tradition mentioned by Physiologus which holds that lion cubs are stillborn. "They must be awakened to life by a roar. That is why the lion has such a roar—to awaken the young lions asleep, as they sleep in our hearts. Evidently, the thought of the heart is not simply given—a native spontaneous reaction—always ready and always there. Rather, the heart must be provoked, called forth. . . " He continues in his commentary to mention modern stillborn lions in their "meat-eating stupor," asleep in front of their television sets. Fifth House planets refer to our children, whether physical, mental (idea-children, such as books), or spiritual. Few Leo parents would allow their cubs—their physical children—to sleep in front of the television. They would be at dance or drama classes after school, or in their rooms working on school projects, developing their creativity.

Like the Leo parent, all of us need to work at finding a fulfilling outlet for the energies in the Fifth House. If this energy, these Fifth House planets, are allowed to sleep until mid-life when transits through the Eleventh House oppose them, a crisis-point may be reached. As a result of the crisis, a bridge is often built from the ego to the Self, which liberates (Eleventh House, Aquarius) the energy of the Fifth House planets. S/he can no longer live in the modern materialist desert, the barren landscape of our times. S/he must find personal meaning, value, the heart's love. The search is sometimes directed by the ego, with its mania, in Leo, for conscious control of the mid-life change, and sometimes in more esoteric, more receptive Leos, the search involves listening openly to the Self. But the crisis, the outer world's challenge to the ego's power, is often the roar that awakens the sleeping lion. If the ego's old approaches to life no longer work in the outer, material world, it is thrown back upon the Self, dependent upon faith and introspection to discover a new identity— a new, more fulfilling way of being.

The mid-life Fifth House crisis of romance or creativity often evokes in my mind the image of the great, powerful lion with a thorn in his paw. The wounded lion is immobilized. Alice Bailey has remarked that a crisis the ego suffers is often the means by which the personality transcends to a higher level and contacts the Self. It is a rite of initiation. In *Problem of the Puer Aeternus*, Marie Louise von Franz, too, speaks of the ego's sense that it is dying, but explains that it doesn't really die as such, but temporarily falls into a pit between two opposites, or feels crucified on a cross formed of two conflicting polarities. In my work with T-Square clients during their 40's or 50's, I often encounter egos that feel pulled apart by the opposites and impelled to break free. This is particularly true of the more rigid, Fixed T-Square clients.

The dreams or visions and the active imagining of this cycle help to clarify matters as the normally extroverted Lion withdraws to reflect, to introspect. S/he emerges, often, a shaman, a compassionate healer, a transformer of others in need.

Mircea Eliade used to tell his students the story of an American Indian, a hunter like many in his tribe, who began to have visions. He rejected the message that he was to become a shaman because such was not his egoic desire. He believed himself quite contented as a hunter. He wanted life to continue in its constant, fixed pattern. He grew ill, however. He had to leave the tribe and dream his dreams in order to be healed. He went through the experience alone, withdrawn. He emerged in touch with the Self, as a healer. He could still hunt if he wished; he could still play the old persona role, but he had touched upon a deeper, more fulfilling talent—the role of healer. His life was richer because of the crisis and the inner change prompted by the Self. He began by resisting, but eventually, because his body forced him to yield at the crisis point, he became receptive to the Self. His later years were lived with the Self, rather than the ego, as producer/director of his actions in the outer world. Willfulness had changed to willingness. His strong emotional nature became the servant of the Self, rather than of the ego. And the center of control shifted so that ego, too, became an instrument of the Self.

Leo is a dramatic, dynamic sign. Fifth House planets, too, share in the drama, the dynamism. One might ask, "Doesn't the vision experience result in inflation when the ego is back to its normal, waking-state consciousness? Doesn't it reinforce the vanity and pride of the Lion?" Here it seems that the Virgo progression helps to add common sense, discrimination, and perhaps most important, humility. Fifth House planets, too, progress into the humble, serviceful Sixth House, which is a healing house for oneself and others. Religions of East and West alike emphasize the need for groundedness after an exalted psychological or spiritual experience. They also stress the need to give the credit to God as the performer of the action, rather than to oneself. "God is the real doer." Leo moves through Virgo as the servant of humanity rather than the egoic personality. This was the case for the American Indian in Dr. Eliade's story and for many clients with Leo Sun, Leo rising or Fifth House planets as well. If Leo has passed through a personal crisis he may attempt integration of the Aquarian polarity in a spiritual community or an organization which helps reinforce his sense of service. (More information on the polarity integration later.)

What, then, is the quest of Leo, the Sun, and the Fifth House? Is it just to sit on stage and receive applause from one's subjects? Or to live one's life around some area of the Fifth House? Be a sports car driver? A professional gambler? An entertainer? A persuasive sales-man? A mother of several talented, individualistic children who run wild (in the opinion of the Capricorn down the street)? To work with children in some way? To run for local office as a Leo leader? To be a benevolent despot or a Leo tyrant with one's Fifth House magne-tism? What is fulfillment for Leo, and is it always derived from the outer world, from the people they successfully and generously rule, supervise, or coordinate?

Leo clients have told me over the years that theirs is a quest to be in control. This reminds us of the first Fixed sign, Taurus, the rider of the bull, who seeks to control his instincts. For Leo, who proceeds from the heart (that's Leo in medical astrology), the issue is self-control—self-mastery is the road to success and fulfillment. For some Leos, the quest is entirely mundane, of course. Like Taurus, they exercise willpower and perseverance, but these Fixed qualities are combined with fiery energy. When we think of Leo, we think of Saint Paul saying, "I have fought the good fight; I have kept the faith; I have finished the course; the crown of justice is restored to me."

In Iran, the Lion Initiation was a major part of the Mithrus cult. Frescoes show Mithrus, or the initiate, riding the lion bareback. This is a triumph of skill and self-mastery, of willpower and courage. In *Labours of Hercules*, Alice Bailey also tells us that Hercules fought the Nemean Lion barehanded in his Leo Quest. The lion ritual sym-bolized bringing under control the inner lion of strong emotional reactions, just as the Cretan bull initiation symbolized bringing the physical instincts under control. Like the esoteric Taurean, the Leo initiate can use his controlled energy either for mundane success or for esoteric purposes. No longer is any part of him fearful or out of control like the Nemean lion "laying waste the land," preventing him from reaching fulfillment.

The heraldic lion is also interesting. The lion seems to have been a popular choice for family crests in the medieval period. T.H. White, in his *Book of Beasts*, mentions that the lion in legend was supposed to be compassionate to his fallen enemy. In England, the Thrale family passed down a story about an ancestor named Sir Henry who, having defeated an enemy in battle, found the man prostrate before him reciting the motto from Thrale's family crest, "I prostrate myself before the lion" (*Sat est protase leoni*), and Sir Henry was induced to practice compassion and let his enemy live.

From stories such as this one, we derive our many sayings about Leo. A lion is not greedy, but leaves off eating when he's had enough for the day. He never eats leftovers. He doesn't get angry unless seriously wounded. He is the enemy of the scorpion, which, like the snake, can kill him with its venom. When the lioness is most fertile, she gives birth to five whelps and then reduces her litter each time by one cub. This last was, to me, perhaps the most interesting point in White's *Book of Beasts*, because of the association of fertility or creativity with the fifth sign, Leo, and the Fifth House. Jung also tells us that the number five is the number of the human hand, which, with its five fingers, is our creative instrument.

T.H. White tells us further about the king of beasts:

> The lion. . . is known as wild because [he is] accustomed to freedom by nature and governed by [his] own wishes. They wander hither and thither, fancy free and they go wherever they want to go.
> . . . "Leon" has been translated into Latin from a Greek root because he is prince of all animals. . .
> Their courage is seated in their hearts, while their constancy is in their heads. . . A lion. . . proud in the strength of his own nature, knows not how to mingle with all and sundry, but like the king that he is, disdains to have a lot of different wives.

The constancy or loyalty of the Fixed sign is also characteristic of the astrological lion, who is no philanderer. This is generally true, I have found, of human lions, though of course, in any individual's chart there are 10 stellar bodies scattered through several different signs and elements.

Myths for Leo are Solar in nature, involve the color gold, the kingship, and the conquest or re-conquest of the throne. We could actually have used the Jason myth for Leo instead of Aries, as it has all these elements. It too is a heroic Solar myth but seems more appropriate for Aries' headstrong nature, Aries' impetuosity, and the short bout of Aries' faintheartedness. Leo demonstrates a more consistent courage and constancy. For that reason, we leave Greece and Egypt for India and the myth of Narasimha, Vishnu's incarnation as the man-lion, and patient Prahlad, the quiet hero. There is an analogous story from the *Book of Judges* in the Bible about Samson and Delilah. The Prahlad story is important because it illustrates more clearly than many other Solar myths the lack of support from the father, seemingly a part of Leo's karma. This lack of parental support frequently is an issue to be resolved on the emotional level during the individuation process—the process of becoming a spiritual adult. I have noticed this struggle in many a Leo client, both male and female lions. In myth and fairy tales, the giant is an exaggerated father symbol, because to a small child, Father seems to be an all-powerful giant.

In this myth, a story from the Indian *Puranas*, Lord Vishnu manifests upon Earth in answer to a prayer. The name of the hero and heir to the throne, whose father preferred his younger brother, is Prahlad, which means "devoted one" or "constant one." In the beginning of the story, Prahlad seemed to his father, the King, to be physically weaker and much less courageous than his brother, and his father appeared to Prahlad to be an evil giant. His father's name was Hiryana-Kasipu, which means "golden fleece" in Sanskrit. (This is reminiscent of Jason's golden fleece in the Aries myth.) His father did not want Prahlad to sit for hours praying to Vishnu, and made sport of his devotion. Prahlad knew that he would lose the throne to his brother and feared that his father, the giant, would have him killed. He prayed to Vishnu to deliver him, spending days in vigil and meditation. Vishnu at first replied that he could not, because Brahma, famous for his boons to the most unlikely people, had promised Hiranya-Kasipu that he could not be slain by man or beast, indoors or outdoors, by weapons made by humans, gods or demons, in daytime or night. To Prahlad, the odds seemed impossible—a giant father and a boon of Brahma which could not be repealed. Still, Prahlad kept up his courage, though his father tried three times to have him poisoned.

Finally, convinced by the determination, faith, and courage of the heir to the throne, Vishnu appeared in the half-man, half-lion form of Nara-Simha, neither man nor beast nor god. He appeared on the patio at twilight, which was neither day nor evening. He sprang out from a porch pillar (neither indoors nor outdoors) and killed Golden Fleece (Hiryana-Kasipu) with his claw, which was not a weapon made by men, gods or demons. The throne then belonged to Prahlad, whose courage and fasting had reduced him to a wraith in the pictures that accompany the story in the *Puranas*. This is true mastery of one's own fears: a threat to the body, and the emotional loss of having Leo's own father disinherit him in favor of a less worthy brother. It is a superb test for the pride of a Lion. One thinks of internal fortitude here because the saddest part is emotional separation from the father, and the difficulty in getting a hearing from Vishnu (God).

To me this is a more heartening story than many of the Greek myths which involve outer rather than inner quests. Prahlad's test involved the emotions, which are so strong in Leo. In the later texts, Prahlad seems to come through as a good and wise king rather than to become a replica of his father. He does not seem to have abandoned his kingdom for wider quests like Jason who in his restlessness sought new worlds to conquer. He does not seem to have succumbed to *hybris*, struggling against his fate, or trying to outshine Vishnu. Like the lion in the merciful story of Sir Henry Thrale, Prahlad's ego did not slay the enemy, though he was the clear victor and the throne was his. It was the Self that freed him. He resembled many a timid Leo of my acquaintance who developed courage and valor, who overcame his/her fears and grew up to become a strong adult Lion. His weak ego transcended to touch the Self through a crisis experience.

In India, there is a great deal of esoteric symbolism to the pillar on the porch because it is said to represent the astral spine, in which is found the key to success—the chakras, or power centers through which yogis, in meditation, direct the life force. The lion-man incarnation of Vishnu burst forth from the power source, the pillar. Of course, this is the inner passage to success, offering access to the "throne" for all of us.

The same symbolism, interestingly, is repeated in the story of Samson in the *Book of Judges*. The events occurred when, we are told, "Israel was without a King." (*Judges* 19:1.) Samson's story is about physical strength and an emotional test. Here the hero, unlike

Prahlad, is physically strong and also unlike Prahlad, popular in the outer world among his kingless people. His enemies (the Philistines) feared that Samson would become a king and make a strong people of the Israelite tribes. They determined to prevent this by discovering the source of his great strength. They sent Delilah, a beautiful woman, to seduce Samson and discover his secret. Samson, although victorious in the outer battlefields, succumbed to his emotions and fell in love with the enemy spy. After telling her several lies, he finally told her the truth—that the secret of his great strength lay in his hair (his lion's mane). She cut his seven locks while he slept and then turned him over to the Philistine men, who blinded him and tied him between two pillars in their prison. Crowds came to laugh and jeer.

Samson prayed to the Lord God with what must have been great concentration, faith and courage: "Lord, I ask Thee only once, let me be avenged on these Philistines. . . " Then he pulled with all his might on both pillars and brought down the whole prison-house (*Judges* 16:30). He overcame with an inner strength, even though his mane had been shorn; he was a Lion. These stories of Prahlad on his fast and of Samson in the enemy prison bring to mind the saying: "His strength was as the strength of ten, because his heart was pure." Both were, in their own way, Leo heroes; they faced tests of the heart, struggle with a Father in one case and Delilah in the other. Both suffered within, yet had tremendous willpower, courage and faith that carried them to victory.

This brings me to an observation. In the esoteric tradition, there is no exaltation in Leo. Several authors feel that the Sun is sufficient. After all, it does symbolize illumination, or individuation, if you're a Jungian. Everything in our Solar System revolves around it. At the mundane level, Apollo's children are destined for center stage and a lot of applause. Their leadership will be recognized. Yet, I think a case could be made based on the Prahlad and Samson stories in favor of Neptune's exaltation in Leo. Neptune refers to faith and sacrifice—the humble surrender of ego control. Neptune seems a natural protection for a hero who might otherwise develop what the Greeks called *hybris*—that arrogant attitude towards the gods, or the attempt to encroach upon their powers which brought one to punishment by the Fates. Hybris often led to the pattern within a hero's family whereby through successive generations one generation repeated the mistakes of the last. A tyrant's son would rebel against his father, take the throne, and eventually become a tyrant himself. Neptune's exaltation refers to giving credit to God (to Vishnu or the Lord Yahweh), thus protecting Leo from the "pride that goeth before a fall."

In sum, then, the quest of Leo is like the Solar Quest of Jason in Aries. Usually, Leo is found in a leadership role in the outer world—staking out his kingdom and conquering it. The kingdom could be a sales territory, an inheritance of land and power or in the world of visual arts, dance and drama. The kingdom could be the whole country—the Leo artist might go on the road and perform. I have several clients who participate in the Leo archetype through the stage.

Often, like Aries, Leo opts for a quest that involves fighting a giant and fearful odds against his success. Sometimes the giant is not a father but a father figure, with a giant's reputation. His or her own emotions appear to be the major test for Leo. As with the other Fixed signs, betrayal by personal friends or family members hits him hardest, and s/he will fight for principle. Yet, Leo is constant, like the Sun in its orbit, or the like the lion in T.H. White's beastiary that appeared on so many family crests in medieval Europe.

Several Leo clients have been really drawn to Jung and his psychology of individuation. Jung himself was a Leo and found the inner quest of the individual for wholeness of particular fascination. To be all we can be, "to strip away the layers of the onion and get to the core of who you are," he once said. That's a quest worthy of a Leo. In the sense that Leo means illumination, all disciples on various paths up the mountain to the Divine are esoteric Leos. So this is, indeed, an important sign. If Aries was a doer and activist, then Leo is a becomer—a personality in the process of becoming him or herself. Every time I see a Leo client, he is "advancing" (as the Egyptians put it in the above-mentioned hymn to Ra). It was Apollo the Sun God who brought spirit to man. Leo has spirit. It's like the song, "You've gotta have heart, lots and lots of heart."

There is a lot to be learned from the Leo archetype in the broader sense because many of us are esoteric Leos regardless of whether we literally have Fifth House planets or Leo energy in our horoscopes. The Solar Path is quite popular in the modern West. It is a more mental path—the path of conscious awareness. The Lunar Path of the Cancer archetype, which is less conscious, is still very popular in India. It emphasizes a passive-receptive surrender to the will of a personal deity and a dependence upon grace. This was Ramakrishna's path to realization through his personal relationship with Goddess Kali. (See Cancer, Chapter 4.)

The Solar Path involves active, conscious participation, or the use of one's own will and understanding—a cooperation with the Divine. It includes the fiery zeal of Leo—the courage of the Lion who goes forth independently and takes risks, who fearlessly faces the adventure of life and makes mistakes, willing to accept the "lion's share" of the responsibility for them. A medieval Vaishnavite philosopher, Ramanuja, used the analogy of kitten and baby monkey to contrast the Lunar and Solar Paths to the goal. The kitten is carried along by its mother; she lifts him up and puts him down. He is totally dependent and totally secure, like a religious person. The baby monkey, on the other hand, is on the Solar Path. He rushes forward independently to experience life and learn from it as soon as he can walk. Both animals are going to grow up and get along in life. They are simply on two different paths, like different human personalities. Those of us who follow the path to wholeness, or to the Self, or to the Divine in an active, conscious, fearless but constant way are a lot like the archetypal Leo. We need to guard against *hybris*, to keep our compassion in victory and our cheerfulness when emotionally wounded. But there's a lot of fun and joy on the Solar Path, too.

My Leo astrology students who are born on the cusp of Cancer and seem more introverted than most Lions will often express an aversion to western psychology. "This individuation process sounds as if it would reinforce the ego! The ego is bad enough already. It's full of desires that will just sidetrack us from our quest for the Self. It pulls us outward into the world of the body and sensory objects." These objections often come from Leos in the eastern religions who have their Sun intercepted, or in the 12th House. This is what I have come to call the lion cub or timid lion pattern. The Lion has not yet learned to roar, but during his long solar procession through Leo or the Twelfth House, or his/her eventual progression out of the intercept, will release his emotions and his creative juices. His/her journey seems more like that of the lion in *The Wizard of Oz* than the usual Leo. His/her timidity is revealed through his aversion to the objective world of the senses, the dynamic world of passion and desire through which ego-consciousness relates.

In my sessions with the timid lions, I usually mention C.G. Jung's analogy about the ego revolving around the Self as the Earth around the Sun, and perhaps give the definition of individuation from his book, *The Integration of the Personality*. It is. . . "a psychological process that makes of a human being an 'individual,'—a unique, indivisible unit or 'whole man'." If we can take back repressed parts of ourselves and become more conscious of them, we can then create more effectively. We will feel alive and vital. Next we can endeavor to integrate the opposites (as the *Upanishads* also tell us to do) and have something worth offering to God—a strong ego-consciousness. Before we can surrender our ego to the Divine (as cusp of Cancer, intercepted, or Twelfth House Leos often feel a need to do) we must first have an ego to surrender. Like a Greek warrior, Leo can experience *arete*, justifiable pride in excellence, without *hybris* (trying to assume the powers appropriate only to God). Jung has covered the issue of ego inflation well in his *Answer to Job*, which is, I think, a good book for the Leo counselor. Job saw himself as a virtuous man with a strong intellect, capable of solving others' problems with his fine advice. Imagine his horror when Yahweh responded to his ego inflation by making certain that the outer world no longer cooperated with Job's expectations, plans, and desires!

Jung remarked that the more conscious the ego becomes, the longer the Shadow it casts in the outer world. Magnetic people like Leos behave in ways that are noticeable to others. But this midsummer sign tends to remain unaware of its own shadow for long stretches of time, till, thwarted as Job was by the outer world, Leo relaxes its conscious control and begins to listen to the Self. Wilfullness changes to willingness and leadership to cooperation. How hard it is to see the shadow at noon on a midsummer day, with the Sun directly overhead. So often the outer world acts to confront Leo with his Shadow, forcing him or her to face the dark side and integrate its positive aspects.

Must Leo's plans be thwarted dramatically before s/he relaxes the ego's control and lets the Self come forward? Not always, Jung tells us in his treatise on the inner alchemy, *Mysterium Coniuncionis*, "because it very often happens that ego-consciousness and the ego's sense of responsibility are too weak and need, if anything, strengthening. . . " Every Leo does not suffer from the *hybris* of an inflated ego. Many timid lions are still struggling to emerge from the unconscious, take back their vitality, their repressed emotions, accept the positive contents of their Shadow in order to become whole and to create according to their unique talents. Those who are born close to the Cancer cusp may find Chapter 4 helpful.

The inner alchemy often involves a mystical marriage, symbolized by the marriage of Queen with King, of the unconscious and the conscious within us, or the feminine intuitive feeling creative side, the Queen, and Logos, the King, the masculine thinking function that we met in Aries and in Gemini. According to Jung, if the conscious mind is unaware that there is an imaginative, creative talent down in the Unconscious, then the ego will deny it. The talent may as well not exist. This is, of course, true for all of us, but it's especially sad for Leo, who has an archetypal connection to the creative Fifth House. Thus the inner marriage between the conscious mind and the unconscious must take place. These two facets of the psyche are not opposed to each other, but are complementary. (If the ego has had a bad day, for instance, the unconscious may send it a pleasant compensatory dream to make it feel more confident.) Thus, an inner marriage is quite suitable. (In Jung's system it is also the Self that coordinates the contents of the Unconscious, that is the center and source of both unconscious dreams and superconscious visions, so integrating the Unconscious takes us closer to the Self.)

How does this work? There are a number of ways. Often the unconscious sends the conscious mind a signal through the body, to get the ego's attention. If Leo's heart is not in his work, he may develop chest pains, which in medical astrology are a clear cut signal, "stop and listen to the psyche. Give it room to make a change in your life, if it sees a need." The conscious mind of Leo, a Fixed sign, tends to resist. One accountant in his late 40's, a cusp of Virgo Leo, told me "I have chest pains every year during tax season. I feel such stress that I am almost unwilling to get up in the morning and go to work." "Your heart is no longer in it," I said, "perhaps you have something else you've been thinking of doing? Something interesting, creative? Something your Leo planets would enjoy and your Virgo planets could study? Something that would give you time out from your stressful job?" "Naw. I haven't any creative talents. It's a good, secure living being a CPA. It was good enough for Dad all those years. . . " He responded with his Virgo stellium which hates risk-taking.

Later, after his heart condition became more severe, he acknowledged an interest in learning computer programming and designing a tax program for the small businessman's home computer. He soon became enthusiastic about marketing it. He was motivated to learn quickly at computer school. The confidence he built through the career change carried over into other areas of his life; the magnetism in his aura was enhanced. He no longer seemed such a timid lion, and shortly thereafter he drew a self-assured woman—his lion's mate.

When the body, especially the heart, sends messages to Leo/ Leo rising, it is important to relax and listen to the instincts, feelings, emotions, intuitions, and other inhabitants of the Unconscious. It's important to be willing to make changes, follow the fiery inclination to take risks, move beyond the settledness of fixity. Not only will Leo live longer, but he'll enjoy life more.

Having spoken of the inner, alchemical marriage of opposites, conscious and unconscious, we come to the topic dear to the heart of most Leos: "Where is my mate in the outer world?" There are, of course, a few Leos for whom the divine romance of the soul with God is the life path—a few renunciants—but the vast majority follow the pattern of the lion in T.H. White's *Bestiary*, who seeks a mate for life. Leo men seem to have an easier time drawing the partner than do Leo/Leo rising women. The sign is very romantic, and quite spontaneous. Quite often the Lioness will call and announce: "I met my soul mate at 10:00 a.m. today; I want to come over tonight for a relationship reading." Yet the Lioness is also quite capable of spending many years alone, nursing her grievances and enjoying proving herself in the outer world, or the inner, introspective quest for the Self. This is especially true after a painful divorce if her pride was wounded.

Men will often admit to feeling intimidated by the Leo/Leo rising woman. "She's so strong and self-assured," said one man of his beautiful Leo rising ballerina. "I love to be seen with her on my arm. Yet, when it comes to. . . you know. . . a commitment. . . well. . . she's so intense, so powerful; I don't know if I could live with her on a daily basis." Another has said, "She manages so well on her own, I don't think she really needs anyone." Leo women seem so competent, almost larger than life to many men (unless they are of the timid variety). Yet, it is very important to Leo/Leo rising women to respect their husbands. A Lioness is seldom happy with a wimpy man.

Attunement to the Water planets in the horoscope has been known to help. For instance, Leo women who have chosen to leave a competitive work environment such as marketing for a more creative, less aggressive profession begin to project a softer, more feminine energy. Men no longer see them as the competition. Instead they appear as lovely, graceful, warm women. The feminine side

(Water planets) come through and men are no longer as intimidated.

Attuning to Neptune's mystical, metaphysical, musical, or meditative talents will also bring out the exalted Neptune virtues of gentleness, kindness, forgiveness, and ability to trust men again if the Lioness has been wounded in her last relationship. The Unconscious may be saying, "Don't rush into another relationship; you may get hurt again." But Fire signs are risk takers who know at heart that if nothing is ventured, nothing is gained. Eventually, the Lioness will risk her pride and take a chance on commitment again.

We come now to the polarity—Aquarius. If Leo represents the individual, shining in his solar glory, then what, if anything, needs to be incorporated from the polarity of Aquarius? I think most of us have heard that old truism that Leo loves the man next door but finds humanity a concept that's a bit too broad to grasp. Here we have the Uranus ruled Aquarius to help him out. If you think of your Leo rising friends and clients, you'll see this at once. They are inclined to choose exotic or unusual looking (Aquarian type) people as marriage partners. The partner of a Leo rising person takes him beyond his own neighborhood into the greater community. Leo, then, surveys a larger territory partly because the partner requires it of him. Leo rising has his own projects—his personal kingdom. But the partner adds a Uranus dimension of volunteerism and through the partner's interests, the Leo Ascendant becomes the chairman of the Aquarian's committee. One Leo rising client told me that before his marriage he thought he had enough responsibility at work. He used to play softball or relax with his men friends. After his marriage his Aquarian lady took him along to all her committees to save the environment and raise money for homeless people. He soon was busier than ever before, but really enjoying himself. He now has more responsibilities outside his job than at work. Actually, he'd like to have more time to spend with the children, but it simply wasn't going to happen for him. "There is satisfaction, though," he told me, "in the work my wife does. I rather like the feeling of contributing. . . of helping in the community at large."

As Aries benefits from integrating Libran energy, Leo benefits from incorporating the Aquarian altruism and airy objectivity. If a problem from work is bothering Leo, he may call an Aquarian friend to discuss it. If the Aquarian can think up a way for the Lion with injured pride to save face and compromise, s/he provides objectivity.

Remember, if you are the spouse, the co-worker, or even his/her competitor, *never* insult Leo. Always leave the king room to save face; never embarrass him in front of others. Scorpios often make this mistake. This, I believe, is part of the difficulty with the square from Leo to Scorpio.

In the *Beasts* book by T.H. White we read, "The snake and the scorpion's venom can poison the lion." In the last part of the Hymn to Ra already quoted, the Sun God confronted the serpent Nak and cast him into the fire. Tapestries and family crests and art often depict the struggle with the lion and the serpent, or lion and bull, and it has often seemed to me, observing it in my clients, that the Scorpio/Taurus polarity is too subtle for our frank, conscious, upfront Lion. The Fire signs are open communicators and thus may resent or become confused by the indirect tactics of Taurus or Scorpio. Aquarius is equally Fixed, but Uranus' Aquarian children are alert, conscious, and good at communication. They can clear the air with Leo and make suggestions for dealing with the other Fixed signs (which Aquarians often find equally frustrating). Like Scorpio, Leo has difficulty trusting a second time if s/he thinks a person has betrayed him/her. Letting go of old slights is a source of pain for the Lion and Scorpion alike.

In summary on the Lion, the Sun, and the quest for emotional control, we should perhaps mention that Leo is constancy (Fixed or persevering Fire), pride and sometimes *hybris* (arrogance), but is less impetuous and more determined than Aries (Cardinal Fire), and has a greater zest for life than most other signs. Archetypally Leo represents the individual engaged in the process of becoming whole. Leo is a leadership sign; we say, for instance, that a successful person is "lionized" at a party in his honor. My experience with male and female people with Fifth House planets, Sun, or Ascendant in Leo, is that they come to the astrologer for personal rather than career insights.

The Sun needs someone to warm up and shine upon. A Leo does not like to be without his lioness, his mate. No matter how successful on her own, or how creative the lioness, she too wants her mate around. Isabel Hickey made the following significant remark in her book, *Astrology, The Cosmic Science*, about Leo rising: "Physical heart problems often result from unresolved emotional problems." Thus, the inner quest for personal, emotional fulfillment is a major issue for most Leos, be they esoteric or mundane. So it's important to check out the transits and progressions involving the Leo client's emotional life even if s/he is a successful prima ballerina, top salesperson, or the mayor.

The emotional reactions of a Lion wounded in love or in the heart, the Fifth House area of life, reveal his level of conscious control and self-mastery. Is he a totally mundane Lion or an esoteric Lion? How merciful is he to the ex-wife who proved to be disloyal and then prostrated herself before him like a fallen enemy on the battlefield? How soon will he be able to trust again in a new relationship? Is the mercy of Neptune exalted in this particular Leo? Has he integrated the Aquarian polarity with its tolerance and cool evaluation? "My ex-wife was human, after all." How soon does he recover from a public challenge that hurts his pride or dignity? Can he rage and roar and then really go away and forget it? Or does he store the memory of the wound away for years?

Phoebus (golden-rayed) Apollo had a motto installed over the main entrance to his shrine at Delphi for pilgrims to read when they came in search of his oracle's guidance. It said, "Know Thyself." Many spiritual teachers through the centuries have expressed that same point: "Unless we first face the person we are (natal chart), how can we expect to become the person we want to be?" How can we fulfill the potential in the personality? How can we reach wholeness (individuation), or how can we find the Self within—reach illumination? A Leo can take his zest for life, magnetism, confidence, courage, willpower and style from one desire to the next and walk away each time feeling empty, or s/he can be master on the throne of his or her own personality, inner ruler of the emotions, director of the drama of his/her life. Alice Bailey tells us the will to rule, the leadership instinct within Leo, must first be used to conquer the raging lion within. Not to kill the lion, but to ride it—to control it rather than be controlled by it. Next, the esoteric Leo develops his will to illumine, and attuned to the Sun as esoteric ruler, his magnetism reaches out to draw to him the right mate and true friends (Aquarian polarity). Bailey sees the esoteric Leo as goal directed (Eleventh House or Aquarius represents personal goals) and purposeful—a conscious planner. (Bailey, *Esoteric Astrology*, pages 288, 91).

There is an almost magical quality to the esoteric Leo. Others see him as an uncommon man—realized, illumined, or divine. To the

Egyptians, the Pharaoh had the inner power to protect the kingdom and to assure its prosperity. He was a magical or divine being. (Campbell, *Primitive Mythology*, pages 167-168.) Leo was the most important time of the year in Egypt—the time of the rains. But sometimes the rains were unpredictable and came during Virgo instead. The Egyptians developed one symbol for this entire magical time of year (Leo/Virgo) and for the Pharaoh's wisdom and unselfish service (Virgo), as well as his leonine courage and inner power—the Sphinx. Fifteen years ago I read about this Leo/Virgo symbol in Dane Rudhyar's *Astrological Signs, The Pulse of Life*, and my unconscious has been processing it ever since.

I'd encourage anyone who is on the Quest of Individuation or Illumination to ponder the Sphinx. She's a powerful symbol of wholeness. She combines the best qualities of Leo and Virgo, and thus, people who have in their charts any of the combinations of Leo and Virgo energy might like to keep her picture around and glance at it from time to time—Virgos with Leo rising, Leo Moon or Fifth House planets; Leo with Virgo rising, Sixth House planets or Virgo Moon; cusp people—the combinations are endless. In the Sphinx we have the constancy or perseverance of Leo (fixity) combined with Virgo flexibility (mutability); we have wisdom and discrimination and prudence (Virgo) combined with courage, zeal, activity, and willpower (Leo). We have the spirit of humble service (Virgo) combined with self-confidence, physical strength and stamina (Leo). We have the cool head (Virgo) and the warm heart (Leo). It's a lot like the Tarot card Strength, because both the Sphinx and the Strength card combine a lion and a virgin—power and innocence. It is also a symbol of personality integration if we think of a conjunction of Masculine (consciousness) and Feminine (unconsciousness) in the virgin and the lion.

All too often the Leo leader automatically presumes s/he knows what's best for his/her followers. S/he overreacts in a moment of crisis and takes them off in a tangential direction, away from the main road to truth. Apollo, God of Truth, rules the Fifth sign and the Fifth House. The desert lion, the Sphinx of Gizah with her knowing smile, her inner truth awareness, seems a fitting symbol for Leo/Virgo. She is rooted in her meditative pose, staring into the Sun calmly, patiently, listening. (Listening, as we have seen in the Aries chapter, is not particularly easy for the Fire sign.) Unlike the Sphinx of Thebes, who sought merely to catch Oedipus in a riddle, the Gizah Sphinx is an inspiration to the weary traveler who unexpectedly encounters her in his/her desert solitude, his/her spiritual dryness. She has an inner directedness. She listens to her soul and to the needs of the collective unconscious, to which her humble, serviceful attitude renders her totally open.

What is this sphinx-like progression through Virgo about for Leo, in practical everyday affairs? At first it may feel like a dimming of the natal Sun's light. One Leo remarked that it seemed to him as if someone had put a basket over his head and left him in the dark. "Is this how it feels to be a Virgo, and if so, will it really last thirty years?" he asked. He experienced a listless feeling, a sort of ennervation that he described as "loss of vitality, and a tendency to worry about health, which I've never done before in my life. Perhaps I'm becoming a Virgo hypochondriac. Then, too, I suddenly have this paperwork job, which I hate. Yet, I seem stuck there, because the part-time hours fit my schedule and I'm able to take classes in the afternoons. Still, it's frustrating. A few years ago I had unlimited energy; I could juggle a full-time job with night school and feel rested every morning. Now, the part-time job is wearing. I want to be through with school and go out and *do* things in life." The Virgo-apprenticeship cycle did bring him the ability to reflect, through practical "dry earth" courses that provided him the skills he would one day need to hang out his own shingle. The ability to wait patiently, work industriously, and learn thoroughly is developed during the Virgo progression. This individual learned what many an Aries discovered progressing through the Earth sign, Taurus—be patient and considerate of others who may not have the vitality that belongs to the Fire signs! Consideration for the feelings and pace of life of the less flamboyant signs comes through the Earth progressions, wherein Fire signs learn to build slowly and well.

Virgo represents the sword of discrimination, the Hermes-ruled mind of the Egyptian seers. Hermes rules alchemy, the inner progress of transformation which came to Greece from Egypt. In the Virgo cycle, sometimes seemingly as spiritually dry as the Egyptian desert, extroverted Leo has an opportunity to introspect and, through a Mutable openness, to become more discerning about his or her heretofore Fixed opinions. Perhaps there's truth everywhere, not just in Leo's own religion, be it Eastern or Western, mystical or psychological. During the course of the Virgo progression, his stubborn dogmatism may dissolve, and many a Leo seems less inclined to confront others with their errors, to try to save others from what Leo perceives to be their delusion. Virgonian receptivity facilitates the spiritual and psychological transformation as Leo becomes able to see his or her shadow, admit to it, and analytically determine which parts of its nature s/he needs to integrate and which to struggle against, as Jacob struggled with the angel. In reclaiming the positive shadow energies Leo usually discovers that his Virgo hypochondria and fatigue diminish. Virgo worry or fussiness over details abates.

Even the menial, quiet, unassuming job that Leo may hold during the Virgo apprenticeship period is helpful for it gives him time out from center stage activity, from rushing about acting and performing in the outer world. Virgo's more subtle, introverted cycle enables him to withdraw into a sort of gestation period. For the first few years of Virgo, s/he may complain of feeling alone, isolated, like a hermit or desert saint of early Christianity, and wonder why s/he is not his/her usual social, extroverted self. However, after accustoming him/herself to the quieter energy, Leo is usually able to go deeper into his/her own soul. Usually co-workers are part of his learning situation. The Leo star is suddenly a member of the band, or just another student of the Master, stuck in a dull grind, a Virgo routinized schedule. If Leo formerly identified with his creative persona, he may feel very much like the Gizah Sphinx, parched and alone in the desert. What has he done lately that's original, that reflects his ego, that's worthy of the applause of his fellow man? Unless he has a Grand Trine in Earth for the progressed Sun to activate, the answer may be "very little."

Virgo, however, learns by observation. Hermes is a good imitator. The master teacher, whether he be artist, singer, or guru, has a ready student in his Leo during this cycle. Leo is at his most industrious, his most conscientious. Leo is learning to be a follower so that one day he can lead, but from his soul, not from his personality, his ego. Virgo is a good progression for growing a soul. Many old habits, entrenched in Fixed Leo from past lives, can be released during Virgo if Leo is willing. Part of the key, however, lies in Virgo techniques. One can observe a mentor all day long, but if one fails to practice his techniques, what happens when the mentor is no longer around to ask "What do I do next?" The techniques may be artistic, musical, healing (Virgo is a health-related sign) research-oriented, but like the Teacher, they somehow become available to him in this cycle.

Ego inflation is, in some cases, a tendency to identify with the persona, "I am the Messiah." Because the natal Sun sign is connected to ego consciousness and power, the strong Leo (not the timid Lion) must often look at himself in terms of inflation. Why is he so impatient during this Virgo cycle? Why should he be hanging out his own shingle more quickly than others? Is the *persona*, the outer I AM all that important? The Virgo cycle, with its quiet energy, usually confronts Leo with this if Leo is spiritually or psychologically aware.

There are many Greek myths of the heir to the throne, the Fire sign hero full of courage and confidence who undergoes tests and overcomes obstacles. The outcome of these stories is always the most interesting part. What does the hero plan to do once he has possession of the throne? Once he is realized, or individuated? Will he be a tyrant king like some of the Greek rulers or a philosopher king? Will he draw others to seek the Divine in themselves? Virgo is all about service. Virgo seeks possession of the inner throne in order to help others, not simply to be more creative and impress the outer world. Edinger, in *Ego and Archetype*, has said that the individuated man doesn't need to prove himself in the outer world, to compete in it, to compare him/herself constantly with others who are successful there. *S/he knows who s/he is!* In the same source, Edinger explains that the inflated ego, however, believes not only that s/he is the Son of God and heir to the throne, but that s/he is "God's *only* child!"

The beauty of the Virgo progression, spiritually and psychologically, seems to be that its service attitude subliminally affects Leo. At the conclusion of the 30 years he may have evolved to the point where, to paraphrase Edinger, he sees himself not as the *only* creative ego on Earth, but as one part of the whole planetary organism. He does not even feel a need to be a conspicuous part.

For a timid Lion who is working on courage, on building an ego identity distinct from his parents' egos or that of his caste, the Virgo cycle works differently, it seems. Here one may have the progressed Sun cross a stellium of Virgo planets like going down a flight of stairs, and with each conjunction to a Virgo planet the client may remark, "I have so many self-doubts and insecurities. I don't know how I can go on. My high school teacher thought I had more writing talent than she had seen in a long time, but it seems I'll always be stuck in a doctor's office, doing x-rays and seating the patient in a waiting room. I feel that I've let the teacher down, but worse yet, I'm letting myself down." With many planets in Earth, this timid Lioness sees time passing and feels overwhelmed. Positive transits come and go and still she does not give up the secure job that she hates and enroll in courses that would give her techniques, skills, and very important, deadlines to turn in her copy to the writing teacher. She has a wealth of material collected from watching the patients in the doctor's waiting room and the doctor him/herself. But without the writing class, she may spend many years amassing information and never translate it from the unconscious to paper. Jungian therapy would help the timid lion in this cycle, but too often he or she will remark from Virgo frugality, "It's too expensive." I recommend mythology; it helps to read, especially about Lions, or heros and heroines.

During the Libra progression, the Leo leaves the dry desert sands of Virgo for the Air. Concepts, objectivity, extroverted social energy and positive self-expression are once more part of his/her kingdom as this cycle accords well with his/her natal Leo energy. From the earliest days of the progression, a symbolic sextile operates. The Lion's question, "Where is my mate?" if indeed s/he is still asking it at this point, is likely to receive an affirmative, "Here I am." Libra is about the marriage relationship. If Leo has worked through some of his/her stubbornness in the Mutable Earth progression, then these years can be the happiest of the incarnation. Libra gives the spirit of cooperation and also warmth that attracts to him people who share his/her values. Leo often retires in Libra around the time progressed Sun sextiles natal Sun. This frees him/her from the tedious Virgo routine that nagged at him/her during the old progression. As a parent, Leo took his/her duties quite seriously in Virgo, especially supervising his/her children's study habits and encouraging them in extra-curricular activities. They may have found him/her demanding, as s/he wanted them to have it all. But in Libra, if grandchildren appear on the scene, s/he will seem quite different—a mellow person with a great sense of humor (Libran Air).

As a creative artist, Leo may succeed in his/her retirement years, when s/he is more relaxed and less anxious to prove him/herself, to a greater extent than ever before. Spiritually, too, after the analytical Virgo cycle, Leo relaxes about his progress on his path and begins to enjoy it. Gone is the striving-striving-striving pressure of his earlier years. In this conceptual cycle, s/he enjoys discussing ideas with others, rather than giving them the benefit of his/her ideas. By hindsight, s/he sees the progress s/he has made over the years, the transformation of old habits and attitudes. It is generally a very positive 30 years.

The Scorpio cycle is ordinarily Leo's last progression. It seems appropriate to leave the Earth Plane in the archetypal sign of death and rebirth. I have very few Leo clients who have lived long into the Scorpio period, so I do not really know a great deal about it. I believe one reason I have so few might be that heart attacks are associated with Leo, and these reduce the lifespan by a number of years. Leos who pay attention to diet, get moderate exercise, have their cholesterol level monitored regularly, keep open an outlet for their creativity (find some interest that their hearts are in) should live on into Scorpio. Previous generations were not as aware of preventive medicine as today's Leo; so today's Leo should live to a ripe old age.

Questionnaire

How does the Leo archetype express itself? Though this relates particularly to those with the Sun in Leo or Leo rising, anyone could apply this series of questions to the house where his Sun is located or the house which has Leo (or Leo intercepted) on the cusp. The answers to these questions will indicate how in touch the reader is with his solar energy, his pride, self-esteem, confidence, courage and his individual creativity.

1. From my earliest childhood memories
   a. I was always self-confident.
   b. I was sometimes confident in myself.
   c. I have always had trouble with self-confidence.

2. If my friends were to be asked about my strongest trait they would say that I was
   a. generous, courageous, a natural actor.
   b. mostly generous but sometimes moody.
   c. mostly withdrawn and thoughtful.

3. When my authority is questioned I
   a. become angry and hurt.
   b. become angry but forget about the whole thing soon after.
   c. become more hurt than angry and have trouble letting go of it.

4. When I make up my mind I
   a. never change it.
   b. am sometimes open to compromise.
   c. am easily persuaded to change it.

5. I consider the weakest part of my body to be
   a. I am generally healthy.
   b. my heart.
   c. my nerves.

6. My greatest fear is
   a. losing the respect of my friends.
   b. not being chosen to head the committee.
   c. discovering I don't know anyone at the party.

7. If I am not progressing in my work I:
   a. quit and free-lance or become self-employed.
   b. keep my job but channel my energy into a sport or hobby.
   c. keep my job and channel my energy into my love life or family life.

8. The greatest obstacle to my success is
   a. from others outside myself.
   b. within myself.

9. I see myself as a well-rounded person
   a. almost always.
   b. about half the time.
   c. not very often.

10. I am considered to be proud and/or vain by
    a. 80% of the people I meet.
    b. 50% of the people I meet.
    c. 25% or less of the people I meet.

Those who have scored five or more (a) answers are highly in touch with their solar nature at the personality level. Those who have five or more (b) answers may need to work in the area of life symbolized by the house that has Leo on the cusp and/or the house where the natal Leo Sun shines. Those who scored five or more (c) answers may be timid lions. You may have been born on the cusp of either Cancer or Virgo. The Sun may be intercepted or in the twelfth house. You may need to integrate such positive solar qualities as confidence, self-esteem, courage, and dignity.

Where is the balance point between Leo and Aquarius? How does Leo integrate Aquarian objectivity into the Lion's personal have planets in Houses 5 and 11. For all of us, the polarity from Leo to Aquarius involves the ability to relate on both the warm personal level and the cool level of objectivity.

1. I consider my ability to relate to children to be
   a. very good.
   b. good to fair.
   c. poor to fair.

2. My approach to life is
   a. through my feelings.
   b. a blend of feeling and analysis.
   c. analytical.

3. I use my creative gifts
   a. whenever and wherever I have a chance to.
   b. when it is beneficial to the group or project at hand.
   c. seldom.

4. When volunteering my time and energy for charitable or civic causes, I consider my talents as subordinate to the needs of the group
   a. 25% of the time or less.
   b. 50% of the time.
   c. 80% of the time.

5. When it comes to my time and energy, I tend to put personal needs ahead of universal causes
   a. 80% of the time.
   b. 50% of the time.
   c. 25% of the time or less.

Those who scored three or more (b) answers are doing a good job with personality integration on the Leo/Aquarius polarity. Those who scored three or more (c) answers may need to work more consciously at developing personal identity (Leo Sun) as they may be looking to the group to tell them who they are. This is particularly true of people with several natal planets in the 11th House. Look at the planets in your creative fifth house. You may need to work at developing them in order to promote the greater good as well as your personal fulfillment. Those who have three or more (a) answers may be out of balance in the other direction. They may be uncompromising, holding to their subjective opinion at the expense of the needs of the group. Uranus represents objectivity, the universal good of the group, altruistic idealism, openness to new information. Study the houses with natal Uranus and natal Sun in Leo. Which is stronger by house position, aspects? Find the houses with Leo and Aquarius on the cusps. These are the areas which provide clues to the integration of the Leo/Aquarius polarity.

What does it mean to be an esoteric Leo? How does Leo integrate the principle of illumination into the personality? Does the Sun express itself on the esoteric as well as the mundane level? Does Leo act as if his ego is the instrument of the Self? Or, does Leo act from the ego alone? Neptune is exalted in Leo. Neptune is the planet of the surrendered will. Every Leo will have both the Sun and Neptune somewhere in the chart. The well-integrated Neptune will help Leo to transcend from ego to the Self. Neptune's receptivity to the Self helps to change willfulness to willingness. Answers to the following questions will help indicate the extent to which Leo has transcended from ego to Self.

1. When I do service or volunteer work I
   a. work well with those I have been assigned to work with.
   b. usually make lots of suggestions but work well with others.
   c. usually find myself in charge.

2. When the vote goes against me and I have to give up my authority I
   a. look at it as a learning experience and accept it willingly.
   b. give in but not as gracefully as perhaps I should.
   c. quit the committee.

3. I consider myself an adaptable person
   a. 50-80% of the time.
   b. 25-50% of the time.
   c. less than 25% of the time.

4. When I act I see
   a. God as the doer. (In my mind I give *God* the credit.)

    b. myself as doing work for *others*.

    c. myself as the doer.

5. When I am frustrated in my desires I
   a. introspect and find my own faults to be the cause of the difficulty more often than not.
   b. have trouble dealing with the frustration but eventually learn from it.
   c. become angry and find fault with whoever is causing the frustration.

Those who have scored three or more (a) answers are in touch with the esoteric Sun. Those who scored three or more (b) answers need to work consciously at changing willfulness to willingness. Those who scored three or more (c) answers need to consciously attune to Neptune (surrender) as a means of transcending from ego to Self.

References

Alice Bailey, *Esoteric Astrology*, "Leo," Lucis Publishing Co., New York, 1976

Alice Bailey, *Labours of Hercules*, Lucis Publishing Co., New York, 1977

Gret Baumann-Jung, "Some Reflections on the Horoscope of C.G. Jung," Spring, 1975

Joseph Campbell, *Primitive Mythology*, Vol. 1 of *The Masks of God*, Viking Press, New York, 1959

Chang Chung-yuan, *Creativity and Taoism*, Harper Torchbooks, Harper and Row, New York, 1970

Jean and Wallace Clift, *Symbols of Transformation in Dreams*, "The Self," Crossroads, New York, 1986

Franz Cumont, *Mysteries of Mithra*, Dover Publications Inc., New York, 1956

Edward Edinger, *Ego and Archetype*, G.P. Putnam's Sons, New York, 1972

Marie Louise von Franz, "The Process of Individuation," Part 3 in *Man and His Symbols*, Doubleday and Co., Inc., Garden City, 1969

Norma L. Goodrich, *Ancient Myths*, New American Library Mentor Books, New York, 1960

Isabel Hickey, *Astrology, The Cosmic Science*, Altiere Press, Bridgeport, 1975

James Hillman, *Eranos Lectures #2*, "The Thought of the Heart," Spring Publications Inc., Dallas, 1981

C.G. Jung, *Aion*, "The Ego," "The Self," Princeton University Press, Princeton, 1959

C.G. Jung, *The Integration of the Personality*, "The Meaning of Individuation," Kegan Paul, Trench Trubner and Co. Ltd., London, 1948

C.G. Jung, *Portable Jung*, "Answer to Job," "Relations Between the Ego and the Unconscious," Joseph Campbell ed., Penguin Books, New York, 1971

C.G. Jung, *Mysterium Coniunctionis*, Princeton University Press, Princeton, 1976

C.G. Jung, *Psychology and Alchemy*, R.F.C. Hull trans., Princeton University Press, Princeton, 1968

H.D.F. Kitto, *The Greeks*, "The Greek Mind," Penguin Books, Baltimore, 1962

"Narasimha-Avatara," Bhagavata Purana (also transl. as *"Srimad Bhagavata"*), part 7, chapters 8-10, Syamakasi Press, Mathura, 1940

Vishnu Purana, part 1, Chapters 17-22, Gorakpur, 1940

Sallie Nichols, *Jung and Tarot, An Archetypal Journey*, "Strength," Samuel Weiser, New York, 1980

Dane Rudhyar, *Astrological Signs, The Pulse of Life*, Shambhala, Boulder, 1978

"Samson," Judges 16: 1-31, The Holy Bible, King James Version, World Bible Publishers Inc., N.D.

E.A. Wallis Budge, *Gods of the Egyptians*, vol. 1, "Hymn to Ra," Dover Publications Inc., New York, 1969

T.H. White, ed., *The Book of Beasts*, Dover Publications Inc., New York, 1984

Edward Whitmont, *The Symbolic Quest*, G.P. Putnam's Sons, New York, 1969

Swami Sri Yukteswar, *The Holy Science*, S.R.F. Press, Los Angeles, 1974

6 VIRGO:
The Search for Meaningful Service

In Leo we experienced the exuberance of full-blown summer. Each year as we enter Virgo, the mood of the Earth itself seems to become more withdrawn, introspective, quieter. Hermes of the autumn leaves is not the same gossipy messenger-god of breezy spring, of Gemini. In considering Mercury/Hermes as Virgo's ruler, several images come to mind—Alchemical Mercurius, Hermes Psychopompous (Guide to Hades), Hermes Trismegisthus or Thoth of Egyptian fame, and the healing Hermes who, like Aesclepius the physician, raised his magical Caduceus-staff to cure the sick or to put them to sleep for the journey to the underworld. Finally, we can visualize Hermes as Mercury retrograding slowly, quietly, redundantly on his orbit. The earthy nature of Virgo seems to provide Hermes the patience and powers of concentration required for his serious healing and alchemical work. As ruler of the Earth sign Virgo, Hermes seems less flighty, more grounded, stable and consistent in his behavior than he was as ruler of airy Gemini.

My first image is of Hermes standing in yellow sulfur fumes with tears running down his face as he turns the Wheel of Transformation. As Hermes spins the wheel, he slowly and patiently accomplishes the impossible and even irrational task of uniting the opposites, reconciling scientific paradoxes or "squaring the circle." Hermes has set his own sign on the airtight vessel; it is hermetically sealed. Within it, nature's (or body's) dross will be purified and nature itself will be changed. Animal (instinctual) nature will be transformed into human and human nature will be perfected to become divine. When the impurities have been sublimated out of substance, after the purified remains have congealed, wholeness is the final result.

189

In the process of alchemical purification Hermes' virtues are those of the Virgo archetype: patience, purification or perfectionism, meticulous attention to technique and procedure, obedience to methodology, industriousness, and most important, humility. Who but a humble godling would persist amidst all those uncomfortable fumes in that toxic, shadowy world? Jung, in *Alchemical Studies*, explains that sulfur is a negative symbol, referring to facing the dark side of ourselves, our animal instincts, which are to be transformed. As a conscious, rational being, Hermes the Mind does not care to face his dark side, yet only when he does face it can his magic flow. Few of my Gemini or Virgo clients are comfortable looking at their animal nature. Yet it is out of the unconscious, rather than from the scientific, rational, conscious mind, that Hermes' magic comes. Magic goes beyond nature's limits; it is supernatural.

When Hermes has dealt with the sulfurous, he is like Ahasuerus, the alchemist who took the stone rejected by other alchemists—a common, lowly, ugly stone, and turned it into the Philosopher's Stone. Hermes can take the common soil of Virgo Earth, humble clay, and fashion from it a work of perfection. My experience of those who participate in the Virgo archetype through either planets in Virgo or Sixth House planets has been that they can do the smallest, most ordinary or commonplace job with such detailed, skilled precision that they make of it an art. Behind many a shy, simple Virgo personality hides magical Hermes.

Our second Hermes image for Virgo comes from a Greek vase. On the vase, Hermes Psychopompous (Guide of Souls) is a luminous young man in perfect physical condition, winged like the Christian guardian angel. He extends both hands outward, intent upon an invisible spirit who will soon be journeying with him to the underworld. As Guide, Hermes seems to represent the bright light of intelligence that will illumine the way for the soul and render the darkness less fearful, more intelligible.

Balancing mind and body, or mind and matter, is central to the Virgo journey. Astrologers from Dane Rudhyar to Liz Greene have referred to it over the years. My own experience has been that Virgo prefers to focus on one thing at a time, to compartmentalize life. For example, my Virgo clients who are in the study or apprenticeship phase of life will neglect the body in favor of the mind. They will put in long hours and pay no attention to diet or exercise. They will forget the annual dental or medical check-up. This phase will often be followed by a swing to the other extreme once they have settled into the structure of a secure job routine. The mind is then neglected while Virgo pursues rigorous hatha yoga routines, fad diets, or long fasts. If mental stagnation sets in at the office, Virgo tends to develop odd physical symptoms and consults the astrologer about health. "Have I a good dentist, doctor, chiropractor, exercise instructor? What does my chart say is wrong with me?" Often it says s/he needs an outlet for the mind. Hermes, even when s/he rules an Earth sign, is a restless planet. S/he needs new facts, new skills, new challenges. In my view, the health, service and study meanings of the Sixth House are all archetypally interconnected. When Virgo feels that his/her work is not useful, or meaningful to him/her, that s/he is no longer learning or growing in some way, his/her body begins to exhibit symptoms as a warning that a change is needed. The body is a barometer of the satisfaction or lack of it in the various meanings of the Sixth House. It's usually the unhappy or the bored employee who regularly calls in sick.

Jung made an interesting point about Christianity's disdain for the body, going back to the Garden of Eden and the "fall." It's interesting that while the eastern religions offer a physical component (hatha yoga) to the development of mind and spirit, the West does not seem to include the body in its spiritual exercises. Perhaps that's why, among my clients, there are so many Virgo hatha yoga teachers. They are seeking a way to balance body, mind and soul that is missing in the western religious tradition. Hatha yoga seems helpful to them in getting beyond the compartmentalizing. Talking to Virgo clients who are in the phase of neglecting the body is very much like an encounter with Woden, the German Hermes, the genii imprisoned in the bottle. These clients are identified with the mind, imprisoned in a sluggish body, worried and racing about in its cage. Grounding for Hermes ruled Virgo often comes with recognition of the need to give the body its due. To me, Praxiteles' beautiful winged Hermes statue is a symbol of the proper functioning of body and mind as an integrated whole. When the bodily instrument is in good condition, winged Hermes can soar off to deliver his idea messages.

The Psychopompous paintings and statues have a more subtle meaning, too. As Guide of Souls, or Guide to Hades, Hermes is one of the few deities able to travel to the underworld with impunity. He alone is free to come and go without any danger of getting stuck there. To the Greeks the underworld meant the resting place of the dead, but to Jung it has an additional meaning—the Unconscious, the land that we roam in our dreams. Hermes Psychopompous had the power, through his magic wand or Caduceus, to put people to sleep for a short time (as he did with the guards in the *Iliad*) or permanently. Thus, through his underworld role, he is a god of dreams as well as a messenger of death.

In *Psychology and Alchemy*, Jung demonstrates through his commentaries on several different dreams that Hermes Psychopompous as Guide represents the light the intellect sheds to illumine the dark Underworld inhabited by the Anima (Animus), Wise Old Man, and the Shadow. For Virgo, clearly Reason would have to illumine this dark world. Hermes the dream figure need not be luminous like the Hermes of the vase and the statues; he may have a dark cape and a black or red beard, or even be beardless and wingless. But he is generally young and swift and knows where he is going. I have often wondered if other Virgos have seen him in their dreams.

The third Hermes image connected with Virgo would be Hermes Trismegisthus (Thoth)—the Thrice-Great Hermes of Egyptian fame—the healer by sorcery and magician who has the power to resurrect the dead. This Hermes, instead of wielding the Caduceus, holds *The Book of the Dead*, which he himself authored. It contains the mantic spells and techniques of his healing art, the same spells he taught to Isis, his disciple. He tends to heal by proxy (through Isis) especially through the throat chakra, using charms and magic phrases, though he has been known to cure with the aid of underworld creatures like toads and beetles. He sometimes is pictured in art as an Ibex bird (Jung mentions that the bird often represents Soul) or an ape-headed god. According to Jung, the ape's head means that Thoth had successfully entered the Unconscious and assimilated those instinctual contents which he considered positive and helpful (that is, assimilated his primitive, ape-like shadow). (*Portable Jung*, Dreams #16 and #22.) The reaction of Greek artists and sculptors to the Thoth ape statue which came to them from Egypt was quite interesting to me because I have had the same reaction from the more squeamish of my Virgo intellectual clients. The rational Greek artists who were so tolerant in reproducing Isis and synthesizing the images of Ishtar and Aphrodite stopped when they came to Thoth. They found his ape's head monstrous. They did not want to imagine their friendly Hermes, the quicksilver mind, the airy sprite, the wind god, with an ape's head.

Finally, we come to the last Hermes image—Hermes as counselor, healer and friend to mankind, Hermes of the Caduceus (magic wand), Hermes the Enchanter. In Gemini, we encountered helpful Hermes in the *Iliad* using his Caduceus to put the Greek guards to sleep so that King Priam could slip past them to retrieve his son's body for burial. But it is in the *Odyssey* that Hermes Psychopompous has real scope for his magic. The *Iliad* was a rather mundane battlefield compared to the realm of the watery unconscious, fraught with unknown dangers and frightening feminine figures for the beleaguered hero to face.

Odysseus, the hero, had wandered the seas for nine years after the end of the Trojan War. Neptune was angry with him because he had forgotten to sacrifice to the sea god (honor the unconscious). Zeus, as a favor to Neptune, had struck Odysseus' vessel with a thunderbolt off the coast of an island owned by a formidably powerful nymph, Calypso. She had saved him, seduced him, and then made him prisoner. She intended to render him immortal and keep him as her lover forever. Odysseus only wanted to find the Feminine in the form of his wife Persephone, and go home to his kingdom, Ithaca. But he couldn't find Ithaca. He had no ship and no guide. Zeus sent Hermes with his magic wand to outmaneuver Calypso. In this long-haired sorceress who sat at the loom in her cave sealing Odysseus' fate into her weaving, Hermes had a worthy opponent. In Hermes' struggle with illusion-spinning Calypso we have a western version of the conscious mind grappling with Maya.

Calypso was lonely for conversation because Odysseus was off weeping over his lost wife. Hermes had a meal with her, charmed her with his words, and persuaded her not only to release Odysseus from the spell, but to help him build a magical raft, provision it with food and drink and give him nautical directions and a protective wind. Then he vanished without even meeting the hero.

Hermes is known as the healer in the village of Tanagra because he reputedly saved the area from a plague by carrying a ram on his shoulders around its outskirts and reciting the right words. The spell had not been forgotten by the time of the Roman Empire, for the traveler Pausanius remarked that villagers were still making terra cotta statues of Hermes and the Ram during the Christian era.

Another Enchanter in the tradition of Hermes is Merlin, the tutor and magician to King Arthur. Those of you who have read *The Crys-*

tal Cave by Mary Stewart are familiar with the legend of his humble birth in a cave (and therefore his association with magic and the unconscious). But an older Arthurian chronicle, *Le Morte d'Arthur* by Sir Thomas Malory actually has Merlin state, "I was born in September and Mercurius is my patron." Merlin's role as tutor to Arthur was to help the young prince find the sword of discrimination (the implement that would empower him), or find the Masculine, just as Hermes had helped Odysseus get his bearings nautically and find his home, his inner Feminine.

Merlin was, therefore, a medieval guide in the tradition of Hermes/Mercurius. Merlin had the Enchanter's personality, a somewhat introverted or "retrograde" personality, a celibate lifestyle, and a reputation for wisdom and supernatural powers. Merlin was selective in choosing his pupils. This seems, also, more typical of the Virgo than the Gemini approach. Gemini is democratic rather than selective with its concepts and its information; Gemini shares with everyone. Many of my Virgo clients are, perhaps because of their shyness, more selective about their clientele as tutors, therapists, astrologers. Both Gemini and Virgo, like Hermes, are skilled at their craft, whatever it is that they choose to do.

Mercury retrograde introduces us all to Virgo-like energy three times a year. The next time Mercury goes retrograde, note the archetypal energy all around us—the sense of patient waiting while we perform humble, routine tasks—the introspection, the industrious planning, or most important, repetition of the old task that was imperfectly completed the first time. On a Mercury retrograde, we wait, we live in the "meanwhile," the alchemical interval during which nothing at all seems to happen. Maybe we're anticipating an event and would like to push the days in the calendar ahead, or maybe we're just waiting for some news, like the outcome of a project (was it well-received or not?). We may go eagerly to the mailbox each day and be disappointed. Or we're reviewing, rewriting, reflecting. A retrograde cycle is composed of many "re"s. How very different this energy is from that of the last sign, Leo. Leo was active, dynamic and most of all, in control. Virgo is Mutable, or passive-responsive to events and circumstances, especially those involved with the Sixth House of labor, health, service and study.

Jung tells us in "Dream Symbolism and Alchemy" that Mercury was *servus*, the servant god. (*Portable Jung*, p. 341.) Prometheus described his rank more harshly and sarcastically, down in Tartarus, when he said to Hermes "I should not have spoken to a slave." (*Prometheus Bound.*) In Dream #14 (*Portable Jung*), the dreamer is in America, which Jung tells us would mean the land of the common man to a European like the dreamer, and he is looking for an employee. It is interesting that Hermes, the man with the pointed beard, appears in this dream, because the dreamer is seeking an employee; the Sixth House represents labor, employees, co-workers, service professions, and of course, the body—which to many Virgos is simply the mind's lowly employee. The Virgo reader may enjoy Alice Bailey's account of Hercules' Virgo test. It emphasizes the retrograde or slow and sometimes frustrating quality of Virgo's timing. Hercules got his assignment wrong the first time and had to perform a second task to redeem himself and learn his lesson. (See *Labours of Hercules*, "Virgo, the Sixth Labour.")

Over the years, so many people with authority planets in the Sixth House have come to me and complained about their employees. "Why do I spend all my time listening to their problems, trying to help them? They are getting free astrology readings, or free therapy, or free dental work, when I should be getting other things done. I adjust my vacations to their schedules. You wouldn't believe how hard it is for me—with the Sun, or Saturn, or Pluto in the Sixth, to be a supervisor!" This seems especially true for clients with Mutable planets in the Sixth House, as mutability reinforces the employee meaning. I have, however, even met managers with Cardinal and Fixed Suns in the Sixth House with the same complaint—"the service, the time and energy is going the wrong way, from me to the employee!" Without planets in the 10th House, they tend to do the serving. It's hard to be business-like about service, or to shift gears and charge a person they are used to paying. Getting an office manager is a good way around it, if one can find the right sort of individual—an administrator who knows how to conserve the boss's time and energy.

The problem of finishing an apprenticeship—leaving the low-paying internship, with its secure, comfortable benefits—is harder for Virgo than for Gemini. Virgo, as an Earth sign, feels secure when it has job structure and tends to stay too long in the same office, or with the same employer, rather than look for a more lucrative or challenging environment. Though both Virgo and Gemini communicate well at job interviews, it is Virgo who asks, "How long do I work here before I get the desk near the window? or the private office? or the sabbatical? or the step raise?" Hermes' Gemini children usually become bored if they stay in the same field, much less with the same company, long before they qualify for any of these benefits. Both signs are skilled and mentally alert, but Gemini is a short-term planner and Virgo seeks something permanent. Gemini would prefer to work with people and concepts, while a Virgo or Virgo rising individual is often just as comfortable in his cave, like Merlin, surrounded by his software discs or his account books, hiding from chaotic interruptions. To Virgo/Virgo rising the data is interesting, but people may seem difficult.

Sixth House archetypal situations (co-worker situations) can also be stressful for Virgo. Other hermit or retrograde positions for the Sixth House would include, of course, the hospital lab and the rare book room of a university library. Not all Virgos, of course, are misanthropic hermits, but the archetype tends to value quiet time and privacy within the workday routine. It helps his sense of efficiency if he has time to get his thoughts together. Virgo prefers to focus on one skill, task, or technique at a time and perfect it, to do one project all the way through to completion. Gemini would be bored without variety and would prefer to learn an entirely new skill than to perfect the old one or to "gild the lily." The Virgo teacher will usually embellish last year's outline for the classroom; Gemini will throw it out and begin anew with a different concept altogether.

Virgo enjoys the sense of continuity to his/her craft; for each day brings him/her delight in learning something new, however trivial it might seem to others. This is also true of many people with Sixth House planets. They often remark, "Today I experienced a breakthrough in my work. If I tried to explain it, it would probably seem insignificant to you; but because of this discovery, my job from now on will seem entirely different to me." The "something new" could be a concept, an approach to the subject or to people, a short-cut in the procedure, or a refinement of the skill itself. But the sense of satisfaction in small discoveries stems from the application of a practical, useful, tangible, concrete technique that will help Virgo in the future. Hermes' Gemini children make these discoveries, too, but they don't really need to apply the concepts—just discovering them and enjoying them theoretically is often enough for airy Gemini. Hermes as ruler of Virgo tends to go deeper into the same field over the years. As ruler of Gemini, he collects information in many different areas.

While Gemini (Third House) is sensitive to any environment,

Virgo (Sixth House) is particularly sensitive to the work environment. Both the Hermes ruled signs react to stress such as deadlines advanced or sudden increase in the workload. Hermes is ruler of the central nervous system and his Mutable children will often leave a situation because of nervous tension resulting from pressure. Virgo professors will leave a more prestigious university for a less prestigious school rather than deal with publish or perish deadlines. Because of their high-strung natures, Mercury-types have been deemed by astrology texts to be better Indians than chiefs, better employees than employers. If they can deal with stress through some other type of energy in the chart—Cardinality, for instance, that can delegate work, or Fire that can say "Don't put that on my desk! Put it on his instead"—they can handle the stress better.

Rewarding work is more important to Hermes' Virgo children than lucrative work, and many employers value them as social workers, researchers, teachers, proofreaders, and health practitioners, because they prefer being useful or helpful to performing more highly paid, non-serviceful tasks. Virgo loves to tidy up the cosmos, patch up the world mentally, physically or spiritually. It is true that Virgo is sometimes overwhelmed by the details and fails to see the forest for the trees. But when it comes to expertise at his craft, it is hard to find anyone better than an experienced Virgo dentist, bookbinder, or other technician who works in small spaces with precision.

When we leave the work environment and turn to the area of social life, there is a big difference between the two Hermes ruled archetypes, Virgo and Gemini. Gemini is *not* a hermit. He is an extrovert, a Peter Pan who wants to soar, a *puer* who fears having his wings clipped. Virgo is ruled by the same free-spirited planet, but as an Earth sign, has more conservative tendencies. An unmarried Virgo will not usually express fear at having his wings clipped when he comes to the astrology reading in his late twenties or early thirties. Rather he is likely to say, "Mother has a point. It would be good to settle down soon, get married, pay off a mortgage, have children, enjoy the benefits of emotional and financial security." Mother's traditional values sound fine to Virgo. "Yet," he concludes, "I like to do things one at a time. I feel that I'll lose out on something in life if I try to do everything at once like work, go to school, have a family. Why give up my potential by getting married too soon? Why not wait until I have my professional identity, and, er, a few years of experience. . . ?" The young Virgo woman says, "Mother is probably right; it would probably be better to have children in my twenties. But working is so much more interesting than staying home with noisy, active pre-schoolers." She may also add, "I'd rather take life one stage at a time than try to do everything at once."

Virgo or Virgo rising still looks quite young in his or her twenties or early thirties, and I can almost see Hermes flitting around in the corners of the room during these sessions on the serious topic of marriage. Hermes seems to be encouraging Virgo to hang loose awhile, rather than give up any of his future options—learn his/her craft, gain his/her experience. Most Virgos excel at waiting, partly because they believe in their potential. There's plenty of time to find their niche in life, their skill or service, which will help to make the world a better, or at least a more efficient place.

Many parents mention that they are worried about the Virgo child. The anti-social hermit phase seems to continue so long that they fear perhaps the late blooming daughter will metamorphose some day into the picture of the Old Maid playing card. One mother told me, "I fear that she will wake up some morning a spinster who keeps cats." Usually it can be demonstrated to the parent's satisfaction, though, that the hermit cycle coincides with some kind of apprenticeship and is not just social maladjustment. When Virgo feels content or competent at his craft, he does develop interest in social life. It has little or nothing to do with chastity versus sex, but is a type of Virgo simplification. How many of my Virgo/Virgo rising clients have remarked over the years, "I could never have been married during my first year of teaching (or nursing, or social work). I went home exhausted, took a nap and opened the books or the briefcase and worked till the wee hours. I couldn't have related to anyone else at home. I simply didn't have the energy." The body (Sixth House) had absorbed too much stress.

A year or two later when Virgo felt competent at the job, could anticipate any problem likely to arise, and knew the logical solution to that problem, it would be easier to find the energy to date or cook a dinner for someone else. Till then Mother was right. She had the cat for company. House Six, after all, is the house of small animals and hobbies. The cat does not require much energy, or bring out the defense mechanisms, like sarcasm or criticism, which Virgo often uses to keep the opposite sex at bay until the apprenticeship period is over.

Virginity is a matter of attitude, not a matter of bodily intactness. Virgo is pure in the sense that it is open and receptive to life. Though my clientele includes many Virgo rising people who remain single into their 40's, most Virgo Sun sign clients tend to marry by the mid-30's.

Virgo in his 30's and 40's asks some of the same questions Gemini brings to the session: "I am bored and restless" (especially during Uranus opposite Uranus close to age 41, when the higher octave of Mercury/Hermes—Uranus—brings out the impatient, rebellious side). "Shall I go back to school and learn a new field? I want to do it quickly, though. I don't have the patience for school that I did in my 20's. Something has to change in my life—the job, the marriage, the location. . . " "I'm tired of waiting."

My average Virgo client has been in a service profession where s/he witnessed a great deal of human sadness over a period of years. Counseling, teaching the mentally retarded, social work, nursing, parole board work, government work with the aged or infirm in the welfare agencies are all Virgo communication jobs. Many think of turning to writing instead of returning to school. Most, however, remark that they would like to learn a new skill which would better compensate them for their time and energy than their present employment but which would still be rewarding. They would prefer a daily routine involving contact with cheerful people for a change. The business world does offer many of the things Virgo seeks, but at the price of bringing greater stress into the life of Virgo than the class-room, hospital, or government office did. It is a trade-off—pressure, deadlines, and positive environments at higher pay versus satisfaction in helping the handicapped, transforming like Hermes/Thoth, the lives of individuals, rather than enjoying a healthy savings account and trips to the Caribbean. Virgo often thinks of self-employment, particularly in consultant work, counseling or secretarial services, but Hermes seems to feel most secure as the Virgo scribe or "herald of the gods," the archetypal employee. A Virgo who tries self-employment may find it is easier to deal as an executive secretary with the chaos his/her boss brings her *every* day than deal with Internal Revenue as a self-employed person, or live with other uncertainties such as the day-to-day worry about whether business will be good or bad, or whether or not his/her health insurance policy is adequate.

It is difficult to choose a Greek myth for Virgo. Persephone seems to fit because she is a late bloomer, yet she lacks the mental energy that most of my Virgo clients have demonstrated over the years. Artemis is independent, like Virgo, and is quite skilled at her craft of archery, but she's too athletic or "outdoorsy." Hera is definitely a marriage goddess. Demeter is the all-powerful Great Mother. Athena is too Cardinal. Aphrodite is too romantic, too physical. Aesclepius' daughter, Hygieia, fits for Virgo but she has no real myth associated with her.

Virgo seems definitely more connected to Egypt than to Greece. In Egypt the rains that flooded the Nile delta occurred somewhat unpredictably during Leo/Virgo, and for the Egyptians the two zodiacal signs converged or overlapped in time and were combined in the same symbol, the Sphinx. The Sphinx seems to me to capture the enigmatic spirit of Virgo (the attitude of sorcerer's apprentice and powerful magician) more fully than anything I've come across in Greek art or mythology. Hermes/Thoth represents Virgo magic and also functions as the sorcerer's tutor for Virgo, and the Isis story is an archetypal drama. The glyph for Virgo (♍), too, comes from the Near East, the Semitic languages. It's the Hebrew letter *mem*, standing for the Virgin with the Tail of the Fish (the Pisces mystical polarity) curled upward. This magical glyph is appropriate for Hermes of the healing Caduceus. Isis, too, is an appropriate Hermes herald, a messenger, an intermediary between man and God. Like her Christian equivalent, the Virgin Mary, Mediatrix of all Grace, Isis draws her power from a male divinity (Thoth) and plays the role of messenger—the ultimate Virgo role. Isis' story is one of humility, efficiency, industriousness, and technical perfection. She brought the secrets of the gods to mankind in order that he be healed and assured of immortality.

Isis was very learned. She studied under the Egyptian Hermes, the mentor god named Thoth, scribe of the sun god, Ra. Thoth taught her the science and art of healing from herbal remedies—chants, use of beetles, toads, and stones—even the ability to raise the dead by the power of Ra. She was a very capable healer, on both mental and physical levels. At her shrines and temples inscriptions announce that those who had slept there received solace from Isis in dreams and were cured of emotional problems. Virgins dedicated themselves to Isis through vows of celibacy while they worked and studied at her temples. She had interesting titles: the Mage (or Wise One), the Enchantress, Lady (Kyria) Isis, She Whose Words Have Power.

In a ceremony which may well have been astrological, initiates were taken through *twelve* chambers in the Temple (House of Isis), and in each chamber a new cape with the image of an animal was tossed over the initiate. He prayed and fasted and emerged from the last chamber onto the Nile to see the Boat of Isis pass him and to feel the peace of Osiris. The initiate was then known as Conqueror of the Seven Planets, which probably meant conqueror of the natal chart, master of his own personality.

Before we study Isis' story, let's consider for a moment what Virgo potential means. The cult statues considered most powerful were not those of Isis standing alone, but holding her child, Horus. In art, the image of mother and child is one of the world's most potent symbols. The statue represents realization (the child) of potential (the womb). The self-sufficient Virgin who stands alone, no matter how wise, is not complete. The new form is the completion. Whether a child or a book or the founding of a Wholistic Center—whatever the creative venture—some tangible new form needs to emerge. The form usually requires a long and painful gestation and labor, such as Isis' sad delivery of Horus. The apprenticeship can involve, for the Virgo client, a mentor who keeps Virgo too long at minimum wage in his office, lab, or school. It can involve struggles with finances and self-confidence, doubts about the mentor, even doubts about the value of the service itself. But in the end, usually after a long gestation period, the esoteric ruler of Virgo, the Mother of Form, the Moon will bring forth her new creation.

Another pattern to observe in the Isis story and in the lives of one's Virgo clients is that of Hermes' twilight deceptions, the trickery that surrounds them, whether or not they actively, consciously participate in it. Things are often not what they seem. Isis' sufferings began when her brother-in-law, Seth, tricked and killed her husband. Isis did not know for certain that he was dead, but in the early stages of her pregnancy she began a long, dolorous journey alone and in disguise as a lowly governess. Think of Isis when you see your Virgo clients disguised as teachers and administrators. Who might this client be? An alchemist in disguise on a lonely journey in a foreign land. The transforming power of speech that belonged to Lady Isis also belongs *in potentia* to these Virgos, living their humble lives. Perhaps respect for the power of the word keeps them from writing and speaking until they have the message just so. This long gestation or apprenticeship seems often to be self-imposed by the Virgo perfectionist.

Isis

Isis and her husband, Osiris, reigned over the Nile delta in Egypt as Queen and King. They were happy and their subjects loved them, but their happiness was flawed by the fact that they had as yet no son to inherit the kingdom. Osiris was popular for introducing arts and crafts to Egypt, and he frequently traveled abroad to teach less fortunate peoples. While he was away, Isis ruled "wisely and well." (Norma Lorre Goodrich, *Ancient Myths*, page 29.) She also kept an eye on her brother-in-law, Seth of the red beard, who was envious and awaited an opportunity to seize the throne.

Once, while Osiris was traveling, Seth and his friends had a casket made exactly to fit Osiris. It was of beautiful cedar and ornamented in gold. When Osiris returned to the delta, they held a banquet in his honor. (Isis was away in the city of Coptos.) After they had been drinking, Seth's friends suggested they all try out the beautiful casket fit for a king. The guests were all too short or too tall except, of course, Osiris. As soon as he stretched out in it, Seth closed it tightly and his friends sealed it with molten lead. They carried it to the Nile and pushed it into the river. Seth rejoiced at being the new ruler of Egypt. Osiris was dead in his 28th year, on a day when the Moon was waning.

While in Coptos, Isis heard of his death and did not want to believe it. She put on black clothing and cut her hair. She walked the banks of the Nile seeking the casket among the reeds where it might have washed up. She wept, for she now realized how deeply she had loved him. Some children told her that the casket had washed up in Syria and was caught in the trunk of a tamarisk tree. King Melkarth of Syria, walking along the river one day, had marveled at the tree and suggested that it be cut down and made into a pillar for his palace. Isis went to the palace, sat on the veranda and put her cheek to the pillar. The palace women came over to her. She taught them how to fix their hair in the Egyptian style. The serving ladies, of course, were then asked by Queen Ishtar who had perfumed and arranged their hair. They told her that a simple Egyptian servant in a white linen dress had taught them. Ishtar sent for Isis and had her appointed governess to her (Ishtar's) child.

Isis grew fond of the baby as she spent a long time in the palace. She would hold him over the fire at night to burn off his mortal dross that he might become immortal. After doing this, she would transform herself into a black swallow and fly around her husband's casket in the pillar, longing to embrace Osiris, longing to have a child of her own.

One night, Queen Ishtar came into the room as Isis was holding the baby over the fire. Ishtar panicked, screamed, and broke Isis' spell, thus depriving the prince of immortality. Isis was forced to tell Ishtar who she really was—Lady of Abundance, Queen of the South (underworld). Ishtar knelt to Isis and then helped her take Osiris' body from the tamarisk tree. The two women wrapped the tree in white linen and placed it reverently in the temple for worship. Isis then took Osiris' body down the Nile on a boat and in hiding, performed secret rites. She was able, under the tutelage of Thoth/Hermes, to resurrect Osiris long enough to conceive the long awaited Divine Child, Horus. She was worshipped as House of Horus or Temple of Horus after her remarkable, magical conception.

Isis did not, however, have a delivery worthy of a Queen Goddess. She was in hiding from Seth, who raged as he sought her up and down the banks of the Nile. Seth had heard rumors that Isis was claiming to be pregnant with Osiris' posthumous child but he refused to believe in a miraculous conception. He believed Isis' child would be illegitimate, but did not plan on taking any risks. Isis knew that he would kill her and the child if he found them. She squatted in the reeds and gave birth like a peasant woman. She was in agony for hours, until finally two gods came with a frog and stone amulets to help her. The child burst forth in a great light—He Who Was Long Awaited, Horus, the Avenger of His Father, Horus the Hawk of the Sun God. His birth took place on the Vernal Equinox, when the Earth was at its most fruitful.

His father, hidden away in his casket, sometimes appeared to Horus and taught him. They discussed weapons and the art of war, because they knew one day Horus would have to fight mighty Seth for the throne.

One day Osiris asked the child, "What is the most glorious action a man can perform?"

"To avenge his father."

"What is the most useful animal?" Osiris continued.

"A horse," said the boy quickly.

Osiris was perplexed, because the lion, which is overhead when the Nile begins its inundation, is usually the favorite animal.

"Why do you prefer the horse?" the father asked the son.

"Because the horse is more helpful in overtaking and cutting off the enemy force. The lion is stronger, but the horse is swifter."

One day, while Isis was in town getting supplies, having left her child alone on a mat to nap, a scorpion came along and stung Horus. Isis returned to find his body rigid and cold, his limbs swelling and his lips white with foam. She felt terror as she picked up her child. She and her sister called out to the sun god Ra with such force that the Disk stopped on its orbit overhead. Ra's million-year-old journey had been interrupted for the first time. Thoth, Lord of Learning and Scribe of Ra, Mentor to Isis, flew down from the boat of the Sun Disk to help.

Thoth had an encyclopedic memory, having written most of the great treatises on magic, as well as mathematics, astronomy and astrology. Even more important than knowing which were the right charms to cure Horus though, was getting the pronunciation right. So as Isis sobbed over the body of Horus, Thoth/Hermes taught her to pronounce the words properly. (E.A. Wallis Budge, *Gods of the Egyptians*, vol. 1, page 408; vol. 2, pages 214-215.) The wound opened, and the venom flowed out. Horus began to breathe again!

"Horus lives! Horus lives!" the crowd shouted.

Thoth returned to the disk boat and Lady Isis received a new title—Mistress of Magic.

Isis gave the magic incantations Thoth had taught her to the temple priests so that no other Egyptian child would have to die of scorpion bite.

Meanwhile, word had reached Seth that Isis' young son was thriving. He heard that Horus was skilled in weaponry and that Horus' magnetism attracted Seth's own warriors away from the palace.

Each night Seth went out ostensibly to hunt but actually to find Horus and kill him. He searched all the caves by the light of the Moon. One Full Moon, he found Osiris' casket, opened it, and cut the body into fourteen pieces. He tossed them into the Nile. Isis found the casket destroyed the next morning. She made a light boat from papyrus and set off down the river to find the pieces. Horus, meanwhile, had been learning black and white magic. He told his mother he would meet her at the temple in Abydos, where the tamarisk coffin had been left. Isis would bring the pieces and they would ritually resurrect him again.

Isis passed many fierce crocodiles on her journey, but they had such respect for her that they did not eat any of Osiris, and since that time, crocodiles have been sacred animals in Egypt. (More about them in Chapter 10: Capricorn.) Isis found thirteen of the pieces, but a fish had eaten the phallus, and she therefore took to Horus a body that was not whole—that had something very important missing.

At Abydos temple, they put the pieces together and added a model of the phallus that Isis had made. They went through many rites over the body on the 14-day cycle of the waning Moon. Only after the rites were concluded could Horus leave to find his uncle and win his throne.

God Thoth came down from the Disk in his messenger/arbiter role to judge the battle between Seth and Horus, between uncle and nephew. Some sources say that perhaps he came because of fore-knowledge that Isis would need him.

Whether or not Thoth had advance knowledge, Isis certainly did need him. First Seth and Horus fought for three days like "great bears." Then Horus managed to overcome and bind his uncle in chains. He took Seth to Isis in triumph and pushing him to the floor, put his foot on the great red head. Then, leaving the Queen to guard his prisoner, Horus left to dispose of Seth's army.

As soon as Horus was gone, Seth began to plead with Isis to let him go. "It's cold and dark in the prison; it's an unworthy place for a great king." And, "Surely the land will recover its fertility faster if you release the king." And, "I am, after all, your brother." When these arguments failed, Seth showed her the wounds Horus had inflicted. Her pity for his condition finally moved Isis and she released him.

Horus, who was an impetuous Aries, (born on the Vernal Equinox), returned to discover that his mother had forgiven and freed the man who had twice murdered his father and deprived him of his throne. Exhausted from battle and furious at the news, Horus drew his sword and, in a fit of temper, lopped off his mother's head. Thoth, however, was standing by and was able immediately to pronounce the right words to save Isis. He replaced her severed head with that of Hathor, the ancient Egyptian cow goddess. Isis then acquired a title of Hathor, an older earth goddess, Patroness of Childbirth.

Together mother and son pursued Seth. Eventually they chased him to the Red Sea. He never returned to Egypt and the prosperity of the Nile Valley was restored under Horus and his four sons who reigned consecutively in truth and harmony.

Isis and Osiris reign as judges of the dead in the underworld. There they greet newly arrived souls and judge them according to the 42 commandments.

At first appearance, this story might seem to be a solar rather than a lunar myth. Horus of the Sun struggles to regain his kingdom from a wicked uncle, just as Jason did battle with his wicked Uncle Peleus. (See Aries, Chapter 1.) But if we take a second look, we see that this tale is really about Isis and the subtle, magical power of the Feminine; it's a Lunar myth. Yet, Isis is not the Great Mother who, by her own power and authority presides over life, death and resurrection, but Virgo the Intermediary—humble Virgo, child and student of Hermes/Thoth.

Virgo is a more subtle autumnal goddess; she does not possess the Great Mother's Shakti. Isis tells Ishtar that she is Queen of the South, the setting sun—the Sixth House, or twilight region of the natural zodiac. We have an insight into Isis' role as intermediary when Plutarch tells us that she is Hermes' daughter (E.A. Wallis Budge, Vol. II, p. 187). She is Virgin and Mother, the intercessor and mediatrix of the gift of divine grace and wisdom. But she remains totally dependent upon Thoth, her Divine Mentor, to bring consciousness to mankind. In this myth, Isis does nothing by her own authority. She is a humble vehicle, the Temple of Horus through which healing techniques come.

The Virgo Goddess studies, waits, prays, has faith (Pisces polarity), and responds efficiently and appropriately in a crisis. Isis shows a mercy to Seth, that comes, we are told, out of "pity for all his human weakness" (Goodrich, *Ancient Myths*, page 39). Yet, for all her quiet humility, Isis wins in the end; the solar figures are not as strong as she. Even Seth is vanquished from the land by her patient, persistent effort.

Isis' son Horus, the Divine Child of Ra the Sun God, owes everything to his mother—his miraculous birth from the seed of his dead father, his survival of the birth process, his protection from Seth's armies in the caves along the Nile, his magical cure from the scorpion sting, the opportunities to learn magic from Isis and the arts of war from Osiris and thus, indirectly, even his victory over Seth and the throne. All this he owed to the Feminine, to his humble mother. In fact, he owed too much for his own ego to handle and in the end he lopped off her head in order to achieve his own freedom and room for personal growth. Thus Horus is able to take the throne and reign of his own power.

In the Isis myth there are many Virgo traits: humility, perfectionism (the words must be pronounced exactly right), efficiency in times of crisis, application of learned skills and techniques for problem solving, intercession for others with the gods (many Virgos hold intermediary jobs in personnel, child counseling, middle management in government, etc.), healing (keeping the body intact). Healing is another issue common to Virgo and also to Isis' quest. First she kept intact the body of Osiris, then she rescued and resurrected the cold body of Horus, and finally, in the case of the enemy, Seth, she was moved to release him. This she did not in order to save the kingdom or because he was a relative, but because he had suffered wounds in battle and should not be put into a cold, dark, dank prison. He should be out in the sunlight, healing. Isis could not bear to be responsible for even an enemy being in physical distress.

In *Esoteric Astrology*, Alice Bailey makes the point that Hermes' duality expresses itself in Virgo as the soul/body dichotomy. The Pisces polarity accentuates the dilemma because it emphasizes renunciation of possessions, sometimes even including one's vitamins, whenever transits oppose the Virgo energy in the horoscope. Thus, an esoteric Virgo can vacillate from emphasis on body to emphasis on soul according to the seasons of the year—the transits through the Sixth/Twelfth House axis or opposite the Virgo Sun/Virgo rising. Healing of body, mind, or soul (psychic healing) is a natural sort of quest for people who participate in this archetype, but Virgo tends to go through periods of doubt. Should she forget or deny the body and work instead on developing Piscean intuition, Piscean imagination, Piscean renunciation? Meditate more? Should she seek monastic seclusion?

The waiting, the hidden life, the serviceful attitude are also characteristic of Virgo. Isis and Osiris waited a long time for a child. Actually they seemed to think they had plenty of time, and thus Horus became Osiris' posthumous Divine Child. Many Virgos wait like Isis or Persephone until mid-life to make major commitment decisions. Isis did not realize until after Osiris' death how much she loved him. Many Virgos do not connect with their feeling function until mid-life or even later when the esoteric ruler tends to surface in the personality.

A Virgo's quiet, hidden life may be spent in academia, hospital or government service, or as a low-paid employee, though he knows he is intelligent and talented enough to move on. Virgo serves a long apprenticeship, as Isis did with Thoth, before she became a Goddess in her own right. Often Virgo/ Virgo rising will ask, "Why does it seem I'm a late bloomer?" I often think of Hermes being of two minds about taking the risk of leaving behind his safe, secure apprenticeship, and of Isis' remark that until Osiris died she hadn't realized how much she loved him or how much she had wanted his child. Until then, life was simply an opportunity for her to learn. She eventually did give birth to her own Divine Child after first helping Ishtar with *her* baby. In this way, Virgo often gives birth to creative projects after playing a supportive (lunar) role in fostering others' creative ventures.

Who, then, is Thoth, the Father of Isis and the god from whom the Greeks derive their Thrice Great Hermes, the alchemist/magician? Thoth is the author of many Egyptian texts on astronomy, astrology and magic. He was self-created. He did the mathematical calculations that determined the placements of the stars in the heavens. He was the inventor of all arts and sciences, the master of law, the master of divine speech and scribe of the gods. He was the author of the all-important funerary books which contained the secrets of immortality. Without his presence and guidance in the next world, the dead couldn't pronounce the words properly. So not only was knowledge of his books required in the underworld; Thoth's personal guidance was needed as well.

The Book of the Dead tells us that Thoth's powers are greater than those of Osiris and greater even than those of Ra. (E.A. Wallis Budge, *I*, page 401.) This was because Thoth himself was the "heart and tongue of Ra," the reason, will, and power of speech of the sun god. Thoth spoke the Word that resulted in Ra's will being accomplished on Earth, in Hermopolis, the city of the nine gods, and in the underworld of the dead. Once Thoth had spoken, Ra's will could not fail to be accomplished; there was no way to change it. The other eight gods depended on Thoth because they were connected to the seasons and it was he whose calculations determined the Solstices and Equinoxes. In the underworld, he was scribe and recording angel and most helpful to new arrivals who needed to face their demons and monsters. Thoth gave them the name of each being, so that when they properly pronounced its name it would become their friend. It would help the new arrivals to enter the Boat of the Millions of Years (Solar Disk Boat) or the Fields of Peace of Osiris.

On Earth, Thoth appeared in times of need, rather like Hermes in Greece, but his is a greater power than Hermes'. Thoth seems to have been less a prankster, and to have exhibited more of the qualities of a shaman. In each story, he has the requisite skill or the technique, as well as the proper healing words. Isis learned, for instance, the tone of voice to use for each chant. Thoth seems to have a genuine connection with esoteric healing and the Sixth House. Hermes' mental, mathematical and verbal or communicative attributes are Thoth's as well. But Thoth has a funereal connotation also—a sort of sextile relationship to Osiris and the Eighth House.

Thoth, like Hermes, is young. He has a crescent Moon atop his head, a Feminine and also an underworld symbol. Artists also represented him as the Full Moon, meaning that he ruled the entire lunar month. He stood by the side of a pillar which supported heaven. A flight of fourteen steps led up the pillar. The steps were of unequal length and depicted the first fourteen days of the month, the first half of the lunar cycle. In some drawings, Thoth faced in two directions, possibly toward spring and autumn Equinoxes.

Thoth had a connection with autumn and winter. He was also called the Dark Eye of Ra that gave off less heat, light and warmth than the bright eye. The black eye of Ra was said to be the New Moon, the Dark of the Moon. Artists' most popular representation of this god, though, seemed to be the stork-like Ibis bird, from which his name, Thoth, was derived. The Ibis was said to have been a most helpful creature in the delta, because it killed snakes and scorpions. Its habit of bending over and wrapping its trunk around itself, tucking its head into its chest, gave it a heart shape. Thus, the heart hieroglyph was used to represent Thoth and conveyed "knowledge and the understanding heart." The role of the Ibis in purifying the area of snakes and scorpions is reminiscent of fastidious Virgo, too.

The Moon, the symbol atop the glyph for Thoth, is also the esoteric ruler of Virgo. Thoth presided over forms in transition, from illness to health (as in Horus' case when he was stung by the scorpion) in the sense of the Sixth House, and from death to rebirth (as in Osiris' case) in the sense of the Eighth. The moon, as we have seen in Taurus and Cancer, represents form. The Divine Child is Virgo's child, the result of a long gestation/apprenticeship period. Virgo, at the mundane level, picks apart data in the process of analysis. In its esoteric sense, the Moon represents fusion, synthesis, and actualization of potential—part of this growth for Virgo consists in incorporating lunar caring or the nurturing we saw in Cancer. In the myth, Isis was a

loving mother to Horus, an example of the esoteric, caring Virgo. A Virgo friend once mentioned that she felt she was growing personally through her counseling business. "Clients seem more like individuals, like people to me now. I used to perceive them as problems to be solved or as interesting articles to be written up. Now I am more caring, more tuned in at the human level." That is the lunar level, too— the level personality.

The quest begins with Thoth's truth, "Knowledge is power," and concludes with his "understanding heart"—wisdom. Some Virgo/ Virgo rising clients have discovered that in abandoning a profession that dealt with analyzing cold data and moving toward an intuitive or imaginative career (integrating the Pisces polarity) that personal growth resulted. Some became counselors who worked with dreams, astrologers, or creative writers and journalists. They became more involved with the whole picture. Formerly, as computer technicians and scientists in their labs, they were dissectors of reality. Meditation, symbolized by the Pisces fish opposite Virgo, is also a key to developing the faith in human nature that goes beyond the rather smug live and let live attitude of many mundane Virgos. Theirs is often a tolerance which implies, "Well, so and so is dead wrong, but I'll let it pass."

"How should Virgo integrate the Pisces polarity?" we might ask of the Sphinx that stands in the parched desert. (See Leo, Chapter 5.) Perhaps it's balancing body and soul in a way that does not harm either one—avoiding hermit-like withdrawal into severe austerities on one hand and obsessive hypochondria on the other.

The *Bhagavad Gita*, (VI: 16-17), says: "Oh Arjuna, the gourmand, the scanty eater, the person who sleeps too much or too little, none of these finds success in yoga. He who with proper regularity eats, relaxes, works, sleeps, and remains awake will find yoga the destroyer of suffering." This passage balances Virgo work routine and asceticism with Piscean rest and relaxation. It means working conscientiously when it's time to work and letting go of the day in the evening—taking a walk on Neptune's beach to enjoy the ocean breezes. It means balancing time and energy spent with people in the daytime with time spent in solitude in the evening, meditating or working on one's own creative projects, nourishing the Divine Child within. One great yogi said that when we are with people we should really be with people, and when we're with God, we should really be with God.

Integrating this polarity means discerning when, in a given situation, Hermes' logic is required to evaluate the facts, and when it's time to let go of logic and follow Neptune's intuition. It also means the ability to temper Hermes' logic with Neptunian kindness, mercy, and compassion. People are imperfect, and when Virgo is too critical, they may become too depressed to improve. As Virgo progresses in integrating Piscean inner peace and faith, many self-doubts disappear. The ego begins to depend upon God more and to rely less on its own resources. In *Anima*, James Hillman defines ego in a way that Virgo can appreciate, for Virgo enjoys tidying up the cosmos. Hillman says that ego is "the trusty janitor that sweeps out the planetary houses." Through Piscean surrender to and dependence upon the Self, the ego will cease taking itself or the daily routine so seriously and do a more efficient sweeping up as a good, faithful servant of the Self. Integration of the polarity also involves balancing Virgo realism with Piscean willingness to give others the benefit of the doubt.

One key to the integration of this polarity might be that both signs are Mutable/receptive. Isis was receptive to Thoth and had total faith in his words. Centuries later, the Virgin Mary was overshadowed by the power of the Holy Spirit and said with total faith and lunar receptivity, "Be it done unto me according to thy Word." (Luke I: 38) She too conceived a Divine Child under miraculous circumstances and gave birth under conditions that any Virgo would find far from perfect. She and Isis both were humble, conscious vehicles for Divine Grace. The Moon as esoteric ruler of Virgo opens the sign emotionally and makes it receptive to Spirit.

When pondering the Virgo/Pisces polarity, the biblical story of Mary and Martha (Luke 10: 38-42) comes to mind. Mary was the sister who took the Piscean approach to Christ, her Master. As soon as He entered their home, she hurried to sit at his feet with great devotion. Martha, the sister who took the Virgo approach, busied herself to make Him comfortable. She probably brought a water basin and a cloth for His Feet according to the local custom. While serving, she noticed her sister sitting, resting, and listening. Martha became quite angry. "My Lord," she said, "You do not seem to care that my sister has left me to serve alone? Tell her to help me!"

Jesus answered, "Martha, Martha! You are worried and excited about many things, but one thing is necessary, and Mary has chosen the good portion for herself which shall not be taken away from her."

Martha's Virgo (serviceful) approach missed an important Piscean truth. We must live in, and enjoy to the full, the opportunities of the present moment. If Virgo becomes too rigid about routine schedules, and takes its service too seriously, too rigidly, then the service profession may become a dictator. It may eventually come to close off Virgo's opportunities for mental and soul growth if Virgo becomes a slave (Hermes as *servus*) to it. Mary's opportunity to open her heart receptively to the Master was a once in a lifetime experience for her. When she chose not to miss it in restlessly rushing about, she "chose the best part."

Many serious minded, serviceful Virgos will tell me that they would like to take a non-business related vacation, a spiritual retreat (Pisces polarity) for instance. But they feel uncomfortable traveling without the appointment book and the practical workshops that are tax-deductible—the usual pattern. On these workshop trips they learn valuable and useful skills to share with others.

But what so many fail to grasp is that *intuition is very practical*. The esoteric ruler of Virgo is the Moon, an intuitive, nurturing planet. A retreat will not only put Virgo in touch with the Pisces polarity by freeing Virgo to meditate and develop the intuition, but will also help to develop the inner strength, the lunar soul resources on which the Esoteric Virgo constantly draws while helping others. Without time in the Virgo routine for meditation. . . without retreat weekends, Virgo may feel burned out on the service profession. Like Mother Theresa of Calcutta, who is a Virgo, many see a great deal of human suffering all day long. Like Mother Theresa, they also need to dip in Cosmic Waters and revive the Spirit—to touch the Soul energy in order to keep nurturing others. Virgos at the mundane level think that facts and information are what the world needs—Hermes' message. Most people, however, seek more than information; they seek inspiration from the counselor. Those Virgos who are true lunar intuitives, true nurturers combine the Hermes' discrimination and magical power to transform, to heal, with the caring nature of the Moon. They encourage others to believe in themselves and develop their resources. Without Hermes' gifts the Moon can foster dependency (see Chapter 4: Cancer). Without the Moon, Hermes' discrimination applied to the patient, client, or student seems a very sharp sword. Virgo can come across as clinical, uncaring, cold.

In *The Problem of the Puer Aeternus*, Marie Louise von Franz discusses ancient Egypt as a civilization in which ideas were considered real or concrete and all else was seen as transitory. The influence of Hermes/Thoth, the idea god, is strongly felt here. The concrete, literal meaning of words and even of their proper pronunciation was important, because of their use in magic—words were causative. Yet, as von Franz points out, this concrete literalism can interfere with our growth. The animus, a woman's inner pessimist, for instance, is concrete and literal in its opinions and the problems it presents sphinx-like, to be solved. A Virgo client who has an afflicted Moon, little Water in the chart and a strong Mercury will often fall into the animus negativity. "There are two alternatives here, two only, and both of them are equally bad." Sphinx-like, such Hermes' types feel that life is an enigma to be resolved. One should observe it and figure out the answer or ask a theologian the question and then the problem will be solved. This path is not very satisfying, because it is devoid of fun, imagination, intuition, and risk taking. If the animus is fearful of making a mistake or a wrong choice then perhaps no choice at all is made at Hermes' crossroads. Time passes and Virgo has regrets about unfulfilled potential. The horoscope's positive elements—Air (sense of humor) and Fire (courage, risk-taking, positive thinking)—can help Virgo move beyond the caution and literal mindedness that tend to sabotage his timing. Integration of the Pisces polarity and tuning in to the Moon will also facilitate growth.

In *Labours of Hercules*, "Sixth Labour," Alice Bailey speaks of the ability of the esoteric Virgo to attune to the Collective Unconscious. Virgos who have cultivated the inner psychic nature as well as their Hermes minds are able to connect to the Masses (Cancer, the Moon). Many are also able to predict the trends for the Collective, especially in the idea world of Hermes. "What workshops will be helpful to people in five years? What books will people want to read in ten?" This, even practically speaking, helps with the perennial Virgo fear for financial security, as a Lunar Virgo knows that the ideas will never run out, that the power to help and draw an audience for their message comes not from workshops they attend in the outer world but from within themselves.

Virgo/Virgo rising readers who would like to tune in more to their lunar side would do well to study the natal Moon by Sign, House and Aspect. Does it connect to the Sun in Virgo? To Virgo rising? To Hermes? I have discovered over the years that many a Virgo rising horoscope has an innate Isis-like healing talent but lacks the confidence in his or her magic to follow through on it. It's safer to be an accountant or a nurse. Developing and believing (Pisces polarity— faith) in one's intuitive, lunar gifts is the first step to developing them through meditation, active imagination, dream interpretation, fantasy reading. To connect with the Pisces polarity, one might try reading a bit of poetry at night before retiring. A bit of inspirational or devotional poetry, not *The Waste Land*. It helps to balance Virgo Earth with Water, to alleviate the desert dryness. Pisces seeks peace of mind, and so does Virgo. Pisces is closer to the Unconscious, the inner feminine. (Virgo might find it interesting to read Chapter 12, Pisces: The Castle of Peace.) Finally, Pisces is all about dreams and fantasies. It helps to have dreams to be happy, even if not all of them are going to come true.

Virgo, in working at developing the Moon and integrating the Pisces polarity, moves beyond Hermes' mundane intellectualism to the understanding heart. When Virgo works from the heart as well as the head, then the Moon will give birth to the inner potential, to the inner Divine Child, and Virgo will become a spiritual midwife to others.

Virgo/Virgo rising spends 30 years progressing through Libra. As Libra is ruled by Venus, goddess of love, many marry during this cycle, particularly the last decanate, or final ten years. (Apparently, by then they have had time to accustom themselves to the Venus energy.) I've often asked Virgos who attended progression classes to describe their reaction to marriage during this cycle. Here are some of the comments from those for whom the progressed Sun formed positive aspects to their natal planets:

"I am so much calmer and happier than I used to be."

"I have relaxed a lot about finances since my marriage. I don't have to make it on my own anymore."

"I think I'm living a much more balanced life."

"If I had known marriage would be such a positive experience I would have married years earlier than I did. I was worried about losing my identity before I found my niche in life."

These words—calm, relaxed, happy, and balanced are Libran words. Many Virgos seem to move from vague dissatisfaction with life toward contentment in this developmental cycle. They develop Libran even-mindedness.

Others, however, experience progressed Sun or progressed

Mercury running afoul of natal Cardinal planets, forming squares and oppositions. They tend to complain in the Libran vocabulary, "It's not fair of my spouse to expect me to do all the housework; I'm tired at night," or "I'd like to keep things harmonious, but I am in a service profession where I listen to people's problems all day long. I don't want to have to analyze him (or her) at night." Or, "I'm tired at night; he, however, has plenty of energy and wants to entertain, or go out socially. We need to compromise and only go out or entertain at home twice a week." "Marriage is about learning cooperation. I wish my spouse would cooperate and do the list of chores I posted on the refrigerator door for him." Here we have many Libran keywords—harmony, fairness, cooperation, compromise (especially other peoples' need to compromise) and listening. These are combined with the Virgo problems of getting the chores done to their satisfaction, time to rest or do office work at home versus social life, the structure of free time in the evenings which the spouse may approach with spontaneity. (As in "Hi honey, you won't mind that I brought these friends home with me tonight? Is there anything in the kitchen we could fix them?") Spontaneity is not a trait that appeals to the average natal Virgo.

Confrontations about money are common during the Libran progression. Budgeting is a Virgo issue. Virgo may not realize, however, s/he is spending a lot more than s/he used to as s/he progresses through Libra. (Often other people notice our progressed changes before we observe them in ourselves—these are unconscious and gradual developments.) Virgo, who thinks himself a financial expert and quite frugal, will accuse the spouse of spending impetuously and unwisely and will be quite surprised when the spouse points out Virgo's expenditures. "Really, did I spend that much money last month? I thought I just bought a few books and records," says Virgo, now a progressed Libran.

Virgo is often a long-term planner. The partner may not be concerned about annuities and retirement funds; s/he may just want to live from day to day. If progressed Sun in Libra forms an opposition to the spouse's natal or progressed Sun in Aries, there may be a power struggle over budgeting versus spontaneous spending, in spite of progressed Libra's concern for peace and harmony. It's sometimes useful to raise these issues in relationship readings. People who have had long marriages may be quite confused by progressed changes in the partner and the partner may be unaware that he is changing.

Venus, ruler of the Libra progression, is a social planet, a friendly planet. Many stellium in Virgo clients tell me that they enjoy attending artistic functions, office parties, and other gatherings more than they used to as several faster moving planets in the stellium travel through Libra. Said one such Virgo rising woman,"I used to sneak out of the office Christmas parties early and catch up on the files. Now, I relax and enjoy them more, forgetting the pile of folders on my desk. I remember when I was first unit manager for my department. A Libran personnel director retired and we had a party for her. People were talking about how well liked she was and I thought, on my way back to my desk, "Humph! Well liked indeed. Does she think life is a popularity contest? At *my* retirement party they are going to say, 'she ran the most efficient unit. She really got the job done. She was so conscientious, it'll be very hard to replace her.' Now, I'd be just as happy if they said, 'She was well liked'." Many Virgo/Virgo rising people seem to be considered by those around them to become better socially adjusted in this cycle. This is especially true if progressed Venus moves from Virgo to Libra.

As an Air sign, Libra is concerned with ideas and concepts. Virgo usually de-emphasizes the concept and emphasizes the content, the data, the material, or the service skillfully performed. Many Virgo/Virgo rising people become more conceptual, less concrete and literal minded and more objective in the progression of Sun or Mercury through Libra. They will remark, for instance, "When I began teaching American history, I was determined to cover every fact and date in the lesson plan. If a student asked a 'why' question, a conceptual question that would hold me up, I would rush through the answer so I could cover the day's material. If he asked, 'Is it true that George Washington and the other founding fathers had slaves and slavery was legal then? How was it justified in the constitution? How did the slaves get here?' I would just say, 'That's how things were in the 18th century' and move on. Now, I would stop and spend time on that. It no longer seems so important to cover the material—to follow the lesson plan slavishly. Concepts are what make it interesting for the students, and for me too."

Or, "My staff in the government agency where I work would complain that I required too much paperwork, too many statistics on the clients, and they had little time left to spend with the clients as human beings when they finished asking all the questions on the forms. The content—the data that goes into planning, into the computers for future analysis and decision making, is important, but maybe I did let it get out of hand. The service we provide is for people. We could come up with new plans, new ideas and concepts, without having quite so much data that duplicated other data, or overlapped. I'm changing my mind about a lot of these things. . ."

Uranus is the esoteric ruler of Libra. It's also the higher octave planet for Mercury, Virgo's mundane ruler. It refers to objectivity on the material, the data, the approach to the service. Virgos with a strong natal Uranus let go of a good many nit-picky or fussy traits in favor of new approaches in this cycle, I find. Uranus is a planet of quick insight. Virgos of an esoteric nature who attune to Uranus in the Libran progression can learn to speed up life's timing by letting go of their nervous worry. "What's missing? Should I go over this again just to be certain it's complete?" Uranus helps Virgo to quickly take in the entire forest, rather than keep sketching the same tree over and again, to perfection.

Many Virgos experience Uranus opposite Uranus in the Libran progression. This transit may take them into a New Age profession, or at least lead them to study astrology, ecology, food chemistry and nutrition, or wholistic healing. Some have investigated living in New Age communities in the Libran progression around the time natal Uranus was under transit. Sometimes, to see if the client is working with the esoteric or mundane ruler during the progressed cycle, I'll ask a mail order client over the phone, "What have you been reading lately?" One possibility is Venus related, "Mostly romantic novels." Or, another, "Books on art. I'm taking classes on flower arranging." A Uranus answer, "Well, lots of astrology and astronomy." Or, "I'm going back to school in computer programming"—a Uranus approach that is not quite New Age esoteric, but close. Uranus rules advanced technology, too. At the mundane level we have, "I'm re-taking my C.P.A. exam for the third time. I know the material, but it's so important to me that I get nervous and freeze up. I can't get through the whole test in the allotted time."

Because Uranus brings objective insights, particularly close to age 40 on the Uranus opposite Uranus cycle, if natal Virgo tunes in to these insights, many old Sixth House habits may be discerned and dissolved. It's better to make a clean break with a bad habit than to make an abrupt break in a personal relationship in this cycle. Many Virgos leave a work environment that frazzles the nerves, only to discover the new environment is just as hectic as the first. Virgos may come through this Libran progression more positive, more Cardinal and less self-critical. Virgo may build in an airy sense of humor, too, if the progressed Sun contacts natal Air planets, and may replace the old perfectionism with Libran objectivity and fairness. Uranus, too, refers to the group. Virgos with strong natal Uranus may emerge from Merlin's cave to participate in the wider community before progressing into Scorpio, a quieter, more reclusive energy.

Spiritually, a sense of calm, equanimity, and serenity can be developed in this phase. These are perhaps the most important gifts of the progression.

If natal Virgo's progressed Sun conjuncted natal Venus while traveling through Libra, then very likely Virgo absorbed some of Venus' warmth and expanded beyond critical thinking toward feeling and relating diplomatically with others. If progressed Sun in Libra formed an aspect to natal Uranus, it is likely that Virgo expanded beyond literal, concrete thinking to broader, more humanitarian idealism. Self-criticism will probably have diminished during the thirty-year Libran cycle, especially if the two rulers of Libra, Venus and Uranus, were both involved in natal Virgo's personality development.

If Virgo has let go of narrowness, self-criticism, constant analysis of feelings and emotions and perfectionism during the Libran progression, then Virgo is ready to benefit from the positive personality traits of the Scorpio cycle. If not, then Scorpio, the sextile sign for the progressed Sun, will reinforce many negative Virgo characteristics. The positive qualities of Scorpio for Virgo involve physical stamina and endurance, magnetism and vitality. Scorpio is ruled by Mars and Pluto, which lend steadiness (Fixity) to the nervous system and dynamic power to the aura. Scorpio is, however, similar to Virgo in that it is hard driving, goal directed, compulsive, perfectionistic, demanding, and for Mercury in Virgo people, conducive to obsessions. It is also rigid in its attitudes and its thinking, unlike natal Mutable Virgo.

Scorpio can reinforce the introverted Mercury in Virgo tendency to withdraw to a cave, hermit-like, or be jealous or suspicious of others. On the other hand, if the natal Virgo has a Grand Trine in Water, the progressed Sun traveling through Scorpio can bring depth to Virgo's work. What are the aspects from natal Mercury to natal

Mars? To natal Pluto? Is either ruler of Scorpio in contact with natal Sun in Virgo? What sort of potential in the natal chart will be realized by Virgo in the thirty-year Scorpio progression? If there is a natal Mercury/Mars square and the person has not dealt with a tendency to cynicism and/or sarcasm in the diplomatic Libran cycle, for instance, then the Scorpio progressed Sun contacting natal Mercury/Mars will tend to make it even worse. If natal Mercury is retrograde in Virgo, for example, the Scorpio progression can bring out self-doubt and self-criticism, as retrograde energy is usually directed inward. Thus, in contrast to the Libran progression, which was more Venusian, the Scorpio progression inclines toward the energy of Mars and Pluto. Many Virgos become totally focused on a narrow goal with laser-like Scorpio intensity. This is frequently the case when transiting Pluto squares natal Pluto during the Scorpio progression. Some Virgos who have natal Mars afflictions become spiteful, impatient and dissatisfied.

The Virgo craftsman who made of his work an art form in Libra is likely to go deeper into it in Scorpio. This tends to be true whatever the service or products involved. As the progressed Sun travels through Scorpio, whether or not it contacts natal Virgo planets in a given year, it is in symbolic sextile to natal Virgo. During certain years it may make aspects to Virgo planets or Capricorn planets, and may trine any planets or angles (Ascendant, Midheaven, Nadir, Descendant) in Cancer and Pisces. If there are natal Scorpio planets in the chart, it will conjunct them. These progressed aspects exert a powerful pull on the unconscious as Earth and Water, the Feminine elements, are important in alchemical changes or transformations because they are the receptive elements. Intuitive, psychic, creative, spiritual energy abounds for those introspective Virgos who consciously work with it in this cycle. Virgo's quest for meaningful service, with its inner satisfactions and its rewards, is within reach as Virgo looks within, at his knowledge, his/her expertise, and experiments with techniques, old and new, in this cycle.

Virgo has more faith in himself in Scorpio, ordinarily. The progressed Sun is ruled by Mars, planet of confidence and vitality. Mars is also a pioneering, discovery, research and development planet. In Libra the progressed Sun was in its fall (opposite Aries). Now, the Sun is better placed for growth in both professional and spiritual work. Those who are involved with communication, Hermes' field, will find Scorpio lends its magnetism to the aura, and its persuasive authority to the words. (One is reminded of the Egyptian myth, of the power Isis' words had when in contact with Thoth. Scorpio is the Eighth House—of magic, transformation, death and rebirth.) If Virgo is open to the unconscious, the nervous system also stabilizes and Virgo is not as worried. The unconscious provides the information and inner resources needed.

Sometimes, if Virgo is too cautious to cooperate with the unconscious, if the progressed Sun makes confrontational aspects to natal planets, or if transiting oppositions (Uranus opposite Uranus, Saturn opposite Saturn) occur, the outer world may push Virgo out of the secure job into the unknown. Or, if the Sun conjuncts or squares Mars, amplified by transits of Mars and Uranus, Virgo may be involved in an accident. The body may take time off so that the mind can re-train itself and prepare for a new direction. The transformation does not always come through gentle trines and sextiles; sometimes it comes as a result of the mid-life opposition transits and progressed squares. Squares and oppositions challenge us to make changes. Easy aspects may pass while we think, "I'd like to take the summer off and write, but I should probably teach instead. . . I have the car payments." If the school administration says "No. You have to take the time off. The money isn't in the budget." Or if the body is in an accident, we may be more likely to get the work done.

It is quite important to watch the progressed Sun's contacts to Mars, Pluto, the Eighth House and the ruler of the natal Eighth house during the Scorpio progression. If Virgo continues in its structured way, Mars and Pluto may take him/her on the Night Sea Journey (See Chapters 8 and 12).

If Virgo is in healing of mind, body or soul, shamanistic dreams or experiences in the outer world may occur at this time. Inner, as well as outer goals can be achieved by Virgo in this phase. Scorpio deter-mination and perseverance are definite assets to those Virgos who have difficulty finishing their creative or educational projects.

I do not know many Virgos who have progressed as far as Sagit-tarius. Those I do know are interested in spiritual service, spiritual study, and in travel. The outer and the inner journeys are the stuff of Sagittarius. This is the progression of Virgo, the most concrete, literal minded sign, into Sagittarius, the most universal, absolutist sign. We have a sense of the potential for the microcosm to expand into the macrocosm—infinity.

Sagittarius is a vital, energetic Fire sign. Two Virgo women who are now progressed Sagittarians told me that never have they felt so alive, so full of energy. One said that she always thought that she would be the type of little old lady who would sit around the hearth fire knitting for the grandchildren. "Well, nothing could be further from the truth. My family hardly knows where I am. I've been to Europe twice since entering Sagittarius." A second told me, "My family thinks I'm mad, but I'm actually moving from Miami to Tel Aviv. It's a dream come true." A third has finished her writing project and hopes that "the world will be my audience." Another, a former teacher, now communicates a spiritual message at her spiritual center. Virgo seems to expand its communicative skills or its audience in this phase, as Hermes flits about restlessly, communicating an inspirational message.

Questionnaire

How does the Virgo archetype express itself? Though this relates particularly to those with the Sun in Virgo/Virgo rising, anyone could apply this series of questions to the House where his or her Mercury is located, the House which has Virgo (or Virgo intercepted) on the cusp, or to his or her Sixth House. The answers to these questions will indicate how in tune the reader is to his or her analytical Mercury.

1. In a conversation I consider what the person says literally more than his intent
   a. most of the time.
   b. half of the time.
   c. not very often.

2. Among my strong points I would list
   a. logic, discrimination and an analytical mind.
   b. helpfulness and consideration.
   c. kindness and sympathy.

3. I prefer to associate with people who are
   a. intelligent and informed.
   b. serviceful and sincere.
   c. caring and nurturing.

4. Some people see me as negative, a nit-picker. I perceive myself as
   a. an efficient, practical troubleshooter.
   b. exacting and concerned.
   c. not at all detail-oriented.

5. Some people would say that I pay too much attention to detail. I consider myself conscientious and thorough
   a. 80-100% of the time.
   b. 50-80% of the time.
   c. 25-50% of the time or less.

6. My greatest fear is
   a. losing my mind.
   b. that I might fall short or fail in my goals.
   c. that all my worst fears will be realized.

7. The greatest obstacle to my success comes from
   a. not seeing the forest for the trees.
   b. poor timing.
   c. inattention to detail.

8. After sacrificing my projects to accommodate others I feel resentful
   a. most of the time.
   b. some of the time.
   c. not at all.

9. When I'm at a low ebb mentally I am also low in energy and vitality
   a. 80% of the time.
   b. 50% of the time.
   c. 25% of the time.

10. When I feel ill the part of my body that is most often affected is
    a. the duodenum—ulcers.
    b. chronic fatigue.
    c. headaches and sinuses.

Those who have scored five or more (a) answers are highly in touch with Mercury, the planet of concrete, logical analysis. If the mind makes the body ill one may be too in touch with Mercury—overanalyzing. It is necessary to build good habits of diet and exercise into one's daily routine. Too often Virgo reads about nutrition and exercise but does not apply the knowledge. Those who scored five or more (c) answers may be moving toward the polar extremity. This is especially likely if there are several 12th House planets or a prominent Neptune. One means of developing Mercury is learning a practical skill.

Where is the balance point between Virgo and Pisces? How does Virgo integrate logic and intuition? Reality and imagination? Though this relates particularly to those with Sun in Virgo, Virgo rising, or a prominent Mercury, all of us have Mercury and Neptune somewhere in our horoscopes. Many of us have planets in our Sixth or Twelfth House. For all of us, the polarity from Virgo to Pisces involves the ability to move from the concrete to the abstract.

1. If my spouse were asked he/she would say that I am
   a. organized but not intuitive.
   b. both organized and intuitive.
   c. intuitive but disorganized.

2. When I stop at the store I
   a. pick up what is on the shopping list only.
   b. get what is on the shopping list and whatever else we might need.
   c. pick up what looks good to me.

3. In my approach to projects at work I am
   a. a technician.
   b. a technician and an artist.
   c. an artist.

4. In my relationships I am
   a. realistic.
   b. both realistic and compassionate.
   c. compassionate.

5. My co-workers probably consider me
   a. analytical.
   b. good at both analyzing and synthesizing.
   c. vague about details.

Those who have scored three or more (b) answers are doing a good job at personality integration on the Virgo/Pisces polarity. Those who have three or more (c) answers may need to work more consciously at developing Mercury in their horoscopes. Those who have three or more (a) answers may be out of balance in the other direction (weak or undeveloped Neptune). Study both planets in the natal chart. Is there an aspect between them? Which one is stronger by House position, location in its sign of rulership or exaltation? Is either of them retrograde, intercepted, in fall, or in detriment? Aspects to the weaker planet can point the way to integration. A profession that involves service, or healing of body, mind, or spirit also helps with integration along this axis.

What does it mean to be an esoteric Virgo? How does Virgo integrate the Moon, its esoteric ruler, into the personality? Every Virgo will have both Mercury and the Moon somewhere in the horoscope. Mercury and the Moon working in harmony will help Virgo not only to bring Hermes' messages to others, but will facilitate the development of Virgo's own creative talents. Esoteric Virgos have developed the Moon as a nurturing planet both in their service to others and their own creative efforts. Having given birth to the project, the esoteric Virgo then learns to let go of his or her attachment to it. Faith in both the Divine and him/herself is characteristic of the esoteric Virgo.

1. When I make my detailed plans for the future, I remember to let go and leave room for God and my creative imagination to intervene
   a. often. When my plans go awry it is usually for the best in the long run.
   b. a good part of the time, though it is hard to let go.
   c. seldom. Sudden changes in plans are depressing.

2. I consider myself a happy person
   a. most of the time.
   b. about half the time.
   c. seldom. I worry a lot.

3. Though I am a thinking type, I am in touch with my feelings, my lunar nature
   a. and I try to understand other people's feelings as well.
   b. and I take my feelings as seriously as my ideas.
   c. but I don't let them interfere with getting the job done.

4. I have strong faith in
   a. both God and myself.

b. God but not myself.
c. neither God nor myself.

5. I would describe myself as
   a. serviceful, nurturing, conscientious.
   b. serviceful, analytical, precise.
   c. analytical, precise, nervous.

Those who scored three or more (a) answers are in touch with the esoteric ruler. Virgo is in touch with the lunar feeling function. Those who scored three or more (b) answers are working on themselves but need to continue. Those who scored three or more (c) answers need to develop the Moon and the feeling function. Faith in oneself and in the Divine helps Virgo to transcend, to let their feelings flow more freely. Lunar surrender helps overcome insecurity, self-doubt, worry and nervousness, the Hermes tendencies.

References

Aeschylus, *Prometheus Bound*, E.H. Plumptre transl., David McKay, New York, 1960

Alice Bailey, *Esoteric Astrology*, Lucis Publishing Co., New York, 1976

Alice Bailey, *From Intelligence to Intuition*, Lucis Publishing Co., New York, 1972

Alice Bailey, *Labours of Hercules*, Lucis Publishing Co., New York, 1977

Francoise Dunand, *Le Culte d'Isis dans le Bassin Oriental de la Mediterranee*, Brill, Leiden, 1973

Franklin Edgerton, *Bhagavad Gita*, Harvard Press, Cambridge, 1952

Marie Louise von Franz, *A Psychological Interpretation of the Golden Ass of Apuleius*, Spring Publications, Irving, 1980

Marie Louise von Franz, *Puer Aeternus*, Spring Publications, Zurich, 1970

Norma Lorre Goodrich, *Ancient Myths*, New American Library Mentor Books, New York, 1960

Liz Greene, *Astrology of Fate*, "Virgo," Samuel Weiser Inc., York Beach, 1984

Joseph L. Henderson, *Thresholds of Initiation*, Wesleyan University Press, Middleton, 1967

Ray Hillis, "To Groom a King: The Legend of Merlin," Lecture given to San Diego Friends of Jung, Feb. 2, 1980

James Hillman, *Anima: An Anatomy of a Personified Notion*, Spring Publications, Dallas, 1958

C.G. Jung, *The Portable Jung*, Joseph Campbell ed., "Answer to Job," Penguin Books, New York, 1971

C.G. Jung, *Psychology and Alchemy*, R.F.C. Hull transl., Princeton University Press, Princeton, 1968

The New Testament, According to the Eastern Text, George M. Lamsa transl., A.J. Holman Co., Philadelphia, 1968

Sir Thomas Malory, *Le Morte d'Arthur*, J.M. Dent, 1930

Sallie Nichols, *Jung and the Tarot*, "The Magician," "The Popess: High Priestess of Tarot," Samuel Weiser Inc., New York, 1980

Alma Paulson, "The Spirit Mercurius as Related to the Individuation Process," Spring, 1966

Pausanius, *Guide to Greece*, vols. I and II, Peter Levi transl., Penguin Books, New York, 1971

Plutarch, *De Iside et Osiride*, J. Gwyn Griffiths ed., University of Wales Press, Cardiff, 1970

Rananuja, *Badarayana: The Vedanta Sutras*, George Thipaut transl., Motilal Banarsidass, Delhi, 1962

Dane Rudhyar, *Astrology, The Pulse of Life*, "Virgo," Shambhala, Boulder, 1978

Wallace Stevens, *The Necessary Angel: Essays on Reality and the Imagination*, Knopf, New York, 1951

Mary Stewart, *The Crystal Cave*, Morrow, New York, 1970

Thrice Great Hermes, (Corpus Hermeticum), Vols. I and II, G.R.S. Mead transl., Hermes Press, Detroit, 1978

E.A. Wallis Budge, *Egyptian Magic*, Dover Publications Inc., New York, 1971

E.A. Wallis Budge, *Gods of the Egyptians I*, Dover Publications Inc., New York, 1969

A.E. Waite, *The Illustrated Key to the Tarot, The Veil of Divination*, De Laurence and Co., Chicago, 1918

Reginald E. Witt, *Isis in the Greco-Roman World*, Cornell University Press, Ithaca, N.D.

Marion Woodman, *The Pregnant Virgin: A Process of Psychological Transformation*, Inner City Books, Toronto, 1985

7 LIBRA:
The Search for the Soul Mate

Libra is the seventh sign of the zodiac. It is the second Air sign and because the third seasonal change occurs in Libra, it is the third Cardinal sign. As autumn begins the Earth becomes quieter, more subdued, withdrawn and peaceful. The mundane ruler of Libra has an energy that is appropriate to the season. She is Aphrodite, Goddess of Love, aesthetics and civilized good taste. She has a son named Eros (love or relationship) and a daughter named Harmonia. She is usually found in the company of the three Graces or the Muses. If we visualize two Roman statues depicting Aphrodite, the shapely Venus de Milo and the Venus of Arles which presents her holding her mirror and staring intently into it, we have an image of this vain and beautiful goddess. Now, if we visualize Athena in full battle dress, or Mars going forth to war, we have a contrast between Libra and its polar opposite, Aries—between the Autumnal and Vernal Equinoxes, between the Seventh House of the natural zodiac and the First.

When we consider the polarity from Aries to Libra, we are observing two Cardinal, or managerial signs. Most students of introductory astrology are quick to acknowledge the active leadership energy of Aries, but many ask about Libra, "Is this one really a Cardinal sign? It seems so quiet, passive, calm and unobtrusive. It's hard to think of Libran people we know as Cardinal." Yet people born at the Autumnal Equinox are just as Cardinal as Aries people.

The Greeks saw Ares (Aries) and Aphrodite as particularly potent deities because they were among the few divinities who could actually *possess* mortals. Ares could possess a man with rage, and Aphrodite with her spell of longing, yearning, and love. This usually happened against the better judgment of the man in question.

231

One interesting thing the Cardinal Goddesses Athena and Aphrodite shared was descent from their fathers, Zeus and Uranus, respectively. Both were motherless goddesses, descended from the masculine, thinking function. Both were self-possessed and in control. In astrology, they each rule a positive or masculine element: Fire (Athena) and Air (Aphrodite). There, however, the parallel seems to end. Athena's birth myth is simple and direct, much like the Fire sign, Aries, with which we associate her (Athena of the Battlefield). She springs forth from her father's head (Logos). Aphrodite's birth myth is much more complex and subtle. Her father, Uranus, had been cast into the ocean, the unconscious, or feeling element, prior to her birth. She was born not from her father's head, but, in contrast to Athena, from his most sensual organs, the genitals. She is thus connected with feeling, with the magic and power of the ocean of the unconscious, and with pleasure. Almost immediately upon her birth, however, she rose from the ocean into the air. The Renaissance artist Botticelli depicted her rising from the sea in his famous work *The Birth of Venus*. The painting is popularly known as "Aphrodite on the half-shell" because it presents her emerging from her seashell. Other artists have depicted her shaking the foam from her hair. It's interesting that Aphrodite began life confronted with a decision, a choice between living in the ocean (the feeling function, the unconscious) and the Air (the objective thinking function, consciousness) because Libra/Libra rising people continue throughout their lifetimes to weigh the pros and cons, to attempt to make balanced decisions upon their mental scales, yet also to evaluate—to make a value judgement—from the feeling perspective (the ocean) as well as that of the theoretical, the logical (air).

In the myth, Aphrodite chose to live in the air. Many Librans follow her lead and orient themselves toward the thinking function. However, they become abstract theorists, rather than concrete factual thinkers like the other Air signs, Gemini and Aquarius. I have many ivory tower professors among my Libra/Libra rising clientele. (One Libran friend remarked that if in fact there had been a college major called Theory of Theory, that would have been his chosen field.) Academic Librans ordinarily have many planets in Air signs. They are conceptual people who enjoy the company of other thinkers and at the same time appreciate a non-competitive environment like the university, an environment where people try to cooperate, to live in harmony. Plato's *Republic*, with its emphasis on the Good, the

True, and the Beautiful, comes closest perhaps to the political realization of the Libran ideal with an abundance of interesting people who enjoy philosophizing, and with the elimination of coarseness, ugliness, war and unpleasantness.

Aphrodite's decision to live in the air was a compromise like so many decisions made by Libra Sun sign/ Libra rising people and people with planets in the Seventh House (Libra in the natural zodiac). She continued to value the oceanic world of feeling. Libra seeks to make the best decision not only for for him/herself, but for others as well. S/he will not ordinarily make a thinking decision that s/he knows will hurt or alienate others regardless of the logic involved. Aphrodite is the polar extremity of Mars and Libra of Aries. While Mars would quickly decide, "Well, I've got all the facts on how this will affect me and I'll come out fine, so I'm going to take action," Libra would take longer to evaluate the situation and give equal weight to such subjective factors as "How would this decision affect others— especially my romantic or business partner? Who, if anyone, would suffer? Does anyone really have to be hurt? Maybe I can wait longer and come up with a better solution that would be harmonious for all of us. I'll keep my options open. New alternatives (theories or possibilities) may occur to me in the meanwhile."

Several planets in Libra, or in the Seventh House, will tip the scales from me toward us over the years to the extent that at mid-life Libra may ask, "Do I have what these popular psychology articles call a dependency relationship? We're supposed to avoid those, aren't we? Have I lost sight of me while balancing the scales in favor of we? Ought I to be irate over this and take an assertiveness class?" Or, "I do seem to be equivocal, to take longer than other people to make my decisions."

The assertiveness training class, or the martial arts class, is often suggested to Libra or the Seventh House personality by a Fire sign friend. They are suggesting *literal* attempts to move to the Aries polarity, to get in touch with Mars. While this is not always wrong, it doesn't always help, either. If Libra/Libra rising is really unhappy, a drastic approach may recharge Mars briefly. Assertiveness training seems to help someone with five planets in Libra, or in the Seventh House, to say no firmly and finally for a short time, but tends to wear off when Libra meets disapproval, when others no longer find Libra pleasant and charming. Libra soon returns to being equivocal and cooperative. If Libra has determined that there is a real problem in the relationship (such as dependency that is eroding self-esteem) therapy will work better in the long run. It's important to ascertain if the individual is unhappy, though, or if the theory in the Collective— about dependency being wrong—has eroded his/her sense of inner satisfaction, completion, or fulfillment in his/her current relationship. Aphrodite is a beneficent planet. There's nothing wrong with sharing, relating, cooperating, making life easier for the partner, trying to make one's corner of the world a happier, more harmonious place. We are all rooted in reciprocity.

Someone with a stellium in Libra, or in the Seventh House, usually will encounter enough Aries confrontation at work where the competition must be faced daily and responsibility (Saturn) assumed. As a benefic planet, Aphrodite does not like to work or to confront. Though natal Mars may be situated in a weak House, it is usually re-charged in the course of confrontational encounters with others during the day. One doesn't ordinarily have to take up running with an Aries friend or accompany him to the shooting gallery to activate Mars. Decisions to stimulate Mars are often made when the adrenal glands are not functioning well or when the Aries part of the body (the head) develops aches or sinus problems. But any new approach to Mars has to feel right or click for Libra.

This brings us to the next point about golden Aphrodite, goddess of love and peace. Though she chose to live in the air, she is primarily a feeling goddess. Other Air signs often ask in class, for instance, "If Libra is an Air sign, why is Libra so subjective, always thinking in terms of personalities? People matter more to Libra than facts and data, than information." Yes, as Paul Friedrich pointed out in *The Meaning of Aphrodite*, she is subjective, and her power is based upon her subjectivity. In astrology she is the principle of attraction as well as the principle of harmony. So many of the relationship questions asked not only by Librans but by clients in general have roots in one major question: "How can I get my Aphrodite magnetism working? How can I draw a good partner?" To accomplish this, thinking signs (especially the other two Air signs and the Hermes ruled signs) need to attune to natal Venus/Aphrodite by House, Sign and Aspect. They need to develop the feeling function and become aware of its contents—their own individual feelings. To tune in to the feeling nature does not mean to become sentimental or frivolous or to acquire Aphrodite's lower nature (sulkiness or phony feminine wiles) as so many thinking types fear, but to develop her magnetism through discovering one's own personal value nature, one's own ability to evaluate others subjectively, rather than attempting a mental approach to others as if the thinking type were entering variables about the romantic partner into a computer.

Academia has reinforced the Air sign orientation to the thinking function by insisting that "objective, scientific analysis always avoids value judgements." It has thus become difficult for thinking types to trust their romantic instincts, their value judgements, to evaluate subjectively at all. This is particularly true of thinking types with Venus/Saturn afflictions in the horoscope. Academia emphasizes the virtues of Athena. Athena is an Aries polarity thinking goddess, a strong solar goddess whose approach is direct and objective. She always behaves in the same detached manner, proceeding from the head. Because Aphrodite, Libra's mundane, instinctual ruler, belongs to both the air and the ocean, she can be objective at work and subjective in relationship. Or, she can consciously change her energy within the relationship once she has attracted the partner. She can become cool, aloof, and distant as easily as she can be warm and sensual. She is an enigmatic goddess—the lovely, mysterious female that men find so alluring. Men cannot figure out an Aphrodite woman in the same way they can understand the behavior of an Athena woman, who is more consistent. Aphrodite is the Libra rising beauty who is warm some days and other days aloof, some days passionate and other days too spiritual to care about the body or sex at all.

This Aphrodite fascination on the part of certain men has often caused Libra rising and sometimes Libra Sun sign women to be surrounded by ardent admirers at a party. Later Aphrodite will remark to the astrologer, "I don't seem to have many women friends. I have almost no married women friends. I can't understand why. . . " She consciously needs to tone down Aphrodite's magnetism. This is also true of women with Venus close to the Ascendant (unafflicted to Saturn). Many other women wish they had this problem. Aphrodite's famous child, Cupid (or Eros), had in his quiver both the golden arrows of attraction and the leaden arrows of aversion. He could inspire emotional turmoil—yearning, longing, love—in, for instance, Jason, when that hero encountered Medea. But he could also produce aversion in Jason for Medea when the task had been finished and Aphrodite (Libra) decided to turn off the spell. Aphrodite's charms are legendary, but the important thing to remember is that she is a powerful goddess who is in control—a Cardinal goddess who can turn off her charm as readily as she can apply it. Paul Friedrich reminds us not to underestimate the Goddess of Love, for she is just as potent as Athena, Goddess of Victory. Her enigmatic Mona Lisa smile appears to be naive, but she is quite shrewd beneath her charming exterior.

The distance, the aloofness, the "cool air" meaning of Aphrodite can be understood if one considers Marilyn Monroe, or similar centerfold models—modern goddesses who display perfect physical form and apparent sensuality, but who are also remote and inaccessible. It is hard to imagine that Aphrodite would remain satisfied for long in any one romantic relationship. She is an ideal, a fantasy, a dream love for many of my male clients who participate in the Libran archetype. No human woman will ever quite equal the dream of Aphrodite, so human relationships are often sadly disappointing and missing something that is very hard for Libra or Libra rising men to define in words. In working with such clients, the astrologer comes to see what Friedrich calls her power to possess others, or what Jung has discussed in *Memories, Dreams, and Reflections* when he talks of the anima (the man's inner feminine) as a rather naive ideal that is projected upon women in the outer world during the initial stages of a relationship. When anima driven men discover that the woman in question is not really Goddess Aphrodite, disillusionment sets in and they venture forth to fall in love with someone new—another anima projection. Here, I think Jungian psychology is useful, particularly for Libra rising men. Dream interpretation, active imagination and introspection about the anima offer perspective. Men with several planets in Libra in the Fifth (romantic/creative) House have, for example, come to understand the anima through rendering of the dream in artistic media, or in poetic form. Aphrodite, after all, is the patroness of aesthetics, so the arts provide a natural outlet for her energies, a natural release for the positive qualities of the anima.

Friedrich's adjective "dewy" as applied to Aphrodite seems most appropriate for describing her influence upon the Libra archetype. Astrologically, we have traditionally used the adjective 'naive' for Libra, but dewy is somehow even better. While Libra, as an Air sign, can be quite logical about areas of life other than relationships (business matters, for instance), when it comes to what Jungian psychologists term the inner, personal Other, relationship and the choice of a marriage partner (the Seventh House choice), airy logic seems to

fly out the door as personal fantasy, dreams, visions and ideals enter to replace fact and reality. One is reminded of Pygmalion, King of Cyprus, who carved his ideal (Aphrodite) in ivory and fell in love with her statue. She came alive for him in answer to his prayer. In their search for the soul mate, many Librans have the Pygmalion approach—projecting their personal ideal upon a human being in the outer world and feeling great disappointment when he or she turns out to be human rather than Adonis or Aphrodite. This is particularly true for the Neptune in Libra generation, as Neptune has reinforced the Pygmalion illusion.

Because the Seventh House is, for Libra, life's major issue, Librans will remark in the course of the reading, "I have a prosperous law practice" or "I have a successful decorating business" but "life is empty. There is no relationship right now. I am out of balance. If I were married or living with someone, then my whole life would be back in equilibrium." The scales (equilibrium) seem intrinsically connected with the partner. Eros (relating), Aphrodite's child with the bow and arrows, seems to follow Libra about the same way he did Aphrodite in myths. If the astrologer says to a disillusioned Libran emerging from a relationship, "But you are so attractive and popular. You'll find someone else very soon," the response is almost always, "Yes, but when will I meet the *right* one?" In looking at these charming attractive people, one thinks of Aphrodite herself, admired by so many and adored by Pygmalion, pining away for the impossible love, Adonis the mortal, unhappy because she couldn't keep the right love forever—for all mortals are destined to die.

Aphrodite had many titles, just as she had many types of worshippers. She was worshipped for her physical beauty, her promise of fertility in marriage, and her knowledge of the arts of love and seduction. Courtesans and others who worshipped her in this way called her by the title, "Aphrodite Pandemos"—"Aphrodite of the common people." We can understand their level of appreciation of her beauty from words which still linger in our own language from this cult: aphrodisiac, pandering and from her son Eros, erotic or eroticism. At her temples, according to Paul Friedrich, young maidens studied the arts of love. They learned about perfumes, oils, literature (especially poetry), and artistic refinement. Friedrich compares their education to that of the Japanese geisha, or the *kama sutra* courtesan of ancient India. He mentions that Hera and Aphrodite presided jointly over marriage. Aphrodite gave the bridal veil (the secrets of love) as a gift at the ceremony; her role was to instruct the bride to keep the groom happy as a companion and giver of pleasure. Clearly, her role in the wedding indicates that she values legitimate marriage as well as romantic and sexual love, though her record for fidelity to her husband, Hephestus, was poor.

Plato and his philosopher friends called her "chaste and pure Aphrodite," or "heavenly Aphrodite clothed in stars." They worshipped her under the title, Aphrodite Urania. Aphrodite Urania is the Platonic friend, a spiritual role many Libran Sun sign people seem to play. Plato's Aphrodite is a subtle ideal of spiritual beauty— beauty that is more than skin deep. Here, Aphrodite is a caring if dispassionate goddess. As Uranus' daughter, she has a genuine concern for humanity, a spiritual nature that is not vain or subject to flattery, like the Aphrodite of the common people. The philosopher who seeks impersonal Truth, as Plato sought the Good, the True, and the Beautiful, appreciates this cosmic Aphrodite. She shines her golden light on all men, whether or not they admire or pray to her. This Aphrodite is often manifest in the horoscope of Libra/Libra rising when Venus aspects Uranus. She may have an entourage of admiring friends, like the more sensual Aphrodite Pandemos, but she is often not interested in marriage, in personal relationship. (She tried it early in life and found it too limiting, too intimate.) Urania seeks a broader circle of friends. She ages more gracefully than the sensual type of Aphrodite, because she does not identify beauty with body, with the physical form. Uranus is a wisdom planet and either lends her true wisdom, or at least the appearance of it, as she gracefully grows older.

Thus, Aphrodite has quite a range from Platonic ideal to physical seductress. Her son Eros, too, represents not only physical attraction, but connections of a deeper, more spiritual nature. Many of my clients who participate in the archetype through Libra Sun, Libra rising or Seventh House planets have the same problem accommodating the two Aphrodites that the ancient Greeks did. After a dissolved marriage, they speak of their intention never to get involved in a relationship again. They express fear of disappointment, of becoming emotionally attached and hurt; they insist that Platonic Divine Love is the answer. They try to shift from the personal to the cosmic Aphrodite. Talking to them at this stage is much like reading Plato on the subject of love. They may continue in a pure, sexless love relationship awhile and prefer being in conversation to being in love, but usually do not remain single for long. The other Aphrodite takes over; her son, Eros, brings out his bow and arrows. Air signs crave companionship. They need to connect with others, often first through the mind, and then eventually, the emotions and the body.

Those who have many Seventh House planets usually experience merging of their identities with the Other in marriage. Many experience a loss of individuality through dependency upon the relationship. Aphrodite, as you may remember from her rulership in Taurus, means value. For a person with Seventh House planets, value is found in the Other and in the relationship. Unless there are planets in the First House (the identity house) or planets in Aries to balance those in the Seventh, an individual may become unable to sort out her/his own tastes and preferences from the partner's. Life has become a shared pattern of joint plans and common interests. Aphrodite and Hera have both been satisfied. The person may even have picked up the partner's vices as well as virtues, including focusing joint energies on solving some problem which began as the partner's but is eventually considered joint—such as alcoholism, gambling or obesity. The Seventh House stellium person, for instance, will tend to say 'we think,' 'we feel,' 'we plan,' and so forth, rather than 'I think,' 'feel,' or 'plan.' Often a woman wearing a bright red dress will tell you her favorite color is blue, though you know she has nothing blue in her wardrobe because it's the color her husband always prefers. It's 'our' color.

One of the saddest sessions an astrologer can have is reading for a client with a stellium in the Seventh House, or Libra rising (even more than the Libran Sun sign) whose longtime partner has been lost. The 'we' has suddenly become an 'I' and yet after fifteen or twenty years of marriage, the person has come to feel as if there is no more 'I'. The separate identity seems to have vanished long ago. Friends try to help and listen, but spending time with friends may seem to revive memories of the 'we' because the friends were 'our' friends, the plans were 'our' plans, the beautiful house was 'our' house, the children 'our' children. The 'I' may have ceased to function independently so long ago that the person feels s/he has forgotten how, and is perhaps afraid to try. Fortunately, strong values are inherent in Seventh House planets, too. If Jupiter is there, faith usually sustains the person until Jupiter attracts a new partner.

If a person has a stellium in the Seventh House and has identified with the relationship, and if the partner is lost not to death but to
another human being through divorce, the astrologer may well be
seeing Raging Hera in his or her office. Hera does not direct her anger
at the spouse ordinarily, but rages about the other woman or other
man in question. The spouse wouldn't have abandoned the relationship of his or her own free will—never. The spouse was part of the
'we'. It was sorcery on the part of the third party in the picture. There
was nothing at all wrong with the relationship itself. This is an amazing phase. An abandoned man will tend to sulk, and an abandoned
woman will not listen to logic either, because her animus, her inner
masculine nature, already knows what happened. It speaks in
generalizations about the husband's vulnerability to spell-binding
Aphrodite and his temporary mid-life crisis. Her animus says in a
cool, logical tone when the rage has subsided, "Of course, he'll return
when he gets over her spell." Or the animus may make a moral judgment. "Why can't modern young women behave themselves? They
ought to know better than to try to destroy someone else's marriage"—
and it follows this up with a long string of logical points. "Even if the
other woman isn't a moral sort of person, she should know that my
husband doesn't earn enough money to support two families comfortably. She isn't even thinking about her own future or children.
She must be very stupid, indeed. Yet she has a college degree. This is
not intelligent behavior for an educated person. . . " And so on.

The woman's animus will often have concrete, definite opinions
which are expressed as absolute truth, and her quotes from authority
("the Bible says" and "my minister says") will present angry Hera in a
totally positive light and obscure the issue, because of course, there
are two sides to every question and every dissolving marriage. In the
case of the woman's thinking function out-of-control, or angry Hera
as animus, Jungian counseling could be a very useful process for
clarifying the situation. The 'I' must again begin to function apart
from the 'we' and the self in contrast to the 'other.' She can then begin
to take her own individual stand apart from her husband's, her
mother's, the minister's or the astrologer's, and base it on personal
values in her individual case, setting aside animus projections, expectations of the other in relationship, and opinions of those around her.
Transits of the outer planets through House Seven in the person's
horoscope may help in gaining clarity or perspective, or the progressed Moon moving through the Seventh, or contacting a natal

planet there, may aid in getting in touch with the Unconscious and gaining the personal awareness that helps in making the decision.

In life's timing, one very important period for Libra would be the years when transits pass through House Seven. It is then that Libra becomes more aware of his/her own expectations in relationships and through newly developed objectivity redefines them. For some of my clients, this period has meant real growth and maturity in understanding the role of another in their lives. This tends to be true whether or not the client is married or in a relationship at the time. If married, then the balance of self and other is likely to occur in the outer world through some change in the nature of the relationship.If single at the time, the understanding and attitude changes are likely to occur within, through dreams wherein anima or animus figures raise the issue of cooperation. Some clients have faced the issue of cooperation versus competition (Libra versus Aries) in business partnerships during these transits as well.

Though Goddess Aphrodite is essentially a romantic, a feeling goddess with more concern for fantasy than nurturing children (one cannot really visualize her changing diapers), she is very fertile. She does have children. Among her progeny are Eros, whom we have already met, the Hermaphrodite (see chapter 3), and Aeneas. Friedrich tells us that according to one myth, when her children were young she left them with nymph nursemaids and went about amusing herself with romantic or artistic pastimes. This accords with the style of many of my young Libran women clients. But the story of her aid to Aeneas was a favorite of the Greeks, a real contrast between Athena, who loved the battlefield, and the Peace Goddess, Aphrodite, who disdained it. This is the major contrast between Libra and Aries: "Make Love, not War." Friedrich draws an important symbolic contrast—Aphrodite was associated in art with the dove of peace and Athena with a predatory bird—the owl.

Aphrodite's son Aeneas was very nearly killed in the Trojan War, but the goddess, looking lovely, smelling of sweet oils and perfumes, every hair in place, sallied forth into the fray and pulled him out of range of Diomedes' weapons. In the process of rescuing him, she scratched her delicate wrist and noticing the scratch, dropped Aeneas to the ground abruptly. She turned to Zeus and complained, "Look at this scratch. Why should I have had to come to a dreadful place like this battlefield? It's unseemly for me to be here in the midst of all this blood and gore. I don't belong here." Zeus, amused at her, laughed and told her to go home and take care of her wound—". . . you were not meant to concern yourself with the matters of war. Go, now, and attend to the sweet tasks of love." Athena, the Victory Goddess, enjoying herself, joked at Aphrodite's expense—"are you certain you didn't scratch yourself fastening that brooch this morning?"

The other gods joined in the laughter because Aphrodite had been caught in such an incongruous situation. Battlefields are, indeed, unseemly places for Libra. Fighting and disharmony are to be avoided. Aphrodite belonged with the Beautiful Ones on Olympus. If anyone has had the occasion to ask an archetypal Libran for help with a messy task, such as cleaning the garage, or clearing up the kitchen after a dinner party, Libra will probably show you the scratch and beg permission to leave or will remember an important appointment. Though Athena's laughter was not kind, many of us have been in a position to appreciate it.

In Aphrodite's defense, we recall that she is a benefic planet, a morning star, shimmering and golden. Benefic planets are not hard workers. In her rulership of Taurus, a Fixed sign, we observed some tendencies to become stuck or rigid, over-structured. With her rulership of Cardinality, we have more flexibility, with the possible exception of the relationship area, where some of her benefic inertia does come through. Many a Libran or Libra rising client will stay for years in what he or she perceives to be a disappointing love relationship rather than divorce the partner. Sometimes, like Taureans, Librans will stay put because of attachment to material comfort or to their standard of living.

In other cases, however, Librans will tell their friends that though the spouse falls far short of the ideal partner, they will stay with him or her because of belief in the marriage commitment—the Seventh House contract. When Libra is really unhappy but as a peacemaker refuses to make waves in the marriage, Saturn is often strongly placed in the individual's horoscope. A legalistic judgment planet, he plays out his exalted role in the lives of many Librans. (More will be said about other meanings of Saturn's exaltation later, but in the area of relationship he stands for serious commitment.) Many friends of Librans have remarked over the years, "X complained so much about her husband that I was delighted to hear she finally separated from the monster. But now she's back with him again." Or, "This Libran friend of mine, who has an impossible, demanding wife, divorced her—but now they are remarrying. It's hard to understand. Then, when I finally met the Harpy, she didn't seem nearly as bad as I'd thought she'd be. She seemed pretty much like anyone else's wife. . . " Often when Libra begins to date outside the marriage, he or she discovers the ex-spouse bears as much resemblance to the ideal love as anyone else, any other imperfect mortal out there. The Saturn reality becomes apparent during the separation. We are all human; nobody is without faults. Several of my Libran clients have divorced and then remarried the former spouse. Aphrodite or Adonis Incarnate is very hard to find.

The Balance or the Scales, the glyph for Libra (♎), represents equilibrium. Originally the symbol may have derived from the point of the balance which the Earth itself experienced at the Autumnal Equinox. The word Equinox means equal days and equal nights, or cosmic equilibrium. In the twentieth century, by the end of Libra, we turn our clocks back to reflect the growing imbalance that begins in Scorpio as the nights become longer than the days. One way to view the Libran seasonal equilibrium might be first to consider the hectic energy of Virgo every year. There is a definite busy season beginning in late August when summer winds down and the earnest, serious back to work or back to school mood strikes. There is a flurry of activity around Labor Day as children are taken, often protestingly, to purchase school shoes and notebooks; teachers draw up lesson plans and many adults return to their work routine. Then, by late September, everyone tends to relax. Children are accustomed to new teachers and new subjects. Mothers have adapted to the new schedule of having the children gone all day, and those mothers who are not working have begun to enjoy their free time. By the last week of September, the beginning of Libra, industrious Virgo is over and a calm, tranquil equilibrium sets in. It is almost as if a hiatus is needed before the Earth moves toward the intensity of Scorpio.

In Egypt, the balance was Thoth's measuring scales which he used in the Underworld to judge the hearts of newly arrived souls. We have already encountered Thoth in Virgo. Like the Greek Hermes, he was a Messenger to the three worlds—the world of the gods, of men, and of the dead (the Underworld). Thoth had *thouhs*, an additional function that Hermes lacked. He was a Judge. Thus, all the traditional associations we make with Libra—Judgement, the Scales and the Book—were also connected with Thoth. It was Thoth who had composed all the learned treatises in Egypt, both secular and sacred, scientific and spiritual. He was Hermes at his kindest, for Thoth had an understanding heart. His hieroglyph was the symbol of the Ibis, a bird which tucked its head into its chest in a heart-shaped stance when in repose. Thoth was thus a type of combined Hermes/ Aphrodite symbol. He had a learned mind and also had heart. He was less the prankster and more the serious magician, like alchemical Hermes. His functions of messenger, healer, and judge made him a natural bridge between Virgo and Libra. The Autumnal Equinox was a time of year sacred to Thoth, the Dark Eye of Ra, who presided over the colder weather and the onset of diminishing sunshine in Scorpio.

For those with planetary energy in the autumn signs from Virgo to Scorpio, the papyrus paintings on the Judgement of Osiris are interesting to study. They reveal a progression from death to resurrection and judgment. There is a reassuring feeling to Thoth's scales and his *Book of the Dead*, with its charms guaranteed to protect Osiris from his own inner fears and other monsters of the underworld. In the papyrus paintings Osiris passes from the skillful hands of Isis, his Virgo wife, to the Libran judgment of Thoth, to his resurrection in Scorpio (the underworld).

Osiris and Thoth as judges, and their book, another Libra symbol, are very important to understanding this archetype. Librans have an inner fairness standard that operates from early childhood. "It's just not fair" is often the first sentence out of the mouth of a Libran babe. The inner fairness value is applied to the adults in his life— parents, neighbors and teachers. Later it is extended to co-workers and supervisors. A Libran at work can make him/herself truly miserable dwelling on the lack of justice around him/her in situations where others are unconcerned or even unaware of it. It's as if Libra goes through life weighing others' hearts on Thoth's scale against the feather of Goddess Maat and finding them wanting. It's often the spouse who suffers most from being "weighed in the balance" however.

Part of the problem in relationships is that Libra's inner judge, who has been weighing others since childhood, is waiting in the wings for the spouse once Aphrodite's romantic courtship period is over. The spouse is human and the strong aversions or dislikes that Libra manifested when told by the teacher it was time to do his/her homework will manifest when s/he has things expected of him/her in a relationship. There are things about the spouse that are simply not likeable, just as in the case of teacher or employer. But we have to cooperate (Seventh House) even with people whose habits drive us crazy. Just as Libra had to do his/her homework whether or not s/he liked the teacher or has to do our job whether or not s/he likes the unfair employer, s/he needs to compromise with the spouse even when the other side seems unfair and s/he doesn't like it. Aphrodite can look around and think, "The grass would be greener at that company, gallery, university—or in that marriage. Maybe I could make a change. Maybe a different business partner or different spouse would appreciate me (Aphrodite) more." The Justice of the Gods is not human justice—and certainly not always Libran justice.

Another interesting thing about Libra is that the Seventh Sign of the zodiac is similar to the seventh day of creation in the Genesis story. "On the seventh day God rested." The other eleven archetypal signs could learn from Libra the wisdom of resting and surveying their creations. We return from a break more relaxed and more efficient. What does a Libran enjoy doing at night? Resting. Unless his or her horoscope contains a prominent Saturn, s/he does not want to take home a briefcase full of papers as an Earth sign individual would. S/he wants to take it easy, to relax. This is why it usually won't work to suggest to a Libran client that since the boss is so unfair and disorganized, perhaps s/he could move on and open his or her own consulting practice, or gallery, or decorating firm. Unless s/he has a Cardinal Cross or T-Square s/he is very likely to reply, "Oh, no! I don't want that kind of administrative responsibility." "But you're so unhappy where you work now; things are so disorganized and inharmonious," the astrologer remarks. "You're a Cardinal sign, after all, and good at management skills. You're also good with people. Why not become self-employed?" "It's too much of a hassle," says Libra. S/he continues to look for the perfect situation, the ideal studio, the ideal business partners.

Still, Libra has an important insight to offer the more compulsive, driven signs. Those who are all work and no play find that their work time is not as creative or as efficient as they would like. We all need time to stand back and just stare into space, like the Libran employee who sits with his feet atop the desk and not a paper in sight as the boss looks in from the corridor. He is thinking, reflecting, in touch with his muse; he is probably developing an idea to present at the board meeting. The boss, though, will have to see and hear it to believe Libra has really been working. Libra often accomplishes his best idea work during long coffee breaks when the mind is roving free, but the Earth signs around him will feel that he makes the job look too easy or that he is probably careless about his work; otherwise it would take him as long to do the same task as it takes them. He needs to let them know about his procedural shortcuts so that they don't think him irresponsible.

The exaltation of Saturn in Libra, one of the better placed exaltations, can come in handy if Libra attunes to it. Saturn refers to inner discipline in the very areas of life that Aphrodite is lazy about—punctuality; self-control (especially about diet and exercise as Libra or Libra rising gets older—Aphrodite has a sweet tooth); assuming responsibility, even if it means saying disagreeable things to co-workers whom Libra is temporarily supervising; professionalism with paperwork (Aphrodite is bored and wants to do creative, not repetitious work); keeping the desk clean; all those dutiful and tedious Earth sign Saturnine things that Libra does not feel are important. However, Libra is Cardinal management talent and Saturn is a professional, ambitious planet. The combined energy of Saturn and Libra can help to offset the sultry Aphrodite's mood when she resents the extra duties imposed upon her.

The negative part of the Saturn exaltation in Libra would be its brittleness, its rigidity, its refusal to be flexible. Justice is a lovely Tarot card, but the Judgment card is much more severe. Saturn in Libra can mean that the harshness, the austerity of the judge comes out; the demanding supervisor can be a judge who lacks mercy, who hasn't the understanding heart of Thoth. It is interesting in horoscopes of Librans to see if Venus (Aphrodite) is aspected to Saturn. If so, very cool air comes across to others, as well as a tendency to judgmentalism, because of the natural power of the Saturn exaltation. If Saturn is strong in the chart, especially if it's in the Seventh House, marriage is seen as a contract to guarantee emotional and/or financial security.

Yet, the practicality of exalted Saturn could also help to balance the idealism and ground the unrealistic expectations of some who participate in this archetype. Saturn is aware that there is really no perfectly harmonious marriage, or truly creative work environment—that *everything* has its flaws.

The understanding heart of Thoth helps modify the judgmentalism of Saturn, as does the objective view of Uranus, Aphrodite's father, the esoteric ruler of Libra. Uranus has an objectivity about life's situations and injustices that helps Libra to stand back and detach rather than yield to Aphrodite, the mundane ruler, when she tries to take things too personally. Uranus, with its tolerance, objectivity and universal friendship can say, "The boss is having a bad day." This depersonalizes Aphrodite's reaction. "The boss is being unfair to me; this is a disharmonious place for me and I'm going to go home early tonight." A more esoteric Libran can resist passing judgment and thus is able to give others the benefit of the doubt.

In his essay "The Feeling Function," the Jungian analyst James Hillman describes marriage as a container for the development of the feeling function through tuning into the Eros values of sharing, relating, and cooperating over time. Marriage could be imagined as a sort of alchemical vessel for personality purification and growth. Falling in love, according to Hillman, means taking a chance and trusting one's feeling judgments. It is easier in our times to quit an employer or move from a locality than it is to leave the marriage partner. Saturn's exaltation in Libra, too, lends a seriousness to the marriage contract. There are few ceremonies or binding rituals left in western society other than this Aphrodite/Hera commitment made in front of the assembled community.

In marriage, even people for whom feeling is the inferior function, Hillman believes, come to accept their own feelings and values because the partner accepts them as they are. In marriage, people can even come to terms with the dependent or clinging side (a side of them the Aries or First House planets hate), a side which is very unpopular in the literature of the twentieth century. When we are in love, Hillman reminds us, we feel young, healed, whole. We are ready to take risks of being hurt or of hurting others for the joys and sorrows that our thinking nature might otherwise seek to avoid. Eros as an archetype offers his strength to Psyche in the myth.

In marriage, however, facets of the personality that remained safely hidden during courtship come to the surface. Each party sees the other's dark side. He or she may be able to hide it at work, but the persona does not protect us from the scrutiny of the spouse. As Marie Louise von Franz remarked in the film interview, *Way of the Dream*, "When the woman's animus meets the man's anima, animosity can appear." In "The Feeling Function," Hillman provides an example we have all observed in couples we know. The man may be really angry at his wife, but his anima tries to smooth things over. So he chooses a romantic, candlelit restaurant for dinner, pulls her chair out politely, lights her cigarette, orders a gourmet dinner and seems perfectly charming and polite. However, he ignores his wife and chats with the waitress, entertaining her, being entertained by her, all evening. His wife is secretly fuming. Later, her animus rages, emotes, asserts itself. He withdraws into moody silence, his anima playing the feminine role to her animus. He has displayed excellent manners while she has behaved in an uncivilized way, ruining a delightful evening. She thinks she has been manipulated. The next day he may gossip and complain about her at work to a sympathetic secretary.

Von Franz said in *Way of the Dream* that it is important to note in a severe argument involving a couple that there may well be four participants including the woman's animus, with its aggressive, opinionated shoulds and oughts and generalizations, and the man's anima, smoothing things over, or retreating into a mood, avoiding controversy, repressing its anger. I have seen this pattern mainly in working with Libra rising clients, as well as some Libra Sun sign people. Gentle, polite Aphrodite as a man's anima can be exasperating and bring out his wife's assertive animus. She makes his decisions when he vacillates and he complains to others that she constantly decides for him. Yet, his vacillation, from her point of view, causes her to take charge by default. Reducing the battle from a foursome to a couple by retracting the anima/animus behavior decharges the energy in the room and makes it easier to deal with the issues at hand. For Libra/Libra rising, or people in whose charts Venus is stronger than Mars by House position and aspects, or people with many Seventh House planets, it is important to express those negative feelings that persist, rather than wishing them away and becoming polite, charming, or distant. Symbolically, negative feelings that are not filtered out can build, in Libra, as kidney stones. The kidneys are the body's filtering system or purifier.

Uranus, as esoteric ruler, may objectify the value system by introducing new people from vastly different backgrounds with vastly different value systems during the course of the marriage. Just as negative or dark qualities hidden in courtship surface after marriage, so also in-laws often become quite visible after the legal, contractual ceremony. The astrologer often sees this coming before the happy couple does, though they're quite certain that their ethnic/religious/ educational differences will not matter an iota. But the Italian mother-in-law-to-be will appear and state, "This is against my better judgment. My son should have a good Italian Catholic wife who will send my grandchildren to parochial schools. It won't work." "Well," the astrologer says, "maybe you, as well as your son, have something to learn from this Protestant girl. Her perspective will surely open to you some new concepts, approaches to life, and values." "Nonsense," says the future mother-in-law, "my better judgment is accurate. Who needs 'new ideas' or 'new ways'? The old values are the true ones, the only values worthwhile." Uranus, the esoteric ruler of the marriage institution, has quite a job ahead of it in introducing mother-in-law to a new perspective. Yet, unless they live on opposite sides of the continent, there are likely to be many occasions for Uranus' radical ideas to permeate both families, producing, one hopes, broad-mindedness, tolerant acceptance and growth. (Arrival of grandchildren on the scene usually helps to harmonize the family.)

Expansion and growth in values is the combined work of both the mundane and esoteric rulers of Libra. Marriage is usually the area where the pressure of the alchemical process operates. "Can't I just opt out of relating and express Aphrodite/Eros in my art?" asks Libra rising. "Isn't there a perfect ten, an ideal partner from a past life out there? A relationship that I can just relax and enjoy? If there is to be no soul mate relationship that won't hurt, and that won't require work (Saturn), maybe I should give up and devote myself to dusting the altar at church—give my romantic nature to God." Libra/Libra rising may attempt this for awhile, but the feeling function usually guides them toward another relationship.

We tend to think in terms of the "battle of the sexes" raging around us in our world of duality where opposites, such as Masculine and Feminine, seem to clash like noisy cymbals. James Hillman thinks it is an insidious cliche to believe that women are naturally, automatically feeling types and men are born to be thinkers. It's insidious because it promotes laziness, and is not conducive to personality integration for the individual of either sex. Each of us as a human being has both a thinking and feeling function to develop. But because we think in terms of opposites, many lazy women allow men to carry the thinking function for them while they establish the family values as feeling types. The men make the mundane thinking decisions, or conversely, men allow their wives and lovers to carry the feeling function totally, including the full responsibility for the relationship. Men do not need to work at it, because they are "not supposed to be feeling types." They can also remain lazy about developing an appreciation for the arts, taste in clothing, confidence in their value system, and their value judgments.

Hillman provides an example of a couple who carry each other's inferior functions in the relationship, which is certainly the easier and more commonly seen, if also the most unconscious method. (It's hard work to try to develop the inferior function when, after all, the spouse ought to be good at it anyway.) Yet, the path to wholeness requires us to exert ourselves. In Hillman's example, a woman pulls a man along by the arm to a concert or into a clothing store. She has chosen the concert and she will select his apparel. Many of us have seen this type of behavior in men's stores and at concerts.

Hillman doesn't go into the couple's background, astrologically. But an astrologer can identify the Venusian/Libran archetype of taste and value in this concrete situation. First he visualizes the Libran as the woman and the husband or boyfriend as a double Virgo computer programmer. She resembles Aphrodite and he looks rather like Mr. Magoo. She belongs in both those feeling environments; she looks like a make-up consultant perhaps. She has developed or educated her superior feeling function, which came naturally with her natal chart. He has developed his thinking function, but he relies upon her judgment. Their behavior seems appropriate to us as we look on. They are feeling and thinking, Aphrodite and her somewhat settled, middle-aged Hermes, a balanced couple.

Now, let's reverse the situation astrologically. He is the Libran Sun sign—a furniture salesman. He is a photography hobbyist, but hasn't developed his taste or his feeling function. He is naturally good with people and does well in sales; he's a feeling type with a good deal of natal talent. This time she is the double Virgo computer programmer wearing trifocals; *she* looks like Mrs. Magoo! She is a natural thinking type who has developed her superior function through specialized education. She subscribes to *Computer Weekly* and has no interest in frivolous fashion magazines. Everything in the store looks over-priced. Other than that, it's hard for her to evaluate it. Her *Consumer Report* cannot provide the data on taste or intangible values she needs in this situation. She bites her lower lip. Society tells her she is supposed to be good at this; she is, after all, a woman. He gravitates to a shirt in a shade of blue that looks especially good on him; he knows what he likes, but defers to her final choice. When it comes to clothing, men are supposed to do that. Later the couple attend the concert. On the way home she asks him for verification: "It was good, wasn't it? I hope so; it was expensive enough." "Well, I liked it," he says, with total confidence in his taste.

Hillman elucidates further the need to develop both the superior and the inferior functions, giving an example from the 'feeling' area of music. Interest in the arts by itself doesn't demonstrate that one is in touch with the feeling function. Nazi death commanders at concentration camps enjoyed Wagner operas tremendously, but they weren't in touch with their feeling functions at all. Nor will every artist have a developed feeling function. An artist may be educated in such thinking areas as mathematics, techniques and structure, but still be working to develop style, originality, form. We cannot generalize about artists and the feeling function any more than we can generalize about women or men.

According to Hillman, we are inclined to look at life dualistically— to perceive thinking and feeling as rival functions of the psyche that must always be opposed to one another, rather like game pieces on the playing field of life. Yet, they are really two ends of the same axis. (In astrology, this is true, too, of Aries/Libra, or First House and Seventh House.) Each of us, Hillman states, is oriented toward approaching life from thinking or feeling—whichever is the superior function. We may endlessly go on refining this function out of balance to the other, if we so choose. A thinking type can always read more and more selectively. A feeling type can always refine his taste or expand his social and artistic contacts, but may leave little time for reading; or he may read indiscriminately, choosing poor materials. The thinker may continue to go through life with very little trust in his taste in art or people, or his value judgments. If the thinker is depressed he may say "I've been in this trivial mood a long time. How negative. It interferes with my aims, my work." But he may not take his feelings seriously enough to ask, "Why am I unhappy?" Therefore, he may go on being unhappy, but singleminded, while the feeling type continues to be wholehearted. Thus, for a balanced, well-rounded, happy personality, it is important to develop and integrate both functions. We could all become wholehearted *and* singleminded.

"Is it necessary to be married to do this?" Suppose you have nothing in Libra or the Seventh House, and a stellium of planets in the First House or in Aries? For you the answer is, "Probably not." You may not care about Other, about the social adjustment; you might feel trapped in a dependent relationship; it may seem as if you would lose your independence and gain very little in return. But for most of us, marriage is a very good alchemical container for the integration of self and other, thinking and feeling, ideas and values. Among my friends and clients are many with Aries Sun/Aries rising who are magnetically drawn to Libra Sun/Libra rising people in business and personal relationships alike. There are also many stellium in the First House individuals who are fascinated with Librans or people with stelliums in the Seventh. This may be a division of function marriage, though. "You be my thinking function; I'll relate to the outer world for you, nurture you, etc." Instinctually, people tend to move toward this balance, it would seem. Many military men tend to choose attractive, artistic Aphrodite women, many of whom literally have Libran planets. Libran men of a theoretical or artistic nature also gravitate toward women with planets in Aries/Aries rising—autonomous, decisive women who organize, administer and schedule their lives for them.

The tendency is for couples to approach personality integration in an instinctual or unconscious way. But the inner work can also be accomplished if, as we become more aware of our behavior patterns, we may consciously choose to develop our inferior function as well as to refine and differentiate the natural or superior function.

We come now to some myths of Libra. One is about judgment, a typically Libran issue, and the others are about two princes who preferred to sit on the sidelines and evaluate their situation rather than fight—Arjuna and Telemachus. They chose to watch the battle as spectators: "I am powerless to act. The battle is already lost, or the situation will resolve itself without me. Doubt is a problem endemic to the Air signs, while the Fire polarity, as represented by Krishna or Athena, impels to action, to a decisive resolution of doubt—toward courage in adversity; beyond likes and dislikes, and in the end to fulfillment of the warrior's or hero's duty (Saturn's *dharmic* exaltation). Mars (Ares), ruler of the polarity, endows Libra with these exact qualities.

The Judgment of Paris myth can be found in Jane Harrison's *Prolegomena* (page 292), Joseph Campbell's *Occidental Mythology* (pages 158-159), and Liz Greene's *Astrology of Fate* (pages 223-225). It's about Libra and choices and also about Libra's desire to please—to be all things to all men and offensive to none. Esoterically, it seems to me to mean that the Libran quest is to reach beyond judgment or choice toward Divine Love—Celestial Aphrodite, or Aphrodite Urania, ideal or pure love.

The judgment myth involved a mortal, Prince Paris, and three great goddesses: Athena, Aphrodite, and Hera. Jupiter/Zeus, whose ways are mysterious to men, had foreordained that a golden apple was to be presented to the most deserving goddess. Hermes was dispatched with the apple to find Paris, who was tending a flock of sheep. Ceramic art, as reviewed by Jane Harrison, shows that Paris tried to run from the choice—the judge role—in the direction of Troy. He wanted to go home and escape the responsibility. In ceramic art, Hermes, however, grabbed him by the wrist and turned him back in the direction of the goddesses. They did not look particularly imposing in the drawing, as Harrison and Campbell pointed out. (You can see Paris and Hermes reproduced in *Occidental Mythology*, page 161.) Aphrodite did not look voluptuous—she looked rather frumpy. In fact, Liz Greene's version of the story has Paris first attempting to cut the apple in three slices, one per goddess, as a fair Libran would do, but Hermes would not let him in. Zeus wanted a choice, a judgment, here. Paris, who wanted to please, was now in a quandary—whichever goddess he chose, two would be furious with him. Each, according to some accounts, offered a bribe to Paris. Perhaps they meant to bestow these gifts out of kindness—or perhaps Zeus wanted a mortal to determine which of their gifts was most valuable—Athena's military prowess, Hera's legitimate control of all Asia, or Aphrodite's gift of love. Paris made the Libran decision—the gift of love. He chose Aphrodite. Hera and Athena, rejected and vindictive, started the Trojan War. They embroiled the Greeks and Trojans, who were delighted to fight anyway. The final straw that set off the conflagration was, however, Aphrodite's gift to Paris of a married woman, the perfect, noble, ideal, and pure—Helen.

This myth incorporates many of the Libran archetypal themes: the desire to avoid making choices, to avoid closing off any options, or alienating any goddesses as friends; the theme that avoiding judgment postpones taking the responsibility that follows upon choice; the theme that for Libra, dejection follows upon the doubt, "What if it

doesn't turn out well?" Often the fantasy of falling for the unavailable love, a married person, appears in Libra's life pattern as well.

For Libra, as for the rest of us, not every decision will have a positive outcome; one has to choose and hope for the best. In Paris' case, he and Helen had nineteen years and three sons together. He and the boys died in the Trojan War, but Helen, daughter of Zeus, was returned to the Greeks. Her people loved and admired her still at the end of the war and wept with her over her suffering.

Her reception was very different from that of the Indian Queen and heroine at the end of the *Ramayana* epic, Sita. This too was the story of an archetypal couple. Rama, the king, and his wife, Sita. Sita, like Helen of Troy, had been abducted to a foreign land where she was held prisoner. The connection had been severed for King and Queen in the case of the Greeks and the people of Rama's kingdom. For the kingdom to be whole once more, the Feminine must be redeemed. Though it took a heroic, courageous king (a strong ego), the emphasis was on the need to reconnect with the Feminine. Thus, these stories are of a vastly different type. The struggles of Odysseus, Rama, and Menelaos seem to be more personal, more value-laden, more intense. To lose Helen or Sita, or for Odysseus to lose Penelope meant a symbolic loss of anima, of soul, for the King and the people. The joy was gone from the kingdom without the lovely Queen. Thus, the Indian people, to be certain that they had their ideal of femininity intact, put Sita through an ordeal of fire. She came through unscathed; she had been loyal to Rama and to them, she was whole.

In our times, when the ideal of love or beauty seems less honored than the patriarchal ideals, the thinking virtues, many women find it difficult to identify with such heroines as Queen Sita or Helen of Troy. They want a more equal partnership. Hera, as legitimate wife of Zeus, the long suffering wife of the philanderer, is unappealing. Yet the supportive wife role, the Seventh House role whereby an ambitious woman helps her husband succeed professionally and fulfills her ambitions through his success—the joint partnership marriage is still popular. Rosalyn Carter and Nancy Reagan are two cases in point. Ms. Reagan made an almost archetypal Seventh House statement, quoted in *Goddesses in Everywoman*: "My life was incomplete until I met Ronnie." The search for completeness through marriage is the Seventh House search. This balance of energy for the Seventh House personality would include, perhaps, not only such goddesses as Hera, and Sita, and romantic Aphrodite, but the Polarity Goddess, integration of Athena. Athena, as ruler of the First House (Logos/ Self), balances the Seventh House (Eros/Other) because she represents the ability to fight for individuality, to avoid losing one's identity by a dependent merging, a total yielding to the feeling of connectedness—through marriage—that is the Seventh House. Athena is a goddess who can discriminate, take a personal stand, act on her decisions, and express anger appropriately—unlike raging Hera. She is a wiser (esoteric) version of Ares/Mars. Her owl, after all, represents wisdom.

Hindu astrologers have pointed out that Libra is the only sign of the zodiac whose symbol does not breathe. The others are birds or animals, a man or two fish—symbols that breathe. But for Libra, we have the scales and the book, two inanimate objects. They are both mental and moral symbols, yet they have no life or *prana* because they cannot breathe. "The letter of the law without the spirit of the law is dead," one could say by way of interpretation. Or one could regard this curious Air sign as life's spectator or observer who fears to make mistakes and accrue bad karma—the Arjuna or the Telemachus who feels the odds against him are overwhelming, so why fight? This view of life as a series of ethical problems which require no physical activity to resolve them seems to lack life, too. Only in the area of romance, when they're in love, does one sense that Libran planets are alive; and there, of course, it may be a fantasy—an impossible dream—an inaccessible love such as noble Helen already married to Menelaos.

I think one key to the lack of aliveness or *prana* may lie in the fact that Thoth, the Egyptian judge, wrote a *Book of Breathing*—a book of apparently esoteric techniques like those the Hindus call *pranayama* —getting the inner current, the life force going. I think another key lies in the fact that Libran, like the other signs, is located 180 degrees away from an active, alive, courageous Fire sign—Aries. Whatever Libra may say about Aries' energy—"It's impetuous. It's ruthless in battle. It's foolhardy. It's reckless." Libra must acknowledge the Aries courage and decisiveness, confidence and vitality.

There are two myths, one from India and one from the Greek *Odyssey*, which seem to demonstrate integration of the Aries polarity by Libran archetypal figures. Their Divine Counselors urge them to practice the usual heroic Aries virtues. Yet the heroic courage once acquired is devoted to redeeming the Feminine.

The first involves the Greek heir to the kingdom of Ithaca—young Telemachus. His father, Odysseus, has been gone since the end of the Trojan War, lost among magical women—witches, sirens and so forth. Odysseus is trying to find his home and Penelope, his wife, his Seventh House partner (the Other), his feminine side. Telemachus has lost any real hope that his father is still alive, that he will ever return. He sits, dejected, watching his mother's suitors—tall, athletic, powerful men who are skilled with weapons, eating his mother's food and living in his father's palace. He thinks, full of sorrow and doubt, "What can I do, a young man like myself, unskilled, inexperienced, one boy against so many? I should just give up. How can I possibly fight? And even if I tried, what if my father is already dead? What's the use?"

Goddess Athena, the family counselor, the spirit of wisdom and inspiration, decides to go to Ithaca and put some life and some courage into Telemachus. She disguises herself as a stranger, a traveler named Mentor, a man "who used to know Odysseus well." She enters the palace and tells Telemachus that his father is indeed alive in the islands and exactly where he can start looking for Odysseus. She then delivers the following lecture:

> ". . . Collect your wits and make a good plan to kill these hangers-on, either by craft or by open fight. Indeed, you ought not to play about the nursery any longer; your childhood days are done. Haven't you heard what a great name Orestes made for himself in the world, the fine young fellow, when he killed the traitor Aigisthos who had murdered his famous father? You too, my dear boy, big and handsome as I see you now, you too be strong, that you may have a good name on the lips of men for many generations. . ."
>
> "When Aethena had said this, away she went like a bird, up the luffer in the roof. In the spirit of the boy she left courage and confidence and he thought of his father even more than before. He understood what it all meant, and he was amazed; for he believed her to be a god. At once he went back to that rough crew, looking more like a god than a man himself." (*The Odyssey*, Mentor Edition, pages 17-18.)

Telemachus was able to believe in himself and rescue his mother (his inner feminine) with the aid of his father (his masculine side). At the end of the story Odysseus, too, not only recovered his courage, but found his feminine side, his loyal Penelope as well. The *Odyssey* and the *Gita* seem deeper, value-laden stories in contrast to many other accounts of egoic heroism.

My favorite story on firing up Libra, however, comes from the

Bhagavad Gita. In the first few pages of this Hindu scripture, there is dialogue between Lord Krishna, an incarnation of Vishnu, and his disciple, Prince Arjuna, the would be hero. The story has an esoteric level to it as well as a mundane emphasis on assimilation of Aries' courage and hope. (The *Gita* is a 200-page discussion on ethics in the middle of an action packed story, the *Mahabaratha*.) Krishna and Arjuna have settled down in the middle of a raging battlefield to discuss yoga practices and values. This battlefield, esoterically, is within us all. "Kurukshetra" it was called—"the battlefield of the heart." The *Gita* tells us to forget about receiving the "fruits of our labors" in this lifetime and instead to do our duty in the right spirit; to move away from petty likes and dislikes; to live a balanced life; to neither eat too much nor too little; nor to sleep too much nor too little. Also, the yogi learns to breathe—to control the life force. "Offer the inflowing breath into the outflowing breath and the outcoming into the inflowing. . . " This emphasis on *pranayama* is reminiscent of Thoth's *Book of Breathings*. It is a full text, not only for those who participate in the Libran archetype, but for all of us.

In the first chapter of the story, Arjuna sits dejected, having tossed away his bow and arrow, his eyes full of tears and compassion for his kinsmen, the enemy forces.

"Why should I kill my kinsmen, and in so doing their children and their grandchildren? It will not bring me peace of mind. Why strike them down in the prime of life? Even if I were to be King of the Three Worlds, not merely an earthly kingdom, what would I gain? How can I profit by the death of kinsmen?"

And again, "Women will be abducted by lower caste soldiers and mixing of blood lines will result and caste itself will be destroyed."

"What if a stray arrow were to kill my own revered archery teacher Drona, who advises my cousins? This would be great dishonor."

"The other side, the hundred sons of Dritherastra, are simply ignorant (Dritherastra meant "blindness") and not evil. How can I slay them—they have done no wrong."

"My bow burns in my hand; I will bare my breast to the enemy; I will not fight."

Krishna responds to Arjuna's list of rationalizations with the argument that there is really no death on the battlefield; it's only the appearance of reality—a shadow play. He says:

> "How hath this weakness taken thee? Whence springs the inglorious trouble, shameful to the brave, barring the path of virtue? Nay, Arjun!. . .

"Forbid thyself to feebleness, if Mars is thy warrior name. Cast off thy coward fit. Wake! Be thyself. Arise! Scourge of thy Foes!

. . . Thou grievest where no grief should be. Thou speak'st words lacking wisdom. For the wise in heart mourn not for those that live nor those that die. . . All that doth live lives always.

"The soul that with a strong and constant calm takes sorrow and takes joy indifferently, lives the life undying.

He who shall say, 'Lo, I have slain a man,' or 'Lo, I am slain,' these both know naught. Life cannot slay. Life is not slain.

"Let no loss be feared. . . faith, yea, a little faith, shall save thee from the anguish of thy dread.

Find full reward of doing right in right. Let right deeds be thy motive, not the fruit which comes from them. And live in action. Labor. Make thine acts thy piety. Casting all self aside, condemning gain and merit; equable in good and evil: equability is Yog, is piety.

. . . Scorn them that follow virtue for her gifts. The mind of pure devotion, even here, casts equally aside good deeds and bad, passing above them. Unto pure devotion, devote thyself: with perfect meditation comes perfect act. . . and the righthearted rise.

This is Yog—this is peace."

("The Song Celestial," *Bhagavad Gita*, Sir Edward Arnold, pages 9-25.)

"Make thine *acts* thy piety!" There is a great deal of esoteric truth here on the blending of Aries Fire and Libran Air—Libran reflection or meditation with Aries deeds and Libran calm and equanimity with Aries strength and courage. Aries' optimistic faith to modify Libran fear of making mistakes—of being unjust or unfair. Uranus, the esoteric ruler, comes through the passage, too. Uranus represents detachment from the pairs of opposites—not only joy and sorrow, but even life and death. Finally, Krishna pleads with Arjuna to detach from desire for the gifts of virtue, or merit—not to worry about whether his deeds be good or bad or if he is to be rewarded for them—but just to perform his deeds as a true Kshatriya warrior who knows his dharma.

Many Libra Sun sign and Libra rising people have Neptune, a particularly idealistic, romantic planet conjuncting them. They are "in love with love itself," and often have difficulty in finding a partner in the real world who can fulfill their expectations. They attempt to put him or her on a pedestal and invariably it cracks. Libra then feels hurt and disappointed. I think people with strong Neptune in Libra contacts to natal planets or to angles like the Seventh House cusp, would benefit from reading Robert Johnson's book *We*. In this very worthwhile treatise, Mr. Johnson takes the reader through the courtly love tradition in medieval Europe and then through the romantic myth of Tristan and Iseult. He identifies two separate Iseults: Tristan's human love and Iseult of the White Hands. She was the imperfect Iseult through whom he experienced great delights as well as sufferings and a sense of betrayal. The second Iseult, Iseult the Fair, was his spiritual guide. She was the impersonal, divine Iseult. She was, like Aphrodite in Plato's philosophy, impersonal Divine Love. She was the perfect soul ideal.

I think it's important for all of us to ponder the Libran archetype, whether or not we have any Libran planets. We live in a culture that emphasizes romantic love as an ideal. It's in the air around us. We all have Aphrodite/Venus in some House of our horoscope and Libra on (or intercepted on) one of our House cusps, too. In those Houses, we deal not only with the Good, the True and the Beautiful, but with meaning, longing and yearning for warmth and companionship. We also, if we are seekers, deal with spiritual aspiration in that house.

Spiritually, we associate Libra, the (ideally) balanced scales, with even-mindedness, an important virtue for the yogi, as well as serenity, calm, and equanimity. Many Librans are cheerful in adversity, cool and collected in times of crisis. They keep their heads when all about them are losing theirs. This inner balance is to be admired and imitated, especially by those whose Mars leads them to overreact, or to react too quickly, out of proportion to the situation. In the *Bhagavad Gita*, Chapter II explains that though the Kshatriya warrior must fight his battles in the outer world, he is to proceed from a state of inner peace. Inner tranquillity, however, does not mean one can sit on the sidelines of the battlefield of life.

Uranus is a liberating planet, a transpersonal planet. It raises the ideal (Aphrodite) to the level of universal beauty, love, truth and value. As an esoteric Libran, Mahatma Gandhi liberated his country from alien rule. His non-violent value, *ahimsa*, was developed in South Africa and India where his courage and faith were tested by the political authorities. He stood by his principles in adversity and won through in the end. He put his political ideal ahead of his own personal relationship with his wife; he risked his peace and harmony at home to achieve a larger goal. His work in integration of the courage polarity (Aries), in manifesting willingness to stand and face the enemy, to act decisively, to believe in himself and his duty, are inspirational to all of us, whatever our level of attunement to Libra, Venus/Aphrodite, or Uranus.

The thirty-year progression through Scorpio is a progression from light, cheerful Air into deep Water. A word of caution to the Libra/Libra rising reader who is entering Scorpio now. Hang on to your sense of humor. It takes a year or two to become accustomed to the new intense, earnest, serious energy. If progressed Sun conjuncts natal Mercury in Scorpio or if natal Libran Mercury enters Scorpio, Libra is likely to experience an urge to study something practical in a focused and disciplined manner. To many Librans, especially those low in Earth, this practical cycle may seem unfamiliar.

"This is so unlike me," says the Libran whose B.A. was in an exotic field like pure mathematics or linguistics or fine arts, political or economic theory. "I'm thinking of taking a course in tax accounting; I'm thinking of becoming an investment broker."

Libran women, those true Aphrodites who have enjoyed staying home arranging flowers, decorating, entertaining, and venturing forth on Sunday to play the organ at church or do flower arrangements, may also become practical. "I'm tired of television and romantic novels. I'm tired of listening to my husband moan over the bills. I think it would restore harmony at home if I earned some money. I'd like to sell cosmetics or be an interior decorator. Is this practical, do you think?"

Scorpio archetypally refers to joint finances as well as one's sex life. Financial careers and domestic harmony seem interrelated. But the discipline of the Mercury transits tends to wear off unless the progressions through Scorpio conjunct natal business planets or sextile natal Virgo planets (precision work). Thus, many Librans will quickly become bored with mundane financial studies, lose interest and quit. Unless Saturn (archetypally exalted in Libra) is strong in the natal chart, sustaining career interest, Libra asks in a year or two, "Why was I interested in accounting or insurance brokers? How odd." There's no scope for the Good, the True and the Beautiful here. Money is, after all, so mundane.

Librans whose progressed Sun or Mercury contacts many natal Scorpio planets may develop an interest in sex therapy, hypnosis, massage, marriage counseling, or a psychology degree. Several Libra

Sun sign men have switched from the legal field to psychology during the progression of Sun and Mercury through Scorpio, conjuncting natal planets in the Earth houses (Two, Eight and Ten).

In relationships, life's major issue for Libra, this can be life's most stressful period if the mundane ruler, Venus/Aphrodite, is in Scorpio. As the Sun and other progressed planets conjunct natal Venus in Scorpio, activating any natal harsh aspects to her, the dark side to Scorpionic Venus is revealed. Her suspicion, possessiveness, jealousy, and fear of betrayal. If Aphrodite thinks she has been slighted or that others are gossiping about her, she can be spiteful, vengeful, and nasty. She wanted to be fairest of them all, the winner of the beauty contest. If she feels she is losing, especially to a younger woman, Aphrodite in Scorpio can fight underhandedly.

Progressed Sun activating the aspects to Venus, or to the ruler of the Seventh House, can find Aphrodite accusing the partner of infidelity. It may not seem to matter to her, really, whether he *is* unfaithful; she superstitiously clings to her suspicions in a compulsive Scorpio manner. Finally, the worn out partner ceases to protest his or her innocence so loudly. This implies to Venus in Scorpio, "Aha! So I was right all along. You've been cheating on me; others know about it. I'm going to sulk, withdraw, or cost you a lot of money." Scorpio is ruled by Mars at the mundane level, which means that Venus in Scorpio may be setting herself up for a reversal, perhaps an accident, or a financial loss of her own.

I usually try to convince the Venus in Scorpio Libran, or Libra rising person, to read the final chapters of the *Ramayana*. In this chapter, after a long marriage, Lord Rama finds his wife a prisoner in the palace of Ravana, his enemy. It seems to him she's been caught in incriminating circumstances though her prison is nowhere near Ravana's chambers. He wonders "what others will think" of the queen's virtue. (Aphrodite is a social goddess. She cares about what others think.) He puts poor Sita, who has been a prisoner for 11 years, through an ordeal by fire. His suspicions proved groundless. Many gods come down to lecture Rama, among them three very powerful, royal gods whom he respects—Indra, Shiva, and Varuna. "She is pure; she is innocent," they cry out as the fire fails to singe her garments. "Oh well, I knew that all along of course. I just wanted this ordeal so other people would accept her too and respect us both," says repentent Rama.

At the end of the story outraged Sita tells him what an unworthy king he is—what a doubting, trivial approach he took toward her, his wife, his feeling side. It is a powerful account. If you have Venus in Scorpio, and if this strikes home for you, you might read it in *Hindu Myths* (Penguin Classics), if your bookstore does not have the entire *Ramayana* text. Betrayal or suspicion tends to become an important issue for those who have Seventh House planets, Libra Sun or Libra rising.

Finally, Aphrodite put Psyche, her future daughter-in-law, through ordeals—four impossible tasks to prove herself worthy to marry Eros, Aphrodite's beloved son. Possessiveness, jealousy, envy of others who are young and fair seems to be an Aphrodite issue. Here, one thinks of the statue of a goddess with the looking glass. Though Aphrodite Urania ages gracefully, because she is detached from the body, this is not always the case for mothers with Venus in Scorpio.

Attitudes, values, and relationships are transformed in Scorpio as love and money, inner serenity and outer confrontation (at work or at home) as Libra and Scorpio interact. Libra is no longer a spectator on the sidelines of life's battlefield or an Arjuna who rationalizes staying out of the fray, in this cycle. Mars, ruler of Scorpio, makes it difficult for Venus to keep the peace. Waves will be made around Libra whether he or she approves or not. The esoteric response is to preserve the inner calm through the turbulent waters of Scorpio—at home and at work. To react calmly inside, though assertively, taking a stand for principle, may be required in the outside world. Pluto brings its transforming energy and victory to many.

The Sagittarian progression, ruled by Jupiter, is a good deal more enjoyable. Like Libra, Jupiter ruled Sagittarius is a relaxed, benefic, positive sign. Progressing through it may seem like a rest for Libra. Travel, spiritual progress, good friends, publication, success in litigation, academic honors are among the advantages of Sagittarius. Librans who have remained in law throughout their professional lives may become judges in this cycle. Libra feels lucky in this cycle, especially if s/he has natal Sagittarian planets for the progressed Sun to conjunct, or a Fire trine for progressed Sun to activate, or grandchildren to enjoy. (Sagittarius, the Ninth House in the natural zodiac, is the grandchildren House.) If natal Jupiter is well-aspected, abundance may come to Libra from investments made during the Scorpio cycle, or from lecture travel, if his Ninth House is populated by well-aspected planets. This cycle may provide an opportunity to give well attended lectures about Libra's theories, as they have been tested and proven over the course of the lifetime. This is not as hard-pressed, or as driven, as the Mars ruled Scorpio cycle, and therefore much more enjoyable. Libra may do and achieve if he so chooses, or as he so-chooses; he is not pressured as much by the spouse or the outer environment as by his own inner nature—his own desires. Like Libra, Sagittarius knows how to have fun. These are some of the best years for Libra. For the hard working professional (Saturn exalted) Libra, these years may be crowned with honors, gratitude, appreciation.

Librans who live on into Capricorn feel more in control, more Cardinal, once again. In that sense, it is a period similar to their youth, when they had very definite opinions and wanted to structure the world according to their theories—except that now many a Libran has the wherewithal to do it in reality. (Capricorn Earth is the world of reality in the mundane sense.) Capricorn, however, is more concerned with final arrangements—wills that dispose of property and other assets, power of attorney, and administrative decisions. Esoteric Uranus Librans may live to see their humanitarian ideals made manifest in this cycle; the community that they have served may name a scholarship fund, a classroom, the wing of an art museum after Libra, or put his name in bronze on the law firm door. The exalted Saturn administrator may enjoy this period, as it brings not only honor, but power and pride in accomplishment. Libra who progresses into Capricorn may enjoy in common with natal Capricorn a delight in passing on to his heirs the values, both tangible and intangible, for which s/he has worked hard all his/her life. He or she may end his or her lifetime as a patriarch or matriarch.

Questionnaire

How does the Libran archetype express itself? Though this relates particularly to those with the Sun in Libra or Libra rising, anyone could apply this series of questions to the House which has Libra (or Libra intercepted) on the cusp. The answers to these questions will indicate how in touch the reader is with Venus/Aphrodite, the goddess of love and beauty; with his or her feeling-nature, his/her instinctual taste and confidence in his or her subjective value judgments.

1. My communication style is
   a. charming and light.
   b. charming when I want it to be.
   c. forceful and direct.

2. When co-workers are not getting along I
   a. always play the peacemaker.
   b. take the side of the underdog.
   c. ignore them completely.

3. Among my better qualities I would list
   a. diplomacy, kindness, confidence.
   b. kindness, tact, cheerfulness.
   c. assertiveness, control, ability to get the job done.

4. Among my negative qualities I would list
   a. indecisiveness, procrastination, vacillation.
   b. vanity, judgmentalism, laziness.
   c. directness, abruptness, harshness of speech.

5. When I am in an inharmonious environment I
   a. am uncomfortable and try to leave as soon as possible.
   b. am uncomfortable but get used to it soon enough.
   c. don't pay much attention to it.

6. My greatest fear is
   a. losing the one I love.
   b. losing my professional status.
   c. losing all my wealth.

7. If asked I would have to say that my taste in music, decoration, art is
   a. very good.
   b. good.
   c. poor.

8. When I come home from work I
   a. sit back (or lay back) and rest.
   b. have a short rest and then do what needs to be done around the house.
   c. start in on my home project right away.

9. The weakest part of my body is
   a. the kidneys, lower back.
   b. the head and neck.
   c. lungs, digestion.

10. When I feel wronged by others it's usually because
    a. they were unfair.
    b. they gave the promotion to somebody else.
    c. they hurt my feelings.

Those who scored five or more (a) answers are highly in touch with their instincts. Those who have scored five or more (b) answers may need to work more consciously with Venus/Aphrodite. Those who scored five or more (c) answers are out of touch with their mundane (instinctual) ruler. They may need to study the House Venus occupies or the House with Libra (Libra intercepted) on the cusp.

Where is the balance point between Libra and Aries? How does Libra integrate the independence, courage, and directness of Mars into the personality? Though this relates particularly to those with the Sun in Libra and Libra rising, all of us have Venus and Mars somewhere in the horoscope. Many of us have planets in Houses Seven and One. For all of us, the polarity from Libra to Aries involves the issue of reciprocity as well as the issue of independence.

1. I am most comfortable
   a. by myself with no ties that bind.
   b. in an equal partnership (each of us does our part).
   c. in a relationship/partnership.

2. When it comes to exercise I
   a. exercise often and hard. (It eases the tensions of the day).
   b. have a balanced program that I try to keep up.
   c. sit down until the urge to exercise goes away.

3. Cooperation is more important to me than competition
   a. 25% of the time.
   b. 50% of the time.
   c. 80% of the time.

4. When in an argument I find it works best to
   a. keep asserting myself until the other person gives up.
   b. make my stand clear and then find some common ground we
      can agree upon.
   c. find a way to compromise.

5. My co-workers probably consider me
   a. forceful and assertive.
   b. compromising but firm where it counts.
   c. compromising and easy-going.

Those who scored three or more (b) answers are doing a good job with personality integration on the Libra/Aries polarity. Those who scored three or more (c) answers may need to work more consciously with natal Mars in their horoscopes. Those who scored three or more (a) answers may be out of balance in the other direction. Study both Venus and Mars in the natal chart. Which is stronger by House position, or by location in its sign of rulership or exaltation? Is either planet in detriment, intercepted, or in its fall? Are there any major aspects between them? Aspects to the weaker planet will help point the way to its integration.

What does it mean to be an esoteric Libran? How does Libra

integrate cool, objective Uranus, its esoteric ruler, into the personality? Every Libran will have both Venus, the feeling planet, and Uranus, the thinking planet, somewhere in the horoscope. The well-integrated Uranus broadens Libra's perspective beyond self and partner to the community at large. Uranus brings detachment, originality, and an expansion of the Libran value system.

1. My ideal spouse is
   a. Divine Mother/Heavenly Father—love on its highest level.
   b. a spiritual woman/man (soul mate).
   c. a woman who is beautiful and caring/a man who is sensitive and handsome.

2. If my spouse were to leave me I would be
   a. saddened for a while but would let go and continue on with my life.
   b. broken-hearted.
   c. crushed, and it would be a long time before I would trust in a relationship again.

3. Service to humanity is
   a. more important than service to self and loved ones.
   b. important for those who are called.
   c. something that doesn't interest me.

4. I use my Libran scales to
   a. seek my own balance between lofty ideals and practical reality.
   b. balance myself and others.
   c. balance out those around me.

5. The purpose of life is
   a. to remake myself, to become able to reflect the Divine.
   b. to keep balance and equanimity through the changes of life.
   c. to change the world where I can and live with what I can't change.

Those who scored three or more (a) answers are in touch with the esoteric ruler. At the esoteric level Uranus' role is to expand

Aphrodite beyond her focus on personality to universal, divine love. Those who scored three or more (b) answers are working on themselves but need to continue. Those who scored three or more (c) answers really need consciously to integrate Uranus in their chart. Tuning in to Uranus allows Aphrodite to refocus her attention from her own hurt feelings and extend her warmth to those around her.

References

Alice Bailey, *Esoteric Astrology*, "Libra," Lucis Publishing Co., New York, 1976

Alice Bailey, *Labours of Hercules*, VII, "Libra," Lucis Publishing Co., New York, 1974

W. Norman Brown, "The Bases of the Hindu Act of Truth," *Review of Religion V*, 1940

Joseph Campbell, "Occidental Mythology," vol. III in *Masks of God*, Penguin Books, New York, 1982

Irene C. de Castillejo, *Knowing Woman*, G.P. Putnam's Sons, New York, 1973

Jean and Wallace Clift, *Symbols of Transformation in Dreams*, "Anima," "Animus," Crossroad Publishing Co., New York, 1984

Colette Dowling, *The Cinderella Complex*, Summit Books, New York, 1981

Franklin Edgerton, *Bhagavat Gita*, VI 16-17, Harvard University Press, Cambridge, n.d.

Hugh G. Evelyn-White, *Hesiod, The Homeric Hymns and Homerica*, Loeb Classical Library, Harvard University Press, Cambridge, n.d.

Marie Louise von Franz, *The Way of the Dream*, Windrose Films Ltd., P.O. Box 265 Station Q, Toronto

Paul Friedrich, *The Meaning of Aphrodite*, University of Chicago Press, Chicago, 1978

Liz Greene, *The Astrology of Fate*, "Libra," Samuel Weiser, York Beach, 1984

Jane Harrison, *Prolegomena to the Study of Greek Religion*, Cambridge University Press, London, 1903

H. Rider Haggard, *She*, Airmont, New York, 1967

James Hillman, *Anima*, Spring Publications Inc., Dallas, 1985

James Hillman, "The Feeling Function," in *Lectures on Jung's Typology*, Spring Publications Inc., Dallas, 1986

Hindu Myths, Wendy Donigen O'Flaherty transl., Penguin Classics, New York, 1975

Homer, *The Homeric Hymns*, "Hymn to Aphrodite," Charles Boer transl., Swallow Press, Chicago, 1970

Homer, *The Iliad*, E.V. Rieu transl., Penguin Classics, New York, 1982

Homer, *The Odyssey*, W.H.D. Rouse transl., New American Library Mentor, New York, 1937

Robert A. Johnson, *We: Understanding the Psychology of Romantic Love*, Harper and Row Publishers, San Francisco, 1983

C.G. Jung, *Memories, Dreams and Reflections*, Aniela Jaffe ed., Vintage Books/Random House, New York, 1965

C.G. Jung, *The Portable Jung*, "Marriage as a Psychological Relationship;" "The Feeling Function," Joseph Campbell ed., Penguin Books, New York, 1981

Emma Jung, *Animus and Anima: Two Essays*, Spring Publications, Dallas, 1981

Karl Kerenyi, *Goddesses of the Sun and Moon*, "The Golden One—Aphrodite," Murray Stein transl., Spring Publications, Irving, 1979

C. Kerenyi, *The Gods of the Greeks*, "The Great Goddess of Love," Thames and Hudson, London, 1951

Walter Otto, *The Homeric Gods: The Spiritual Significance of the Greek Religion*, Moses Hadas transl., Beacon Press, Boston, 1954

Pausanius, *Guide to Greece I and II*, "Aphrodite," Peter Levi transl., Penguin Books, New York, 1979

Jean Shinoda-Bolen, *Goddesses in Everywoman*, "Hera," "Aphrodite," Harper and Row, San Francisco, 1984

Murray Stein, "Hephaistos," in *Facing the Gods*, James Hillman ed., Spring Publications Inc., Irving, 1980

Valmiki, *Ramayana and the Mahabaratha*, Romesh C. Dutt transl., E.P. Dutton, New York, 1910

E.A. Wallis Budge, *Egyptian Book of the Dead*, Dover Publications Inc., New York, 1967

8 SCORPIO:
The Search for the Transformation

We now leave the balanced, orderly world of Cardinal Air (Libra) for the turbulent swampy waters of the underworld (Scorpio). Every year in Scorpio the Earth passes through its transition from autumn to winter and symbolically, we make our descent into Pluto's Underworld: the Eighth House of death, transformation, and rebirth. When we think of late October, Halloween comes to mind. The word *Halloween* is a contraction of All Hallowed's Eve and refers to the night before the Christian feast of All Saints' Day. On Halloween in medieval times, people went to church to pray for the souls of the deceased who were not included in the category "saints"—the inhabitants of the Christian Underworld. During the Middle Ages, many superstitious people believed that those who had not died in peace left the cemeteries on Halloween and wandered about restlessly. In modern times, we have left behind most medieval superstitions, but we still celebrate Halloween. We open our doors to children dressed as skeletons, ghosts, goblins, witches and other ghouls who threaten, "trick or treat!" How appropriate for Scorpio! The mood is nocturnal, lunar, and funerary.

The mundane rulers of Scorpio are Mars and Pluto. Pluto, appropriately, is Hades, Lord of the Greek Underworld. Pluto rules the unconscious depths of the Scorpio or Eighth House personality, with its residue of instinctual drives, emotional attachments, and compulsive-obsessive tendencies carried forward from past lives to the present. According to Alice Bailey it is Mars, not Pluto, that functions as esoteric ruler of Scorpio. This is understandable if we consider Mars as the principle that impels a person to take positive action—the

273

inner Kshatriya warrior who stands and fights against sulky moods; who sets fire to the old "seeds" of negative ideas and habit patterns instead of sitting by watching them sprout, or watering them again this lifetime.

Mars also makes sense as esoteric ruler if we consider it in its retrograde phase, as the introverted, sublimated instincts consciously focused upon a specific goal. Thus, in Scorpio, Mars is not the outspoken, direct planetary ruler we encountered in Aries (see Chapter 1), but a much subtler energy. His inward-turned fighting spirit is quite suited to performing the alchemical task of killing King Ego (often depicted by alchemists as a lion) in order to free the Soul (represented as the Elixir of Immortality or the Philosopher's Stone in its pure form—free of dirt and debris of the lower Eighth House—Scorpio nature). If we look upon the alchemical transformation as psychological growth or personality integration, then the sublimated Mars is quite suited to the task. An intense, focused Scorpio-will directed by Mars' dynamic thrust is capable of achieving a major breakthrough this lifetime. I have seen many examples of this movement from the darkness into the light in the lives of clients with planets in the Eighth House, Scorpio Sun sign and Scorpio rising.

In *Astrology: A Cosmic Science*, Isabel Hickey speaks in particular of Scorpio as a pivotal lifetime for the individual, during which he will either progress or retrogress, become angel or demon. My own client work has verified her point many times. There are many angels born with Scorpio rising, Sun, or Eighth House planets, but there are also some lower-consciousness types. It is important to look to the aspects natal Mars makes in order to determine the level or the battlefield on which the Kshatriya warrior is fighting. Is he dealing with his own inner shadow (the karmic residue at the depths of his own Eighth House) or is he fighting with others, on life's outer battlefield in a selfish, vindictive manner?

Because Mars and Venus meet on the axis from Scorpio to Taurus, the aspects between these planets will be important. On the mundane level the issues of the Eighth House (joint finances), such as battles fought over alimony or inheritance, will be quite revealing of the client's level of awareness. The lower-consciousness Scorpio/ Eighth House individual will use the vocabulary of sex and money (Mars and Venus/Houses Eight and Two) at the session. "My spouse betrayed me sexually, so I'm going to fight him for his money—every cent of it!" Or on the Taurus end of the spectrum, "My spouse betrayed me so I'm going to stay with him for financial security but withdraw sex and spend all his money!" This is "tit for tat" consciousness, equating love and money.

If Pluto is afflicted to Venus and/or Mars, then power and control, karmic obsession and inflexible will are also factors. If the Lunar Nodes (karmic points) are involved in the Mars/Venus/Pluto aspects, this pattern of behavior has been going on for centuries. One always hopes that attitudinally the couple will be able to transcend the karmic pattern this lifetime, will become conscious of the futility and the boring redundancy of returning to Earth with the partner on the same old battlefield. Still, if Pluto is involved by aspect, letting go of the habit is not easy even for those who have become conscious of the pattern.

To the ancients, Taurus and Scorpio were connected with light and darkness, respectively. The Pleiades constellation rose in Taurus and set in Scorpio. The Eye of the Bull meant enlightenment in Asia, and was also a positive symbol, a symbol of hope to the ancient Greeks, Mayans, and Egyptians. (See Chapter 2.) Plutarch, the Roman writer, in *De Iside et Osiride*, alludes to the funerary customs of the ancient Greeks during the autumnal setting of the Pleiades. In Scorpio the days became shorter and it seemed the sunlight waned as well, giving an underworld feeling to the season. Because of the connection between the rising Pleiades and light in Taurus in contrast to the setting Pleiades and the darkness of Scorpio six months later, the axis from Taurus to Scorpio became associated with integration of light and darkness, consciousness and the unconscious, rebirth and death. The Uroboros (the snake biting its own tail), which was the alchemical symbol of the transformation, referred not only to the mundane calendar year, but esoterically to life, death and rebirth as well. In Egypt, the old Apis bull would be sacrificed in autumn, but each spring a new Apis bull would be found in Taurus and the resurrection of Osiris would be celebrated anew.

Esoterically, Taurus represents the birth of value or meaning. However, before a higher level of awareness, a better value system, can be born in Taurus, Scorpio must first release or kill the old, outworn desires, attitudes, concepts, and in particular what James Hillman called those "hounding ideas." (See his essay on Ananke, or Necessity, the Greek Goddess who ruled the Underworld, the consort of Chronus the Time Serpent.) Ananke is not something outside ourselves but, though she has no form, no image, no altar, is within us archetypally just as Mars, Venus, Saturn, and the other gods and goddesses are within us. We feel her presence through the House with Scorpio on the cusp—the Underworld House, and the House where natal Pluto resides. We become aware of Ananke especially through Pluto's limits, his frustrating natal squares, the desires we seem driven toward yet cannot have.

The hounding ideas may have been around as voices in our minds for lifetimes if they are especially strong. The inner voices of our fixed Pluto squares precondition our happiness and seem to have the power to make us miserable. Even if we succeed in the other eleven Houses of the chart, but we fail in Pluto's House spiritually, psychologically, or financially, the unconscious keeps reminding us "your partner isn't perfect," or "you don't have a partner yet" (Pluto in the Seventh). "Yes, you're doing all right in life, but you can't be happy till you're free, till you're self-employed" (Pluto in the Tenth). Sometimes the House with Scorpio on the cusp, when transited, brings these inner voices to the surface of consciousness. We can make ourselves miserable dwelling on the area where Ananke/Pluto, the underworld deities, have set their frustrating limits. It does little good to blame God or Fate or others. We have cultivated our Fixed squares in past lives.

Since an entire generation has Pluto in Leo (1938-1956), the drive-to-individuation sign (see Chapter 5), this compounds the problem for them. Leo can represent the heroic ego at its most selfish. Pluto in Leo squared Mars, for instance—one mundane ruler of Scorpio squared the other—can be painful. But the square aspect lies inside oneself. It's like Hephestus' fiery forge, down in the underworld, burning steadily. The person wants his power to be free, to individuate, to achieve his desires in Mars' House, Pluto's House, the Aries and Scorpio Houses, and it seems really slow going to an impatient Mars-ruled Scorpio/Scorpio rising person. Strong emotions are hermetically sealed in the alchemical bottle, waiting for time (Chronos, Ananke's husband) to pass, to release the energy to heal. The progression of Mars out of orb to Pluto often effects this release.

What should one do in the interim, while waiting for wisdom? Scorpio/Scorpio rising individuals do not want to talk about it. The counselor has to respect this. Relatives may come to the astrologer and say, "My Scorpio should come and talk to you, or talk to a therapist, but I can't make him/her do it." In his essay on Ananke, Hillman refers to Sigmund Freud having called psychology "the talking cure." Astrology also involves talking, though more on the part of the astrologer. The Scorpio client may well prefer not to open up his private pain to outsiders or, skeptically, may not feel that this will do any good. One Scorpio woman with several Eighth House planets in square to the Sun told me that she had installed some mattresses against the walls of her gatehouse. She went there and yelled and screamed to release the energy, the frustration of her Pluto in Leo squares. Then she felt better, temporarily. She said, "I've tried talking to therapists. My intensity frightens them. Or they ask me how I feel. I know how I feel. I feel furious that I am powerless to have my life the way I want it." She added, "The Tibetans are right. Talking doesn't cook the rice. It doesn't change anything at all."

I saw her later, by chance, when the Mars/Pluto square had progressed out of orb to a full degree. She said, "I feel better, but it isn't anything I did; it's God's grace. I was able to let go of my own pain. I knew nobody could do it for me, and nobody could. I dismantled the screaming room as I haven't needed it in a long time." Her behavior reflected a genuine breakthrough in consciousness. King Ego, the Lion, yielded to the Self. Now she does things for others in the House her Pluto occupies. She has a great deal of compassion because of her own inner struggle. She continues to hold, as many Scorpios do, that talking doesn't help at all, that airing a problem feeds the fire, the emotion.

The Eastern tradition accords with their perspective. In the astrological tradition, time (Ananke's consort, Chronos the Wise Serpent) is also a healer. Sometimes, observing the faster-moving planet progress out of aspect to Pluto helps provide hope to the client. Sometimes, though, the aspect may take another ten years to progress out of orb and the client would not be inspired to hear this. Air is objective clarity, the developing of conscious awareness, but many people with Eighth House planets prefer to stay in the Unconscious and when relatives attempt to drag them to the astrologer or the therapist, it's important to remember this. People may want to do the inner alchemy at their own rate—to accept Ananke's limits.

What then of *fate*, of the inescapable givens of Goddess Ananke in Pluto's House or the House with Scorpio on the cusp? In the Gospels, there is a story that Christ told of a man possessed by a demon, a very Asiatic sounding story, because the Orient has many such parables about driving out desire. Christ said that a man was tormented by a

demon who possessed him, so an exorcist came and drove it out. But the man in question did not replace the empty spot left by the demon with anything else, and thus it was later able to return with seven demons stronger than itself. The hounding idea that Hillman mentioned, or the desire that is frustrated—"I must have him (or her) to be happy, yet he (or she) does not want me," or, "I must accomplish Y to be fulfilled, yet Y is the one thing I cannot do"—is the sort of Plutonic demon we mean here. Hercules, in the "Scorpio Quest," (*Labours of Hercules*, Labour 7), kept kneeling in the mud, strangling the hydra's heads, but a new one would grow just as fast as he killed an old one. He finally made the hydra conscious by lifting it from the mire (Eighth House, Underworld) into the clarity of daylight (consciousness), and it died immediately. Conscious understanding of the nature of the demon is the first step. (Some people identify it, label it, and then do no more with it in this incarnation. "Oh, that's a hydra's head or that's an obsession; that's a demon.") But, one has to stop feeding it, nurturing it, watering it, brooding over it and dwelling upon it. Then, as Christ said, one has to replace it with something positive. Taurean openness to God's grace is an important part of the process of releasing and eliminating the negative compulsion or hounding idea.

As an archetype, Taurus is warm, open, trusting, honest and sometimes gullible. Scorpio, its polarity, is withdrawn, secretive, and at its worst is negative or cynical, devious, suspicious and manipulative. Esoterically, this has meant that through Taurus we are hopeful and through Scorpio we face our fears, including our fear of death, as the Buddha faced his fears under his Bodhi Tree, when the serpent came and coiled itself around him seven times. Taurus represents attachment to form and Scorpio's work is to transform, to change and refine the form. Taurus is structured Earth and Scorpio is amorphous, murky Water. Yet, the two signs have in common the Fixed mode, which is resourceful, persevering, stubborn, magnetic and powerful. Both signs are industrious, striving, and productive. At the esoteric level, both refer to the struggle for liberation or immortality, a powerful will to transcend, to conquer fears and doubts and reach the goal. Both signs have the inner strength, the stamina and willpower to become whole, to face the darkness and discover the Self.

Esoterically, both are on the values axis in astrology (Houses Two to Eight); both seek what is real, what is of genuine quality. As "deep Water," Scorpio has an intensity and an earnestness to it that causes many lighthearted Air signs to marvel. Perhaps this Scorpionic earnestness derives from an unconscious awareness that this is a pivotal lifetime on Earth. Beginning with childhood much past-life karma will be resolved, either consciously or unconsciously. Nothing is frivolous; everything is important to Scorpio. A lifetime with Sun, Moon, or Ascendant in Scorpio can be much like cleaning out the Augean Stables of the accumulated debris of incarnations. Scorpio faces the challenge of habits entrenched for lifetimes which are difficult to transform. This is particularly true if there are many planets in the other Fixed signs. Through the Fixed squares and oppositions, attachments to people, ideas, principles, or to one's work, must be confronted. If, as Hindus believe, we choose our time of birth freely, then Scorpios are brave souls. Mars gives them a good deal of courage, as well as a passionate nature.

One other general point should be made about Scorpio before turning to specific symbols, and that is the psychic nature of the Eighth House and the Scorpio archetype. If we are alerted to that now, we can more easily discern the depth of the Scorpio myths later. Those born with Scorpio planets, or planets in the Eighth House, have an uncanny instinctual awareness—the gift of the psychic hunch. Whether it manifests through dreams, through imaginative work, or even business intuition, there is power behind an Eighth House planet, a Scorpio planet or Ascendant—power to attune to the underworld. Information slips through to conscious awareness from the unconscious in an almost uncanny way. A Scorpio boyfriend once remarked to a client out of the blue, "Where were you yesterday morning at 10:00 a.m.? I called you for some reason, and when you didn't answer the phone, I just knew you were at breakfast with an old lover." She was. And never before in her memory had this friend called at 10 a.m. on a weekday, nor had the old lover ever before been in California. A businessman with several planets in dry (unimaginative) Earth once remarked at a party, "Well, I would never go to an astrologer. That would seem weird. But something odd goes on in my business. I'm a stockbroker, and I get all the news on the market and analyze it intellectually, and then I just let it sit in the back of my mind overnight. And the next day, even if the logical thing would be *not* to buy the stock, based on the facts, I somehow 'know' it's a good one and I go ahead and act on the hunch. And I persuade others to do so. If I know, then I know, and that's that. I wish this worked in my love life—this uncanny power to tell the good from the bad—but it only seems to work in my investment business. Where do you think that comes from?" I thought it came from the location of Earth sign planets in his Eighth House, and sure enough, later when he was curious enough for his wife to order the horoscope, that was it. He was a "stock market prophet," though it would sound weird to him to put it that way.

Premonitional dreams, also, come through the psychic energy of the watery Eighth House. One is in touch with the unconscious, without even trying to be. That natural attunement to the dark side has its pros and cons; many people with Eighth House planets feel confusion about what to do with the energy and many are apprehensive. "If I try that, is it bad karma? Will something else in my life die, like a relationship, if I'm successful with this new use of my Eighth House planets, of my Scorpio energy?" This is the Taurus/Scorpio cycle—an old chapter of life sometimes ends so that a new one may begin. It is almost as if people within the Scorpio/Eighth House archetype experience what the fertility cultists in ancient times believed—"Something (in me) must die so that something else can be born." A Scorpio who is conscious of the inner cycles of growth and transformation may be protective of his new ideas as he crosses a psychological threshold; he may choose not to communicate his inner feelings at all. He'll discuss the weather with us, and that's about it. This can be frustrating for his marriage partner.

The symbols for Scorpio are quite diverse. Each of the Fixed signs is symbolized by a powerful creature. The Taurus bull represents physical stamina, the Leo lion willpower or emotional stamina, and the Scorpio symbols psychic energy or power. Scorpio is more subtle energy. If we think, for instance, of the serpent, a common Scorpio symbol, we think of Genesis II:1, in which ". . . the serpent was more subtle than any beast of the field. . . " Here, we have two possible interpretations. Subtle can mean devious or cunning, like the serpent in Genesis, or subtle can also mean something rarified, or elusive, like the *kundalini* current in the astral spine—subtle power, the yogis call it, which is also represented as a coiled serpent (*kundala*) in the coccyx area. Thus, any myth with a snake or serpent in it could have a devious meaning to it—as in the usual interpretation of the Genesis Garden of Eden myth, where the devious snake is cursed in the end and must crawl on his belly and eat dust forever after. Or, we can be tipped off by the presence of a snake that the myth is very subtle in the sense of deep, that the myth will be about a higher Scorpio experience—psychological transformation, enlightenment or immortality. In the Clifts' book on dream symbols, for instance, to be bitten by a snake often symbolizes becoming conscious. (See *Symbols of Transformation in Dreams*, Chapter 12.)

Artistic representations of spiritual initiations often have serpents standing by as guardians. The Demeter frieze at Eleusis near Athens is one example, but all over the world groves or sanctuaries were associated with the fertility goddesses and were guarded by the snake consort. The Cretan High Bronze Age statue of the fertility goddess holding out her arms with a snake in each is an example. Crete was a center of ritual initiation. (See Taurus.) India, Persia and mainland Greece also associated bulls, snakes, and the goddess with cult initiations. The python was a snake sacred to Apollo's oracle at Delphi. If the python came at once to receive its food from the maiden, then the omen was good; if the python did not appear immediately, it was bad. The serpent was the prophecy vehicle, the guardian, or the consort of the Mother and a powerful aid to Her in the Bronze Age, but the Shakti, or magical power, was the maiden's or mother's.

Campbell informs us that the symbolism shifted in the late Bronze Age and early Iron Age from the Goddess and Mother Right to the male Sky Gods and the patriarchy. No longer did the Goddess herself have the Shakti; no longer was she the lead character in the initiation stories. In the Age of Heroes, phallic symbolism prevailed. In at least one story about death, resurrection and immortality, a serpent (in the form of Zeus/Meilichios) became the central figure. Campbell tells us that Zeus took upon himself the shape of a serpent and sought out the maiden, Persephone, in her Cretan cave. One day, Demeter went away and left her daughter there in the care of two serpent guardians to work on her wool tapestry of the universe. Zeus slithered in, united with Persephone and left. The result of their union was the immortal Dionysius, Lord of the Mystery Cult, who was born in a humble cave, killed, and resurrected. (*Occidental Mythology*, page 18, figure 8.) We have here a myth about a serpent including death, resurrection and immortality—a myth replete with symbolism for Scorpio and the Eighth House.

This positive myth about the serpent power behind the birth of the great Dionysius is interesting, according to Joseph Campbell, because it is such an exception in Western tradition, where serpents were at best humble or lowly guardians. It was unusual to see All-Highest Zeus take on the lowly form of a snake. Yet, in the mystical traditions of both East and West, the serpent has been viewed as a symbol of spiritual transformation and psychic attainment. It could slough off its skin and assume a new form, just as our immortal souls would do after the body's death. (See T.H. White, *Book of Beasts*, p. 187.) The snake thus symbolizes Scorpio power at both the lower and higher levels. Some Scorpio rising or Scorpio Sun sign people might be at the level of the snake in the Garden of Eden—deceitful and manipulative, while others might use the power to transform themselves, as Zeus did, in order to give birth to the Divine (Dionysius).

It's true though that negative snake symbolism was more common in the West. The Greek word for any large serpent was *draconta*, a category inlcuding pythons, hydras, anacondas, the Gorgon, the Medusa, and any dragons from whose jaws heroes rescued maidens. Flying lizards that killed with their tails and breathed fire, "making the air around them ardent," were also included among draconta. (T.H. White, page 165.) Heroes projected their fear of the Dark Mother and her mysterious nocturnal powers over life and death upon these dragon-like or many-headed beasts.

Wherever the patriarchy conquered in the late Bronze or early Iron Age, according to Campbell, the Earth Mother assumed the shape of a hideous Dragon or Monster in the eyes of sky gods and human heroes.

The hero, conscious of his free will and personal responsibility for his actions, challenged a form which appeared to him to be the evil darkness left over from a more primitive age—the feminine, the magical unknown, the contents of the unconscious. The imagination and the instincts became manifest in his personal Medusa, Gorgon, Hydra, or in the case of All-Highest Zeus, his Typhon. In other words, the Hero challenged the contents of the Eighth House—death, the underworld, and with it, his Feminine side. In certain myths, if he saved the Maiden, his own personality could be reborn or redeemed.

The battle of Zeus and Typhon as presented in *Occidental Mythology* (pages 22-25) should be quite interesting to anyone who has ever asked him/herself, "How do I face my fears, especially the fear of my own mortality? How do I confront my lower nature in order to become transformed, liberated, freed from all this darkness within me? Do I try to deny it? Do I try to kill it altogether, like Zeus did

Typhon?"

Typhon, we are told, was the youngest son of Mother Earth (Ga). He could still be the world ruler had Zeus not challenged him on behalf of the Olympian Sky Gods, the Greeks tell us. Typhon was an enormous Titan, half man and half snake. He stood so tall that his head "knocked against the stars." He was so broad that "he could stretch his arms from sunrise to sunset." From his shoulders grew a hundred serpent heads, all flashing fiery tongues. White fire flashed from his many eyes. Voices from within him sent out vibrational sounds the gods could understand, but also powerful lion roars, bulls' bellows, and dog bayings so loud that the mountains echoed.

The earth shook beneath Zeus' feet on the mountaintop as he cast his lightning bolt at Typhon. The sky lit up over the waters with the Titan's fiery breath and with the flames his eyes shot at Zeus:

> The ocean boiled, towering waves beat upon . . . the coast; the ground quaked; Hades, Lord of the Dead, trembled; and even Zeus himself for a time was unstrung. But when he had summoned again his strength, gripping his terrific weapon, the great hero sprang from his mountain and, hurling the bolt, set fire to all those flashing, bellowing, baying, hissing heads. The monster crashed to earth, and the Earth Goddess Gaea groaned beneath her child. Flames went out from him so hot that much of the Earth dissolved, like iron in . . . the flaming forge . . . of Haephestus.

The body was consigned to Tartarus by Zeus and the Olympian gods replaced the Titans.

Typhon's imagery is that of Mars' heat and fire, watery prophecy (the eyes), power (size, strength, and the voices of bull and lion), and the serpent, the Great Mother's son. Zeus had quite a shadow in the Titan. There was a good deal of positive as well as negative energy in Zeus' unconscious. What makes it an Eighth House experience, similar to what people see in nightmares or what they perceive when they meditate and recognize the darkness within themselves, is that the experience is temporarily unsettling. "Zeus himself, for a time, was unstrung," and the ocean boiled. A boiling ocean is a marvelous Scorpio image. Scorpio has been called "boiling Water" in contrast to Cancer and Pisces, the other, milder Water signs.

Once again one thinks of the Biblical phrase appropriate to Mars ruled Aries—"and the violent bear (the kingdom) away"—but this time Mars ruled Scorpio is fighting his shadow in an inner battle, whereas Aries' confrontations usually take place in the outer world. Here Zeus fires his light into the darkness as an actual lightning bolt.

Zeus' patriarchal approach to the unconscious was, "kill it and toss it into Tartarus and let Logos take the throne." Let the conscious, waking state mind rule! Zeus' light was more than his inner darkness (the Titan) could bear, and the Feminine, Ga, the Earth Mother, groaned. Turning against the gifts of the Feminine, rather than assimilating some of them, such as Prophecy—challenging the fighting instinct of the Earth Mother's child, is probably not our wisest course. The Titans can still fight back from Tartarus. The unconscious instincts, if repressed, will rebel. They are very subtle, in the case of Scorpio, and very powerful. It is better to give them their due, to direct them into a positive channel, than to deny them altogether.

We won't go into all the scorpion symbolism. If you are interested in the use of scorpions in Egypt, you can read "The Sorrows of Isis" in *Egyptian Magic* by E.A. Wallis-Budge, or his commentary on *The Egyptian Book of the Dead*. In the Gilgamesh epic, as well as in the Isis story, scorpions,like serpents, are ambiguous symbols. Some appear as helpful guardians of the Goddess; yet, a scorpion stung Isis' child, Horus the Avenger. He died and she resurrected him with magic. (See Chapter 6.) Yet, the Egyptians revered the Ibex because it killed scorpions in the Delta. In Egypt the scorpion, like the serpent, had both positive and negative connotations.

Small creatures like scorpions and vipers are often the most dangerous, possibly because men and larger animals are unable to see them and might step on them accidentally. Because of their poison, it is essential to watch for them when walking barefoot along a jungle path at twilight. Yet, even the poisonous side of the Eighth House and the eighth sign of the zodiac has a positive feature. The krait is the smallest viper in South India; it is about as long as the index finger, yet it is India's most deadly snake. Its venom can paralyze the central nervous system almost as soon as it strikes. Yet krait venom, when distilled, is also a proven cure for certain diseases of the nervous system. Once again, a Scorpio symbol is associated with both death and healing.

The Eagle is said to be a higher symbol for Scorpio than the serpent and to represent the more highly evolved souls born at that time of year. That is, a Mafioso who dies wanting revenge on an enemy (a lower-evolved type) would be a Scorpio at the snake level; but a higher-quality soul who could forget, or at least forgive, and work at forgetting what the enemy did to him, would be at the Eagle level. The second person does not crawl on his belly and eat dust. He is not intentionally cruel, nasty or criminal. He is still a bird of prey, though.

The Eagle is as important in heraldry as the lion and the bull; many families chose it for a crest emblem. It flies higher than any other bird so it is said to be the most powerful creature in its domain, the air. It also flies the fastest. When the ancients said, "The Eagle flies closest to the Sun," or "The Eagle looks upon the face of Apollo, the Sun God," they may have meant that Scorpio has a strong chance of reaching illumination (the Sun). It has a very wide perspective on the Earth from its vantage point, its eyrie. The Eagle is also the enemy of the snake, the instincts, the dark or shadowy side. It lifts the snake out of the murky water and in some myths, destroys it. In one Indian legend, Krishna converted a *naga* (water snake); he first killed it, then he danced upon it and resurrected it. In a version of this myth, Krishna even left his footprint on one of its five heads so that Garuda, Vishnu's snake-killing Eagle, would see Krishna's mark and leave it alone in the water. (J.P. Vogel, *Indian Serpent Lore*, page 89.) This legend of Krishna and the serpent king always appealed to me because the serpent had five heads and five is the number of creativity. Krishna did not kill the creativity; he just drained the venom, or transformed the snake's attitude, and let it live. It's better to cooperate with the dark or unconscious creativity that lies beneath the surface of the water than to kill or repress it completely.

The Garuda-bird is pictured in the *Mahabaratha* killing serpents, for those of you interested in art. The Eagle and the Snake appear together on the Mexican flag; they are a popular theme. When the serpent is out of the water and in the air (the Eagle's element) he can be killed or tamed. This is similar to riding the bull or the lion in Chapters 2 and 5. Repressing the serpent, tossing him down into Tartarus, seems to make him more toxic.

Repressing the feelings and instincts rather than communicating about them is a problem many Scorpio clients seem to face at the Eagle level of evolution. They are aware that the Shadow is there, and they also have the willpower to repress it. Some also fear friends and associates might not be very understanding if they discovered the depth or the negative contents of the Scorpio unconscious. People with several Eighth House planets often feel the same way. Saturn's transits through Scorpio have brought out emotional toxins in the form of physical symptoms involving the bowels, especially.

Such diseases as cancer of the colon, constipation and, in older clients with the square to Leo planets, heart and circulatory problems have appeared. Communication, or symbolically, Air, is a way to release some of the energy and lift the serpent out of the murky waters. Scorpio/Scorpio rising, who has natal planets in Air, may find it helpful to discuss the problem with a loved one or an objective counselor. Sometimes, psychological counseling, working with the emotions, will even help stop the spread of a disease which otherwise will eventually have to be cut out through the surgical meaning of Scorpio and the Eighth House.

In *Anatomy of the Psyche*, Edinger discusses the alchemical process called *sublimatio*, which has nothing to do with the Freudian definition of sublimation, but rather is the reverse. In alchemy the vessel was cool on top but hot on the bottom. As the purified elements rose from the heat on the bottom, they adhered to the top. In this way, sublimation led to objective perspective, and because it involved a process of ascending, it brought man closer to eternity. Discussing one's pain often takes the lead (the Saturn element) out of it and the person's heavy depression abates. Air is the mercurial quicksilver-like element in alchemy. I find that it has to be a serious minded friend, astrologer or therapist for Scorpio/Scorpio rising, or the Eighth House client. They do not want to be cheered up or jollied out of the depths by a Pollyanna entertainer type. Edinger mentions that elevator dreams, wherein a person ascends, are *sublimatio* dreams. Those in which the elevator descends, however, are *coagulatio*; they bring him down to earth and ground him after a desire achieved, a success in the outer world, a vision or inner satisfaction, has inflated the ego. *Sublimatio*, then, is part of the process of releasing energy from the Eighth House, akin to the Eagle lifting the serpent from the murky waters.

There is also a type of bird related to the Eagle that we call the Vulture. If an archetypal Scorpio has a negative attitude most of the time, if he is constantly a suspicious type, he is at the Vulture level. T.H. White tells us that the Vulture, like the Eagle, flies high over the Earth and has a good view; but rather than enjoy the beauty of what he sees below, he looks only for carrion, for decaying corpses in a world where life is thriving. Most of us have known participants in this archetype who see death and destruction everywhere and seem to be always looking for the negative. No matter how wonderful, how exciting the news you tell them, they consistently respond with something dreary that depresses you. This cynical type of Scorpio is even more aware of others' flaws than Virgo; he is a true misanthrope.

Beginning astrology students sometimes ask, "What do you do if a very low consciousness Scorpio Sun sign type, a real Snake, turns up for a reading?" The answer is, "I usually manage to screen out these types over the phone, and I don't have to see them." As soon as you have the birth date over the phone you know the Sun sign. You can sound the person out about the focus of the session. If he or she says, "I want to find a time to sue for divorce when I can really take my spouse for every penny," or "I sneaked into the personnel office and found the data in my worst enemy's file. Can you provide some days for me that will be really terrible for him?" Or "I've been into black magic for awhile and thought I'd see what I could do with astrology, so I want to start by having my own chart done. . . " These people can all be screened out.

A few manipulative people with Scorpio rising or Eighth House planets get through the filter and appear. I stick pretty much to these ground rules. You, of course, will find others that work for you:

1. As an Earth sign, I attempt to dry out their Eighth House Water, to place them on dry land, the land of reality. This is similar to the alchemical process called *coagulatio*, when the sediment filters itself out of the solution—after the unconscious dissolving of the personality during *solutio*. I try to be concrete, pragmatic, factual, practical, grounded. My favorite line is, "As an Earth sign, I want you to leave here having your money's worth. We don't really need to go off on these tangents with other people's horoscopes you've brought along (the people they are trying to manipulate).

2. They hear voices. They have seen visions of World War III or earthquakes in China. "You may have picked up something on the astral plane that will happen in the distant future, but today we should talk about your purpose in coming here. Mars is going through your Third House; is your car in good repair? Saturn is transiting through your Sixth; are you getting enough calcium? Nutritious food?" It's not a good idea to swim in their Eighth House with them.

3. If they tell you your last five lifetimes as a favor to you, will you then do them a favor and point out just a few weak spots, vulnerable areas, in the chart of someone else they happen to have with them? "No. This is your reading. I am not looking for a regressionist today. That other person will have to make his own appointment. Do you have questions about your chart?"

4. They've learned hypnosis quickly, and they enjoy massage because there's such power in their hands. In rebirthing/regressing/massaging they've noticed that afterward the person they have treated leaves energized, but they are wiped out. Explain the law of karma: As ye sow, so shall ye reap. To steal others' energy may well result in returning to Earth in a weakened body oneself.

5. Try to lift the snake out of the murky waters. Introduce the Air element—objective clarity, perspective. Or try to put him in touch with his sense of humor if he takes his magnetism/power too seriously. Many people with Eighth House planets are "stuck" in an ego-position, where they can no longer laugh at themselves. They are all-powerful saviors carrying those around them. Appeal to the Air planets in the chart. "What have you read lately that was positive? Inspirational?" If there is an Air void I usually do not bother with this approach; they have their own peculiar sense of humor.

6. Look at the social planets (Venus and Jupiter). Is this a misanthropic Snake? Has he any friends? Does he feel alienated?

7. Ask about the body, the elimination system, constipation.

8. Look at the spiritual planets (Jupiter/Neptune). Is he open to meditation? To burning the seeds of his karma with his concentration (which is usually quite good) before they sprout and cause him to become more locked in by Ananke next lifetime? If he's receptive (has mutability at all prominent), recommending your spiritual center/temple/church may be worth a try.

In Scorpio, the body is usually the alchemical laboratory. While the Aquarian or the Virgo may fight a mental battle, as Alice Bailey points out in *Esoteric Astrology*, Scorpio carries the struggle into the physical form—the depths of the instincts, emotions, passionate drives. This seems to dispose many Scorpio/Scorpio rising personalities to study or to practice psychology, which is concerned with the depths as well as the heights of human experience. To my Scorpio/Scorpio rising clientele, Osiris' ladder to the underworld is more interesting than the mystic's ladder to the stars, to joy, bliss, and other such frivolous experiences. In the view of many Scorpios there is little passion at the heights. This tends to be true for religious, as well as psychologically oriented Scorpios. They would rather speak of the final ultimate issues—death, resurrection, judgment, and the afterlife, than lesser topics. Like the lower Scorpio, the esoteric Scorpio has a strong will, a passionate nature, desires and ambitions. S/he is not simply concerned about sex, money, comfort but with the more subtle tests—power, suspicion, betrayal, mental cruelty, and pride.

The ego is already well formed in a Scorpio story, such as the Sumerian Gilgamesh myth. It no longer needs to prove itself as in the cases of the earlier, heroic signs discussed in the first six chapters of this book. Scorpio knows who s/he is and sees to the depths of his/her own nature, as Gilgamesh saw his instinctual side, his twin, Enkidu the beast, who was his equal in strength. They wrestled each other to a stalemate, then embraced and became friends. Enkidu, however, being mortal, died. Gilgamesh was then inconsolable. He focused on the Quest for Immortality, the Quest for Soul, a more serious, deeper quest than the quests for success in the outer world.

To resurrect Enkidu, Gilgamesh entered upon a dark, dangerous journey into the polluted waters of the Unconscious. When he reached his destination, the caretaker of the herb of immortality assigned him a task—to stay awake seven nights; but he failed this test. The caretaker's merciful wife awoke him on the last day or he would have been a total failure, rather than a partial success. She directed him toward the herb. He dived very deep and found it, though his lungs nearly gave out in the effort. He then set it down while he rested. A water snake was attracted to its pungent aroma and ate it. He did not have the strength to dive again. Yet, he had found it, had demonstrated that it existed. Also, Gilgamesh was not selfish; he did not eat it, but planned to keep it for Enkidu and other mortals. He had found his Soul, his immortality, but not for selfish reasons.

He had failed to stay awake, to be conscious; he was not ready to keep the herb. In Chapter 11, Aquarius, the story of Perceval's quest for immortality is recounted. He too failed the first time. I think these two stories of partial success are important for the esoteric Scorpio who may be discouraged with himself—the Scorpio with a strong

Saturn or many planets in Earth whose ambitions are not easy to accomplish—the Scorpio who like Gilgamesh feels driven, compelled. If he is not fully conscious of the scope of the task, if he is not ready in the sense of awake and alert, he may meet with partial failure. His will is strong enough to win a victory in this lifetime if his motives are unselfish and if the requisite faith is there. This refers not simply to his faith in himself or his pride in his own will to overcome. Many Pluto ruled Scorpios have infinite faith in themselves, yet have little faith in the Divine, and are alienated from their fellow man. Or as in the case of a Scorpio woman now deceased, they are suspicious, hostile, resentful and bitter toward those around them. This sense of separateness from humanity often contains an element of selfishness that prevents progress on the spiritual path.

The woman to whom I refer denied to herself that there was any problem with her health for a long time. Eventually, she sought the help of physicians (getting second and third opinions). They told her that the cancer had spread to the bones and it was too late to help her. She was suspicious of them and furious. "These doctors are incompetent and expensive. I have spent my entire inheritance on them. I am now in such excruciating pain that I can barely drag myself to the University three days a week to teach my class." She tried osteopaths, chiropractors and healers but told me, "before I spent money on these people I knew, of course, there was a good chance they were all charlatans and quacks."

"It sounds as if you haven't much faith in anyone outside yourself," I said.

"It has been my experience that many people are untrustworthy," she said. "Then, too, I have found that the only person I can rely on is myself. It's always been that way. I've been a loner since my divorce at a very young age. Relating to others is not my forte."

I had mentioned on the phone that astrology might not be able to shed much light on her situation at this advanced stage in the disease, but I would certainly be willing to see what, if anything, I could do. What I saw was a very strong, driven Saturn, hostility to family (including the two children of her brief marriage, raised by their father) and frustrated professional ambition. Her instincts and emotions seemed to be digging in like ingrown fingernails.

At the time I met her there had been a series of clients who were relocating, so I had been working with Astro*Carto*Graphy®* tech-

---

* Jim Lewis' Astro*Carto*Graphy workshop, February 7–9, 1986, Laguna Beach, CA

niques. I wondered if a healer would turn up in some location on her progressed Astro∗Carto∗Graphy® map, so I spent some time with it before she arrived. It was clear, however, that she no longer had the faith or the openness to trust physicians. Still, where there's life there's hope. Perhaps there would be a city where she could live long enough to work out some of her emotional problems.

When she arrived, she began asking about good dates to win her lawsuit with her employer, the University, and to pass the real estate exam. "I really hate the department chairman," she exploded. "While I was in the hopsital he hired a young woman to teach part-time, instead of using that money for me. Her salary was to have been my step raise money. I could have retired at a higher rank with more money in my disability pension. He felt it was necessary to have her teach my course while I was hospitalized, and I can understand that—temporarily—but I'm back now and he can let her go. Walking into the building is draining. He hates me because of the lawsuit. *She* hates me because I went after her job. I feel their hostility in the halls, but I can't afford to quit."

"Well," I said, "the cost of living would be a good deal less in one of these other states. California is an expensive place to live. Maybe if we looked at the Cyclo∗Carto∗Graphy® map you could find a place to live where life would be less hectic for you. It sounds as if you are driving to work in excruciating pain, to a building where you feel angry vibrations."

"No. I am used to California. I couldn't live someplace cold. I'm not accustomed to winter anymore. I just need some dates to pass this real estate exam. I could drag myself around a few days a week and sell property; I am very persuasive. I know I can do this. But I am in such pain that it's difficult to remember the paragraph I just finished reading. Still, it helps to have these concrete facts to memorize for the exam. It takes my mind off the body. I know I need this job to supplement disability retirement. Retiring at this present rank won't be sufficient; I have given all my savings to these incompetent doctors."

"I wasn't going to suggest anyplace cold to live," I told her. (The map had come out strongly in southern latitudes.)

When I suggested three cities, she looked at me warily. "That's uncanny! Did my friend who referred me to you, tell you where my sister and my sons are living? I've always been a loner. My sons feel I abandoned them when they were small, but there was little else I could have done. As a young woman, noisy children drove me crazy. . . ."

She felt a good deal of resistance to seeing her family again. I often wondered about her after the reading. Would she live long enough to take the real estate exam in January? Then, the Christmas card I sent her was forwarded to Texas and returned to me stamped "deceased" by the post office. At least she had gone to see her son and perhaps had released some of the pent-up emotions connected to her past.

Shortly after her card was returned, I read about fate or Necessity (Ananke) in Hillman's article (mentioned above). According to Hillman, Ananke is sometimes connected with the marrow of the bones. This woman had a strong Saturn (bones) as well as a strong Scorpio will. The faith planets (Neptune and Jupiter) were weak in the chart. A high percentage of Earth and Water planets contributed to her tendency to repress the emotions and to wait too long to get help, denying that there was a problem which her will alone could not handle. I also thought of the subtle tests of pride, ambition, and will to control connected with the more conscious Scorpio personality in Bailey's *Esoteric Astrology*. Her Mars was a true warrior; it would fight the outside world to the end and make its own separate way in life. But the inner battles remained unresolved and the body suffered at the very depths—the marrow of the bones. Though her field was depth psychology and she was as intent, serious, and earnest as a human being could be, she was also uncompromising. Peace of mind seemed less important than setting the limits. "I won't live in a certain climate," "I won't give in on the lawsuit. These people should be punished for the way they behaved toward me, if nothing else." In her case, I did not try to relate to her through my own Earth element as I would the client with an Eighth House stellium in Scorpio (double watery influence) for she was already overly dry and pragmatic herself. I attempted to work with the faith and trust planets in the chart, though they were weakly aspected. I felt a deep sadness at her death, but I also felt that, like Gilgamesh and Perceval, this life was a partial success. She had made a great effort and she would do much better next time.

Alice Bailey makes the point that the Scorpio/Scorpio rising personality must face the depths as well as scale the heights. Having seen the depths, Scorpio must decide how to proceed. Bailey calls the residue of past life tendencies at the roots of the personality the Dweller on the Threshold (of consciousness). The soul, she terms the Angel. The Angel meets the Dweller and they battle. (This is reminiscent of Gilgamesh's struggle with Enkidu, or in the Old Testament, Jacob's struggle with the stranger.) If the soul (the Angel) comes forward to triumph over suspicion, hostility, resentment, and other pent-up emotions, great progress will be made this lifetime and Scorpio is able to share the result of his own struggle, his discovery of the herb of immortality (the Soul) with others. Many of my Scorpio clients in the fields of psychology and religion endeavor to do this—share with others the fruits of their own life-experience or transformation. They become spiritual or psychological shamans, or shamans who heal others physically.

Shamanism is intrinsic to the Scorpio archetype. I think it's interesting that at this point in time so many of my clients with Scorpio rising/Scorpio Sun/ Scorpio Midheavens are becoming interested in shamanism and that Jungian analysts are approaching shamanism through the dreams of their clients. Dreams contain elements of this ancient (or archaic as Mircea Eliade called it) healing science—ladders, death and rebirth, guardian spirits. The right to die with dignity, for those who cannot be healed, has been defended by many of the great shaman healers from Mother Theresa of Calcutta to Elizabeth Kubler Ross, who has a Scorpio Midheaven and powerful Eighth House planets. There is a good deal of interest in the Books of the Dead, Tibetan and Egyptian, with their techniques of chanting mantras into the ears of the dying, to carry them forward into the next life. The quality of death is emphasized by C.G. Jung in "Stages of Life," (*Portable Jung*) as he believes that the entire last half of the lifetime is a preparation for death. The Eastern religions attach particular importance to the last few moments of life. The individual should be fully conscious, for if he does not achieve liberation this lifetime then these moments determine his next birth. The Guru, or the Lama guide, or the spirits of the ancestors (in the American Indian religions) attend the dying individual as his soul journeys to the next world.

Because there is currently such interest in shamanism, especially on the part of those whose physical illnesses lie beyond the scope of medical science's present knowledge, it seems important to clarify some points about it. The shaman is not just any medicine man or woman. Most tribes have others who perform more facile cures with herbs. The shaman is a "specialist in the soul" (Mircea Eliade's phrase). S/he has definite techniques, a type of apprenticeship (through dreams, wherein s/he may be taught by the ancestors, or through experiences, which are severely tested by the tribe's current shaman, whom s/he may someday replace) and visions powerful enough to convince the tribe. S/he can enter his/her trance at will. As a soul specialist who has experienced his or her own immortality, s/he can accompany the souls of the dying (those beyond cure) because s/he knows quite well the path they are to take and the dangers on their journey. His or her soul soars like an eagle (for that reason eagle feathers are the symbol of many shamans). It has powers beyond the world of opposites. Physically shamans can withstand extreme heat or cold, or leap great distances, or demonstrate clairvoyance or dance for hours without signs of fatigue, even when in their sixties.

Many shamans have been ill, or close to death, and have had dreams resembling those Jungian analysts describe from their patient records. The body decays to the skeleton, which is then boiled and purified, or washed, cleaned and reassembled. The feverish person (or dreamer undergoing a psychological change) is thus reduced to prima materia (the bare bones) while his or her soul looks on, unharmed. The spirits of the ancestors teach the shaman candidate how to heal the sick.

In one dream which Eliade recounts, the ancestor took the feverish youth to a large cauldron and bade him test the water. It was lukewarm, which meant that the boy would recover. The ancestor explained that in treating others he should return in trance or dream to the cauldron and test the water. If it were boiling, the person would not recover, but he would need to be prepared for death. If the water were hot to lukewarm, the patient would recover after a struggle with the illness. If it were tepid to cold, the patient would recover fairly quickly.

Dreams of healing and transformation, which the Jungian analyst Joseph Henderson calls "initiatory," can be found in his books, *Threshold of Initiation* and *Wisdom of the Serpent*. Also interesting are the dreams on snakes and consciousness in *Symbols of Transformation in Dreams*, by Jean and Wallace Clift, who are also Jungian analysts. Today we attribute direct experience of God through dreams and visions to the remote past, the era of the Old Testament. Yet, even in our own times, many continue to have such shamanistic intiatory dreams, to be called to the transformation during a time of intense physical suffering or emotional crisis. Many a Scorpio rising/Scorpio Sun sign client undergoes his test of faith, the day when his own willpower, or his bodily stamina, is not sufficient to conquer disease or depression. S/he feels powerless or out of control. If s/he responds to the crisis with faith in God and his physicians—spiritual, physical, or psychological—s/he helps with his healing. When, however, s/he reacts with pride and skepticism—when s/he refuses to allow God room in the healing process, the cure is likely to be slow, arduous, painful, and sometimes even unsuccessful. Christ once told a Samaritan man who fell to his knees in gratitude, "Your faith has healed you." (Luke 17: 18-19). Faith is a key factor in the Eighth House healing crisis, whether it is physical, spiritual, psychological, or even financial in nature.

The final type of Scorpio is a rare bird—the Phoenix. S/he has been through the fire this lifetime; s/he has burned away the dross like an alchemist and transformed his/her baser nature into gold. Sometimes the fire is a long childhood illness or an emotional wound— the death of a beloved relative or the denial of a cherished goal. Instead of becoming bitter, cynical and vengeful like the Vulture or the Serpent, s/he passes through the crisis and resurrects him/ herself from the ashes of his/her burnt nest. Often, as a result of his/ her trauma he goes through a conversion experience. S/he may come across a homeopathic cure for his illness and dedicate him/ herself to homeopathy; s/he may go through analysis and find the process so rewarding that s/he becomes a therapist and helps others as s/he was helped. Or a spiritual transformation might result from his/her crisis; s/he may benefit from the teachings of a certain Master and feel called to share it with others. At an astrology reading, the Phoenix can easily be distinguished from the Eagle because when s/he begins to speak about a relative, co-worker, or neighbor s/he doesn't express fear, suspicion, or envy. S/he doesn't ask about the other's vulnerable areas, but asks instead "How can I help this poor, suffering person?" (Often, however, help means how can I convert, convince, persuade this person to my own viewpoint? How can I change him?)

In *Esoteric Astrology*, Alice Bailey cites St. Paul, the apostle, as an example of the higher Scorpio, the Phoenix. His style demonstrates the passion, the zeal, the power of persuasion that astrologers associate with Scorpio. He also went through a personal transformation. After being knocked off his horse he was transformed from persecutor of Christians to true believer and active advocate of the gospel, travelling from Jerusalem to Spain and Italy preaching the word. St. Paul's epistles employ the life or death vocabulary of Scor-

pio. "You must kill everything in you that belongs only to earthly life—fornication, impurity, guilty passion, evil desires, and especially greed, which is the same thing as worshipping a false god," he writes in Colossians 3:5. He encourages his reader to change, to take off the old man and put on the new. He speaks of a need to cut loose from old habit patterms. "When I was a child I spoke as a child, I understood as a child, thought as a child; but when I became a man I put away the things of a child" (I Corinthians, 13:11). He addressed the Scorpio issue of vengeance, quoting from the Old Testament, "Vengeance is mine, saith the Lord" (Deut. 32:35; Paul to Hebrews 10:30), and giving very spiritual advice on the subject: "If your enemy hungers, feed him; if he is thirsty, give him drink, for in so doing you shall heap coals of fire upon his head" (Romans 12: 19-20). This would certainly force the enemy to think, to awaken. He saw his enemies as the world, the flesh, and the Devil, but wrote most frequently of the flesh, the enemy within, in the manner of an esoteric Scorpio. The spirit is willing, but the flesh is weak, and interferes with the best of our intentions. "Those things that I want to do, I do not do; and those things that I would not do; those I do" (Romans 7: 14-25).

Alice Bailey comments that St. Paul's view of the body as enemy of soul influenced Christian thinkers in future centuries. He also believed in celibacy, as do many of my esoteric Scorpio clients. St. Paul held that whereas a married man or woman must seek to please the spouse by spending time in worldy concerns, the celibate can serve God alone. St. Paul was a man of great faith in God's will, rather than his own. He also evidenced humility, which is a sign of the Phoenix, rather than the Eagle. He lamented to the end of his life that he would always be the lowest of the apostles, because he had once persecuted Christians.

Because s/he has been through so much in his/her own life prior to his/her transformation, the Phoenix may be fanatically zealous to save others. Scorpio may, when s/he finds his/her faith in a religious philosophy, psychological system, or physical healing technique, want to convert his/her family, friends and everyone s/he meets for the first few months. If they run from his/her zeal, perceiving him/her as a lunatic, s/he may feel isolated and Scorpio-like, withdraw from them still further. But a true Phoenix will not long remain a hermit, for s/he wishes to serve others. And too, s/he has respect for others' intelligence and others' free will; his/her efforts to convert them will not be arrogant or self-righteous. The true Phoenix is generous with his/her time and resources. S/he does not become a total recluse caught up in his/her own personal projects, meditation, visions. S/he is Mars active and helpful to those in need. There is no longer any suspicion, pettiness, jealousy or possessiveness in the Phoenix/Scorpio. S/he has met his/her shadow like a warrior, fought and made peace with it.

The Phoenix has been through a good many tests consciously and has learned from his/her mistakes. Alice Bailey says that Scorpio is the sign where major tests and spiritual initiations occur. The lower Scorpio (Snake) who lives life only on the sensate level is tested through sex, power, comfort and money. In this sense, s/he has a lot in common with the lower Taurean who lives in the desire nature. The lower Scorpio is not very conscious of the results of his/her actions, so s/he strikes out violently at his/her enemies. The Eagle is more conscious. S/he may consider doing something mean or cruel to an enemy, but is not as prone to act on the idea. S/he is more positive in his/her motives and his/her mind is more in conctrol than his/her emotions. S/he is not inclined to be cruel for the sake of cruelty, as a Snake would be.

If Pluto is afflicted in the Eagle's chart, s/he may be tempted to be devious and manipulative, but s/he does not react unconsciously; s/he struggles with his/her suspicions, doubts, jealousies, obsessions and premonitions. When s/he acts s/he usually has a great deal more foresight than the Snake. The Eagle and the Snake both like intrigue and mystery. It has been my experience that when they have extra-marital affairs, for example, they enjoy the planning of the rendez-vous, the intrigue, mystery and secrecy, as much as the sex. They are not tuned in to the law of karma, or thinking of the consequences of their actions. The Eagle enjoys power in relationships, business, and community affairs. His/her tests are frequently tests of power. An Eagle is capable of sublimating sex and putting the energy into his/her business for a long period of time. The higher Eagle is a would-be Phoenix, a disciple who is working on transformation. S/he introspects about life, death, retribution, illumination, immortality or liberation and his/her own baser tendencies. S/he works on controlling his/her sarcasm, modifying his/her rigidity and resistance to change, letting go of his/her suspicions and jealousies, and s/he moves toward a more Taurean receptivity to grace. S/he tries to look on the bright side rather than be so vulnerable to doubts and watery depressive moods. The Eagle, like the Snake, is a risk-taker; his rulers are Mars and the planet of obsessive-compulsive drives, Pluto. The Eagle's risky ventures are usually well thought out in advance, however, unlike the Snake's risks, which stem from sensual desires.

The Eagle disciple, or the would-be Phoenix, may confront his/her shadow through an eastern religion or a monastic approach that tries to sublimate the "snake of sexuality" for spiritual purposes. Many with Scorpio planets seem unaware that confronting the ego's power drive is just as important for the transformation as confronting sex. Joseph Campbell tells a story of Alexander the Great, Conqueror of the World, in India. One day he and some of his more philosophically minded companions of high rank in the army, along with a historian and a scholar, decided to find a yogi and study Indian philosophy. They found a group of men sitting in the cross-legged lotus position in the blazing sun on some boiling hot rocks. They told the teacher about the ideas of Socrates, Aristotle and Pythagoras. The yogi admitted there was merit to Western philosophy, but asked why Seekers would be wearing such clothing. The yogi thought it inappropriate for a philosopher's disciples to wear the trappings of high birth, rank, learning and power. To the yogi, this was ego. To transcend form, the identities that distinguished them in the eyes of the world, they would first need to remove all their clothes, sit naked and uncomfortable on the rock, and go within through meditation. Alexander and one or two others did remove their clothing and headed for the rocks, according to Campbell, but the rest of the Greeks taunted them with laughter and abuse (*Oriental Mythology*, p. 277).

This story about removing the outer layers of form seems to fit Scorpio very well if we consider that Scorpio lies opposite Taurus where the Moon, Mother of Form and of attachment, is exalted. Scorpio means transforming and mastery of the inner habits—the lunar side; but it means conquest of the ego's desires, the solar tendencies, as well.

On his journey, the would-be Phoenix learns not only to open up to grace like a Taurean, but he also learns to be less resistant to others' suggestions, less rigid in meeting change. His sword, or ally, is the courage of Mars, but in attempting psychic surgery on his habits or lower nature, the Eagle often acts like Zeus going after Typhon with violence—with a vengeance. The would-be Phoenix hears a minister speak, or reads a Scripture and decides to rid him/herself of all his/her vices overnight—to give up smoking, drinking, meat eating and sex. A week later s/he becomes severely depressed with himself. Like Zeus, s/he magnifies the demon within out of proportion and attempts to shine too much light into the darkness too quickly. S/he next experiences the Hydra effect. Like Hercules lopping a head off the Hydra, Scorpio finds that another head (habit or desire) appears to replace it. Doing violence to the contents of the Eighth House tends to produce this phenomenon. As a child of impatient Mars, Scorpio needs to learn patience from Taurus, his/her polar extremity. It took lifetimes to acquire some of these habits. They cannot be lopped off overnight.

Taurus also represents hard work which Scorpio, too, appreciates. Rather than brood in solitude about his distressing struggle with the inner Hydra or his fleeting existence on this earth—"only 70 years left of this lifetime to reach illumination"—many a Scorpio yogi would be better off performing useful tasks in the world rather than sitting all day long in a Himalayan cave nursing his/her depression. Eventually the darkness becomes more accustomed to the light rays shining through and begins to dissipate. Then one day the Phoenix, arising from the ashes, meets an Eagle and thinks, "I too used to have those same negative or suspicious thoughts that this Scorpio person just expressed." Or, like the Buddha, he thinks "I used to fear Death, but now I have no fears—I have seen the Light." When Scorpio says, "I used to. . . " it indicates growth has taken place; s/he has left more of the darkness behind.

Finally, we come to the myth of Prometheus. Half man and half Titan, he seems more human than Olympian Zeus or Prince Mahavira (Buddha) and perhaps for that reason we can identify more with his level of awareness and his plight. Prometheus fits nicely into the Scorpio pattern: he has a devious mind; he likes to take risks (such as stealing the secret of fire from the gods and passing it on to mortals); he enjoys power struggles, having challenged the Greatest Ego and authority on Olympus, All Highest Zeus; and he is a courageous Mars person. But he is no impetuous Aries hero. He is fixed to the point of rigidity. He is willing to spend 30,000 years in Tartarus, down in the underworld chained to a rock, awaiting the visits of Zeus' blood-red Eagle who comes to feast on his liver. Here we have God's Eagle, or Fate, feasting on the part of the body ruled by Jupiter (Zeus), the liver.

Hillman tells us that Ananke (Fate) was also associated with the liver. In our times the liver is associated with toxins, the residue of improper dietary habits. Symbolically, the liver contains emotional poisons, things that the unconscious has stored up—such as resentment, hostility, and the urge for revenge. Yet, the blood red color of the Eagle indicates that the victim is in the final stage of his purification. Blood red is the second to last alchemical stage. The next stage is gold.

According to the playwright Aeschylus (*Prometheus Bound*), Zeus would gladly release the Titan if he would reveal the secret of Zeus' fate. Zeus will lose his throne, just as Chronos and Uranus did before him, when a certain son is born to overthrow him. If Prometheus would give Zeus the name of the woman who will give birth to the son, then Zeus could avoid her; the child would never be born, and Zeus could postpone his fate. But Prometheus would gladly wait 30,000 years just to spite an enemy whose justice he finds unsatisfactory. This is real fixity. Prometheus is very strong willed. He prefers his private hell to communicating with an enemy, revealing his secret, or compromising. He goes through years with the blood red Eagle picking at his wound and Zeus' messenger, sarcastic Hermes, trying to persuade him to be reasonable. A Scorpio who is this stuck cannot be reasoned with. One simply has to wait for him to see the Light, for him to let go of the slight, to forgive and forget.

In one scene from the play, Hermes pleads with Prometheus to compromise because Zeus and Poseidon have backed down. They are no longer planning to destroy the Earth, along with Prometheus' beloved human race, with earthquakes and floods. Still he won't yield. Zeus decides that even if this pest Prometheus does give up the secret, he must remain in Tartarus till someone else is willing to take his place on the rock and finish out his sentence.

Karolyi Kerenyi, in *Prometheus*, makes the following important point: the Titan must accept the fact that his own limited understanding of justice is far removed from that of Zeus, and the reality in this situation is that Zeus, not Prometheus, is the being on the throne in Olympus. Though he would gladly suffer for humanity if he could get them better fate, better quality justice, he cannot obtain it. After his 30,000 years in Tartarus things would still be the same for humanity. Justice (Cosmic Law) will not change. The All Highest may occasionally revise a plan, like destroying the Earth, but God's justice is not justice as humans perceive it. So human suffering will continue, regardless of Prometheus' decision. Finally, Prometheus agrees to tell the secret to his mother, Themis, the Prophetess and advisor to Zeus. He chooses an indirect way of communicating and of saving face. (He suspects she already knows the woman's name anyhow and she does. It's Thetis.) Instead of marrying Thetis himself, Zeus arranges her marriage to Peleus, who is a mortal, not a god, and thus temporarily escapes his fate.

Prometheus remains in Tartarus until Hercules comes along to chase the Eagle and provide him with a replacement—someone else willing to suffer for others—Chiron the Wise Centaur, whom we will meet in Sagittarius.

Scorpio spends 30 years progressing through the following sign of the zodiac, Sagittarius. If there are natal planets in Sagittarius, his/her indirect, behind-the-scenes approach to life may change dramatically as the progressed Sun or Ascendant cross the natal outspoken Sagittarian energies. The vocabulary Scorpio chooses may incline toward Sagittarian keywords—justice, fairness, integrity, sincerity, ethics. Scorpio may set forth on the Quest for Wisdom, for objective Truth that we associate astrologically with Sagittarius (see Chapter 9), especially if s/he is a higher consciousness Eagle or a Phoenix who has passed through his/her period of trials by the time s/he arrives at the Sagittarian cycle. (Scorpios born in the last few days of their natal sign may go through their inner crisis in Sagittarius, rather than Scorpio, as they would progress into Sagittarius when only a year or two of age.)

Sagittarius is a Mutable or adaptable sign and thus an important phase of development for Scorpio. The individual will ordinarily learn to compromise with others in this cycle if s/he is to learn the art of compromise at all. This is particularly true of the Pluto in Leo people with Fixed squares (tendencies going back many lifetimes) in the horoscope. The Sun or Ascendant in fiery Sagittarius will sooner or later trine the Pluto, bringing opportunity in the Houses involved to expand beyond Plutonian dogmatism, opinionatedness and rigidity. Sagittarius is not only adaptable, but is fortunate, auspicious. It is ruled by Jupiter, the Guru planet in Hindu astrology. In this cycle, the higher Eagle or the Phoenix will incline toward St. Paul's philosophy that the worldly wise lack true wisdom. The lower Scorpio inclines to view Jupiter as luck rather than wisdom, or as philosophical idealism. S/he may expand financially through his investments (often in international companies, service, products). S/he may speculate, gamble, or wheel and deal in both the Second and Eighth House issues—love and money. Several Scorpios have worked with Jupiter's lucky energy activating natal Fire planets by trine to become upwardly mobile. They have divorced the old marriage partner to wed the boss's daughter, or the boss! The astrologer can observe these tendencies in less-evolved Scorpios with benefic planets in the Fifth and Seventh houses, activated by progressed Sun or progressed Mars/Venus into Sagittarius, contacting these benefics. Jupiter's opportunities can be sought out on both the mundane and the esoteric levels. The older texts will mention opportunities to meet attorneys, people in import/ export, and the affluent in general on transits and progressions through Sagittarius. People from foreign countries, journalists, or people in communications professions at all levels enter the lives of Scorpio in this period. Esoterically, they introduce Scorpio to a wider spectrum of ideals, concepts, viewpoints. They enlarge his perspective beyond traditional religion or its dogma.

Travel to spiritual places, or for academic or spiritual purposes, may open to Scorpio in this phase—travel that forces him to confront any rigid opinions s/he may have held about certain racial, religious, or ethnic groups. Sometimes these opinions go back more than one lifetime. Sometimes, too, the ideas relate to a social group rather than a racial or religious background. One Scorpio woman whose husband was transferred to California during this progression remarked, for example, "My parents back in the Midwest looked down on military people socially. Since moving here, I discovered that on the whole they are just like everyone else, they're certainly well travelled, and in some cases they're even better educated.

I have seen an expansion beyond the fixed opinions of childhood relatives among my Scorpio clients under the influence of the Sagittarian progression. I am reminded of St. Paul's lecture wherein he universally identified and said, "I am a Roman. I am a Jew. I am a Greek."

Sagittarius is a communication sign. Many a natal Scorpio works hard to develop his powers of self-expression in Sagittarius. Opportunities often come between the age of 36 (the Jupiter return) and about 42 (Jupiter opposite Jupiter) to lecture to groups or to train younger people in their profession. Initially many resist the opportunities. "I've always preferred to work behind the scenes, to schedule others' travel itineraries, others' lectures. Now I'm asked to do these things myself. I don't know. Part of me would rather stay home and be quiet." But, if the progressed Sun in Sagittarius forms harsh contacts to natal Mutable planets in Virgo, or opposes Uranus in Gemini, others may insist that Scorpio share his approach, his expertise, the shortcuts that he has worked out. This seems especially true for the Scorpio shaman, the nurse, massage therapist, psychologist, or spiritual initiate. If s/he is without planets in Fire or Air to sustain the challenge of this progression, Scorpio may prefer to hide his or her light under a bushel. This is sad for the rest of us, who stand to benefit from the depth, experience and focus Scorpio has brought to bear in his/her specialized field during the first forty years of life.

As a respite from communicating (speaking or writing) Scorpio may enjoy vacationing in the wide open spaces, like the Sagittarian Centaur, Chiron, who roamed the forest freely. He may acquire a desert home or a mountain retreat with a deck which has a panoramic view of nature, unimpeded by hectic vibrations of commuter traffic, tall buildings, anxious people. The panoramic view helps him to put life into perspective, as s/he combines the Sagittarian growth-phase qualities with his natal determination, drive, intensity, and need for solitude. If s/he fights the inner battle of Pluto square Pluto (age 42-45) which usually involves a frustrated personal desire, or the combustible nest of the Phoenix catching fire from within, this outdoorsy retreat is a wonderful place to relax alone with his thoughts, to re-energize body, mind and soul. He can also get some exercise out in the wide open spaces, climb mountains, hike long distances, get in touch with his instincts.

For Scorpios who have the Fixed Cross or Fixed T-Square, involving the heart and circulatory systems (planets in Leo/Aquarius), exercise is essential as they get older. There is a type of Scorpio woman who is very much like Goddess Artemis and who instinctively seems to know this. Artemis was a virgin goddess who lived in the forest and disappeared quickly into the brush if her solitude was threatened. She was quite independent and quick with a bow and arrow. She was tough minded and merciful; she would shoot her arrow at the dying and put an end to their suffering. Wounded animals, women in childbirth and others received her death arrows if they could not be healed. Many a Scorpio woman resembles brave Artemis, lean and athletic, going about her business skillfully with precise focus on the target ahead. There was nothing squeamish at all about Artemis.

As a 30-year-cycle, Sagittarius is a good deal more easy going, procrastinatory and mellow than natal Scorpio. The ideas, concepts, ideals, scope of the vision—even the concept of God is expanded during this cycle. As the years go by, Scorpio seems less intense and more relaxed, more willing to socialize at night than bury him/herself in his/her work. Those whose natal Saturn (professional ambition) is not strong by House and aspect may even seem less ambitious, more playful (Jupiterian). They may opt to do short-term projects rather than assume long-term responsibilities. In the Fire progression, Scorpio learns like a Fire sign from acting, doing, confronting.

Those who emerge from this progression having assimilated the positive, optimistic Sagittarian approach to life with Sagittarian flexibility and Sagittarian idealism have tuned in positively to Jupiter. I have seen Scorpio assimilate natal fiery planets during this phase and write motivational, inspirational articles. The determination, focus, and persuasive magnetism of the natal chart has been lifted up from the depths to the heights in this cycle. His/her pleasant rather than skeptical personality will attract good friends to him.

Next comes the 30-year Capricorn progression. This will enhance natal pragmatic, suspicious, withdrawn, judgmental tendencies. If the flexibility and optimism of Sagittarius has had little impact, or if Scorpio has not learned to relax and enjoy his/her free time, the pressures of the Capricorn cycle can be difficult. He may forget how to laugh at him/herself, for Capricorn takes its role, or title, quite seriously. He may become a very demanding supervisor, a petty tyrant, in the view of his underlings. Capricorn is an authority figure, and Scorpio may become part of the conservative establishment in this cycle. If s/he has a strong, professionally ambitious natal Saturn, then the Capricorn cycle will likely fulfill his expectations in the outer world. If s/he has not developed a Sagittarian philosophy, an objective system to which s/he adheres, then pragmatism, the philosophy of "whatever works is fine with me," may become his approach in Capricorn. Natal Pluto, the mundane ruler, is a power planet. Scorpios born between 1946-48 who have this conjunction of the natal and progressed rulers in Leo in square to natal Sun may become cynical, even paranoid, if others threaten their power. There's a ruthlessness to the lower consciousness Snake when he's cornered or threatened by a younger competitor.

Among other body parts, Capricorn rules the bones. Several Scorpios in my clientele have had bone cancer during the Capricorn progression. Their emotions ate away at them. They planned and schemed, leaving little room for God to act. Jupiter, ruler of Sagittarius, is not only about confidence, and the quality of the philosophy or the message Scorpio would share with others, but about his/her faith—does he have any? S/he has had 30 years to grow a soul—to develop faith.

The Phoenix is not simply concerned with the title on his/her office door, with power and influence in his/her chosen profession, with belonging to the right country club or owning property to pass on to his/her heirs. S/he is more concerned with civic duty, his/her role in the community, his/her dharma in the broader sense. Sometimes Scorpio seeks political office in this cycle, as both the natal and progressed Suns are connected with power. Sometimes, too, s/he may work behind the scenes for a candidate whose philosophy of government approximates his own. Or s/he may support a community organization that provides a vital service in which s/he believes and has an interest. Esoterically, Capricorn is associated with the elderly. Scorpio may help his/her parents in their old age or s/he may donate time and energy to the needs of the elderly of his neighborhood.

Scorpio may not have taken much interest in children early in his or her life. Mars' biological energy may have been sublimated into career or a celibate religious vocation. Sagittarius cusp Scorpios who progress into Capricorn during their late 30's often discover a strong desire to become parents. (Capricorn and the Tenth House are on the heredity axis). So the question, "Will I be able to have a child?" may come up for them for the first time around the age of 37 or 38. This is particularly true if the Sun progresses through the Fifth House or the progressed Moon passes through House Four or Five. This is a major lifestyle change for the woman who may have dealt with children only through her profession and cherished her privacy at night, or for the Scorpio engineer or computer person who loves nothing more than to retreat to the solitude of his den for uninterrupted hours with his discs or his blueprints. Perhaps Pluto square Pluto will come along early (it's usually closer to mid-40's) and delay or frustrate the desire if Scorpio is on the Fifth House cusp or Pluto affects it by transit. Or, Saturn transits may delay the birth. This will give the person time to invite nieces and nephews for the summer and see if this lifestyle change is really desirable, as opposed to the Big Brother program or Sunday School teaching. One Scorpio schoolteacher told me, "You know, I had my niece for the summer but when fall came I discovered that it was good to come home to peace and quiet, to read the Bible and meditate. I'm not suited to motherhood." The Saturn delays gave her time to consider whether it was the right decision for her Scorpio stellium.

I have not had many Scorpios who lived long into the Aquarian progression. Those who did seemed to revert to their natal opinionatedness or rigidity. Relatives, for instance, would comment, "Mother is so stubborn in her old age. Of course, she was always "fixed," but she is now so rigid it's hard to find a cleaning woman who will stay with her beyond the third appearance." Scorpios who have worked throughout the Capricorn progression may find themselves quite bored when health problems force them to slow down and stay home. Mars is accustomed to being active, making decisions, earning money. If the progressed Sun contacts natal Air planets, mental curiosity and a sense of humor keep Scorpio alert and healthy. Otherwise, the Scorpio loner may lament that relatives do not often phone or come to visit. This Scorpio may regret not having made more effort to socialize in the past. His/her relatives are used to thinking of him as a workaholic who never seemed to need them. Other, more positive thinking, cheerful Scorpios seem to enjoy this cycle, which gives them an opportunity to read about new discoveries, attend New Age lectures, or spend time with like-minded friends.

Many of my self-employed Scorpio/Scorpio rising clients do not adjust well to retirement. They are similar to Mars ruled Aries in that they are accustomed to making decisions, exerting influence, contributing in the outer world. The less-evolved Scorpio, who had not developed his inner resources in meditation or introspection (the inner work that can be done while sitting still) may be restless and crotchety.

Many of my driven clients have the natal Fixed T-Square configuration. This structure may be activated with transits, or the progressed Sun in Aquarius may trigger it, bringing circulation problems, chills or (in opposition to natal Leo planets) a heart attack. Early heart attacks reduce the life expectancy for Scorpio. Preventive medicine, which includes attention to diet, moderate exercise such as walking, and regular monitoring of cholesterol levels, helps promote health. Even more important, perhaps, is faith in a higher power, oneself, one's family and friends. If Scorpio holds on to negative memories and emotions, his heart, symbolically speaking, also suffers. Elimination of all the old heartaches from his/her memory will help to keep him strong in body, mind and spirit.

Questionnaire

How does the Scorpio archetype express itself? Though this relates particularly to those with the Sun in Scorpio or Scorpio rising, anyone could apply this series of questions to the Houses where Mars and Pluto are located or the House which has Scorpio (or Scorpio intercepted) on the cusp. The answers to these questions will indicate how in touch the reader is with Pluto, his power drive, and Mars, his passion.

1. When the conversation becomes too personal I become uncomfortable
   a. most of the time.
   b. 50% of the time.
   c. 25% of the time or less.

2. When I am given a project the most important thing to me is
   a. getting the job done.
   b. seeing that I get credit for it.
   c. making sure I don't offend anyone.

3. I prefer to work where
   a. there is no interruption.
   b. there are a few others involved.
   c. there is a lot of social contact.

4. When something is on my mind I
   a. keep it to myself.
   b. tell one or two others that can keep a secret.
   c. let everyone know.

5. Among my negative qualities I would probably include
   a. moodiness and stubbornness.
   b. a tendency to criticism.
   c. a lack of consistency.

6. When I feel threatened I
   a. fight back as hard as I can.
   b. withdraw within and brood.
   c. look for a convenient way out.

7. The greatest obstacle to my success comes from
   a. within myself, self-doubt.
   b. the outside world—circumstances beyond my control.

8. My greatest fear is
   a. my deepest, darkest secret will be found out.
   b. loss of my independence.
   c. others wouldn't like me.

9. I feel the weakest part of my body is
   a. the colon.
   b. my stomach.
   c. my throat.

10. Important in my life are such Mars/Pluto concerns as sex, power, control and privacy. These are
    a. very important.
    b. moderately important.
    c. not important at all.

Those who have scored five or more (a) answers are highly in touch with their instincts. Those who have scored five or more (c) answers are moving to the polar extremity on the instinctual level—their Mars is not allowed to express itself properly. Is natal Mars in the Twelfth House? Is it retrograde? Is it intercepted? It is important to work consciously with the positive aspects to Mars to help it express such instincts as courage, direct communication, vitality, positive or optimistic attitude.

Where is the balance point between Scorpio and Taurus? How does the Scorpio integrate transformation/personal resources? Though this relates particularly to those with the Sun in Scorpio or Scorpio rising, all of us have Mars and Venus somewhere in our horoscope. Many of us have planets in the Eighth or Second Houses. For all of us the polarity from Scorpio to Taurus involves learning to balance others' values with personal power and security, change and transformation with stability.

1. When my spouse plans a social event that is important to him/her I attend it for the sake of my spouse
   a. 25% of the time or less.
   b. 50% of the time.
   c. most of the time.

2. When I stop at the store I pick up the brand my spouse/roomate requested rather than a cheaper version of the item
   a. 25% of the time or less.
   b. 50% of the time.
   c. 80% of the time or more.

3. When somebody asks me to do a favor that I really don't want to do or I really don't have time to do
   a. it is easy for me to say no.
   b. I usually say no but feel bad later.
   c. I have trouble saying no.

4. If asked, my spouse would probably say
   a. that I lack warmth and tenderness.
   b. that I am warm as well as passionate.
   c. that I am warm and tender but not very passionate.

5. When it comes to partnerships (joint investments)
   a. I would rather go it alone.
   b. I believe in equal participation and equal gain.
   c. I feel better with a partner than in an independent venture.

Those who scored three or more (b) answers are doing a good job with personality integration on the Scorpio/Taurus polarity. Those who have three or more (c) answers need to work more consciously on developing natal Mars in their horoscopes. Those who have three or more (a) answers may be out of balance in the other direction (weak or undeveloped Mars). Study both Mars and Venus in the natal chart. Is there an aspect between them? Which is stronger by House position or location in its sign of rulership or exaltation? Is either of them retrograde, intercepted, in fall or in detriment? Aspects to the weaker planet can point the way to its integration.

What does it mean to be an esoteric Scorpio? How does Scorpio manifest Mars at the esoteric level, as a Kshatriya warrior? How does Scorpio come to terms with Ananke/Pluto? Every Scorpio will have Mars and Pluto somewhere in his chart. The answers to the following questions will indicate the extent to which Scorpio is reacting at the esoteric level.

1. When someone has done me a misdeed I
    a. have faith that it is for the best and will promote growth and learning in me.
    b. have faith in myself. My reputation can be cleared.
    c. return tit for tat.

2. In Pluto's house, or the house with Scorpio on the cusp, when I can't have my desire, I
    a. let go and do my work.
    b. find frustration is high but try to accept it.
    c. find that I can't be happy without it.

3. The word "control" means to me
    a. self-control—work within myself (meditation, analysis, journal writing).
    b. helping others to control themselves.
    c. to be in control of the environment I inhabit.

4. Suspicion is something that
    a. draws the very circumstances feared.
    b. may be unwarranted but skepticism is healthy.
    c. I live with daily.

5. I experienced a crisis that I thought would finish me. By hindsight I see
    a. that it was the best thing for my personal growth; God's grace was with me.
    b. that I somehow found the strength to get through it.
    c. it proved that I could depend only on myself.

Those who have scored three or more (a) answers are in touch with the esoteric ruler. At the esoteric level, Mars' role is to react courageously but not vindictively, returning tit for tat. At the mundane level, Mars is an ego planet, but at the esoteric level the Scorpio has sufficient faith in God as well as his own resources. Mars does what he can and leaves the rest to the Divine. Those who scored three or more (b) answers are doing their inner work but need to continue. Those who have scored three or more (c) answers need consciously to develop a balance between faith and personal effort. Pluto, through the crisis process, helps Scorpio develop his faith in a higher power.

References

Aeschylus, *Prometheus Bound*, E.H. Plumptre transl., David McKay, New York, 1960

Alice Bailey, *Esoteric Astrology*, Lucis Publishing Co., New York, 1976

Alice Bailey, *Labours of Hercules*, "Labour VIII," Lucis Publishing Co., New York, 1974

Taylor Caldwell, *Great Lion of God: A Novel Based on the Life of St. Paul*, Ulverscroft, Leicester, 1976

Joseph Campbell, *Masks of God: Occidental Mythology*, vol. III, Penguin Books, New York, 1982

Joseph Campbell, *Masks of God: Oriental Mythology*, vol. II, Penguin Books, New York, 1982

Jean and Wallace Clift, *Symbols of Transformation in Dreams*, Crossroad Publishing Co., New York, 1984

Edward Edinger, *Anatomy of the Psyche, Alchemical Symbolism in Psychotherapy*, Open Court, La Salle, 1985

Mircea Eliade, *The Myth of the Eternal Return*, Willard Trask transl., Pantheon Books, New York, 1965

Mircea Eliade, *Rites and Symbols of Initiation*, Willard Trask transl., Harper and Row, New York, 1958

Mircea Eliade, *Shamanism, Archaic Techniques of Ecstasy*, Willard Trask transl., Princeton University Press, Princeton, 1964

W.Y. Evans-Wentz ed., *The Tibetan Book of the Dead*, with Psychological Commentary by C.G. Jung, Oxford University Press, London, 1960

Marie Louise von Franz, *A Psychological Interpretation of the Golden Ass of Apuleius*, Spring Publications, Irving, 1980

Jeff Green, *Pluto, The Evolutionary Journey of the Soul*, Llewellyn Publications, St. Paul, 1986

Liz Greene, *The Astrology of Fate*, "Scorpio," "The Astrological Pluto," Samuel Weiser Inc., York Beach, 1984

Joseph L. Henderson, *Thresholds of Initiation*, Wesleyan University Press, Middleton, 1976

Joseph L. Henderson, *The Wisdom of the Serpent, Death Rebirth and Resurrection*, G. Braziller, New York, 1963

Isabel Hickey, *Astrology: A Cosmic Science*, Altieri Press, 1970

James Hillman, *Facing the Gods*, "Ananke and Athene," Spring Publications, Irving, 1980

C.G. Jung, *Memories, Dreams and Reflections*, Aniela A. Joffe ed., Vintage Books, New York, 1965

C.G. Jung, *The Portable Jung*, "Stages of Life," Joseph Campbell ed., Penguin Books, 1981

Karolyi Kerenyi, *Prometheus: Archetypal Image of Human Existence*, Ralph Manheim transl., Pantheon Books, New York, 1963

George M. Lamsa ed., *The New Testament According to the Eastern Text*, A.J. Holman Co., Philadelphia, 1968

Marc Robertson, *The Eighth House, Sex, Death and Money*, A.F.A. Inc., 1979

Jean Shinoda-Bolen, *Goddesses in Everywoman*, "Artemis," Harper and Row Publishers, San Francisco, 1984

James Tatum, *Apuleius and the Golden Ass*, Cornell University Press, Ithaca, 1979

J.P. Vogel, *Indian Serpent Lore, or Nagas in Hindu Legend and Art*, Indological Book House, Varanasi, 1972

E.A. Wallis Budge, *The Egyptian Book of the Dead*, Dover Publications Inc., New York, 1967

E.A. Wallis Budge, *Egyptian Magic*, "The Sorrows of Isis," Dover Publications Inc., New York, 1971

E.A. Wallis Budge, *Osiris and the Egyptian Resurrection*, vols. I and II, Dover Publications Inc., New York, 1973

T.H. White, *The Book of Beasts*, Dover Publications Inc., New York, 1984

Parmahansa Yogananda, *The Divine Romance*, S.R.F. Publications, Los Angeles, 1986

9 SAGITTARIUS:
The Search for Wisdom

Each year around November 20, we who live in the temperate zone experience the entry of the Sun into Sagittarius. To the astrologer this 30-day period is a cheerful, optimistic, lighthearted interval between two of the zodiac's most earnest, serious-minded, striving signs—Scorpio and Capricorn. To me it has always seemed perfect synchronicity that here in the United States our Thanksgiving holiday falls in Sagittarius. We celebrate our gratitude for being alive, happy and healthy as together with friends and family we count our blessings. This jovial festival of overeating is truly in the spirit of All Highest Zeus, or Jupiter, as the Romans called him, the ruler of Sagittarius. Had he been invited to an American home, Zeus would really have enjoyed himself at the groaning board on Thanksgiving Day.

On our archetypal journey around the zodiac, when we reach the ninth sign and the Ninth House we have emerged from the murky, swampy waters of the Scorpionic Unconscious, having faced our fear of death and probed the depths of feeling and emotion. Now, in Sagittarius, we bask once more in the sunlight of a solar Fire sign and again experience conscious, extroverted energy. Traditionally astrologers have associated Sagittarius with Spirit, expansion of awareness, aspiring to greatness, and the ability to motivate, inspire, or "fire up" others. These grandiose associations fit not only individuals born into the sign, but people with Ninth House planets, too. Inspiration is offered through such Ninth House professions as college teaching, writing, and the ministry. The publishing and advertising industries also accomplish the work of the Sagittarian archetype through disseminating information and sometimes, one hopes, wisdom as well. Motivated salespeople have the zeal of ministers when

317

they're at their best, and they too participate in the Ninth House archetype. In my own client experience, however, the major concern of the archetype as I have observed it has been practical moral philosophy and ethics. Law, an important Ninth House field, involves the practical application of ethics to concrete cases, for example.

There is a sense of playfulness to Sagittarius. It's rather like the stage in alchemy where hard work is over and there is the joy of spontaneous growth. In her book *Alchemy*, Marie Louise von Franz speaks of the clashing together of unconscious and conscious forces, followed by a peaceful plateau which she likens, as a stage in alchemy, to a child playing in a beautiful garden. Many who participate in the Sagittarian archetype through Sun sign, rising sign or prominent Jupiter in the horoscope have this sort of playful approach to life and tend, as a result of expecting good things to happen to them, to draw many positive experiences in the course of the lifetime. The experience of the ninth sign can be very much like this image of the playful children in the paradise garden after the hard work of the Scorpio stage or the descent into the Unconscious.

The number nine means completion, perfection, or purity of thought. The ninth sign tends to resemble the peak of the alchemical process, the completing or finishing up of the work that Von Franz cites from the Arab alchemist known as "Senior," which is "the washing of the seven stars nine times," or until they were totally spotless, perfectly clean and shining white in their purity. The seven stars meant the totality of the horoscope. The Sun, Moon and the five planets from Mercury through Saturn were known collectively as the seven stars and together with their Aspects, Signs and House placements, comprised the individual personality. During his alchemical process, the conqueror of the seven stars had succeeded in mastering his/her instincts, frustrations, desires, bad habits and other obstacles to realization of the Spirit. What remained was the washing up, the polishing process, the ninefold cleansing. I often think of this stage in alchemy when a client with a stellium in Sagittarius tells me of his/her blissful, grandiose dream and how easy it will be to make the dream manifest. Perhaps it will be—for him or her. Perhaps s/he has already completed the long journey through the first eight signs and now has arrived at the end of the process—the washing up and polishing.

When the Arab "Senior" speaks of the number nine symbolically in terms of perfection and completion, or finishing up, he is quite consistent with the esoteric writers of Greece and India. The number nine is a peak number to the Pythagoreans and the Greeks referred to the totality of the Olympic Gods sitting in assembly as the Nine—the Ennead. The *Navamsa* (Sanskrit for number nine) is still identified with completion and perfection in India. When an astrologer looks for a life partner for a given natal chart or when someone seeks to learn what inner work or life mission is his or hers, the circle is divided by nine, and the planetary degrees in the person's natal chart are grouped in 40-degree angle relation to one another to determine the completion or perfection chart. The Greeks had nine Muses, and the Christians had nine choirs of angels standing closest to perfection— the unity of the Godhead.

The glyph, or symbol, for this archetype is the arrow ($\nearrow$). The phrase "straight as an arrow" describes perhaps the most important keyword that beginning astrology students learn for Sagittarius— bluntness, directness in speech. This directness is usually, like the arrow, sharply pointed. Sometimes it is amusing in a "foot-in-mouth" sense and sometimes it really wounds the target.

One foot-in-mouth remark that comes to mind is the greeting of a Sagittarian guest as she hugged her hostess whom she hadn't seen in several years: "How good to see you again, Martha, and *my God how fat you've gotten!*" But the arrow can also be intended to wound, especially if Sagittarian planets are accompanied by a few spiteful Scorpio planets in an individual horoscope. No chart is a pure, isolated archetype. Every personality is a blend of diverse energies. Thus, a Sagittarian whose Hermes/Mercury or communicator planet is in Scorpio may dip his arrow in Snake venom.

Beyond the Sagittarian communication style, however, straight as an arrow has another important meaning. A person who is straight with us is sincere, honest, truthful, above board. S/he's a person who is known to keep his/her promises. Regardless of the circumstances, his/her word is his/her bond. This is the pure archetype. Though Sagittarius expects this behavior of other people and tries to live up to the code himself, his arrow often lacks follow through. His promises are frequently not kept in the generous spirit in which they were intended because his energy is too scattered or over-extended; he's signed up for too many projects to complete them all. This is why myths about the art of archery are so applicable to Sagittarius. This archetype needs to practice concentration and focusing before shooting his/her arrows or making his/her promises.

In ancient Greece, India, and traditional Japan, archery was an important psychological and spiritual discipline. The student developed patience and presence of mind, but even more importantly, s/he learned to flow with the action—the process of releasing the arrow at the target. In the motion of releasing the arrow, the mind and body of the archer were one with the bow, the arrow, the motion and the target. Mastery of archery was, therefore, in ancient times a type of self-mastery. The heir to the throne who was also the winner of the archery competition, the Master, was deemed worthy to rule the kingdom. Arjuna, in the Hindu epic, the *Mahabaratha*, and Odysseus in the Greek *Odyssey*, were two such archer kings. In our own time, Eugen Herrigel, author of *Zen and the Art of Archery*, spent four years in Japan on this path to self-mastery. Herrigel's years in Japan brought him an understanding of the sacred doctrine of archery which very few Westerners have been privileged to experience. One quote from his Zen archery Master sheds light on the technique:

> Your arrows do not carry because they do not reach far enough spiritually. You must act as if the goal were infinitely far off. For master archers, it is a fact of common experience that a good archer can shoot further with a medium-strong bow than an unspiritual archer with the strongest. It does not depend on the bow, but on the presence of mind, on the vitality and awareness with which you shoot. In order to unleash the full force of this spiritual awareness, you must perform the ceremony differently, rather as a good dancer dances. If you do this, your movements will spring from the center, from the seat of right breathing. Instead of reeling off the ceremony like something learned by heart, it will then be as if you were creating it under the inspiration of the moment, so that dance and dancer are one and the same. By performing the ceremony like a religious dance, your spiritual awareness will develop its full force!

Archery is thus both a spiritual science and an art form. It is both mental and active, just as Sagittarius is Mutable and fiery. The Master says that the archer's goal must be seen as distant or far off. It's better to overshoot the target at first than to repeatedly have your arrows fall short of it—that can be discouraging.

With its confident belief in future greatness and the larger goal, Sagittarius sets a good example of vision and inspiration to the polarity sign, Gemini, and the square sign, Virgo. Both these Hermes-ruled archetypes tend to be short-sighted in comparison to Sagittarius; they are involved with the details of their craft and all too often do not go beyond craft to creativity, to enjoy the inspiration of the moment, to dance the uninhibited dance and passionately become one with the action. Hermes-ruled signs tend to worry too much about making a factual mistake whereas Sagittarius is able to relax, as the Zen master encouraged the archer to do, and enjoy the process. Many a Sagittarian client has said to me, in the vocabulary of the archer, "Well, that idea didn't work out, but I gave it my best shot and now I'm going to forget about it and go on to the next one." How happy most Virgos and Geminis would be if they could let go of the problem and move on rather than do prolonged mental post-mortems on the imperfections of the plan.

The art of archery also includes some modifications of the Sagittarian telephoto-lens view of reality. There is occasionally a need to apply the precise, accurate, Virgo/Gemini lens, to zero in on the target. It is this lesson which enthusiastic, energetic Arjuna, the young heir to the throne in the Hindu epic, had to learn. His overview of the big picture needs focus. Prince Arjuna and his four younger brothers applied to the learned Brahman, Drona, the Archery Master for acceptance as students. Drona, though, was an old man who considered his time very valuable; he no longer took on just any nobleman as a disciple. The brothers thus had to qualify as students through a session whereby they each took hold of the bow, showed him their stance, and answered his questions.

The youngest brother held the bow and concentrated. Drona asked, "What do you see?" He replied, "I see the mountain across the valley, the sky, the trees, and a bird on one of the treetops." "No," said Drona, "you do not pass. Get down." The second brother took his place with the bow. "What do you see?" asked the Master. "I see the sky, the mountain, a tree, a bird on its limb and you, out of the corner of my eye, Master." "Sorry," said Drona, "you fail. Next!" The third brother said, "Master, I cannot see you, but I hear your voice; I see only the tree, the limb and the bird." "Step down," said the Brahman, "for you also fail." The fourth brother saw only the limb and the bird, but he, like the others, didn't succeed. Finally Arjuna, having observed his younger brothers' scattered concentration and focus, took the stance and picked up the bow. "What do you see?" asked Drona. "I see only the bird, Master," said Arjuna. "Look again; concentrate harder," he was told. "Ah! I see only a spot on the center of the bird's forehead!" "Very fine. Release the arrow. You will be my student!" said the Master.

Thus, the long view, which comes naturally to Sagittarius, must be tempered with the precision corrective lens, or focus of Hermes—concentration. Both the telescopic and the microscopic views must work together in the Art of Archery, or as the Japanese Masters called it—the Sacred Doctrine. This is an important key to integrating Houses Three and Nine, or as the older textbooks called them, the lower (factual, technical) and higher (abstract) minds.

It's been my experience that education is a major part of the Sagittarian Path. The Master Archer must find his Drona and develop a trained mind. It's a pleasure to meet a Master Archer who has persevered in school long enough to benefit from the discipline and learn to organize his thoughts—to filter them through his head before blurting them out. A businesswoman client once told me she was exhausted from spending the morning interviewing two Sagittarian job candidates. Neither had been exposed to much formal education; both had opted to live life rather than to finish school. She said, "They were like forest fires that had gotten out of control. They were both so enthusiastic about the job opportunity. They made so many positive but inappropriate suggestions for changes in the position I was considering them to fill. They spoke in a disorganized, disconnected manner, starting to discuss one area of the job and then interrupting themselves to discuss another. It was as if they were coming at me from six different angles at once. Some of the ideas were good, but the presentation was terrible. I had to ask each of them at the end, 'Did you really take time to read the job description? To think through what you were going to say before coming in? Your ideas are interesting, but do you really understand what this job entails?' "

Without training in presenting their large ideas, Sagittarians can indulge in Gemini-like babble, which tends to work against them in the business world. They also tend to overgeneralize. Mental training is required to learn to think sequentially, as well as imaginatively—to learn to read the actual document (i.e., job description) in front of them, rather than to read between the lines or read too much into it.

This brings us back to the issue of centering, of quiet concentration in the archery lesson, and to the practical logic of Earth. The person who participates in this archetype can benefit from planets in fixity to stabilize the personality, from Saturn in a strong house or from a number of planets in the Earth signs (Taurus, Virgo, or Capricorn). Perhaps this is why Alice Bailey in *Esoteric Astrology* has Earth as the esoteric ruler of Sagittarius. The wisest Sagittarians I have met, those who are spiritual as well as spirited, and the happiest too, manifest in their everyday lives a practical, common-sense wisdom. Earth represents structure, organizing ability, commitment and responsibility. It's true that higher education can help focus or train the mind in some of these areas (like presenting one's ideas in such a way as to meet the job description), but even more important, it seems to me, is life experience—the progression of the Sun through Capricorn. Every Sagittarian has a thirty-year progression through Cardinal Earth where, often through the business world, he or she actively learns about reality through trial and error, like the other fire signs. Unlike the Air sign spectators, fire needs to be a *doer*, not an observer of life.

One such fiery activist was Hercules, a hero we met in the Aries chapter. Hercules was a sometime student of archery, whose teacher was Chiron the Centaur. The story of Hercules and his beloved friend and teacher adds another dimension to our understanding of Sagittarius—the generosity of the Sage. Chiron seems to have had a broader background than Drona, the Archer in the Hindu epic. He was also a scholar, a teacher, healer and adviser renowned for "just judgments." His physical form was most unusual. As a Centaur, he had the head and torso of a man, but the body of a horse. (*Bulfinch's Mythology* informs us that in no way did Centaurs seem monstrous or ugly to the Greeks, because they really loved their horses.) Chiron and his fellow Centaurs inhabited the forests of Thessaly, a wild part of the country, where they "roved free." If we visualize all these gigantic horsemen riding through the forest, we can readily understand the "don't fence me in" nature of the archetype, and especially of the Sagittarius rising, the bachelor Ascendant.

It should be observed that there were many different types of Centaurs, just as there were many different types of Sagittarians. Not all of them were as wise or as well-rounded as Chiron; in fact, he stood out in the crowd—or horde. Bulfinch tells us that many of the Centaurs were "rude guests." At the wedding feast of Hippodamia, for instance, one of them lost control, yielded to his passionate nature, dragged the bride off by the hair and attacked her. Several others followed his example. Jung sees the horse as a symbol of "instincts out of control," or the unconscious dominating the conscious mind, and this story of the wedding feast seems to bear him out. Yet in the *Upanishads* the horse is a symbol of the Cosmos (the Self). Chiron clearly represented the mind in control of the instincts, or riding of the horse. A kindly and educated Centaur, he apparently had aimed higher in life than the others. Yet, in his encounter with Hercules, even Chiron was vulnerable in the horse part of his body—his leg.

One day Hercules the Hero was passing through Thessaly on the way to a challenge, or task, when it occurred to him that Chiron might have some useful advice for him if he were to stop for a visit. He was impatient, however—(this *is* a Fire sign story)—and he did not want to wait with nothing to do while Chiron and the others roamed the far end of the forest. He demanded that the Centaur on duty open the wine and give him some. The scent of the wine at once reached the other Centaurs and they were furious. Either a thief had taken what was theirs without permission or an enemy approached their territory.

Hercules panicked when he heard the sound of their hooves tearing towards him. He could not see at all in the cloud of dust the horde had raised. He was extremely frightened that he would be trampled to death, so he instinctively fired a volley of arrows skyward. He did not take aim or concentrate, but wanted only to warn them— to let them know that the Great Hercules was there. Then, disconsolate, he discovered that one of the stray arrows had hit his friend and beloved teacher, Chiron, wounding him in the leg. Because Hercules had dipped the arrows in the Hydra's blood, an especially potent poison for which there was no antidote, Chiron, the wounded physician, could not heal himself. Chiron, so educated, so intelligent, so knowledgeable; Chiron, tutor to the famous healer Aesculapius; Chiron, the Immortal, could not stop his own wound from aching miserably.

Chiron, however, possessed a generous Sagittarian disposition. As an Immortal, he could not die, but offered graciously to retire to the underworld and trade places with Prometheus, so that the thief of Fire could be released. As Chiron departed for Tartarus, Hercules went sadly on his way, regretting the impatience which had prompted him to demand the wine. Like fiery Aries, Sagittarius is not good at patiently waiting, and often has trouble postponing gratification. Hercules knew that had the wine not been opened, the Centaurs would not have smelled it and there would have been no stampede. He vowed never again to shoot an arrow defensively without first tak-

ing careful aim and waiting till the dust had settled and the enemy became clearly visible. The Greeks record that eventually Chiron's wound did heal in the underworld and he ascended to take his place in the skies, in the constellation of Sagittarius.

In my acquaintanceship with this archetype, I have known many wise but wounded Chirons as well as many an impatient, impetuous young Hercules. When it comes to other people, the wounded Chiron can be a most effective, insightful counselor, for Apollo did give him the gift of prophecy. But when it comes to his own wound, the wise Sagittarian who serves others well prefers to avoid facing the issue as long as possible. Fire signs are very adept at projecting blame—the arrow, after all, is a projectile. It isn't enough to blame the outer world for the wound. "It's my husband's fault, my mother's fault, my boss's fault," etc. Fixing the blame on Hercules doesn't really accomplish anything constructive where healing the wound is concerned, even though Hercules may be the guilty party. To relieve the pain, Chiron had to descend into the underworld (the unconscious) with his instincts for his healing. Fire signs are often impatient with the inner process and break off their own counseling prematurely. They prefer to live in the outer rather than the inner world. The Ninth House, after all, is a Fire House, full of pleasant, distracting activities, travel, workshops, courses, conversations, books. Tartarus (therapy) is not a pleasant place for the Sagittarian to be for long periods of time. It is easier to say, "I have diagnosed myself as cured. The wound will go away if I change my outer environment—go back to school, go into sales instead of teaching." But in a new environment, the same old horoscope will continue to manifest (the wound to hurt). It takes patience, time and often another physician to heal a deep wound. Chiron had to spend time in Tartarus.

In her book *Alchemy*, Marie Louise von Franz says that washing the seven stars nine times means that the transformation may take nine or ten years of therapy. During the process one detaches oneself from projecting one's seven planets on the outer world. One learns that his complaint about his angry boss means that he is not in proper touch with his *own* Mars. If one complains about the type of relationship partner he consistently draws in the outer world he is projecting his inability to manifest his *own* Venus properly. Because the Sagittarius often projects his/her own problems, it may take him/her several angry bosses or difficult relationships to discover the pattern behind his/her projections and seek help. Sagittarius is greatly concerned with freedom, and to be free from these imprisoning projections, able to go about his/her life consciously and spontaneously, is well worth the effort expended in the alchemical purification.

Wisdom results from the practice of detachment and introspection tempered by compassion. Jupiter, ruler of Sagittarius, is exalted in Cancer, the archetype of the Great Mother. In Chinese art, Kwan Yin Bodhisattva, embodiment of Wisdom/Compassion, rides upon clouds wielding her bow and arrow to make war upon Evil. The wise and merciful mother, however, does not make war upon the evil-doer but only upon Evil itself. This is an important lesson for the Sagittarian to learn from the exaltation of its ruler in compassionate Cancer. The higher Sagittarian incorporates the wisdom and compassion of Kwan Yin in his/her efforts at right action.

At what, then, does the higher Sagittarian shoot his/her arrow? What is the highest target at which s/he could aim? The answer, I believe, is Truth. This is what Zeus, in his highest manifestation, meant to the Greeks, and this is what is implied in the Sagittarian search for honesty, sincerity, integrity and just judgment.

Why do we associate the search for Truth with the Sagittarian archetype? To answer these questions we must make the acquaintance of All Highest Zeus, later known to the Romans as Jove or Jupiter. Jupiter is not only the mundane ruler of Sagittarius and the Ninth House but, because of his grandiose nature, Zeus the All Highest exerts so strong an influence that no other planet could be exalted in his sign. The Sagittarian, like his ruler, manifests *big* virtues and *big* vices. The same would generally be true of an individual born with a Ninth House Jupiter, or Jupiter in Sagittarius.

Carolyi Kerenyi in *Zeus and Hera* tells us that when Zeus first appeared in Greece (most likely from Egypt or Babylon) he was felt as a force or Sacred Presence. No artists were needed to represent him. All Seeing Zeus was everywhere, on the hilltops, falling as a gentle rain or seen in the night sky as lightning or thunder. Zeus of the day sky was recognized by such positive omens as the flight of his eagle overhead or a sudden change in the weather that revealed his presence. Zeus of the night sky was a more frightening force. Zeus' presence was particularly felt in fires. In the dark caves of Crete and on the wild hilltops of Thessaly, the ancient Greeks felt Zeus' presence and protection in their camp fires. In every Sagittarian there is a spark of Zeus' sacred fire. Zeus and Theos (God) are one and the same. From the word Theos we derive the word enthusiasm. In every Sagittarian client—even those who seem to burn like forest fires out of control—there is this pure spark of Zeus' enthusiasm. There is an impulse to get on with it, to make progress toward the goal. Most twentieth century astrologers can easily relate to the positive traits of Jupiter/Zeus and to positive key words for Sagittarius.

Like the ancient Greeks we are aware that Jupiter is the great benefic. Like Venus, the lesser Benefic, it shines with a bright light. The ancients knew that Jupiter was the largest planet in our solar system. Today we know that it is the most massive and that were it only a bit larger it would be a Sun, the center of its own solar system, with planets revolving around it. Therefore we can easily appreciate the positive key words the Greeks attributed to Zeus—magnanimity, majesty or power, beneficence, abundance, spirituality, gravity, joviality or optimism, justice, truth, wisdom, etc. Modern astrologers can easily relate to Homer's Zeus who manifests in the *Iliad* and who was called the Counselor, All Seeing Zeus and Zeus the Wise. This would be the archetypal ideal.

In *Psychology of the Planets*, however, Francoise Gauqelin points out that the negative Jupiter key words rather than the positive were found to correspond to Jupiter strongly placed by House position in individual charts. Some of the negative key words she lists are: arrogant, proud, negligent, embarrasses others, overly optimistic, wasteful, verbose, extremist, provocative, extravagant, not critical, fanatical, lazy, irresolute, self-loving, pompous, ostentatious, opportunistic. These are the qualities that appear in the myths of Zeus of the Dark Sky who thundered at his enemies and did not spare the lightning bolts. The myth of Zeus' battle with Typhon has been related in the Scorpio chapter. Here we saw the arrogant, fanatical side of the All Highest. Rather than learn from Typhon (integrate his shadow) Zeus let fly his lightning bolt and killed his opponent, the son of Mother Earth. Liz Greene tells us in *The Astrology of Fate* that in Sagittarius, "fanaticism is generally closely linked with deep inner doubts." I also have found that when Sagittarians strike out with brutal force (Zeus' thunderbolt) they often do so from fear. Zeus was terrified of Typhon (his own nightmare). The Sagittarian client, rather than introspect about his own inner fears, will indulge Zeus-like in overreactions in the outer world. Zeus of the Dark Sky, the storm god, is the paradoxical side of the Sagittarian personality, the ill-tempered

side which acts out with the lightning bolt—reacts out of proportion to the crime committed against Zeus' Tribunal. (Zeus was known as the God of the Violent Hand because of his extreme temper.)

Especially appropriate for the Sagittarian stage of purification is Zeus Sykasios, a kingly figure who holds a cornucopia (abundance) and sends forth his royal Eagle messenger. We met this blood red eagle in *Prometheus Bound*. The Eagle went each day to the underworld to consume a bit more of Prometheus' liver, to purify him and purge him of his emotional toxins. Homer also tells us in the *Iliad* that Zeus was connected with sulphur, the alchemical purifier. Zeus washed things in sulphur and once destroyed a tree with his lightning bolt, leaving a lingering sulphur odor.

During their "sulphurous" thirty-year progression through Capricorn many Sagittarian clients have undergone a symbolic purification. They have developed their Saturn sense of planning, sharpened their focus on the goal at hand and developed a more realistic sense of their limitations where time, energy and money are concerned.

In *Please Understand Me*, Keirsey and Bates refer to the "work ethic" versus the "play ethic." The work ethic is quite saturnine (Capricornian) and the play ethic is more jovial (Sagittarian). By nature Sagittarius seems more inclined to keep his/her options open, resist fixed deadlines on his/her projects and to prefer spontaneity to long-term planning. As a Fire sign, the Sagittarian likes the project itself (the action) and not the preparation, maintenance, or clean up—s/he tends to disappear and let those parts of the project remain undone. During the Capricornian progression the Sagittarian encounters the work ethic at every turn. There is a Saturnian introspectiveness to the Capricorn progression, which enables Sagittarius to come to terms with Zeus of the Dark Sky and work with the negative Jupiter traits— procrastination, poor preparation, lapsed deadlines, etc. I have among my clientele several Sagittarians who have never been required to earn a living. (Some have inherited wealth; others have been supported by the spouse.) They have never been exposed to the work ethic in the form of an employer. They have lofty ideals which are out of proportion to the limits of their time and energy. One such Sagittarian mentioned that she would like to finish her degree but she didn't know where to start. Before her marriage she had taken a hodge-podge of courses—those that she enjoyed. She had not, however, taken many of the required courses. Twenty years later she wasn't any closer to her degree though it was still among her goals.

Another Sagittarian remarked that she knew her house was cluttered. In the abstract she would love to have her garage all cleaned out so she could move some items from the house to the garage. In fact, however, time went by and the clutter increased. When asked about it she said, "I don't know where to begin. Whenever I think about all the steps involved—sorting, pricing, calling the newspaper to advertise, making cookies for a garage sale, etc.—well, I am so exhausted just thinking about it I have to sit down."

Esoteric astrologers have rightly pointed out that Sagittarius has great aspiration and lofty goals but that it is weak on the follow-through. Often the Sagittarius perceives the goal as so distant that the first step seems insurmountable. One question or comment astrologers often hear from Sagittarius is "I don't know where to start." It has been my experience that the Capricorn progression has shown them where to start and how to maintain their progress. After the thirty-year progression through Capricorn the individual has learned through his/her association with the business world to develop common sense. S/he has a greater awareness of the practicality of his/her goals and the method by which to achieve them—to handle deadlines, to deal with stress, to adjust to the work routine. Those Sagittarians who have been self-employed during this progression have learned to deal with such details as employee paperwork, government forms, billing and collections and meeting licensing requirements in their field, but it has been painful in the extreme to many of them. However, they have developed what Jung would call groundedness.

The Sagittarian on the threshold of progressing into Aquarius says to the astrologer, "I am bored to death. I have achieved what I set out to accomplish in the outer world"—travel, academic success, recognition, even affluence. "Something's missing, though. Shouldn't I be happier in my personal life? I've been putting all this energy into the outer world but I feel my life is incomplete." What I usually say is, "take courage; you are beginning a long progression through Aquarius." Whether the Sagittarian client is married or single as s/he begins his Aquarian progression s/he tends to shift his energy away from the outer world of career and focus it upon relationship. Aquarius, like the other Air signs, is concerned with communicating and relating to others, but is more concerned with an egalitarian friendship. This does not mean that as soon as Sagittarius progresses into the new sign, he or she will suddenly want to bake cakes and clean up the house. It does mean that s/he will suddenly aspire with his usual lofty idealism to find a partner who shares his goals, who communicates well, who gives him/her lots of space, who shares his world view. In many cases the new partner likes to travel and is affluent.

In the first five years of the progression through Aquarius I have noticed a pattern develop. The Sagittarian would ask, "When am I going to meet a rich man (rich woman)?" They're seeking Jupiter in the outer world. They would like to marry their ruling planet (the guardian angel, the principle of abundance, the horn of plenty) and have it take care of them. I sometimes ask, "What are *you* going to bring to this relationship for which you have such high standards?" As they progress deeper into Aquarius they become more Fixed and tend to settle down in their personal relationships and become more realistic in their expectations. The Aquarian progression provides fixity of purpose and helps them with follow-through. As they progress into Aquarius many seem better able to manifest their dreams here on Earth. They seem to come closer to their Truth, which each Sagittarius perceives in his own way.

To the Greeks, All Highest Zeus was primarily regarded as the upholder of the Cosmic Order, Cosmic Law, Justice, Truth and Virtue. Zeus presided over promises made and oaths taken before witnesses. We know from Homer's *Iliad* that Zeus punished perjurers by sending them to Tartarus. Hermes tells us in *Prometheus Bound* that Father Zeus does not love a liar and "to speak false is unknown to the mouth of Zeus." Not for Zeus or Sagittarius the glib rationalization of airy Gemini, its polar extremity. For the ancient Greeks as well as the ancient Egyptian and Hindu civilizations thought and speech were causative. Therefore, when Hermes (Gemini's ruler) taught his son Autolycus spell-binding, or the imaginative art of giving false oaths, he was diametrically opposed to Zeus' instinct for truth. Scheming Geminis (Hermes) are 180 degrees away from Sagittarius (Zeus).

In her book *Alchemy*, Marie Louise von Franz describes this instinct for truth, which I have seen operate in so many of my Sagittarian clients. She says that anthropologists have found among primitive tribesmen a strongly developed sense for determining when someone was lying or concealing the truth. An informant would tell the anthropologist that a wealthier fisherman had offered what sounded like a good opportunity to go out with him in his new boat. Yet the man would refuse to go because he knew that though the other fisherman spoke well he was not a good man. Von Franz says that in our sophisticated modern culture we have lost this instinct for truth. Yet, I often see it in my Sagittarian clients. And, like Zeus, they "do not love a liar."

One young woman with several planets in Sagittarius mentioned matter of factly that she had broken her engagement because her fiance told her one lie. To him it was a little white lie told because he didn't want to hurt her feelings. But to her it reflected a deeper insincerity. She said, "If he lied to me once he will do it again. If he lies about small things he will lie about big ones too." She had picked up on the lie instinctually.

Zeus, sitting on his tribunal, does not weigh the words but instinctively knows the truth or falsity behind them. In the Gemini chapter we have already come across Zeus' ability to see through Hermes' imaginative alibis in the case of Apollo's stolen cattle. Alice Bailey tells us in *Esoteric Astrology* that Mercury (Hermes) is weakened in its power in Sagittarius. This has seemed really true over the years with my Sagittarian clients. I do not mean that they are unintelligent; rather that facts, logic and particular circumstances (situation ethics) are irrelevant. Like Zeus himself many Sagittarians through their instinct for truth can look beyond the Gemini facts, no matter how beautifully organized, and see the fallacy. That is what makes this archetype so appropriate to the courtroom environment.

Like Zeus, Sagittarians have a strong sense of justice. So many times while listening to them describing their feeling of outrage at what has been done by a supervisor to a fellow employee I am reminded of a biblical quote from the Beatitudes, "Blessed are those who hunger and thirst for justice sake, for theirs is the Kingdom of Heaven" (Matthew 5:6). As extroverts, Sagittarians often crusade on others' behalf or attempt to set others' wrongs right. Their view of justice differs from that of Libra. While Libra is concerned with fairness, with a mental balance of the scales, fiery Sagittarius is coming from the emotions and the desire to act—to *do something* to right the wrongs in the environment. While Sagittarian spontaneity definitely has its advantages, Pythagoras, who loved Zeus above all else, said that justice must be tempered by prudence. He considered prudence the greatest mental virtue, essential for a balanced life. It's possible for Sagittarius to get a reputation as office troublemaker for constantly crusading.

Justice in the abstract is an important part of the Sagittarian quest for truth. Pythagoras tells us that justice is the most important of his four virtues and is contained in the other three: prudence in thought, courage in action, and temperance in matters involving the senses. He tells us that justice is "a hope that can not deceive us." For those on his Path of Truth and Wisdom the justice card in the Tarot deck is an appropriate symbol for meditation. For Pythagoras, justice had more in common with harmony than with compensating the victim. It was not a mathematical process of exacting an eye for an eye and a tooth for a tooth. It was a matter of upholding the Cosmic Order. Zeus was an Absolute Judge. Yet, the Tarot card Justice is very feminine. She wields a sword representing discrimination in one hand and holds a scale in the other. Like the Goddess Athena, she wears a helmet symbolizing courage. She stares straight ahead as if, detached and impartial, she sees beyond the facts and personalities of the litigants to Truth itself. Thus, she seems to blend masculine courage and discrimination with the feminine feeling for truth. She seems to say that justice is indeed a hope that can not deceive us. She seems to say "take justice to heart and look within; judge yourself rather than seek righteous retribution from others."

Astrologers often encounter litigious clients—those who repeatedly seek compensation in the courtroom. They often come to ask for good dates to go to court. Cosmic Order would be better served if the litigants would seek to restore harmony rather than seek financial compensation. It has been my experience that a litigious attitude tends to involve the client in a vicious circle of lawsuits. It has also been my experience that litigation produces avarice, one of the vices Pythagoras warns against.

To the Greeks, Father Zeus was not simply a just Judge; he was also a merciful Father. He forgave Prometheus with Sagittarian magnanimity. Zeus does not hold grudges. Neither do Sagittarians. They are quick to anger and quick to forgive. Though the city of Ilium, the capitol of the Kingdom of Troy, was filled with his loyal and devoted followers, Zeus listened to the prayers of one Greek mother for her son, changed the course of the battle and allowed the Greeks to destroy Ilium. He was nothing if not Mutable. Zeus' myths were full of surprises. He had a love of freedom reminiscent of the Sagittarian personality. He traveled widely. His myths are Panhellenic.

Zeus, then, first appeared to the Greeks as an impersonal god with tremendous power who could strike suddenly with his bolt in the night, or as a reassuring presence that could be felt on the mountaintop during a pleasant picnic lunch. It was Zeus' moral power that upheld the kingship and the social order on Earth. The kings derived their authority from Zeus and were in turn expected to live up to their responsibilities, keep their oaths, as well as protect their subjects from danger. Xenophon, for instance, according to Carolyi Kerenyi, had a dream from Zeus that offered him the kingship—a destiny dream. Thunder shook his house and lightning hit close by so that the whole house was bathed in light. And he knew that Zeus "stood behind him and wanted him to have the power."

Zeus was Sender of Dreams and Wise Counselor for many mortals, but especially for kings. Plato, in the first book of the *Laws*, recounts a legend from Crete, Zeus' birthplace, where he was particularly revered. The kings of the Minoan dynasty, according to the legend, met once every nine years with Zeus near the cave where he was born and were inspired in their lawmaking. Plato tells us that while these meetings took place the Sun stood still overhead and there was a feeling of rest, of peace, of timelessness. The impression one has of Zeus as an impersonal spirit is, to my mind, similar to the one certain Christian sects have of the Holy Spirit, who is also a presence rather than a personal deity, and who is also called Counselor.

Zeus' free spirit attitude, as well as his role of protector of the social order beyond the home and personal life seems to have carried over and influenced the attitude and lifestyle of so many of my Sagittarian clients. Not only do they crusade against injustice and discrimination at work, seek to defend and protect the meek or the victims in the environment, but their spouses often complain to the astrologer that this dedication to larger goals keeps them away from the family for a good deal of time or that they uproot the family and take it along on one of their crusades. The spouses see a devotion to the impersonal or larger world at the expense of the personal home and hearth.

Many Sagittarians see themselves as catalysts, people who bring the world together—make it smaller by their contacts and in their work promote a larger human understanding between nations. A faculty wife, married to a Sagittarian professor who is such a catalyst, once remarked, "He thinks it's great to have had three sabbaticals in ten years and to have dragged all of us to three countries where we knew not a word of the language. He's helped many foreign students come here, but what about our own children—what will they know of their country? He feels they've had tremendous advantages to have seen the world, how other people think and act at their ages, but what about the friendships they set aside at home—how children *here* think and act?" Personal desire to see the larger picture, expand their own horizons, and wanderlust are as much a part of Sagittarius' motivation as the dedication to "making the world a better place," of course.

A man married to a Sagittarian teacher made a similar comment: "I knew she wasn't very domestic when I married her. She doesn't cook and we have to hire a cleaning woman or we'd be sticking to the kitchen floor, but what really bothers me is that she keeps putting off having *our* family—having children—so she can continue to teach other people's kids and be free to spend every summer in Europe traveling with her women friends. I did think when we got married that she'd eventually want her own family, but she likes showing her European slides to the kids in her geography class too much, I guess." Well, showing slides of Europe to American children is a way of bringing the world together. Zeus, after all, wanted the Greeks and the Trojans to get along together. (He actually seemed fonder of the foreigners—the Trojans—than of the Greeks, if the truth were told.)

A client once asked about her Sagittarian husband, "Do you think all of his cross-country business trips are really necessary? Sometimes I think he just uses them to avoid me and the children. I think we make him feel claustrophobic." I replied that yes, there *is* a certain restlessness to the sign and to its ruling planet, Zeus/Jupiter, which is associated with space and with motion in astrology—with a need to go the distance and cover the miles, to experience as much of life as possible, and that I think the trips release a lot of energy for him, quite apart from the business involvement. She was a feeling type and wanted him home, to relate to her, and found this difficult, but the Centaur roaming through the wide open spaces is part of the archetypal journey for the Ninth House and the ninth sign. Many clients with Ninth House planets have regularly taken a year or two off from work, traveled abroad and returned to find another job with another company. To them travel has been much more important than the supposed benefits of long-term employment with the same firm.

Many Sagittarius rising clients have been unable to satisfy the desire to travel prior to retirement, but have always dreamed of being totally mobile in a van or camper and really free to see the country upon retirement. If the spouse doesn't share the yen for faraway places and would rather be within sight of the grandchildren, this creates retirement problems. My client experience with this particular "don't fence me in" ascendant is that the wide open spaces beckon and the client enjoys spending his or her free time in the forest or the mountains, much like a Centaur. Often marriage is delayed until the wanderlust dwindles in mid-life (often the forties), or a home in the mountains is found as a second residence so the Jupiterian personality can be free to think amidst nature, away from the hectic pace of city life and the concrete jungle.

We come now to an interesting question about impersonal Zeus, the free spirit. How was he at forming close relationships with others? Had he really the desire to settle down with Hera and have a family or was he happier single? Homer and the later Greek writers of mythology seem to be telling us that he was quite promiscuous. They cite a long list of affairs and illegitimate children, and an angry consort, Hera, as evidence. Yet, I have never come across a promiscuous Sagittarian who did not have deceitful aspects in the chart or many Scorpio planets that loved intrigue and mystery (the planning of the affair as well as the sexual passion). Further, there would seem to be a real paradox here if we have the upholder of ethics, truth, honesty and morality involved in breaking his word and failing to keep his own law—live up to his own marriage contract.

It would be logical to assume that if Zeus were a fickle sort of god, then Sagittarius would be inclined to marital disloyalty, undependable conduct, or promiscuity. Pythagoras told his followers not to think such things of Zeus, and not to read Homer's epics, because they were full of slander about the gods, particularly Zeus. Having read Pythagoras, I looked further at the interpretations of the Zeus myths and found a good explanation in Kerenyi's *Zeus and Hera*. According to Kerenyi, Zeus was a free spirit who remained a bachelor for a long time after his arrival in Greece, but the mythmakers finally married him off to Hera, the Great Mother, most widely worshipped of all the Greek goddesses. The mythmakers apparently sought to have an archetypal couple—King and Queen, Father God and Mother Goddess, so they tied Zeus down with a wife. (Kerenyi's interpretation seemed logical after reading the accounts of the same process occurring in India, where Lord Shiva was married to all the goddesses in South India by various mythmakers and thus included in the goddess worship through his new tie to the older deities.)

Some of the first representations of Zeus to be found were images in the Hera temples of Samos and Attica, the most important cult sites of the Great Mother. In Samos, for instance, terra cotta statues were discovered of Hera and a bearded youth (Zeus) standing next to a royal bed. Similar statuary was found in Attica. In Samos the marriage of King and Queen, Father and Mother was celebrated annually by Hera's devotees, just as today in South India one can see the re-enactment of the wedding between Lord Shiva and a local goddess, Meenakshi, at Madurai Temple. In Greece as in India the mythmakers began by attributing power to the Feminine, extended it to an archetypal couple where god and goddess were equally powerful, then in the Age of the Heroes, shifted the power to a patriarchal Father God.

What was the wedding really about? One can understand Zeus and Hera providing legitimacy to the human king, lending their support from Mt. Olympus to the moral order here on Earth, but what, if any non-political meaning did the wedding have? The cult titles provide very interesting clues. Zeus was known as Hera's Right Thundering Husband, and after the ceremony she was called completed Hera (Hera Teleia) and Zeus was called Bringer of Completion (Zeus Teleios). The Greeks thus envisioned that marriage brought about a perfection or completeness. Much was made of the concept that both were purified and perfect beings, so that the Ninth House of the gods bestowed perfection on the Seventh House—the human institution of marriage. In astrology we have a sextile relationship between Houses Seven and Nine. In Indian astrology the Ninth House is the marriage house—the soul mate house where completion takes place between the masculine and feminine as they merge in marriage.

We have seen in the Libra chapter that the spiritual ideal is often projected upon the partner. We hope that the marriage ceremony will complete our lives and help us to perfect or balance (the Libran scales of the Seventh—marriage house) our own energies. Even today many of us envision marriage as a completion through union with our ideal partner—the anima or animus in its positive manifestation. This idea of "completed" and "bringer of completion" from the Zeus and Hera wedding seems similar to the Hindu theory of the soul mate. Hindus who subscribe to the Soul Mate theory believe that each of us is seeking the other half—the part of his or her soul that split off centuries ago to take rebirth in many bodies, male and female, and experience life to the fullest. Some lifetime, according to this theory, each of us will meet the other half of its own soul and merge once again into completeness. The Zeus-Hera completion, then, may have had a deeper spiritual (Ninth House) meaning besides its political meaning of legitimizing a local king and queen, or even legitimizing human marriage as an institution.

Thus, depending upon one's reading of the mythology, Zeus either found his soul mate or his nemesis in Hera. Perhaps it was a mixture of both, as it seems to be for so many of my married Sagittarian clients. The restlessness of the All Highest was contained, restricted. He was claustrophobic perhaps. Still, it is hard to believe that he was fickle or lacked integrity, honesty and commitment to Hera. In Homer's epic, Zeus and Hera seemed a pretty incompatible couple. She, the All Powerful Great Mother, has been reduced by Homer to a nagging shrew, and All Highest Zeus to a henpecked husband. There is still something to be gleaned from the author's poetic license with mythological tradition though. He has Zeus threaten to hang Hera up by the heels as punishment if she won't keep quiet.

Though Mutable, Sagittarius is a Fire sign and does have a temper. Sagittarians really do not like coming home after a day's work wanting to play and instead being presented with someone's petty list of grievances or things to do before they've had a chance to let off steam by going to the tennis court or the gym, bowling, joining a pal for racquetball, etc. Exercise is a better outlet for working off the day's outrages than being told to fix the old refrigerator.

Ptolemy mentioned "rest" as an important keyword for Jupiter/ Zeus. It means both peace and relaxation. Sagittarian parents, like Sagittarian spouses, have a difficult time coming right home to unpleasantness instead of rest and relaxation. One Sagittarian parent called me in a state of extreme outrage after her clash with her son's teacher. She said, "I came home after a miserable day at work to a message on my answering machine. I didn't listen to all of it but the gist of it was that Andy's teacher had kept him after school as a punishment for something I knew he could never have done. I had to drive clear across town to get him myself and I was fuming. How could she treat my child like that? Would you believe, after I gave his teacher a piece of my mind, I found out he had really done what she had said. She told me that I was presumptuous, arrogant, pompous and had clearly not bothered to listen to the whole phone message. The worst part was that Andy—the little wretch—thought I had embarrassed him. He told me that he wanted to fight his own battles and that the teacher would probably hold my yelling at her against him. He ought to be glad that he has a mother who sticks up for him."

My own immediate reaction to the story was that the Sagittarian client's outrage over a supposed injustice interfered with her usual instinct for truth. Of course any mother, regardless of her date of birth, has difficulty being objective about her own child. Before wielding the sword of justice, however, it is important to get the message, to get all the facts in the situation. Often the Fire signs err by acting before all the facts are in. In this case her son had a valid point—he should be empowered to fight his own battles. This client's story reminded me of Father Zeus over-reacting to protect his son, Dionysius.

When Dionysius first appeared in Greece, a very stubborn king, Lycurgus of Thrace, refused to worship him for what he, Lycurgus, considered to be very good reasons. Dionysius was at first frightened of Lycurgus and took refuge in the sea. Later, feeling more courageous, Dionysius came back to capture Lycurgus and put him in a cave. After some time Lycurgus emerged from the cave with great respect for the god whom he had mocked. It was at this point that Zeus heard that his son was being treated with disrespect by a mere mortal. Furious at the news, Zeus immediately went to Thrace and struck Lycurgus blind. Like most mortals who felt the wrath of Zeus of the Dark Sky, Lycurgus died soon after. The other gods told Zeus that they felt he had overreacted. On several such occasions Apollo took Zeus aside to calm him when he was outraged against injustice. This myth of Zeus and his son seems an amazing parallel to my client and her son. Like the client, Zeus did not investigate the situation in Thrace before he took action. He was unaware that Dionysius had already fought his own battle; she was unaware that her child had been "justly" punished.

Though all of the Greek Zeus myths were associated with the Roman Jupiter, his role as *pater* or Father was the most important by Roman times. In Latin, Jupiter is *Iu-pater* or Heavenly Father. His moral force and his association with truth telling and the keeping of oaths were seen by the Romans as the source of his power. Our expression "by Jove" comes from the old Roman oath in Jupiter's name. In his moral role the Roman Jupiter is similar to Yahweh who gave Moses the Ten Commandments. The Zeus who was a free spirit to the Greeks became the arbiter of the moral law of shoulds and oughts to the Romans. Zeus, both of the Dark Sky and of the Light Sky, seems to have been assimilated when Christianity became centered in Rome. Zeus of the Dark Sky seems to manifest in Christianity as the righteous retribution by which the Father casts sinners into an eternal hell. (This Christian hell differs greatly from Tartarus, the Greek hell, where those who offended Zeus were purified and eventually obtained release.) Zeus of the Light Sky seems to fulfill the role of the Father's forgiving nature in Christianity. As Zeus progressed from Greek to Roman and on to Christian times he seems to have become more rigid. He seems to have lost a lot of his mutability. Yet, like Zeus Sykasios, Zeus with the horn of plenty, the Christian Heavenly Father provides both material and spiritual abundance.

In our study of the Sagittarian and Ninth House archetype we have discussed higher education, travel, justice and the instinct for truth. One major issue remains—Spirituality. Many older astrology text books referred to the Ninth House as the House of Religion. My experience with this archetype has resulted in a somewhat different understanding. I think that in the twentieth century we could call it the House of the Way of Life. Just as Zeus had many different titles and was worshiped by people at many different levels of understanding, there are many types of Sagittarians and many levels at which the Ninth House can be experienced. One meaning is ethical morality. A client with several Ninth House planets, for instance, asked, "Do the Eastern religions have an ethical or moral basis? Do they have something like the Ten Commandments?" I told her yes and mentioned Patanjali's *Yoga Sutras*. Her understanding of the Ninth House was purely ethical. The esoteric writers such as Alice Bailey and Isabel Hickey interpreted the Ninth House somewhat differently—a religious philosophy of the Self, spiritual visions, the wisdom upon which one bases one's actions in practical life situations. Ninth House wisdom is based upon the instinct for truth.

This is similar to the path of Jyana Yoga (wisdom and truth) in India. When it is accurate, it is wonderful to behold. An example would be the wisdom of Solomon. Following instinct rather than logic, he decided between two mothers, each of whom claimed the same baby. "Cut the child in half and give half to each mother." This practical wisdom was based upon innate understanding of what a real mother would do in that situation—give up her child so that it could live. In this particular case, Solomon's instinct for truth was right on target. The other Mutable signs often fail to understand Sagittarius or people with Ninth house planets. They see such decisions as totally arbitrary and irrational. A Gemini or Virgo attorney who had prepared a complex brief for Solomon's court would have been furious. Even when certain that the truth instinct is accurate, Sagittarius would do well to look over those briefs just in case.

The Ninth House is the third Fire House and completes the Fire Trine from body (Aries), individual soul (Leo), to spirit (Sagittarius). This is an experience that goes beyond adherence to religious dogma, listening to polished sermons in church on Sunday, or performing rituals with a distracted mind. Most of my Sagittarian clients would much rather experience Truth by communing with nature on Sunday than hear Truth interpreted for them by a minister in a stuffy church. There is an opinionatedness or arrogance and a narrowness to Sagittarius and the Ninth House which is quite paradoxical if one thinks in terms of spirit (universality) and the expansiveness of Jupiter. Liz Greene called it fanaticism. Francoise Gauquelin, while discussing Jupiter, mentioned arrogance. I attribute the paradox in the behavior of individual Sagittarians or Ninth House clients and the tolerant broad-minded Jupiter ideal to the underlying zeal, the crusading spirit, of the archetype itself. In practice, it's all too easy to mistake one's own truth for the Whole Truth.

So often individual clients have blind spots. In the case of Sagittarius or people with Ninth house planets a blind spot topic will come up in the course of a conversation, the individual will quote an authority figure from childhood or college days, or a scripture as the authority, to the effect that nothing good can be said about a particular sect, race, political philosophy, or sometimes a New Age philosophy like astrology. If the Ninth House is the House of the Philosophy of Life it can all too frequently be the House of "my philosophy alone is true, all others are fallacious."

A few examples of this would be: "My college professor told me thirty years ago that astrology was just superstition. Therefore I certainly won't waste my time on it. I get angry when people take it seriously." This individual adheres religiously to his atheism. (He has four planets in the Ninth House.)

Another said, "After reading the Freud-Jung correspondence, I was completely turned off by Freud. He has no depth whatsoever. I resent having to take courses in Freudian psychology to qualify for state licensing."

Two examples from non-Western religion: "As a Buddhist whose goal is liberation from the cycle of rebirth I am really amused at the Christian Heaven—such delusion. These people are as simplistic and as superstitious as the illiterate peasants in my country."

"My Master told me not to study or perform the hatha yoga exercises because they make use of the body and you can't take it with you when you die. Those people are really wasting their time."

Sagittarian zeal can be blind. My impression is that the purification work of the Ninth House involves a Jupiterian expansion of consciousness beyond all petty narrowness, beyond the residue of bigotry from childhood in this life or even, if the Ninth House planets are in Fixed Signs, beyond the bigotry of past lives. The antidote to misplaced zeal, opinionatedness, and pompous behavior lies 180° away in Gemini. Hermes, Gemini's ruler, deals in facts rather than emotionality and knows that there is truth in every philosophy.

We all participate in this archetype. Even if we have nothing in Sagittarius or no planets in the Ninth House we have Jupiter in some House of the chart. We might ask ourselves about that House, "Am I a bit smug about my talents? Does it make me really outraged if I am challenged in that House? Will I fight blindly to protect my interests there? Do I rest on my laurels at times in that House? Do I just philosophize and dream about future achievements in this House? It has been my experience that a person needs to have total faith in the issues of Jupiter's House, that s/he must struggle against a tendency to procrastinate or wait for good things to happen without putting forth much effort.

Pythagoras says that knowledge, especially useful knowledge, will prevent mental laziness, sharpen our discrimination and lead to wise judgment. I think this is important for understanding the working of the learning/communication axis from Gemini to Sagittarius:

> Thy judgment, therefore, sound and cool preserve, nor lightly from thy resolution swerve.
> The dazzling pomp of words dost oft deceive, and sweet persuasion wins the easie to believe.
>
> Golden Verses, #22

Sagittarius as a Fire sign seeks to take action on its decisions, to reach resolution, to move beyond Gemini's hesitant stance at life's crossroads. (Airy Gemini can go on contemplating both sides of a decision until the opportunity has moved on to knock at someone else's door). Yet, Sagittarius often brings heat rather than light to bear on a subject. Pythagoras' sound, cool judgment is 180° away, in the opposite sign, waiting to be intregrated. Useful knowledge to Pythagoras included the study of ethics and philosophy to enhance discrimination, develop objectivity, and learn to analyze data as an Air sign would naturally do. If Sagittarius is unschooled in logic, s/he can go through life the enthusiastic, unwary prey of glib lower Gemini salespeople. Lower Sagittarius, the lazy mind, listens to the Trickster, the lower side of Gemini, which is capable of editing or distorting facts and putting together what is on the surface a beautiful, logically constructed sales presentation. A lazy Sagittarian, an impulsive buyer will say, "Why should I go to the library and read *Consumer Digest* or shop around elsewhere? This is obviously a very smart salesperson who has done the comparison shopping for me already. S/he knows his/her product. S/he's right. All the yuppies have these things and I need one, too. I'll just sign the contract to buy it and then I can get out of here and go to the mountains for the weekend." "Haste makes waste," however, and the next morning s/he will be on the phone a long time trying to get out of the contract instead of going to the mountains.

Sound and cool judgment would be the polarity reaction. If the Sagittarian had taken Logic 101, s/he would have been warned against phony statistics, arguments from authority (all the yuppies have bought these) and glittering generalizations. S/he would analyze not only Madison Avenue ads in the course (eat this breakfast cereal because a famous baseball player eats it) but also his own thinking. Do I dislike the Japanese because my father fought in World War II? Do I form my philosophy of life on the basis of authorities' views or do I analyze their views and form my own—politically, religiously, etc.? Education in Ninth House topics is especially useful knowledge. Pythagoras also recommended music (harmony) and mathematics as expansive fields which engendered objective thinking.

Sagittarius could profit from the last part of the Pythagorean verse, "do not lightly from thy resolution swerve." Too often people will say of Sagittarius, "I was so impressed with that person when I first met him/her. S/he was so persuasive, zealous, convincing. I was sure s/he would pursue our cause in City Hall and get us a fair settlement, but s/he seems to have pooped out. Our St. George got distracted and never made it to the dragon's den." Leos, particularly, have remarked over the years that they can't take Sagittarians very seriously. When Sagittarians get all excited about something, Leo thinks they're Fixed or resolved (the way a Leo would remain), but they're not. The progression through Aquarius adds Fixed resolution and airy objectivity to the individual with Sagittarian or Ninth House planets.

Truth and wisdom are the goals of philosophy, the Pythagorean Spiritual Path, but not reason for its own sake. Jupiter is not Hermes the student, the scribe. Pythagoras tells us, "the reasoning art to various ends applied, is oft a sure, but oft an erring guide." For that reason, he says, it is important to choose "wise and virtuous friends" and not be stubborn, but listen objectively to their counsel and forgive them their faults so as to preserve the friendship. Strife, according to Pythagoras, lies in everyone's bosom waiting to be aroused, so one should not use words to arouse it in others, but rather to restore harmony. We undergo difficult experiences sometimes in order to learn, but Jove (God) is not malicious—"he does not afflict the good." In times of difficulty, "from Wisdom seek relief, let her healing hand assuage thy grief" (verse #19). Then "Thy wounded soul to health thou shalt restore, and free from every pain she felt before" (verse #66).

Right Reason (Gemini) lies opposite Right Action (Sagittarius) and integrating them is the function of the learning/communication axis, Houses Three to Nine, as well as of the Gemini/Sagittarius archetypes. To this end, Pythagoras gives us further guidance in his symbols or aphorisms at the end of the Golden Verses:

"Keep the Vinegar Cruet far from you." (verse #29) Vinegar to Greeks is the gall of satire. Proper use of reason should not involve putting down others with sarcastic remarks intended to wound.

"Avoid a two-edged sword." (verse #40) To the Greeks this meant a slanderous tongue. We are instructed to avoid gossipy, slanderous people.

"Stir not up the Fire with a Sword." (verse #5) Say nothing to inflame people who are already at odds with each other.

"Sow Mallows, but never eat them." (verse #13) Be mild in judging others but not in judging yourself.

In reflecting on these aphorisms, I looked around at a dinner party. Sagittarius was philosophizing expansively and very generally on a topic he really knew nothing about. He was getting people's attention but I doubt he did much harm. The next morning few of them were likely to remember what he had said. Gemini, however, at the other end of the table, was making funny but sarcastic remarks at someone else's expense. She was great entertainment but the remarks were direct, specific and likely to be remembered. This behavior exemplifies lower Gemini and lower Sagittarius. Pythagoras tells us not to speak "beyond our knowledge" and to "be just in word and deed." For their first five years at Pythagoras' school the disciples were known as "hearers" and were not allowed to speak at all. In the sixth year those who were considered ready were initiated and were allowed to teach. This five-year period of silence might seem extreme today. But the Gemini/Sagittarius axis often chatters, and listening is an important part of communication. Also receptivity, opening the channel to wisdom, is facilitated by silence.

Truth (Wisdom) is the philosopher's goal. We cannot reach the truth by telling lies like Hermes the Trickster, by communicating the facts in a selective way or making ourselves look good at someone else's expense.

"When Fools and Liars labour to persuade, be dumb, and let the Bablers vainly plead." (verse #23)

"Let no Example, let no soothing Tongue, Prevail upon thee with a Syren Song, To do thy Souls' Immortal Essence wrong. Of good and ill by Words or Deeds exprest, Chuse for thyself, and always chuse the best." (verses #24-27)

Truth is more than the adding up of Gemini facts. For Pythagoras, truth was the goal of the ethical or philosophical path. Zeus, or "the mystic Four" (our glyph for Jupiter (♃)) was the key. In the Golden Verses, Pythagoras tells us that the mystic four is the "source of eternal nature and almighty power." It is "what bounds the parts and unites the whole." It is the four seasons—the totality of the year, and the four virtues. It is the Four Ages of Man—infancy, youth, adulthood, old age, the totality of his life. The Four is also called the Quaternion. C.G. Jung points out in *Psychology and Alchemy* that this quaternion is the "psychic space" of the unconscious which appeared in many individual's dreams. It may refer to the four functions of the psyche: thinking, feeling, intuition and sensation, or to the process of integrating the inferior function.

Pythagoras and his disciples also practiced dream interpretation and quite probably experienced the sacred psychic space themselves. In astrology we have the Quaternity of four quadrants within the horoscope. We orient ourselves in reading charts and reading dreams according to where the planets are within the quadrants. In dream study we begin to interpret from the quadrant in which the dreamer stands and then trace his movement through the others. Like the Pythagoreans and the dreamers Jung studied, astrologers also have a quaternion of four elements: Air, Earth, Fire and Water. The Four is seemingly universal. American Indian rituals are often centered around a sacred place laid out to the four cardinal points and in China the square quaternion mandala represents the Earth Mother who gave birth to the cosmos. It has long served as a Buddhist meditation symbol.

Pythagoras believed that the word Zeus was a mantra which meant Light (enlightenment) but more importantly that it was a "mystik" or causative mantra—the first principle, power or energy which created the cosmos. Pythagoreans invoked Zeus' name before beginning their day or any important project. They sought to contact the Source of creative power and energy. Esoteric astrology preserved the hidden teaching of Jupiter and the Four not only in the glyph but in Jupiter's exaltation in the Fourth House and in the fourth sign.

In astrology, we normally use transiting Jupiter to answer questions about moves and long-distance travel—about motion in the outer world. However, apparently the esoteric tradition experienced Jupiter through dreams and meditation as inner space, as what Jung called psychic space. In India, Jupiter is known as Guru by astrologers. In the House where our Jupiter sits, and in the House with Sagittarius on the cusp, if we can transcend such negative traits as pride, extremism (immoderate behavior) or arrogance and replace them with the Pythagorean virtues of temperance, prudence, humility and justice, we are on our way to the goal. We already have God's blessing to help us through Jupiter's presence in that House.

The gifts of Jupiter (including wisdom and understanding) listed in the *Golden Verses* and the commentaries are similar to the gifts of the Holy Spirit in Christianity. The Leo Quest for the individual Self resulted in an experience of wholeness and personal creativity. Pythagoras' Path of Purification expands beyond the individual Self to universal Spirit and to immortality. The Sagittarius experience completes the Fire Trine of Body, Soul and Spirit.

The Four is a solid cube. In Pythagorean geometry it is the first solid figure. It meant Earth or matter to the Greeks and to the Chinese. Matter is solid ground—the foundation, cornerstone, or Nadir. Earth is the esoteric ruler of Sagittarius. Through his philosophy of balance, called the Golden Mean, Pythagoras sought to ground his young disciples, those fiery, Mutable, freespirited seekers. In the *Autobiography of a Yogi* Paramahansa Yogananda tells of his first experience of the Spirit of God as inexhaustible Bliss. When he came back to Earth after the vision, his Guru, Sri Yukteswar said, "much yet remains for you in the world. Come; let us sweep the balcony floor; then we shall walk by the Ganges." Yoganandaji said that his Master was teaching him the secret of balanced living—keeping one's head in the clouds and one's feet on the ground.

There are three Earth signs. The first, Taurus, refers to value. The esoteric teaching was: Esteem thine own soul above all. Do nothing in word or deed to wrong the soul. On the mundane level, Taurus means "be neither a spendthrift nor avaricious." Virgo, the second Earth sign, represents humility. In aphorism #50 Pythagoras says, "When it thunders, touch the ground." When Jupiter (God) expresses anger through someone in our environment, instead of instinctively yelling back, respond with humility—touch the ground. Capricorn, the third Earth sign, relates to advance planning. One's dreams cannot be realized without this. Earth also relates to the body. The Golden Mean involved daily exercise, abstention from meat eating, sufficient rest, and "prudent supply of the body's needs."

When esoteric astrology texts speak of Sagittarius as Spirit or we think of Sagittarius as the final stage of an alchemical purification, it sounds almost too easy. Zeus himself walked about for two or three months with a painful limp before giving birth to his divine child Dionysius whom he had carried in his thigh. Stories from Hindu and Old Testament sources as well as Greek myth link the hip or thigh, the Sagittarian part of the body, with gaining wisdom and understanding.

Liz Greene has found a correlation between her Sagittarian clients and hip injuries. I have noticed among my clientele a general correlation between painful out-of-joint hips and the need to take time out from work to reflect, to gain understanding, ponder one's philosophy of life, or get in touch with the Spirit within. I have especially noticed among elderly clients lacking in inner focus this tendency toward hip problems or sciatica.

Whether one works on the purification through meditation, introspection, or dream interpretation, the process often begins with an injury to the Sagittarian part of the body—Chiron's wound.

In *Genesis* 32: 24-30 Jacob dreamed that he wrestled an entire night with a strange man (angel) and only at daybreak, when the stranger touched Jacob's hip and threw it out of joint, was he able to win the fight. At the end of the dream, Jacob asked the stranger for his blessing and received a new name—Israel, prince over men. He named the place of the dream Peniel which meant "I have seen God face to face and my life has been preserved." Afterwards, we are told, Jacob "halted upon his thigh," like Zeus and the centaur Chiron.

Jupiter represents not only Truth, Wisdom, and Justice, but also our birthright to happiness. One of the most beautiful lines in the *Golden Verses* is ". . . Joys on Joys forever shall increase; Wisdom shall crown thy Labours, and shall bless Thy Life with Pleasure, and thy End with Peace." (verses #31, 32)

Questionnaire

How does the Sagittarius archetype express itself? Though this relates particularly to those with the Sun in Sagittarius or Sagittarius rising, anyone could apply this series of questions to the house where his Jupiter is located or the house which has Sagittarius (or Sagittarius intercepted) on the cusp. The answers to these questions will indicate how in touch the reader is with his Jupiter, his expansive nature, his Sagittarian instincts.

1. My communication style is straight as an arrow—direct and to the point.
   a. Usually.
   b. Most of the time.
   c. Seldom.

2. When I am under pressure I tend to lose my temper
   a. 80-100% of the time.
   b. 50-80% of the time.
   c. 25% or less of the time.

3. I fail to see the value of such negative virtues as humility, prudence, moderation, and temperance.
   a. Most of the time.
   b. 50% of the time.
   c. 25% of the time or less.

4. Among my better qualities I include honesty, integrity, fairness, optimism, and generosity.
   a. Usually.
   b. About 50% of the time.
   c. 25% of the time or less.

5. Among my negative qualities I would probably list procrastination, lack of follow-through (I am enthusiastic at the beginning of a project but I get sidetracked easily), and going to extremes in spending, eating, and over-commiting myself on

group projects.
    a. 80% of the time or more.
    b. 50% of the time.
    c. 25% of the time or less.

6. My greatest fear is
    a. being the victim of injustice.
    b. that I will hurt other people's feelings.
    c. that someone will see my dark side.

7. The greatest obstacle to my success comes from
    a. those around me.
    b. within myself.
    c. circumstances beyond my control.

8. I feel the weakest part of my body—the part that causes me the most trouble—is
    a. the hip, the sciatic nerve, or the liver.
    b. my feet.
    c. neck and shoulders.

9. Important to me are such Sagittarian interests as travel, some form of gambling (stock market, race track, Las Vegas, bingo), philosophizing, affluence.
    a. Very important.
    b. Moderately important.
    c. Not important at all.

10. I see my job as
    a. something I do to pay the bills between vacations.
    b. well suited to my personality; my job allows me a lot of travel.
    c. a major priority in my life.

Those who have scored five or more (a) answers are highly in touch with Jupiter on the mundane level. Those who have five or more (c) answers may be moving toward the polar extremity, Gemini, and need to be more expansive. If Sagittarius does not perceive itself as generous, social, or as preferring play to work, natal Jupiter may be retrograde or in the Twelfth House. This tends to produce an emphasis on metaphysics rather than extroverted social activity.

Those of you who answered (b) to question number seven are aiming the archer's arrow inwardly. Saturn is most likely conjunct, opposite, or square your Jupiter.

Where is the balance point between Sagittarius and Gemini? How does Sagittarius integrate the factual data into the grand picture? Sagittarius has been accused of overlooking his immediate neighborhood—what transpires under his nose—to follow what goes on in distant countries. Though this issue relates particularly to those with Sun in Sagittarius and Sagittarius rising, all of us have Jupiter somewhere in our horoscope. Many of us have planets in the Ninth or Third House. For all of us the polarity from Sagittarius to Gemini involves the ability to synthesize and to analyze data—to integrate the data into the whole picture and to communicate well with others.

1. When I lay out a new project I visualize the whole picture as complete. I relax about it. I schedule a lot of breaks so that I return refreshed to the job. I don't worry about the small details—I usually leave those to other people.
   a. Never.
   b. Some of the time.
   c. Most of the time.

2. I believe that "situations alter cases."
   a. Usually.
   b. Sometimes.
   c. Never!

3. I like to travel
   a. short distances only.
   b. both short and long distances.
   c. overseas—long distances.

4. I am more interested in the letter of the law than the spirit of the law
   a. most of the time.
   b. 50% of the time.
   c. I don't distinguish between the two.

5. My higher education includes
   a. some education beyond high school.
   b. a bachelor's degree.

c. a graduate degree.

6. Though I make new friends easily, it seems hard to keep the old ones for very long. I find this is the case
   a. never.
   b. sometimes.
   c. often.

Those who have scored three or more (b) answers are doing a good job with personality integration on the Sagittarius/Gemini polarity. Those who have three or more (c) answers may need to work more consciously on developing natal Mercury in their horoscopes. Mercury/Hermes was the "friend and companion to mankind." (See Gemini chapter.) Those who have three or more (a) answers may be out of balance in the other direction (weak or undeveloped Jupiter). Study both Jupiter and Mercury in the natal chart. Is there an aspect between them? Which one is stronger by house position or location in its sign of rulership or exaltation? Is either of them retrograde, intercepted, in fall, or in detriment? Aspects to the weaker planet can help point the way to its integration.

What does it mean to be an esoteric Sagittarian? How does Sagittarius integrate practical earth, its esoteric ruler, into the personality? Sagittarius will progress through Capricorn and become more grounded through the responsibility of business and/or parenting. After the sense of adventure winds down, some Sagittarians become more interested in esoteric matters and look within rather than focus their energy primarily in the outer world. Sagittarius' ruler, Earth, has given this archetype discipline, concentration and grounding in order to focus and overcome the restlessness which distracts the archer from his goal—Spirit. The answers to the following questions will indicate the extent to which Sagittarius is in touch with his esoteric ruler.

1. Rather than plunging headlong into the fray I take time to get the facts and analyze before I take action
   a. 80% of the time or more.
   b. about half the time.
   c. 25% of the time or less.

2. If I were to be perfectly honest I would have to say that my bluntness of speech, when it occurs, hurts others
   a. almost always.
   b. about half the time.
   c. hardly ever.

3. I think that the sustained effort that I make every day towards the goal is
   a. just as important as understanding the meaning of the goal.
   b. not quite as important as understanding the goal in its entirety.
   c. definitely not as important as the vision in its grand scope.

4. My decisions are based on common sense rather than impulse
   a. 80% to 100% of the time.
   b. 50% of the time.
   c. 25% of the time or less.

5. I agree with and practice justice, prudence, temperence, and moderation in both speech and action
   a. 80-100% of the time.
   b. 50% of the time.
   c. 25% of the time or less.

Those who have scored three or more (a) answers are in touch with their esoteric ruler. Those who scored three or more (b) answers need more work at integrating practical Earth, at approaching situations with less impulsiveness and more prudence (combining right action with right understanding). Those who answered (a) to questions four and five, however, may have Jupiter retrograde or in House Twelve. In the case of question four they may lack spontaneity and consider themselves financially unlucky, especially if there is a harsh Saturn/Jupiter aspect. In the case of question five, they should not only focus on ethics and philosophy but may need to make a greater effort in the material world. If Jupiter is turned inward (retrograde), positive aspects from other planets are often a key to developing Jupiter's social and financial magnetism.

References

John Blofield, *Bodhisattva of Compassion: The Mystical Tradition of Kuan Yen*, Shambhala Publications, Boston, 1978

Arthur B. Cook, *Zeus of the Dark Sky*, Biblo and Tannen, New York, 1965, Vol. 2

Arthur B. Cook, *Zeus of the Light Sky*, Biblo and Tannen, New York, 1965, Vol. 1

M. Dacier and N. Rowe, *The Life of Pythagoras with His Symbols and Golden Verses*, Samuel Weiser Inc., York Beach, 1981

Francoise Gauquelin, *Psychology of the Planets*, Astro-Computing, San Diego, 1982

Liz Greene, *The Astrology of Fate*, Samuel Weiser Inc., York Beach, 1984

Eugen Herrigel, *Zen in the Art of Archery*, Vintage Books, New York, 1971

Isabel Hickey, *Astrology: A Cosmic Science*, Alteri Press, Bridgeport, 1970

C.G. Jung, *Psychology and Alchemy*, Princeton Press, Princeton, 1968

David Keirsey and Marilyn Bates, *Please Understand Me,* Prometheus, Nemesis Books, Del Mar, 1978

Carolyi Kerenyi, *Zeus and Hera: Archetypal Image of Father, Husband and Wife*, Princeton Press, Princeton, 1975

Sallie Nichols, *Jung and Tarot: An Archetypal Journey "Justice"*, Samuel Weiser, York Beach, 1980

Thomas Taylor, *Theoretic Arithmetic of the Pythagoreans*, Samuel Weiser Inc., York Beach, 1983

Marie Louise von Franz, *Alchemy*, Inner City Books, Toronto, 1980

Paramahansa Yogananda, *Autobiography of a Yogi*, The Philosophical Library, New York, 1946

References to Zeus in Other Chapters

Gemini: "Myth of the Judgment of Hermes"
Scorpio: "Zeus and Typhon"

10   CAPRICORN:
The Search for Dharma

The Sun enters Capricorn each year at the time of the Winter Solstice, December 21 or 22. As the days grow darker and colder the mood becomes more serious. T.V. and radio announcers exclaim: "Hurry! Only five shopping days till Christmas." People everywhere, faces creased in concentration upon their lists, brush past each other muttering, "I should pick up something for my neighbor in case she appears with a gift for me." "I must get the 'under ten dollar present' for the office exchange on my lunch hour or it'll be too late. . ." "I have to find a present for Great Aunt Edna this year. Last Christmas I forgot her and felt so guilty. She's 92 and she won't be around to celebrate many more Christmasses." "I feel so torn at holiday time between my duty to my parents and my duty to my children. My folks will be disappointed if we don't go to Florida, and yet so much of the fun for the kids is rushing out to use their new ice skates with their friends Christmas week. They can't do that in Florida." "I wish I weren't a working mother at holiday time. The kids are growing up so fast and they should be experiencing family traditions. I'd love to be home to decorate and cook for them and read them Christmas stories, but, there's so little time."

At the mundane level, the Capricorn archetype can be recognized every year in conversations about shoulds and oughts, conflicting family duties, traditions, growing older, and an overwhelming feeling of being under pressure because "there's so little time." One can almost see Chronus, or Saturn, as the Romans called him (Father Time) standing to one side holding his hour glass, or his sickle, while people make these Winter Solstice remarks. Capricorn as an archetype is about continuity of family life, including family memories and

357

traditions, land, possessions, and other inheritances, duties, personal and collective ambitions and all those 'should have dones' in the past that emerge from the unconscious en route to grandmother's house or condominium for holiday dinner. "Maybe I should have joined Dad's law firm instead of becoming a journalist 30 years ago. Dad would have been so proud and happy. But I, personally, am a happier man as a journalist" (conflict of personal and collective family ambitions). Or "Maybe I should have lost the 20 pounds I vowed to lose last New Year's. I know Aunt Edna will think I have no will power whatsoever." Or, old resentments emerge—"Uncle Harry should have loaned me that money I needed for tuition 10 years ago. I'd be independently wealthy by now if he had. Now he'll ask *me* for a loan for one of his wild schemes—but I won't have any money to give him. It's his own fault."

Competitiveness is as much a part of the Capricorn archetype as introspection and old memories. For many of us family competitiveness can be easily seen if we look up and down the dinner table at the family members seated between the Matriarch and Patriarch. Two sisters, meeting for the first time in a year, scrutinize each other, mentally scoring points. The elder is unmarried and is now a year closer to thirty. She is dismayed that the younger has had yet another baby, delighting Mother and Dad with another grandchild. The younger envies the elder her fashionable clothes, her recent promotion, her summer in Europe, her freedom.

Material wealth is, at the mundane level of Capricorn, an important measure of success, ambition fulfilled by the zodiac's most striving sign. Great Aunt Edna, at the end of the table, may keep the scorecard for the family. Suddenly, Auntie will fix her gaze on a college-age boy and clear her throat, *"Ahem!"* in a voice surprisingly loud for a frail old lady. "Well, Roger, did you complete your degree, find a worthwhile job, marry that Angela and buy a house? You told us last year that you were finally 'getting it all together'? I'll bet you are still living with your parents and going to school though." "Er, yes, Aunt Edna," says blushing Roger in a small, quiet voice inappropriate for someone six feet five inches tall. "Things are underway, in progress, though." "Hrummph," says the matriarch, "My grandson and his wife bought a new $200,000 house last year, presented me with another great-grandson and invited me on their trip to Rio de Janeiro which the company gave him for selling so much insurance. I'm getting a bit too old for carnival, but Arthur certainly is doing well for himself." Sadly, Great Aunt Edna herself is a symbol of the sands running through the hour glass of mortality. Several family members are thinking "she certainly is looking a lot older this year."

The Capricorn archetype includes every concept, sense and meaning of time, from the most abstract Hindu, Mayan, and Greek ages of the gods, aeonic time, to the concrete calendar year and the lifespan of an individual, personal longevity and mortality. Two of the symbols chosen to represent the Winter Solstice and Capricorn, the crocodile and the tortoise, long lived and slow moving as well as hard shelled (durable), reflect the association of Capricorn with life and death and with survivalism. Until the discovery of root crops and refrigeration in the last 200 years, people and animals died in large numbers during winter because of food scarcity. Symbolically, souls, which the Greeks believed to have descended through the Womb, or Gate of Cancer in fertile summertime, departed in great numbers through the Death Gate of Capricorn during Winter Solstice. The same concepts prevailed in the tropics where hot, dry winds parched the soil in wintertime. Thus Saturn, with his sickle, was said to cut down the infirm and the elderly in winter, to perform his grim reaper task during Capricorn.

Though we in the modern western world are no longer tied to the fertility cycle like agricultural peoples, the symbolism has remained. During Winter Solstice we still celebrate the "death" of the old calendar year. If, for instance, we recall the line from the Christmas carol, "The Earth in solemn stillness lies," we'll recognize a very ancient mood describing the Winter Solstice. . . the Sun "makes its station," or appears to stand still overhead as the days grow shorter, and there is a hushed sense of anticipation to the Earth itself.

In the liturgy of several Christian religions there is a season called Advent, during which families open a window in an advent calendar every day or light candles on the advent wreath as a sign of hope. This mood of anticipation is a reflection of the faith with which the ancient world awaited the coming of spring thaw long before Christianity. Solstice meditations are still popular among astrologers around the world as a means of tuning in to the quietude, faith, peace, and inspiration of the solemn stillness.

Those who do not understand the patient, quiet waiting of the Solstice season often come to readings in December through January complaining about the loneliness they feel inside. Everyone seems to be rushing off to parties, indulging in consumerism, getting into debt with expensive purchases. There seems to be nothing deeper than this gross materialism they see around them. Many people become depressed over the emptiness. I notice among my clients a higher incidence of suicidal phone calls in December through January. It's not so much that they feel left out of the festivities but that they feel disconnected from family and tradition, from their roots.

One lonely client made a really insightful statement: "Christmas is for children, for families. I think I feel isolated because I haven't any children to celebrate with." "Why," I asked, "is it just for children?" "Because they're innocent—spontaneous. A child is simply happy to have a package to open. A six-year-old's face lights up when he sees it. He doesn't stop to analyze it as his parents might: 'How much did Auntie pay for this?' He doesn't think 'uh oh, I only gave her a card I made myself that cost very little and she bought me this expensive gift'. . . not at all. The magic is still in the holiday for the child. But when his mother opens my gift her face wrinkles up cautiously, and I can almost hear her thinking something like, 'She paid more for this than I paid for her gift. She must be doing better financially than I am.' And she'll become depressed, she won't enjoy the gift, after all that analyzing. So, as a single person who is happy most of the time, Christmas is the only time of year I feel that something's missing from my life—kids."

The client has pointed out something important, for the Solstice is about the juxtaposition of old age and youth. C.G. Jung, for instance, saw the archetypes of the old man and the child as polar opposites. If Saturn is not a Wise Old Man but a senile, rigid symbol it has become too grounded, stuck in the mud—depressing. Attitudinally, Jung recommended that we never lose our childlike sense of fun, that we not become academically knowledgeable or unwise, rigid, over-structured, sterile in our thinking or unable to respond spon-taneously. Customs and traditions can become like petrified wood—hard, brittle, limiting. The *puer* (eternal youth) within us balances *senex* (our rigid Saturnian traits) in its eager openness and curiosity, faith in the future, flexibility. When Capricorn or Cancer parents com-plain about the hectic pace of life interfering with their customs at holiday time I am often secretly glad that *puer*, the family child, puts them in touch with change and forces them to become less rigid about holiday planning. Parents, in their own personal growth proc-ess, approach the mid-point of life (age 40-45, Saturn opposite Saturn), attain a level of material success and tend to stultify—to

become patriarchs and matriarchs, to resist change or feel too many
regrets about it. ("If only I didn't have to work outside the home... if
only I didn't have to rush about chauffering the kids to Christmas
pageants at three different schools. I'd have *time* to do the old-
fashioned things.") Children keep them young, living in the present,
and hopeful about the future. Senex and puer, as polar opposites,
have a lot to learn from each other.

There is so much *senex* in the air at Solstice time, so much planning on the part of authority figures, of teachers and parents who
want everything to be perfect for children, that perhaps we adults
need to pause in our industrious preparations for perspective and
observe *puer*, the child himself, his eagerness, his enthusiasm, his
anticipation, rather than weighing him down with lines to memorize
for the school play. Perhaps puer can help us not to take the Solstice,
and ourselves, so seriously. There must be an important spiritual
message here because Christ has said, "Unless ye become as little
children, ye shall not enter into the Kingdom of Heaven."

It seems, however, that this message was archetypally out there
long before the coming of Christ, or of Jung's helpful puer category.
On December 25, about a week after the onset of Solstice, the feast of
Mithrus the Divine Child was celebrated from Persia to Roman Bri-
tain. The Archbishop of Canterbury made a decision to build churches
on the sites of the Mithrus cult and to set the feast of the Christ child's
birth on December 25th, thus preserving the Feast of the Child for us.
And yet, for the Mithraic cult, with its focus on meditation and spiritual
initiation, the feast of hope and anticipation celebrated during the
darkness of winter was not only the external event of Mithras' entry
into the world, but the internal birth of the divine child within the soul
of each initiate. We have a Saturnine duty to ourselves, as well as to
our families, to the inner as well as to the outer world, to Spirit as well
as to Matter in this important season of solemn stillness.

Whether we light advent or Hanukka candles to illumine the
darkness with hope, it's important to find time to explain to children
the inner meaning of the rituals; otherwise the rituals tend to become
empty forms. As in the Hebrew tradition, the Macabbee brothers lit
candles and rededicated the temple in the outer world, and we could
remind each other, and our children, especially, that we are re-
dedicating our inner temples as well.

Carl Jung put it very well when he said that each of us is responsible for his own "inner manger." This would seem to be the real,

esoteric meaning of Solstice time and of the Solstice meditations. We are all striving to give birth to the inner child, the Self, in the manger of our hearts and to nurture the Divine Child. Too much dashing about in the outer world can distract us from our inner work at this introspective time.

The annual mood shift from jovial Sagittarius to Saturnine Capricorn is a striking contrast apparent to the astrologer who does Solar Return (birthday) readings between Thanksgiving and Christmas. First he sees a long succession of Sagittarians who affirm, "I just know this is going to be my lucky year. I'm about to realize all my dreams and have a lot of fun." They are followed by a series of Capricorns who appear close to their Winter Solstice birthdays and affirm the reverse: "Gee, I'm depressed. This time of year is a bummer. Every year when my birthday comes along I realize that I'm another year older; I think of all my ambitions that have yet to be achieved, and compared to other people life seems to be going at a snail's pace for me. I don't know whether I'm a late bloomer or a failure. When, if ever, will my luck and my timing improve? Why are there so many hurdles and delays in my life when things seem to happen so quickly and easily for others?"

The issues of luck and timing are the issues of the planets Jupiter and Saturn, respectively. These are the rulers of Sagittarius and Capricorn. Unless Sagittarians have Jupiter badly afflicted and Saturn is stronger than Jupiter in their charts, they tend to identify with the Great Benefic and see life in a positive way. Theirs is the philosophy, "every day in every way I'm getting better and better." Capricorns, on the other hand, tend to see life not in terms of luck or progress (Jupiter) but in terms of timing and their own limitations (Saturn). Fifteen years of observing this contrast in attitude while doing readings between Thanksgiving and New Years has convinced me, personally, of the truth of the power of positive thinking. If, in a jovial spirit, we believe that the cosmos is a cornucopia of good things, and that Heavenly Father Jove offers an unlimited supply of fame, fortune, health and joy to us, his deserving heirs, we are likely to draw these things to ourselves. But if we consider ourselves the hard working but undeserving heirs of Saturn, a cold Father who judges us harshly and focuses on our limitations, not what we actually accomplished but what we should have accomplished more perfectly, more thoroughly, more rapidly, we tend to draw more of Saturn's tests, hurdles, delays, and frustrations because we are looking for them—pessimistically expecting them.

The Greeks were aware of the Saturn principle: "Know thyself, accept thyself, be thyself." They encouraged the individual to face his own limitations in terms of physical stamina (not everyone could be an Olympic champion), artistic talents, intellectual prowess, but as their art testifies they were mainly a jovial people. It was during the Roman empire that classical art became more rigid, derivative and structured, that duty to the collective became more important than the individual's philosophical search, that government-sanctioned cults became the official religion and that Saturn seems to have triumphed over Jupiter. The fatalistic Stoics were more concerned with limits than expansion, with fate than growth and cast a Saturnine pall over philosophy and astrology alike. The Sophists in the Roman period were more concerned with rhetorical style than meaning or truth. Finally Christianity, with its rites, dogma and church structure, developed during the Roman Empire and took on the flavor of Saturn—God the Father on his Judgement Seat. As astrologers, we are struggling even now to bring back the balance between Saturn as duty and Jupiter as joy. The aspects between these two planets in the natal chart are very important. Their House positions, signs, and relationship to the individual's Sun, Moon, Mercury reveal whether he or she is spontaneously attuned to the duty or joy philosophy. Usually a Saturn/Mercury person will see a water glass as half-empty, a Jupiter/Mercury person as half-full. Clearly, we need both Jupiter and Saturn in our lives, that's why we came to Earth through Time (Saturn) and Space (Jupiter); but most of us have a pattern of attunement to one and underdevelopment of the other.

Often the astrologer, especially the beginning astrologer, is so preoccupied with giving out information to the client on luck and timing that he doesn't tune in to how the client is going to receive the information. What is the client's philosophy? Is it jovial or saturnine? It's important to listen to the client. If he has a stellium in Capricorn with a square to it from Saturn and the astrologer says there's a wonderful opportunity (Jupiter transiting the Ninth/Tenth) abroad for him, will he take it? Or will he stay with his father's (Saturn) company for the good of the Collective (family), as a dutiful son and good provider for his children? Most likely, to know about the opportunity would lead such a client to frustration and resentment (Saturn square) at the Collective to which he feels bound, rather than movement in the direction of the opportunity in the outer world.

The Saturn/Jupiter dimension of a horoscope will also give the counselor a feeling for introversion/extroversion. Astrologically, Fire signs, like Sagittarians, are usually considered extroverts, but imagine a Sagittarius who is progressing through Capricorn and who has a natal Saturn/Jupiter square. He can direct his Jupiterian social energy into business contracts and appear quite serious and subdued for a Sagittarius—even introverted. He might even be in a workaholic phase (almost a contradiction in terms for playful Sagittarius) and need to be reminded to take time out for exercise and hobbies. It's important to check the Saturn/Capricorn archetype out before presuming Fire or Air sign people to be wild extroverts.

There is a good discussion of the work ethic versus play ethic in *Please Understand Me*, by Bates and Kiersey, and though it is not called the Saturn/Jupiter balance it is quite similar. A person who looks at life through Jupiter will most likely play first and procrastinate where his work is concerned; do the report the night before he is scheduled to present it. The person who is attuned to Saturn's work ethic will be inclined to start on the report as soon as it's assigned to him, over-researching, over-preparing and putting off play. "I can't go in for social life; I have to stay home and work on this report due in three months." If s/he had a better balance between play (Jupiter) and work (Saturn) s/he would likely give a better, more relaxed presentation. Both extreme Jupiter and extreme Saturn people feel stress; the procrastinator is rested till the night before the report, but pushes his/her body very hard in short spurts, so neither imbalance is healthy.

Attitude is very important in healing the body. If we accept disease as our fate (Saturn) and resign ourselves to it, it will probably conquer. But if we procrastinate about changing poor health habits, the results of this jovial pattern will catch up with us in the end too: "I'm going to quit smoking tomorrow; I'm good at quitting smoking; I've done it 200 times in the last two years." Good intentions (Jupiter) without discipline (Saturn) can lead to lung cancer in the long run. For all the above reasons, it's important to check out the Jupiter/Saturn orientation in clients' horoscopes.

The ancients had a better understanding than we do of the importance of Jupiter and Saturn because they concentrated on the meaning of what to them was the outermost edge of the solar system—

the orbits of these two planets. Since the 1700s, when the first of the trans-Saturnian planets, Uranus, was discovered, we have lessened our emphasis on Jupiter and Saturn in the West as we strove to grasp the subtle meanings of the new "mass" or "impersonal" planets. In present-day India, the trans-Saturnian planets are used by few astrologers in chart interpretation, and Jupiter and Saturn retain their deeper meanings. They are seen as impersonal forces, not only in the sense that their transits rule the Collective (the Nation or its Ruler), though that is part of it, but in the sense that the time (Saturn) and place or latitude and longitude (Jupiter), through which an individual's soul comes to Earth, determines the working out of his karma. Why come to Earth at a certain time and in a certain city? Why not some other century, some other city or village? The chart, with its opportunities and timing (limits), represents the map the soul has chosen prior to coming to Earth to work out its karma, an attempt to fulfill one or more desires left over from his most recent past life. In the last few seconds of that life, I was told by several Indian astrologers, a person regretfully thought, *"If only I had . . . ,"* and that sentence, completed, established the next horoscope. Perhaps s/he chose to come to Earth in a home where music was valued, where there was an emphasis on education, or chose a family with political power, or wealth, or just a loving home where everyone lived to adulthood. Whatever was lacking was potentially achievable. The support for the desire was there in the life circumstances. At this point I asked, what if I had thought, "If only I had worked harder or had more discipline?" "Ah!" said the astrologer, "There's your First House Saturn, in square to your Sun." To me this was an important discovery—we set our own limits and our own discipline when we chose our Saturn placement.

We live in a time when so many of us tend to blame the Collective. "I was raised in a strict religion—not enough joy." Or "My family had such tremendous expectations of me. There were two senators in the family and I was expected to follow suit." Or "All the women in my family were teachers, so I didn't think about a different career till I was 30 years old." Or, "The women in my family were expected to have children and stay home from work; it's *their* fault I'm so frustrated at 40—still at home with kids under the age of six." Well, according to the Hindu philosophy, "Not so."

Carl Jung contributed to our understanding of Saturn in a woman's chart with his concept of the animus, her masculine side and its expectations. Facing the animus can be pretty depressing for a mother who is home full-time with small children. The animus wants to be active in the man's world—the marketplace—thinking, competing, striving, achieving. Women who are at home full-time often come to a reading complaining that "men, especially husbands, are free to accomplish professionally, while women, especially mothers, are not." One Capricorn Sun sign woman came in around the Solstice for her annual update quite critical of her husband. "He has such an enjoyable life, practicing his profession, while I, who am just as educated as he, am stuck at home nursing three small children through the flu, watching my own skills get rustier by the day. The walls are closing in on me." Some also make critical remarks about women professionals who have children, yet who work full or part-time outside the home: "Just look at my sister (or my college room-mate)—her place (duty) is in the home with her pre-school children, but she leaves them at a daycare center with strangers and goes to work. Why did she have them in the first place if she wanted to neglect them and go to work?"

While the astrologer can make some suggestions based upon Jupiter transits which help provide outlets for the claustrophobia (the Saturn feeling of the walls closing in during Winter Solstice—flu season) through service to the community and the social contacts with adults, I find that Jungian analysis is a real help, too. If such an educated woman feels claustrophobic and rusting away at home, it often seems due as much to her own animus' perfectionism as to the patriarchal society against which she rants and rails—her husband, or others. One such Supermother, down with the flu and feverish her-self, insisted on making four costumes for her children's Christmas pageants in addition to cooking, decorating, shopping and serving at church. She said, "My mother always had time to make our costumes for holiday plays, so I ought to be able to do it for my kids, too." Jungian analysis helped her to distinguish between herself and her mother—between the 1950's (her own childhood) and the 1980's (her children's childhood) and to gain a more realistic understanding of the limits of time. Mainly though, analysis helped her to distinguish between what her animus expected of her and what the members of her family expected. Their standards for the Perfect Mother were much lower than her standards for herself. Now when she comes in for her birthday update she makes fewer criticisms of other working women with small children, and of her husband. She still can't let herself work outside the home, but she sees that Motherhood won't always be her career and that in a different life cycle she will be back using her talents in the marketplace again. As a thinking woman, her Jungian work with the animus has helped her as much as the understanding of the Saturn/Jupiter life cycles through astrology.

In India, where life moves at a slower pace, it seems somewhat easier to understand the positive qualities of Saturn. Even saturnine perfectionism has its purpose if we think in terms of the evolution of the Soul on its journey to perfection and of the Biblical admonition, "Be ye perfect as your Heavenly Father is perfect." It takes the Soul a long, long time—a whole series of lifetimes, to the Indian mind—to accomplish that! Dharma, then, astrologically represented by esoteric Saturn, is about the Soul's evolutionary journey, over time, toward oneness with and freedom in the Divine. Within this long journey there are Saturnine lifetimes of repaying old debts and ambitiously working off desires, and Jupiterian lifetimes of harvesting past-life merit. A Jupiterian lifetime, I was told in India, "is a lifetime to rest." I often think of that in horoscopes where Jupiter is in Grand Trine to Sun and Moon in the Earth Houses and draws success and charts where Saturn is in T-Square formation in the Earth Houses, meaning hard work and discipline, but in the long run, success. The person with Saturn in the T-Square would be said in India to really be doing his dharma and in the end to have led a more victorious life than the person with the Jupiter Trine, unless he became too depressed and gave in to despondency. His test is often one of Faith, of Jupiter, the ruler, in India, of Pisces, the sign of faith that moves mountains. There is then an esoteric balance between Saturn (duty, or Dharma) and Jupiter as faith in the grace of Guru. Both are necessary to be victorious, to move forward in this incarnation on the spiritual path.

Both Jupiter and Saturn are goal-directed planets and if we can make proper use of their energies, if we can bring them into balance, goals can really be reached. Jupiter's faith and self-confidence, positive attitude and progressive impulse toward the future, combined with Saturn's patience over time, consistent application of elbow grease and hard work, even when the going gets rough and the road seems dark, when restlessness or boredom set in, can guide us to liberation. People whose charts are very earnest and hard working, very Saturnine, often forget that as Hindus would say, "God is the Doer." Reality, this world, is "too much with them," and they tend to forget that Jupiter, the grace of God and Guru, is as important as doing their dharma perfectly. In the west, Christian theologians have long debated over which is more important to attaining the Kingdom of Heaven, faith or good works. In Hindu astrology, Jupiterian faith and Saturnine dharma are equally important.

Taken together Jupiter and Saturn rule the four outermost signs representing the end of the astrological year—Sagittarius, Capricorn, Aquarius, Pisces. Esoterically speaking, the last four signs and the last four Houses are considered the most impersonal areas of life. They are also the areas over which our egos have the least conscious control. Esoterically, these energies are said to carry us beyond our limited, selfish individual ambitions, enable us to serve the masses and touch the Infinite. The outer planets and the signs which they rule are said to represent Universal Truth (Sagittarius), Universal Government (Capricorn), Universal Humanity (Aquarius) and Universal Divine Love (Pisces).

In the last chapter we reviewed the mythology of Zeus/Jupiter, the Divinity of Space or Location, and now it's time to see what can be gleaned from the myths of Chronus/Saturn, Lord of Time. Macrobius, a Roman writer, tells us in *The Saturnalia* that Chronus, the Greek God, originated further east, that his art and mythology are closely associated with the Persian Sun-God Mithrus. The Greeks appreciated beauty rather than the grotesque, and it is amazing that they accepted these ugly funerary statues of open-mawed, devouring lions, that the Mithrus Lion would be assimilated with their own Time God, Chronus. But at second glance, the devouring lion statue reveals symbolically the power of death, the fate with which we mortals must contend at the end of our days.

Macrobius explains the symbolism of the Chronus Lion to his Roman contemporaries as if its full message had been lost by his period, the late Roman Empire, even though the Lions were still carried in funeral processions. He tells us that the lion is always surrounded with a circular form, either the circular river of time, Oceanus, or the snake eating its own tail, the Uroboros. The lion is mortality, but the circular form is immortality, infinity. There are always two faces to Chronus—time and eternity, in the art of the Greeks and the Persians. The lifespan of a human being is just one face of eternity, and therefore there is hope. The River Oceanus, according to Macrobius,

is really the Earth's Ecliptic, the point where time meets infinity. It flows on forever, carrying the zodiac within it.

Hope to the Greeks and the Mithraic cultists lay in the fact that after being devoured by the Lion (death), souls would take on new forms, like the Uroboros snake changing his skin, and drop through the ecliptic, through the signs and elements (the zodiac) it contained, taking on ever new personalities, opportunities, moving forward. This larger picture of the Lion surrounded by Uroboros or Oceanus is, I think, a good meditation image not only for people born during the Solstice (Capricorns) or those with Capricorn rising who are afraid of time passing them by, but for all of us in the House where natal Saturn sits. When we face delays, frustrations, limitations on our desires, or we feel burdened by time like the picto-glyphs of the Mayan Day Gods, carrying time as a burden in their backpacks, we can visualize the Uroboros around the Lion of Mortality—there's plenty of time, for everything unfolds in due time, or as the Book of Ecclesiastes has it, "For everything there is a season, under Heaven." When we are in the midst of a Saturn year and time drags, our ambitions in the outer world seem thwarted or challenged, our desires put on hold by the cosmos or we feel the Winter Solstice doldrums, melancholy and negative introspection set in, this larger vision of time as a face of infinity is helpful.

The Greeks had another artistic representation of Chronus that I like as a symbol for transiting Saturn; it's a very fragile, almost humorous dragonfly, just barely resting on the edge of a surface as if about to take flight. Two of its wings are downward, as if settled, and two are moving skyward. Here we have the transitory nature of mundane Saturn; *sic transit gloria mundi* (so passes the glory of this world). This dragonfly Saturn is light, and clearly not fated to remain forever. If we can remember this dragonfly we can retain some humor in the midst of a Saturn year, though we feel unsettled or fearful, perhaps of the future. When the year is over Saturn will take flight and Jupiter will not be too far behind. (Age 29 may be a Saturn year, but age 36, a Jupiter year, will come along too). Clients with Saturn in T-Squares or the Angular Houses or undergoing Saturn opposite Saturn (challenges from the outer world), or Saturnine depression, can recall the Chronus Dragonfly, the transitoriness of most earthly ambitions: why allow ourselves to become depressed? We can control our reactions, our attitudes even when we cannot control the outer world.

This background from art and from Macrobius is helpful in understanding Chronus. So many of my students and clients have been appalled at their first encounter with him in Great Books Class—a father who eats his own children seems pretty repulsive, indeed, in our literal minded twentieth century. The idea of a god dethroning and dismembering his father, as Chronus did Uranus, seems just as abhorrent. Both stories are central to the Journey of Capricorn/ Capricorn rising people, however, and to many of us in the House where our natal Saturn lies. The writings of Carl Jung shed much light upon the psychology of the Fatherhood of Chronus.

There are many types of Fatherhood, and in some ways Chronus/ Saturn represents them all. The King or Emperor, for instance, was, historically, the Father of his People. It was universally believed that if he did his duty well, made and enforced wise laws and protected his subjects from outside attack, his kingdom would prosper. The Russian Tsar was known as Little Father, and the first United States President as the Father of his Country. In Indochinese art perhaps the idea of Divine Kingship is most graphic, though, as the Khmer Emperors stand next to, and turn, the Wheel of Dharma for their subjects. If they have done their duty well, the inscriptions refer to them as Dharma Rajas, or even Deva Rajas (God Kings, Divine Kings) after their deaths.

Saturn, then, is associated with Government, and with Divine Law in its proper fatherly guise. The Roman *paterfamilias*, who ruled a large community-household with absolute power, was also a father figure on a large scale, as was the medieval Baron who was father as well as sometime tyrant to those on his Manor. A patron of a Renaissance artist was as beneficent a father to him as is, in a looser sense, today's college professor who not only trains his students in their craft but often finds funding for them during college years and beyond.

Though we still deal with Saturn through authority figures such as politicians, policemen, internal revenue agents, motor vehicle licensors, college administrators and professor who seem to have power over us in Saturn years (or officious bankers who can turn down our loan papers), the first association most of us have when we read the myth of Chronus dethroning his Father the King is with our own personal father.

Patricide was a terrible crime to the ancient Greeks, as well as to us in the 20th century. The Furies punished it and considered it as serious as perjury. Why then did Chronus the Titan, the lucky seventh son, depose and dismember Uranus, his father and king of the gods? What is the psychological message behind it? Jung has an excellent chapter—"Stages of Life" in Vol. III of his *Collected Works*—that sheds much light on the dark subject of Chronus. Chronus was the youngest son of Uranus by Mother Earth. She gave her son Chronus a deadly flint sickle and urged him not only to free the rebel Cyclopes but to prevent future injustice by killing Uranus.

Jung tells us that a kingdom cannot prosper under a senex ruler (a senile, decrepit, rigid tyrant) or a ruler whose subjects perceive him as a senex. In myths of kingship there seem to be two alternatives for the tyrant after he is challenged by rebellious youth—either the heir to his throne or the young hero passing through the land. His first alternative involves learning from the experience, regaining his physical strength and mental capacities lost as a result of the fight, and changing his attitude in the direction of justice, becoming a Wise Old Man. The second alternative, more common in myth and in life, involves the defeat of the senex tyrant by the young hero or heir and the beginning of a New Age for the Kingdom.

The timing was right for Chronus. The 2,400 year reign of Uranus had come to an end and Mount Olympus was ready for a New Age, a new king, the heir to the throne. His intuition (the Earth Mother) told him to proceed and take action; he was given his tool, the sickle. The way he did it still seems gory to the modern reader, though. He cut off Uranus' phallus and threw it along with the rest of his body into the ocean. In Western psychology we are used to thinking of the phallus as a symbol of sexual potency, and by extension a symbol of power in general, but in the East the primary meaning of the phallus is Creative Power, and Divine rather than human creativity at that. In the East, dismemberment symbolizes the extension of the deity's creativity into the world. Multiplicity emerges from Oneness. Dismemberment enables the One, the deity, to experience life in a variety of forms.

The End of the Age is always characterized by a decline in creativity, so Chronus performed a useful task in releasing Uranus' creative flow. He brought about the birth of Aphrodite as she sprang forth from the Ocean. Fertilized by Uranus, she was called She Who is Born of the Foam, and proved to be exactly what Chronus needed, and also what any client with Capricorn planets, Capricorn rising, or strong Saturn aspects needs to this day—gentleness, warmth, free-flowing feelings, aesthetic values, the ability to relate, to love (eros). In the esoteric tradition, Isabel Hickey, Alice Bailey and others have written of Aphrodite/Venus as the antidote to Saturn in the individual horoscope. We will return later and pick up the thread of this theme.

King Chronus did not seem any kinder to the Cyclopes than to his Father. They were sent right back to hell as soon as they began to stir up trouble for the new king. At the end of the age he proved reluctant to yield power gracefully to his heir, Zeus/Jupiter, even to using his role as Father Time against the gods, as well as mortals, and devouring his potential sons and heirs. The youngest, Zeus/Jupiter, was rescued by his mother and sent to safety in a Cretan Cave.

In Cancer (Chapter 4), we had the duty to the feminine, especially to Mother. In Capricorn, we meet duty to the masculine, the conflict of aspirations, goals and expectations between Father and Son, or, in the case of a woman who has Capricorn/Saturn strong in her chart (especially her Tenth House), Father and daughter. Though at first glance the myth of reclaiming the throne from Father seems to be a replay of the Leo Quest (see Chapter 5), there is one important difference. Solar-ruled Leo, archetypally speaking, has from early childhood plenty of confidence in himself and his direction; he isn't inwardly as dependent on Father's approval as Capricorn. He isn't willing to wait patiently for Father to retire gracefully or die or wait until the Earth Mother comes forward with the means to take action and permission to act. He doesn't seem to feel the same conflict of duties that Dharma-ruled Capricorn feels. Capricorn/Capricorn rising and Angular Saturn people are so often in inner conflict over what they perceive as duty to Self, duty to Father, and duty to the collective (Society).

Sons and daughters in this Capricorn Archetype have made the following remarks, for instance: "I had a very good offer from another corporation when they recruited at our college, but it would have meant really disappointing my Dad. He financed my education and, well, it's always been understood that I'd one day go to work in his company. It's a small company without much scope for my education, without much excitement, but I'll go there a few years and see what happens"(Capricorn rising). (He is still there after 15 years. He has very little decision-making power and will always be the boss's son or junior to the employees. His father is 75 and still in charge.)

"I know it's funny to meet a 50-year-old woman CPA. My Father survived the depression and told his children, 'become a CPA like me and you'll never starve, no matter what happens to the economy.' Well, I've never starved, but I do look around at my women friends doing interesting things, creative things. I've always wanted to try my hand at interior decorating . . . I'm a Libra . . . but it isn't a secure job." (Saturn in the Tenth House. After her father's death, she studied design and is now doing part-time work through furniture stores, enjoying life more.)

Yet another Tenth House Saturn, a male client, had a father-figure, rather than a father:

"Professor X has been a father to me. When I was a scared graduate student at a huge university he took me under his wing and recommended me for all kinds of grants. Even found me two jobs after I graduated. Taught me everything I know. I revised his last two books and was mentioned in the preface, but I'll never be an ac-knowledged expert while he is still living. I'll always be known as Pro-fessor X's student. If he'd ever retire, I could be hired at *his* university, but I don't foresee that happening." (Professor X is emeritus, but still going strong at age 77.)

To be still thought of as "junior" becomes difficult for adult Cap-ricorns after the Saturn return, where so many seem to get in touch with their own expectations and aspirations. A client recently fought to leave his father's restaurant business at this point (age 29) and suc-ceeded. We worked with the House his Uranus was in (his unique-ness, his originality). Saturn and Uranus share rulership of the house with Aquarius on the cusp, which is activated, or opened along with the Capricorn house the Saturn return year. He chose to manage a health spa, applying his old expertise (Saturn) to his new (Uranian) environment. He feels terrible about the estrangement from his father, but is succeeding at the new job and receiving recognition for his own creative talents already, by age 33, from customers and reviewers.

Recognition by the Collective is as important as Father's approval; some sort of compromise often enables Capricorn to find both. This is still, of course, the quest in the outer world; the internal quest seems to come during the later years of the progression through Aquarius/ Pisces. Creativity is a key though the next step seems to be through the House with Aquarius on the cusp or the House of natal Uranus. There is a genuine message in the myth of cutting off the phallus— proving to Father that one is just as gifted, original, creative as he was.

Jung gives an example in Volume VIII of Father's approval (or lack thereof) holding up adult growth that is similar to one I have often encountered with women clients. Jung's woman patient could not find a husband because nobody would measure up to Father's standards for her. I see this often with Angular Saturn, especially the Tenth House Saturn. On the surface the women seem married to their jobs and eventually many of them find a man a lot like dear old Dad, but others are single till his death. Women with the Saturn/Sun conjunction tend to have the same pattern—strong father identification, a personal career Father would approve of, or eventually marriage to a man in the same field of work as Father.

If Saturn is more strongly placed by Sign, Aspects, or House position than Aphrodite in a Capricorn rising chart, this pattern of old issues from past lives to be resolved with Father seems to be present. Even in charts where the Sun sign is romantic—Libra, Taurus, Pisces— there seem to be old (Saturn) issues for Capricorn rising to conclude with Father before entering Aphrodite's world of romance and relationship.

In Volume VIII of the *Collected Works*, Jung writes of the sad plight of the son or daughter whose father lives too long, like the Old King. This person is stuck in the puer phase of life, unable to become an adult, form a new family, find Aphrodite, discover personal aspirations as distinct from family expectations, or move forward toward personal goals. Yet, if the Capricorn archetype is strong in the chart, he wants to move on and take his place in society as a Cardinal person, a leader, a responsible taxpayer, though he feels stuck in the child role in the family into which he was born. As Jung points out, people are living longer now. There are a lot of fathers going through the third Saturn Return, few of whom felt ready to yield power and gracefully retire after the second Saturn return, in their late 50's.

Fathers of children in the Capricorn/Saturn archetype often describe their sons and daughter as diligent but late bloomers, not-too-creative people who are somehow still financially dependent upon Dad into their forties. They seem to feel what Jung said in Volume V, that there is something of the parasite in the puer. But often duty to father has so limited the scope of the child's creativity, or his experience managing money (Dad makes the decisions in the corporation) that the child has never had a chance to prove himself a responsible Capricorn/Saturn person. If strings have been attached to financial aid, or other help Dad provides such as the job in the firm, such strings often need to be severed with the flint sickle from the Chronus myth.

Sometimes on the Saturn return or Saturn opposite Saturn, a Capricorn/Angular Saturn client will bring in his father's chart in an effort to understand him better and approach the issue of his need to cut the strings, to enter the larger world. Often the father turns out to be a Wise Old Man who was mistakenly perceived as rigid Senex. If he is really Senex, it then becomes necessary to let go of resentments. By Saturn opposite Saturn, in the forties, it becomes easier to perceive Father not as the All Powerful King, but as a human being who is growing older and who, most likely, feels dependent himself. He does not want to lose his heir. Two gifts of Saturn are patience and introspection. If father and child are both going through their returns together (age 29 and age 56) or within a year of each other, both feeling lonely and alienated, a serious talk can often help them begin a new cycle together as two adults.

For Tenth House Saturn people, Saturn opposite Saturn may mean the death of Father, especially if he is seriously ill at the time. (Transiting Saturn makes its opposition from the Fourth House, the House of childhood authorities.) Some clients have felt freed and immediately changed their life direction (Tenth House), set down Father's standard to pick up their own banner. Sometimes, though, there's a Saturn delay because the Tenth House Saturn son or daughter has so deeply identified with Father's view, has internalized it in the unconscious. The Libran woman cited above, for instance, had wanted to do something artistic for years, but it took her a full seven years from Saturn opposite Saturn and her father's death to gradually phase out of the CPA job.

Letting go is usually difficult for us in Saturn's natal House. I admire those of my clients who can yield the throne and flow gracefully into the changes in that House during Saturn opposite Saturn. (It helps, of course, if natal Saturn is in a Mutable sign.) Most of us established ourselves later in life in the House of our natal Saturn (experienced the Saturn delay), faced many fears and insecurities there as young adults, and worked hard to provide ourselves a cushion, or a security blanket, in that House. (Few people have *no* harsh aspects to natal Saturn.) Most have climbed uphill like Capricorn mountain goats in the Saturn House as well as the Saturn ruled House (the one with Capricorn on the cusp). Then, during Saturn opposite Saturn in mid-life the outer world challenges us to let go rather like the hero is challenged by the Old King in myth. And most of us say, "I don't want to yield the throne, or share power. I put a lot of effort into that area of life—it's my Dharma. I was just beginning to feel good about the control I had there." Others of us, usually those with Saturn in Mutability, or Saturn in a progressive thinking sign like Fire or Air, say "I was getting bored anyhow. New doors will open. I have plenty of faith in the unknown future." Many intuitives have already begun to phase out old attachments even before the transit begins.

Some people live in fear of Saturn transits, partially because they don't like to let go of the past, but partially also because they live at the level of mundane Saturn rather than esoteric (serviceful, dharmic) Saturn. Clients who have read cookbook astrology texts often come to the reading worried: "I'm going through the mid-life Saturn opposite Saturn," or "I'm going through transiting Saturn opposite my Sun or Moon or Mercury. Will I lose money, power, status, property, spouse?" Saturn as the Cross of Matter can mean that attachment to these mundane things interferes with true happiness. "I sure hate my job, but I wouldn't give it up for anything. It pays a lot and if I stick it out another 15 years I'll retire with company stocks and bonds, a good pension and insurance program. If I stick it out even another few years I'll have a month's vacation instead of two weeks. If I start over at my age it won't be easy to find an equivalent job. I'll be three months without medical insurance. . ." This is mundane Saturn working against happiness, planning as if we were to be here on Earth for eternity. One doctor's wife said, "I'll admit I'm sticking with my marriage mainly because of the lifestyle. The children and I hardly ever see my husband, and when we do he's a heavy handed authority figure, but financially we depend on him and the structure (Saturn) of the family is important."

The first client was fired in a departmental reorganization during Saturn opposite Saturn and was miserable for six months, then found something he liked better. In the second case the doctor left his wife on Saturn opposite her Seventh House Sun and she is now much happier with her second husband. Saturn simplifies our lives by dissolving things we hang onto that don't really make us happy, so that we can get on with life. One sees this constantly as an astrologer. Saturn is the greatest of teachers for those of us who are observant. How we react to Saturn transits indicates the level of our attunement.

Do we see Saturn as esoteric Dharma or as a mundane malefic?

We can all go through years of feeling like the Christian master carrying his cross uphill, slipping and falling but rising to keep moving on, in the House of natal Saturn. The Christian image comes to mind because Saturn's glyph (♄) is the Cross, and the material world seems a harsh place in these years, especially if natal Saturn is in an Earth (business) house. We can feel persecuted as Christ was by the world. But if we have made mistakes we can learn to reflect, intro-spect, and reappraise our conduct and our attitudes in Saturn years. Are we resting on our laurels? Are we tempted to say, "Let this Cup pass from me; I want to remain as comfortable as I am now. I don't want any changes"? Do we let go and accept the future challenge, the Quest for the Cup (the Grail, the Aquarius progression)? Christ's de-pression in the Garden of Gethsemane and his surrender to the will of His Heavenly Father (not his personal, mundane Father) are important developmental phases in the life journey that is Capricorn—the journey we all undertake in Saturn's house. Out of Capricornian depression often comes a period of reflection, of introspection on our Dharma, on what Christ called "the need to be about the Father's business." Perhaps the depression occurred because we concen-trated exclusively on our own mundane business instead. Jung, too, sees a period of depression as the forerunner of an insight, or of a period of enhanced creativity.

Saturn transits often teach the student of esoteric astrology about the nature of his true Dharma. That may well be its real cosmic function. If we have strong Saturns, we make many Capricorn com-parisons, in terms of black and white, right and wrong, concretely assigning rank to ourselves and the people around us—"I am doing more work than X" or "I've already learned from that situation; I shouldn't have to do it over again; let someone younger do it." Tran-siting Saturn often grounds us by putting us back into an old occupa-tion, an old friendship, a past situation, so we can break free of our smugness and those comparisons that we sometimes make to the detriment of others. Even the ability to make these Saturn com-parisons comes in handy though, if by hindsight, introspecting about the past when confronted with a Saturn decision (especially occupa-tion) we can say, "I used to think less tolerantly (or more judgmen-tally) when I knew those people or worked in that environment 7 years ago, 14 years ago, etc." We can often see our progress by hindsight if we compare ourselves with ourselves as we once were rather than with other people. Someone with real Saturn wisdom remarked once in my office: "This would have been the ideal job offer for me 7 years ago. This would have fit all my aspirations and desires at that point in life. But I'm not that person (persona) anymore. That's not what I'm supposed to be doing now." He turned down the job offer but took one that paid less but that he enjoyed more—a challenging position. It was a position where he felt less secure because he wasn't yet knowledgeable in all areas, but one with a future where there was a great deal to be learned.

The temptation of Christ on the mountaintop after his Transfiguration and realization of His Heavenly Father is significant not just for people with "top of the mountain" Tenth House planets, but for all of us. The gifts that the Devil offered were clearly mundane. After his experience of His Heavenly Father, Christ knew that ruling the world was not his dharma; he was very clear on the nature of his Kingdom and of His work. The rest of us who lack what the Vedas call the lightning flash of illumination are not as clear as Christ was about our dharma, but if we develop our intuition (Cancer Fourth House polarity) through meditation we can get more of a fix on what it is. Saturn opposite natal Saturn or our Ego (Saturn opposite the Sun) helps us to clarify it through the process of comparison too. "Am I now the person I used to be? Is there still growth or joy in the current or the past life direction?" Saturn, like Jupiter, provides perspective, but does so more concretely.

Early in our lives we need to put down roots, to build foundations in natal Saturn's House. We need to take a stand in order to feel confident, to overcome our insecurites or sense of limitation. In their book *The Grail Legend* (p. 207), Emma Jung and Marie Louise von Franz inform us that medieval artists often depicted Saturn with a hollow wooden leg. As an example, they refer us to Figure #223, "Saturn" in Carl Jung's *Psychology and Alchemy*. In this illustration Saturn's wooden leg begins at the knee, which is especially interesting to the esoteric astrologer. The knee is the body part most directly connected to Saturn in medical astrology and therefore central to the message of the archetype. (Saturn also refers to bone and cartilage in general, to coverings and hard substances like hair and nails—but the knee is the major connection.)

The question, then, becomes: Have we by midlife taken such a strong stand (perhaps, too, a hollow, defensive stand) in the House where Saturn sits that we can no longer "bend," like the Saturn in Figure #223? Have we become calcified, rigid, like petrified wood in that area of life the Saturn house represents? Isabel Hickey in *Cosmic Science* links bending with Christian humility. She points out that Christians kneel in prayer. In so doing, they symbolically acknowledge God's part in their success and de-emphasize pride in their own merits. I often think of this when some of my most competitive clients complain of nagging pain in the knee from college days when they played football. These are men who are strong Saturn or Capricorn/Capricorn rising types.

Attainment in Saturn's House (or the Tenth House, Capricorn's natural zodiac House) serves its purpose in fulfilling desires, building security and confidence into life and personality, but by mid-life pride, smugness, judgmentalism, and negative comparisons with the less fortunate or the lazier can manifest. If we must take a stand in our youth, we must also bend in mid-life. If our attitudes become unappreciative, hard, self-righteous, we can become subject to hardening diseases of joints and arteries. (As co-ruler of Aquarius, Saturn affects the circulatory system.) An attitude of rigidity can result, over the years, in physical brittleness.

All of us can introspect about what we're proud of in the sign and House where Saturn sits, about whether or not we acknowledge that God and other people have helped us get there and express gratitude appropriately, or whether we are smug and self-righteous in that House or the affairs of that sign. Medically, if we look at our Saturn sign, we can tell the part of the body that is suceptible to weakening if we're too proud. (Saturn in Aries—"I can do it alone; I don't need any help." Migraines, sinuses, etc. Saturn in Cancer—pride in family, or embarrassment because family is not as affluent, educated or socially respectable as we'd like. The stomach, the female organs, etc.) For most of us, this is worthy of introspection.

Another interesting question to ask about the affairs of Saturn's House or the House with Capricorn on the cusp is: how comfortable am I in admitting I'm wrong? Those of us who lived during the Nixon years watched the unraveling of a Presidency because a Capricorn with a Zenith Saturn (actually a Ninth House Saturn, but still a Zenith position Saturn according to the Gauquelin research) could not admit publicly that "A mistake was made. Those close to the seat of power, my advisors that I myself selected, made an error." Readers who do not have Capricorn politicians among their clientele can study the archetype in Noel Tyl's books, *The Expanded Present* and *Integrated Transits*. These provide extensive commentary on Nixon's early career, presidency, and resignation. The President's counsel John Dean wrote a book on the Nixon Administration called *Blind Ambition*, an appropriate title for a Saturn ruled Presidency.

The pain Nixon experienced over his failure to defeat Ms. Helen Douglas in the California race unleashed a gamut of dark Capricorn emotions—denial, defensiveness, paranoia. He lashed out at the press, that eternal shadow of the candidate which follows him everywhere. "Now you won't have Richard Nixon to kick around anymore" became a famous phrase and is similar to the childlike remarks my adult Capricorns often make when success is not forthcoming in the outer world. The Shadow attacked him severely, particularly in the post-Watergate congressional hearings. Still, Mr. Nixon denied using poor judgment or having any part in the cover-up. In his resignation statement, his final speech, he spoke about his advisors Haldeman and Ehrlichman as "two fine public servants" hounded by the press for no apparent reason. The hearings revealed that he had an enemies list (paranoid behavior) with several journalist's names on it. After the resignation he was hospitalized within a short time for the leg disease phlebitis. The rigid stand he took, his inability to face reality, his ungroundedness led to the collapse of the administration. Finally, there is a twist at the end of the story, for Richard Nixon is presently regarded by important members of his political party as an Elder Statesman—a Wise Old Man to be consulted as a foreign policy expert on China.

Some lessons of Saturn transiting the Midheaven are: "Pride goeth before a fall"; do not take short-cuts to power or protect those who are in error. Admit mistakes. What is covered up will very likely surface for others' viewing.

We now leave the mountain goat to consider a vastly different Capricorn coat, playful Pan. At first glance it would seem as if these two contrasting forms of the Capricorn Goat are polar extremities; that the same sign could not embrace both types of behavior; the same human being (Capricorn client) could not swing from one to the other in the course of a single lifetime. But such is not the case. Pan often hides behind the surface of the Mountain-Goat who dutifully appears at his responsible job every day, and the aspiring Mountain

Goat may lurk beneath the surface of the Pan the perennial adolescent who refuses to settle down. The Saturn Return (age 29-30) may induce a shift from Pan to the Mountain Goat. The Aquarian progression, or a Uranus transit, may mean a shift in the other direction, from the Mountain Goat to Pan.

Who is Pan, the woodland deity so beloved of the Greeks, the Romans, and especially of repressed Victorians? (His admirers in nineteenth century England were legion—Elizabeth Barrett Browning, among them, wrote of him). Pan is everything that the Nixon-type Mountain Goat is not; where Nixon was controlled, repressed, bitter, defensive, denying his human side (his capacity for error), Pan is spontaneous, acts upon his instincts compulsively, is joyful and free-spirited. Pan cares not a bit for the Top of the Mountain, and has opted out of the competitive marketplace. He shuns the city and lives beyond its boundaries in caves, grottoes, forests.

Pan is Nature. Pan in all of us is the body, with its drives and its wisdom. In living beyond the boundaries of the city Pan also lives beyond the limits of conventional morality, the mental ethic of the straight world. It seems to make no sense to him, to be totally irrelevant. He is not image-conscious like the mundane Capricorn Mountain Goat. Society's opinion of him matters not at all. What matters are nymphs; Pan is always chasing these wisps of cloud on whom he projects substance or reality, but they fail to satisfy him. He also falls in love with Goddess Echo and becomes quite frustrated to discover that she's only the sound of his own voice. Thus Pan, like the Mountain Goat, suffers frustration in Aphrodite's realm, Eros, relating, Love.

Though Pan as Body or Nature seemingly wants to relate to Spirit, (the ethereal cloud nymphs), in fact he has chosen to chase that which he can never catch, that which he can never commit to. He thus has preserved his own freedom from responsibility, puer-like. In "An Essay on Pan," James Hillman tells us that Pan and Aphrodite (true love) are two levels of consciousness that cannot meet. Pan, says Hillman, "knows only what the five senses can tell him. He is in goat consciousness." Aphrodite is Love; Pan is lust. The two cannot relate. We see this clearly represented in art by a statue in the Acropolis Museum, where Pan approaches Aphrodite seeking an embrace. Disdainfully, distractedly, she hits at him with her sandal. She does not take him too seriously; she is not afraid of him at all. She is gentle, fair skinned, refined, anointed with Olympian perfumes.

Pan has sharp horns, black skin, hairy thighs, an erect phallus, and a strong goat odor, according to Homer (*Ode to Pan*). He has in common with the Mountain Goat, then, frustrations with the elusive Aphrodite (relationship), loneliness, and sensitivity to slights.

Pan is open, honest, truly his uninhibited self. When he has no prospect of catching his insubstantial love, he reveals himself as a true friend, providing solace through the healing wisdom of nature that is unique to him among the gods. His friend Psyche (the human soul), for instance, suffered from unrequited love for Amor, who seemed lost to her forever. She was about to drown herself; she was *not* about to ask Pan for a commitment. He was totally safe in spending some time with her. His wise counsel pulled her out of her despondency, for Pan (body) knows the joy in simply being alive, of living in the moment. In touch with Pan (her body), Psyche became convinced that the Sun would rise again, that a better day would dawn tomorrow, that her attachment to Amor was deep but not worth giving up her life. The story of Body's advice to Soul, of Psyche, Amor, and Pan is worthwhile reading for anyone suffering Psyche's plight. It can be found in the tragi-comedy *The Golden Ass* by the Roman Sophist Apuleus, who became a disciple in the Isis cult. (It is well written and full of puns, as when Apuleus apologizes to the reader for the times when his main character becomes "a pompous ass.")

The Pan goat then spends time with safe members of the opposite sex who do not expect a commitment. He listens to their problems and offers good instinctual advice. Sometimes he or she lives outside the boundaries of conventional society by frequenting gay bars (if the Ascendant is in Air or Fire, the Sun is in Capricorn and Saturn isn't Angular, this is a definite possibility) or just indulging in the singles scene, biding his or her time till the Mountain Goat within makes itself heard. Another way to live beyond the boundaries and get in touch with Body is to experience the call of nature and leave the city behind for the bucolic life of the countryside. Usually the Pan-goat is more of a loner than a joiner of rural communes, until the Aquarian progression when New Age communities begin to appeal. Often he builds himself a cabin miles from other people and attunes to nature within and around him.

His attunement, then, is to Mother Nature. Like the Mountain Goat, he suffers disappointment in his relationship with Father. While many Mountain Goats seem to feel that Father's expectations are too high, most have been provided with a mature, responsible masculine role model for mundane living, mundane aspirations. The Pan-Goat, in my experience, often has had no strong Father to serve as an example in his childhood. His father may have been a Hermes type, restlessly drifting through life dreaming big dreams but not fulfilling them. Pan grew up helter skelter with only his five senses and his instincts to rely upon. The wisdom of the body is no small thing, however. So often the Pan/Capricorn will tell me that his body told him to leave a situation or to move from a geographic area and he acted upon it. In that sense, the Psyche part of us does need to listen to the Pan part—to Saturn as our bodily, instinctual reaction in the areas of life that natal Saturn rules.

One client who heard Pan's flute calling and acted on his instincts—with positive results—related this story: "I was driving home from work one day in rush hour traffic. I was thinking over a remark made by a senior partner in my firm, that I was destined to become a judge at a very young age if I kept going as I was then—I had such potential. Then I thought of my old friend from law school days telling me I should join his firm. It had unlimited financial potential, offered me scope for my talents, a lot more responsibility, a lot more pressure, too, of course. I suddenly became very depressed. My leg began to cramp. I turned on the classical music station on the radio. Around me diesel fumes blackened the sky. Suddenly I had an anxiety attack, an experience not just of claustrophobia, but of real panic. I suddenly knew that I *had* to get out of the city right away, find a cabin in the woods, cut wood for the stove, get out of the rat race. Listen to music, just *be* for awhile—find out who I really am, what life is all about. So I did it. My wife, my old school friend, the senior partner all thought I was completely mad. But it was the best decision I ever made. I'm convinced that my instincts saved my health, maybe even my life, at that point. It was really out of character for me though, to act on impulse; I've always been a planner, a strategist about life."

He heard the call of "The Great God Pan," as Plutarch called him. After his encounter, he left behind the boundaries of the conventional world—the mountain top, the image or persona (previously so all important to him) to get in touch with Nature, with Pan. Pan's environment of trees and plants, lakes and clear skies is quite healing. What is interesting, though, is that Pan spoke in the pandemonium of rush-hour traffic, and "panicked" him with an anxiety attack. In spite of logic, he followed his instincts, listened to his body. In his case, and several others like it, the bucolic life was a temporary phase. It resulted in introspection and reflection on personal values. He felt less like a mechanical goat climbing the hilltop. He got in touch with his imagination, his creativity. Later, articles and eventually a novel resulted from the time off experience.

For others, Pan's call is more permanent. The nature of their aspiration changes. They seek a simple life as an environment for spiritual, rather than mundane, mountain climbing. During the Aquarian progression they find people of like values in New Age communities, where their leadership talents surface in the new environment, and they have a good deal to contribute in structuring, organizing, teaching others. If these people are put back into an urban area for a few days visiting relatives, Body (Pan) immediately complains about the air, water, and noise pollution. They'll speak of the healing of the trees, the fields, or the mountain streams. They continue to nourish both Pan and the Mountain Goat in the countryside.

What of the lecherous Pan who seems to thrive on urban night life as a swinging single? The raunchy old goat who seems identified with the body's desire nature on its lowest level—compulsive cravings leading to addiction to alcohol or drugs? The Capricorn who tries to starve his aspiring mountain goat for years on end and behaves like a repressed Victorian breaking out of conventions—out of his archetypal mold? If this state goes on too long, there are definite risks, definite dangers because, in the company he keeps, Pan is a lot like Dionysius (see Chapter 12, Pisces), god of wine, sex and song. Meaningless affairs, insubstantial loves like Echo or the nymphs, are not really satisfying. Loneliness ensues for the urban Pan as it does for the hermit Pan out in the country. Pan the motherless child feels empty, feels that something's missing. The year of the Saturn Return, of the encounter with Father Time, often brings about a shift toward the direction of the Mountain Goat. Ambition surfaces.

Clients involved in the "old goat" lifestyle have been told by their bodies to leave the bar scene at age 29-30, for that world is partial to youth. Several have told me, "My hair is thinning, and I'm feeling over the hill. There are all these teenagers out there now with young bodies and firm muscles. I look in the mirror and ask myself, where are you going from here? You've no roots, no property, no lasting relationship. You've no proof that you can succeed in anything. I'm so depressed."

In that word "succeed" one hears the voice of the Mountain

Goat. In the rest of the statement one hears Father Time (Saturn) trying to settle the person down for the long run, opposing Pan, who wants him to live in freedom, in the moment. This is not a change that happens overnight. If the client has an Angular Saturn, or several harsh natal Saturn aspects in the chart, the depression may lead to counseling that works a complete change. He begins in the early thirties to find his work, his service or Dharma. He becomes his own Saturn, developing discipline, seeking to be responsible and grounded. Saturn also means be realistic—stop chasing nymphs. Saturn tries to persuade the Pan Goat to take on adult commitments during the Return and the years following, not only in work but in relationship.

There is danger in tarrying too long in Pan's world. The Greeks considered him the God of epilepsy and madness. Hillman's book treats the connection between Pan and nightmare in the sense of dreams. But in waking-state conscious reality a person can live a Pan nightmare too if the spiritual aspirations of the Mountain goat are lost through exclusive homage to Pan.

Hospitalization for substance abuse close to age 29 has been a pattern with my Pan Capricorns. Others have dealt with memories of Father's role in their childhoods which surfaced on the Saturn Return and led them into therapy. One such client, in describing his impressions (projections?) of Father seemed to be describing his afflicted Saturn. This sounds like Senex itself.

"My father was a workaholic, an inhibited person with a sour expression on his face who never seemed to have any fun. He was always correcting me for some minor thing I did wrong. He was a perfectionist. A petty tyrant in his office and a major tyrant at home. If you can't measure up no matter how hard you try, why try at all? I can see now that I gave up, opted out of the competition."

Here, father seems outwardly successful, but inwardly unhappy. Others' fathers were less outwardly successful: "My dad seemed to think he was a failure; life had passed him by. Like me, he was sensitive. He couldn't be ruthless with people. He drank and brooded. I tend to do that, too."

In most cases, depression, introspection, reflection have all characterized the Return year and had a favorable outcome in the case of the Pan Goat. For others, it takes longer to release old habits, to program new ones into the behavior. And yet, the depression is an important phase of the journey. Listening to the body is also important for people with harsh Saturn aspects. If Saturn is in the Sixth House (health) or rules it, or if it is near the Ascendant or in the First House and there are harsh aspects, the body often forces a person to take time out and reflect on the questions so many clients have asked: "Where am I going?" "Why this emptiness?" In dealing with the body—listening to it—there is a similarity in the Saturn Return experience of the Mountain Goat and the Pan Goat. Whether totally driven (Mountain Goat) or seemingly unmotivated (Pan) both goats tend to encounter Father Time through the body, and to try to make peace with him. Whether the old habits are Pan related, or Mountain Goat related (workaholic perfectionism), great strides can be taken to go beyond their limits.

A very few also transcend mundane Saturn and move toward esoteric Saturn in the period between age 29-34. These Capricorns make statements like, "Dad's approval, society's approval no longer matter. I know now that my real Father is the Divine. My relationship with the Divine is the source of my strength; it's His (or Her) approval and His (or Her) will that matter." Father, father figure or mentor have lost their power, their authority. During these years the Saturn limits in the Unconscious—guilt, fear, conflicting duties, lack of confidence in the life-direction begin to disappear for the esoteric Capricorn.

Capricorn rising and Capricorn Sun sign women and women with Angular Saturns also often go through a version of seeking Father's approval; hungering for a relationship with him that he often lacks the developed feeling nature to offer them. Because Capricorn tends to be conservative, traditional at heart, they often marry close to 29 and choose a man Father would definitely approve of. If they wait till age 29 to marry, an older man, a man "established" in his work, a safe or Saturnine man is often selected. But their judgment is not always accurate. Sometimes a man who appears to be a pillar of the community (Saturn) turns out to be flawed, to be disappointing. So many astrologers have had the experience of hearing women who married close to age 30 mentioning that the husband turned out to be cold, neglectful or "too busy for me" with the result that though they had opted for financial security, they felt emotionally deprived. By hindsight, they tend to remark, "If only I had not married out of loneliness; if only I had waited."

Thus many astrologers recommend to single women with strong

Saturns, Capricorn planets, Capricorn rising, "*Wait* till you're 31 or 32." When the lonely settling in Saturn cycle is over, judgment will improve. There are other archetypes in the horoscope which require satisfaction; Capricorn/Saturn is not the only factor in the personality, though it sometimes feels like it when you're close to 30. What about warmth—the Libra/Taurus/Venus archetype? What about wit, friendliness, communication? The Mercury/Gemini/Uranus/Aquarius archetype? What about passion? Mars/Aries/Pluto/Scorpio archetype? To someone with many planets in Air signs, the Saturnine partner may already seem dull within a year of the return. By hindsight she may remark seven years later to a girlfriend, "He's so stuffy; he never has time to go and do things. I guess I married him out of loneliness. I can't imagine what else would have possessed me." This is sad.

Sometimes during the Saturn Return it helps a woman with a strongly developed animus, such as a well organized, perfectionist school teacher, to get in touch with nature—with Pan. I'm not recommending she do it through the bar scene of course; that only brings more emptiness—the feeling of being all alone in a crowd. Rather she could take time off during her summer vacation to leave the world of Logos for the countryside. A change of scene, if nature abounds, is often grounding, healing. Retreats spent in an environment of peaceful gardens and waterfalls, visits to friends in rural communities or relatives who are supportive and live outside the big city, who may be Wise Old Men, or Wise Old Women, often has a healing, peaceful effect. The individual in such a positive Pan environment can take time out to introspect, reflect on what is important to her personally, not to Society, Mother or Dad. To sort out one's own adult values is an intrinsic part of the return—to know thyself, as the Apollo temple message admonished. Otherwise there's a tendency for a single Capricorn/Capricorn rising person to choose a partner who would be ideal for the community, for professional joint projects, for fitting into the socio-economic group but who can be wrong for her—and she, after all, is the one getting married.

Pan's simple, natural environment can strengthen the ability to get in touch with the instincts, with Body, as the antidote to the animus' constant thinking, analyzing, planning, ranking. Pan does not want her to go through life as a repressed, dour, constantly striving perfectionist who shuns fun, and who can never make a mistake.

Pan is an important god because integration of Body, Mind, and

Soul is an important quest for all of us, not just Capricorn/saturnine people. Even Socrates found Pan important in his quest to know himself and supposedly wrote this prayer:

> Beloved Pan, and all ye other Gods who haunt this place, give me Beauty in the inward soul; and may the outward and inward man be at one. (From Plato's *Phaedrus*.)

Even to the Capricorn Goat who is in touch with his instincts, Aphrodite may seem frustratingly elusive till the mid-thirties, unless the Venus/Libra/Taurus archetype is strongly influential in the chart. (People with Venus conjunct the Sun in Capricorn, or conjunct Capricorn rising, for example, will appear to others as much warmer, as more gentle, loving, and charming, as more kind than the usual Goat.) It's important for the astrologer to find the Saturn/Venus aspects in the horoscope and determine if there is a conflict in the client's mind between Love (Venus) and Duty (Saturn). If there is a harsh natal aspect, then the progressed chart can provide insight into the timing for flowing with romance. When Venus progresses out of inconjunct, square or opposition into trine or sextile to Saturn the tension lessens and the person often feels as if the gate to Aphrodite's domain is opening to him or her in the outer world. Progressions are connected to our inner readiness to say yes to life; to transcend our natal insecurities, fears, and self-limitations; to open up to opportunity in the outer world.

Single clients with natal Saturn/Venus hard aspects often think, "That's an attractive person; I'd like to get to know him or her, but right now my duty is to my elderly parent (Saturn), my career (Saturn), or to my child from an early marriage (Saturn)—to my specialized graduate study (Saturn) or to my ascetic, hermit-like search for God Alone (Saturn). There's no time to engage in frivolous things like relationships at this stage of life." There's no time for Aphrodite, because Saturn feels a need to focus all his energy on a higher Duty. Or, as an unconscious voice from the past, he whispers, "It wouldn't work. It didn't work the first time for you, so it won't work now." Or, "Relationship didn't work out happily for your parents, so why should it work for you?" Or, like a perfectionist, "You'd have to lose 20 pounds before anyone would find you attractive. You'd need a hair transplant, you need to wait, to put Venus on hold." Poor Aphrodite, Saturn outranks her.

One esoteric author, Isabel Hickey, says that the major lesson for Capricorn/Capricorn rising is the lesson of unselfish love, of Venus exalted in Pisces. Logically speaking, the conditions will never be perfect, the client will never be a perfect 10 nor is s/he likely to find a perfect 10 in the outer world to marry. We live in a flawed human world, but that is no reason to close ourselves off from others with strong walls and a deep moat (Saturn's defenses). Isabel Hickey describes the search of Capricorn rising for a sympathetic, empathetic mate as the search for an ideal mother. (Capricorn rising has Cancer, the Great Mother, on the Seventh House cusp.)

I've looked for this pattern in the lives of my clients with the Saturn ruled Ascendant and found it to be remarkably true. Yet women with Capricorn rising tend to be ambitious for the partner as well as for themselves. They may fall in love with a gentle soul who is loving, spiritual, kind, and supportive and enjoy having him around the house. But if he proves too sensitive to take criticism, to compete and succeed in the outer world, his Capricorn rising wife may also find it difficult to respect him. If there are children it is especially important to her that the couple be financially secure. Many women with this Ascendant put their energy into their own work; they really marry Cancer on the Seventh House cusp in the form of their nurturing type profession.

If Saturn is a judgmental, critical, perfectionist planet, why then is he exalted in Libra and in the Marriage House (Seventh House) which are both Aphrodite ruled? Perhaps this call to unselfish love is a challenge to blend and balance (Libra) the worlds of love and duty; to think and plan (Saturn) yet be open to flowing with someone else's approach; to compromise, to co-operate (Venus); to be receptive (Venus); to be kind (Venus) while patiently learning through relationship (Saturn in Libra or the Seventh). The truth to the exaltation, the power in the placement of Saturn in Libra or the Seventh House has been demonstrated again and again in my work through clients who appear for a reading close to the first Saturn Return, the second, or even the third.

It seems difficult to balance the inner and outer worlds of Venus and Saturn—of subjective happiness and objective success. The intensity and obsessive force with which Saturn in the Seventh House clients ask the question, "Something's missing from my life. Where's my mate?" close to one of these returns is amazing to behold. (Capricorn Sun sign and Capricorn rising clients ask the question around age 29, 56, or 86, too, but their intensity pales in comparison to the exalted Saturn people.) The search for the partner is so similar to what Jung would call the search for Wholeness, or what the yogi would term the search for true Dharma (Saturn). As they bring in several relationship charts to the astrologer that year, they express both their need to proceed scientifically, and their fear of making a mistake about something this important. Exalted Saturn seeks guarantees that the marriage will work, that it will endure. Saturn seeks contracts carved in granite. Objectively, the astrologer can do the relationship on a point system and conclude, "This is better (or worse) than the last relationship chart you had done," but it seems somehow inappropriate to rank people in Aphrodite's romantic domain. The astrologer can almost feel the Goddess Herself standing in the wings, covering her mouth with her hand and giggling when the client with the Seventh House Saturn asks, "On the scale of 1 to 10, how does this relationship fare? And is the wedding day absolutely free of difficult aspects?" We are all somewhat this intense, perhaps, in the House our Saturn sits in, but the exaltation seems especially powerful. Maturity and deepening personal values characterize the year following Saturn's return. What others think becomes less and less important, seemingly, on each Return, even what Family thinks.

The Seventh House Saturn exaltation also is connected with ego inflation. This usually comes out through the uttering of Saturn comparisons. My spouse is a doctor, a dentist, a vice president, or an officer in the armed services. One client had been in my office less than five minutes when she sat down for the reading. Her first words were, "Of course, my husband is a four-star general." Of course! Who else would she choose with Saturn in the Seventh? Saturn in the Seventh seeks status through Other, through the partner.

Men with Seventh House Saturns tend to be equally proud of their wives. "I can delegate anything to her, forget about it, and it will be done well. She's the best-organized person I've ever met. She's the perfect hostess, wife and mother (the social roles again). But who is she as a human being, and has he noticed? "Would you describe your wife as a happy person, a warm, loving person, a fulfilled person?" "Eh?" he asks, long pause. "Warm? Don't know. Never thought about it. I could ask the children what they think, I suppose. She's a strong woman. Very civic minded. Good-hearted sort—does a lot of committee work, that type of thing, if that's what you mean." (This man had a Venus/Saturn square, no planets or Angles in Taurus or Libra, and a Tenth House stellium with Saturn in the Seventh, so he's an almost archetypal exalted Saturn man. Nonetheless, interesting.)

Mars is the planet exalted in Capricorn. This placement in an individual's chart can also mean different levels of aspiration at different stages of his life. In youth, for instance, it can mean that his energy (Mars) is applied ambitiously (Capricorn) to the pursuit of a purely materialistic, selfish goal in Mountain Goat fashion. Then later in the same lifetime, the person may shift his energy toward a socially conscious emphasis, such as giving up a lucrative law practice and accepting a local political office with a small salary attached to it. This shift in emphasis may occur in the Aquarian progression. Then, later still, during the Pisces progression, Mars in Capricorn may turn inward and ambition may turn to spiritual aspiration as an interest develops in Jungian psychology or meditation. This position of Mars lends energy to the individual's other planets in Capricorn which take time to mull things over cautiously.

Esoterically, of course, we need to remember that Mars is a "me first" type of energy. It helps to ask oneself with this placement, "Who, other than me, will benefit from me getting to the top?" Or in the case of women who have the exaltation and are not working outside the home, "Does my husband really share my ambitions? Am I perhaps using my Mars in Capricorn to push him into roles he doesn't really care about just to satisfy my own Mars? Does *he* want to be a vice president?" Later in life, if the woman is not using Mars in her own career, she may need to ask these same questions of her adult sons. "Are they happy? Am I expecting a success for them that they don't really care about themselves?" Fortunately, in the West, women are able to work with this energy and ambition in their own lives, rather than project it upon their husbands and sons.

Astrology students who have children in the Capricorn/Capricorn rising archetype often ask the practical question, "How can I put the little one in touch with Aphrodite early in life, so he or she won't be such a late bloomer romantically? Can I speed up the attunement to Aphrodite's realm? My child is so serious." One way is to be warm with the child, even if he or she doesn't seem very demonstrative or is embarrassed at being hugged in front of his or her playmates. Show the child that demonstrating affection is normal and that he or she is loved for existing as well as for achieving in school or performing well in extracurricular activities. If the parent has some Libra/Taurus, or a strongly placed Venus, this comes naturally as does exposing the child to beauty and the arts. The parent will, with the Aphrodite archetype strong in his own chart, naturally keep an attractive, nicely appointed house. The parent will probably have friends who talk around the child about aesthetics, from music to the visual arts, photography, architecture, and so forth. The child will naturally be taken along to art openings, concerts, museums, and plays or ballet. He or she will grow up believing that adults consider Aphrodite's aesthetic world a valid realm, a realm worth knowing about, spending time in, and soon will come to feel relaxed, refreshed, and stimulated by it.

Another method is to work with the House the child's Venus is in, the sign and aspects. Find some area of aesthetics the child will succeed at (important for Capricorn) and enjoy. Value the success. Let him or her experiment with color in decorating the bedroom or choosing clothing. Avoid having Father convey to the child that the aesthetic world is sissy stuff and he should instead be practicing baseball every night, as Capricorn is sensitive to father's approval. Do not let him become a technically perfect performing robot. Emphasize style and originality. In *The Pregnant Virgin*, Marion Woodman warns against the tendency to become a performer, an achiever, a competitor, because one loses touch with the Body and the instincts. It can lead to anorexia or bulimia. Emphasize enjoyment and relaxation.

Your little Capricorn will most likely have a long memory. If he recalls having spent many evenings with you, his parent, at concerts and plays, he is likely to gladly accompany his wife later as an adult. If he lacks the memories, if the world of aesthetics is unfamiliar to him, he may feel uncomfortable there. He may cast sad longing looks behind him at his briefcase on his way to the concert with his wife, and see the evening as a duty to be endured.

It's been my experience of Capricorn/Capricorn rising that those whose parents introduced them to Aphrodite's realm early in life had an easier time with the second phase of development—adolescent socializing with the opposite sex. They also tended to choose more refined (Venusian) friends, and through their friendships, to develop the spiritual values of Aphrodite—harmony, co-operation, kindness, the ability to give others the benefit of the doubt, charm, and thoughtfulness of others.

Does your child enjoy his or her recreation time, or is the time spent struggling with a competitive challenge, something to be perfected? If he or she constantly chooses the challenge, the pattern can be set for later in life—sports can be seen as stressful rather than relaxing. (We all know the Capricorn adult who, while the rest of us are enjoying the game, is perfecting his backhand—the man who never seems just to enjoy the game and leave the court refreshed.) I was visiting a friend one Saturday when her ten-year-old was just leaving, tennis racket in hand and determined look on her face. I asked the young Capricorn, "How do you really feel about tennis?" "I sure hate it," she said, "but I practice a lot and I'm getting to be very good at it." I was glad she felt successful, but I somehow wished that when she had free time from her strict parochial school she could use it to delve more deeply into something she enjoyed.

Another example is that of a teenage Capricorn boy who pulled up his bicycle to the steps of his house, got off and began unpacking ten science books from the basket. He seemed to be half-listening to his mother and the neighbor lady, talking on the porch. The neighbor said of her young son, "it cost us a lot of money to replace the Smith's bay window after Jerry broke it with his baseball, but of course, kids will be kids." The teenager paused on his way up the steps, turned to his mother and asked, "Mom, was I *ever* a kid?" Here we see the saturnine philosophy, "Life is real and life is earnest" expressed quite early in life.

It seems particularly important for parents of children with Capricorn rising to expose them to the arts, because these individuals tend with their innate practicality to specialize early in life in such dry (less imaginative) fields as medicine, research, business, urban planning, or political science. An acquaintanceship with the creative arts or music will help them understand and socialize with people outside the confines of their narrow field, as well as enrich them personally.

Many of my clients have benefitted from reading *The Holy Science* by Sri Yukteswar Giri. In this beautiful book he develops the theme that although Dharma is a mental virtue and an important virtue at that, for health and happiness in mind and body there is a still more important virtue—*Shraddha*, or heart's love. Through the efforts in the outer world of career these women have already fulfilled collective duty—or dharma, their own and their parents' expectations, but in their personal lives there's the feeling that something or someone is missing. Swami Sri Yukteswar says that those of us who feel burdened by life rather than joyful are out of tune with nature and therefore do not attract the right partner or the right circumstances for personal and spiritual progress. Sometimes the body seems unable to heal itself; the central nervous system is too excited, and sometimes there is no peace of mind. If this is the condition, the virtue to develop (which sounds like Venus in Pisces) is Shraddha, the attunement to God and Guru through doing what is natural, going with the flow. People whose lives are too structured, too rigid or saturnine have gotten out of the habit of flowing with nature.

The Jungian approach is similar. If we identify with the persona or the role we play in the course of our work, we become inflated and unhappy. We lose our spontaneity, our attunement to nature. We lose our contact with the Self and with it, our innate peace. The persona could be supermom as well as superboss—it doesn't matter. It is still a persona, an outer direction that overwhelms the inner. If instead, according to Jung, we listen to the inner guidance of the Self and begin to follow it, we will observe a healing of body and mind, and soon even the outer world, through synchronicity, will begin to fulfill our needs as well. In this view of moving from the inner world toward the outer, Western psychology and Eastern spirituality are very close.

Having spoken of the need to develop Shraddha through attunement to God and Guru, Sru Yukteswar returns to the subject of Dharma. He says, "Affectionally follow the Guru's teaching." He continues with a practical discussion of yogic diet and the do's and don'ts (Yamas and Niyamas) of the Hindu scriptures. What he says is very similar to the New Testament teaching. "If you love me, keep my commandments," or Paramahansa Yogananda's remark, "Learn to behave." These two things are necessary: love (Venus/Aphrodite) and keeping the commandments (Saturn) out of love. But at the end of his book Sru Yukteswar again gives precedence to Shraddha: "He who cultivates love . . . is on the right path."

The philosophy of Jung and the Eastern sages is refreshing because it gives value to Eros in an age preoccupied with material success and the outer world. What we do (our outer work) is so often perceived as more important than who we are (our inner selves). Jung sees mid-life—the period beginning from age 40-45—as important for refocusing our attention on who we are, as we feel the outer "doing" to be insufficient for happiness. I find that this is particularly true in the charts of Capricorn/Capricorn rising and Angular Saturn people. From mid-life on Eros begins to be taken more seriously.

They seem to preside, Chronus-like, over the birth of Aphrodite, their own feeling nature.

Though the Greek Chronus mythology contributes a great deal to our understanding of the Capricorn archetype, the Roman Empire seems to have been much more attuned to it than the Greeks. As a people devoted to their search for the Good, the True, and the Beautiful, the Greeks expressed the values of Zeus and Aphrodite, the benefic planets, in their art and philosophy. They did not preach the sterling qualities of Chronus at the expense of Zeus. We have only to read Plato, Plotinus, and Pythagoras and to contrast them with the Roman writers, the Stoics, sophists and the Skeptics—with Cicero and Livy—to see this. Then, of course, we also have the legacy of the monuments, elegant vases, sculptures and columns, in contrast to Rome's utilitarian roads, aqueducts and military arches, the aesthetic versus the functional or practical.

While the Greek upper classes read such inspiring writing as Iamblichus, Pythagoras' chief disciple, on the joy of the soul in the presence of God, the Roman upper classes were supporting a "practical, unimaginative, patriotic" official religion "fostering civil and domestic virtues." This was a "cold and formal" state religion of which each family was a little church, according to Professor S. Angus, in *Mystery Religions*. (See pp. 31-45.) The household, which included not only a large joint family but servants, or freedmen, and slaves, obeyed the *paterfamilias*' decision in disputes. The head of the family had the right of life and death over all but his own wife, according to Roman law. There was a shrine to the family guardian spirits, the *manes*, and formal worship was obligatory. This religious dryness of patriarchal Rome, as well as its bureaucratic government, is quite saturnine in nature. Though there were many gods on the ritual calendar and the state list of approved cults, the major Roman festival was the Saternalia, celebrated on the Winter Equinox.

Who then was the Roman Saturn? What was his mythology, and what can we find in it to amplify our understanding of the Capricorn archetype?

In the Roman myth, Saturn arrives in Italy by sea. Janus, the Italian king, meets his ship and welcomes the god ashore. Saturn then presents Janus (from whom we derive our month of January) with a set of laws and the gift of prophecy. Henceforth, Janus becomes known as a shrewd and wise leader; his decisions are viewed as based no longer upon tradition and the past, but also upon his predictive knowledge of the future. Some Roman artists represented Janus with two heads. They were not commenting that the king was shifty or two faced, but rather as Macrobius explains, that he possessed a grasp of the continuity of time, one head facing backwards into the past and the other forwards into the future. Still other statues depicted Janus facing in four directions, the Cardinal points of the compass, and staring into space like an all-seeing Hindu deity.

In expression of his gratitude to Saturn for the gifts of prophecy, agricultural techniques and law, which the god had brought to Italy, King Janus minted a coin. The symbol he chose to commemorate Saturn was the ship upon which Saturn arrived. He could have chosen instead a tablet of laws or an ear of corn, but he preferred the sea to emphasize, perhaps, the original connection of the Lord of dry land and dry laws with the fertile waters of the ocean, with prophecy and creativity. We have in the symbolism a sort of reconciliation or balance of the opposites of Earth and Water.

Thus, in both Greece and Rome the Chronus/Saturn mythology is associated with continuity over time (past, present, future), a Golden Age of rule by good laws, a type of creativity (Aphrodite, gift of the sea, and the gift of prophecy), and the bringing of order out of chaos. This dual theme of time awareness and hunger for order is instinctively important to the Capricorn archetype, as borne out in the lives of my clients. After questions about long-term planning and timing come questions on how to establish efficiency and order in their own lives and Cosmic Order in the world around them. Those of you who are astrologers and have looked at the charts not only of Capricorn Sun signs and of Capricorn rising people, but also the charts of those with the Saturn/Ascendant trine or Saturn/Midheaven trine will know what I mean by the natural talent for organizing, administering, and management that favorable Saturn aspects bring to the personality. And you will know of the questions and frustrations such managers have in relating to others who lack their organizing gift at home or at work.

When, for instance, a person with Capricorn/Saturn personality traits sees my small apartment for the first time with books, notebooks, and papers scattered about in disarray, he cannot help but remark, "How can you stand living in all this clutter?" After hearing the explanation, "It's only temporary—it's because of the book I'm revising. In about two years this will be over," he says. "Oh, I see." What he sees is that short-term disorder is painful, but, if there's a purpose to it, endurable. (Two years ahead would be long term to a fiery personality, but short term to Cardinal Earth.)

A Capricorn Sun sign person, a Capricorn rising, or an Angular Saturn person (Saturn in Houses 1, 4, 7 or 10) may have difficulty restraining himself from organizing the life out of projects, organizing the spouse's schedule within an inch of his or her life, or so thoroughly organizing the children's routines that they have little time left over to lay back and stare at cloud formations or to stop and smell the roses. The urge to manifest cosmic order, to establish efficiency, simplicity, perfection around them so that others can better learn, perform, or accomplish their goals, can be so strong that it strikes others as sheer bossiness.

My favorite anecdote on the Capricorn penchant for law and order is the story told by a Sagittarian woman: "To me, as to a lot of other Fire sign people I know, driving a car is fun; it's an adventure. I know several Capricorns, though, who seem to think it's a dreary procedure fraught with moral lessons. They can be so darn pompous behind the wheel.

"Last month I was a passenger in a car driven by a Capricorn friend. He was waiting in a parking lot—it seemed forever—for this parking space. When it was finally available, some jerk suddenly pulled around the corner from the other direction and took it. Can you imagine?

"Well, I'd have yelled 'Idiot!' and hit my horn and told him, 'that was my space; I was here first, I had a right to it. It's not fair. But not the Capricorn. He turned to me quite calmly and asked, 'Did you see that?'

"'Sure it was an outrage. Go ahead and yell at him. You'll feel a lot better,' I said supportively.

"But instead of yelling at the jerk, he made me listen to a long, boring sermon on the rules of the road—who yields to whom and three other rules the car broke besides taking the parking place. Unbelievable how these Capricorns can be."

So often Sagittarius and Capricorn will react like this to the same situation; the Jupiter-ruled personality tends to see the issue as one of rights or fairness while the Capricorn tends to see it as one of duty under the law.

The association of the law and the mountaintop comes through the Old Testament strongly. One good example would be Yahweh's gift of the law (10 commandments) carved in stone on Mt. Sinai. Because of Yahweh's role as Supreme Lawgiver and Covenant Maker, Jung and other authors have seen in him a saturnine god. However, all over the world gods were said to dwell on mountaintops and make known their decrees. Kings emulated the gods by building their palaces, as well as their temples, on high ground, even when the terrain offered no mountains. In Cambodia, for instance, wats and palaces alike were built on hills. In the death inscriptions on monuments, Khmer Emperors were sculpted standing next to and apparently turning the Wheel of the Law (Dharma) and were called Dharma Rajas if the kingdom experienced peace and prosperity during their reign. Some of the more important emperors were called Deva Rajas (god kings) or, having reached Oneness with the Void, Chakra Vartin Buddhas (Wheel-turning Buddhas). Again there is the symbolism—the Law, the Lawgiver and the Top of the Mountain (the 10th House).

The difficulty with the God King, though, is that "absolute power can corrupt absolutely," as Lord Acton supposedly said. Strict Justice that is not tempered with mercy can be a real burden for the subjects to bear. Capricorn has Cancer as its polarity sign, ruled by the Great Mother, the Moon. One major aspect of the Mother is her Mercy (see Chapter 4, Cancer, Kwan Yin) which tempers Capricornian strict Justice. The Greeks and the Romans alike worshiped her through her son Pan, among other forms. Where Saturn was associated with Kingship, the Arcadian shepherd god Pan was connected with the common people, bodily instincts, and pranks.

Macrobius also informs us that the week of the Saturnalia was a great social equalizer. Servants ate at the table with the Master and were served by his wife. The death of Tyrant Winter was celebrated and duties were replaced with days of rest and feasting. This had the impact of reversing saturnine social roles and conventions so that the upper classes realized they were "as much at the mercy of fortune as their slaves." A commoner was selected to play the role of King Saturn for the week, but we do not know how far his powers actually extended. In antiquity King Saturn was probably killed at the end of festival, but by the first century AD animal sacrifices had been substituted. Fertility and renewal of the Earth with the coming of spring was the theme.

The Romans, for instance, believed that "high noon is Pan's hour." This meant that anything could happen then; it was a time for surprises. If there was a lull in the conversation the Romans would say, "Pan must be here; it must be close to high noon." Pan, who could thwart man's best laid plans with his flute music and induce a crowd to panic seems to have functioned as a natural balancing force to serious Saturn, ruler of the Tenth House planning energy. Astrologically, people born at noon are Tenth House Sun sign natives, and as such are part of the Capricorn archetype. Yet they especially, it would seem, come under the authority of Pan, ruler of their birth hour. I have often observed that regardless of where in the zodiac a Tenth House Sun sign person is born, if s/he takes himself too seriously, becomes too judgmental, too controlled, too austere, too brittle or rigid in his standards for him/herself and others, s/he's likely to be touched by Pan's interference with his/her plans. This is the client who says, "Just when things were perfect for me and I was made a vice president, an Arab bought the hotel chain and replaced me." Or, "Just when I finally had power to make policy, I was transferred to another state and had to start all over again." Pan often waits for the right moment, the culminating moment, archetypally, because the Zenith House is about culmination. The first year of the Aquarian progression, if it coincides with some Uranus transits through either House Ten or Eleven (personal hopes and dreams) can often hit the natal Capricorn Sun in the Tenth (a double correspondence to the archetype) very hard by upsetting longstanding plans. The more rigid the person, the harder s/he takes Pan's blow, or so it seems.

We have met two of the Capricorn goats—the hardy, aspiring, Mountain Goat and the seemingly unmotivated Pan Goat. A third, equally important and somewhat more esoteric goat remains to be encountered—the Scapegoat. His existence is implied in the story of the final banishment of Chronus at the end of the Golden Age. Like the other aeonic lords before him, Chronus refused to retire gracefully at the end of his 2,400-year reign and had to be overthrown by his son, in this case Zeus (Jupiter). As a result of my client work I have come to see the banishment of Chronus as connected to the Jungian Scapegoat archetype, and as central to the life journey of the Capricorn/Saturn archetype. Macrobius tells us in *Saternalia* that there are several versions of the banishment locale. Some sources, for instance, have Chronus banished to the North (the cold?) while others say "the wilderness" or "the Isles of the Blessed." The theme of the Banishment is consistent in all the versions.

The concept of the Scapegoat as a collective projection device is very old, especially in Africa, Asia and the Near East. Primitive tribes have for centuries been observed to capture a wild animal and through ritual, project their guilt and fears upon it in an attempt to propitiate or atone to a local deity. Sometimes the animal would be slaughtered on the altar of the god or goddess, and sometimes it would be banished, like Chronus, to the Wilderness, carrying away with it the evils of the tribe. Afterwards, it was hoped that the deity would no longer look with anger upon his people but would protect them instead.

The concepts of sacrifice and atonement associated with the Scapegoat ritual were important, for instance, to the Israelites. On the 10th day of a certain harvest festival they would bless and send forth a sacrifical goat, having projected all their collective evils upon it. The Greeks and Romans also knew of the Scapegoat, whose blood upon their altars was acceptable to Chronus/Saturn as a substitute for theirs.

In my practice of astrology I have found definite parallels between the life of the Capricorn goat and that of the psychologist's Scapegoat. If one listens carefully to the vocabulary of the Capricorn or Capricorn rising client, or the client with Saturn on the parenting axis (in House Four or Ten) one will hear a great deal about sacrifice of personal interests, goals, and lifestyle for the good of the tribe (family), about suffering that seems unjust to the person and often even voluntary banishment. As a California-based astrologer I have met many a client with a Fourth House Saturn who has given up on the lack of appreciation received in his natal place, stopped speaking to his family, and fled to sunny California (the "Isles of the Blessed?"), vowing never to return to his ungrateful homeland.

The scapegoat feels unloved, alienated, neglected, and dumped on in his childhood, much like the Fourth House Saturn personality in whose chart the heavier elements (Earth and Water) dominate. We are, after all, supposed to receive our *nurturing* in our childhood. The Fourth House is the Moon's domain, but with a Fourth House Saturn the child usually ends up with the responsibility to do the nurturing, to provide in some way for the family, to get a job outside the home while quite young and contribute to the finances, if a man, or to do a good deal of the housework or be emotionally supportive toward a disfunctional parent if a woman.

The most common reaction I have had over the years from Fourth House Saturn clients was, "Poor Mother. She had such a hard life. I tried so hard to take care of her." Or, "Poor Dad, he wasn't able to cope. His personal integrity was impeccable, but he fled from controversy at every opportunity. We kept moving—I didn't have a solid home life or any friends. I felt rootless."

An amazing number of my Fourth House Saturn clients have delved into psychology texts in an attempt to understand the Scapegoat experience and have done so with great intensity. They usually bring in the chart of one or both parents and their own theories. Women who were the family's only child will tell me the theory, "An only daughter is the same as a son; you carry a great burden of parental ambition. You might as well write 'junior' after your name." Another client said, "Here's this book on being born as the middle child in the family. Middle children are neglected and unappreciated. The older sibling is smarter, the younger is cuter. What do you think of that?" Yet another client, the youngest child in his family, told me, "More statistics on people like me should be collected. Youngest children have so many pressures. My older brothers put me through college and I have to be a medical doctor whether I want to or not. I have to be 'my son the doctor, my brother the M.D.'"

One Capricorn rising, Fourth House Saturn woman told me that her mother had post partum depression after the birth of her younger sister and was unable to do any housework. "My father didn't help us at all. He could have hired a cleaning woman. He had plenty of money. But I did all the housework and was everyone's emotional support person. All I ever received as feedback was that the starch in the shirt wasn't up to par." She stayed in her natal place many years, but now that her siblings are adults she doesn't have any family ties. "I wouldn't want to get married. It's too much work. I have already raised a family." In this case, the scapegoat archetype is really apparent—the personal sacrifice, the atonement to her siblings for her parents' neglect of them, and voluntary banishment to the wilderness, the wilds of desert solitude. (She literally moved to the desert.)

A Saturn in the Fourth House man also relocated to California and not on speaking terms with his family, says, "I put my younger relatives through school. They just seem to drift through life irresponsibly. If I let them know my address they'd still find me to ask me for money or try to move in with me." He, too, sought to understand the Scapegoat lifetime, the difficulties in giving and receiving affection that seemed to result from his childhood.

One client summed up the experience well. "With my Angular Saturn I felt loved for doing things for people or for achieving professionally; I never felt loved just for being me. Nobody offers to listen to me, to do things for me." This is a family pattern they may find hard to reverse in adult relationships once it's become internalized. I've found that the Saturn Return year is a key time to get in touch with this behavior pattern. How the adult Scapegoat himself sends out signals! "Give *me* the responsibility! I'll do a good job. I can handle it." One great Master, Paramahansa Yogananda, said, "We are all rooted in reciprocity." Other people need a chance to reciprocate; to do things for us. If we, however, are uncomfortable with compliments and interrupt them, or cut them off, they'll give up and quit trying to praise us, nurture us, or help us with the housework. They'll think, "Gee, I'm in her way; she'd rather do it herself. I don't do it to her satisfaction anyhow." The Saturn in the Fourth person, through his or her own efficiency and capability or unwillingness to watch someone do the job badly, may metamorphose into a tyrant in the home of his or her relatives in old age, into the very tyrant he tried so hard to serve in childhood.

Perhaps the hero who seizes the throne in youth and ends up as a tyrant king in old age is a theme we all need to watch in whatever House our Saturn lies. Hindu astrology warns people with Saturn in the Fourth not to expect too much of their own children lest they end up lonely in their old age. In *Autobiography of a Yogi*, Sri Yukteswar said that he never expected anything of his disciples, thus he was never disappointed in them. I think that is also true of parenting; if nothing is expected of a child, then it cannot disappoint the parent. That, of course, is easy to say but hard to practice. Dr. Bruno Bettelheim, a child psychologist, suggests that parents resist the impulse to create the child they would like to have, but relate instead to his abilities and help him become the child he wishes to be. (*A Good Enough Parent*, 1987). Astrologically, working with the child's natal chart facilitates this process.

In the Orient, people still consider it an honor to be the child who has the opportunity to take care of his parents in their old age, and in India, people with a Fourth House Saturn or Capricorn rising will be given this information by the astrologer: "I am delighted to tell you that you will have the privilege of having your parents in your home until their last breath, though I am sure you have other relatives who would dispute with you for the honor!"

Most of my North American clients would not feel quite the same way about it. They feel that they have a need to be independent, to pursue their own path, or their own process in their own distinct household, rather than a joint family compound. They tend to feel that their success in the outer, material world is sufficient repayment to their parents for the advantages they received in childhood. According to Jung, a certain independence of the Collective furthers our development toward consciousness. Yet one of his students, Marie von Franz, remarked in both *The Way of the Dream*, a film interview, and her book *The Grail Legend*, that we suffer in our times from rootlessness. Connection with family, with the land (Capricorn is also property), as well as contact with the Self, further our growth in consciousness. The positive meaning of Capricorn rising, or natal Saturn on the hereditary axis (Houses Four and Ten), or a Capricorn Sun, is the groundedness of Cardinal Earth, the solid foundations in family relationships—the lasting memories.

I try to get as much information as I can on the parental charts of a client going through the Saturn Return, and sometimes even the second Saturn Return, in Houses Four and Ten. This gives me an idea not only of how the client perceived childhood, but what the parent was really like, what the client's roots were really like. The client is often flooded with memories during the second and third Returns and finds it important to sort out the karmic pattern. If therapists can benefit from seeing not only the patient, but from interviewing the patient's parent, when he or she is available, then surely astrologers can benefit from asking about the birthday, at least, of the client's parent with whom he believes he has the karma and the more painful memories to release.

Clients with the Saturn/Capricorn archetype strong in the personality tend to use the vocabulary of debt repayment when speaking about their childhood and early life this incarnation: "I must have worked off my karma from the last 500 years before age 28," is a popular attitude. "I read a book about reincarnation which helped me to accept a lot of things," said one client. "It said that if I concentrate really hard I can begin to attract positive people and circumstances into my life." True. Concentration is an important key, and Saturn excels at that. But Jupiter's faith is also important—faith in oneself and in the Divine. If the subconscious keeps saying, "the depressing past is going to repeat itself, so what good is all this positive thinking/ affirming going to do someone who is doomed (in whatever house his Saturn is in)?" then the past does tend to repeat itself, and the same type of negative persons and circumstances tend to reappear.

It also seems important to remember to relax and give God some scope for action or for surprises in life as well. If through such thorough planning as Saturn does (building for eternity), one feels like Atlas with the weight of the world on one's shoulders, there isn't much room for God and Guru to step in! Someone with a Mercury/Jupiter square (and very little Earth) might say, "The responsibility isn't mine. If I fail it's someone else's fault. God should do it all for me. When will my luck change?" But the pessimistic person with a Mercury/Saturn square takes on too much responsibility, blames him/herself too much and often hasn't left God enough room to maneuver. He has some advantages over the Mercury/Jupiter square person though— patience, a good memory, an awareness of how to get from Step A to Step B to Step C, and being practical; being grounded in reality helps a good deal in day to day life.

Jung said that when there is bitterness in a person there is no wisdom. He hasn't really learned anything from the past, from his suffering and his mistakes. The alchemists had a watery process called *solutio*, which dissolved forms, obstacles, limits, frustrations. In *Anatomy of the Psyche* Edward Edinger discusses dreams in which people have undergone the alchemical *solutio*, been in a flood, or swimming, or in a bath, and dissolved their obstacles from the past. *Solutio* was followed by an opposing process, earthy in nature, called *coagulatio*, or drying out from the solution.

Salt is a wisdom symbol in the Pythagorean and the alchemical traditions. The alchemists would dry out salt water and taste the salt residue. If it came out pure white and was not bitter, the alchemist had true wisdom, but if it was bitter, the alchemist would throw it out and start over. Christ once said to His disciples, "you are the salt of the Earth, but if the salt loses its strength, then what will Earth be salted with?" They had the wisdom, and in spite of persecution, obstacles, all sorts of suffering, had to keep it from losing its strength and/or becoming bitter. I think that Capricorn is the salt of the Earth, but often struggles hard to release a residue of bitterness. S/he endures periodic depression or melancholia (especially during Winter Solstice) and if in the end his salt is pure rather than bitter his/her lifetime has really been victorious. All of us have Saturn in some House of our charts and Capricorn on some cusp, so the issue is universally important, too. We could all be wise or expert through proper use of our Saturn: if it only could be developed as the Wise Old Man or Woman part of us, rather than solidify as the rigid, hard, bitter Senex.

Concentration, meditation, and discussing feelings (Cancer polarity) with an analyst can help where the issues of Saturn's House are concerned. It's interesting to read in *Saturnalia* about the day during the Solstice festival on which the Goddess Angerona was worshipped. In honor of those who suffered silently and endured their pain, her mouth was sealed. She banished anxiety and mental distress, and those who concealed their suffering felt great joy on her festival day when, in the temple of Voluptes, her statue was unbound at the end of the Saturnalia week.

In *The Scapegoat Complex*, Sylvia Perera makes several important psychological points. As a child the Scapegoat lives under the shadow of his ancestors; it is difficult for his ego to separate out from what he perceives as the needs and expectations of the adults in his family. The child tries to be perfect, to compensate for whatever the adults around him/her seem to him/her to lack. S/he lacks the feeling of belonging, of having roots in the family. Through his/her perfectionist struggle, the child tries to please one of his parents, perhaps hoping for the impossible, because that parent may also be a Scapegoat, an emotionally undernourished person, unable to express approval or affection. The grown-up Scapegoat later goes off into the wilderness carrying in his unconscious the burden of the collective's guilt and suffering—trying to redeem it with his/her efforts in the outer world but feeling inwardly s/he hasn't measured up.

Perera remarks that the theme of the Scapegoat who carries on his or her back the collective evils of the human race is central to Western civilization. We have the examples of Christ and the Babylonian Goddess Inanna. (For Inanna, see Perera's *Descent of the Goddess*.) Christ wandered in the wilderness and was sacrificed on the cross as an atonement to Yahweh for the sins of his people, and the Babylonian Goddess was impaled on a stake for hers. The Scapegoat is not simply a Western archetype, however. We know from the *Bhagavad Gita* that Hindus believe Lord Vishnu incarnates on Earth to rescue humanity from the evil of ignorance whenever there is a Dark Age. Then there is the story of Buddha's sacrifice of his earthly kingdom to seek out the wilderness, practice asceticism, and find for humanity a way out of the cycle of desire, suffering, old age, death, rebirth. Perhaps the most impressive descent of the Savior/Scapegoat comes from Mahayan Buddhism, though. The Bodhisattva has taken a vow not to seek his own final liberation until the last blade of grass on Earth has been redeemed. It would seem that the Scapegoat archetype is universal (for East and West at least) in scope.

Perera sees perfectionism as a call to Spirit. We are called to find our inner roots within our own souls. Yet in youth so many Scapegoat children mistake the inner call for a need to fulfill the aspirations of a parent in the outer world. The Scapegoat pattern of undernourishment at the feeling level (at the roots or Nadir of the personality) can be passed on from parent to child through several generations. I have found the Capricorn archetype—especially the Ascendant and Saturn on the heredity axis—to work in this manner. It is very important to develop self-esteem and to nourish one's Inner Child; otherwise, striving constantly for outer success seems to result in feelings of emptiness regardless of the trappings one attracts in the Tenth House— fame, money, power.

Perera perceives the wilderness as a safe place into which the Scapegoat flees to release his negative emotions such as guilt, fear of rejection ("Won't others treat me the way my family does?"), a sense of failure at not measuring up, or even anger at the poor thing for whom the Scapegoat has been compensating—the parent who cannot cope. She says that the safe place is often the therapist's office, as the Scapegoat receives the empathy and emotional support to deal with these feelings. I think it could also be the home of a good friend or an astrologer's office. (I have had several clients with Capricorn Sun, Ascendant or Angular Saturn tell me that they felt safe in my office.) Without this safe place, a modern Bodhi tree under which he can sit, without the time spent in the wilderness, the perfectionist may indefinitely postpone getting in touch with his emotions (Cancer polarity). Otherwise he can continue performing his duties in the outer world, keeping his personality together on the surface of reality, practicing denial that anything's wrong until the fall from the mountaintop occurs.

By hindsight, years after this fall in the Tenth House (or outer world) Capricorn will sometimes admit it was the "best thing that ever happened to me." At the time of the fall, however, when the astrologer or counselor sees the client, s/he feels as if s/he's been plunged from the Zenith into the unknown, and that it's a very long drop till s/he hits bottom. At the Nadir (Cancer), s/he has time out to get in touch with his/her feelings, emotions, intuition, instincts (the Feminine); and to experience the empathy, support and nurturing s/he needs. Temporary confinement is sometimes necessary. Supportive people in hospitals, mental health clinics, or substance abuse programs are sometimes part of the nurturing. An institutional mother can represent the Great Mother archetype in our society, and support groups can seemingly replace supportive families. In the Solstice darkness before the dawn, the process of falling can seem like a winter nightmare. Capricorn, accustomed to thinking in terms of the collective's "image" of him/her (his or her persona), learns after the fall who s/he is without it and wonders how society will regard him/her without his/her title, or his/her aura of authority. In the safe place and during the time out in the wilderness, s/he can find his inner direction (Cancer), or foundation (Nadir) rooted in the psyche. Often s/he will lose his/her fear of vulnerability and eventually be able to express his/her true feelings to others.

I have by way of example an almost archetypal story of a Capricorn Sun sign client undergoing the Aquarian progression which made him more susceptible to the sudden shocks of Uranus transits. He had invested his paternal inheritance in a small business. For fifteen years (two Saturn cycles of seven years) it had prospered, but suddenly bankruptcy loomed on the horizon. No more loans were forthcoming; there was no purchaser in sight. No matter how hard he worked, or how many hours he agonized, there seemed no way out of the feeling of failure—of losing his birthright.

In addition, he seemed to think of himself as a Dharma Raja standing near the wheel of responsibility and turning it to assure the prosperity of his little kingdom, protecting his subjects. These are his words, or a close paraphrase of them:

> I felt terrible the day I had to tell my employees the business was in bankruptcy. They would have to look elsewhere for work. I couldn't meet the payroll beyond the first of the month. Here, these people had been coming to me for salary advances when they needed them; they were used to Christmas bonuses; and they were really dependent upon me. It was awful for me.
>
> But, you know it turned out well. They cheered me up and a couple of them even told me that they'd wanted to look for jobs elsewhere but didn't have the heart to do it. They knew how I valued loyalty, and felt

they owed me, so they couldn't quit when obviously orders were dropping off and I was in some sort of slump. I had expected them to be stricken, but they just sort of shrugged, and some of them were. . . not glad, but relieved, even though I couldn't guarantee there would be a new purchaser soon, or that if there were, that s/he'd keep them on. It turned out okay for me. I was allowed to keep $100,000, which I used to go into business with an old friend. Meanwhile, I had six months to do nothing, so I took a few seminars on the friend's product, read some of my wife's Jungian books that were around the house, went to a retreat at a Benedictine monastery. The thing that made this so much easier was my family's reaction. My wife and kids clearly believed in me, more than I did in myself. They were very different from the family I had as a kid, where nobody seemed to believe in me. I'd forgotten how important the intangibles are in life, like religion, and family, and learning from making mistakes.

When I had time to reflect, I could see how silly I'd been—too busy to enjoy life and appreciate the intangibles. I also realized that I didn't lose anything really important. At first I felt I had let my father down, but I'd worked hard 15 years; taken care of dependent siblings, doubled the money he'd left me. The capital in the new venture is all mine. Now there's no connection with Dad. I feel free.

Many Capricorns have expressed this feeling of freedom during the Aquarian progression. It's almost as if Uranus, ruler of the progressed Sun, liberates them from the inhibiting feelings of undue caution and insecurity which delayed their timing earlier in life; from a nagging need to prove themselves; from mundane priorities which took up much of their time; from petty narrowness. Uranus seems to render them more receptive to new opportunities, both inner and outer.

The Capricorn Scapegoat has, it would seem, a definite advantage over the purely mundane Mountain Goat who has ruthlessly climbed over his competitors in pursuit of his ambitions of personal glory. From childhood, the Scapegoat has developed the habit of serving others. His/her wound, as Jung would term it—the lack of nurturing in his/her early life that left a "hole" in him—will make him/her less judgemental of others than the Mountain Goat, who can be quite snobbish toward the unsuccessful people of this world. Jung has a good point. The wounded healer is a better, more compassionate counselor than the healer who has never suffered in his own life.

When the Scapegoat emerges from the wilderness with his self-esteem intact, in touch with his instincts, emotions, and intuition, he will be better prepared than the outwardly successful Mountain Goat for the Aquarian phase of the journey, which Isabel Hickey called, "service to that Great Orphan, Humanity." The Scapegoat, who always tried to make the world a better place for his/her own family, can move beyond it in a wider circle of influence, according to the nature of his/her talents, not just his/her persona, but the fullness of his/her personality—*who* s/he is—according to the contents of his own Aquarian Grail Cup (see Chapter 11).

My experience with Capricorn/Capricorn rising clients moving through the Aquarian progression has been that they tend to build upon past experiences, skills and credentials, reflecting Saturn's meaning of continuity and duration over time, rather than choosing a totally different field, though this of course depends upon what other archetypes appear in the individual chart. Capricorns with social work credentials tend to become New Age counselors; those with teaching experience to become New Age teachers (many in astrology); those with a research background tend to shift from an oil company to the ecological movement, but to continue with research; those who were managers in corporate work tend to enter non-profit corporations, or to become leaders in New Age communities; those who were involved in mental or physical healing work continue (but in wholistic rather than traditional medicine) learning massage, vegetarian nutrition, or healing through visualization.

Though these changes build upon past interests, they tend to reflect the nature of the Eleventh House, rather than the Tenth. In the natal Capricorn phase the client thought in terms of proving himself competent and drawing fame, fortune, power. In the progressed Aquarian cycle he moves toward such Eleventh House issues as humanitarian or voluntary service, spiritual communities, working with friends, fundraising for schools, civic organizations, cultural facilities, scout troops. Mundane concerns like status and financial security are no longer his primary considerations, as the emphasis shifts to the intangible rewards. Personal hopes, dreams, and wishes are more likely to find fulfillment as Capricorn stops worrying so much about what other people think and relaxes.

My favorite example of happiness that comes from letting go of others' standards and living one's own is that of the Capricorn Sun sign widower who had moved deeply enough into Aquarius for the progressed Sun to aspect natal planets in Air. With this newfound ability to socialize with people of diverse socio-economic and educational backgrounds, and the newfound Aquarian independence, he chose to re-marry. On his second Saturn Return (age 56) he told his grown-up children, grandchildren, and 80 year-old father about his choice. They were horrified that he would marry beneath them, someone uneducated, totally unsuitable, someone who wouldn't fit in at the country club. He had known her for three years and felt, "It's my choice. I'm the one who's marrying her. But I guess I used to be pretty insecure. Up till now, it would have been very hard for me to marry someone my family strongly disapproved of—the boss, my friends and all—their opinion really mattered. Now I figure—who cares what they think!"

Capricorns who are not in the upper educational, or socio-economic group often have a form of reverse snobbery that they, too, seem to outgrow in Aquarius. They tend to make remarks like, "I didn't used to like my wife's friends—those eggheads who read these books on metaphysics and Jung. But now I can see that they're okay. I'm feeling more tolerant, maybe?" They, too, tend to be able to relate to those outside their own background in Aquarius.

Though the tolerance that develops in Aquarius is positive, it is still a Saturn ruled sign, and a Fixed sign at that. Growth seems as external in Aquarius as it was in Capricorn, though more unselfishly motivated. In the progression through Pisces, Mutable Water, the growth direction is inward. Capricorn's natal introspective or reflective focus is enhanced. The personality is often withdrawn from the public eye (Houses 10 and 11) into the Self (House 12, solitude). Many clients suddenly write poetry, begin to enjoy music, or to ask the astrologer where to go to study meditation and visualization techniques. They seem to be moving dramatically from the circumference of the Wheel of Dharma to its hub, its quiet center. Because it is often the last stage of the lifetime journey for Capricorn/Capricorn rising people, it is connected with preparation for the afterlife, the transition from time to eternity, from Kali's Creation Dance to Shiva's inert, blissful state of meditation on Mount Kailash.

During the Pisces progression many Capricorn clients begin for the first time to take their intuition as seriously as they formerly took their logic. This, of course, will be especially true if the client has Twelfth House planets or a strong natal Neptune—reliable intuition. Saturn is a sensate planet, deriving its data from the world of experience, of phenomena. Pisces tends not to take that world very seriously, at all. So the Pisces watery progression dissolves some of the narrowness of Saturn's approach to decision-making.

In her book *Alchemy*, Marie Louise von Franz views Saturn as

Sol Niger, the alchemical shadow of the real Sun, a black Sun of literal-mindedness and brittle, concrete thinking, inclining to justice without mercy. One has a sort of mental picture, reading *Alchemy*, of Saturn/Capricorn opposite Kwan Yin (Mercy Goddess)/Cancer. In the waters of the Pisces progression many Capricorns begin to believe, to trust in the non-literal world of Neptune, to visualize, to meditate, to let go of the sensate function enough to see through time into eternity. As a result, they are able to let go of the strict justice code and give others the benefit of the doubt, through Piscean compassion— to integrate Kwan Yin and Saturn, seeing that the rule can be modified in individual cases.

Von Franz also pointed out that sensate types take clock time very seriously, worry about punctuality and the passing of time, demonstrated, she observes, by the fact that they keep looking at their watches all day long. Intuitives, on the other hand, have very little awareness of clock time passing. This seems true to me, for many of my clients with Neptune strong, or several Pisces planets, it's as if they live in eternity. Time passes while they work on their projects and they don't care. Often they don't even wear watches. Of course, many Capricorn/Capricorn rising clients are retired from business life by the time they progress into Pisces and have no real need to be glued to their watches. Still, it is interesting to observe the differences in their attitude toward time as they become involved in more creative pastimes.

As Pisces is the last sign of the zodiac, the Night Sea Journey (see Chapter 12), it is perhaps appropriate that so many clients passing through it have read books on the afterlife—reincarnation, dreams of death and dying, visions of eternity by those who died on the operating table and returned to life. The favorites are still the *Tibetan* and the *Egyptian Book of the Dead*, however, for Capricorns among my clientele who are undergoing this progression.

The crocodile, an Egyptian time and eternity symbol and a Hindu symbol as well, is associated with Capricorn. Alice Bailey sees it as a higher level of evolution for Capricorn than the Mountain Goat, though to me this is unclear. Capricorns seem to move back and forth integrating many levels of goat and crocodile in the course of one lifetime. A Mountain Goat can be greedy, ruthless, selfish in his ascent of the mundane mountain, but then can become a Father who is a devouring crocodile keeping his sons in thrall with long-term promises of financial advantage or power. Thus the crocodile is not always a higher phase. The crocodile is a complex symbol, and fits into the Piscean progression because of its connection to spiritual transformation and the last stage of the journey. This is also its dream meaning. It still occurs in clients' dreams as a guardian of the Underworld, just as it did in the *Tibetan Book of the Dead*. In both Egyptian and Hindu mythology there are two crocodiles, one as yet untransformed (mundane) and one which is united with the Divine.

In India, Capricorn was symbolized by the Makara and the Kumara. Makara literally is the number 5—the five senses. The Makara crocodile is similar to Pan—greedy, caught at the level of sensual desire. He is also hungry for power, like the Mountain Goat on the way to the top. Through transformation, initiation, receptivity to the Divine, he becomes Kumara, the White Dragon Crocodile. Like the lunar goddesses, the wise white Crocodile can take on any shape. He has lost his thick, hard skin—his body. The Dragon is a wisdom symbol in India and the Far East. Through his transformation, the Wise White Dragon, Kumara, conquered Maya and with it, rebirth. Leaving behind the world of the senses, he entered into the eternal Bliss of Oneness with Shiva, sitting quietly in meditation posture. In the West, the lore of Capricorn contained a pure white Unicorn, a similar symbol to the White Dragon. The Unicorn was a type of transformed Pan whose double horns, or desire nature, had become a single horn through focused meditation. The unicorn had hidden powers connected with his purity of consciousness and his magical horn.

The Egyptian Book of the Dead, like the Hindu transformation story for Capricorn, has two crocodiles. They stand at the gates to the underworld, the afterlife. The glyphs for the redeemed and the untransformed crocodile are exactly the same.

Capricorn symbols are connected to the Feminine in every culture I have studied; it seems almost a psychological ultimatum. Integrate Cancer! In the late Roman Empire, the cult of the Magna Mater, Cybele, was introduced at the insistence of the masses. When imperial troops were hard pressed during the Punic Wars, her black, magical meteor stone was brought by sea to Rome in 209 B.C. The ship was met by Roman officials and women devotees. Cybele's followers kept up their insistence that she be granted a temple within the city until 191 B.C. when it was finally completed. Devotees came to Cybele's Palatine Hill Temple on pilgrimage from all over the empire. Thus was the balance established between Saturn and the Moon.

The Pan Goat becomes a Unicorn who is always pictured standing with a Virgin or as having his head in her lap. The crocodile lives in the Waters (Feminine), as well as on dry land (Capricorn Earth). Esoterically, he can change shape like a lunar goddess. He is also connected with higher knowledge, or initiation, with the Wisdom Goddess.

From Greece to Egypt, China and India, true Wisdom is symbolized by the Goddess, the lunar shape changer. The Grail Messenger Sophia, who takes the Celtic hero through the Gates to the castle, is one side of Wisdom, as she is young and beautiful. She, too, changes shape. Yet she is also the ugly old hag (the land in its parched, infertile state during the king's illness). She is wisdom in adversity. The hero must embrace the hag, the dark side of the Moon, the part of wisdom that tells us things about ourselves we would rather not hear. We too must accept all sides and powers of the Feminine, all phases of the Moon, Kali's truth and Kwan Yin's mercy and compassion. This is the path to Sapientia, to the goddess who was guide and goal of the alchemical transformation. Von Franz sees Sapientia as the feminine soul trapped in matter, as the indwelling spirit in nature, in each of our bodies, which must be sought and in alchemical terms freed. In alchemy Saturn was seen as an androgynous planet like Mercury. Though in our time we have difficulty understanding Saturn/Capricorn as feminine, it does make sense if we consider Earth as the alchemists apparently did, as the sign of Sapientia's imprisonment within the material world, where she waited to be found and liberated. The next stage of the journey for the Capricorn personality, Aquarius, focuses upon this very issue of freedom.

Clearly we need to honor both Saturn and the Moon within our charts and our lives and not only when we play a parenting role to our children. The balance of discipline and compassion is quite important, for without the creative waters of the feminine, our lunar side, Saturn's work can seem dry and stale. But without our Saturnine deadlines, routines, structures, sense of practical reality, sense of timing, our creative side often goes unfulfilled. Saturn provides the channel for the flood of Cancerian imagination. A driven person may treat himself like a Senex tyrant but a lunar type who lives entirely in her moods and feelings may treat herself like a self-indulgent mother.

Neither is the path of wisdom.

Alice Bailey perceives Capricorn esoterically as the sign of the initiate. In *Labours of Hercules* she explains that by initiation she is not referring to a ritual involving a spiritual teacher but to the everyday sacrifices that we encounter through Saturn's testing (Capricorn labour). In the world of Maya, living the dance of Shiva and Kali, of the isolated Saturn hermit and the dark phase of the Moon, we face our unconscious fears, our inner limitations, delays, and our outer conflicts with others. Freedom results (symbolized by Shiva's son Ganesha, the remover of obstacles). As the inner and outer obstacles drop away freedom is gained from within and with freedom, power. The Aquarian archetype manifests a power that is based upon soul freedom. Dane Rudhyar says that it may well be the most powerful sign in the zodiac. (See his *Astrological Signs*.)

Bailey also remarks in *Labours* that a true initiate, one who has passed through darkness and found the light within, will never tell others he's an initiate. This sense of silence about his progress is characteristic of the esoteric Capricorn, whose life consists of service and suffering. In our own journey through the House that Saturn is in or the House that Saturn rules, we may go through several phases in the level of our aspiration, mundane and spiritual. If we do reach the top of the spiritual mountain, where Body satisfies its yearning for Spirit, where Sapientia is freed, we will then perhaps understand the mysterious esoteric glyph for the sign the Goat Fish (Greek, goat dolphin). We would be beyond the dance of Kali, the world of form and Maya; we would have spun off the Wheel of Dharma, of time. We would no longer need to return to Earth, turn the wheel like karma yogis lifetime after lifetime, taking ourselves and our work so seriously. Esoteric writers have a tradition that the glyph for the sign Capricorn (♑) is veiled, and that we cannot understand it until we have become initiates. Perhaps like the Goat Fish, it represents receptivity, total openness to the divine. Surely it combines the qualities of the Pisces fish with the industrious dedication of the Mountain Goat, a spiritual aspiration that involves total Pisces faith in the divine.

Questionnaire

How does the Capricorn archetype express itself? Though this relates particularly to those with Sun in Capricorn or Capricorn rising, anyone could apply this series of questions to the house where his Saturn is located or the house which has Capricorn (or Capricorn intercepted) on the cusp. The answers will indicate how in touch the reader is with his Saturn (discipline, sense of limitations, ambitions, timing).

1. When told of an opening for a management position with a good deal of responsibility, though not totally knowledgeable about the job, I
   a. send my updated resume after a thorough consideration of the opportunity.
   b. usually let it pass.
   c. ignore it totally. I don't want a lot of responsibility.

2. When I go home after a confrontation at work I
   a. analyze the situation for a few minutes, maybe tell my spouse about it to see what s/he thinks, but I don't brood for long.
   b. spend the whole evening rehashing the scene in my mind. I think of what I should have said to defend my position.
   c. put it right out of my mind, enjoy a good dinner, watch TV, have a few drinks, or go out for recreation.

3. I feel more secure socially with
   a. people from my own office or my own background.
   b. conservative people—types who won't embarrass me.
   c. original, creative, fun people.

4. If I were to make a list of the people I respect and admire most, I would include a majority of
   a. reasonable, dependable people with common sense.
   b. old friends, people I am comfortable with.
   c. imaginative, exciting people though I don't consider myself one.

5. I think I am over-cautious
   a. 50% of the time.
   b. 80% of the time.
   c. 25% of the time or less.

6. My greatest fear is
   a. loss of status, power, the respect of others.
   b. everything.
   c. being thought of as a boring person.

7. On my day off I
   a. follow plans made ahead of time so I can get the most satis-
      faction out of it.
   b. clean the garage or do the lawn, etc.
   c. let things happen spontaneously.

8. I think the weakest part of my body is:
   a. I am generally strong of body.
   b. the bones, especially the knees and the lower back (coccyx).
   c. I get infections easily.

9. Most important to me is
   a. organization.
   b. security.
   c. fun.

10. My usual pattern is to
    a. rise to the top of the organization.
    b. stay in a secure position.
    c. avoid responsibility.

Those who have scored 5 or more (a) answers are highly in touch with Saturn as discipline and ambition—if 8 or more, closer to an inflated Saturn at the mundane level. You need to have more fun. Those who scored mainly (b) answers are more in touch with Saturn as the principle of limitation or inhibition. You need to work more with the Fire (confidence element) in your chart, or your Mars and Jupiter (rulers of Fire signs and of confident signs). Those who have scored mainly (c) answers are in touch with Pan rather than the Mountain Goat and probably need to work more with Saturn as discipline and practical aspiration. The (a) and (b) people may need to integrate Pan more for balanced living—give the body some rest and exercise.

Where is the balance point between Capricorn and Cancer? How does Capricorn integrate his inner and outer worlds? Though this relates particularly to Sun in Capricorn or Capricorn rising, all of us have Saturn and the Moon somewhere in our horoscopes. Many of us have planets in the Tenth or Fourth houses. For all of us the polarity from Capricorn to Cancer involves balancing discipline with nurturing, satisfying others with personal satisfaction, career responsibility with personal life.

1. When I am in an argument with a parent or older relative over something I really want to do
   a. I find that I defer to the person if their disapproval is really strong.
   b. I consider what the person says carefully but in the end make my own decision.
   c. I do what seems best to me without really considering the person's objections.

2. In relationships with close family and friends
   a. I think that love is most important.
   b. I think that love and respect go hand in hand.
   c. I think that respect is most important.

3. In early childhood (before age 7) I considered an adult in my family to be
   a. a "poor thing" who couldn't cope with reality and needed my help.
   b. a loving disciplinarian.
   c. a person who had all the answers and must be obeyed.

4. As a parent I would
   a. put love ahead of discipline.
   b. temper discipline with love.
   c. put discipline uppermost.

5. If I were an employer I'd value uppermost in my employees
   a. loyalty, sensitivity, compassion.
   b. loyalty, dependability, reasonability.
   c. loyalty, organization, conformity to the company image.

Those who have scored three or more (b) answers are doing a good job with personality integration on the Capricorn/Cancer polarity. Those who scored three or more (c) answers may need to work more consciously with developing the natal Moon in their horoscopes. Those who have three or more (a) answers may be out of balance in the other direction. They may have a weak or underdeveloped Saturn. Those who answered (a) to questions (1) and (3) may tend towards the Scapegoat archetype.

What does it mean to be an esoteric Capricorn. How does Capricorn integrate Venus (love) and Saturn (duty) into the personality? Every Capricorn will have both Saturn and Venus somewhere in the horoscope. Well integrated Venus adds warmth and kindness to mundane Saturn and helps in the development of esoteric Saturn. What is the level of aspiration (Saturn) in the horoscope? The answers to the following questions will indicate the extent to which Venus softens and expands the personality.

1. I make my decisions based on
   a. the facts weighted by concern for everyone involved.
   b. concrete adherence to the letter of the law.
   c. what is most expedient for me.

2. In the house of natal Saturn or the house with Capricorn on the cusp I find mostly that
   a. I consciously make use of Saturn's concentration, patience and endurance.
   b. I find that others consider me an expert or an authority figure.
   c. I'm aware of all the delays, frustration, limits and obstacles.

3. I am a wheel turner
   a. in my inner world through meditation.
   b. in both my inner and outer worlds.
   c. in the outer world through my career.

4. I perceive Saturn transits in my life as
   a. an opportunity for learning and spiritual advancement.
   b. something I will understand later by hindsight.
   c. something to be endured until Jupiter comes along.

5. My initial response when told that I must make drastic changes in Saturn's house, or the house Saturn rules is:
   a. I try to welcome change as a manifestation of Cosmic Order.
   b. I feel initial resistance but eventually adapt to the change.
   c. I resist change and find adapting extremely difficult.

Those who have scored three or more (a) answers are in touch with the esoteric ruler. Those who have scored three or more (b) answers need to work more consciously at understanding Saturn as a planet of opportunity. Those who have three or more (c) answers need work in identifying with esoteric Saturn.

References

S. Angus, *The Mystery Religions*, Dover Publications, New York, 1928

Alice Bailey, *Esoteric Astrology*, Lucis Publishing Co., New York, 1976

Alice Bailey, *Labours of Hercules*, Lucis Publishing Co., New York, 1977

Bruno Bettelheim, *A Good Enough Parent: A Book on Child Rearing*, Alfred A. Knopf, New York, 1987

John Blofield, *Bodhisattva of Compassion: The Mystical Tradition of Kuan Yin*, Boston, 1978

Edward F. Edinger, *Anatomy of the Psyche*, Open Court, La Salle, 1985

Edward F. Edinger, *The Christian Archetype: A Jungian Commentary on the Life of Christ*, Inner City Books, Toronto, 1987

Edward F. Edinger, *Ego and Archetype*, G.P. Putnam's Sons, New York, 1972

W.Y. Evans-Wentz, *The Tibetan Book of the Dead*, Oxford University Press, London, 1960

Peter A. Fraile S.J., *God Within Us: Movements, Powers and Joys*, Loyola University Press, Chicago, 1986

Liz Greene, *Astrology of Fate, "Capricorn,"* Samuel Weiser Inc., York Beach, 1984

Liz Greene, *Saturn: A New Look at an Old Devil*, Samuel Weiser Inc., York Beach, 1978

Hesiod, *The Homeric Hymns and Homerica*, Harvard Press, Cambridge, 1954

Isabel Hickey, *Astrology, A Cosmic Science*, Altieri Press, Bridgeport, 1970

James Hillman, "An Essay on Pan," in William Roscher, *Pan and the Nightmare*, Spring Publications Inc., Irving, 1979

Jolande Jacobi, *The Way of Individuation*, Harcourt, Brace and World, Inc., New York, 1965

Carl G. Jung, *Psychology and Alchemy*, Princeton University Press, Princeton, 1968

Emma Jung, *Animus and Anima*, Spring Publications Inc., Dallas, 1985

Emma Jung and Marie Louise von Franz, *The Grail Legend*, Sigo Press, Boston, 1980

A. A. Macrobius, *Commentary on the Dream of Scipio*, Columbia University Press, New York, 1966

A. A. Macrobius, *The Saturnalia*, Columbia University Press, New York, 1969

Patricia Merivale, *Pan the Goat-God, His Myth in Modern Times*, Harvard University Press, Cambridge, 1969

Sylvia Perera, *Descent to the Goddess*, Inner City Books, Toronto, 1981

Sylvia Perera, *The Scapegoat Complex: Toward a Mythology of Shadow and Guilt*, Inner City Books, Toronto, 1986

Dane Rudhyar, *Astrological Signs; The Pulse of Life*, Shambhala, Boulder, 1978

James Totum, *Apuleus and the Golden Ass*, Cornell University Press, Ithica, 1979

Noel Tyl, *The Expanded Present*, Llewellyn Publications, St. Paul, 1976

Noel Tyl, *Integrated Transits*, Llewellyn Publications, St. Paul, 1976

Marie Louise von Franz, *Alchemy*, Inner City Books, Toronto, 1980

Marie Louise von Franz, *Number and Time*, Northwestern Press, Evanston, 1974

Marie Louise von Franz, *Time, Rhythm and Repose*, Thames and Hudson, London, 1976

Marie Louise von Franz, "Way of the Dream," a film festival, Windrose Films Ltd., Toronto, n.d.

Maarten J. Vermaseren, *Cybele and Attis—The Myth and the Cult*, Thames and Hudson Ltd., London, 1977

E.A. Wallis Budge, *The Egyptian Book of the Dead*, Dover Publications, Inc., New York, 1967

Frank Waters, *Mexico Mystique: Coming of the 6th World of Consciousness*, Swallow Press, Chicago, 1975

Marion Woodman, *The Pregnant Virgin—A Process of Psychological Transformation*, Inner City Books, Toronto, 1985

Paramahansa Yogananda, *Autobiography of a Yogi*, Philosophical Library, New York, 1946

Swami Sri Yukteswar, Self-Realization Fellowship Press, Los Angeles, 1974

Heinrich Zimmer, *Myths and Symbols in Indian Art and Civilization*, Princeton University Press, Princeton, 1972

11 AQUARIUS:
The Search for the Holy Grail

The Sun enters Aquarius around January 21 each year and remains until about February 21. Aquarius is the last of the four powerful, magnetic, opinionated Fixed signs. *Symbolically*, Aquarius is the ideal man, often artistically depicted as an angel, an immortal messenger to mankind from the gods, a perfected being who has liberated himself from the limitations of time and space (the orbits of Saturn and Jupiter) so that he can fly between Heaven and Earth with his lofty concepts. Angels inspire, guide, instruct, guard, protect, and sometimes struggle with us to convince us to do the right thing. They can appear suddenly with a momentous message, as Gabriel appeared to Mary; they can guard the gates of Paradise as they did for Adam and Eve; they can manifest with swords and trumpets on Judgement Day or dispute with each other as did Lucifer and Michael. They are definitely superior beings, intermediaries between God and man.

In Asia, the Bodhisattva is an angelic looking perfected being who is also an intermediary, a guide, or savior to mankind. Many Aquarians have the generous disposition of a gentle bodhisattva. Others are fiercer angels who fight for principle. In them we recognize the courageous nature of the Leo polarity. Here, as with the other eleven signs, so much depends on the level of consciousness and upon other energies in the individual horoscope.

Aquarius is an Air sign and as such has a mental approach to life and decision making in the beginning stages of his life journey. The age at which Aquarius progresses into Pisces, a Water sign, will be important in determining a shift in approach from the mind (Air) to the heart (Water feelings). Many students who come to astrology from Tarot are certain that Aquarius *must* be a Water sign because they're familiar with the Tarot Card, Temperance. Temperance is very Aquarian looking. A winged angel pours from a higher urn (realm of the gods) into a lower urn (realm of mankind). "How can this Water Carrier, this generous angel with his bottomless cup filled with the waters of life, be an Air sign rather than a Water sign?" the new student asks. He says, "You must have got that wrong. Why, I have so many moody Aquarian friends who have 'watery' talents, like music. Surely it's a Water sign?" "No, trust me," I respond, "it's ruled by scientific Saturn and mental Uranus; it's an Air sign. Look to see if your Aquarian friends have progressed into Pisces. There are many Aquarians with cusp of Pisces births who have some natal Pisces' talents as well."

During the Pisces progression, many Aquarians not only become conscious of their Piscean imagination, artistic and musical side but also become involved in such Piscean escapism as alcohol and drugs (negative Neptune escapism). Alice Bailey tells us in *Esoteric Astrology* that the line of demarcation between Aquarius and Pisces is not firmly drawn, that the two tend to blend together. This is also clear from the drawings of the Zodiac of Dendera, wherein the major Solstice seasons are not the Cardinal signs, but the Fixed signs Leo/Virgo and Aquarius/Pisces, which take up a large portion of the Egyptian zodiac. February to March was the flood season in the Nile River Valley. Torrential rains assured the fertility of the delta and a bountiful harvest later in the year. Yet, no planting could be done till the waters subsided in late March or early April. People retreated indoors while the wind whistled, and the waters cascaded wildly downriver, forming whirlpools. Flood season meant time out from worldy work.

Like the ancient Egyptians, clients born in February or March often feel flooded by the world around them—the sensations, perceptions, information, possibilities and pitfalls. They occasionally need to go within, withdraw from the world and assimilate; let the waters soak into the ground and fertilize it while the torrent of stimuli pours over them. They feel that a bountiful harvest is sure to occur later, in the future, as a result of this fallow or dormant period. It's small wonder that intuitives who study astrology associate the Aquarian Water Carrier with the Water element, and have difficulty thinking of it as a mental Air sign; there are so many similarities to Pisces, that other rainy season sign.

Pisces and Aquarius are also the two most altruistic signs in the zodiac. A person born with many planets in these two signs may well be a Seeker after the Holy Grail, Omar Khayyam's blissful cup. Yet, s/he is not a Seeker for personal, selfish motives. True, s/he does want to experience his or her own immortality, his or her own soul and the Divine, but s/he usually also sees him/herself as the messenger guide whose main motivation is to find the cup and pour it out upon the parched land for the rest of us, to help us revitalize, to guide us on our way to the inner kingdom.

Though Aquarius usually doesn't withdraw from society for long periods of time, being more extraverted than Pisces, more concerned with friendship, social interaction and his Eleventh House community volunteer activities, parents of Aquarius often wonder when their offspring will find his or her niche in life, when he will stop acting out, rebelling, and join the rest of us here on Earth. Questions frequently asked by parents of Aquarians are: "Why is s/he so rebellious? Will s/he always be a bachelor? Won't I ever have a grandchild? In the process of finding herself, will s/he ever find herself a job or a profession? Why is s/he so restless? Why is s/he always asking why? The rest of us just accept life as it is. Is s/he just running away from responsibility?"

In Greek mythology Uranus is, literally, Heaven—the sky above, an impersonal force of nature. His wife Ga, the Earth mother, seems to balance his airy nature and ground him in reality. Uranian Aquarians look skyward and tend to be utopian souls unless they have many planets in Earth, Capricorn Rising, or a strong Saturn in the chart. They want to live spontaneously in the here and now and they usually express disdain for the grubby routines of the workaday world with its balanced budgets and its pension plans. Uranian Aquarians, especially those with many Air planets in the chart, will ask, "Why is it necessary to hold a dull job? To get married and take on all that responsibility—mortgages, kids' orthodontal bills, tuition fees? *Why* go through all that; what is the *purpose* of it?" Clients with an Angular Uranus (House 1, 4, 7, or 10) have sometimes asked these questions, as well. The Earth plane is a Jupiter/Saturn world, a world where we function in time and space, but Aquarians seem to be trans-Saturnian souls from beyond the orbit of Jupiter and Saturn, angels who've dropped in to visit from some Aquarian paradise, from Uranus' Heaven beyond Saturn's gates. As "fixed" personalities, Aquarius

Sun sign and Aquarius rising children need to learn to compromise their rebellious natures somewhat, to bend to the rules of the Earth plane in order to survive and function here. Unless they can do this, they'll have difficulty leading the rest of us to their blissful Grail.

How does one approach the rebel angel? It is easier to understand Aquarius once we grasp the difficulty involved for that sign in the integration of the two mundane ruling planets, Saturn and Uranus. These are such different energies—Saturn, with its limiting, structuring function and Uranus with its electrical impulses, forever destroying structures that are in decay and need to be replaced. Their lives seem a constant process of tearing down old models, tossing out old concepts, and starting over again from scratch.

The Saturn delay factor can sustain Uranus if both planets are equally strong in an Aquarian Sun sign/Aquarius rising chart. The perfectionistic nature of Saturn (see Chapter 10) takes responsibility very seriously, and in an Angular House will quite often delay commitment, giving Uranus time to experience life, and to ask why—a question that, as we will see, is central to the Grail Quest. Terrible consequences result in the grail story if the seeker forgets to ask the right question at the right time. Life, to my Aquarian clients, seems very much a matter of asking the right questions; so there seems to be a genuine affinity between the sign of the Cup (Holy Grail), Aquarius, and the legend itself.

For Aquarians, choosing the right guide and companions for the quest is vitally important. Aquarian children in particular want to be friends with everybody and are not always very discriminating in their choice of associates. When they reach their teen years, peer pressure and popularity become paramount in their lives. I would suggest that parents of Aquarians who lack the discipline of a strong natal Saturn, an Earth sign rising, or Earth planets, monitor their children's friendships carefully in these years. A Grand Trine in Air to the Sun in Aquarius can render a teenager especially vulnerable to going along with the crowd, as this trine often means taking the path of least resistance.

Saturn, the principle of cosmic order, duty, limitation, Father Time, authority figures, and obedience to the collective's standards was for centuries the *only* mundane ruler of the sign Aquarius. To this day, if we observe even a radical Uranus Aquarian, a young person who once had a blue mohawk hairstyle, as he nears the Saturn return (age 29-30), we are likely to observe the unconscious pull of Saturn, his other ruling planet. Parents of Uranian/Aquarians will find it interesting to watch changes occur in their children close to these years. The rebellious Aquarian tends to become quite serious, more Saturnine and less Uranian. Peter Pan (Uranus) encounters Father Time (Saturn) and seeks to settle down (Saturn) rather than fly through the air (Uranus). The Uranian/Aquarian close to age 29 will begin to think in terms of shoulds and oughts, property (Saturn), his duty to society and the opinions family members have of him.

The Saturn ruled Aquarian, the conservative child, may also go through a shifting of energies close to age 29, because at that time transiting Uranus trine natal Uranus may put him in touch with his New Age ruler. If so, parents may be shocked to see their formerly steady Saturnian Aquarian leave his specialized career or graduate program for some New Age field that isn't very lucrative. Or s/he may go off on a trip with some new and unusual friends—people who seem innovative but lazy. Some Aquarians take up with musicians who use drugs, and tell their parents that the new associates are very spiritual. Since Saturn/Aquarians tend to have parents in the more austere, rigid, or dogmatic religions, this change of behavior comes as a shock as New Age people would not seem spiritual to them.

If you, the reader, have Aquarian planets or Aquarius rising in your horoscope, but do not identify at all with the rebellious, radical innovator Aquarian; if you have no interest at all in New Age religions or New Age healing, you might go back and re-read Chapter 10 on the Capricorn Wheel Turner. (Please study the questions at the end, too.) This archetype may describe your life journey better than Aquarius, especially the first 42-45 years of it. If you are a Saturn/Aquarian though, when you reach Uranus opposite Uranus, your New Age ruler may, through sudden changes in the outer world, put you in touch with your natal Uranus. This chapter may mean a lot more to you at that point in your life.

If you are unsure whether you are a Saturn or Uranus Aquarian, especially if some of your friends are wildly liberal and trendy in their choice of apparel and others are conservatives who dress like bankers, you might want to read through the following list of questions and determine whether you identify more with Saturn or Uranus:

1. a) I was an "old child" in elementary school. I tried earnestly to please my teachers.

      b) As a young child I was a very playful (Peter Pan) type. Also I could be quite rebellious if adults didn't explain why to my satisfaction.

2. a) When my parents met my friends, my main concern was whether my parents would approve of them.
   b) When my parents met my friends, my main concern was whether my friends would find my parents stuffy or not.

3. a) My taste in clothing has always been conservative.
   b) My taste in clothing tends to be more flashy and always has as long as I can remember.

4. a) Titles and credentials are very important to me.
   b) I think life experience is more important than a degree any day.

5. a) I like to discuss ideas that have practical applications.
   b) I can sit and theorize by the hour.

6. a) My outlook on life is cautious and serious.
   b) My outlook on life is positive—tomorrow will be better than today.

7. a) I often have Sunday dinner with relatives when I'd rather not because I think I should.
   b) I often tell relatives I can't have dinner with them on Sunday; I have things I want to do with my friends.

8. a) I see myself as a disciplined person. I nearly always finish what I start in life.
   b) I'd much rather start something new than finish something old that is boring.

If you identified with (a) more often than (b), you are a Saturn/ Aquarian. Yours is a traditional, conservative nature. You're concerned about what authority figures think—parents, teachers, supervisor, credential granting boards. If you identified with (b) more often, yours is a more progressive, Uranian approach to life. You are more restless and easily bored; you enjoy new ideas, and have a "freer" personality. You are not identified with your work (Saturn) to the point that you cannot move on to something new and learn from it.

If you came out half and half on the series of questions, you need to find a way to honor both mundane rulers, Saturn and Uranus, the security loving and the questing facets of your personality. Both are scientific planets. Clinical psychology, salaried by a government agency rather than financially risky private practice, would be one way to honor both. Research in a lab affiliated with a hospital or university where grant money was forthcoming would be another. Saturn would enjoy security and prestige and Uranus would have scope for discovery. You could become a humanitarian (Uranus) authority figure (Saturn), a New Age minister. Or during your free time, you could volunteer (Uranus) in community service (Saturn, collective) and eventually become a highly respected chairperson of the board (Saturn). Uranus needs to be honored through discovery of new concepts, ideas, friends, organizations. Saturn needs the old roots, friends, property, values, as well. It is a delicate balance. Both planets are scientific, and clinical/analytical. Both are concerned for the collective, but in different ways. Uranus is anxious to grow, to live in the now, while Saturn seeks to protect *past* traditions. Building a resilient foundation, or structure, through diverse types of friends, duties and life experiences contributes to this balance.

Though many of my Uranus/Aquarian clients prefer not to settle down and marry till their early to mid forties, there is an important connection between Aquarius and the marriage issue. Uranus is the esoteric ruler of Libra. Through this bond between the two signs, one sees a real change in the lives of free-spirited Aquarians after marriage. They tend to be more balanced and less nervous, more relaxed and happier in general. It's hard for Aquarians to understand how marriage, which in youth they fear will mean giving up their freedom and their quest, can in fact sustain that freedom. In marriage they will have not only moral support for their hopes, dreams, and wishes, and a companion (a friend for the Journey), but material support as well. In our age, marriage usually brings a second income into the household. This second income enables the Aquarian the freedom to quit a boring job or leave a hectic work environment which consumes his outer strength, so that s/he can spend less stressful moments getting his ideas down on paper for his articles, his lab experiments or in the Piscean progression, music scores, poetry or philosophical, instead of technical, essays. As Uranus the Sky God became grounded through his marriage to Ga the Earth Mother, so have many Uranus/

Aquarian clients become grounded through their marriages.

Though astrologers are not in agreement on the planetary exaltation in Aquarius, I think it's Mercury. In the esoteric teaching, Uranus is the higher octave of Mercury and the two work very well together. Mercury is quick in Aquarius and also objective. It settles down to learn (as Aquarius is Fixed) and calms its restless nature. It is more altruistic and eager to share—to communicate insights rather than keep them to itself. Perhaps most important, though, people with Mercury in stimulating Aquarius are impelled to learn, almost forced to work toward becoming more conscious, aware—to work toward their own growth. Hermes (Mercury) is a guide to the alchemical transformation, a sexually neutral planet capable of flying off to heaven or descending into Hades to rescue souls. As a mental healer, Mercury in Aquarius often works a sort of alchemical magic, going beyond the mundane Hermes logic of the finite mind to flights of pure insight. Intellectual understanding becomes Fixed or solidifed into changed behavior. Mercury in Aquarius is very persuasive and very lucid. It's a good placement for the New Age—or any age.

In Chapter 10 we studied the scapegoat archetype theme of banishment into the wilderness. We thought about it in terms of natal Saturn's House in our charts and the House with Capricorn on the cusp. Now, in Aquarius, we come to an equally serious, profound subject—the dismemberment of Uranus. Uranus' own son, Chronus, used his sharp sickle to cut off his father's vital organ, the phallus, and toss it into the sea. The phallus symbolizes, of course, reproductive creativity, but even more importantly it symbolizes power. The theme of being abruptly or suddenly dismembered, being cut off from one's source of power, cut off from the group, one's trusted friends, comes up again and again in the lives of Aquarius, Aquarius rising and people with Uranus in strong House positions, such as on the Ascendant (abrupt loss of personal power in the group), in the Fourth House or the Seventh House (parent, child or spouse cuts the person off), or the Tenth House (employer cuts the person loose and discards him suddenly).

On first impression one might think, "Well, if Aquarians are so fond of their freedom, so independent, why would they care about being cut off? Why is the dismemberment so painful?" There are two reasons Aquarius is vulnerable. First, as Fixed signs Aquarians care deeply about loyalty, fidelity, trust. Second, because of their connection to the friendship archetype (House Eleven) they identify with those who share their ideals. Not the old-fashioned, traditional collective or the birth family (that would be Capricorn/Saturn), but the friends and the family they themselves have chosen, who share their unique slant on life and often their New Age vision.

One client with a very strong Uranus remarked, "Why? I just don't understand it. I had served on that Board for years and when I was out of the country they simply voted me out. Cut me off without any explanation. I wasn't even around to defend myself." It's hard to answer an Aquarian's "Why," as those of you who are astrologers well know. I could only return to the myth of Uranus itself. Aphrodite, the fairest, loveliest of the goddesses, sprang from the foam, taking birth from Uranus' severed creative member. His dismemberment resulted in the appearance of something rare and beautiful—the Goddess of Love. Into the life of the client dropped from the board by her friends whom she had trusted, a new opportunity, a new birth, a new humanitarian service was coming. If she had still been busy with the old friends and the old responsibilities she might not even have seen it coming, or if she had, surely, with her dedication to her old friends she would have rejected it.

The Great Mother fashioned Chronus' sharp flint sickle and gave him permission to use it on Uranus. The intuitive function (or the feeling function) gave permission for the painful, bloody severing process. The rational mind, the inflated side to Mercury exalted in Aquarius, tries to figure it out but fails, because the intuitive function (Divine Mother) is not logical, and it is She who stands behind Chronus holding the sickle. All we can say is, be aware—there *is* an opportunity coming.

Jupiter (opportunity) is the esoteric ruler of Aquarius. God stands behind the abrasive, painful severing blow of the friend. You may no longer be a member of the old Board, but you can, with the combined freedom and universality of Jupiter/Uranus, create your *own* unique humanitarian work, destined perhaps to be more universal in scope than the old work. (Jupiter/Sagittarius is universal perspective.) Combining Jupiter and Uranus (the esoteric and mundane rulers of Aquarius) is the work of the New Age.

The shock of betrayal by a friend in a New Age environment often hits Aquarius very hard. One client said, "I'd have expected such intolerant behavior from the strict religion I was raised in, but to be rejected by my New Age friends who I'd always thought shared my ideals . . . "(to meet intolerance in the Montessori School, holistic health center, or on the Board of the New Age Church), ". . . is incredible." It does seem paradoxical until we remember that people, even in New Age environments are human, and have human weaknesses.

Transiting Uranus, when it brings its sudden and unexpected electrical shocks, is likely to get our attention quickly. Rather than remaining in a state of withdrawal though or asking God, "Why me? What did I ever do to deserve this?" like a whiny child, it's important to detach and remain alert for the new opportunity. In the wake of the Uranus change, opportunity usually appears just as suddenly as the old situation changed. In *The Astrology of Fate*, Liz Greene tells of Carl Jung's rapid shift from the position of heir to the throne in Freudian psychology to loss of the friendship of his mentor and father figure, Sigmund Freud. He suddenly fell from his position as foremost disciple of the great man to *persona non grata* in the group. Lonely, suddenly friendless, isolated because of his innovative ideas and the direction he chose to follow, he went on alone. He gave the Western world back its roots in alchemy, astrology and esoteric Christian symbolism as a result of his ten-year study of the occult. Had he kept his place of honor and authority among the Freudians, we might never have had analytical psychology, or Western psychologists who honor the Self and the Divine. A Leo with the courage to say, "I don't have faith that God exists; I *know* it," in a film interview, Jung also had Aquarius rising—the broad-minded, Uranian ability to seek Truth everywhere, from Eastern philosophy to the myths of the American Indians, including areas that Freud considered worthless or taboo. But it was this very Uranus-ruled ingenuity that paradoxically cost him his friends, a sad plight for someone with an Aquarian Ascendant. What an opportunity his sharp severance from the body of the Freudian group brought to the rest of us.

The Aquarian phase of the spiritual journey is described symbolically in the Gospels. The story of Christ's last few days on Earth can be pieced together from the accounts of the Evangelists. First, we have the introduction of the archetype of God as Divine Friend, in John 15:13-15:

There is no greater love than this, when a man lays

down his life for the sake of his friends . . .

Henceforth, I will not call you servants, because a servant does not know what his Master does; but I have always called you my friends, because everything that I heard from my Father, I made it known to you.

He asked his Heavenly Father that his friends be allowed to experience his state of consciousness and know what he knew. (John 17:24. Lamsa translation from the Aramaic.) Luke tells us that there was an Angel in the Garden of Gethsemane, sent to strengthen him, and then, using the symbolism of the Cup (Aquarius), quotes the surrender of Christ to His Father's will, his sacrifice in drinking the bitter cup of his destiny for the sake of his friends and those who will come later.

Oh Father, if you will, let this Cup pass from me, but not as I will, but as thy will be done.

And there appeared to him an angel from heaven to strengthen him.

And he was in fear, and his sweat became like drops of blood and he fell down upon the ground.

Then he rose up from his prayer, and came to his disciples and found them sleeping because of distress.

And he said to them, 'Why do you sleep?' Rise and pray that you fall not into temptation.' (Lamsa, N.T. Luke 22:42-46)

Matthew tells the story slightly differently, giving a greater sense of the pathos. Christ says:

My soul is sorrowful even unto death, wait for me here. and watch with me. (Matthew 26: 38)

But they are unable to stay awake. In Matthew's version, Christ returns twice from his meditation to attempt to rouse his friends, and then the third time decides to let them remain unconscious as it is nearly daybreak now. At the end of the story another "friend" Judas appears and betrays him right there in the Garden with a kiss of peace.

Here we have compressed into a few verses the whole of the Aquarian archetype: the bitter cup, representing God's will, which our minds cannot fathom at the time—the sacrifice for humanity (for one's friends, present and to come), the angel to strengthen the will and the lesson of conscious awareness. Wake up! Be alert! (The lesson of transiting Uranus.) This imagery, even to the drops of blood falling to the Earth, was later assimilated into the Grail legends of Christianity and Islam. Christ as Cup Bearer, holding the chalice of blood red wine and performing a magical transformation of wine to blood at the Last Supper continues to the present day in the Mass. Red, of course, is the color of courage, of self-mastery, of the hero who has been tested and has proven himself. It is the fearlessness of Leo, the integration of the polarity to Aquarius. But the subordination of one's *own* will to the will of God for the greater good of the group, the transition from willful human to Angel, Avatar or Bodhisattva—that is the work of Aquarius.

Other legends, from Vedic India of the Divine Nectar in the cup (*amrita*), of the ambrosia of the Gods in Zeus' cup on Mt. Olympus, and of the magical Celtic cauldron, which lingered on in Shakespeare's Macbeth, where his three witches chant and stir to affect their spells exist, but it is hard to find a scene more poignant than the Gethsemane surrender to illustrate the Aquarian story. In the end, only God, as Divine Friend, is totally dependable. Humanity needs to be served, true, but individual friends can be very fickle in our hour of need. In the Celtic story of the Fisher king (the version with Gawain as hero) there are two Grails—one Cup of bitter, poisonous liquid and one cup of Immortality. The hero must dispel illusion or hallucination (Maya) and choose correctly between them. If we see Aquarius as a dual sign, like Pisces and Gemini, these two Grails are fitting symbols.

A Uranus transit, whether conjunction, square or opposition, may catch us unaware and present us with a bitter chalice, but the Cup of Vitality, Bliss and Immortality awaits us, too. We may, like the Christian Master, fear the future and sweat drops of blood but the Father does send his Angel of Strength to those who are awake.

I have many clients who take a look at the Bitter Chalice—the sudden severance from job, or spouse or roommate or child, or professional or spiritual group—and feel stunned; who prefer to sleep and wait for the nightmare to end, for the telephone call that says, "Come back. I made a mistake." Raging against faithless friends doesn't help. Christ actually had to entrust his entire work to Simon Peter, who betrayed him three times before daybreak. And yet the work went on after the Crucifixion, in spite of the weakness of the human instruments.

Ralph Waldo Emerson wrote that if we want to have friends, we must first be friends. Though it may be difficult, it seems important to be there for our friends who consider doing wild, erratic things on Uranus transits. Listeners are appreciated when a bolt of electricity has suddenly struck. Sometimes an objective friend can help clarify the next stage of the journey as people try to find their way through the dark forest to the Castle of the Holy Grail. A supportive friend can be like a strengthening Grail Angel.

The *Rubaiyyat* of Omar Khayyam is replete with symbolism on the Blissful Grail, one sip from which will turn our desert wasteland into a Paradise. It's interesting that he chooses to begin his long poem with three verses on the importance of consciousness, of being alert. The Muezzin, before cock crow, calls "Wake up! Wake up! But where are all the drowsy worshippers? Why are they not breaking down the door of the 'Tavern' where the sacred wine is kept?"

Uranus, more than any other transiting planet, forces us to hear the Muezzin's call from the tower, to wake up. Sometimes it seems that must be its major cosmic purpose. On transits like Uranus opposite Uranus, we learn objectivity and detachment quickly, through the natal Uranus House and that with Aquarius on the cusp, as well as the House transited. If we don't stay awake, if we sleep or take flight, we're likely to miss what the Sufis call the Angel bearing the Grail. In that case, we might see only the bitter cup and miss the blissful one.

One irritated client, nervously biting her nails on Uranus opposite Uranus, told me of her fears for the future now that her husband had left. She had determined on the flight reaction: "I'm selling the townhouse and taking all his money and going to Europe to spend it!" This flight reaction occurs frequently, but is not really conscious behavior. Peter Pan liked a change of scene, too, but this alone doesn't always solve the problem. The woman had been embarrassed in front of her friends—couples she and her husband had socialized with over a period of years.

The airplane is a modern freedom symbol. Jungian analysts have told me it means freedom in dreams, but I've seen it mean freedom in real life during the mid-life crisis years. Uranus escapism often involves moving toward the waters in the Aquarian Urn as if they were one's personal fountain of youth—abruptly leaving the past behind by moving cross-country, or even abroad. By hindsight, two or three years later, the person who has responded erratically to the Uranus opposition wonders, "Why in heaven's name did I give up everything I had built up over the years? My suburban house, my job, my friends, my spouse, my children?" Especially if the chart is full of planets in the heavy elements, Earth and Water, it's important to reflect rather than to react impulsively in a Uranus year. The past (what Saturn has built) is important. Charts strong in the lighter elements (Air and Fire) are less likely to have hindsight regrets about taking flight with Uranus, but they too may wonder "Why?" and "What if I had stayed?" It's best to wait till Uranus ends its contact and moves a full degree away before making a major break or lifestyle change.

My own approach when a client is experiencing Uranus opposition Uranus or Uranus transiting the Sun or Midheaven is to ask: "What have you been really excited about or stimulated by lately? There must be a group, a New Age field of study or an individual you've recently met that you'd really like to get to know better." Often a new friend that comes into the person's life is a catalyst or a guide to the Grail. This does not mean that the new person or interest will be a permanent part of the client's life. He or she may vanish suddenly, like the Grail Angel, after delivering a message or an insight. The challenge, the contacts, or the philosophy expounded by the guide may, however, remain important for years to come.

Uranus transits, if constructively used, may be productive time out from mundane, routinized living, to detach, gain perspective and look more objectively at the world through different and clearer lenses. Old acquaintances, habits, circumstances, jobs and environments suddenly look different to us. As a result of the time out and the new people met during the Uranus year (usually age 41-42) many people find their second wind, or envision a second Grail full of new hopes, dreams and wishes, and change course for the second half of life, exploring new territory.

Jung says in "Stages of Life" (Collected Works, VIII) that many women may shift from home and inner focus toward the outer world, and many men in the opposite direction, from career in the outer world to the quest for the purpose in life, the inner search. Many clients dare to take risks on a Uranus transit that they would not have ventured to take any other year. "I was fired anyhow; I had nothing to lose," said one man with an Angular Uranus and Aquarius on his Midheaven. He moved from his work in the computer communication field toward his hobby, writing science fiction stories. He has done well. Working at home has given him freedom to schedule his own life, independence from authority, and an opportunity to earn a living with his ideas and concepts. All of these are Uranus' advantages.

If we look at the year as an adventure, a chance to experiment, to learn, to take some risks, then freedom, independence, and a focus on our own ingenuity or originality can really pay off. But we have to be fearless, use our natal fiery confidence, integrate the Leo polarity. Moving into the Unknown Future courtesy of Uranus has many cautious Earth and Water sign clients sweating blood for awhile, dealing with stress and anxiety, and then discovering that they enjoy the chance to go for it.

Community service is another mid-life change both men and women clients have enjoyed, since Uranus rules the volunteer. Others, housewives who sought to make their mid-life change by moving into the outer world and collecting a paycheck, have used past volunteer experience on civic boards as a means of gaining employment with the Chamber of Commerce or other local organizations. Men who have climbed to the Top of the Mountain (see Chapter 10) and feel bored, or stressed out on the Uranus year, may make a sudden break with the old job and find something more interesting, challenging and serviceful to do. All the Uranus keywords come into play when advising a client in mid-life. The natal Uranus and the House it rules (Aquarius cusp) can provide the astrologer with many ideas on things that would excite the client and enable him to use Uranus' nervous energy productively to develop the Eleventh House goals, hopes, wishes, aspirations. Eleventh House planets and the natal planet ruling the Eleventh house cusp should also be studied.

I have been amazed at the number of introverted bowl charts (charts with all the planets in the bottom hemisphere) who move toward extraversion in their early to mid forties, when Jupiter, Uranus, and Saturn all oppose their natal positions in the bottom of the bowl. On the other hand, many extraverted people with the majority of their planets in the Zenith Houses (Nine and Ten) discover a fondness for quiet evenings spent reading at home. Some even consider moving the office into their homes in order to spend more time with family during the oppositions of the outer planets transiting the bottom hemisphere in their mid-40's. Some of them have considered taking early retirement because they have peaked in the Zenith

Houses and want to "live long enough to enjoy my success," or ask, "Who needs high blood pressure and potential heart attacks from all this rushing around?"

Many clients, men and women, have asked me about training to become psychologists on the Uranus opposite Uranus cycle, especially when it fell within a year of Pluto square Pluto (depth psychology). Though the mind can assimilate concepts rapidly on Uranus transits, this is not a patient period. Long-term academic programs may appeal at first but people in their forties tend to become restless and drop out after the initial enthusiasm has waned. It's important to look at the staying power in the whole chart—Saturn discipline, Fixed signs, T-Squares versus Grand Trines, and so forth—before advising a long program. Building on past skills and experience and adding some new seminars in new areas of interest work for many people in this cycle.

For high strung clients who are severely stressed out in mid-life, a period of time out in a peaceful environment may be suggested. A search for the Blissful Grail of the Sufi poet Omar Khayyam could involve a stay in a quiet retreat house with a garden (so many of the Sufi poets have gardens, even in the titles of their books) while pondering the next stage of the journey, the second Grail which brings hope and renewed vigor to body and soul. One could take along books on current interests, New Age philosophies, New Age sciences, healing, world brotherhood communities, any Aquarian interests the individual has. It's hard to sit still and meditate after a Uranus shock, but if one can do that, the vision of the Angel and the Grail (who may manifest as a human being with an idea or an opportunity) should not be long in coming. Then one has to reflect still longer till the last passage of Uranus by opposition and consider, "Do I really want this opportunity, this break with the past?"

Thus, Uranus transits bring us awareness of the need to take a new direction in the Grail forest of life, occasional breaks with old associates so that we may encounter new ones, and Cups, sometimes bitter and sometimes blissful. They are, on a deeper level, about our faith in God or Goddess as Divine Friend and Guide during periods of change and sometimes of upheaval, about a second wind or a second birth.

One word of caution on stressful Uranus transits: the body, too, is a cup, a vessel. It houses the Mind (so important to Aquarians) and the Spirit! In Uranus years we need to give what Omar Khayyam called the clay pot, the body vessel, its due in terms of rest and relaxation as well as moderate exercise. Uranus rules the central nervous system together with Mercury, exalted in Aquarius. The B vitamins are helpful in the balance of the nervous system, and we might do well to add food rich in these vitamins to the diet.

Uranus, as God of ether or Air, also rules the oxidation of the blood, as well as its circulation. Many Aquarian Sun sign people intuitively know when they need to add garlic or chlorophyl tablets (blood purifiers) to the diet or to add a pinch of cayenne pepper to fruit juices. If we're fortunate enough to live near the ocean, we can always take a brisk walk and inhale deeply, bringing oxygen into the system. Aerobic dance, of course, is excellent for the heart and circulation, but if a person is in the mid-life cycle and has not done much exercise, it's best to get permission from the doctor before impulsively signing up for a strenuous program at a health club. Stretching exercises also help keep the blood vessels supple. Because of its sudden, drastic energy Uranus is associated with cramping, spasms and even epilepsy. Hatha Yoga relaxes the muscles and helps prevent circulatory problems and cramping. If you are interested in yoga, you might inquire, too, about *pranayama*. This technique helps to purify and oxydize the blood, the body, and is good for the soul, too.

At a recent astrology conference, Eileen Naumann, the medical astrologer, mentioned it takes the blood a great deal of oxygen to metabolize starch, and that low starch diets tend to work out well for Aquarians. She also mentioned that many Aquarians crave salt, which is esoterically interesting, because in the alchemical tradition salt is wisdom (see Chapter 9). Perhaps the craving is symptomatic of the search for wisdom, Jupiter's gift. Anyhow, she recommends checking for glaucoma if Aquarians feel pressure on the eyeballs and have a salt craving.

Aquarius also rules the ankles. I have observed many clients who, rushing about on Uranus opposite Uranus in a preoccupied manner (or on transiting Uranus squared Mars) fell and sprained or broke an ankle. Here, the key is be alert, be aware. Broken or sprained ankles may also be related to psychological denial, though I have no way to prove this. Clients who tell me, "My husband and I are only *temporarily* separated," rather than look at the truth—his permanent living arrangement with his girl friend—tend toward ankle sprains on Uranus transits. It is definitely an awareness transit. We *need* to become conscious, whether we want to or not. Resisting the new direction, or trying to hold on to the past, can lead to an accident in a Uranus year. If we do not move forward, the outer world seems to push us ahead anyhow, against our will.

Saturn Aquarians, as they get older, may suffer hardening of the arteries, osteoporosis, or other diseases usually connected with Capricorn (see Chapter 10). Uranus Aquarians are more likely to welcome progress and to deal positively with change, and therefore seem less likely to suffer health problems connected to rigid attitudes (Saturn).

We turn now from events and changes in the outer world, mundane Aquarius, to the inner world, the Quest for the Grail. It begins with a pure knight (attitudinally pure, not necessarily physically pure in the sense of celibate) in search of his soul. Contained in the search for the soul are the experience of immortality, the Divine, and a desire to save the kingdom, which is parched, infertile and dying along with the Senex King whose vigor—mental, physical and spiritual, is fading away. (For a review of the Senex King, see Chapter 10.) There are two colors (in different versions of the Grail story) for this initial stage of the journey. Sometimes the pure knight is white, and sometimes green. Green, of course, refers to the fact that he's a total novice at the task; he has no idea how difficult it's going to be, and he has a great deal to learn. The colors come from Western alchemy as influenced by the Islamic alchemists. As Indries Shah has said, the color scheme is much more vivid in the Orient than in the West, and helps us to visualize the journey.

Peredur the Welsh boy (antecedent to Perceval in the French story and Parsifal in the German version) lived with his mother on the edge of a thick, dark forest. One day he wandered into the forest a short distance and saw a flash of silver. Eagerly, he ran home to his mother's cabin and told her, "Angels! I saw a whole crowd of angels on horseback!" She laughed and said, "No dear, those were knights, not angels. King Arthur's Knights of the Round Table inhabit the forest. It's a dangerous, enchanted place where things are not what they seem. I want you to stay out of it."

"Well, tell me about the knights, then. What does a knight do? Where does he go?" Peredur's curiosity and imagination knew no bounds. But he had to wait several years to run away from home and enter the forest because he was very young. He knew his mother would never approve of him going into the forest by himself, at any age. So he would eventually have to go without permission and over her protest.

Peredur had no other friends besides his mother. Thus they had been quite close, and it was a difficult leave taking. As he crossed the bridge to the forest she ran after him, weeping. She collapsed in a swoon on the bridge, but he did not look back. He was free. In the forest there would be friends, adventures, and some sort of quest, though he did not really understand quests at that point. Peredur was a very green apprentice knight.

To be green is to be an innocent, to live on a day to day, moment to moment basis. In *The Grail Legend* the authors, Emma Jung and Marie Louise von Franz, tell us that innocents, or children and primitive peoples, live for the moment, by their instincts and do not attempt to set themselves long-term goals, or to follow through on a plan of action. They live in the situation at hand, spontaneously deciding what to do next, ready to drop the fishing rod and go hunting on a nice day if a friend comes by and offers the opportunity. If the weather is good, the game plentiful, the season right, why not? It's only adults and civilized people who feel compelled to make plans and follow through with them.

Uranus/Aquarians have the innocence, spontaneity and the restlessness of young Peredur. They too see life as an adventure which will have a positive outcome. (They'll tell you that the New Age will be wonderful, not that the future will bring nuclear war.) Like Peredur, the primitives, and Great Sages everywhere, they live in the moment. This approach to life enables them to make a good many scientific discoveries because they see things today the rest of us would miss while we were planning for the long run, or tying up the loose ends of yesterday.

Omar Khayyam, former mathematics professor and calendar rectifier, wrote in the *Rubaiyyat*: "Ah, but my computations, people say, reduced the year to better reckoning? Nay, 'twas only striking from the Calendar Unborn tomorrow, and dead Yesterday." (LVII)

Green, through its connection with learning, is a good color for Aquarius. The authors of *The Grail Legend* connect green with the sensate function, because it is an earth tone. It symbolically refers to healthy vegetation and animal life and to life in general. It is the opposite of the parched earth, which is a dry red-brown or dry black, symbolically dead. When the ailing kings in legends and myths were magically restored to health, the land outside the castle would immediately become green again.

If green is connected with the Earth and with grounding the electricity of Uranus, it is small wonder that so many Angular Uranus people have difficulty finishing apprenticeships with dull teachers; the electrical current resists being grounded. It's hard for alert and highly intelligent Aquarian children to be in learning situations where others move at a slower mental pace and many are tempted to drop out of formal education and get on with life's experiences. There is a similarity here to Sagittarius (see Chapter 9), which is also ruled by an expansive, free, restless planet.

The Uranus/Aquarian reader will be much more interested to know the esoteric meaning of the color green than its mundane meaning, however. (The mundane world with its competitions, tests, long-term goals and its need for grounding and responsibility seems boring to him or her.) Esoterically, green is the color of the emerald, the highest among the precious gemstones. To the alchemist the emerald is the equivalent of gold among minerals. Hermes Trismegisthes, legendary Egyptian sage and patron of alchemy, chose the emerald as his stone and engraved his secret teachings on emerald tablets. Healing is facilitated by the color green. Thus, whenever Gawain or Peredur/Percival attempted to repair a broken magical sword or heal a king, a green cloak would be placed over them in the Grail Castle.

Green, connected with the search for objective truth, is a very important color in Islamic alchemy. In the Islamic Grail tradition, the Grail Stone was originally an emerald in the middle of Lucifer's forehead, at the position of the third eye. (It was similar to the precious pearl at Shiva's third eye in Hinduism.) When the Angel of Light, Lucifer, was engaged in his fight with Archangel Michael, the emerald loosened and eventually fell to Earth as Lucifer himself fell into Hades. In the Persian tradition it had reposed in a revolving temple, a sort of astronomical building set to move with the seasons and the constellations. It was, however, stolen and taken to Wales, where it was supposedly hidden in a cave or in an invisible castle. The Grail Stone was the alchemical philosopher's stone of magical powers; it could grant wisdom and immortality, as well as confer perpetual youth on those who were privileged to gaze upon it. Hearts yearned for the Grail. It was carried by a lovely maiden on a green cloth, the almarach, which rested on a golden dish, rather than inside a chalice. The stone, the Ka'aba, and the almarach, represented the hope of mankind. Christianity also viewed green as the color of hope and of the Holy Spirit, through which power, wisdom, immortality and many other spiritual gifts are obtained.

Practically speaking, as the color of mutable Hermes, who traverses the three worlds (heaven, hell and earth) with his messages, green is a transitional color. One can wear it anywhere—into the introverted forest or out again into the extraverted real world. When Peredur enters the forest as a Green Squire, he makes a major life transition. Years later, after wandering in circles seeking a castle located just minutes from his starting point, conquering enchantment (Maya, illusion) and finding his Psychic Center (Self, Spiritual Purpose, Inner Voice), he exits the forest wearing the Green Cloak of Hope. He makes another major life transition as he brings the message of hope to humanity: "Everyman can do what I have done." The message of hope seems to be the real message of the Grail. One does not have to be a king or a knight of royal blood, or a great master; we are all sons of God. The ordinary man can become the Grail Angel. This, too, is the message of the New Age.

Peredur, then, as an innocent gifted with a talent for asking good questions, was quite green. He would soon feel overwhelmed by the sophistication and luxurious living of the collective, the Society of the Round Table. But as he entered the forest, he fully expected to enjoy his apprenticeship as a green squire. Like Peredur, the Uranus/Aquarian/Aquarius rising personality welcomes a new learning situation enthusiastically, sure of his gift for asking the right questions and his ability to learn quickly. The green phase involves the stimulation of meeting new people, situations, ideas and concepts, performing altruistic service and making discoveries. When he enters his forest the Uranus Aquarian thinks, "All one has to do is find the right group—like-minded friends—and learn whatever it takes." Performing feats of derring-do with Arthur's knights, saving damsels in distress, and righting wrongs would, after all, be altruistic service. The green learning phase is always fun at first; it's only when the newness wears off and the Aquarian wants to be free to try out his own unique ideas that boredom sets in.

As we enter the dark green forest of the unconscious with Peredur, it's helpful to keep in mind the House of natal Uranus, its contacts to other planets in the chart, and the House with Aquarius on the cusp.

Uranus is our inner Peredur, our awakening consciousness. Uranus represents our curiosity, our need to respond to new challenges and mental stimuli, our personal hopes, dreams and wishes, our altruistic ideals for humanity, our restlessness, our rebelliousness, the perverse instinctual response of the human mind. "I won't listen to the Wise Old Teacher. If he says take the left path at the fork-in-road, I'll take the right. New territory is always more interesting to cover."

Peredur had hoped to meet knights and make friends right away, but soon discovered that the forest is a solitary place. Whether or not he liked it, in the forest of the unconscious, each knight is alone with his own Quest. To emphasize this point, Cistercian monks who reworked the legend and Christianized the symbolism came up with a new condition. In their version, the Grail Knights had to disperse before entering the forest. Each had to find his own path into the dark and airless place and his own path out. While in the forest, they would collect as a group and have common experiences, each working with his own talents and personality traits. (See Joseph Campbell, *Flight of the Wild Gander*.) Thus, the Grail Knights were only loosely bound to the Group through their oath of loyalty to King Arthur and the common values of the Code of Chivalry. How like the threshold of the Age of Aquarius this Cistercian view is. There are so many different Seekers after Truth, each taking his or her own solitary path into the forest, each with his or her own personality, talents, ideas and ideals, yet each participating in the overall plan to further human knowledge, human awareness in the New Age.

After wandering a long time, Peredur encountered an old man. "Where are all the knights?" he asked. He was told that King Arthur was having a banquet at his castle and the knights and ladies were feasting, watching jousting contests, and amusing themselves royally. Though he must have been eager to join in the fun, Peredur decided to stay with the old man and learn about the Code of Chivalry. What would be expected of him at the castle? And what *was* the Quest? What *was* the Grail?

The old man looked at Peredur and saw a boy in simple rustic apparel without much refinement, a diamond in the rough who would need a great deal of work to be presentable at court. He invited Peredur to stay and study with him. The teacher then explained that one had to earn one's place at court. It helped to know someone there, to have a patron, of course (Gawain later became Peredur's patron), but it was also essential to understand the Code. According

to the Code of Chivalry, if the would-be knight requires a suit of armor and a horse (neither of which Peredur owned), and a sword, he has to earn them. He cannot borrow these things while the owner is asleep or indoors. This would be neither courteous nor fair. Courtesy and fairness were two major virtues bound up with the oath of Chivalry. Another virtue was obedience. Under the oath, Peredur would be bound to obey King Arthur. For the moment he could practice obedience by obeying his teacher, the old man.

Peredur could earn his armor, sword, and horse by obeying Arthur's command to right a wrong. If Arthur required him to punish a wayward knight and he could defeat the knight in a fair sword fight, Peredur would be entitled to appropriate the man's possessions. To avenge the king, a virtuous knight or a lady was, after all, to restore the Cosmic Order. (See *The Grail Legend*, Emma Jung and Marie Louise von Franz.) For the Grail Quest, sincerity and loyalty to the task were essential. Knights who were not sincere, whose motives for seeking the Grail were not absolutely pure, were not eligible. An egotist could not even see the Grail Castle, shrouded in mist; s/he would walk right past it. So, sincerity and loyalty (refusal to become sidetracked from the goal) were the most important Grail virtues. Integrity too was important. Performing compassionate deeds, such as protecting maidens and the poor, helped one to merit the right to enter the Grail Castle. One also had to speak the Truth and honor all his vows.

"But how will I recognize the Grail Castle if I see it or know I'm approaching it, if it's hidden in the mist?"

"The Fisher King is usually outside in the middle of a lake. Though he is served every day from the Grail of Immortality, still his wound does not heal and he can no longer stand, walk or lie down comfortably. His servants carry him out to the lake not far from his Castle, where he enjoys fishing. If you see him there and make a favorable impression—though it is unlikely you could do so at this point—he will invite you in. Watch your manners at the banquet table and do not be overwhelmed by all the luxurious things you will be seeing for the first time. And *do not* plague him with personal questions about the Wound and the Grail. He will be your host; be a kind and courteous guest. Don't talk so much, try to listen. Try to learn."

"Where *did* he get the wound," Peredur asked.

"Legend has it," said the teacher, "that instead of marrying the Maiden whose name was on the Grail, his destined mate, he fell under the spell of the Lady in the Castle of Pride (Chateau Orgeuilleuse), and he would not give her up. One day, a heathen foreigner came along and stuck his poisoned spear into the Fisher King's side. Since then, the only way to staunch the flow of blood and ease the pain is to place the magic lance on the wound. It draws out some of the poison and the Immortal Grail keeps him alive, but his condition does not improve. He is an unworthy king. A Perfect Knight will come along one day and heal his pain or else replace him as Grail King."

"Where did the Grail and the magic lance come from?" Peredur asked.

"Legend has it that Joseph of Aramathea, the same man who gave his own tomb to Christ, took the Chalice used at the Last Supper to the Crucifixion and after the Roman soldiers had left, held it under Christ's wound to catch a few drops of blood. He then took the lance which the Roman soldier, Longinus, had used to pierce Christ's side, along with the Grail, to the Island of Patmos. There his son Josephus supposedly gave it to an English Saint who brought it here and hid it in Wales, first in a cave, and then in the Grail Castle."

"How will the Perfect Knight be able to heal the King, if the Grail and the Lance, these magic relics, cannot?" asked Peredur.

"Through sympathy and compassion," said the old man. "You must sleep now. In the morning we have much to study."

But Peredur got up in the night and wandered on his way, trying to recall which path the old man had told him to take when he reached the fork in the road. Until the Grail Castle appears in the mist, he thought, I might as well seek out King Arthur's castle and get on with my adventure. No sense in staying forever with the Old Teacher. Like Peredur's mother, he would probably *never* want to let the boy move on. Or so it must have looked to the restless green squire.

He took the wrong path at the crossroads and got himself lost. He met a beautiful woman there, a young cousin on his mother's side of the family. She thought she recognized him and asked him his name. Peredur thought very hard, "My mother calls me *bon fils* (good boy) and sometimes *beau fils* (handsome boy)," he said.

"No, no," she smiled. "What is *your* name, your *own* name?" He thought again. "It's Peredur, the Welshman," he finally recalled, smiling at the insight into his identity.

"Oh, Peredur. I'm your cousin, your mother's niece. Are you lost?"

"Yes, I'm looking for King Arthur's Castle. Did I take the wrong fork in the road for it?"

"Yes, but this is a fortuitous meeting. I am told the Grail Castle is nearby, though I have not seen it, that it's on this very path. You must hurry and go there, Peredur, for we haven't much time left. The land, as you can see, is dying. My Knight, to whom I am betrothed, is very ill. You must find the Castle, for your mother has told me you have purity of heart. You must remember to ask the question: 'What is the Grail, and whom does it serve?'" (Other versions have, "What are these drops of blood on the lance?" Since Peredur asked neither question, it doesn't seem to matter which is the "authentic" version.)

"Oh, no," said Peredur, "you do not understand. My teacher, to whom I must remain obedient, told me to keep my questions to myself in the Grail Castle and concentrate on sympathy and compassion, for these are the virtues that will heal the Fisher King."

"Well, he's wrong," said the girl with total self-assurance. "You must ask the magic question and then he will be free. The land will recover and my knight will live; we'll be married and live happily ever after." She gave him directions to Arthur's castle. Instead of returning to the crossroads he wandered along the Grail Road, however, wondering, "Who is right? The girl or the Teacher?" The ambiguity that comes with too many sources of information seems as difficult for Air signs as does making clear cut decisions. If we consider the glyph for Aquarius (≈), it seems as dual as Pisces or Gemini. The issue of integration or balancing of opposites is thus important on the Aquarian Journey.

Suddenly Peredur looked up and saw a lake in the forest with a boat in the middle of it. In the boat there was an elegantly attired but very unhealthy looking man holding a fishing rod. He must then be on the outskirts of the Grail Castle near the lake. Servants dressed in silk with gold embroidery darted about attending to the king's every need. Peredur might, if he approached them, be invited to enter the castle. He might be given a chance to heal the king. Such was, in fact, the case. Before he could adjust to the strangeness of it all, he found himself actually inside the Castle seated at a long banquet table watching a procession of 26 maidens bringing in the Grail. (In some of the Celtic versions there are two Grails, and two Grail Maidens in the procession.) The table automatically replenished any food that was being eaten and one of the Grails automatically refilled any empty cups, without ever seeming to empty itself. Each guest tasted the type of wine he preferred, though it was all poured from the same source. Peredur was astonished at the Enchanted Castle. (Joseph Campbell says that he was at the fabled Table of the Celtic King, the Welsh equivalent of Neptune, Manaddwyn. At this magical table even the animals served as the main course came to life again the next day. Manaddwyn's Grail was the ambrosia of Immortality. See *Flight of the Wild Gander*.)

There was a hushed, expectant moment as a maiden put a green silk cloak over Peredur and all attention was focused upon him. He felt great sympathy and compassion but said nothing. On his way to his room in the Castle, when the others had retired for the night, he saw the wisest, kindest, most remarkable old man on a royal couch in a back room, the Real Castle Builder, the Real Grail King in perfect health. Thus, there also were two kings in the Celtic version. It was a study in a world of magical illusion.

So ends the Welsh version, with the implication that Peredur did no wrong and even that the King had been healed through his sympathy and purity of heart and compassion. T.W. Rolleston, author of *Myths and Legends of the Celtic Race*, believes that Peredur was a properly obedient young man and that for a curious youth he did a fine job of passing his test of self-restraint. He showed courtesy, sympathy, and compassion. According to Celtic sources, these so-called knightly virtues were well-known in Wales long before the English introduced Codes of Chivalry and other artificial devices in the belief that they were civilizing pagan barbarians. Later, the French and German versions treat the Welsh account as a fragment of the Grail story, and a pagan, superstitious fragment at that.

Joseph Campbell, in *Creative Mythology*, feels that Peredur repressed his own instincts; he should have asked the Grail question in the Castle, regardless of what the Teacher had counseled. This is a good point too, because on the Path of Awareness (Individuation), we are supposed to be alert and ask questions, to live life consciously. In *The Grail Legend*, Jung and von Franz remind us that the values of Christian Chivalry were the collective's values, and that at the time Peredur/Perceval desperately wanted acceptance at the Round Table, to belong to the Group. Obedience was an important virtue he had been taught. To be rebellious, or as astrologers would say, to behave in Uranus fashion, would have been inappropriate since it would not have won him acceptance, or so he thought at the time. Only *later* does he express anger at both the obedience rule and at others who gave him their questions to ask, and only later does he begin to seek the Grail in *his own way!* Only later does he express anger at the God of Chivalry, and at the collective's judgment of his failure in the Grail Castle, separate himself from them, take his own vow, formulate his own questions, and continue on his journey alone.

Omar Khayyam wrote in the *Rubaiyyat* about his youth:

> Myself when young did eagerly frequent Doctor and Saint, and heard great argument about it and about, but evermore came out by the same door where in I went.
> With them the seed of wisdom did I sow and with my own hand wrought to make it grow; and this was all the Harvest that I reaped, I came like water and like wind I go. . .
> Up from earth's center through the Seventh Gate I rose and on the Throne of Saturn Sate and many-a-knot unravelled by the Road, but not the Master Knot of human fate. . . (XXXI)

Peredur/Perceval must have had similar thoughts about his Teacher when he awoke under a bush in the spot where the Grail Castle had stood the night before and rubbed his eyes. He had kept silence in the Castle and now the land about him looked parched. Sitting on the ground not too distant from the bush was a young girl, totally bald, holding a dead knight on her lap. Clearly, his compassion and courtesy had failed to heal the poor Fisher King. This part of the forest was dying.

"Come no closer," she called out, "for this is a dangerous place."

Suddenly, they recognized each other, "*You,* from whence have you come?" she asked.

"Cousin," said Perceval, "you had helped me find my name. You used to have such lovely brown wavy hair. What happened to you? I come from the Grail Castle," he added.

"Don't lie to me," she sobbed. "If it were anywhere near here I would have seen it by now."

"One does not always find what he is seeking as he expects to find it," said Perceval.

"The land is dying, My fiance is dead. My hair fell out. You did not ask the Grail question, then, while you were there? You had no pity on that king or on the rest of us?"

"Well," said Perceval, "I was counseled not to ask questions. But maybe the Teacher was wrong? Anyhow, I can ask the Grail question on my next visit to the Castle. Let me tell you about the banquet table. I saw the most marvelous things. . . "

"Oh I can't stand to look at you, I hate you so much. Don't you see? Each knight is allowed only *one* chance to enter the Grail Castle.

You can't go again; that's the rule. You have lost all honor. Everyone will just loathe you." She turned her back on him and went off to embalm her knight.

This was sad news for a man who valued friendships, and who had hoped to be well liked at Court. He continued on his way to Arthur's castle, as Gawain had arranged an invitation for him. In fact the White Knight rushed out to greet him, embraced him and wrapped him in a silk cloak with an emerald clasp.

They had barely entered the castle when Cundrie the Sorceress entered, riding her Castilian horse. She was an ugly old hag who was anxious to deliver bad news to Arthur. "Son of Uther Pendragon," she shouted. The King looked up. "Today the Round Table has been dishonored. The Code is no more. Perceval, son of honorable parents, will be condemned by the council when this news is out. That fool went to the Grail Castle and had no care at all for the Ailing King. He did not even ask after his health." She turned to address Perceval, "Your brother Feirefiz who is black and white (of mixed European and Arab blood) is performing deeds of chivalry more noble than yours. He is coming to the Grail Castle and will put you to shame."

Issuing an invitation to the Castle of Marvels, where contests could secure the hearts of 400 beautiful maidens, "for all adventure is wind compared to what might be gained there through love," she rode out. Gawain and some of the others decided to go to the Castle. Moodily, Perceval announced he had no time for such things as romance.

Per-ce-val (French for 'through the center') felt shame and embarrassment at Cundrie's words and was astonished that people seemed to believe her, but he felt no guilt. He felt only anger that his Teacher had misled him. Obedience was not then as important as asking the questions. His cousin had been right. He felt confusion too. He muttered to himself, "Why me? I have performed many good deeds; surely I deserved better than this?" Gawain, still his friend, asked him to go along to the Castle of Marvels and forget the whole thing. Perceval, however, entered into a dark mood and vowed, "I will not sleep two consecutive nights in the same place until I find what I am looking for. I will find my own answers (follow my own instincts) and I will get back into that Disappearing Castle and heal the King. I don't care if there *is* a rule about one visit per knight. He became a true knight-errant, a wanderer, like so many of my Aquarian clients who are confused or angry or both, at the solutions Teachers have given them—"old" approaches that have seemingly failed. Free spirits, they wander in search of their personal Grails.

Everywhere he went he encountered people who laughed at him. Even on the outskirts of the forest, in a remote hermitage, the hermit, while being fed by Angels from a chalice, said, "I heard the oddest story about some unfortunate fool of a knight who got into the Grail Castle and didn't ask the right question. Did you hear that one?" Percevals' embarrassment, his feeling of dismemberment, of being cut off from the body of the group, is also a theme in the lives of many Uranus/Aquarian young people: "My friends all got invited to a certain party (or accepted at a certain school) and I didn't. I feel like the 'reject' in the group." The stone that is rejected, however, will become the cornerstone, according to both the alchemical, and the orthodox Christian tradition.

Perceval told the hermit he was furious with God. God ought to allow a knight more than one entry into the Grail castle. He had nothing to confess in the way of sins, nothing to feel guilty about. After a few days, however, he admitted he was the foolish knight in the Grail Castle.

"Nothing to feel guilty about? And what about my late sister, your mother?" he asked. "She died the day you left her for the forest nearly five years ago. You of course wouldn't know that, since you've never tried to visit her, though you've been within a mile of her cottage many times." Suddenly Perceval felt great sadness.

His mood became less relaxed about finding the Grail and more grim, earnest, driven. And the Castle became harder and harder to see. Some days, though, he wondered if it was beginner's luck when he had so easily found it. Maybe he would *never* see it again.

Perceval left behind his gullibility, his naive belief that God would be bound to reward him immediately for his good deeds and that people would naturally love him just for gaining entrance to the Grail Castle. He learned a very important Uranian lesson through his suffering. He must detach himself from others' praise and blame and at the same time continue on performing his good deeds, doing his best.

Many a Uranian client has come to his reading protesting, "I've been through so much for others, and feel so underappreciated. I gave away my entire inheritance to needy friends within ninety days of receiving it. I was sure that later, when I needed money for something, one of them would have it, and would quickly come forward to help me. They all refused. Some of them will always be poor, and can't help it, and I understand that. But others are doing well financially and are now in a position to help, yet they won't. This is so discouraging."

Or, "I thought when I donated several thousand dollars to the foundation that they would offer me a position on the Board, or at least some sort of job. But they responded, 'Thanks for your money, but we don't think you have the expertise we need—sorry!' I'm astonished, and very, very disappointed."

Or, "When I gave all my funds to the spiritual group, I was certain that I could attend their workshops and retreats for free from then on and perhaps go to Asia on their tour, but they told me I have to come up with more money to pay for these things. If you gave all your money to God, isn't God then going to take care of you through His organization. Through your friends?"

"Aye, there's the rub," as Shakespeare would say. Eventually, the Uranian will get his reward, but here on Earth we function within time and space, and we face many Saturn delays. As Perceval told his cousin, when she complained about not being able to see the Grail castle, "things are not where you expect them." Things do not happen when we expect them, always, or through the people we are expecting to befriend us. We can only go on doing our dharma, as the *Bhagavad Gita* tells us, without expecting to enjoy the fruits of our labors.

In the meantime, we have to earn our living and save enough from our charitable contributions to pay for such self-development needs as holistic healing courses, astrology readings, pilgrimages, creative workshops, retreats, Jungian therapy. One double Aquarian client told me her quite detailed dream about a "castle shrouded in mist." She said that in this dream she wanted very badly to get across the bridge into the castle, "but there were all these silly mundane tasks I had to do first, like take out the garbage and balance the checkbook. Can you imagine?" Yes, I could, and I suggested she take this interesting dream to a Jungian analyst, who could surely provide a great deal of insight and amplification.

"Hmmm," said the client, "therapy is really expensive. I'd have to get a full-time job to afford it, and I can't imagine having one of those long enough!"

Freedom and independence are Uranus/related issues. Any Aquarian who is financially dependant on someone else too long wants to move on for awhile, to be free. The green phase (Earth) emphasizes prudence and planning ahead. Often the Biblical parable of the wise and foolish virgins awaiting the coming of the Divine Bridegroom occurs to me when I think of my Uranian clients. In this parable there were five wise virgins who had enough oil to keep their lamps burning and five imprudent or foolish virgins who did not. One evening, at midnight, someone called out, "the Bridegroom is coming; go and greet him." The Virgins rose and went to get their lamps.

The foolish ones said to the wise ones, "Give us some of your oil, for our lamps are going out."

Then the wise ones answered and said, "Why, there would not be enough for us and you; go to those who sell and buy for yourselves."

And while they went to buy, the bridegroom came; and those who were ready entered with him into the wedding house and the door was locked. Afterward the other Virgins also came and said, "Our Lord, Our Lord, open to us!"

But he answered and said to them, "Truly I say to you. I do not know you." Be alert, therefore, for you do not know that day, nor the hour. (Matthew 25: 8-13.)

This parable emphasizes not only alertness, but the need to occupy ourselves with the trivial and the mundane, to have enough oil on hand. Those who do not put sufficient energy into the mundane world are often treated like the foolish virgins in the parable by others who refuse to compensate for their needs. Paramahansa Yogananda also focused upon balanced living when he spoke of the importance of keeping our heads in the clouds but our feet on the ground.

At this point in the story the color scheme changes from green to red. One reason may be that the Earth near the Grail Castle is dying, turning a parched reddish brown. Another may be that since the death of his mother, whom he missed but did not try to visit, Perceval had neglected his feeling function. In *The Grail Legend* we are told that in mythology red is the color of an unintegrated feeling function. When Perceval is more in touch with his feelings, his dark mood will be dispelled and the world will seem a happier place for him. Relaxing, he will discover that the Quest, too, becomes easier.

Because we are moving from green (Earth) to red (Fire) and the integration of the Leo polarity, some background on the symbolism of the red stage is required. It's important in the Aquarian Journey because Aquarians seem very independent. Their Cup is bottomless and pours out its generous gifts to all. They do not seem to need anyone else to come along and refill it. The Lion, however, the polar extremity, is not a solitary creature. The passionate Lion needs a mate. (See Chapter 5, Leo.) Aquarius seems to hear the rumble of a different drummer, but if the path he follows leads to arid Logos, he may feel some of the same emptiness discussed in Chapter 10. To Aquarians approaching the Saturn Return who feel lonely, Wolfram von Eschenbach's poetic account of Perceval's encounter with Conduire Amour is especially recommended. In Wolfram's version of the Grail story, she vows herself to be his "friend and eternal companion." This is the ideal type of partner for Aquarius, an Eleventh House person who is friend and companion on the Quest. Over the years, so many Aquarians have told me that the spouse (or if they are too restless to remain settled down in marriage, the ex-spouse) "will always be my best friend." We will return to Conduire Amour later.

While the green phase, a mental Hermes Phase, was about learning, the red phase is about doing, acting, feeling and becoming. It's about integrating the Leo virtues, while taking care not to integrate the Leo excesses at the same time. The squire, having mastered the Code of Chivalry (or at least memorized it), hones his sword play and other skills, vows his oath to King and Quest, sets forth to earn his sword, armor, and knightly title. In alchemy the red phase is about purifying the dross for its final transformation into gold, the end result of the work.

In real life, the red phase means entering the fray with passion and enthusiasm, joining in the competition, performing great deeds, winning the respect of one's fellows through demonstrating one's courage. Sometimes the knight is wounded and bleeds, or causes others to bleed while proving himself (thus the connection of the red phase with blood). Esoterically, if the knight is of a higher consciousness, he bleeds for others as Christ did, feeling the pain of suffering humanity and opening the way to Paradise for them. Sometimes, like the Fisher king, his wound bleeds because of his own pride or stubbornness. In life there are years of pain and sorrow, as well as years of great joy and happiness; therefore, the red or blood color is symbolically used to indicate human emotions, passionate feelings.

Red objects often symbolize desire or yearning and are inter-preted according to the reader's level of consciousness. The red wine in Omar Khayyam's *Rubaiyyat*, for instance, can be interpreted as an inducement to get drunk and forget your problems or as symbolic of a soul in an altered state of consciousness, drunk in the ecstasy of union with God. Victorian readers saw hedonism in the *Rubaiyyat*, but a Bengali (Hindu) reader, used to the symbolism of wine and rap-ture in mystical poetry, would see what the Sufi author intended. The red rose also appears often as a symbol of yearning for love, human and Divine. Its strong sensual fragrance can refer to sexual passion, or the opening of its petals (the human heart) toward Spirit. On both levels we have a powerful feeling symbol.

The color red is also associated with spiritual, as well as material, power. In India, power is Shakti, the Great Goddess, who keeps the world of Maya in existence by her passionate, creative, wild dance. She is sometimes called Kali, the Dark One, but when her force, her power, is revealed, artists paint her dark red. This spellbinding power of Maya is what Perceval encountered in the red-cloaked Star Lady who tried to bind him to her with seductive ruses.

When the knight has passed through the alchemical oven or the battlefield, has faced his strongest emotions and gotten in touch with his deepest passions, he acquires this power. Desire, pain, pleasure, anger, and other strong emotions are very powerful. The cerebral Aquarian becomes human, becomes Whole, when he experiences them during his red phase on the battlefield, and also in contact with his Anima, his feminine side. In the green phase the *mind* is sharp-ened, but in the red the *heart* is opened.

The knight loses his innocence during the red phase. He may, like Perceval, feel shame or embarrassment, or he may feel anger. If, like Gawain, he has always been a spotless White Knight, he may be totally shocked when he meets his first anima figure and falls com-pletely under her spell. The cycle of heightened emotions may seem not only confusing, but evil, totally opposed to his better nature, to his mental control. Many Aquarians are more like Gawain than Perceval, purely cerebral. Scientists, academics, angelic minsters tend to live in a mental ivory tower. They have never integrated the Leo polarity; they have not yet gotten in touch with the Heart (Leo), the emotions. Thus, when the Spellbinder comes along and flatters them and appeals to their messianic side with "Help! I'm a damsel in distress," it's easy for them to rush down a side path, forgetting the knightly vows, abandoning the Quest—the road to the Grail Castle, and because they are good with ideas and concepts, to rationalize their behavior. The tests of the red phase are Leo tests of pride, loyalty, fidelity, power abuse, lust and courage.

Both the Fisher King and Gawain were overwhelmed by their emotions and fell under the spell of the lady from the Castle of Pride. She offered them power, or she appeared helpless, or she appealed to their lust—she has innumerable wiles. They were previously detached, objective seekers. But they soon found themselves entranced, prisoners in Chateau Orgeuilleuse in her beautiful boudoire. The Fisher King, for the sake of the Lady in Red, refused to marry the Lady whose name appeared on the Grail for him, his destined mate. Because of his pride and his stubborn self-will, his wound ached and bled. He could neither walk nor stand nor ride nor lie comfortably. Only a totally pure young knight could deliver him from her spell, possibly by asking the right questions, but also by being alert to her wiles himself, beyond her magic. The spotless Gawain spent a long, long time in her boudoire, distracted from his Quest.

Many an Aquarian, male and female alike, has been flattered and entranced by someone outside the marriage and gone off to wander down a back road in the forest with the new person. Later, several have sadly said, "If only I had not done that. My spouse was the one meant for me." It sounds very much like the Fisher King, who had the destined name on his Grail and continued to bleed for not admitting it. The Spellbinder seems to prey on people with unintegrated feelings, those who live in their heads to the exclusion of their hearts. The practical Saturn Aquarian usually exerts control, self-restraint, and keeps the structure of his marriage together. He resists the Spellbinder, generally, but still needs to work with the feeling function. The Uranus Aquarian is more likely to fall victim to the Spellbinder's flattery but also more likely to open his heart in the process.

Perceval the green young squire was in a hurry to prove himself and desirous of having his own horse, sword and armor. The arrogant Red Knight was quite capable of defeating Perceval, but made the error of failing to take him seriously. He knocked the lad off a borrowed horse with the shaft of his sword, but before he could ride off the agile Green Knight drove a sword through the eye of the Red Knight's visor. This was Perceval's first deed for Arthur. He put on the armor over his Welsh costume, refusing to compromise his background. He had a new mask, an identity to grow into.

The Red Knight had been courageous but arrogant. According to Joseph Campbell in *Creative Mythology*, he owned nearly as much territory as King Arthur and contentiously disputed some of Arthur's land. He had attended a banquet at Camelot Castle and, making a gesture of defiance for all to see, walked out with his goblet. This was a symbolic way of saying, "I intend to take what I believe to be mine." Perceval had seen him leaving in an uproar and followed him, knowing this to be an opportunity. He would be well thought of if he succeeded in avenging Arthur's honor.

The news was, however, a long time in reaching Arthur. Nobody had witnessed the scene (except one of Perceval's many maternal cousins). Whenever he was seen in the forest, he was mistaken for the knight whose armor he wore. After his failure at the Grail Castle, Cundrie the Sorceress was later to say, "Yonder Red Knight is a phony disguised as a valorous knight. He who disgraces the Round Table. A fool in Knight's clothing."

Action, then, is associated with the red phase. Deeds to help humanity, especially those in distress. An outward surge of energy. Also, of course, anger. Anger at the Red Knight on Arthur's behalf, anger at God for not helping him in spite of all his good deeds. Anger at the rule a knight has only one chance at the Grail. Later in life, the extroversion winds down with the progression into Pisces, and faith replaces the need to perform good works. Feelings and intuition are trusted at least as much as the intellect, the inner Grail more important than the outer object.

At the end of the red phase comes the red and white. This duality of heart and mind, passion and purity, male and female must somehow be reconciled or, as the Jungians would say, integrated, for Perceval to become a whole person. In Chivalry, the Perfect knight was not an ideal scholar or monk, but a flesh and blood hero who had found a noble lady to love and a worthy enemy against whom to measure himself. (The quality of his enemy was seen as an index to the quality of the knight's own level of consciousness.) The Egyptian alchemists, like the Celtic peoples, saw the need for a Seeker of Pure Truth (White Light) to be in touch with his feeling nature (the red). Sufism, too, stresses a need to seek both the light of Objective Truth and to develop the heart of a lover.

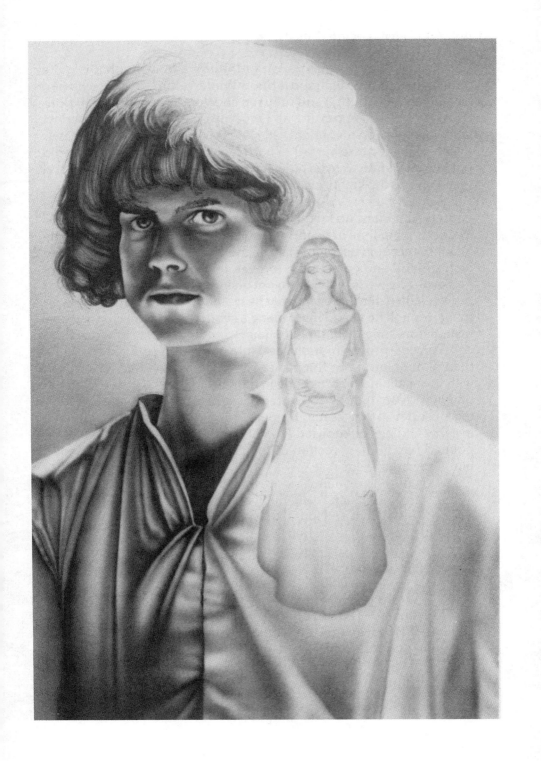

A symbol of the integration of the red and white that is quite familiar to us from childhood is Snow White, in the fairy tale, who had clear white skin (purity) and ruby red cheeks and lips (passion). Conduire (to guide) Amour (love), Perceval's Lady, also had a perfect white complexion and bright red cheeks. When he met her, she was despondent because her father had given his word to a knight she did not love that she was to be his in marriage. She was a genuine damsel in distress, as the knight was about to lay seige to her castle when Perceval arrived. Perceval performed a feat which I have seen many Uranus Aquarians do for their newfound friends. He delivered her to freedom in her time of need, then quickly went on his way before any attachment could develop, or so he thought. She, however, vowed to be his friend and companion forever; to marry no other knight but Perceval. She waited while he went off in search of the Grail. She had perfect faith in him, knowing that he would return to marry her eventually, though he would meet many a seductive sorceress and water-nixie before they would meet again.

Perceval proved more successful at integrating the red and white than either Gawain or the Fisher King. Though he had a close call with the spellbinding Star Lady in the red cloak, who also vowed her undying love to him, he converted her to his quest. Instead of remaining prisoner in her castle, he persuaded her to lend her intuitive insights and occult knowledge to his cause. In the end, she not only pointed him in the direction of the Fisher King's lake but provided him a rowboat to cross it.

As Nature personified, we are told in *The Grail Legend*, the Lady in the starry red cloak really did want him to succeed in his quest, once she tested him and found that he could not be distracted from it. Perceval passed her test when he remained loyal to his Guide in Love (Conduire Amour), the only human anima figure he encountered, interestingly enough, who was not related to him through his mother. The male teachers with all their wisdom could not help him as she could. She was his Sophia, his wise guide to the Heart.

The quality of a man's anima figure, his Guide to Love, like the quality of his best enemy, is an indicator of his level of consciousness. Conduire Amour's faithfulness and friendship speaks well for Perceval. For his part, his loyalty to her was an important part of his inner transformation.

Immediately after his service to Conduire Amour, Perceval was to meet his second friend, Gawain. Wolfram invented a poignant scene for the meeting of the White Knight and Perceval, now the Red Knight. After leaving Conduire Amour, Perceval rode through the forest, blanketed with snow. Overhead, he saw a hawk seize a goose and watched a drop of its red blood fall upon the fresh white snow. Mesmerized by this vision of the red on the white, Perceval entered into a deep trance.

Meanwhile, news had reached Arthur's camp, a few miles away in the forest, that the Red Knight, Arthur's sworn enemy, had been sighted in the vicinity. Arthur dispatched Gawain to kill the Red Knight as an example to others. As Gawain approached Perceval, he noticed that the Red Knight was "in a love trance." Gawain did not charge him. That would not have constituted a fair fight. Instead, he dropped a yellow scarf on the red spot. (Yellow was originally a separate phase of the alchemical process, but by the Middle Ages, it had been dropped.) Yellow, the color of discrimination (Virgo is connected with yellow stones, for instance), brought Perceval back to reality. He removed his helmet and shook his head in the sunlight. When Gawain saw his face, he realized that this was not the real Red Knight; this was a younger knight in the Red Knight's armor. The two rode off together and soon became friends.

Perceval thus went from moody solitude to finding two very good friends, Conduire Amour and Gawain. Surely this was better than achieving popularity with the numerous Knights of the Round Table. This is also a common Aquarian discovery; a few good friends can mean more than a great many acquaintances. The German author seems to imply that the red and white phase has ended, that feeling has been integrated. Perceval recovers from his anger at God, yet never returns to his mother's religion. He develops trust in his two new friends and his own inner voice as he continues on to the next stage of his journey, the integration of black and white.

Before going on to this dilemma, however, while on the subject of close relationships and the Leo polarity, it's important to interject a word about feelings and the courage it takes for Aquarians to discuss them in other than analytical language. Here are two remarks quoted from teenage children of Aquarians about their parents—remarks which will pretty well speak for themselves. Then, on to the next stage of Perceval's journey. If you are an Aquarian parent and these anecdotes strike home, you might read the Leo chapter (5) on the fifth sign and the Fifth House—children.

This story was related by a fourteen year-old girl:

> My mom makes me so mad. She's a double Aquarius. She refuses to talk about any topic where feelings or emotions are involved. It's like she's scared or something, so she changes the subject. She brings these weird strangers home to dinner partly for protection—so she won't have to discuss anything personal with us.
>
> One day I had a problem I really wanted to discuss with her alone. By the way, she's a brilliant person—I value her ideas and suggestions. So at breakfast I thought, "I'll make an appointment with her so we can talk."
>
> "Mom," I said, "since everyone else in the house will be gone tonight, could I talk to you alone about something? Could we just have dinner by ourselves?"
>
> She put down her toast and said, "It sounds intense."
>
> "Not all that intense," I said, "I just wanted to talk while we had some privacy."
>
> Well, at 4:30 she called. 'Will you set the table for 3 and put dinner in the microwave, please? While standing in line at the bank I met the most fascinating woman. I want you to meet my new friend because she's had such an interesting life. Bye, dear.'
>
> Somebody she just met always seems more interesting to her than her own kids. I put the stuff in the microwave, set the table for the two of them and went over to my boyfriend's house for dinner.

A similar story, from a teenage boy with an Aquarian Sun sign dad, is a slight variation of the same theme:

> I shouldn't be jealous of all these other people Dad is always helping, but darn it, I am. My earliest memories are of Dad being slapped on the back and thanked by people from civic organizations for his fundraising work. He helped provide food for the boat peoples' kids and college scholarships for poor peoples' kids and 'big brothers' for orphaned kids, but what about his own kids? Did we ever see him? No! He was always going out at night to some meeting or other to save the world. But what can you say against somebody everybody in your town looks up to as an Angel of Light?

In completing his red phase the Uranus Aquarian Angel has demonstrated his humanness in developing heart, tuning into feelings and emotion. He also moved a step closer to Wholeness, or Individuation, in Jungian terms, through integration of his feminine side when he fell in love with a human anima figure, Conduire Amour, and vowed loyalty to her as his Guide.

In Wolfram's version of the story, Perceval lives out the integration of the human and angelic, or Leo and Aquarius, to the point of having children with Conduire Amour. Joseph Campbell (*Creative Mythology*, p. 565) says something of Perceval's strength which is important for all of us in the search for individuation, on the threshold of the Age of Aquarius, the Age of Man: "there is no fixed law, no established knowledge of God set up by prophet or by priest, that can stand against the revelation of a life lived with integrity in the spirit of its own brave truth. . . ."

It was the awareness of this truth, even during the darkness of the Middle Ages, that made the Grail legend and its secret orders like Wolfram's own Knights Templars so popular. Campbell points out that although priests everywhere performed the transformation of wine into the Blood of Christ for the masses still, this delegation of the transformational work to the clergy was not enough for many seekers. This would seem to be the case today, too, as we enter the New Age and church attendance is declining. There is a tremendous magnetism, a great power to the personality that has integrated this polarity, transcended Time and Space, and stands at the last threshold—the gate of the Grail Castle itself.

We know that Perceval had lost all sense of Space and Time in the enchanted forest; he wandered in circles five years without visiting his mother, whom he missed, though he was within a few miles of her cabin on the edge of the forest. He was also chided by a group of knights and ladies for not being aware it was Good Friday, for not sheathing his sword and going barefoot to confess his sins. He told them that he had not known for a long, long time what day or week it was; he was only conscious that it had been about five years since he entered the forest.

The last threshold for the ego to cross is the hardest for a Uranus Aquarian, though—the finite mind. The Aquarian path is the path of the question "Why" and of intellectual quibbling, analyzing, categorized into black and white. Yet, the *Upanishads* inform us that Soul cannot unite with Spirit in the Vision of the One until these mental limits have been transcended. Like the orbits of Saturn and Jupiter, Uranus' mental orbit stands between us and the experience of the Grail Castle: immortality, life, love, energy, bliss, wisdom and beauty. Gaining access to the Grail Castle, recovering Paradise for humanity requires a surrender, a faith, a type of intuitive groping that is altogether beyond the orbit of mental Uranians. The Magic Castle with its collapsing drawbridges and spinning gates that confound the human mind is a very Neptunian world. It is a good thing that Perceval is still wearing the clothing of the simple Welsh Peredur under his sophisticated armor, because of his primitive instincts and superstitious faith in his intuition, his compassion for the kingdom rather than his concern for his own status at the Round Table will count in his favor the second time around. Yet he has also learned to be alert and to follow his own inner voice—to be true to himself.

In moving from the unification of Masculine/Feminine or Thinking and Feeling (the red and white) stage to the reconciliation of the black and white duality, Perceval begins a work that is quite frightening to the scientific Uranus person. He meets entities that are impossible to classify ethically as either black or white, entities that are clearly there to help him advance regardless of what they say or do. This encounter with what Jung calls the "contents of the irrational unconscious" is quite disturbing to a mentality that would rather dismiss anything with which his intellect cannot deal as mere superstition, silly and unreal. (So many scientific minds avoid the occult because of their own superstitious fears, make remarks against fields that they have never studied themselves, behave in what they themselves would otherwise call an unobjective way when discussing, for instance, astrology.)

Almost immediately after the red and white alchemical integration, the color scheme changes to black and white. Emma Jung and Marie Louise von Franz see this as a Christian dilemma. Christianity, it is true, did not admit to being flawed at all but projected its dark side on Muslims during the Crusades and fought evil as coming entirely from outside its own ranks. But one could say the same about Islam, Judaism and Zoroastrianism, all of which split off the good (white) from the evil (black) in their theologies. Only mystics were able to see, as Indris Shah pointed out in *The Sufis*, that good and evil, black and white are intertwined everywhere, in the same people, the same events and circumstances. To the mystic, without night we could never appreciate the Sun or daylight. It is through the contrast of light and dark that we learn.

Perceval does not understand this at first, however. He tries to act according to what the collective has taught him. This, after all is the rational way to proceed. In the Age of Chivalry, when one encountered a Black Knight one was pretty much bound to stop and fight, just as when one encountered a White Knight one could, logically, trust him. A Black Sorceress like Cundrie would, supposedly, never have anything positive to say; she would always be a bad omen. And the Holy Grail Maiden from the Castle would surely be an ally in the Quest. He was to learn differently, as strong Uranus people do, when this categorizing approach failed. Fortunately, he was conscious enough to catch on and shift away from logic to follow his intuition about the black and white as he drew closer to the Castle, where, like Alice through the Looking Glass, he discovered that things were not what they seemed.

Many Aquarians will ask, "Why did that psychic give me such good advice two years ago and such bad advice this year? I was sure she was a good psychic. Now this time, I wonder if she deliberately tried to mislead me?" It often comes as a shock to Uranus Aquarians that the black and white are intertwined; the same person can have a good day and later have a bad day when her intuition is off center. Or, perhaps two years ago the individual was crystal clear (white to translucent) but this year is undergoing changes in her own understanding, her own consciousness, and seems darker. It has little to do with dark intentions, with good or evil, as the black and white co-exist in us all.

This is an important alchemical stage, reconciling the black and white, not only for those of us who inherit Western religious views wherein theologians have split off the dark and light into good and evil, but for those of us who stand on the threshold of the Age of Aquarius, a mental energy age. The mind tends toward a black and white judgmentalism and we must learn to rely on our intuition about people and circumstances (even the same people in new circumstances) as much as upon our logic.

If we dismiss the black as evil we then split off our shadow side and find it hard to learn from life's events. Wolfram, with his alchemical background, invented many half black (half Muslim) blood relatives for Perceval who had some very important things to say to him; it's fortunate that he listened rather than saying, "You're an embarrassment to me. What if a knight from Arthur's court should find out we are related? Go away quickly." Racial tolerance is an important positive feature of the Aquarian personality. But tolerance of blackness, when interpreted as an ethically *wrong* opinion, is a different matter. Aquarians have said over the years: "I can tolerate her right to hold wrong opinions, but I certainly wouldn't want her around my children. She might influence them. So, I split off from her totally. Nothing to be learned there." That's unfortunate, because then there *is* nothing to be learned there, for the Aquarian.

On Perceval's journey, totally black figures like the Dead Knight, who occasionally emerged from his grave to practice jousting with passers by, were not real threats to Perceval, just distractions. Seeing the Black Knight, Perceval followed the Code and stopped to fight him. This distraction gave a White Knight, sent by the Grail Maiden from the Castle itself, a chance to steal the Star Lady's white stag and hound. Even the Holy Grail Maiden could conspire to prolong his quest. She may have thought Perceval unprepared and unworthy at this point, since he had failed to ask the question. She did not want another unworthy king in the Grail Castle, as the kingdom had suffered a good deal under the current wounded king!

Jung and von Franz interpret the white figures as defenders of the status quo at the waning of the Age of Chivalry. They have a vested interest in keeping things as they are until, at last, the strong knight that they await comes along. (By this time Gawain, too, has failed in the Grail Castle, but that is a different story.) The collective will try to hold itself together to resist the New Order until it is strong enough to take charge. Perceval had to learn this difficult lesson, taking refuge in his awareness (Uranus) and his intuition (Neptune-Pisces progression). He could not let appearances delude and distract him or deter him from the Quest. He came to understand that everything, seen and unseen, rational and irrational, was there to further the Quest, and that once he had helped the Ailing King, everything would be all right. The Grail Maiden would be his friend again.

The chessboard represents the game of life. Powerful white forces confront equally powerful black forces on a black and white field denoting an apparent ethical dilemma. In his first encounter with a magical chessboard which formerly belonged to the sorceress Morgana, Perceval was checkmated three times in a row, each time by the same invisible opponent. Frustrated, he went to the window to throw the pieces away. He didn't want to play anymore. The Star Lady came in and stopped him.

I have met many a Uranus Aquarian who wanted to throw away the chess pieces and opt out of the game of life, feeling frustrated over a temporary checkmate (set back in the outer world). Several have felt suicidal over the mind's inability to cope with, or to understand, why events happened, why their hopes and ideals seemed doomed to failure. Unlike Perceval, they were not up to immediately continuing the game; they were unready to risk another checkmate. But within the Grail Angel archetype, hope is constantly renewed from the Cup, and after some time out from life they were soon back in the game, facing those gray areas that the mind will never fully grasp. They seemed more surrendered, more humbled, more prepared for the next stage. (Because of his humility, Perceval, unlike Gawain, was not seduced by flattery and trapped in the Castle of Pride. Thus, he succeeded in the end.)

During the Pisces Progression, which is connected with surrender to the Guide and to God, as well as the Grail, whether the Aquarian relates to the Wine as lower Neptune intoxication, or as the Divine Bliss of spiritual ecstasy, he usually suspends asking his questions and says with Omar Khayyam:

> You know my friends, with what a brave Carouse I made a Second Marriage in my house; Divorced old barren Reason from my Bed, And took the Daughter of the Vine to Spouse.
> For 'Is' and 'Is-not' though with Rule and Line, And 'Up-and Down' by Logic I define, Of all that one should care to fathom, I Was never deep in anything but wine.
> (*Rubaiyyat* LV, LVI)

The shift from reason (Uranus) to Neptune (wine, or ecstasy) has much to do with the introverted shift away from House Eleven (goals) toward House Twelve (solitude, meditation) and sometimes occurs when Neptune square natal Neptune follows quickly upon Uranus opposite Uranus, or during the motion of the progressed Sun from Aquarius to Pisces. Omar Khayyam himself made a mid-life career shift from mathematician and calendar reformer to Sufi mystic, much to the annoyance of his fellow professors, who could not imagine why he would go off to sit at the feet of some uneducated Sheik (Spiritual Guide). This search for the lost Paradise, for the return from exile, need not literally coincide with Uranus opposite Uranus in the lives of scientific Aquarians, but often does.

Perceval also sees a lady on a black and white horse (the instincts are two kinds—good and bad), birds overhead, some black and white (souls are of either type), and humans of mixed races. Perhaps the most interesting black figure is the Sorceress Cundrie, with dark magical powers, yellow teeth, a humpback and a gossipy tongue. It is she who tells Arthur and his court that Perceval failed on his first attempt at the Grail Castle and is not really the powerful Red Knight but a phony in disguise. Yet, it is the same Cundrie who appears at his final bridge (transcendence) to the Grail Castle. On her black hood are twelve white turtle doves and an embroidered Golden Grail. It is when they see Cundrie on her Arabic steed riding with the young hero that the servants of the Ailing King shout, "we are delivered!" Cundrie is the other side of the lovely young Grail Maiden and apparently she's an older, wiser side.

Caitlin Matthews' essay "Sophia, Companion on the Quest," (in *Table of the Grail*) presents Cundrie as Lady Sovereignty, the land itself, the Earth Mother and the kingdom about whom Perceval is really concerned. She is the type of bewitched old hag who is transformed into a beautiful young princess in Celtic fairy tales by a hero of pure heart who sees through appearances and loves her. Intuitively, Perceval values her aid in the Grail Quest in spite of her harsh way with him at court. He trusts her help across the hazardous bridge and in defeating the guardians of the Old Age who try to keep him out of the Castle. It is partially because of his trust in Cundrie, as well as his love for Conduire Amour, that he wins through. The spell will be lifted from the castle if he asks his question—if he is *both* conscious and compassionate enough.

Perceval, interestingly, has remained true to his Welsh heritage as well as what was useful in the British Code of Chivalry. He values Cundrie's magic and is not afraid of dangerous revolving bridges that rotate as he tries to cross them or of bridges that collapse behind him. He retains his Celtic sympathy, yet on his second entrance, having transcended (bridged) the opposites, he is determined to ask the right question. In the German version the poet Wolfram has him encounter his noble black and white (Muslim) half-brother Feirefiz on the final passage over the mirrored bridge to the Castle Gate. (The mirror is also our view of self, objectively speaking. It is a good Uranus symbol for awareness. The outer world is our mirror at any stage of our journey—the outer perspective on, or confirmation of, our progress.)

Perceval sees a black and white knight and begins to fight with him. Then, suddenly, he recognizes that it is his noble half-brother, the Muslim, Feirefiz. Feirefiz, too, has won access to the Grail castle. Once inside the Castle, Perceval realizes that he can see the Holy Grail Stone (it's a stone, not a chalice, in Wolfram's version, but it lies on a gold dish on the almarach, held by the Grail Maiden). Happy that he is not blinded by its light, as was Sir Lancelot, who was not yet ready for the experience, Perceval turns eagerly to share the majestic vision with Feirefiz. His half-brother, however, is unable to see the Grail at all. He is spellbound by the blue eyes of the Grail maiden— totally entranced.

A second maiden comes forward to explain to Perceval that Feirefiz has not been initiated (baptized a Christian), and thus he cannot see the Grail. Gingerly, Perceval explains that the Muslim must accept the Holy Trinity (which must have seemed polytheistic to him) before he can see the Grail. Feirefiz asks only, "Is *she* a Christian? (meaning the Grail Maiden). If so, and if she will then be able to marry me, I'll gladly be baptized." The Grail Stone tips over to fill a Baptismal Font and Feirefiz is initiated. It is interesting that inside the Castle, love alone seems to matter.

It's very much like what Omar Khayyam wrote about his altered state of consciousness, his intoxication with the Divine Wine, which took him beyond the world of the Islamic theologians:

Lately by the Tavern Door agape, Came shining through the Dusk an Angel Shape Bearing a Vessel on his Shoulder; and he bade Me taste of it and t'was The Grape.

The Grape that can with Logic Absolute The two-and-seventy jarring sects confute; The sovereign alchemist that in a trice Life's leaden metal into Gold transmutes.

(LVIII and LIX)

Feirefiz and Perceval together went to the Grail Table and watched the Grail Procession. This time, Perceval insisted that he be allowed to ask his question before eating or getting involved in anything else by way of distraction. The ailing King had the green cloak brought for him but insisted that he first mend a broken magic sword. (Gawain, in another version, had previously been in the Castle and failed to fix the sword.) Perceval fixed it, but the King said seriously, "I'm afraid the crack is still visible where you repaired it. You did not succeed!" Perceval sadly but humbly accepted that and began to ask his question anyway. After this demonstration of humility, the king laughed and sprang up, healed. The land instantly turned green around the Castle, even before Perceval finished asking. He had been conscious, humble, and compassionate. He had been loyal to his Guide (Conduire Amour). He had transcended duality. He had earned the answer to his question, which included the secret that *he* was the heir to the Grail Throne with all its powers. The ailing King was his mother's brother. Though it was his destiny, he could not simply inherit the Grail Castle and its treasure; he had to earn it, to be worthy of it. Otherwise the castle would have had another wounded, ailing King, who had not transcended red and white or black and white. But Perceval, through his inner transformation, had not only inherited the Castle's treasure, but had avoided the ailing King's wound.

We come now to perhaps the most interesting question for the New Age. What did Perceval do with the Power, with the Grail Treasure, the magic stone (or chalice)? In Wolfram's version he served on a Grail Brotherhood Board, composed of other Grail Kings who had been Self-Realized before him, for the good of humanity—this sounds very Aquarian. The French monastic author had him retire to a hermitage for a few years until the death of his maternal uncle, the King whom he had healed and freed. Perceval then ruled from the Castle and after awhile was ascended into heaven, taking the Grail with him. Jung and von Franz believe this meant that the author did not know how else to end the legend but to have the contents of the unconscious (*The Grail*) return to the unconscious (heaven) rather than remain on Earth as powers we could all access. In other words, the Middle Ages were not ready for the message. (Wolfram wrote several hundred years later than the French monastic.)

In other versions, in later centuries, a new mini-legend was added to the structure. Judas' seat, permanently vacant since the death of Christ, had been awaiting the approach of the Grail Knight and the Treasure (the Grail) to restore harmony. Perceval left the Grail castle and took the treasure back to the Last Supper Round Table where it belonged. We thus have a complete mandala, the circular table, with the treasure in the center. In *Psychology and Alchemy* (p. 181, figure 88), Jung has a representation of this Table. Humanity will benefit from the completion of the Table, or so we assume.

On the threshold of the New Age, it seems that once again the unconscious contents of the Grail are seeking to become conscious so that the final bridge will transcend religious dogmatism and lead to a more direct experience of the Divine. Grail Angels seem to abound and bring pieces of the message through channels to mankind. We must develop our Uranian awareness though and stay awake, be alert to what all this means, for surely the black and the white are intertwined. Sincerity, integrity, courage, humility and the other Leo/Aquarian virtues are reemphasized, and one must determine when to ask questions and when to surrender the mind's limited, or narrow need to understand everything along the way. The Neptunian virtues of faith, intuition, compassion and sympathy for the dying kings of the old age are also important. Inside the castle one is in a Neptunian world totally beyond the mental orbit of Uranus. (See Chapter 12, Pisces.)

The Pisces progression is important in the life of an Aquarian. He can develop psychic, meditational abilities at this time, or he can waste it in the lower cycle of Neptune—drugs, alcohol, escapism. He can move through the arts into an appreciation of the aesthetic value for Neptune and try to bridge the Grail Castle from there. Because the Piscean progression is a quieter, more introverted cycle, Aquarius, who wants to help humanity (his friends) may not understand how to function during it, as he is accustomed to more extroverted energy. The Aries progression will ordinarily feel more comfortable, as it is mental, active, and extroverted again.

Aquarians in this cycle often remark that they have so much more physical energy than ever before, though it sometimes comes quite late in life. This gives them strength to be Grail Angels, too. I have met only a few esoteric Aquarians who lived into the Taurean progression, but each of them told me he or she "felt privileged to have seen the realization of the dream—the manifestation on Earth in solid form (Taurus) of a fellowship program for scientific research, of a foundation for community service to the poor, or of the spiritual organization to which they had dedicated their lives." In the Taurean progression, Aquarius returns to its natal Fixity, feels a familiar sense of conviction about his principles, the quality of his work, of his chosen life path that is a joy to see.

It seems that during the Pisces progression the inner work is accomplished; thus, at this stage, it's important for Aquarius to surround himself with good friends and guides—people who bring out the best in Aquarius. It is during this phase that Aquarians often become less interested in Old Age sciences, and seek to become involved in New Age studies. Guides are often found in the Pisces progression. Caitlin Matthews' essay in *Table of the Grail* concludes that Sophia, or Sapientia the Wise Guide will constantly remind us of the Lost Paradise, of the inner treasure from which we are exiled, and intensify our search for it, rather than distract us from it with idle, tangential side quests. With intuition reinforced in the Piscean progression Aquarius is likely to choose a guide who will show him what he needs to know, though it may sometimes be painful to hear.

Aquarius, with its innate desire to serve mankind and be popular, needs to be careful around guides who are too flattering. Cundrie, the black witch with the white turtledoves on her hood, was valuable because despite her gossipy nature, she told the truth as she saw it, bluntly. Conduire Amour was, of course, an Ideal, a guide to life, to the heart qualities. The Grail maiden, who wields the treasure, may represent purity of motive. One wants to find the Grail for others, as well as for the sake of one's own realization. This altruism, and the humility that is disinterest in Ego status, augmented by Piscean compassion, wins out in the end.

While in the Old Age doing and achieving were valued by the collective (the old ideal of dharma, as defined by one's parents and religious authorities) the New Age seems to hold more to Individual Realization, and to respect what Joseph Campbell calls "people of integrity who adhere to their own truth." The Grail, as vessel, cauldron or stone, is a feminine symbol. One hopes that feminine values will be important in the Age of the Grail vessel; that *who we are* will be as important as *what we* accomplish, scientifically or otherwise.

The Castle of the Grail is the "heaven that lies within" in the Biblical teaching. Christian parables about the Inner Kingdom often use imagery that strongly resembles the Buddhist—for instance, the "pearl of great price," and the "jewel in the lotus" (of the heart). In both systems, the inner treasure is the most important, and is hidden. (In Christ's parable, it is referred to as buried in a field. Again this field is most likely the human heart, which is also Omar Khayyam's "tavern," according to Mr. Bjerregaard, the Sufi commentator.)

The Chandogya Upanishad says, on the subject of Castles:

> In the Center of the Castle of Brahma,
> Our own Body,
> There is a small shrine, in the form of a lotus-flower
> and within can be found a small space.
> We should find who dwells there and
> Want to know him. . . for the whole universe
> is in him, and he dwells in our heart. (Penguin edition)

One can sympathize with the Frenchmen who attempted to conclude the Grail legend after the death of Chretien de Troyes! It's a personal search for Love and Light, as the Sufis put it, and a search for objective Truth—that seemingly elusive Uranian goal. Like the Fisher King with his rod in the Lake, we must go within (the lake of the unconscious) and fish, as well as ask our questions of Guides in the Outer World.

Sri Yukteswar, in *The Holy Science*, tells us that from the time of Galileo to the beginning of Dwapara Yuga in 1899 (the Skanda, or 200-year bridge between Kali Yuga and Dwapara Yuga), mankind became more conscious of electricity and the workings of electrical currents. He predicted that in the new Yuga (after 1899) scientists would rapidly advance in their understanding of electricity and its uses. In the same book, he speaks of the electrical intellectual body sheath. There are five sheaths we must penetrate to find the Self and the next to last one is the mental electrical. Beyond that sheath is Chitta, the heart's love, the Self. Since 1899, as Sri Yukteswar predicted, mankind had become increasingly knowledgeable about electricity and has rapidly invented many useful things.

It is interesting that Uranus was discovered in 1781, and that it rules electricity and the electric mental body. Synchronistically, Benjamin Franklin conducted experiments in grounding electricity with lightning rods and kites close to the time of the discovery of Uranus.

Neptune was discovered in 1846 as scientists had observed that something (Neptune) was pulling upon Uranus, and causing irregularities in its orbit pattern. This pull that Neptune exerts on Uranus is esoterically quite interesting. It means that the erratic but insightful planet, Uranus, has its mental energy pulled upon by a psychic planet, a planet connected from earliest times with the ocean (the unconscious), from the Celtic world to Greece to the Orient. The most conscious, rational energy is pulled upon by Neptune. Yet, the one is altruistic (Uranus) and the other compassionate (Neptune), so there's a commonality here, as well.

Neptune perhaps tries to open the orbit of Uranus (in which so many New Age people dwell) to the psychic, the imaginative, the power of the unconscious contents. The glyph of Pisces (♓), it has been suggested, is two worlds, the sphere of Heaven backed up against the sphere of Earth and connected with a silver cord. Then the psychic energy and the rational energy can influence each other, or seep together perhaps, through the cord that links them. If we look at the lives and the world view of people with some natal planets in both Pisces and Aquarius, or with contacts of both these outer planets to Sun, Moon, Ascendant strong in the personalities, this pull can be seen. We have an otherworldly soul, a Grail Angel in such cases, who may not understand the Old Age at all, but who will live a productive life in the new one. In the Grail castle, Heaven and Earth came together and God descended to contact Humanity. We hope that the bridge from the Age of Pisces to the Age of Aquarius will witness this as well. Alice Bailey says in *Labours of Hercules* (Aquarius), that Christ's eleventh commandment, "Love thy neighbor as thyself for the love of God" will represent the bridge between the two Ages.

In what sign is Uranus exalted? Which is the best House location apart from its own Eleventh House? As Hindu astrologers have pointed out, it's only been 200 or so years since the planet's discovery, scarcely sufficient time to make a determination. Yet, it's always interesting to speculate. My own client experience has led me to conclude that the Third House is a quite powerful (exalted) position for Uranus. I have, over the years, met many brilliant, innovative people with Uranus in the Third, which is of course, Gemini in the natural zodiac.

One could make a strong case for Uranus in Gemini as the exaltation from the social impact of the 1960's generation alone. This very verbal generation reached adulthood during the idealistic years of the Kennedy presidency and sought to volunteer their time in programs like the Peace Corps and Vista. Later, during the Johnson administration (the Great Society domestic programs), they went to college and graduate school in record numbers, preparing themselves to make the world a better place through social work, teaching, and other professions involving communication (Gemini). Many of them were liberal to the point of radicalism. Those who were not fought the Vietnam war with similar idealism and conviction. (This generation is still fighting the war through the American movie industry twenty years later, seeking to understand it intellectually now that the dust has settled.) Many Uranus in Gemini clients sought an outlet for humanitarian idealism in World Brotherhood Communities during the 1970's. Group consciousness was advanced in these communities where like-minded people (Uranian "friends") gathered to meditate and serve. Many are still living in the rural areas year round, but greater numbers are, in the 1980's, returning to urban environments to communicate their message on the cusp of the New Age. The psychic contents of the Grail will likely pour forth to mankind as a result of the efforts of this generation.

Clients with Uranus in the Third House (Gemini in the natural zodiac) manifest many of the same characteristics as the Uranus in Gemini generation. They tend to be idealistic, future oriented, positive thinkers (unless Saturn is involved by aspect or Capricorn is strong in the natal chart), interested in New Age awareness and alternatives. This is a clinical, scientific placement. Many are doing research and development projects, making discoveries in out-of-the-mainstream systems of education and psychology, as well as New Age sciences. Several are interested in research in the structure of crystals as background for subtler techniques of New Age healing. These people are on the cutting edge of innovation and discovery for the New Age. The negative effect of the Third House exaltation is restlessness (unless Uranus is in a Fixed sign), impatience with the red tape of academia in the Old Age and a tendency to scatter the energy. In the individual horoscope planets in Earth or Fixity will help to ground the Uranian current.

Though astrologers have not had the opportunity to study people with Uranus in Virgo, we can tell from the power of Uranus in the Sixth House that this, too, is a likely position for the exaltation. Here, Uranus' insights can strengthen a mundane house, bringing genius to a serviceful area. The combination of Uranus and Virgo, altruism and service, is auspicious. Virgo Earth (House Six in the natural zodiac) grounds the erratic currents of Uranus and facilitates practical application of its ideals and insights better than the airy Gemini placement. Many clients with a Sixth House Uranus have had nervous tension (the health facet of House Six) in the aura until they could, in fact, find a way to apply their Uranus to out-of-the-mainstream education or healing, find a product or service that provided an outlet for Uranus.

Regardless of the position of Uranus in the chart, people are coming to the astrologer more frequently now to ask, "What is my work to be in the New Age?" This question seems to be the modern equivalent of "What is the Grail and whom does it serve?" To an extent, Uranus' House, Sign and aspects in the individual horoscope can help formulate the answer. More important, however, is the intuitional level, the level of awareness in the querant. Did he ask what his work was to be, for instance, or did he ask what his *important* work was to be, implying that he expected the Grail Angel to descend, through the astrologer or through a psychic, and supply it so that he could then become acknowledged as a New Age leader overnight? If the latter, then there may be too much Old Age materialism and competitive mentality left over in this person. In spite of his high intelligence and stimulating ideas, he may be in for a rude awakening. Others probably will not take him seriously, at least not for long.

In *Labours Of Hercules*, Alice Bailey states that those who have not suffered much themselves in life, those Uranians who have had it too easy, are not ready to move beyond the egotism of the Old Age. They are still seeking personal recognition as leaders; they are not thinking impersonally about what's good for the group, for humanity.

Too fascinated with themselves, they are still caught up in the desire nature. (See "Aquarius," p. 88 of *Labours*.) They need to transcend the Leo or Solar philosophy in which they are the Sun and others are the planets orbiting around them to expand towards a universal attunement to the greater good. (Jungian psychologists have said the same of healers. People who are themselves wounded are better able to counsel others in pain.) Yet, it would also seem that Uranians in their humanitarian expansiveness still require Leo's ability to see an individual's need—the exception to the Universal Rule. The line between Uranian detachment and indifference is sometimes finely drawn.

Jupiter, esoteric ruler of Aquarius and of the New Age, adds kindness and compassion to the high mental principles and scientific objectivity of Uranus. It helps Uranus expand his brilliant mind in a positive direction rather than to expand or inflate his Ego. As the classical ruler of Pisces prior to Neptune's discovery, Jupiter is a spiritual, generous-natured planet. It brings love, as well as light. But Jupiter and Uranus are future oriented, free spirited, spontaneous, and concerned with objective Truth. Both operate on a universal, mass-consciousness level. Both are associated with illumination. (Zeus with the lightning bolt; Uranus with electrical current.) Jupiter, however, is Guru in Hindu astrology. Jupiter fills Aquarius' Cup with Ananda (joy or bliss) and brings him peace of mind—freedom from intellectual quibbles. (See the *Rubaiyyat, in toto*.) We live in an exciting period, as these two planets move in trine to one another in 1987. We are rapidly advancing into the Age of Aquarius.

With these two rulers of Aquarius in trine overhead, Soul is coming forward in many Seekers and taking charge of the personality. In the mass consciousness, too, there are signs of greater awareness of, and interest in, the coming age. People have been interested in dream messages and mythology for many years, of course, as well as in meditation. But a remarkable movie, immensely popular, revealed the receptivity of the mass consciousness to the symbols of the New Age, and especially the Grail. "Raiders of the Lost Ark" not only did well at theaters, but continues to be purchased for home viewing on VCRs. The theme is quite similar to the Quest for the Grail. The Ark is a lost treasure that connects Humanity to the Divine, a spiritual source of power and abundance, a type of Grail. It, too, is a link between God and his chosen ones, formerly kept in a sacred place,

Solomon's Temple (similar to the Holy Grail Castle). In "Raiders," the hero and heroine faced great perils with even greater courage to recover the treasure. The characters also went through some inner changes as a result of their search.

Currently, channeling is extremely popular. A great many mediums are putting people in touch with entities from various Ages, planets, even levels of consciousness, including Angels. The Archangel Michael is one Source. This, too, is reminiscent of the Grail Angel and his message of hope for the future of mankind and of the joy he brought. People seem so much more open now about their search for a direct experience of God, or at least indirect contact with a heavenly Messenger. They have all types of questions to ask, Aquarius-like, ranging from the ultimate purpose in life to the name of the soul mate and the future of their finances. It seems so much more exciting than Sunday Service at the "Old Age" Church.

The difficulty, if there is one, with a trine overhead between two educational planets like Jupiter and Uranus, is the sheer abundance of messages and messengers, some of which seem to conflict with others. After awhile it's important to pull back, to detach from all the outer information into one's center and listen to one's own Inner Voice. This alone can validate the outer information; then, one can assimilate and apply it. For New Age people who are in touch with the Inner Voice, the time is ripe to participate, according to their Uranian talents in the service of the New Age, because mass awareness, readiness, receptivity, is building.

Questionnaire

How does the Aquarius archetype express itself? Though this relates particularly to those with the Sun in Aquarius or Aquarius rising, anyone could apply this series of questions to the House where his Uranus is located or the House which has Aquarius (or Aquarius intercepted) on the cusp. The answers to these questions will indicate how in touch the reader is with his Uranus, his ingenious/willful mind and his altruistic instincts.

1. As a child, adults considered me rebellious because I asked the question "why"
   a. Almost always.
   b. Some of the time.
   c. Hardly ever.

2. I value freedom
   a. most highly.
   b. somewhat.
   c. not very highly.

3. I get along with people from all sorts of social, educational and economic backgrounds. I consider my behavior broad-minded
   a. 80% of the time.
   b. 50% of the time.
   c. 25% of the time or less.

4. When my ideas are challenged others see me as uncompromising and willful
   a. 80% of the time.
   b. 50% of the time.
   c. 25% of the time or less.

5. When under stress the part of my body that causes me most trouble is
   a. I'm generally healthy.
   b. Central nervous system.
   c. Ankles or circulation.

6. My greatest fear is
   a. rejection by my friends.
   b. not being invited to a function most of my friends were attending.
   c. not being clearly understood.

7. The greatest obstacle to my success comes from
   a. circumstances beyond my control.
   b. within myself.

8. Important to me are such Aquarian interests as group projects, friends, and freedom. These are
   a. very important.
   b. mostly important.
   c. not very important.

9. I am considered quite inventive or original by
   a. 80% of the people I meet.
   b. 50% of the people I meet.
   c. 25% of the people I meet.

10. As a young person I fantasized about doing great things for humanity through a scientific discovery, philanthropic organization, or the ministry, etc. This was a
    a. strong desire.
    b. moderate desire.
    c. I don't remember such a desire.

Those who scored five or more (a) answers are highly in touch with Uranus on the mundane level. Those who have scored five or more (c) answers need work in the House where Uranus resides or rules. Those who answered (b) to question number seven need to work at formulating their questions properly as they pursue the Quest.

Where is the balance point between Aquarius and Leo? How does Aquarius integrate the Lion's Heart into his analytical kingdom? Cosmic altruism and the ability to relate to the person next door. Though this refers particularly to those with the Sun in Aquarius or Aquarius rising, all of us have Uranus and the Sun somewhere in our horoscope. Many of us have planets in the Fifth and the Eleventh

Houses. For all of us, the polarity from Aquarius to Leo involves the ability to relate on both the universal and the personal levels.

1. When something is bothering me personally I
   a. keep it to myself.
   b. sometimes discuss it with my friends.
   c. talk about it until it stops hurting.

2. Though I am the first one to volunteer my time for a charitable or civic function, I am apt to overlook the needs of those closest to me
   a. 80% of the time.
   b. 50% of the time.
   c. 25% of the time or less.

3. I take the opportunity to use my creative gifts
   a. seldom.
   b. half the time.
   c. nearly always.

4. I consider my ability to relate to children to be
   a. poor.
   b. fair.
   c. good.

5. My approach to life is
   a. mostly analytical.
   b. a blend of analysis and feeling.
   c. through feeling.

Those who scored three or more (b) answers are doing a good job with personality integration of the Aquarian/Leo polarity. Those who scored three or more (c) answers may need to work more consciously on developing natal Uranus in their horoscopes. Those who have three or more (a) answers may be out of balance in the other direction. Study both Uranus and the Sun in the natal chart. Which is stronger by House position, or by location in its sign of rulership or exaltation? Is either in detriment, intercepted, or in its fall? Are there any major aspects to the Sun? Aspects to the weaker planet will help point the way to its integration.

What does it mean to be an esoteric Aquarian? How does Aquarius integrate expansive Jupiter, its esoteric ruler, into the personality? Every Aquarius will have both Uranus and Jupiter somewhere in the horoscope. The well-integrated Jupiter adds compassion to the analytical Aquarian personality. Answers to the following questions help indicate the extent to which Aquarius is in touch with Jupiter.

1. I consciously try to be loving as well as analytical in my personal relationsips
   a. most of the time.
   b. some of the time.
   c. hardly ever.

2. I make my decisions based upon intuition as well as logic
   a. 80% of the time.
   b. 50% of the time or more.
   c. about 25% of the time.

3. If I am cut off (dismembered) from my friends, I
   a. keep on going forward with faith.
   b. retreat for awhile and brood on human fickleness.
   c. keep my "creative ideas" to myself in the future.

4. My motivation in working for humanity is
   a. the result of my contact with the Self.
   b. in part for personal glory and part for the good itself.
   c. to impress others and win friends.

5. When I do service for an organization I
   a. work well with all for the common good.
   b. try to compromise.
   c. always serve in my own way.

Those who have scored three or more (a) answers are in touch with their esoteric ruler. Those who scored three or more (b) answers need more work at integrating Jupiter's flexibility and consideration. They may need to get more in touch with their intuition through the House where Jupiter resides and the Houses Jupiter rules—Sagittarius and Pisces. Those who scored three or more (c) answers should study their natal Jupiter. Is it intercepted, retrograde, in fall, in detriment? Jupiter rules two Mutable signs and facilitates compromise and cooperation in Fixed Aquarius.

References

Alice Bailey, *Esoteric Astrology*, Lucis Publications, New York, 1976

Alice Bailey, *Labours Of Hercules*, Lucis Publications, London, 1977

C.H.A. Bjerregaard. Hafiz Edition of the *Sufi Interpretation of the Rubaiyyat of Omar Khayyam*, J.F. Taylor and Co., New York, 1902

J.C. Cooper, *Chinese Alchemy: The Taoist Quest for Immortality*, Aquarian Press, Wellingborough, 1984

E.A. Burtt, *Teachings of the Compassionate Buddha*, Mentor Publications, New York, 1955

Joseph Campbell, *Creative Mythology*, Penguin Books, New York, 1968

Joseph Campbell, *Flight of the Wild Gander*, Viking Press, New York, 1969

Mircea Eliade, *Yoga, Immortality and Freedom*, Princeton University Press, Princeton, 1969

Edward Fitzgerald, *The Rubaiyyat of Omar Khayyam*, Eben Frances Thompson, Boston, 1899

Emma Jung and Marie Louise von Franz, *The Grail Legend*, Sigo Press, Boston, 1980

Caitlin Matthews, "Sophia, Companion on the Quest," in *Table of the Grail*, Rutledge and Kegan Paul, London, 1984

John Matthews, "Temple of the Grail," in *Table of the Grail*, Rutledge and Kegan Paul, London, 1984

The New Testament According to the Eastern Text, (George M. Lamsa, transl.), Philadelphia, 1940

Sallie Nichols, *Jung and the Tarot*, Samuel Weiser, New York, 1980

T.W. Rolleston, *Myths and Legends of the Celtic Race*, Constable Press, London, 1985

Indries Shah, *The Sufis*, Octagon Press, London 1984

The Upanishads, "Chandoyga Upanishad," Penguin Press. New York, 1975

Swami Sri Yukteswar, *The Holy Science*, Self Realization Fellowship Press, Los Angeles, 1974

Heinrich Zimmer, Myths and Symbols in Indian Art and Civilization, Princeton Press, New Jersey, 1974

12 PISCES:
The Search for the Castle of Peace

The Sun enters Pisces between February 19th and 21st and remains until about March 21st. Pisces is the last of the four Mutable signs—Mutable Water. As the cosmic ocean of infinity, it is boundless and universal, for as William Blake wrote, "Who shall bind the Infinite?" Sensitive, caring, and adaptable, Pisces is the last sign of the zodiac, the last of the Twelve Houses, and the end of the astrological year. Spiritually, the Pisces lifetime is about dissolving of attachment without losing contact with feelings of kindness and compassion.

Though our modern zodiac represents Pisces as two fish swimming in opposite directions, through the ages many cultures chose the dolphin to symbolize Pisces. The dolphin was sacred to three different gods—Apollo, Poseidon, and Dionysius. Because the dolphin was known for its helpfulness to man, its kindness, its mercy, and even for its healing qualities, it seems an appropriate choice for Pisces. Two dolphins swimming in opposite directions are painted on the walls of the queen's chamber in King Minos' palace in Crete. Similar dolphins appear on the zodiac wheel far away in the ruins of Wadi-Hesa, near Palestine. Dolphin lore must have been widespread and popular in the ancient world for dolphins to turn up in the desert, so far removed from the sea that few people would ever have had occasion to see one.

In the Greek story of Telemachus, son of the epic hero Odysseus, we hear of his rescue from drowning by a dolphin which was then chosen to appear on the family shield. In Homer's beautiful "Hymn to Dionysius" we read that pirates captured the young god thinking him a prince's handsome son. They tried to bind his hands and intended to hold him for ransom. Dionysius broke free and turned their masts

487

to grape vines. He then threw the pirates overboard and turned them into dolphins. Even to this day dolphins are said to retain a memory of their former lives as men and congregate around ships, helpfully directing little fishes into sailor's nets. As three Greek gods held the dolphin sacred, few Greeks would harm the creature. In the Near East, however, dolphins were supposedly used in homeopathic remedies. Thus they were linked to healing, and Pisces to a healing sign.

In Roman times, Pliny told the story of the boy and the dolphin, which connected the sea creature to death and the afterlife. This story evokes such a powerful image in the unconscious that even today we see fountains featuring the boy and the dolphin. In Pliny's story, a small boy, very likely an orphan, went each day to feed a dolphin and enjoyed a ride on its back. One day when its human friend failed to appear, the dolphin went in search of him. It finally found the child, drowned. The dolphin brought the boy to shore and remained with him to die itself. On Greek funerary vases, Hermes, Guide to Souls and the dolphin appeared together, the two friends to mankind who aided departed souls to find their way in the afterlife.

The dolphin's is a peculiarly Piscean type of kindness, for it lay down next to the boy and died. It did not distinguish between its own life, its own interests, and the boy's. In the cosmic ocean of feeling, there are no boundaries, no limits between one creature and another. A Pisces hearing a friend tell of his pain will soon be in tears along with the friend out of sympathy and empathy. If Pisces lies down and dies with the person rather than distancing himself mentally (establishing boundaries) it becomes difficult to help the friend find a solution or a way to cope with the problem.

So it seems important when a Pisces friend or client says, "I want to find a compassionate profession and help suffering humanity; do you think I would be a good psychologist, or a good astrologer?" to look for the Air element in his or her chart. Can the person distance himself from others' pain? Is there objectivity? Is there a clear, unafflicted Mercury (the polarity of Neptune). Or, if Neptune is in an Angular House (1, 4, 7 or 10) or if it aspects the person's Mercury, Sun, or Moon, it may be better to ask him, "Do you feel drained when people tell you negative things about their suffering or their pain? How would you feel at the end of an entire day of others' problems? Or a week? Several years? This merging with others' moods and feelings, if it is already tiring to Pisces/Pisces rising, is likely to prove

discouraging and exhausting when Pisces sees the sadness a social worker, astrologer, psychologist, or other counselor encounters. A Pisces with his Mercury in nearby Aquarius, however, will have the requisite objectivity.

Before dwelling, as we must, on the issue of duality, so important for the Pisces archetype, one point needs clarification. Pisces/Pisces rising is idealistic. It cannot betray a strong feeling or intuition without tremendous anxiety or guilt. This is true no matter how ambivalent or even how extremely wishy-washy this dualistic Mutable sign appears to be to others. This is an absolutist personality at heart. I think the following story of a close encounter between two absolutists proceeding from vastly different altruistic philosophies illustrates this well.

Many years ago an Aquarian man who was going through his Pisces progression (see Chapter 11) became quite interested in music and began to attend concerts regularly. At a post concert party he met a woman, an attractive Pisces harpist, and invited her to dinner. They dated for about three months and discovered that they not only had a common interest in music but also shared a mutual idealism, a desire to make this world a better place. One evening, as they were discussing the wedding date, she happened to ask, "by the way, what do you actually do all day long? I know that you're a laboratory scientist, but I can't really imagine what that means. I have no background in the sciences."

"Oh," he said, "well, right now we're involved in a very interesting project doing research for a company that manufactures shampoo. The company wants to be sure the product won't hurt people's eyes or cause allergies, so they have us testing it on rabbits. Rabbits, you see, have particularly sensitive eyes, so if rabbits aren't adversely affected by the shampoo, that means most likely that people won't be, either. . . "

She cut him off abruptly. "What? You mean your job is to squirt poisonous chemicals into the eyes of defenceless animals? Such cruelty. Well, forget it, our engagement is off. I certainly wouldn't be comfortable with you anymore, knowing your work was so sadistic."

The man was totally bewildered when he called to cancel his appointment with me for the relationship reading. "Why can't she understand? I mean, I explained it to her. Why can't she distinguish between animals and people? Isn't it better for a rabbit to suffer than a human child, for instance? How can we have new inventions or progress if we can't test the products? I told her, 'I love animals too. I have two dogs of my own, but you have to distinguish between pets and lab animals.' Well, I'll get her to discuss it over dinner and make her understand. . . ."

He, of course, approached life and fulfillment of his ideals through the mind, Mercury and Uranus. She, as a Pisces Sun sign with a Mercury/Neptune opposition went at life very differently. She approached life through her feelings and impressions as an artist would, not as a scientist who makes objective distinctions between different life forms. The Aquarian was not willing to drop the project for her and she, though ordinarily Mutable, had become adamant.

This is what I mean by Piscean absolutism. If something is intuitively felt to be wrong, Pisces becomes uncomfortable with those involved in it. The Pisces harpist, for instance, said when she called to cancel the same appointment (unaware her fiance had already done so), "I thought he and I had common values, but no matter how hard he tried to rationalize his cruelty to animals in altruistic vocabulary, it won't work. We could never live together."

Thus, though we perceive Pisces as quite adaptable and without boundaries, as constantly merging its own ego into the ocean of people and circumstances around it, Pisces can and does draw lines based on its own intuitive grasp of black and white, right and wrong. Pisces forms strong value judgments. Pisces also does a good deal of its learning when forced to grapple with life's shades of gray. Aspects to Mercury, if positive, will indicate an ability to distinguish and discriminate, unless, of course, there's a strong Mercury/Neptune aspect in the chart of the Pisces Sun sign or Pisces rising, reinforcing the universality of thinking, the mental merging tendency.

The Pisces harpist eventually married a fellow musician. Over the years, their home has come to resemble a shelter for stray animals, and stray people, too. In astrology, the Piscean concern for the underdog is legendary. Many Pisces/Pisces rising children begin early and bring home strays from school—"poor things" from either the human or animal kingdom. As s/he grows older, Pisces continues to be vulnerable to people who represent themselves as underdogs and then turn out not to be as needy as they seemed. One Pisces man of high consciousness remarked, "I know I have a need to be needed, and it makes me pretty gullible to people with a sob story, like my latest house guest. But if they fool me and I lose financially, or emotionally, because of them I still feel all right about it in the end. It's my good karma, and it's their loss if they go through life taking advantage of others."

The archetypal Pisces fish, then, swims in the ocean of life, conscious not simply of his interconnectedness with human beings, but with all life forms—plants, animals and people. It is this wider sense of belonging to the great chain of being that distinguishes Pisces from, for instance, Aquarius, which is a universal sign also but has a mental connectedness to humanity, rather than a feeling of connectedness with all life. Recently I spoke with a Pisces father, elated because he had won the custody suit and had his two-year-old daughter back with him. He said, "Next I think I'm going to take custody of my ex-wife's plants. People shouldn't have plants if they're just going to let them die. I was always the one who watered them. Plants have souls too." Other Pisces have said, "People shouldn't have children if they're going to neglect them and stick them in day care centers. It makes me so mad. And the way the horses are treated at the ranch near mine. I called the animal welfare society and complained about the absentee owners."

This universality, swimming in the ocean of life, connects Pisces to Dionysius as ruling deity. Dionysius, the shape shifter deity, did not limit himself to appearing in human form but appeared in Euripides' play "The Bacchae" as all the powerful animals that rule the Fixed signs—the Lion, the Serpent, the Bull. He was worshipped as the vine, that is, literally identified with it, and with the trampled, suffering grapes that had been harvested. No other Olympian god seems to have had his range, his universal scope, his willingness and ability to spontaneously appear anywhere when the devotees called.

Astrologically, Pisces is the sign of the actor or the chameleon who can play any role in any stage setting or environment of life. As patron of tragedy, theaters all over Greece were dedicated to Dionysius. It is interesting that though comedy and tragedy were both enjoyable forms of entertainment in ancient Greece, and each of them in its own way produced a catharsis, an emotional release, that tragedy was considered the deeper art form. Tragedy put people in touch with stronger emotions. It is the tragic mask of Dionysius that the counselor who encounters Pisces discovers in his office. In the Dionysius cult, the god spent several months each year in the underworld following the wine harvest and left behind the mask as a sign of his presence in the temples. The tragic mask was venerated as the god himself.

When the client comes for a session, I often have the impression that though the mask (body) is there, and the actor goes through his tragic story performance, the soul energy of Pisces isn't present, it's down in the underworld or out in Neptune's orbit, somewhere beyond time and space that's much more interesting than the Earth plane. Perhaps, too, Pisces is abstracted because it takes so much energy to effect the release of the imaginative, unconscious talents from Hades. The dream state, too, is part of Hades, a type of antechamber, wherein Pisces seems to accomplish a great deal. Dreams are often more real than the waking state world to Pisces/Pisces rising because the ego is not there to censure or criticize; Pisces is in a more direct contact with the Self. I use a lot of allegory, symbolism and myth in working with Pisceans whose work is involved with the arts, music, acting, decorating, and other creative fields. Images seem to work better than concrete terms, analogy better than fact.

What was Dionysius doing in the underworld during those months when he left the mask behind for the devotees? He tried to rescue Semele, his mother, who was stuck in Hades as punishment for her hubris, her pride and presumption. As the son of God and man, of Zeus and Semele (his mortal mother), Dionysius was engaged Pisces-like in the effort to integrate spirit and substance, soul and body, divine and human natures. He very much wanted his mother to be liberated and worshipped, to be forgiven for the tragic mistake she made when she was seven months pregnant with him.

After Semele fell in love with All Highest Zeus and conceived Dionysius, the Divine Child, Zeus' wife Hera became jealous and resolved to destroy Dionysius. It was not simply that she envied Semele, for a mere mortal was no real threat to the Queen of Heaven, but rather that Hera could foresee what the birth of the Divine Child would mean for the established order on Mt. Olympus. She knew that Dionysius would introduce the vine to mankind and in return would receive Mankind's worship and gratitude at the expense of the other gods. His Ascendancy would mean the end of the Old Age; he would introduce the Age of Pisces in Olympus and on Earth. The Age of Pisces was to be an age of grace, redemption and compassion, when God himself would become a Fisher among men. Hera's vision proved accurate. Dionysius, according to Karolyi Kerenyi, was worshipped for 1,000 years in Europe and the Near East. His cult was then replaced by that of another Divine Child, Christ Jesus, a Redeemer whose mystical message was similar to that of Dionysius—compassion, communion, grace, unity with the Divine, and redemption through sacrifice (death of the ego and the descent into the unconscious (hell) to liberate souls who were stuck there).

Hera went to Earth to the palace of Thebes and found Semele's nurse. She gossiped with her and suggested that the Queen of Thebes had not seen Zeus lately; perhaps he no longer loved her? Also, he had never appeared to her in his transcendent form. Surely Semele ought to feel lonely and miserable about these things. She ought to demand that Zeus appear and satisfy her needs. Semele's nurse took this negative gossip right to the Queen and convinced her to act upon it. This is an important part of the story for the Pisces archetype, which is very impressionable and needs to guard against believing, absorbing, and acting upon negative rumors or gossip.

Zeus tried to explain to Semele that she was not ready to see him in all his glory, in his shining body of light, but she remained unconvinced and insistent. Apparently, the Queen of Thebes gave way to her emotions and failed to understand her lack of spiritual development—the inner work that was required of her before Zeus could appear to her in that way. In her self-pity, Semele kept nagging, prodded on by the nurse, who in turn was pressured by Hera.

Finally, Hera's scheme worked. Zeus appeared in the palace in his body of light. Semele was immediately blinded and then began to burn. Before her body dissolved into ashes, Zeus managed to save Dionysius, and taking the premature infant, had him sewed into his thigh to absorb Divine Wisdom, which is mythologically located there. (See Sagittarius, Chapter 9.) Several months later, Dionysius' second birth took place from Zeus' thigh. This popular theme of the second birth appeared as a motif on many vases, because the twice born nature of the Divine Child, who united humanity and divinity in his person, touched the Greek imagination powerfully. This is also significant in the Orient, where the upper castes who take the sacred thread initiation are called the twice born. In Christianity, too, people are said to undergo a second birth, or to be born again into the nature of God after the initiation of baptism.

Dionysius' birth put him into the position of intermediary between mortals and immortals. He was quite concerned that his mortal mother be respected among the gods and the Greeks alike. This was difficult because both gods and Greeks considered him an illegitimate child. Euripides' fine play "The Bacchae" centers around the theme of his efforts to win respect in Thebes for his mother and for himself.

In astrology classes we have read the play and found just about every Pisces keyword in it. It's a good exercise for astrology teachers and students. Dionysius' childhood was lived in fear of Hera who sought to destroy him and drove his nursemaids insane. Ino, his maternal aunt, drowned herself and her child when Hera put her into a daze and she walked into the ocean. He also learned to "play the feminine role," developing his feelings, emotions, imagination, and intuition at an early age, as his nurses dressed him in girls' clothing to disguise him from Hera. Thus he had a confused childhood—orphaned, hiding from a powerful Goddess, surrounded by women and madness. He wandered off to play with goats and satyrs (to wallow in the sensate function) and discovered the vine, which can be interpreted on the mundane level as drunken debauchery, and on the esoteric level as divine bliss, the ambrosia of the gods.

Dionysius was timid, fearful and hypersensitive as a child. Hypersensitive, he feared confrontation with King Lycurgus and hid beneath Lake Lerna for a long time before he felt secure enough to come out and demand that the king show him the respect due a Great God. (See Chapter 9 for the entire story, and the part his Father Zeus played in it.) He was similar to Pan, in that he was comfortable outside the boundaries of society. He was also comfortable on the sea and under the lake waters. His connection with the unconscious (Water) or the underworld was a major part of the cult cycle; he and Apollo divided the ritual year at Delphi between them. Late winter and spring belonged to the risen Dionysius who emerged from Hades with his resurrection message of hope and joy. His appearance was a harbinger of the Earth's rebirth as the Sun rose and melted the last of winter's snow.

Though we must emphasize the compassionate meaning of his annual trip to the underworld (to visit Semele and liberate her soul), we must also acknowledge another level to the journey, an inner meaning. Visits to the creative unconscious, as C.G. Jung has pointed out, refresh the spirit and put us in touch with our feelings, psychic development, and intuition. The spirit needs its dormant period of apparent inactivity in the outer world to restore itself. This is an important issue for the archetype of Pisces, Neptune and the Twelfth House, the solitude House. Time spent in the unconscious—whether the dream state, the meditative state, the afterlife vision state or just secluded in our rooms reading, writing, working on projects by ourselves, gives the spirit rest, honors the creative side of us. When the wine culture season ended, his descent into the underworld must have meant for his devotees that he had disappeared to do some of his most important work so that he could bring them increased blessings as a result of his dip in the waters of life (the "other side") when he reappeared in the lunar month of February/March. The Earth itself rested in winter; so did Dionysius. Then, as the first flowers crept up miraculously through the last of the melting snow, while the women who led his cult cried out for him, he suddenly appeared in the wine culture regions of Crete, Greece and the Near East.

Walter Otto, in *Dionysius, Myth and Cult*, several times mentions immanence, the *presence* of the Resurrected Dionysius, as it comes through the joyful songs of the cultists and the Orphic hymns. In particular, the faces of women rapt in ecstasy at his appearance, as described by Karolyi Kerenyi from the Greek vases, are not in drunken stupor but full of inner joy. Different regions of the wine country celebrated his rites according to their local calendars, but the Anthesteria celebration, the awakening of Dionysius by the women nursemaids of the divine infant, occurred usually in late February and, according to Kerenyi, no later than March. This would correspond to our astrological sign Pisces.

In several regions he made his annual appearance by sea, as in the Homeric hymn to Dionysius; he arrived on the pirate ship after having first turned the pilots into dolphins. Athenian women went to a nearby seaport and met his ship, which was on wheels, and in a long procession they pulled it many miles into the city. In the procession all the Dionysian symbols were carried—the ivy, the winter blooming plant that dualistically grew first toward the shade and then reversed itself and grew to the sunlight to produce its berries; the phallus carved of his sacred fig wood, to indicate restored life, fertility and productivity for the new season; the underworld mask, the opposite of the phallus, which represented death and the other side, and many musical instruments. The women then prepared their secret rites which involved a communion service, and the mixing of water and wine.

It is interesting that out in the countryside the men celebrated the Dionysian feast differently. Theirs was the mundane version. They toasted each other till they were all quite drunk, sang songs and had a rustic good time. Some were said to dress like women and sneak into Athens to try to mingle with the women and discover what they were doing at the Sacred Mysteries. This custom of dressing like women may also have been an enactment of the Dionysian myth, wherein the nurses had dressed him as a little girl to protect him from Hera's revenge. This theme appears in "The Bacchae," too. Dionysius, angry that King Pentheus (whose name means full of suffering) of Thebes refused to honor Semele's memory, or to acknowledge Dionysius' divinity, dresses the king in a woman's clothing and leads him to the sacred rites, places him high in a tree, aims the branch, and shoots it into the midst of the women. Pentheus is then torn apart by his own women relatives, including his mother. Women's clothing would seem to mean, in a sense, receptivity to the divine and surrender of our will to that of God or Goddess. This is the theme of the story of the Garden of Gethsemane: surrender of human will to the divine. In most religions, the soul is feminine and receptive to the spirit of God. Pentheus refused to surrender to god (Dionysius) and as a result was torn apart by his own feminine side: his mother.

Dionysius' cult also involved, at least in Athens, a Divine Wedding between the queen of the city and the risen god. On the eve of this wedding little girls were pushed into the air on swings, as close to heaven as they could get. Sometimes their envious little brothers imitated them and were pushed as well. Kerenyi describes the preparations for the Divine Wedding from a wall painting, but the artists were forbidden to paint the actual marriage; this was part of the secret cult. The queen of the city was, symbolically, Ariadne or the receptive human soul, and the deity was Dionysius the Savior God. The sense of the presence, or immanence of Dionysius must have been strongly felt throughout the city on the eve of the Sacred Wedding. At the mundane level, for those who were not religious, it also was a hopeful celebration of the prosperous new year in viticulture.

It is interesting that throughout the Dionysian myth and cult, as Walter Otto demonstrates so well, the symbolism is always dual. This is the age of Piscean duality. Dionysius is a Divine Child with nursemaids, or a young adult on a pirate ship. But on the underworld vases he's a bearded old man, a guide to the dead. His phallus represents life, yet in the same procession, his mask means death. As the harvested grapes, he suffers death on the wine press, and yet he rises every year with renewed vigor. Pentheus, because of his willful resistance, suffered dismemberment. Yet to those who approach him with faith, to those who surrender to his grace, like Ariadne of Crete (see Taurus, Chapter 2), Dionysius offers comfort and ecstatic joy. Dionysius is really the god of emotional extremes—agony and ecstasy, suffering (Pentheus) and bliss. He offers prosperity and success in this world and also happiness in the afterlife (underworld). He dresses as both a boy and a girl, combining the Masculine and Feminine. Because he is the twice born, he combines the nature of man and the nature of God. Even his wine symbol can be taken on two levels—as the gift of wisdom, the blissful cup of Omar Khayyam (see Chapter 11), or as the drunken, lethargic energy of the lower consciousness. Plutarch explained that the Greeks toasted an oath with wine because "in wine is truth" (in vino veritas), yet they were well acquainted with its negative effects, such as loosening the tongue to reveal secrets, too.

With Dionysius' cult, the Age of Pisces begins, and on the same soil where Dionysius was worshipped (Tyre and the surrounding area), Christ preached many of the same lessons—humility, resignation, surrender to grace and God's will, receptivity, honoring the Divine. He even drew on the old Dionysian viticulture symbols for His parables. "I am the vine, you, the branches." The issue of dualism which developed during the Age of Pisces with the Dionysius cult is even more strongly apparent in Christianity. In Aion, C.G. Jung devotes many pages to the theme of good and evil in the history of Christianity. He mentions that various zodiacs had used only one fish to represent Pisces prior to the advent of Christianity, when the two fish swimming in opposite directions became popular in Christian art. He said that theologians saw evil merely as the absence of good (privatio bono), in the sense the color black hasn't any color on its own merits, but is just the absence of color. The work of reconciling, or at least understanding the duality of good and evil is an issue central to us right now as we stand at the end of the Piscean Age.

I have often thought of the black and white duality, watching Piscean clients swing back and forth like pendula between extremes of behavior at different periods of their life—from alcoholism to religious asceticism, from promiscuity to the ashram where strict celibacy is practiced, from heavy drug use to substance abuse clinics, and sometimes back again. Neptune/Bacchus/Dionysius is not a rulership of moderation, but of vast mood swings. The sea of life is also the sea of emotionality. Many Pisceans drift with the current. Yet, many also intuitively know when to reverse the current, to seek out a cleansing environment, surround themselves with positive thinking people and attune to the higher meaning of Neptune. For the dual and the Mutable signs, environment is always very important, for they are impressionable types.

Duality can be observed in the lives of Pisces over a period of years as they swing, like the Athenian maidens, from the ground into the sky and back again. But in the short run, in any given month, I also think Pisceans can benefit from having their biorhythms done and observing mood swings. Life for them seems like a Dionysian rite of the agony and the ectasy, joy and suffering. I have, for instance, one Pisces friend who will call to cancel our lunch appointment every time there's a calamity somewhere in the world that appears on her television during the evening news:

"I couldn't possibly go out and indulge myself in a restaurant when people are trapped underground in the Mexico City earthquake. (Or starving in Ethiopia, or flooded-out in Bangladesh.) I just don't think I could enjoy myself. Watching that sadness has made me unable to swallow food."

"Well, why not call the TV station that had the documentary and ask for the phone number of the relief organization. Maybe they can tell you where to send a contribution and that will help you release some of this sadness."

"I don't know. Maybe I could do that. Anyway, I can't go today."

Three weeks later, the same Pisces will call again to invite me to lunch and tell me about her latest shopping expedition. "I'm so excited! I want you to see my new ultra-suede jacket. I just cleaned out my savings account and bought it on the spur of the moment. I guess because today I'm feeling good about life. $450 is a lot to spend on something that isn't real suede, but it's lightweight and comfortable. I feel good in it and I just love it."

It always takes me a moment to absorb the fact that this is the same woman who three weeks before could not manage to spend five dollars on herself at a salad bar. Today she's delighted to spend $450 on herself! (Pisces men have these same mood swings but they are more likely to buy themselves different kinds of toys on the spur of the moment—sailing or surfing equipment, stereo equipment, etc.)

One thrifty man married to a Pisces woman with a strong (Angular) Neptune told me that she's a shopping mall fish. "When I pick her up on Saturday with all her packages, I observe a lot of those mall fish swimming through the crowd or relaxing by the fountain. My wife's astrology books usually depict Pisces as mystical or psychic or religious. What happened to my wife?"

Actually, though, if this man were to look at the packages he would find that most of her purchases were for others. On the typical shopping orgy the Dionysian credit card addict acquires a few expensive articles for him/herself and then remembers the needs of others. Pisces is more likely than any other sign in the zodiac to shop for others first and him/herself second. Because Venus is exalted in their sign, Pisceans can have expensive tastes, but Venus also seeks value or quality for her money. (See Chapter 2, Taurus, on Venus.) Pisces, as a paradoxical dual sign, is also capable of saving money for *big* projects, such as decorating the house or collecting art when Pisces is interested. Ascetic saving cycles are usually followed by spending sprees or sometimes temporarily interrupted with shopping binges if a favorite store has a major sale.

Is there such a thing as a thoroughly selfish Pisces, an out and out materialistic consumer who puts him/herself first? Yes, there are selfish people in *every* sign. But Pisces feels guilty about spending exclusively on Pisces when there are needy people out there and sooner or later will grow tired of the emptiness of accumulating possessions for personal use and comfort. In the esoteric section of this chapter, a contrast will be made between the search for the earthly paradise and the search for the castle of peace. The earthly paradise is often an important phase in the growth process of Pisces, but tends to dissolve during the 50's and 60's, the decades when relationships, particularly, grow through changes.

Establishing the Earthly Paradise is an important dream for the greater part of my Pisces/Neptunian clientele. They seem to gravitate toward building walls around the paradise garden, and strong ramparts within it to protect themselves and their loved ones from the pressure of emotions, vibrations, and depressing energies floating in the sea of life beyond its gates. The mountaintop is often an ideal place for the earthly paradise home, or (here in California) a cliff overlooking the sea of infinity. But dry land is also an important concept, land that is high and dry is preferable in myths and fairy tales. (Across from every Water sign in astrology we have an Earth sign representing reality or groundedness as the polarity to be integrated.) For Pisces, it is particularly difficult to find one's personal identity if one is always merging into the vibrations of others. The earthly paradise home is thus a beautiful, comfortable retreat for self and family, and for those guests whom Pisces invites in to indulge with lavish hospitality. The homes of so many Pisceans, beautifully landscaped and furnished, are like the paradise gardens in myth. I often think of Coleridge's poem about Xanadu when visiting my Pisces friends:

> In Xanadu did Kubla Khan
> A stately pleasure-dome decree:
> Where Alph, the sacred river, ran
> Through caverns measureless to man
> Down to a sunless sea.
>
> So twice five miles of fertile ground
> With walls and towers girdled round:
> And there were gardens bright with sinuous rills,
> Where blossom'd many an incense-burning tree;
> And here were forests ancient as the hills,
> Enfolded with sunny spots of greenery.
>
> A damsel with a dulcimer
> In a vision once I saw:
> It was an Abyssinian maid,
> And on her dulcimer she played,
> Singing of Mount Abora.
> Could I revive within me
>
> Her symphony and song
> To such a deep delight t'would win me,
>
> That with music loud and long,
> I would build that dome in air,
> That sunny dome! Those caves of ice!
> And all who heard should see them there,
> and all should cry, Beware, Beware!
>
> His flashing eyes, his floating hair!
> Weave a circle round him thrice,
> And close your eyes with holy dread,
> For he on honey-dew hath fed,
> And drunk the milk of Paradise.

This poem, allegedly written under the influence of two grains of cocaine (how Dionysian!) describes the kind of enchanted paradise garden many Pisceans have built. The mood is Neptunian, other worldy, and dualistic. On the one hand, there is great beauty; on the other, an implied sense of danger, for a charmed circle is drawn around it, rather as mandalas are drawn in the Orient in circular form to protect the center, to shut out evil spirits. The maid with the dulcimer is an underworld, magical figure, evoking a mood. The caves are also Dionysian. He hid in them often in youth, running from Hera. There is a magic to the place. It's safe for those who understand it, and are invited in. It's a place to retreat, out of the ocean (the unconscious), but still, though an airy (conscious) dome, full of mystery. One can almost see Aphrodite, rising out of the sea into the air and entering this lovely pleasure dome.

In astrology, bringing the unconscious' contents into manifestation, creating from the sea within us, is symbolized by the emergence of Water signs onto dry land into a lovely airy or sunny place, like this Garden of Xanadu. (In the Scorpio life journey, the Eagle lifts the Serpent from the murky waters into the Air, or makes its wisdom manifest in the conscious, rational world.) Pisces attempts to do this in building its airy, spacious, but mysterious pleasure gardens or earthly paradises, aware that the lady with the dulcimer (the ominous) can creep at any moment, too, and that charmed circles, prayers and affirmations, are necessary against her siren song, which might lure a family member into danger. One needs one's firm roots, one's home garden, from which to create.

I have found that the more needy the Pisces felt in childhood, the more lavish and impressive the paradise garden he attempts to construct as an adult. Pisces clings to his dreams and fantasies and uses his imagination to embellish them. Eventually he draws the resources he needs to manifest them on Earth. (For Pisces women, this sometimes translates into drawing a rich husband—Prince Charming on his white horse.) Children whose early life was similar to that of Dionysius—children who felt abandoned, lonely, or as if adults failed to honor them as they deserved to be honored, tend to build very lavish material castles. They tend to fill the safe with stocks and bonds, insurance policies, savings passbooks for the rainy day ahead and surround themselves with valuable, beautiful objects. They are deserving. Anyone who enters their castle can see it.

One client, a septuagenarian who recently died after a successful career in the entertainment industry, told me of her childhood in Hollywood during the Great Depression. "Some people in the movie industry were still going strong even in the early 1930's. My father had been able to give my older sisters and brother a lot of private lessons. He had more money when they were small. When I came along, however, he was unemployed. I envied the children around me, and my brothers and sisters, too. They were not nearly as attractive or as talented as I, and yet life seemed to offer them all the advantages I lacked. I really felt deprived. When I attended Hollywood High, one particular girl who was quite homely arrived every day in her father's limousine, had all the smart clothes she wanted and the admiration of the teachers. Her father was important, famous, and still earning a lot of money for those days, while the rest of us were scraping by. This girl had any sort of private lesson she wanted— dance, drama, make-up, fashion consultations. I really hated her. I guess what I really wanted was her father, someone like that to save me and take care of me. So, I got married, early and often. Influential men, men with contacts, took care of me. And I did well. I knew I was attractive and talented. Still, there was an emptiness. You're never really sure if it's your talent or your patron's help that's behind the success, for one thing. You still don't quite have faith in yourself. It took me a long time to feel secure.

Then I began charitable work. I felt guilty that others had so little when I had so much—other children who had talent and no means of developing it. I felt better. But I was still a lot like the character in "Flashdance," that welder/ballerina who performed in discos and said that she couldn't wait to get out on the stage, be one with the music and the motion, and disappear. Acting is like that—a way to disappear by becoming someone else. Then, later, without the make-up you look in the mirror and wonder who you are. Life is so strange that I came full circle and had a chance to help that other girl (the one in the limo from Hollywood High) when her fortunes reversed after her husband's lingering illness. I felt a lot better after that. Life itself is a type of movie.

This woman had a magnificent pleasure dome, but in the last few years of her life she used it for meditation and charitable foundation consultations. She had become dissociated, detached, from the needy little girl she used to be and the possessions she had required to feel secure. For many decades, though, she seemed to oscillate like a pendulum from insecurity to security and from lack of confidence to faith.

The Aries progression, with its positive energies, its self-confidence and vitality is a real help. Even the body seems stronger in these years. One can compete, confront, succeed in the outer world. From these thirty years of progress comes faith in oneself. This is the supreme gift of Aries. Aries also strengthens Pisces in the courage to say no without feeling guilty—the courage not to foster dependency. Others will not grow if we do all their inner homework for them. This cycle brings the courage to be resigned only to that which, as a progressed Aries, you cannot fight to change about life and yourself. Pisces learns to surrender to God's will, as Christ in the Gethsemane Garden, but not necessarily to other people's will, to all the craziness in the environment around them. Pisces can too often follow the path of least resistance, passively, but the active Aries progression should bring a change in habit so Pisces no longer endures such nonsense in the outer world and stops being a doormat.

The material paradise tends to be secured in Taurus, as in Aries one is often too busy doing or competing (in the 1980's anyway) to enjoy the fruits of success. Venus rules the Taurus progression, enhancing the charm and magnetism of Pisces. People are drawn toward Pisces, wanting to help him succeed, expressing their gratitude and admiration. Taurus, as a Venus sign, strengthens the bonds of relationship.

Thus, in the thirty years of the Taurus progression, Pisces settles down into the earthly paradise garden and establishes it as a safe place for its loved ones. Karmic attachments from incarnations are worked through in this phase with more contentment, for life is not as hectic. Often Pisces has a feeling of deja vu familiarity with spouse, children, in-laws, nieces, nephews, grandchildren. Many of these souls have been around for incarnations. Pisces spontaneously takes care of or sacrifices for children and grandchildren, often at great personal inconvenience in the Taurean phase, for Venus is a warm ruler. I have observed many a Pisces take in grandchildren, even if it meant giving up his/her own creative interests or cutting back on his/her schedule. I have seen them move cross-country to bail out children or nieces in trouble. It is very different from the Aries or the (later) Gemini cycle!

Pisceans have often asked in readings, "Why did I draw this particular person—daughter-in-law, mother-in-law, or 'blacksheep child?" Symbolically, as the last sign of the zodiac and the last house (number 12) Pisces either consciously or unconsciously works at concluding leftover karma; they often have past-life closets to clean. Also, Dionysius, as we recall, was born from his father's thigh—the thigh of All-Seeing, All-Wise Zeus. Pisceans, we hope, have garnered sufficient wisdom in past lives so that, like Dionysius, they often know how to adapt to the situation, to reach that difficult person. I have seen this wisdom demonstrated many times over in the case of clients with a culminating T-Square to the 12th House. Transits through the T-Square open a Pandora's Box to them of unresolved situations from past lives, yet they somehow muster the faith and the fortitude, as well as the wisdom, to cope with it all. It's as if God somehow knows exactly how much we can handle in any given lifetime. His grace and the strength of the human soul are amazing to behold.

So, though we may sometimes be tempted to think, "Pisces people are materialistic consumers," or "Pisceans are spacey, flaky poets; souls too sensitive to compete in the real world," or "Pisceans are true Dionysians, given to wine, women and song and pretty wishy-washy and vacillating in their decision-making," or "Pisceans are paradoxical; one never knows what mood he'll find one in. . . " or "Pisces are immoderate, over-reactive types. . . " we must also realize that they proceed from the heart, not the head. Many of them are accomplishing work of real value in this incarnation, especially in the area of human relationships. Their inner work is not always visible to the rest of us, but is quite visible to the Divine and those who benefit from their unselfish love.

When the earthly body temple dissolves at the end of our allotted time here, it won't really matter whether or not we accomplished our mundane Tenth House goals, whether or not we achieved name and fame, material success or social status. Others will forget this in a very short time. What *is* of value will be our efforts at relating to others. (Venus' exaltation refers to value in relationship.) Were we kind, understanding, and forgiving of those who treated us badly? Were we good to those who, in the words of one Piscean client, "seemed to act from the day we first met as if I owed them something?" (Perhaps, in a case like this, something was owed from another life.)

The Age of Pisces teachers, from Dionysius, to Buddha, to the Christian Master, all seemed to preach this gospel of sacrifice and unselfish love. Dionysius saved his mother and Ariadne, and Christ, of course, saved sinners. Mahayana Buddhists have the ideal of the Bodhisattva, who vows to return to Earth until each blade of grass is liberated. Christ and the Buddha both told the parable of the prodigal son, about the need for mercy and forgiveness even in cases where it is seemingly undeserved or unmerited. Both taught compassion through their similar versions of the Sermon on the Mount—that we must try to help others without becoming inflated or developing Messiah complexes. "Because the first shall be last, and the last first" in the *real* castle beyond the earthly paradise. Edward Edinger put it well when he said, in *Ego and Archetype*, that the message of the Beatitudes seems to be that "blessings come to the non-inflated personality." (p. 144-45) Humility seems central to the Age of Pisces teaching—obedience to the commandments, to the Master, faith, grace and redemption, surrender and resignation to the Divine Will. All these truths are to be found in the revelations of Age of Pisces teachers.

Piscean compassion and forgiveness comes through in the Lord's prayer and throughout the New Testament we are told to "turn the other cheek," "forgive our neighbor 70 x 7 times" (i.e. to Infinity), and to "Love the Lord thy God with thy whole heart, mind, strength, and will and thy neighbor as thyself, for the love of God." This needs to be emphasized because Pisces as an absolutist sign has a tendency to view the world in terms of black and white, and in making moral judgments, to cut off the prodigal, or the black sheep from the family fold. Moral outrage might seem the righteous approach in the heat of the moment, but after 10 years of not speaking to the relative or ex-spouse, Pisces may do a reappraisal. The black sheep is most likely still a sinner; cutting him off did not really cure his delusion. Perhaps it even demonstrated to him that religious people are lacking in charity. Surely the Buddha and the Christ did not intend for us to leave this impression. (The Good Shepherd, for instance, would leave the 99 and go in search of the one lost sheep.)

Pisces can be similar to Cancer, another watery sign, when it comes to letting go of past hurts and old memories. "Sigh. He hurt my feelings in 1928. How can I forgive him in 1987? He cut me to the quick. Poor little me, insecure person that I used to be then. . . " But, no longer. If Pisces has grown, perhaps the other person has grown, too, and, if not, an affirmation, "Bless that soul; I forgive him," won't cost Pisces anything. There is no need to bring him back into Pisces' daily life, but it helps Pisces to let go of the old resentment.

Many ex-spouses of Pisces, as well as estranged relatives, have remarked over the years, "I'm sorry to have been cut off from my cousins (or my children). I'd have kept in touch, but because the Pisces would first insist that I return to her church, or drop all my friends in the band because they do some drinking, and I considered this emotional blackmail, I dropped the people I care about rather than pay it." In many cases, Pisces' righteous attitude deprived the children of parental visits, and her children, as they got older, resented mother for keeping father away, or for the negative things she said about him. For sensitive people, these are touchy issues. But keeping relationships as harmonious as possible seems to be part of the archetypal Piscean karma. Pisces planets, and Angular Neptune, have a flowing, mediator role in family life. It seems important to play it positively, rather than negatively.

Letting go of one's negative memories or at least refraining from inflicting them on one's children is another issue. An Aries astrology student, herself a grandmother, told the following anecdote:

"I was sitting in the living room, flipping through a magazine. Mother was sipping her tea in a nearby armchair."

Suddenly she said, "I was just thinking about the time you disappointed me so badly."

"Oh, were you?" I asked, putting my finger into the magazine to mark my place, "and which of the many times I let you down might that be?"

"Sigh," mother began, warming to the subject, "the time you got that 'B' in algebra back in high school, remember? The child next door to us managed to get an 'A' and I was so embarrassed!"

"Oh, sure, mother," I said, reopening my magazine. "But isn't it remarkable that here we are still discussing it when I'm a grandmother and you're a great grandmother."

While the students were thinking about her story, the Aries laughed and summarized, "It's a good thing I'm a Fire sign. These guilt trips mother lays on us seem to sail right past me. My sensitive Cancer sister, though, internalizes them. I'm sad for her. It is hard on her self-esteem to think she's a disappointment to someone she cares so much about."

Before leaving the cycle of the Taurean progression and the study of Venus' exaltation in Pisces, here are two other issues we might ponder at the end of the Age of the Fishes. C.G. Jung raised one in *Aion* when he said that Aphrodite in exaltation could be a "sensual, lascivious and vain" fish (p. 112). Many astrologers who have observed clients with this placement in the chart have also noted that through this sensuality the client becomes increasingly lazy and fickle, while at the same time deluding him/herself that he or she is very spiritual. It is such a temptation to use the magnetism of this exaltation, the allure and the seductive charm on the opposite sex that the client gets stuck at the mundane level, the personality level, and does not advance in soul development. The client deludes him/herself while others meanwhile, are saying, "How fickle that person is. I feel so sorry for that person's family. How can s/he be so shallow?"

By way of example, I would cite three remarks I have heard many times over from Venus in Pisces clients:

"I know that my boyfriend is married, but his wife is so abusive. It's perfectly obvious that she is ripping him off emotionally and financially and I'm going to have to rescue him." (Messiah complex? This is the Avatar archetype.)

Or, "I haven't asked my girl friend to leave her husband. I believe in universal free love. I don't understand why her husband would be so old-fashioned, petty and narrow-minded about it? Why we should have to sneak around? Why can't we both share her love?"

Or, "I just read this New Age book that explains that since my newfound soul mate and I were married in ancient Egypt, *I* knew him first; *I* was there ahead of his present wife, so it's okay for us to be together again this time. I'm sure I can convince him of this. I'm much prettier than she is."

I am not speaking just of people with exalted Venus from the entertainment world, or of politicians with groupies (though Venus in Pisces is a common placement for them as Venus' magnetism makes them universally popular), but about the ordinary man or woman with an inflated Venus operating at the mundane level.

The second issue is this—in *Flight of the Wild Gander*, Joseph Campbell says that the mandala of values is dissolving around us. The Old Age authorities are no longer respected; lip service may be paid to the Ten Commandments on Sundays, but people's actual behavior indicates that the Mosaic Law is no longer taken seriously. We in the counseling professions have long been aware of this. Those old Piscean inhibitions, fear and guilt, no longer keep the majority of people obedient. For one thing, according to Campbell, few really believe in the doctrine of eternal hell anymore. This is not all bad; now people can approach the Divine from more positive motives such as love and the desire to serve.

Freedom, the supreme Uranus/Aquarian value, is here to stay.

In the Western world, at least, people have grown braver and are less afraid to follow their own path, their own consciences, and take responsibility for their own mistakes. But there is a danger—Uranian depersonalization of love can become indifference to the feelings of others; freedom can be misconstrued as license to hurt others—those old-fashioned, narrow-minded, possessive, petty monogamists, for instance. While a client with Venus in Pisces who is using a spiritual vocabulary but living life at the mundane level is saying "Ooooh. Yesterday I met my soul mate. He's married *but . . .*" I scan the chart and find Neptune, that great deluder, the mundane ruler of Pisces. Sometimes it sits on the Heredity Axis (near the Nadir or Zenith) and the person is very needy emotionally, and perhaps out of touch with her feeling nature altogether, living in the romantic imagination. Sometimes in childhood, a parent (usually the father) was lost to death, divorce, alcohol, religious idealism (Neptune in the Tenth—he was never home, he was out saving the world) or withdrawn, moody escapism (he felt like a failure—a man with great gifts who was unappreciated by the common herd). Because the parent was somehow not there in body, in mind, or in spirit, Venus in Pisces is living in the imagination, desperately seeking its ideal and attracting insubstantial partners, partners who, like the missing parent, are in some sense not there for them. The Venus in Pisces wants to live in Coleridge's pleasure dome in Xanadu, where life is easy and there are no responsibilities.

My approach to the person is through Earth or Air: either an attempt to get the person out of the Water (fantasy, wishful thinking) onto the dry land of reality, or into the cold air of objective truth. It depends on the element strongest in the person's chart which appeal is likely to find favor. Often with Neptune on the Fourth one can say, "You're very protective of your own home environment, aren't you?"

"Absolutely," is the usual reply. (This person is sensitive to the surrounding vibrations and wants a peaceful, lovely home.)

"Um. How would *you* like it if someone tried to destroy your beautiful castle; to hurt you at home where you are most sensitive and most vulnerable? Think back to your childhood, to how you felt at home. This new soul mate of yours . . . does he have small children?" This universal love surely extends beyond the couple, to the others in the situation. Xanadu, in Coleridge's poem, has its hidden, unconscious dangers—its dark caves as well as its sunny spots. It helps to point to some of these.

Fortunately, when the exalted Venus or the Sun in Pisces progresses into Taurus some of its dual restlessness settles down and the unconscious seems more comfortable with a less complicated life. The yearning for mystery and romance that in many cases led to duplicity tends to dissipate. For one thing, the person is much older now. Sensuality is waning, and there is increased competition from younger attractive and charming people. The Taurean virtues—loyalty, constancy, devotion—become more appealing. Often the person whose progressed planet in Taurus sextiles its natal position in Pisces will make such statements as, "Now I actually understand these possessive and jealous types who wanted to cling to just one love. I've grown quite attached to my partner and I don't know what I'll do if s/he dies first. This is the kind of attachment that I was always running from and now it's caught me."

In *Esoteric Astrology,* Alice Bailey points out that Venus is exalted in one dual sign (Pisces) and the esoteric ruler of another (Gemini). Its work is to harmonize, balance, or reconcile duality through relationships. Sometimes the mundane Pisces tries to do this balancing by having two simultaneous romantic relationships, two loves at once. But the esoteric Pisces, the one in whom the soul has come forward to lead the personality, has the Divine as primary love.

Few people with Venus in Pisces who are stuck at the mundane level seem happy in their personal lives, at least for long. At holiday time, for instance, I often receive suicidal telephone calls from despondent fish. They sit and weep in their apartments while thinking about their married lover enjoying a family dinner elsewhere. For romantic Pisces, this is the emotional Nadir, a genuine Dionysian agony. They look about the apartment at all the expensive mementos and gifts which in their emotional neediness they had mistaken for signs of real love. If they can learn from these Nadir Moments to look through Neptune's smokescreen and see that real love is not free, nor can it be bought or sold, they can break free of the fantasy life—the weekends in Xanadu with the prince or princess. Many Pisceans, however, prefer fantasy to reality. They spend a good deal of time imagining the perfect mate, rather than working to change themselves to become a good mate for somebody. It's important to stay with therapy no matter how painful the mirror is! It's also important to put faith in the Divine, rather than into the material world, which, as the forest sages of India have always said, is the real illusion.

Reality, then, is not the Xanadu castle of the imagination, but the Interior Castle of inner peace, about which St. Theresa of Avila wrote in the 16th century. The road to this castle is the real road to romance, the divine romance between God and the human soul.

We come now to the integration of the Virgo polarity for Pisces or the integration of the solitude (House Twelve) and service (House Six) axis. Since St. Theresa of Avila's own life journey involved the opposition of the two feminine planets (Venus and the Moon) on this polarity, those who are seekers and whose planets fall along this axis would very likely benefit from reading her book, *Interior Castles*. She has much esoteric information about such Virgo/Pisces issues as illness and hypochondria, peace and anxiety, melancholy (or "dryness"), how to tell a true vision from an imaginary vision or a fantasy, whether or not people who crave solitude to meditate should give up acts of charity (service). She discusses whether or not it's wise for the sick to obey a spiritual advisor who thinks attempts to concentrate and pray are harmful to the health, how to feel calm and peaceful instead of confused about decisions, and how for those who are really attuned to God even business decisions go well. (As an administrator, she had numerous business decisions to make for the order.) This is a very practical book because so many questions that trouble clients and friends with planets on this polarity are covered by someone who lived with and worked through the Virgo/Pisces issues.

Anxiety, health (mental and physical), the mundane versus the spiritual—shall I do as Christ commanded, "leave all and follow him?" Shall I try to live like the "lillies of the field?" These are types of questions clients ask. So many say, "I have no energy." Even with her Aries Sun Sign which we associate with vitality, St. Theresa had a terrible time with health. She recommends courage as an important virtue for the path to the seventh dwelling at the center of the castle. This is another important issue—I often find myself looking for the percentage of Fire (courage) in the horoscope of a client on the Virgo/Piscean axis.

The seven dwellings in the castle parallel the seven chakras in the Oriental tradition. She even discusses the breathless state— mostly, though as something not to be alarmed about. Each of the first six dwellings has a closed door and a guardian, familiar from our dreams and from Jungian lore. Her guardians are the faculties, the senses, the mind, the imagination and feelings. God dwells in the 7th room, in the center of the circle. There is no real door between the 6th and 7th chambers. The souls who reach the 7th center want only to do God's will. As surrendered minds and wills who are concerned only to please God, they discover that He, in turn, wants to make them happy, too. He removes all their fears, provides for their needs, and the Divine romance concludes with a happy ending—union of Soul and Spirit.

In our own times we have Shirley MacLaine with the Moon/Venus opposition from Virgo to Pisces and a definite message for the end of the age. Unlike St. Theresa, however, Shirley is a Taurean with an extroverted lifestyle. In the Old Age, St. Theresa lived a cloistered life while the Inquisition perused her books keeping an eye out for heresy. On the cusp of the New Age, Shirley has free and full access to the media. She has documented her search with a series of books that are in themselves a study on the workings of Venus in Pisces at every level—artistic, psychic, romantic dualistic, and spiritual.

Communication, especially writing, is definitely a good way to integrate the Virgo/Pisces polarity. Many people with Twelfth House planets are afraid of exposing their ideas to criticism, so journal writing is an excellent way for them to develop Mercury, the self-expression planet. If Twelfth House planets have free reign to express themselves on paper, eventually they will feel confident communicating in public. I have many writers, as well as psychics and Jungian dream interpreters with Twelfth House planets. They give free rein to their intuition, their imagination, their fantasy nature in these areas. The work is not only therapeutic for them, but others too are inspired, entertained, or even healed by the release of Twelfth House psychic energy.

What happens if an imaginative Neptunean doesn't develop Mercury, ruler of Virgo, through writing, or through communicating in his business? There are definite dangers here. Alice Bailey speaks, for instance, in *Esoteric Astrology*, of the low-grade medium. This is a Piscean who has no Virgo energies, who has never developed the mind (Mercury) and who, in addition, may have some Cancer planets. This is an open or receptive person, a natural medium. But this sort of person is a negative fish, always predicting gloom and doom, seeing bad omens everywhere, scaring people rather than inspiring them. They usually advise people about what to avoid on the material level, or how to attract with animal magnetism, but they have limited powers of telepathy and clairaudience. They are impressionable, but are not discriminating. They do not really know how to interpret what they see. Many feel controlled by the environment and feel a helpless sense of self-pity. It is important for Pisces to keep its sword of discrimination honed, to be conscious of negativity in the environment and do battle with the obstacles in life when necessary.

Mercury also has to do with the facts and the details, which so many Pisces clients have told me (or their spouse or parent) "are irrelevant." But *are* they? One Piscean mother told me that she was worried about her serious-minded, concrete and literal thinking nine-year-old Virgo daughter. "She's always making lists for me and attaching them to the refrigerator with magnets," said the Pisces. "I wish she'd relax and learn to stop and smell the flowers. Anyhow, one morning I was making lunches for everyone and I happened to be throwing away an empty mustard jar. As I passed the window, a ray of sunlight suddenly caught it, and oh it was so beautiful. My arm stopped in mid air and I called out to my Virgo, 'Come quickly and look at this. It's like a lovely stained glass window.' "

"Oh mother," she said, shaking her head. She walked purposefully over to the refrigerator and wrote mustard on the grocery list. "Would you please stop spacing out and remember to put things on the list when you run out? Otherwise the five of us will have very dry sandwiches tomorrow for lunch."

I had to laugh because her little Virgo's behavior was everything she'd said—concrete, literal, terribly mundane. Yet, facts *do* have a place. I am also reminded of facts as an antidote to wishful thinking, or Virgo/Mercury as the polarity to Pisces/Neptune. A woman with many planets in Pisces once said, "Why do Virgos always have to be so critical—play the devil's advocate? It's compulsive. One burst my balloon again today at work. I was telling the others in the cafeteria about my latest boyfriend when she walked in.

"How many times has *this* one been married?" she asked.

"Er, four," I said.

"Four. Well, has he finished his analysis? Is he employed?"

"He explained it to me. His first wife died and the rest were just attempts to find someone as perfect as the first. He left his analysis because it was too expensive and he *is* employed."

"Well, I thought you said that *you* paid for dinner on your last date."

"He just forgot his wallet, that's all. I don't know why I have to justify myself to you anyway; you're always so negative."

"This Virgo told me that she wondered how I could be so astute in business—apart from the detailed work—and so obtuse in my personal life." This, too, is a function of Piscean duality.

Pisces wants to believe in a new relationship; to operate on faith and intuition about others' characters. Pisces can attempt to be businesslike at business, but doesn't want to be businesslike in romance. Actually, even in business, many a Pisces has attributed his success to the subjective, personal interest he takes in every client. "Every client is a friend—someone I care deeply about, or at least that's how it seems to me." The Virgo polarity person is a logical strategist— analytical in both business and personal life. He tends not to suffer the emotional lows of feeling Pisces, but not to experience the Dionysian joys of Pisces, either.

Virgo as the polarity sign may play devil's advocate not to hurt Pisces, but rather because Virgo sees Pisces as a poor thing—a suffering wishful thinker. Virgo hopes to help Pisces see the new romantic partner more clearly before Pisces falls in love again. It's usually too late, though. Pisces is so quick to fall in love. Virgo's perspective is that of the Vedantist's prayer, "Lead us, oh Lord, from the Unreal to the Real." Virgo brings clarity to Pisces.

Apart from facts, detailed precision, discrimination, logic and strategy, what can Mercury contribute to Pisces? A sense of conscientious service. Pisces can play (smell the flowers) well, be creative, artistic, imaginative, but often in an otherworldly way, not really understanding what needs to be done technically (from a Mercury skills angle) in a particular case. Pisces sees the overall task in a vague, general perspective way. Virgo is realistic, practical in its approach, follows the routine from step A to B to C and usually comes up with the solution through an uninspired but workable procedure. While watching Virgo reading the manual of operation, Pisces is perhaps thinking "I guess I'll go out in my boat Saturday if the weather's nice," or, "I guess I'll stop at the mall on the way home." Statistical courses, or bookkeeping courses, though Pisces/Neptune hates them passionately, are good for developing precision thinking skills.

Pisces and Virgo can flow together as practical idealism or compassionate service. Both are Mutable, impressionable signs though. This means that they will both adapt to the "needs of the underdog," setting policies and then immediately altering them for the first special case that happens along. This would be fine if the person with many Virgo/Pisces or Sixth/Twelfth House planets did not harbor any resentment, but over the years he tends to feel victimized or martyred, the supreme underdog himself. Pisces, for instance, asks, "What about my creative projects? I spend so much of my time supportively nurturing my family, friends and students or clients but what about me? With all this compassionate service, there's no time left over for me." "I wish I could afford to send my kids to the same camp where my patients and clients send theirs, but I can't. It makes me mad, too, as some of these people owe me a lot of money."

Or, "I really wanted to go on that pilgrimage tour to Asia but I can't afford it. Why is it all these people I serve are able to afford it, when I'm not?"

I usually point out that the last time I spoke to Virgo/Pisces (or Twelfth/Sixth House) he or she had mentioned the intention to set a few policies and stick to them—no installment plans, new fees to be charged for after hours phone consultations, fees for cancelled appointments, etc. But, did they stick to their new policies? No. Each person with an excuse was a special case, and since they made an exception for Joe, then, it followed that they'd have to make the exception for all of Joe's referrals.

Or, the Virgo/Pisces need to be needed came up. "I didn't want to alienate anyone who needed help; I'm here to serve." And the same person continues, "What makes me mad, though, is the years go by and I get nothing done on my novel. My poems still aren't revised... My thesis is still unfinished..." No, these haven't materialized by themselves, one actually has to follow through using his fixed planets. "Monday is my day for my own projects; I can't come in to the office then." And mean it when people who are used to finding wishy-washiness about his new policies really press him.

If Pisces, especially, finds itself feeling victimized, taken advantage of, or abused, it's better to use the Fire or the Fixity in the chart to assert him/herself than to go on feeling bitter or disappointed or to become increasingly listless and negative. Many who think themselves quite spiritual have somehow lost sight of God as the real Doer. When they are back in touch with that reality once more, it's amazing how the energy level improves.

We come now to an interesting issue raised by Liz Greene (indirectly) in *Astrology of Fate*, "Pisces." Many of you who are reading this chapter, certainly many Pisces men, will be wondering by now, "Well, what about me? I have the soul of a poet, or an artistic nature, and here I am stuck in the mundane world in a 9 to 5 service job with a Virgo sounding title."

I have many a Pisces client who meets this description. Many Water Grand Trine people, for instance, would be doing very well for themselves if this were the Renaissance instead of the cusp of the 21st century. They would be court musicians, portrait painters to Grand Dukes, royal architects and sculptors. But the Grand Dukes have been replaced with bureaucratic government agencies which, of course, prefer to patronize scientists who are likely to find a cancer cure, improve a bomb, design new artificial organs or the ever smaller microchip. In short, the Uranians are in vogue, not the Neptuneans. Eventually, we hope that the Piscean psychic healers will earn a decent living, but in the meanwhile, many a Pisces is stuck at the Virgo polarity, the other end of the service axis.

Why do they pretend to be so rational, these Pisceans, Liz Greene asks in *Astrology of Fate*. Why not show their intuition and feeling nature to the rest of the world? Perhaps, for one reason, because it's very difficult to market these kinds of talents in our period. And Pisces enjoys its comforts; it is not a sign to starve in a garret while all around them others are eating well. Or, at least, not for long! Pisces is a materialist fish joined with a silver cord to the psychic-spiritual fish. The glyph of the two fishes linking Heaven with Earth is concerned with keeping body and soul together, on the Earth plane, and with that occasional trip to the shopping mall!

The Mutable signs are gifted in the areas of communication and of people skills. Pisces is intuitively talented in reading between the lines, in answering the question that remains unasked but is in the air at committee meetings. Pisces is a natural caretaker. My Piscean clients are found in a lot of the same sorts of jobs as Virgos—Sixth/Twelfth House service jobs, hospitals, schools, clinics, prisons, social work agencies, various types of transformational therapies, in particular any job where nurturing applies to the service. Appearing between age 30 and 40 at an astrology reading, though, they usually remark, "This profession is tedious, depressing. The building is sterile looking. There are so many rules that I cannot apply my personal ideas, my intuitions, my tender loving care. I'd like to do something more creative." They hate the routine, the paperwork, and the bureaucratic pressures. They don't want to continue wearing the Virgo mask.

Pisces women seem to have it easier, as there are things that they can do to get out of the rational, specialized Virgo niche. They can, for instance, try sales, a people-oriented communication job, and obtain a 50% discount on their apparel at their favorite store in the mall (if there's an opening). They can study art history, the Japanese tea ceremony, and other things that interest them. They tend to perceive their job as helping out or supplementing the family income even when they earn nearly as much as their husbands and can thus make the shift to having fun with it more easily than Pisces men, who often feel guilty about taking a position that doesn't pay as well as the Virgo job they hate.

Many Pisceans find themselves able to shift toward more creative work in their 40's or 50's, and most, if pressed, will acknowledge that they benefited from living through the dull cycle of Virgo work in the professional or business world. Living in the real world of time, space, and logical problem-solving brought them out of the watery unconscious onto the dry land (Virgo Earth). Their own schedules became much more organized after having worked for someone else.

One Piscean woman called me in great spirits the day she quit her hectic job at the newspaper. Her last child had flown the nest and she had gone to the garage for her old manual typewriter.

"Let me know how the novel goes," I said, excited for her.

She called about a month later. "You know, I've been writing 8 to 12 pages a day. I have to admit that you were right when you told me that newspaper stint was good for me, though at the time I was furious with you for saying so. I wanted you to encourage me to go back to watching the soap operas and reading romance novels at home. When I was home in those days I would occasionally stare at a blank sheet of paper for a moment, get scared, and call a friend for an hour long chat. Then I'd go out to lunch with another friend or out for coffee.

On that job I got used to deadlines—squeezing my ideas into small spaces around others' columns at the last minute when there was some local news to add; defending my material at the top of my lungs to that insensitive boss and polishing the paragraph the first time through because I only had a few minutes. Before I went to work at the paper, I thought writing was like English Composition 101 in college but I had no professor at home to assign the topic and the deadline, so I did nothing. Now I think of it as work and say to myself in the morning, 'You can have your coffee break after you've finished four pages,' the way I did at the paper. And I'm not afraid of criticism or rejection anymore; I really toughened up. And those impossible co-workers are becoming characters in the novel. Where on earth would I ever have met people like them if I had quit and gone home with my tail between my legs?"

Where indeed? The Virgo cycle may seem draining to Pisceans without any natal Virgo planets, or without any Sixth House planets, but patience, please, it's definitely character building. (Apparently, if you're an aspiring writer it can be character building in more ways than one.) On the other hand, if you are a Pisces who has three or four Virgo planets opposite the Sun sign, your mundane job can seem perfectly natural, even creative, to you. You have more going for you in Virgo than Pisces. This is often true of Pisceans who work in banks and brokerage or insurance offices; they tend to have the Virgo/Pisces polarity on the money axis, Houses Two to Eight.

Integration of the Virgo polarity, then, is not often a conscious choice for Pisces but tends to happen unconsciously through the job, especially through interaction with co-workers and pressures inherent in the routine. It is somewhat similar to the progression of Pisces planets through earthy Taurus. A settledness occurs in the Taurus cycle. Possessions and people are accumulated. Then, all of a sudden, in the midst of the rootedness, changes occur in the outside world. Children grow up and move away, or the partner is sometimes transferred to another city, meaning that Pisces is suddenly uprooted just when everything is going so well. Sometimes, it's the loss of the partner to death or divorce. Pisces often feels like Dionysius pursued by Hera, who is trying to drive everyone around him mad. Or, like the dolphin in the story who wanted to lay down alongside his dead friend and die.

What is the cosmic purpose behind this stage of the journey, the night sea crossing? In this phase Pisces feels swallowed up by forces or circumstances beyond his control, as Jonah felt when he was swallowed up by the whale, or Hiawatha felt when the great fish Mishe-Nahme swallowed him, canoe and all:

> In his wrath he darted upward,
> Flashing leaped into the sunshine,
> Opened his great jaws, and swallowed
> Both canoe and Hiawatha.

Down into that darksome cavern
Plunged the headlong Hiawatha,
As a log on some black river
Shoots and plunges down the rapids,
Found himself in utter darkness,

Groped about in helpless wonder,
Till he felt a great heart beating,
Throbbing in that utter darkness.

And he smote it in his anger,
With his fist, the heart of Nahma,
Felt the mighty king of fishes
Shudder through each nerve and fibre. . .
Crosswise then did Hiawatha
Drag his birch-canoe for safety,

Lest from out the jaws of Nahma,
In the turmoil and confusion,
Forth he might be hurled and perish

Severed from attachments to people, places or possessions, Pisces faces the unfamiliar and the unknown courtesy of Pluto, the sign's esoteric ruler. The big fish or Jonah's whale, or the wave that engulfs Pisces in his dreams, or the loss of the loved one, the beloved city, the beloved possessions, are all symbolic of Pluto's work dissolving the cord that attaches the spiritual fish to matter. The whale or the flood in our dreams is the transformational process, the Pluto process.

If Pisces has already developed his intuition, and is, through the workings of grace and faith, already attuned to his soul nature, it is easier for the ego to let go of worldly attachments and believe that out of this painful experience spiritual growth will come. Pisces will draw closer to the Divine. It is easier to cease trying to do or act or achieve in the old familiar ways in the outer world of matter and withdraw into the waters of the psyche. If Pisces tries to swim against the current of these withdrawal planets, transiting Neptune and Pluto, he meets only inner confusion, disorientation in time and space and feelings of fear about the sense of aimlessness during this phase.

When I see clients who have had dry land flooded out from under them, who have lost their bearings and feel that they are uncomfortably drifting with the current, I attempt to remind them what real inner fortitude they possess. Pisces/Pisces rising and the Twelfth House planets' personality when in touch with their inner center are able to be more resourceful than most of us. This is a lifetime when they can touch the Infinite by descending into their own souls. (The wisdom of lifetimes is stored, for instance, in the

Twelfth House.) Pisceans who meditate, or who say the rosary or practice some other devotional technique regularly have seen glimmers of insight and may already know about the treasure to be found in the underworld.

In *Gilgamesh*, the hero brought the elixir of immortality up with him for humanity. However it was stolen from him by a snake (Pluto) again because humanity wasn't ready to have it. In the Hebrew tradition, when Jonah reached the other side he emerged from the belly of the whale with his pearl of illumination and was then able to share prophetic insights with others. Hiawatha, too, emerged with a treasure, a fish oil which could calm troubled waters for his future descents to the underworld.

There is an important message here. In these Semitic paradise gardens a snake is always present. So often the Piscean, Pisces rising or Twelfth House stellium client comes to the reading expressing anger and disgust at this situation. "Just when everything was going perfectly, just when the landscaper had finished work at our new home, we heard we'd been transferred to Saudi Arabia." The snake had again appeared in the midst of the paradise garden. Yet, without the snake in the garden there would be no story. Imagine Milton trying to write *Paradise Lost*, for instance, without the snake, his main character. Adam and Eve would probably have gone on living their passionless lives and raising colorless descendants. Without the snake there would be no sin, and without the sin, no need for a Messiah, no need for Christ with his Age of Pisces message of universal divine love.

Would the Pisces client have learned as much from living in the newly landscaped paradise garden as from the Saudi Arabian experience (which the family perceived as exile to the desert wilderness, the extreme polarity of Paradise). Probably not, because fate (Pluto, the spiritual ruler) deemed it was time to move on. The snake appears as a harbinger of the transformation. But it's not easy. It's not a resigned following of the path of least resistance, which all too often is the path Pisces takes. It involves a change of attitude—the need to work on oneself. But Jonah's whale, or the exile transfer to the desert, can be like the transcendent bridge to the Grail Castle wherein the treasure lay. It takes courage to be swallowed up into the unknown, to cross the bridge, to transcend the personality and its desires, even the desire to keep the status quo as a form of negative peace. This is a common Piscean desire.

In the late 1980's Pluto and Neptune are transiting the early degrees of Earth and Water, so their withdrawing influence is especially working upon people in the early decanates of Pisces to draw them into deeper water, to remind us all that this world is only transitory and that attachment to it can easily be dissolved. Also, these rulers of Pisces point toward deeper truths, eternal truths in the depths of the cosmic ocean.

It helps if the counselor can identify the hidden (Neptune/Pluto) talents in the chart as the client enters upon the night sea journey, particularly if he or she has just suffered a loss in personal life, for the psyche will need time to heal. Whatever outer form the inner work assumes—Jungian therapy, art, journal writing, meditation—something productive is likely to emerge from it if a positive channel is found for the introspective energy. Sometimes the astrologer can help the client recall a personal dream which has been set aside or neglected since childhood or early youth. Progressed Neptune aspecting a personal planet, especially natal Sun or Moon, can often provide important clues, as can the Pisces House and the Scorpio House, ruled by Pluto, the esoteric planet that helps Neptune transform the psyche.

If the client will take time out from business as usual to listen to the Soul, to listen to God on these cycles, much can be gained; but too often wool gathering is confused with meditation, or petitioning God is confused with listening to Spirit in meditation. Alice Bailey is adamant about this in *Labours of Hercules*, "Pisces." Neptune is not about apathy or feeling good in meditation, but about hearing and acting upon what God tells us to do in the outer world—acting from the inside (the Spiritual Center) outward. We need to let go of the planning, strategizing, intellectualizing energies of Hermes and shift to Hestia's approach. The Venus in Pisces, or Sun in Pisces, client who has already satisfied his emotional needs in the earthly paradise garden is often ready, on a Neptune cycle, to look for the interior castle of Hestia, the peaceful goddess.

In *Goddesses in Everywoman*, Jean Shinoda-Bolen describes the role of Hestia, goddess of the hearth. She represents the homemaker, the mediator and connector within the family, the household's nurturer. Hestia had an inner intuitive certainty that does not depend at all upon the mind but flows from the heart. She does not need to remember facts or details or adhere to a schedule, but delights in timeless contemplative tasks like folding the laundry, arranging flowers, setting and clearing the table as if for a ritual dinner. She does not need to function in time and space. She creates a beautiful, peaceful sanctuary for the household. She is a universal goddess too, as brides establishing their own homes were careful to bring her along on the wedding day by moving some of the hearth fire from the parental household to the one they were establishing. Beyond that, colonists who moved from Greece to Italy and even further brought along the hearth fire as a link to the home culture. She was an international catalyst. Yet, according to Shinoda-Bolen, she preferred to remain anonymous, hidden. She stood aloof and removed from the gossip and intrigues of the Olympian Gods, detached from the outcome of the Trojan War. When it was time for Dionysius, God of the New Age, to take his place on Mount Olympus, she humbly ceded her position to him without any fuss.

It would seem that Hestia is the soul within us, our center, or spark of hearth fire. Though Hestia's fire gave warmth and light to the Greek household; though she was a compassionate and supportive family goddess; she remained self-contained, content within herself. Her happiness did not depend on others' conduct, or upon whether her desires were fulfilled in the outer world because she had an inner calm, an inner peacefulness, an inner knowing that nothing or no one could disturb. She seems to represent universal, impersonal, unselfish Divine love, and therefore to be a fitting symbol of the Spiritual Fish.

Many of my clients seem to be groping about, looking for Hestia on Neptune transits. They want to stay home and tend the hearth. A common response among those who are familiar with the writings of Carl Jung is, "the psyche is no longer cooperating with what I'm doing in the outer world. I'm withdrawing my savings, quitting my job, and going into analysis. The inner world beckons. It's night sea journey time." Several clients with Twelfth House stelliums have checked into mental health clinics for time out to accustom themselves to Neptune. (The Twelfth House is the confinement house.) Others, spiritual seekers, have told me, "The material world holds no value for me. Who needs it? I'm moving to an ashram" or "I'm moving to India."

A common response for people who are not involved with Jung, yoga, or some other system of introspection and growth in awareness is to drift with the current. The surrender is not conscious on their part, they may vegetate in front of the TV with junk food and alcohol, take recreational drugs and go to their jobs hungover. People at every level of awareness come to the reading feeling confused, especially if

Neptune moves across an Angle in the chart or transits a personal planet. Tracy Marks' recent book, *The Astrology of Self-Discovery*, has a very fine section on dealing with this confusion. I will not duplicate her information here. She has a good point about the psyche needing rest in our stressful times. And television, of course, is not all bad; it may be the mildest form of Neptunean escapism. It can, however, become addictive.

My own clientele tends toward motivated, even driven personalities. Here I refer not only to those driven to achieve material success, but also to the spiritually driven. "I must get myself into the Interior Castle this lifetime." For this personality type, Neptune's truth is difficult to grasp, because Neptune's message is "Relax. Let go and let God have some room. Resign yourself to the idea that maybe you won't get there this lifetime, quit striving so hard, and then maybe you will get there after all." Neptune's message of faith and resignation is hard for Westerners in our period to hear. Though the major religions teach attunement to God's will—faith, devotion, and surrender—we are somehow too busy to hear it until Neptune transits come along and we are in a different dimension; our efforts in time and space don't work anymore, and then we remember faith. "Ah, yes. I'm trying too hard. I'm rushing around in the enchanted forest looking for the Grail Castle but it's invisible. If I sat still for a while and simplified my schedule, maybe the fog would clear, and I could see it!"

When our planning, thinking, Hermes-mind approach fails, we can try to get answers from the psyche and the intuition (Neptune/Pisces). We can begin to accept these answers as just as practical as the answers the intellect offered and even more useful on the Neptune cycle than Hermes' ideas. The Greeks put Hermes (the pillar or column) outside the door and Hestia inside the home. Both were necessary, but the rational mind is the last guardian to the interior castle to be overcome. Theresa of Avila discusses this need to transcend the mental guardian during the Neptune cycle.

The confused client who appears on the Neptune cycle may not be a spiritual seeker, and of course, we need to answer the questions he asks, coming from *his* level of awareness, rather than try to convert him to *our* philosophy against his will. I usually point out that a new dimension of the personality is coming forward, that the energy is withdrawing for some creative purpose (rather than try to tell a skeptic that the soul is coming forward), and I usually ask, "Is there something you've always wanted to do but wouldn't let yourself take time away from work to enjoy? A relaxing hobby that you can withdraw into? Your son is old enough to handle the family business, and you've proven yourself successful—why not move in the new direction? It would be better for you than all that alcohol, which is hard on the body. If medical astrology indicators point to the liver, I may mention it in this part of the session.

If the astrologer proceeds this way, of course, the client's spouse may call later to complain: "What did you say to my husband? He put our 40-year-old son in charge and bought a yacht. I'm furious with you. I hate the water." Or, "He bought a lot of brushes, paint and canvasses and took an apartment by the seaside. He hasn't painted since college, 25 years ago." So, we take risks encouraging people on Neptune transits. But Neptune is *about* taking risks and opening up new inner dimensions. There are many different ways to get in touch with the psyche. C.G. Jung demonstrated the usefulness of art in connecting with the Self in his works on mandalas.

Very intense professional women who may be out of touch with their feeling nature altogether go through many changes on Neptune transits. They may feel romantic for the first time close to age 40 (Neptune square Neptune) when Neptune trines a Capricorn Sun or Moon or sextiles Scorpio planets. "What's happening to me? I don't really care about my career. I could actually marry this person and be 'just' a housewife." (A Hestia.) That's a frightening change for her. She thinks she's losing her mind. She's not used to emotional surrender, to going with her feelings, trusting them. She's always been "under control." Scorpio and Scorpio rising professionals and people with Tenth House stelliums tend to go through similar changes on Neptune transits. Understanding how to enjoy life more with less control is a Neptune lesson, but they often have a perfectionist nature and they're afraid of making mistakes. They don't understand feeling lazy, feeling romantic, or sometimes, feeling anything. Neptune suddenly floods them with feelings of all sorts. Intense people with a background in metaphysics will understand that the Soul is coming forward, but the Capricorn Vice President or other career administrator may have difficulty with or even be frightened by that news.

During Neptune transits many Capricorn or Scorpionic women administrators appear for readings who otherwise would be skeptical towards astrology or have no interest in it at all. Now that Neptune has their attention and they find themselves avoiding evening meetings after work, they wonder what's going on and find themselves open to strange and occult things like astrology, through which to seek clarification. It helps to sound such clients out on their metaphysical background, and after gauging how open they are, suggest some books on the interior journey. If the dreams are frightening, or at least active, Jungian analysis is another option, of course. It helps to have a list of analysts in your area who are suited to working with these intense professionals during a cycle of great change.

I have found that people who are compulsive workaholics are compulsive in other areas of their life, too. If the Neptune years are not passed in a spiritual, creative or introspective way, they may become the alcoholic years, even for someone formerly very controlled. My own approach to this Dionysian tendency, when I observe a compulsive client suddenly withdrawn, spending time alone at home and avoiding the rest of the world, is to say, "you know, you have two years left of this transit. If you keep eating and drinking at this rate for two years and sitting rather than going to your exercise class, you'll really berate yourself in 1990. You'll be attending AA and Weight Watchers a long time to get yourself back together. Why not redecorate at night instead of gorging? You'd have a sense of accomplishment in 1990; your house would be all finished. Your sense of color and design is quite good right now."

Intense personalities in the structured health professions may find respite under Neptune transits in the unstructured New Age healing programs, attending short-term workshops on crystals and healing, aura reading, phrenology, etc. This is especially likely if Twelfth House planets are transited. Those with natal Piscean and Twelfth House planets may wish to finish the creative writing project that's been in the attic for years. The night sea journey holds many options that they might not have taken seriously at any other time in their lives—if they are psychologically ready to take some risks and are courageous enough to make the descent.

Many Pisceans acknowledge that there are pearls of wisdom in the cosmic sea of the unconscious, and that they would certainly like to dive for them like Gilgamesh (or Hiawatha, who made several descents), but they are afraid of losing their minds and never getting back out into the waking-state consciousnesss. The unconscious is the extreme polarity of the rational mind, its natural complement, as Hestia complements Hermes in Greek mythology. Many Pisceans operate in the course of their workday almost exclusively from the

Hermes/Virgo polarity—that is, those who are not in Piscean professions, such as artists, musicians, entertainers, full-time housewives. They have a secret yen to dwell in Hestia's peaceful, uncomplicated, non-competitive world, but they are living at the Hermes' polarity much of the day.

One Pisces Sun sign hospital worker said, "I'm afraid I'm losing my mind. I cannot recall facts and details. Hours go by and I don't know where they went. I all of a sudden don't want to get out of bed in the morning and go to work. This is not like me at all. I always keep to my schedule. When will this be over?" The disorientation in time, space and memory will often continue for some time, however.

In Book VI of the *Iliad*, Homer refers to "mad Dionysius" and his frenzied followers. Aristotle spoke of the fine line between genius and madness. In his book *Dionysos*, Karolyi Kerenyi mentioned that people who have been in the unconscious depths working creatively often have a mad look in their eyes, not unlike the look of abstraction in the eyes of the women in Dionysian art. They are in an altered state of consciousness. It's small wonder, then, that Pisceans who are living at the rational Virgo polarity feel fear of madness when their ruling planets, Neptune and Pluto, beckon to them to embark upon the Night Sea Journey in the belly of Jonah's whale, across a vast and uncharted sea.

In *Symbols of Transformation*, Carl Jung speaks of the need for the conscious mind to fight its way back to the material world after its stay in the unconscious. Astrologically, this makes a good deal of sense because Pluto, Lord of the Underworld, has dissolved the cord connecting the two fishes, the material and the spiritual. The spiritual fish is thus free to swim in his own element, which makes him ecstatic. (This is true whether the element is seen as creative or spiritual by Pisces.) Therefore, he is often none too happy to return to what the rest of us call the real world of matter.

Jung describes his own return from the night sea journey in the final three chapters of *Memories, Dreams and Reflections*. He floated over India and the Near East and had many beautiful visions. He approached a temple, but was told he could not stay, for it had been decided that his work was not yet finished. He would have to go back to Earth, to his physical body. He was not overjoyed at the thought of re-entry. Most heros struggle to get back to waking state consciousness. In mythology, they light a fire in the dark belly of the sea creature, shining light into the unconscious, illuminating it. Or, like Hiawatha, they take their fists to the heart of the Big Fish. It ejects them on dry land, and they are back among us with their insights. Yet, making many journeys to the blissful world of the unconscious seems to weaken the desire to return, for there is joy, beauty, peace, light, wisdom, and rest on the other side.

In the yogic tradition, the personality, when caught up in soul ecstasy, sees itself as a wave upon the ocean of life and wishes to merge forever in that ocean. In his earlier writings Jung rejected the oriental philosophy of the extinction of the ego as something that would not appeal to the heart of a westerner (or assuredly, of a Leo, interested in individuality above all). His visions are recounted in some detail in *Memories, Dreams and Reflections*, published posthumously. In the final chapters of *Memories*, Jung discusses swimming in the stream of life and losing all fear of death. He seems as assured as the yogis of India, based upon his own experiences of the afterlife and of God that consciousness never dies.

Jung's stay in the hospital had begun with an injury to his foot (Pisces), followed by a heart attack. When he awoke after his afterlife experiences, he was furious with his doctor for saving him. He missed the other world, where he and others were without boundaries and had conversed simply by exchanging thoughts. Each night he was in ecstasy and each morning he awoke in his hospital bed without any interest whatsoever in what went on outside his window, in this world. He disliked having to adjust to a "compartmentalized world" in which "box-like" people went about on separate business. He could not get the doctor for whom he had had great respect to listen to him. He had seen the doctor's subtle body on the other side, and knew that if the man did not get more rest and take care of himself, he would soon die. The doctor did, in fact, predecease Jung, who recovered and entered one of his most fruitful writing cycles.

In his withdrawn state, his interest in this world waning, Jung seemed to be in the state of mind similar to Hiawatha's when he made his final conscious descent into the underworld, beyond the horizon, into the sunset of the afterlife. Before leaving, Hiawatha said to his Mother, Nokomis, the Great Mother of the Eternal Waters:

> I am going, O Nokomis,
> On a long and distant journey,
> To the portals of the Sunset,
> To the regions of the home-wind,
> Of the Northwest Wind, Keewaydin.

One long track and trail of splendor,
Down whose stream, as down a river,
Westward, westward, Hiawatha
Sailed into the fiery sunset,
Sailed into purple vapours,
Sailed into the dusk of evening.

Thus departed Hiawatha,
Hiawatha the Beloved,
In the glory of the sunset,
In the purple mists of evening,
To the regions of the home-wind,
Of the Northwest Wind, Keewaydin,
To the Islands of the Blessed,
To the kingdom of Ponemah,
To the land of the Hereafter.

Questionnaire

How does the Pisces archetype express itself? Though this relates particularly to those with the Sun in Pisces or Pisces rising, anyone could apply this series of questions to the House where his Neptune is located or the House which has Pisces (or Pisces intercepted) on the cusp. The answers to these questions will indicate how attuned the reader is to compassionate Neptune/Dionysius.

1. In a conversation I often respond to what a person is thinking or feeling rather than to what he actually says
   a. most of the time.
   b. some of the time.
   c. hardly ever.

2. Among my strong points I would list empathy, sensitivity, and generosity. These apply to me
   a. 80% of the time.
   b. 50% of the time.
   c. 25% of the time or less.

3. I prefer to associate with people who are
   a. refined and affluent.
   b. kind and considerate.
   c. intelligent and informed.

4. Some people see me as hypersensitive—always getting my feelings hurt. I perceive myself as
   a. quite sensitive to criticism.
   b. moderately sensitive to criticism.

5. When I get in a mood I stay there
   a. all day long.
   b. a couple of hours.
   c. I don't get into moods.

6. My greatest fear is
    a. that all my worst fears will be realized.
    b. that somebody in my immediate family will be hurt.
    c. that I might fail in my goals.

7. The greatest obstacle to my success comes from
    a. feeling guilty.
    b. complacency.
    c. over attention to detail.

8. After sacrificing my own creative projects to help others I feel resentful
    a. most of the time.
    b. some of the time.

9. When I am at a low ebb emotionally I am also low in energy and vitality
    a. 80% of the time or more.
    b. about 50% of the time.
    c. 25% of the time or less.

10. When my intuition tells me to take action I follow it
    a. most of the time.
    b. some of the time.
    c. hardly ever.

Those who have scored five or more (a) answers are highly in touch with Neptune, the planet of the unconscious. Though you are sensitive, intuitive, and compassionate by instinct, you may be following the path of least resistance. It's important to develop conscious control of moods and feelings for improved health and vitality. If you answered (a) to question (3) you may be a material fish who is compensating for a needy childhood by seeking Jupiter in its mundane meaning of abundance. Those who have scored five or more (c) answers are moving toward the polar extremity (Virgo) on the instinctual level. Their Neptune is not coming through. Attunement to Neptune is developed through such creative activities as music, the arts, writing, meditation, visualization, and design.

Where is the balance point between Pisces and Virgo? How does

Pisces integrate fact and logic? Fantasy and reality? The creative imagination and the disciplined routine? Faith and discrimination? Though this relates particularly to those with Sun in Pisces, Pisces rising, or Neptune prominent by House position, all of us have Neptune and Mercury somewhere in our horoscopes. Many of us have planets in the Sixth or Twelfth House. For all of us, the polarity from Pisces to Virgo involves the ability to go from the intuitive to the concrete.

1. If my spouse were asked s/he would say that I am
   a. disorganized and intuitive.
   b. both intuitive and organized.
   c. organized but not intuitive.

2. When I stop at the store I
   a. pick what looks good to me.
   b. get what is on the shopping list and a little something extra.
   c. pick up only what is on the list.

3. In my approach to projects at work I am
   a. an artist.
   b. a technician and an artist.
   c. a technician.

4. In my relationships I am
   a. nurturing.
   b. both loving and realistic.
   c. realistic.

5. My co-workers probably consider me
   a. vague about details.
   b. good at both analyzing and synthesizing.
   c. analytical.

Those who have scored three or more (b) answers are doing a good job at personality integration on the Pisces/Virgo polarity. Those who have three or more (c) answers may need to work more consciously on developing natal Neptune in their horoscopes. Those who have three or more (a) answers may be out of balance in the other direction (weak or undeveloped Mercury). Study both planets in the natal chart. Is there an aspect between them? Which one is stronger by House position or location in its sign of rulership or exaltation? Is either of them retrograde, intercepted, in fall, or in detriment? Aspects to the weaker planet can point the way to integration.

What does it mean to be an esoteric Pisces? How does Pisces integrate Pluto, its esoteric ruler, into the personality? Every Pisces will have both Neptune and Pluto somewhere in the horoscope. Neptune and Pluto working in harmony will help the Soul come forward to take charge of the personality. Acting together, these two outer planets work to dissolve attachments to people, places, and possessions, to liberate the surrendered Soul from the bonds of Matter.

1. To me resignation means
   a. surrender to God's will.
   b. accepting what you can't change.
   c. expect the worst.

2. I have strong faith in
   a. God and myself.
   b. God.
   c. neither God nor myself; I'm a fatalist.

3. I deal with my inner fears and inhibitions by practicing
   a. meditation, devotion, affirmation, and/or attending religious services.
   b. positive thinking whenever negativity manifests around me.
   c. frankly, I want to hide under the bed.

4. When it comes to having control over my worries and anxieties I can honestly say
   a. I am doing well! I'm much less disturbed than I used to be.
   b. I have made some progress and am still working on myself.
   c. I guess I could say that there has been some progress made but by no means enough.

5. Changes in the extreme (death of a loved one, divorce, uprooted by job transfer, loss of much-loved possessions) affect me deeply
   a. but by hindsight I can see the ultimate good that emerges.
   b. and I find it hard to adjust, but after some time I get back to living and do the best with what I have.
   c. to the degree that all I want to do is escape.

Those who have scored three or more (a) answers are in touch with the esoteric ruler. At the esoteric level Pluto's role is to free Pisces from attachment during the night sea journey. Those who scored three or more (b) answers are working on themselves but need to continue. Cleaning out past memories/resentments is of vital importance during Pluto's night sea journey. Jungian analysts can provide skilled, objective, and professional help during this process. Those who have scored three or more (c) answers really need consciously to understand Pluto's energy in their chart. Pluto should put you into contact with your inner resources in time of crisis, help you face your worst fears and transcend. Though you may view Pluto as a malefic planet, its prime objectives are transformation and transcendence. It helps to understand that change is inevitable and that resisting lengthens the very process of psychic healing it is trying to bring about.

References

John Armstrong, *The Paradise Myth*, Oxford University Press, New York, 1969

Alice Bailey, *Esoteric Astrology*, Lucis Publishing Co., New York, 1976

Alice Bailey, *Labours of Hercules*, Lucis Publishing Co., New York, 1977

Joseph Campbell, *Flight of the Wild Gander*, Viking Press, New York, 1951

Sri Daya Mata, *Only Love*, Self-Realization Fellowship Press, Los Angeles, 1976

Eleanore Devine and Martha Clark, *The Dolphin Smile: Twenty-Nine Centuries of Dolphin Lore*, MacMillan Co., New York, 1969

Edward Edinger, *Ego and Archetype*, G.P. Putnam's Sons, New York, 1972

Euripides, "The Bacchae"

George Ferguson, *Signs and Symbols in Christian Art*, Oxford University Press, New York, 1959

Nelson Gluek, *Deities and Dolphins, The Story of the Nabataeans*, Farrar, Straus and Giroux, New York, 1965

Erwin R. Goodenough, *Jewish Symbols in the Greco-Roman Period, V*, "Fish, Bread and Wine," Pantheon Books, New York, 1956

Liz Greene, *Astrology of Fate*, "Pisces," Samuel Weiser Inc., York Beach, 1984

Isabel Hickey, *Astrology: A Cosmic Science*, Altieri Press, Bridgeport, 1970

James Hillman, "Dionysius in Jung's Writings," in *Facing the Gods*, Spring Publications, Irving, 1980

C.G. Jung, *Aion*, Princeton University Press, Princeton, 1959

C.G. Jung, *Memories, Dreams and Reflections*, Aniela Jaffe, Ed., Vintage Books, New York, 1965

C.G. Jung, *Psychological Types*, Princeton University Press, Princeton, 1971

C.G. Jung, *Symbols of Transformation*, Princeton University Press, Princeton, 1956

Barbara Kiersey, "Hestia, A Background of Psychological Focusing" in *Facing the Gods*, Spring Publications, Irving, 1980

Karolyi Kerenyi, *Dionysos*, Routledge and Kegan Paul, London, 1976

Tracy Marks, *The Astrology of Self-Discovery*, C.R.C.S., Reno, 1950

Tracy Marks, *The 12th House*, Sagittarius Rising, Arlington, 1977

Walter F. Otto, *Dionysus, Myth and Cult*, Indiana University Press, Indiana, 1965

Jean Shinoda-Bolen M.D., *Goddesses in Everywoman*, "Hestia," Harper and Row, New York, 1984

Theresa of Avila, *The Interior Castle*, Kieran Kavanaugh, O.C.O., transl., Paulist Press, New York, 1979

Heinrich Zimmer, *Philosophy of India*, Pantheon Books, New York, 1951

Glossary

Air: The element associated with thinking, communicating, mental idealism, scientific curiosity, a cheerful attitude, and a sense of humor. Karmically, the area of relationship is the Air issue; each Air sign and Air house (3,7,11) is associated with a different type of relationship— siblings (3), marriage and business partners (7), friends and organizations (11). Air is ungrounded idealism. Persons with 50 percent or more of it incline toward Jung's *puer/puella* attitude. The 3 Air signs and 3 Air Houses are catalysts, or connectors; Gemini, Libra, and Aquarius connect people with ideas and concepts, and people with other people.

Angular: Sharp energy. A dynamic or Cardinal point in the horoscope. We are *aware* of angular energy while we might flow with or relax about non-angular energy.

Angular Houses: A term referring to the houses immediately following the Angles or Cardinal points of the horoscope (Houses 1,4,7 and 10). Each Angular House begins a new quadrant.

Angular Planets: Natal planets in Houses 1,4,7,10) or in close proximity to these Angular cusps but in Houses 3,6,9,12.

Angular Transits or Progressions: The motion of any planet, Node, etc., over the cusp of an Angular House, impacting a new quadrant of the horoscope and suggesting that a person focus attention on that quadrant.

Archetype: A model or prototype. In Plato's philosophy, the original idea from which any existent material thing has been copied. The archetypal idea must first exist as a model; no substantial thing can exist without it. (See Introduction for C.G. Jung's modern use of the term archetype.)

Aspect: Geometric relationship between the planets (or planets and angles); psychological dialogue between the planets (or planets and angles). A hard aspect (known as an affliction in the older texts) would be 90 degrees (square), or 180 degrees (opposition). The square is energetic and frustrating energy within oneself that pressures a person to do something with the energy; an opposition is pressure from the outer world, often confrontation. The awareness aspect—inconjunct or quincunx (150 degrees)—is one that clients tend to notice nagging at them by mid-life. Other major natal aspects, softer in nature, are the free-flowing isosceles triangle (the trine—120 degrees), often a talent from a past life which may be a relaxing hobby this lifetime, and the "lucky opportunity" aspect (sextile—60 degrees). The conjunction (2 planets, or a planet and an angle, within about 7 degrees of each other) in the natal horoscope helps a person to focus his or her energy. It may be either hard or soft according to the nature of the planets (or planets and angles) involved. A conjunction of Moon/Jupiter, Jupiter/Venus, Jupiter/Neptune would be soft. Mars/Uranus, Saturn/Sun would be hard. There are also many minor aspects not mentioned in this book.

Axis: (See diagram on pages *xix* and *xx,* "The 6 Polarities of the Natural Zodiac.") There are 6 axes passing through the wheel of the horoscope, or 6 polarities to integrate. They are: self/other (Houses 1 and 7), values/resources (Houses 2 and 8), communication/transportation and travel (Houses 3 and 9), heredity axis (Houses 4 and 10), personal creativity/community volunteerism (Houses 5 and 11), service/solitude (Houses 6 and 12). The nature of the planets on these axes indicate the approach to personality integration, or the balance of opposites.

Cardinal: One of the modalities or qualities, known in certain Hindu texts as *rajas,* or the dynamic initiating energy that gives life to new projects and has the power or authority to manage others, to give direction, as the cardinal points of the compass direct the traveler. Each season and each quadrant begins with a Cardinal sign. The Cardinal signs are Aries, Cancer, Libra, and Capricorn.

Communication Axis: Houses 3 and 9 also involve learning, travel, and time and energy balance between close relatives (siblings) and distant relatives (in-laws, grandchildren). Do we learn and/or teach close to home, in our own neighborhood (3rd House) or through distant travel, publishing our ideas, studying out of town, abroad (9th House)? Do we develop and expand our concept of the Divine as adults (House 9), or are we stuck with our early education concepts (House 3)?

Cusp: The edge. The degree along the ecliptic that marks the beginning of a zodiac sign and divides it from the preceding sign. In Sun sign astrology, a person born in 29 degrees Taurus would be on the cusp of Gemini. A person born in 29 degrees of Cancer Ascending would have a cusp of Leo Ascendent. The cusp of a house is the degree of the ecliptic on its edge, but there are many different mathematical formulae (systems) for calculating the houses of the chart. Intuitives who are sensitive to the motion of the progressed Moon can often feel it cross a cusp. They may, accordingly, use their own life experience to choose the house system that works for them.

Detriment: The position a planet is in when placed opposite the sign it rules. For example, the Moon rules Cancer and is in detriment in Capricorn. The detriment is a weak placement in one sense because the planet lacks affinity for the sign in which it's placed, but in certain cases the detriments seem to have more conscious control. People whose Moon is in Capricorn may be melancholy and disinclined toward giving and receiving nurturing (the Moon's strong point), but they are also more in control of life (consciously) than Moon in Cancer people who proceed emotionally from unconscious feelings and psychic intuition. Venus in detriment has a similar conscious control. The magnetism of the detriment planet seems weakened to some degree. A thinking planet in an impulsive, active sign (Mercury in Sagittarius) or an unconscious, intuitive sign (Mercury in Pisces) doesn't work normally; it loses some clarity and precision. But if aspects to it are good, it will function positively in an unusual way. (Uranus trined Mercury will have ingenious ideas.)

Ecliptic: The Sun's apparent path around the Earth. The ecliptic plane contains the 12 signs, so that in Plato's philosophy, souls coming to Earth to be re-born had to pass through the ecliptic at some point—one of the 12 signs.

Esoteric Ruler: Soul ruler, as opposed to mundane ruler, or ruler of the personality. Through conscious attunement to the esoteric ruler we can transcend our instinctual limitations and our separateness from our fellow man and let the creative energy of the cosmos flow through us without ego-obstruction. (For a list of esoteric rulers see the chart in the Introduction).

Exaltation: Placement of a planet in a sign that lends it a particular type of magnetism; there is an affinity between the sign and the nature of the planet. It is important to become conscious of the way in which this magnetism operates—the message the exalted planet sends to others. For example, Venus in Pisces—victim? or messiah? (See Introduction for more examples.)

Earth: The sustaining element that gives form and stability to all the other elements. Earth molds the Divine spark of fire into concrete manifestation. It is solid, grounded. Earth signs (Taurus, Virgo, and Capricorn) act as containers for others around them, as Earth contains the other elements. It's the "heavy" element; people with fifty percent or more planets in Earth may undergo cycles of depression, unless air is also present, such as Ascendent in Air.

Elements: The four fundamental substances necessary for physical life in Western astrology—Fire, Air, Earth, Water. Polarity integration occurs in the elements as across from every Air sign is its polar opposite, a Fire sign. Air/Fire involves integrating thinking/doing. Across from every Earth sign is its polar opposite, a Water sign. Earth/ Water integration involves a balance of structure, reality, and responsibility with free flowing feelings, fluid imagination, and psychic intuition. People low in one of the four elements may learn by drawing to themselves others with planets in that element.

Fall: A planet placed in the sign opposite its sign of exaltation is in its sign of fall. Its nature is out of sync with the nature of the sign it is placed in. Venus, for instance, is an open, sociable planet in exaltation (in kindhearted Pisces). In fall (in Virgo) she becomes narrow or petty or insecure and perhaps venal, if afflicted. She may help others (Virgo), yet resent the fact that others do not seem to see her as very deserving of help. Some Hindu astrologers see planets in fall as indicators of past-life debts to be repaid.

Fire: The element that enlivens the other 3—enthusiasm, inspiration, dynamism, self-confidence, restless and sometimes impetuous activity. A horoscope with fifty percent or more planets in Fire signs/ Fire houses is a restless impatient hero on his quest, a pioneer; s/he may lack sensitivity and/or groundedness.

Fixed: One of the three modalities inclusive of the signs Taurus, Leo, Scorpio and Aquarius; Houses 2, 5, 8 and 11. Fixed signs and houses stabilize the work begun in the preceding Cardinal signs/ houses. Fixed signs are intense, persevering, powerfully magnetic, resourceful, loyal to friends and principles. They are also rigid and resistant to change; therefore, they are connected with *tamas* (inertia) in Hindu astrology.

Grand Trine: Usually occurs in one of the four elements. Three or more planets are located 120 degrees apart, as a planet in Taurus, Virgo, and Capricorn (same element, Earth) each 120 degrees from each other. A person with a Grand Trine in Earth would "land on his feet" financially this lifetime without having to struggle. A person with a Grand Trine in Air would communicate well socially and learn easily without necessarily choosing to spend time on an advanced degree. A person with a Grand Trine in Water would attract emotionally supportive people in his/her life. A person with a Grand Trine in Fire would enjoy sports, adventure, travel, outdoor work. This can be a lazy structure as the person with a Grand Trine doesn't feel challenged to work with it this lifetime.

Heredity Axis: Houses 4 and 10. Planets in these houses through their dialogue with the rest of the chart describe early childhood impressions contributing to self-esteem or its absence. For example, Venus and Jupiter in the 4th House with soft aspects generally means contented home and ethical parents. Saturn conjunct Moon in the 4th House with harsh aspects generally means a financially and/or emotionally insecure parent. Neptune in the 4th afflicted can mean an artistically or spiritually unfulfilled parent who, perhaps, drank.

Intercepted: A sign that is wholly encompassed within a house but does not appear on the cusp. Intercepts run across the entire polarity axis, so that, if for instance, Taurus is intercepted in House 3, Scorpio will also be intercepted in House 9. Intercepted signs operate in the unconscious; a chart with several planets in intercepted signs will have a powerful creative unconscious if s/he can access it. Accessing is often done when a person is removed from the environment into which s/he came to earth and is given time out to get in touch with the intercepted planet(s) as transits/progressions trigger the intercept.

Midheaven: The cusp of the 10th House derived from the position of the Sun at local noontime. Prior to the mid-forties, the Midheaven sign represents ambition and aspirations, urge for honor and recognition, status or prestige. Planets close to the Midheaven describe the parent who helped establish these aspirations. (See Heredity Axis.) Transits to the Midheaven are important not only for career events but for personality development. Transits will square the Ascendent/ Descendent axis and oppose the Nadir. After the mid-forties the 11th House cusp becomes as important as the Midheaven for a Conscious Seeker.

Modality: (Also called mode, or quality.) Modality is a major category in astrology, like the Elements. There are three types of modality energies that refer to ways of being, acting, and reacting. They are Cardinal, Fixed, and Mutable. The hard aspects (squares and oppositions) usually occur in the modalities. The Grand Cross or the T-Square, in the modalities with their sharp angular energy, impel us toward growth and change.

Mundane Ruler: The planet associated with the sign's unconscious, instinctual drives—the drives of the ego personality as it attempts to build self-esteem and/or win recognition through the sign and its ruler, to build a persona and manifest its earthly desires as an isolated self without awareness of Self or Spirit. (See also esoteric ruler above, and the list of mundane rulers in the Introduction.)

Mutable: One of the three modalities. It is a flexible/adaptable energy that lends the personality an ability to compromise. Mutability communicates well and is a reflective element, promoting growth and learning; thus it has been associated with *Sattwa* (wisdom) in India. It is said to spark Cardinality and activate fixity. Too much Mutability in a horoscope can result in a wishy-washy personality that theorizes constantly, scattering energy and not finishing projects. The Mutable signs are Gemini, Virgo, Sagittarius and Pisces; Houses 3, 6, 9 and 12.

Nadir: The bottoming-out point—physically and emotionally—for the horoscope (opposite the Zenith). This bottoming-out feeling accompanies slow-moving transits from the end of the Third House to the midpoint of the 4th House.

Passive planets: The Moon and Venus were considered passive planets in Ptolemy's astrology. Medieval alchemists and astrologers considered planets in Earth and Water signs (feminine signs) as passive/receptive in balance with Fire/Air, masculine and active.

Polarity: (See pages xix and xx.) One of the six axes of the horoscope wheel consisting of 2 houses or signs—a continuum from Earth/Water or Air/Fire to be brought into balanced perspective. Self meets the outer world or Soul meets Spirit along these axes.

Progressions (secondary): A calculation of the symbolic motion of each natal planet through time, representing the development of the natal personality over the years as its potential unfolds. Progressed planets aspect natal planets, natal angles, and each other. The Sun is the creative self; the Moon is feelings, emotions, psychic growth; the Ascendent is body, etc. (See Introduction for a discussion of the progressed Sun.)

Quadrant: One of the four quarters of the horoscope defined by the cusps of the four Angular Houses. Each quadrant comprises three houses. Transits through the quadrants activate Houses 1-3 or independent personality growth; Houses 4-6 or home, children, skills, service; Houses 7-9 or partnership, joint investment and publicity; and Houses 10-12 or soul growth and/or public influence.

Receptive Signs: The Yin signs—the quieter Earth and Water signs which are more introspective, less extraverted.

Retrograde: Term used for a planet which appears from Earth to be going backwards on its orbit through the zodiac. For planets involving business contracts this means delay and confusion. For travel planets, retrograde motion may mean schedule changes or delays. Retrograde motion is useful for catching up on correspondence, re-reading insurance policies, housecleaning, etc. *Natal* retrograde planets are slower to act, less conscious than direct planets.

Rising Sign (Ascendent): The constellation coming up over the horizon in the natal place at the time of birth. The degree of the rising sign will reflect the exact moment of birth. The rising sign is very important because it is associated with our pattern of acting and reacting, and our attitude, which goes deeper than the persona (the appearance, the mannerisms, and the impression we make upon others). The rising sign is also linked to the body's health.

Ruler: (Lord of the sign in older texts.) The planet assigned to a sign based upon its affinity or familiarity with the sign's qualities. (See Mundane Rulers above, and also chart in Introduction.)

Trans-Saturnian Planets: The planets beyond Saturn's orbits—Uranus, Neptune and Pluto. The outermost, slowest moving planets in the Solar System. They linger in our lives long enough to make a *real* impression!

Transit: The passing of a planet through a sign of the zodiac, over an angle of the chart, or over a natal planet.

T-Square: Two planets in opposition to each other with a third planet at a midpoint between them. T-Squares are usually found in the modalities. They are probably astrology's most dynamic and restless aspect. When desires and ambitions wind down at midlife, this becomes a powerful structure promoting perspective and personality integration.

Values and Resources Axis: Houses 2 and 8. Represents personality integration through learning to compromise the interests of self and partner in the areas of sex and money. Compromise and sharing is a higher expression while tit for tat is a lower expression of this axis.

Void: Absence of an element in the horoscope with the resultant need to compensate for it. A person with no natal Air planets and no planets in the Air Houses (3, 7, or 11) would take courses and seminars constantly. No Water planets nor planets in Houses 4, 8, or 12 would mean a compulsive nurturer by profession and/or needy in personal emotional life.

Water: Of the four elements, the unifying element that provides feeling and emotion, empathy and sympathy. The Water Houses (4, 8, and 12) are the psychic houses. Water also involves the aspect of psychic intuition. Water signs Cancer, Scorpio and Pisces feel deeply and often provide an empathetic environment that nurtures and sustains those around them. Too much compassion may result in an energy drain and eventually in cycles of withdrawal for the more sensitive, watery personality.

Zenith Area: Houses 9 and 10 of the natal chart. Natal planets in these houses tend to be ambitious Zenith planets. Transits through this part of the chart tend to bring culminating success to a hardworking person. The spouse tends to feel neglected at the times of these transits.

STAY IN TOUCH

On the following pages you will find listed, with their current prices, some of the books now available on related subjects. Your book dealer stocks most of these and will stock new titles in the Llewellyn series as they become available. We urge your patronage.

To obtain our full catalog, to keep informed about new titles as they are released and to benefit from informative articles and helpful news, you are invited to write for our bimonthly news magazine/catalog, *Llewellyn's New Worlds of Mind and Spirit*. A sample copy is free, and it will continue coming to you at no cost as long as you are an active mail customer. Or you may subscribe for just $7.00 in the U.S.A. and Canada ($20.00 overseas, first class mail). Many bookstores also have *New Worlds* available to their customers. Ask for it.

Stay in touch! In *New Worlds'* pages you will find news and features about new books, tapes and services, announcements of meetings and seminars, articles helpful to our readers, news of authors, products and services, special money-making opportunities, and much more.

Llewellyn's New Worlds of Mind and Spirit
P.O. Box 64383-088, St. Paul, MN 55164-0383, U.S.A.
* * *

TO ORDER BOOKS AND TAPES

If your book dealer does not have the books described on the following pages readily available, you may order them directly from the publisher by sending full price in U.S. funds, plus $3.00 for postage and handling for orders *under* $10.00; $4.00 for orders *over* $10.00. There are no postage and handling charges for orders over $50.00. Postage and handling rates are subject to change. UPS Delivery: We ship UPS whenever possible. Delivery guaranteed. Provide your street address as UPS does not deliver to P.O. Boxes. UPS to Canada requires a $50.00 minimum order. Allow 4-6 weeks for delivery. Orders outside the U.S.A. and Canada: Airmail—add retail price of book; add $5.00 for each non-book item (tapes, etc.); add $1.00 per item for surface mail.

FOR GROUP STUDY AND PURCHASE

Because there is a great deal of interest in group discussion and study of the subject matter of this book, we feel that we should encourage the adoption and use of this particular book by such groups by offering a special quantity price to group leaders or agents.

Our special quantity price for a minimum order of five copies of *Archetypes of the Zodiac* is $44.85 cash-with-order. This price includes postage and handling within the United States. Minnesota residents must add 6.5% sales tax. For additional quantities, please order in multiples of five. For Canadian and foreign orders, add postage and handling charges as above. Credit card (VISA, MasterCard, American Express) orders are accepted. Charge card orders only ($15.00 minimum order) may be phoned in free within the U.S.A. or Canada by dialing 1-800-THE-MOON. For customer service, call 1-612-291-1970. Mail orders to:

LLEWELLYN PUBLICATIONS
P.O. Box 64383-088, St. Paul, MN 55164-0383, U.S.A.

Prices subject to change without notice.

THE HOUSES
Power Places of the Horoscope
Edited by Joan McEvers

The Houses are the departments of experience. The planets energize these areas—giving life meaning. Understand why you attract and are attracted to certain people by your 7th House cusp. Go back in time to your 4th House, the history of your beginning. Joan McEvers has ingeniously arranged the chapters to show the Houses' relationships to each other and the whole. Various house systems are briefly described in Joan McEvers' introduction.

Learn about house associations and planetary influences upon each house's activities with the following experts:

• Peter Damian: The First House and the Rising Sun
• Ken Negus: The Seventh House
• Noel Tyl: The Second House and The Eighth House
• Spencer Grendahl: The Third House
• Dona Shaw: The Ninth House
• Gloria Star: The Fourth House
• Marwayne Leipzig: The Tenth House
• Lina Accurso: Exploring Your Fifth House
• Sara Corbin Looms: The Eleventh: House of Tomorrow
• Michael Munkasey: The Sixth House
• Joan McEvers: The Twelfth House: Strength, Peace, Tranquillity

0-87542-383-3, 400 pgs., 5-1/4 x 8, illus., softcover $12.95

FINANCIAL ASTROLOGY
Edited by Joan McEvers

The contributors to this popular book in Llewellyn's New World Astrology Series have vast financial and astrological experience and are well-known in the field. Did you know that new tools such as the 360 dial and the graphic ephemeris can help you spot impending market changes? You owe it to yourself to explore this relatively new (and lucrative!) topic.

Learn about the various types of analysis and how astrology fine-tunes these methods. Covered cycles include the Lunar Cycle, the Mars/Vesta Cycle, the 4 1/2-year Martian Cycle, the 500-year Civilization Cycle used by Nostradamus, the Kondratieff Wave and the Elliot Wave.

• Michael Munkasey: A Primer on Market Forecasting
• Pat Esclavon Hardy: Charting the United States and the NYSE
• Jeanne Long: New Concepts for Commodities Trading Combining Astrology and Technical Analysis
• Georgia Stathis: The Real Estate Process
• Mary B. Downing: An Investor's Guide to Financial Astrology
• Judy Johns: The Gann Technique
• Carol S. Mull: Predicting the Dow
• Bill Meridian: The Effect of Planetary Stations on U.S. Stock Prices
• Georgia Stathis: Delineating the Corporation
• Robert Cole: The Predictable Economy

0-87542-382-5, 368 pgs., 5-1/4 x 8, illus., softcover $14.95

URANUS: Freedom From the Known
by Jeff Green

This book deals primarily with the archetypal correlations of the planet Uranus to human psychology and behavior to anatomy/physiology and the chakra system, and to metaphysical and cosmic laws. Uranus' relationship to Saturn, from an individual and collective point of view, is also discussed.

The text of this book comes intact in style and tone from an intensive workshop held in Toronto. You will feel as if you are a part of that workshop.

In reading *Uranus* you will discover how to naturally liberate yourself from all of your conditioning patterns, patterns that were determined by the "internal" and "external" environment. Every person has a natural way to actualize this liberation. This natural way is examined by use of the natal chart and from a developmental point of view.

The role of Uranus within relationship dynamics is explored with the use of synastry and composite charts. This will show you how the archetype of freedom from the conditioning in relationships can be experienced.

The 48-year sociopolitical cycle of Uranus and Saturn is discussed extensively, as is the relationship between Uranus, Saturn and Neptune. With this historical perspective, you can see what lies ahead in 1988, a very important year.

There is much to be gained from Jeff's insights and he makes it both entertaining and informational. You will be digging into all of your charts to discover the nature of Uranus' role in each after reading this book.

0-87542-297-7, 192 pages, 5¼ x 8, softcover   **$7.95**

OPTIMUM CHILD
by Gloria Star

This is a brand new approach to the subject of astrology as applied to children. Not much has been written on developmental astrology, and this book fills a gap that has needed filling for years. There is enough basic material for the novice astrologer to easily determine the needs of his or her child (or children). All it takes is the natal chart. A brief table of where the planets were when your child was born is included in the book so that even if you don't have a chart on your child, you can find out enough to fully develop his or her potentials.

In *Optimum Child* you will find a thorough look at the planets, houses, rising signs, aspects and transits. Each section includes physical, mental and emotional activities and needs that this child would best respond to. It is the most comprehensive book yet on child astrology. This one is definitely not for children only. Every parent and professional astrologer should read it thoroughly. You should use it and help your child develop those talents and potentials inherent in what is shown within the natal chart.

This book will also help you, as an adult, explore and discover how your childhood experiences have shaped who you are now. It will open your eyes to your own potentials, still untapped, and where your own blocks to fulfilling those potentials have developed. You can become the person you were meant to be.

0-87542-740-5, 360 pages, 6 x 9, softcover   **$9.95**

HEAVEN KNOWS WHAT
by Grant Lewi

What better way to begin the study of astrology than to actually do it while you learn. *Heaven Knows What* contains everything you need to cast and interpret complete natal charts without memorizing any symbols, without confusing calculations, and without previous experience or training. The tear-out horoscope blanks and special "aspect wheel" make it amazingly easy.

The author explains the influence of every natal Sun and Moon combination, and describes the effects of every major planetary aspect in language designed for the modern reader. His readable and witty interpretations are so relevant that even long- practicing astrologers gain new psychological insight into the characteristics of the signs and meanings of the aspects.

Grant Lewi is sometimes called the father of "do-it-yourself" astrology, and is considered by many to have been astrology's forerunner to the computer.
0-87542-444-9, 372 pgs., 6 x 9, tables, charts, softcover $12.95

THE BOOK OF GODDESSES & HEROINES
by Patricia Monaghan

The Book of Goddesses & Heroines is a historical landmark, a must for everyone interested in Goddesses and Goddess worship. It is not an effort to trivialize the beliefs of matriarchal cultures. It is not a collection of Goddess descriptions penned by biased male historians throughout the ages. It is the complete, non-biased account of Goddesses of every cultural and geographic area, including African, Egyptian, Japanese, Korean, Persian, Australian, Pacific, Latin American, British, Irish, Scottish, Welsh, Chinese, Greek, Icelandic, Italian, Finnish, German, Scandinavian, Indian, Tibetan, Mesopotamian, North American, Semitic and Slavic Goddesses!

Envisioning herself as a woman who might have revered each of these Goddesses, Patricia Monaghan has done away with language that referred to the deities in relation to their male counterparts, as well as with culturally relative terms such as "married" or "fertility cult." The beliefs of the cultures and the attributes of the Goddesses have been left intact.

Plus, this book has a new, complete index. If you are more concerned about finding a Goddess of war than you are a Goddess of a given country, this index will lead you to the right page. This is especially useful for anyone seeking to do Goddess rituals. Your work will be twice as efficient and effective with this detailed and easy-to-use book.
0-87542-573-9, 456 pgs., 6 x 9, photos, softcover $17.95

CHIRON
by Barbara Hand Clow
This new astrology book is about the most recently discovered planet, Chiron. This little-known planet was first sighted in 1977. It has an eccentric orbit, on a 50-51 year cycle between Saturn and Uranus. It brought far-sightedness into astrology because Chiron is the *bridge to the outer planets,* Neptune and Pluto, from the inner ones. The small but influential planet of Chiron reveals *how* the New Age Initiation will affect each one of us. Chiron is an Initiator, an Alchemist, a Healer, and a Spiritual Guide. For those who are astrologers, *Chiron* has more information than any other book about this planet.

- Learn *why* Chiron rules Virgo and the Sixth House.
- Have the necessary information about Chiron in each house, in each sign, and learn how the aspects affect each person's chart.

Chiron is sure to become a best-selling, albeit controversial book in the astrological world. The influences of Chiron are an important new factor in understanding capabilities and potentials which we all have. Chiron rules Healing with the hands, Healing with crystals, Initiation and Alchemy and Alteration of the body by Mind and Spirit. Chiron also rules Cartomancy and the Tarot reader. As such it is an especially vital resource for everyone who uses the Tarot.

0-87542-094-X, approx. 300 pages, 6 x 9, charts   **$9.95**

Llewellyn's Personal Astrological Services
Llewellyn offers a variety of specialized charts and readings tuned to your exact needs. Write for our catalog for a complete listing.

Simple Natal Chart
Computerized chart based on your exact time and place of birth. Tropical/Placidus House system unless otherwise stated. Please give time, date, year and location of birth (please include county as well as town and state).

APSO3-119   **$5.00**

Detailed Natal Chart
Personalized chart reading by a professional astrologer focusing on one area of your life (you specify). Please send along a detailed letter describing your concerns. Give all birth data as described above.

APSO3-102   **$65.00**

THE LLEWELLYN ANNUALS

Llewellyn's MOON SIGN BOOK: Over 400 pages of valuable information on gardening, fishing, weather, stock market forecasts, horoscopes, planting dates, and instructions for finding the best date to do just about anything! Articles by prominent forecasters and writers in the fields of gardening, astrology, politics, economics and cycles. This special almanac, different from any other, has been published annually since 1906. It's fun, informative and has been a great help to millions in their daily planning. **State year $4.95**

Llewellyn's SUN SIGN BOOK: Your personal horoscope for the entire year! All 12 signs are included in one handy book. Also included are forecasts, special feature articles, and an action guide for each sign. Monthly horoscopes are written by Gloria Star, author of *Optimum Child*, for your personal Sun Sign and there are articles on a variety of subjects written by well-known astrologers from around the country. Much more than just a horoscope guide! Entertaining and fun the year around. **State year $4.95**

Llewellyn's DAILY PLANETARY GUIDE: Includes all of the major daily aspects plus their exact times in Eastern and Pacific time zones, lunar phases, signs and voids plus their times, planetary motion, a monthly ephemeris, sunrise and sunset tables, special articles on the planets, signs, aspects, a business guide, planetary hours, rulerships, and much more. Large 5-1/4 x 8 format for more writing space, spiral bound to lay flat, address and phone listings, time-zone conversion chart and blank horoscope chart. **State year $6.95**

Llewellyn's ASTROLOGICAL CALENDAR: Large wall calendar of 48 pages. Beautiful full-color cover and paintings. Includes feature articles by famous astrologers, and complete introductory information on astrology. It also contains a Lunar Gardening Guide, celestial phenomena, a blank horoscope chart, and monthly date pages which include aspects, Moon phases, signs and voids, planetary motion, an ephemeris, personal forecasts, planting and fishing dates, and more. 10 x 13 size. Set in Central time, with fold-down conversion table for other time zones worldwide. **State year $9.95**

Llewellyn's MAGICAL ALMANAC: This beautifully illustrated almanac explores traditional earth religions and folklore while focusing on magical myths. Each month is summarized in a two-page format with information that includes the phases of the moon, festivals and rites for the month, as well as detailed magical advice. This is an indispensable guide is for anyone who is interested in planning rituals, spells and other magical advice. It features writing by some of the most prominent authors in the field. **State year $7.95**

TRANSITS IN REVERSE
by Edna Copeland Ryneveld

Have you wondered about whether you should take that trip or ask for that raise? Do you want to know when the best time is for a wedding? How about knowing in advance the times when you will be the most creative and dazzling?

This book is different from all others that have been published on transits (those planets that are actually moving around in the heavens making aspects to our natal planets). It gives the subject area first—such as creativity, relationships, health, etc.,—and then tells you what transits to look for. The introductory chapters are so thorough that you will be able to use this book with only an ephemeris or astrological calendar to tell you where the planets are. The author explains what transits are, how they affect your daily life, how to track them, how to make decisions based on transits and much more.

With the information in each section, you can combine as many factors as you like to get positive results. If you are going on a business trip you can look at the accidents section to avoid any trouble, the travel section to find out the best date, the relationship section to see how you will get along with the other person, the business section to see if it is a good time to do business, the communication section to see if things will flow smoothly and more. In this way, you can choose the absolute best date for just about anything! Electional astrology has been used for centuries, but now it is being given in the most easily understood and practical format yet.

0-87542-674-3, 320 pages, 6 x 9. $12.95

THE WOMEN'S SPIRITUALITY BOOK
by Diane Stein

Diane Stein's *The Women's Spirituality Book*, is a work of insight and a much needed addition to women's magic and ritual. Beginning with "Creation and Creation Goddesses" she enthusiastically informs the reader of the essence of women-centered Wicca, using myths and legends drawn from a variety of world sources to bring her work to life. Non-patriarchal myths and tales intersperse the first half of the book, which leads the reader through the yearly progressions of rituals in some of the most complete descriptions of the Sabbats ever published.

The second half of the book is a valuable introduction to visualization, healing, chakras, crystal and gemstone magick. Subsequent chapters cover "transformational tarot" and Kwan Yin.

Diane Stein's *Women's Spirituality Book* is a tool for self-discovery and initiation into the Higher Self: a joyous reunion with the Goddess.

0-87542-761-8, 300 pages, 6 x 9, illus., softcover. $9.95